Sybex's Quick Tour of Windows 95

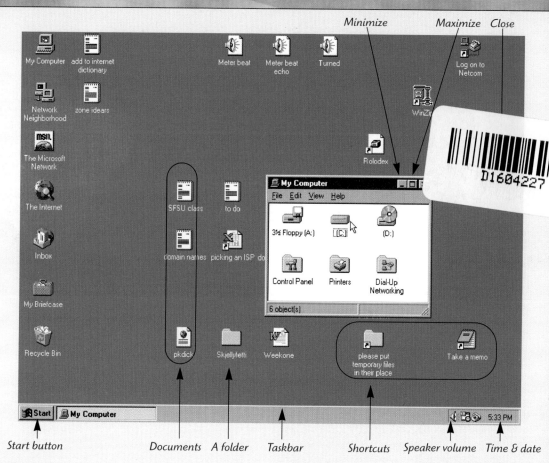

Minimize   Maximize   Close

Start button   Documents   A folder   Taskbar   Shortcuts   Speaker volume   Time & date

The Desktop *is where your programs, files, and shortcuts reside.*

My Computer *allows you to browse the contents of your computer, open folders, open documents, and run programs.*

Network Neighborhood *gives you direct access to other computers (and shared resources, such as printers).*

The Microsoft Network *dials up your connection to Microsoft's online service.*

The Internet *starts up the Internet Explorer, a World Wide Web browser (available only with Plus!).*

Inbox *starts Microsoft Exchange and opens your inbox, so you can see if you have any new mail.*

My Briefcase *is a new feature for keeping documents consistent as you move them between computers.*

Recycle Bin *makes it easy to delete and undelete files.*

The Start button *pops up the Start menu, from which you can run just about every program.*

The Taskbar *displays a button for every running program.*

Create **shortcuts** *on your Desktop for frequently used programs and documents.*

Every window has a **Minimize, Maximize** *(alternating with Restore), and* **Close** *button. The Close button is new; the others just look different.*

FORMATTING A FLOPPY DISK

To format a floppy disk, first double-click the My Computer icon. Put the floppy in the disk drive. Then right-click the 3½ Floppy icon in the My Computer window and choose Format. The Format dialog box appears.

If you want some density other than the standard 1.44MB, click the Capacity drop-down list box and choose another option. To give the disk a label, click in the Label box and type one. Then click Start.

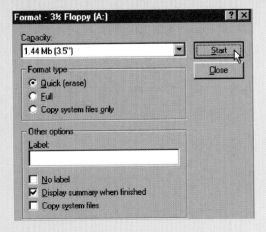

USEFUL KEYBOARD SHORTCUTS

TASK	KEYSTROKE
Get help	F1
Quit a program	Alt+F4
Pop up shortcut menu for selected item	Shift+F10
Pop up the Start menu	Ctrl+Esc
Cut a selection	Ctrl+X
Copy a selection	Ctrl+C
Paste a selection	Ctrl+V
Delete a selection	Delete
Undo the last action	Ctrl+Z
Select all items in window	Ctrl+A
Refresh a window	F5
Open folder one level up from current one	Backspace
Close a folder and all its parents	Shift and click Close button
Rename a selection	F2
Find a file starting with current folder	F3
Delete a selection without putting it in Recycle Bin (be careful!)	Shift+Delete
View a selection's properties	Alt+Enter or Alt+double-click
Copy an icon	Ctrl+click and drag
Create a shortcut from an icon	Ctrl+Shift+click and drag

Sybex Inc.
2021 Challenger Drive
Alameda, CA 94501
Tel: 510-523-8233 · 800-227-2346

SYBEX® Fax: 510-523-2373

© 1995 SYBEX Inc.

CHANGING THE WAY WINDOWS 95 LOOKS

You have all kinds of control over the appearance of Windows. You can get to the Display Properties dialog box to change the look via the Control Panel, but the easiest shortcut is to right-click in any empty area of the Desktop and select Properties. The Display Properties dialog box comes up with the Background tab selected.

- *Choose a desktop pattern or wallpaper design.*

- *Choose **Screen Saver** to select a screen saver or stop using one.*

- *Choose **Appearance** to change the look of the windows and dialog boxes.*

- *Choose **Settings** to change the color palette or screen resolution.*

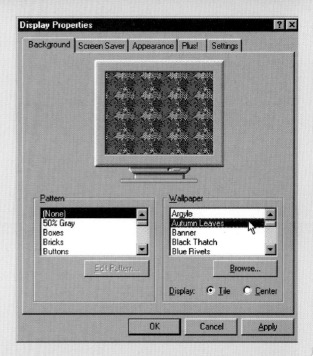

SETTING UP YOUR PRINTER

No one likes having to set up a printer, but Windows has made it fairly unthreatening. Choose Start ➢ Settings ➢ Printer (or open My Computer and double-click Printers). Your Printers window will open.

- *To modify an existing Printer, right-click it and choose Properties.*

- *To create a new Printer, double-click the Add Printer icon and follow the instructions in the Add Printer Wizard.*

- *To change the default printer, right-click a printer and choose Set as Default.*

Sybex's Quick Tour of Windows 95

Just press the Start button to do almost anything.

Running a Program

To start a program, click Start ➤ Programs, choose a program folder (if necessary), and then point to a program.

- Choose a program or program group from a submenu.
- Reopen one of the last 15 documents you've worked on.
- Change the way Windows is set up or add a printer.
- Search for a missing document, folder, or program.
- Get online help.
- Run a program directly, the old-fashioned (DOS) way.
- Turn off or restart your computer.

Putting a Program, Folder, or Document on the Start Menu

First, open the folder that contains the program you want to put on the Start menu. Then click the program icon and drag it onto the Start button. (If you want to get a look at the hierarchy of the programs on the Start submenus—so that you can move things around—right-click on the Start button and choose Open.)

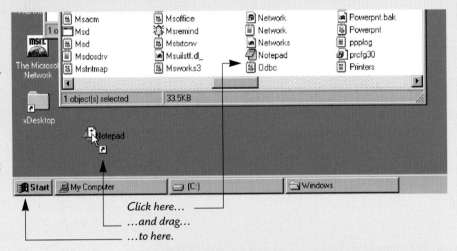

Click here...
...and drag...
...to here.

Finding Files and Folders Quickly

Unlike Windows 3.1's cumbersome Search command in the File Manager, Windows 95 has a simple-to-use Find command. To try it, select Start ➤ Find ➤ Files or Folders.

Type the name of the file you're looking for (or just part of it), then click Find Now.

A window will open, showing the files as Windows finds them.

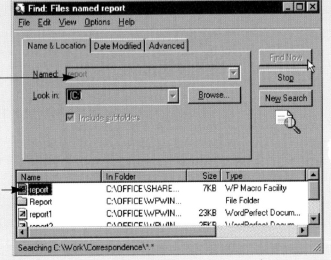

Sure, Windows 3.1 enabled you to use the mouse to scroll, click menus, and interact with dialog boxes, but now just about every feature of Windows can be clicked on (with either button), double-clicked, and/or dragged.

Selecting Things

Click most things to select them. Shift-click to add all intervening items to a selection. Ctrl-click to add an individual item to a selection. Click and drag to lasso and select several items (click in an empty space before starting to drag—otherwise, you'll drag the item itself).

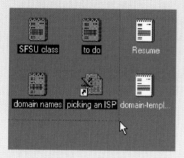

Right-Click Dragging

If you click with the left button and drag, Windows 95 will either copy the icon (for example, when dragging from or to a floppy) or move the icon (for example, when dragging from one folder to another).

For more control, right-click on an icon and drag it. When you release the mouse button, a menu pops up.

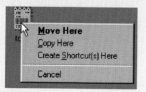

Things You Can Right-Click On

Right-click on an item to pop up a shortcut menu. Every icon's shortcut menu has Properties as its last choice —each object on your computer has a set of properties associated with it, which you can view or change.

■ **My Computer**

Explore displays a File Manager-like view of folders and files.

■ **Any folder, document, or program icon**

Send To sends documents directly to a floppy, printer, or fax machine.

■ **The Start button**

Open lets you make changes to the Start menu.

■ **The Recycle Bin**

■ **The Desktop**

Arrange Icons sorts them by name, type, size, or date.

New creates a new folder, document, or shortcut on the Desktop.

■ **The Taskbar**

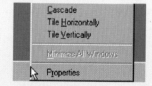

■ **A Taskbar button**

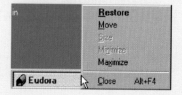

■ **Undo** After you move, copy, create a shortcut from, or delete an icon, the next time you right-click anywhere you can undo your last action. The menu will have a choice like Undo Move or Undo Delete.

One of the best new features of Windows 95 is shortcuts. Each shortcut you create takes up only a small amount of disk space, but can save you time and energy by opening a program or document that you'd otherwise have to hunt around for. You can recognize a shortcut by the little doubling-back arrow in the bottom-left corner of its icon.

Putting a Shortcut on the Desktop

There are many ways to do this. If you have a document or program already visible on the screen and want to create a shortcut to it on the desktop, right-click on the icon, drag it onto the Desktop, and then choose Create Shortcut(s) Here. You can also start from the Desktop when the "target" of your shortcut-to-be is not readily available.

Right-click on the Desktop, select New, and then Shortcut.

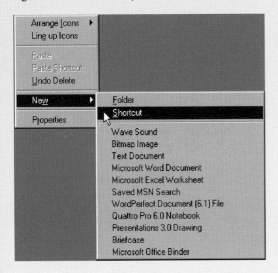

This brings up the Create Shortcut wizard. If you don't know the command line for the program you want, click the Browse button. This brings up an Open-style dialog box; work your way through various folders until you find the program you want to make a shortcut to. Then click the Open button, click Next (or type a different name for the shortcut and click Next), and click Finish when you're done. Voila! Your shortcut appears on the Desktop.

Making a Keyboard Shortcut

Once you've created a shortcut icon, you can also set up a keyboard shortcut to launch the program (or open the document) automatically.

Right-click the shortcut icon and choose Properties. Click the Shortcut tab in the Properties dialog box, click inside the Shortcut Key box, and then press the keyboard short-cut you want. It will appear in the box as you press it.

Shows the default folder for the program

Controls how the program's window appears when you first run it (other choices are Minimized and Maximized)

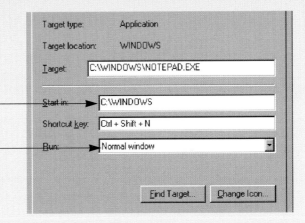

MASTERING

CORELDRAW™ 6

MASTERING

CORELDRAW™ 6

SECOND EDITION

Rick Altman

SYBEX®

San Francisco ■ Paris ■ Düsseldorf ■ Soest

Associate Publisher: Amy Romanoff
Acquisitions Manager: Kristine Plachy
Developmental Editor: Melanie Spiller
Editor: Carol Henry
Project Editors: Neil Edde and Malcolm Faulds
Technical Editor: Dean Denno
Desktop Publisher: Deborah A. Bevilacqua
Production Coordinators: Ron Jost and Alexa Riggs
Indexer: Matthew Spence
Cover Design: Design Site
Cover Illustrator: Gary Priester, Black Point Group

Library of Congress Card Number: 95-70849
ISBN: 0-7821-1802-X

Manufactured in the United States of America
10 9 8 7 6 5 4 3 2 1

CD Warranty

SYBEX warrants the enclosed CD to be free of *physical defects* for a period of ninety (90) days after purchase. If you discover a defect in the disk during this warranty period, you can obtain a replacement disk at no charge by sending the defective disk, postage prepaid, with proof of purchase to:

SYBEX Inc.
Customer Service Department
2021 Challenger Drive
Alameda, CA 94501
(800) 227-2346
Fax: (510) 523-2373

After the 90-day period, you can obtain a replacement disk by sending us the defective disk, proof of purchase, and a check or money order for $10, payable to SYBEX.

Disclaimer

SYBEX makes no warranty or representation, either express or implied, with respect to this medium or its contents, its quality, performance, merchantability, or fitness for a particular purpose. In no event will SYBEX, its distributors, or dealers be liable for direct, indirect, special, incidental, or consequential damages arising out of the use of or inability to use the medium or its contents even if advised of the possibility of such damage.

The exclusion of implied warranties is not permitted by some states. Therefore, the above exclusion may not apply to you. This warranty provides you with specific legal rights; there may be other rights that you may have that vary from state to state.

Copy Protection

None of the programs on the disk is copy-protected. However, in all cases, re-selling or making copies of these programs without authorization is expressly forbidden.

To our player to be named later, who, by February of 1996, will either be a baby boy or a baby girl.

Acknowledgments ▰ ▰ ▰ ▰

Some things in life aren't supposed to be easy, and that certainly holds true for CorelDRAW books. It proves to be an impossibly large task to cover in one book, however large, all of the programs that make up the CorelDRAW suite. Photo-PAINT deserves its *own* book. So, it seems, does the new DREAM3D module. PRESENTS isn't exactly utility software, either.

I remember so clearly the strategy sessions I held with my editors and publishers back in 1992 and 1993, when CorelDRAW was just beginning to grow into the giant it is now. Corel then had the chutzpah to include several other programs with DRAW—such as screen capture and image-cataloging software—and had also thrown in typefaces and clip art. "Well, what do we do now?" one editor wondered aloud. "Write a bigger book," I responded. "Maybe we need to go to 500 pages." Does the phrase "cooked in your own grease" come to mind?

In a moment that shall live in personal infamy, I did indeed suggest that my CorelDRAW book be expanded to include the program's own expanding horizon. The rest, of course, is history, as the *Mastering CorelDRAW* title at Sybex has led a charge of books that have spiraled upward in girth, first flirting with and now surpassing the four-figure mark in page count.

Am I complaining? Yes…no…maybe…I'm not sure. There is little question that authoring a book this size about a program of this breadth is an undertaking of preemptive proportion. Since I began trying to keep up with software that reinvents itself every 12 months, my summers have never been the same. On the other hand, I don't try to take this on by myself, and am grateful for the chance to work with a very talented and spirited group of collaborators who contribute in word, art, advice, and/or inspiration.

As always, in the pole position is my partner for life and wife Becky, who coordinates all the disparate elements of this book that, under her deft care, somehow become a whole. It's only fair that she's indulgent and tolerant in this project—you should see the size of her PageMaker book…

Making her second appearance in this latest edition is my friend and colleague Sue Blumenberg. She wrote the chapters on outlines and fills, and undertook the savage job of coordinating, collecting, organizing, and documenting the Companion CD. I knew she'd be good at it; she expertly manages the chaos of the two conferences that I direct for CorelDRAW and Ventura users each year. By comparison, the CD project was easy.

In his third appearance in the *Mastering CorelDRAW* series, Byron Canfield's contributions are sprinkled throughout these pages. They include embellishments to our sunset drawing in Chapter 6, and pearls of wisdom about halftoning in Chapter 29. Not to mention the mammoth effort to contain an overview of DREAM 3D in Chapter 34.

Speaking of efforts, Wayne Kaplan's gigantica about DRAW's new print engine can be found in Chapter 27, and his prose and drawings are sprinkled throughout Part V, Effects and Affects.

And we had numerous writers and artists making their debut, led by award-winning DRAW artist Gary Priester, who designed the drawing on the cover and contributed two chapters to our Doing It section.

Other significant contributors were

> Ken and June Reeder, who explained styles and presets and described the new PRESENTS module.

> Wil MacDonald, who wrote with authority in the Effects and Affects section and then sank his teeth into the Photo-PAINT story.

> Matthew Lecher, who cut his CorelDRAW teeth on last year's edition of *Mastering CorelDRAW* and this time shares the making of his work, *The Lighthouse*.

Valerie Lennox, who takes us through the production of *The Dragon Lord*, 1995 winner for best animation in Corel's World Design Contest.

John Shanley, who tells all about importing and exporting, Windows 95 style.

And Norm Tiedemann, who covers a variety of CorelDRAW utilities, including FontMaster, Capture, and the installation procedure.

My tag team of editors—Carol Henry on prose and Dean Denno on facts and figures—performed up to their usual excellent standards, despite conditions that proved to be treacherous at best. We couldn't then, but we can now look back and laugh at our startling midsummer discovery: More than halfway through the writing of this book, Corel changed the interface so significantly that almost all of the illustrations and about half of our writing had been rendered null and void.

Special thanks go out to the team at Sybex, led by project editor Neil Edde, who inherited his position at halftime and nonetheless did a terrific job of keeping all the pieces together. Other significant players include desktop publisher Debi Bevilacqua, Production Coordinators Ron Jost and Alexa Riggs, DTP Technical Coordinator Molly Sharp, and Technical Assistant Dan Schiff.

I owe a debt of gratitude to approximately 750 users who came to our seminars and two annual conferences over the last 12 months. Your feedback, experiences, suggestions, positive attitude, and overall good humor and cheer fuel my creative fire.

Finally, I must acknowledge our good and great friends Gregory and Pamela Bohlmann and Steven and Jenifer Turnbull, with whom Becky and I enjoy many vacations, outings, and evenings out. Countless times over this past year, they tolerated the intrusion of my notebook computer on our social events. They forgave me when I showed them the Pinball game for Windows 95.

Rick Altman
Lead Author

CONTENTS
AT A GLANCE

Table of Contents

PART II   **LIFE IN AN OBJECT-ORIENTED WORLD**

Introduction ▰ ▰ ▰ ▰

"So how big is that book going to be this time around?" my father asked. Readers of previous editions might remember my story of his reaction when I told him that my upcoming book was to be over 1,000 pages. He called me a Jewish word that loosely translates to my being nuts.

"This one's going to be even bigger," I replied. "Does this mean that I'm meshuga again?"

"Not again," he said. "Still."

Father does seem to know best, but if I'm meshuga, think of how you'd describe Corel, the Canadian company that brings new meaning to the word *ambitious*. The engineers there have once again outdone themselves with the sixth iteration of DRAW. In terms of depth of features, breadth of scope, consumption of hard drive space, and as always, swiftness of development, CorelDRAW 6.0 furthers Corel's position as the most proactive company in the graphics business.

Indeed, CorelDRAW is the clear and obvious leader in Windows-based drawing and illustration software, and it has reached this position with both a whimper and a bang. Beginning with modest attempts to ride the coattails of then-ringleader Ventura Publisher—with unspectacular utilities for Ventura users to create headlines and logos—the Canadian-based Corel gradually set its sights on a previously underrepresented market: people who want to create art with their computers. Today, this market is at the center of desktop design and electronic illustration, and Corel has much to do with this sharply refocused dimension of computing.

What Is CorelDRAW?

Even those in the know are looking forward to this book's writing team botching the answer to the question, what is CorelDRAW? Is it a program that allows you to work with refined curves and objects to produce precise artistic effects? Is it a powerful typographic engine for the creation of logos and other text-based work? Is it actually a collection of several programs, each covering a particular sector of the graphics industry? Or is CorelDRAW just a tool for driving book authors crazy? (Five pages down, 995 more to go....)

The fact that CorelDRAW is actually all of these things underscores the impression this program has made in its community. One way or the other, the applications in the box of software known as CorelDRAW assist you in the creation of modern-day graphics. They are the tools with which you can create

- Full-color illustrations
- Complex drawings
- Logos
- Fancy headlines
- Three-dimensional renderings
- Photo-realistic images
- Surrealistic images
- Charts, graphs, and pictograms
- Slide shows
- Animation sequences
- Sound bites and film clips
- Libraries of clip art
- High-quality drawings from low-resolution originals

CorelDRAW is actually DRAW, Photo-PAINT, DREAM3D, PRE-SENTS, OCR-TRACE, MOTION3D, DEPTH, and a small army of smaller programs. In varying degrees of detail, this book will cover them all. Six pages down, only 994 to go...

CorelDRAW Is for Drawing

If there are users out there who have purchased CorelDRAW for the sole purpose of creating slide shows, bar charts, or animations, we haven't met them yet. Many users do occasionally turn to the expertise of the other CorelDRAW modules, but what they really bought Corel-DRAW for was one primary function: to draw! Day in and day out, the colorful and now-famous balloon icon is what receives the majority of double-clicks. This lopsided popularity is not lost on us—in fact, we agree, and the lion's share of this book is devoted to DRAW, the flagship product. One of these days, a book proclaiming itself "the definitive reference for Corel's other modules" might reach the shelves, but this isn't it.

Is DRAW easy to use? You're holding a very thick book in your hands and that ought to tell you something, but a majority of users are of the opinion that, yes, DRAW is very easy to pick up and begin using. In fact, Corel owes its phenomenal success in large part to that intangible and mystifying quality we call intuitiveness or user-friendliness. DRAW is one of those rare programs that makes itself look easy. The menus make sense, the screen icons seem at home, and most of the functions and dialogs invite you to try them before forcing you to retreat to the User's Manual.

Don't fool yourself, though. This software can take you to positively dizzying heights. The richness of its color palettes, the intricacies of its fill patterns, the layers of detail heaped upon its special effects, the mind-boggling power behind its print and export engines—all this can lead to early retirement for users, readers, and authors alike. But traveling DRAW's long and winding road is not the dreadful journey it is with some programs. Our job is to smooth out the bumps in the road, but we take no credit for making your first few steps easy. The software has already seen to that.

For Whom Does This Book Toll?

As lead author, I like to think that any CorelDRAW user on the planet will enjoy the pages of this book. The fact that I won't try to convince you of that is a sure sign that I have no future as a marketing consultant. From my on-going series of CorelDRAW seminars—at which I meet several hundred users every year—I have defined a clear profile of you, the mainstream user: You produce lots of one-page fliers, logos, and small brochures, and you do not necessarily have a professional background in the arts. You want to develop a better understanding of CorelDRAW's tools and functions, and learn the hidden treasures that allow for faster and more efficient operation.

This book is written with the following users in mind:

- Technical illustrators, who want to reduce the amount of busywork involved in producing diagrams, charts, and simple drawings

- Amateur and budding designers, who strive to develop an eye for good, clean, simple designs

- Desktop publishers, who need a better understanding of DRAW's text-handling capabilities, both inside and outside of Ventura (DRAW's new industrial-strength document publisher)

- Commercial artists, who might be auditioning the new version of DRAW for producing their next double-page spread

- Fine artists and illustrators, who have no patience for a book that tries to teach them their business, but want to sharpen their CorelDRAW skills and their understanding of its tools

- Brand-new users looking for a book that neither talks down to them nor leads them slowly by the hand, but rather arms them with information and gives them the practice they need to become self-sufficient

- And prospective users, who want to get a sense of what CorelDRAW is all about before they make their purchase.

How to Use This Book

It says something about a book's scope and length when the book comes with instructions to itself. ("To use this book, start at the top of the page, read from left to right, and turn pages with your right hand…") But really—since this text addresses users at distinctly different levels of knowledge and skill, you need to know what is what, where, and for whom. We include both tutorial and reference material, and when necessary, we specify right away any chapter that is either for beginning or more advanced users.

Part I, "A New Era of Desktop Graphics," is an introduction to the software in general, and Chapter 3 is about version 6.0 in particular. If you've never before produced a drawing on your own, you'll want to make stops at Chapter 5, "Quickies," and Chapter 6, "From Start to Finish: Creating an Illustration."

Part II, "Life in an Object-Oriented World," explores the lifeblood of DRAW: curves, nodes, outlines, and fills.

Part III, "Working with Text," covers—you guessed it—your work with text in DRAW: paragraph and artistic, fancy and conservative, fast and slow, good and bad.

Part IV, "Have It Your Way," explores the improved functions of styles and templates and the brand-new, ultra-exciting customizable interface.

Part V, "Effects and Affects," features the stellar performers found under the Effects menu, which are responsible for the more artistic (and sometimes not-so-artistic) effects possible with DRAW.

Part VI, "Doing It!," showcases some of the finest work ever achieved with DRAW, including prominent winners in Corel's Annual Design Contest.

Part VII, "The CorelDRAW Freeway," exposes DRAW as the expressway it is, with emphasis on its exits and entrances—namely printing, color and prepress theory, importing, and exporting. It ends with our Annual Export Torture Test in Chapter 31.

Part VIII, "The Supporting Cast," provides a focused and authoritative look at the other modules in the box, including the new-and-improved Photo-PAINT and the brand-new DREAM 3D.

No Time Like the Present

We know that many CorelDRAW users are a bit gun-shy about new releases of this software, given the pattern of bugs and initial instability established in the 3.0 and 4.0 releases. And we know that many of you rely on books like this one to help you make that buying decision.

For these reasons, we're grateful for our standing policy of writing the introduction after writing the main body of the book. We started this project in the summer of 1995; much has happened since then, including another frenetic period of beta testing during which Corel's engineers turned out new releases almost daily.

Photo-PAINT breaks into the major league of image editing, with a significantly overhauled interface and collection of tools and effects. DREAM 3D angles to be the go-to application in the quickly emerging niche of 3D rendering. PRESENTS hopes to compete against the presentation programs found in all of the major suites.

Most of you are more interested in the fate and fortunes of the main module, DRAW, and we don't have to tell too many veteran customers about what we will affectionately refer to as the ".0 Curse." Most versions of DRAW leave the starting gate without a wheel or two, in need of a maintenance release before they can hit stride, and we don't find DRAW 6.0 to be an exception. The late-summer release ushered in an autumn of discontent for many users, who found themselves scratching their heads over mysterious glitches, unidentified floating objects, and unceremonious ejections from DRAW and even Windows 95 itself. The knight in shining armor—Maintenance Update No. 1—arrived with the New Year and addressed many of the more egregious bugs and bombs.

On behalf of my entire writing team, we hope you enjoy the book. Now if you'll excuse us, we must begin work on the version 7.0 edition…

A NEW ERA OF DESKTOP GRAPHICS

We used to think that the notion of a computer book being over 600 pages was absurd. Then we met CorelDRAW, the program that seems to stretch into infinity in both its breadth and its depth. As the program extends over all known horizons, this book does, too. Here you'll find analysis and discussion to soothe even the most savage DRAW power-user.

But we are getting ahead of ourselves. Across 1,000 or so pages, there is plenty of time for discussions on advanced usage. This first part of the book is devoted to new users, occasional users, and even prospective users who are still in the throes of a buying decision.

Part I is an introduction to the software, but it is much more than just a tutorial on how to click the right buttons. We intend to provide insight into what CorelDRAW does, why it does what it does, and how it does it. Except when we state otherwise, these first five chapters assume only modest familiarity with CorelDRAW.

1

The Foundation of CorelDRAW

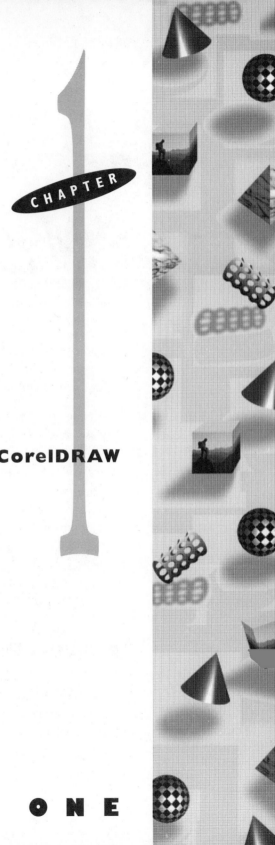

We remember it as if it were yesterday—the day that Corel-DRAW 1.0 was first released. Up until then, the closest things to illustration software were unremarkable paint programs and nongraphical applications that required you to describe the effect you wanted, instead of drawing it. CorelDRAW was one of the first Windows-based drawing programs to take hold.

Today, nearly ten years later, CorelDRAW is one of the giants of the industry in terms of customer base, stature, and the sheer volume of programs that are included in this one product.

It is no mystery to us why this is so. From its inception, CorelDRAW was the most approachable, the most inviting of the drawing and illustration programs. Its army of users covers virtually all corners of the graphics community: from fine artists to illustrators to technical artists; from freelance designers to desktop publishers; book publishers and newsletter editors; signmakers, T-shirt designers, and logo creators; secretaries turned designers; well-meaning but unartistic managers…and even your lead author's three-year-old daughter! Granted—becoming proficient with CorelDRAW might be a challenge; but more than two million users will attest to the fact that playing around with, developing a feel for, and even getting the hang of this program is not difficult at all.

Drawing versus Painting

When we first started offering our one- and two-day seminars for CorelDRAW users, we were surprised to discover how many users did not understand the essential qualities of the two broad categories of illustration programs. Today, three years later, we still encounter hundreds of users who are unclear on the concept, because many electronic artists simply take for granted what these programs do in the background. When you get past all of the jargon about Béziers, pixels, halftones, and clipping paths, graphics programs produce art in one of two ways: They produce curves, lines, and other distinct shapes that are based on mathematics; or they produce dots. At the core of it all, everything that comes from graphics software is curves or dots.

The one characteristic that distinguishes vector-based drawing programs like DRAW, Adobe Illustrator, Deneba Canvas, Micrografx Designer, and others is their own particular degree of intelligence. When you draw a circle in one of these programs, the circle has a set of properties—an identity, if you will. It has a radius from the center, a circumference, a set of x- and y-coordinates, an outline, and an interior color. If you change the appearance or size of the circle, DRAW still knows that the circle is a circle.

Painting programs, on the other hand—such as Photo-PAINT (included in the CorelDRAW box), Adobe Photoshop, and Micrografx Picture Publisher—are not nearly as smart. In fact, they're pretty dumb, but don't think of that as an insult. Their primary job is to lay down pixels on a screen, no questions asked, just as a painter would place paint on the canvas. The circle you create in a paint program is simply a collection of pixels, perhaps millions of them, lined up in rows. Taken together, the dots might happen to look like a circle, but there are no properties identifying it as a circle.

When You Have to Choose…

When buying graphics software, it's unlikely that you would choose *either* a vector-based *or* a paint program. Most businesses need the services of *both,* because whether dumb or smart, both types of software play important roles. That is precisely why every copy of CorelDRAW includes DRAW (the drawing program) and PAINT (the painting program).

If You Need Clip Art   Turn to DRAW and the gaggle of prefab clip art images on the CorelDRAW CD. Because vector drawings can be edited so easily, DRAW is the perfect tool to produce simple art from scratch or to modify existing art.

If You Need to Scan Photos   That's a job for PAINT or your own favorite paint program. The undying virtue of bitmap images is the extraordinary level of control they offer you. *You* decide how small each dot is to be (that is, how high the resolution is), and *you* can change the color of every dot that makes up the image.

If You Need to Capture and Refine Computer Screen Images
Here, as well, give the nod to your paint program, coupled with a screen capture program (such as CAPTURE, included in the CorelDRAW box). When you take a picture of your screen, it is stored as a bitmap. Although this bitmap is not as detailed as most photographs, you can still edit all the way down to the dot level.

If You Need to Set Lots of Type   Hightail it back to DRAW, where all the fidelity of your typeface format is honored, including letter spacing, tracking, kerning, and hinting.

If You're Producing Technical Drawings   Once again you're in DRAW's domain, where you can achieve utter precision, razor-sharp lines, and can scale, reshape, group, and duplicate individual objects.

If You're Creating Logos, Flyers, Brochures, or Ad Layouts
Chances are good in this case that you're going to want both DRAW and PAINT, because today's electronic art often contains text and other vector-based objects integrated with a scanned image. DRAW can be your Grand Central Station for such projects, because it allows you to import bitmap images into a drawing. But DRAW can only *place* bitmap images. It can't edit them—for that, you have to send them back to PAINT.

The Magic of the Curve

We may be guilty of a bit of oversimplification, but the cornerstone to DRAW can be summed up in one word: *curves*. The essence of DRAW is its ability to create curves, in stark contrast to what a paint program does.

This bears repeating: Paint programs work with hundreds of thousands or even millions of tiny dots, which together form an image that registers with your brain. But the paint program doesn't know that they are supposed to look like something—that happens practically by accident.

On the other hand, DRAW is more intelligent about the basic elements it uses. DRAW understands the dynamics responsible for an object's shape; it is not just a collection of pixels or dots.

As a result, vector art is quite lean. Bitmap images, in contrast, can get big in a hurry. With all of those dots to cart around—as opposed to the nice, neat set of mathematical instructions that describes an object— bitmap images can quickly commandeer your hard drive, especially with four-color images. Figure 1.1 is a drawing of President Clinton's family, produced in DRAW. The curves and fill patterns that make up this image will require barely 100K of disk space, but if it were converted to a bitmap image, you'd be looking at a minimum of 500K for a low-resolution rendition, and as much as 5MB for one in full color.

No question about it, if you choose your paint program to produce work that is better suited for your drawing program, you'll hear about it from

1.1

Rendered as vector
art, the Clinton
Family is a lean,
100K DRAW file.
Described as bit-
map art, this same
image grows to at
least 500K and
likely more.

your hard drive. And if you decide to go all out and use a professionally scanned photograph of the Clintons *and* the First Feline standing in the Oval Office, you're talking about really high rent: 10MB to 40MB.

You'll read a lot about curves throughout this text, especially the so-called *Bézier curve* (see Figure 1.2). It's named after the man who discovered the dynamic relationship that exists between a starting point, an ending point, and the two control points that determine the path taken by the curve from start to finish. You don't need to understand the intricacies—just know that Bézier curves get the credit for just about everything that CorelDRAW does right.

1.2

The magic of the Bézier curve

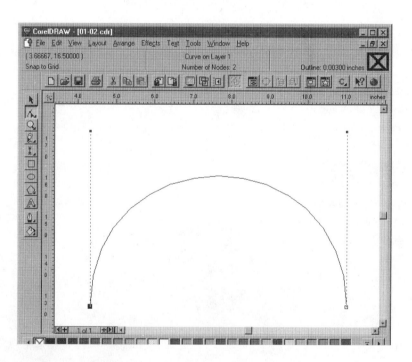

CorelDRAW Is Greater Than the Sum of Its Parts

Like most sophisticated graphics programs, CorelDRAW hits its stride when you apply a few of its special effects on otherwise simple objects.

Creating a few ellipses like the ones shown at the left of Figure 1.3 may not be cause for celebration, but you will really begin to turn heads when you unleash the higher-octane features. There's Blend, which transforms one object into another, and Trim, the tool responsible for creating the sprocket in the center of Figure 1.3. Extrude is what produced the depth-defying effect for the finished sprocket. There's Radial Fill, which gently changes the fill color from one to another, and Rotate, Envelope, Weld, Distribute, Trim, PowerClip—the list goes on. As Figure 1.3 shows, the relationship between simple objects and powerful effects might be the marriage made in electronic heaven.

1.3

CorelDRAW's special effects steal the headlines every time.

Typefaces: The Final Frontier

To many, the most impressive part of CorelDRAW is the control it gives you in handling text. A mind-boggling number of typefaces ship with the product. Its typographic engine allows for the setting of a typeface in point increments as small as .1, and for rotations in equally fine steps. In short, CorelDRAW allows you to manipulate text on your electronic drafting table just as you would other objects, using all the same special effects.

Historically, DRAW's text prowess has been responsible for two things: pure joy on the part of eager users accustomed to having substantial constraints on their ability to manipulate type; and horror at some of the less-than-stellar efforts foisted upon the user community by those same eager but artistically challenged users. Many users start out blissfully unaware of the skills required to effectively pilot the software, and indeed, CorelDRAW users' contributions to the Desktop Publishing Hall of Shame are substantial. Perhaps this is the inevitable price to be paid for software so inviting that practically anyone can use it.

On this last point of irony, we will close this introductory chapter. CorelDRAW has made a name for itself as an artist's tool despite the fact—maybe *because* of the fact—that a majority of its users are not artists. This demographic distinction is not lost on us, and our intent in this book is to speak to the practical, pragmatic demands of mainstream CorelDRAW users. We do not hope to convert you into brilliant artists, and we believe one of the strengths of this book is that we don't try. Rather, we hope to broaden your understanding of the software and help you become more efficient and productive.

♣

In our ongoing series of seminars, we have met thousands of skilled CorelDRAW users who turn to the product for technical work, simple logos, sketches, headlines, and other projects that don't require formal training in the arts. These power-users enjoy the continuing search for better and faster ways to pilot the software. We have also encountered accomplished artists (those who really do the program justice) who wouldn't know a keyboard shortcut if it landed on their foreheads. Users in both categories will benefit from a more complete understanding of the inner workings of CorelDRAW, and that is what we intend to deliver.

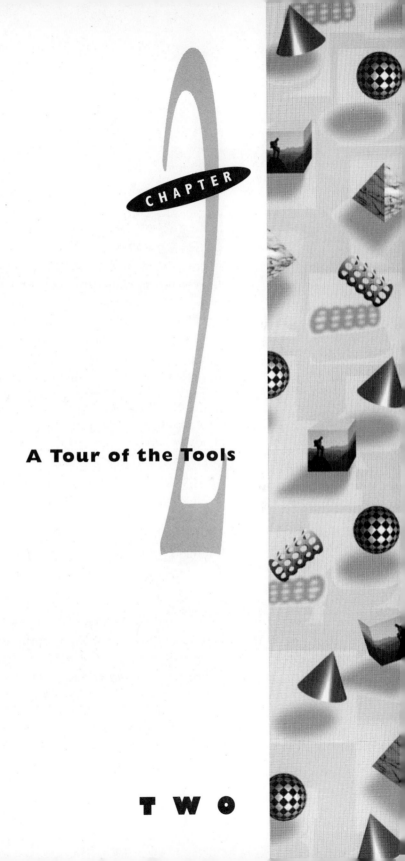

CHAPTER

A Tour of the Tools

TWO

Most long-term users are amazed at how differently each version of CorelDRAW operates from the previous one. Corel's team of engineers seem to work eight days a week through the entire calendar year to come up with a bevy of new features, and usually at least one entirely new application, every 12 months. Chapter 3 will focus on what has changed in version 6.0; here in this chapter we'll also look at what has stayed the same. From one version to the next, CorelDRAW's essential look and feel—its heart and soul, really—have remained unswervingly consistent. This chapter is for new or occasional CorelDRAW users seeking an overview of the program.

As in most Windows programs (95 and earlier), all of the CorelDRAW modules consist of menus that you pull down, dialog boxes that you invoke, and tools that you click. Most of the functions, across all the CorelDRAW modules, can be accessed from both keyboard and mouse. In this regard, we will likely harp a bit throughout the book on our favorite hotkeys, as we believe them to be invaluable when you want efficiency and economy of motion. (And what's fair is fair, so we'll also complain a bit about some very strange key mnemonics, and others that are inexplicably absent.)

AUTHOR'S NOTE

CorelDRAW 6.0 is a 32-bit application that was not designed for, nor will it run under, Windows 3.11 or earlier. It will run only on Windows 95 and Windows NT.

Surfing the Interface

This chapter is akin to the couch-potato activity of cruising via remote control every single one of the television stations offered by your cable provider. We won't stop long at any one of them—we'll surf.

Figure 2.1 shows the essential interface for DRAW, the main module of the CorelDRAW suite of programs. Your screen might look slightly different from the one we show here, because video cards, color palettes, your preferred Windows Display Properties, and your screen resolution all affect the appearance of Windows applications.

2 . 1

DRAW may overwhelm you with its depth, but its interface has remained clean and uncluttered since version1.0.

The 11 rectangles along the left side of the work area make up DRAW's *Toolbox*, providing access to the most common commands and functions of the program. The *Standard Toolbar* below the menus offers shortcuts to other frequently-used commands, including your favorites; you can even add custom commands that you create yourself.

NEW FOR 6

Corel added the Ribbon Bar to DRAW in version 5.0 and it immediately became controversial. Some thought it was a productivity enhancement; some thought it just got in the way and consumed valuable work space. This question will likely get resolved by users of DRAW 6, thanks to the intelligence Corel has added to its new Toolbars. You can decide which functions go on the Toolbars and which ones don't; you can even remove them altogether. Now that you can personalize and customize the Toolbars, we suspect most of you will come to like using them.

DRAW owes much of its success to its clean interface. Even if you have never used a drawing program, we bet you can draw a blue rectangle in DRAW for the first time without too many wrong turns. And once you know the most basic of maneuvers—click on the tool, move to the page, click and drag, and click on a fill color—you are all set to create not just rectangles, but ovals, text blocks, lines, stars and other polygons, and free-form objects. In mastering this maneuver, you also automatically know how to zoom in on parts of your drawing, group and ungroup objects, and change the basic shape of curves.

All these operations result from one set of motions:

1. Click on the desired tool.

2. Move your cursor out to the page.

3. Click and hold Button 1 on your mouse.

AUTHOR'S NOTE

> We try to avoid "dexteritism"—discrimination on the basis of one's dexterity, that is. So instead of the terms *right-click* and *left-click*, we prefer *Button 1* (the primary mouse button, the left one for most users) and *Button 2* (the secondary mouse button). Unfortunately, however, Microsoft has officially coined and sanctioned *right-click* as the term for clicking Button 2 to invoke a context-sensitive menu, and so it will be hard for us to avoid using that term. Nonetheless, when it comes to plain old clicking or clicking-and-dragging, we'll use Button 1 and Button 2 to keep them distinct.

4. Drag the mouse across the page.

5. Let go of the mouse button.

We're only exaggerating a little bit when we say that once you have learned this procedure, you have learned about 90% of the motions required to drive the program. Of course, knowing how to press on the accelerator doesn't give you license to drive a car, and we readily acknowledge that the tool is not capable of creating fine art on its own. For that matter, total expertise with DRAW won't turn you into a fine artist if you aren't one already, and this is a point that we will continue to drive home throughout the book. Becoming a capable DRAW user requires vision, good judgment, experience, and practice, practice, practice. Couple that with a knowledge of the arts, and you're on your way to becoming a successful electronic illustrator.

The Supporting Actors

Many parts of DRAW's face are leased from Windows 95 itself. Like practically every Windows program, all of the CorelDRAW modules include

- A title bar listing the name of the application and/or the particular file opened, with Minimize/Maximize/Restore/Close buttons to control the DRAW window

- A menu bar that provides access to most of the program's functions and commands

- Scroll bars for moving to other parts of a drawing, and page icons for scrolling through pages (if a drawing contains more than one)

- The DRAW balloon icon at the top-left, for quickly sizing and closing DRAW or the current window

It would be nearly impossible to find a Windows program today that *doesn't* offer File, Edit, and View as its first three menu choices, or that doesn't offer some sort of button or toolbar with icons that provide shortcuts to commands and functions. DRAW is no exception. DRAW's menus work just as any Windows 95 user expects—but not quite as a Windows 3.1 user wou,d expect. That is, you can pull down a menu by clicking it once, or by pressing the underlined character in combination with the Alt key. But unlike Windows 3.1, you can move the cursor across menu choices to automatically highlight them. When the one you want is highlighted, click again to invoke it. (By the way, keep your eye out for those underlined letters. They keep you informed about keystroke alternatives to using the mouse.)

The Status Bar   You can choose to display the *status bar* immediately below the menu bar, or below the on-screen color palette at the bottom of the window. DRAW uses this six-sectioned area for communicating with you.

The status bar in DRAW 6 gets quite a shot in the arm. Suffice it to say that when Corel says "status," it means it. As Figure 2.2 shows, you can instruct DRAW to deliver a dizzying amount of information about the objects on your page, the configuration of DRAW, and your system in general.

One of Figure 2.2's messages is "Curve on Layer 1." At first glance, this might sound like a secret code; actually, DRAW is being specific about the type of object you are working with (rectangle, ellipse, polygon, text, or a free-form curve) and where it is in DRAW's layering system. You select objects on the page by clicking them, and when you do, they grow small black handles around their perimeters. The selected shape in Figure 2.2 is a curve, and you can see the selection handles around one of the leaves in Figure 2.2. Remember what we said about curves in Chapter 1: Without them, life as DRAW knows it would be impossible.

Toward the right end of the status line, DRAW gives you information about the interior and exterior of the selected object. In this example, DRAW indicates that the interior of the leaf has a certain fill pattern, and an outline that is colored black and set at a thickness of .007 inch.

2.2

DRAW's informative status bar stops just short of reporting stock prices and ballgame scores.

The rectangle at the far-right end of the status bar changes dynamically to reflect the properties of the currently selected object. If the leaf were red, so would be the rectangle. And if the outline were red and 3 points thick, the line around the rectangle would change to reflect that. When objects overlap, sometimes the only way you can tell which object is selected is to watch this little box in the status line. Continuing with our automobile analogy earlier in this chapter, staying mindful that this representative box is akin to using your rearview mirror: It's an excellent habit to develop and will no doubt save you someday from major trouble.

The Scroll Bars   DRAW's *scroll bars* operate just like those in most other Windows programs, and the horizontal and vertical scroll bars operate identically. There are three ways to scroll the screen: You can scroll little by little, by clicking on the small arrow buttons on either end of the scroll bar. You can scroll a lot at a time, by clicking on the gray part of the scroll bar (on your system, the scroll bar may be a different color). Or you can scroll any amount you choose, by clicking and dragging the small rectangle (the *scroll button*) inside the scroll bar.

NEW FOR 6

> **Experienced DRAW users may find themselves using the scroll bars far less often than before, thanks to the new panning feature that allows for quick movement around the page. See Chapter 3.**

The Color Palette   At the bottom of the screen you'll find the *color palette*, which provides you with a very easy method of changing the interior fill or the outline color of a selected object. Because most color palettes have many more colors than can fit on the screen, the palette area works like a scroll bar to give you access to all the palette's selections. The × button at the left end is for the quick removal of a fill or outline. One palette serves both the outline and the fill, thanks to the fact that PC mice have two buttons. If you click on a color or the ×

with the primary mouse button (usually Button 1), you change the interior fill of the selected object; click with the other mouse button, and you change the outline.

The color palette, the status bar, and the on-screen rulers can all be toggled on and off, via the View menu. The Toolbox, as well, is controlled on the View menu, using the ToolBars item (the Toolbox is treated as a special toolbar). And the page border is toggled on and off using a check box in the Layout / Page Settings dialog. By controlling all these screen elements, you can make a dramatic change in DRAW's appearance, as shown in Figures 2.3 and 2.4.

2.3

The DRAW interface with all its essential parts intact

Understanding Dialog Boxes

When you issue commands for actions such as removing the status bar or the color palette from the DRAW interface, you are performing the

2.4

The **DRAW** inter-
face without the
status bar, Toolbar,
rulers, color pal-
ette, page border,
and Toolbox

next most common maneuver in the program after the click-and-drag: pulling down a menu and then choosing one of its functions.

Clicking on a menu choice will generally produce one of two results. It will either trigger an on/off toggle—as in showing and hiding the on-screen rulers—or it will activate a *dialog box* in which a collection of controls resides. (We use the term *dialog* for short.) Menu choices that invoke dialogs are all followed by three dots (an ellipsis), indicating there is more to the story. Figure 2.5 shows the result of choosing Tools /Options. This dialog (formerly the Preferences dialog) controls the way many of DRAW's elements behave and appear on screen.

Since version 5, CorelDRAW has used "tabbed dialogs," in which electronic file tabs along the top of a dialog box indicate the various places you can go. In Figure 2.5, you know you are looking at the General settings because the tab of this page is raised up a bit higher than the others.

2 . 5

A typical dialog
with fields for en-
tering values, check
boxes to click on
and off, and tabs
for displaying other
pages of the dialog

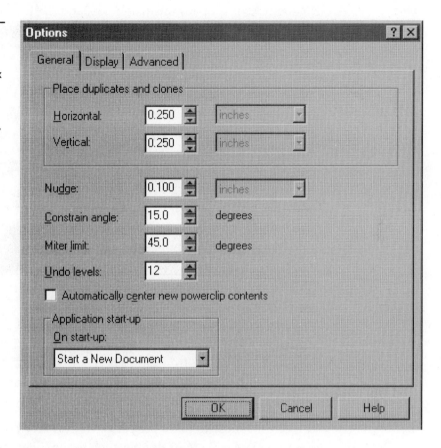

Remember, it makes no difference to DRAW how you open this dialog.
You can use your mouse, clicking once on Tools in the menu bar and
then on Options. Or you can press Alt+T for Tools and then P for Options. Or you can mix and match your keyboard and mouse actions;
DRAW doesn't care.

Because the route to this Options dialog is heavily traveled by regular
DRAW users, the developers assigned a *hotkey* to it: Ctrl+J. DRAW's
hotkeys provide you with instant access to a dialog or command without having to pull down a menu. Whenever you want to access the Options dialog, typing Ctrl+J will do it, no questions asked. Hotkeys are
particularly handy if you just want to check a value for a setting without

changing it. Ctrl+J opens the dialog box, and the Escape key closes it, ignoring any changes you might have made.

INSIDE INFO

> All of DRAW's keyboard shortcuts to dialogs are shown on the menus with their functions. For instance, pull down the File menu and you'll see Ctrl+S associated with the Save command. A variety of "hidden" keystrokes exist, as well, that have special jobs when used at specific times. All told, there are about 150 different hotkeys across the entire program—including such obscure gems as holding down Alt to select an object by touching it; and pressing Ctrl while rotating an object to constrain it to 15° increments.

Understanding what all of DRAW's controls mean can be tricky, but changing them is easy. DRAW lets you navigate with the mouse or the keyboard within almost every dialog. As you can see in Figure 2.5, every field, check box, and button can be accessed with a keystroke (remember those underlines). So if you're going to change, say, the Undo Levels setting from 4 to 8, you have three choices:

- Use the mouse to place the cursor in the entry box, press Backspace to erase the 4 or double-click to highlight it, and then press 8.

- Press Alt+U to highlight the box and press 8 to enter the new value.

- Click on the little up-arrow spin box to increase the value until it reaches 8.

No surprise here—our preference is the second option, using the keyboard. We believe that nothing is faster or easier on your hands and wrists. Try all three and judge for yourself.

WATCH OUT!

When entering values in number fields, make sure to set the unit of measurement first, and *then* change the number. If you do it in the wrong order, DRAW might yell at you. For instance, let's say one of the fields for Place Duplicates and Clones (in Figure 2.5) is measuring in inches, and you want to set it to 70 points. If you enter 70 and then change the measuring unit to points, DRAW thinks you want to convert 70 inches to points. The resultant number, approximately 5,040, will be not quite what you had in mind! So be sure to set the unit of measurement first.

Exploring the Toolbar

We barely mentioned DRAW's Toolbar in the last edition of this book, and in most of that book's screen images the Toolbar was not visible. In fact, we just couldn't get that excited about a little button that saves a drawing, since File / Save or Ctrl+S do that just fine. Vertical screen space on a 640×480 display is far too valuable to waste on redundant controls, we thought.

But we are singing a different tune about CorelDRAW 6. The user now has the ability to determine what goes on the Toolbar and where the Toolbar resides. You can now position the Toolbar anywhere on the screen, add and remove functions, or drag tools from the toolbox to the Toolbar. Chapter 3 offers a preview, and Chapter 15 has the full story.

Working with Roll-Ups

Corel invented these cute little quasi dialogs for version 3.0, and they quickly became a big hit with users. *Roll-ups* perform many of the same functions as conventional dialogs, but roll-ups are much more interactive. For instance, they don't necessarily disappear after carrying out a command as conventional dialogs do. And because of roll-ups' diminutive size, you can place them right next to the object in question for quick mouse action.

NEW FOR 6

DRAW users are used to their roll-ups remaining on screen after each use, but now you can change that. Each roll-up has a little control that Corel calls a *push pin*. When the pin is pushed in (the default state), the roll-up persists after each use until you close it. When the push pin is pushed out, the roll-up acts like a dialog and goes away after it is used. Also new to version 6.0: Roll-ups can be grouped together to reduce screen clutter.

Figure 2.6 shows one of the many roll-ups available to you in DRAW. This one has just presided over the blending of one character to another. Instead of clicking an OK button to enact a change, you click on the Apply button. And instead of disappearing promptly, this roll-up sticks around, making a series of tweaks a much friendlier task.

Exploring the Toolbox

The tools that make up the toolbox are the electronic lifeblood of DRAW. You can create hundreds of complete drawings using just these tools and no menu commands (except Save!). Following is a brief rundown on each tool.

The Pick Tool

The Pick tool acts as home base for DRAW. It is the tool that you use to select objects before altering them, and it is the active tool every time you start the program. You can select an object by clicking it with the Pick tool, or by dragging across it with a marquee (see Chapter 4).

2.6

Blend is a typical CorelDRAW roll-up, in that it packs a lot of commands into a compact space and remains on screen until you close it.

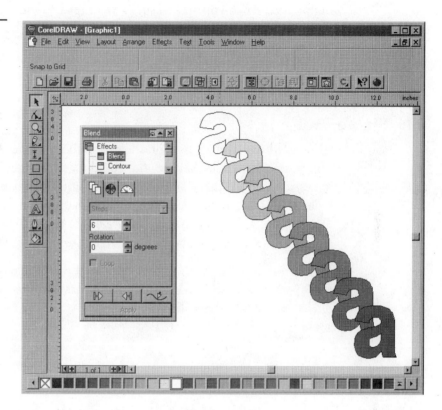

INSIDE INFO

When you drag a marquee around an object or group of objects, you must make sure to completely surround them—*unless you know the new DRAW 6 secret shortcut:* Hold the Alt key while dragging your marquee, and you need only touch an object with the marquee to select it.

However you decide to select an object, once it's selected you also use the Pick tool to move and/or resize it. Most advanced DRAW users take this tool so much for granted that they may not even know its name. They might describe it as "that thing at the top that is always highlighted when you aren't using anything else. You know, the one that pretty much does everything." That about sums up the Pick tool.

Hotkey: the Spacebar, most of the time. When you are editing text, it's Ctrl+Spacebar.

The Shape Tool

Also called the Node Edit tool, the Shape tool presides over parts of an object, not the whole. Where you would reach for the Pick tool to move or resize an entire curve or a whole string of text, the Shape tool provides access to a part of the curve or one character in the text string. The parts of a curve are called *nodes*—hence this tool's other moniker— and by adjusting a node you can change the essential shape of a curve.

In addition to node editing, the Shape tool can edit and kern selected text characters, crop bitmaps, round the corners of rectangles, and turn circles into arcs and pie slices.

Hotkey: F10.

The Zoom Tool

The Zoom tool is one of the most essential aids to creating and editing illustrations, because it lets you work in the optimum magnification. The Toolbox offers you quick access to the Zoom In tool—with which you drag a marquee around the area you want to magnify—and the new Panning tool. The other Zoom commands are available from the View Manager, reached by double-clicking on the Zoom tool, or from the Zoom Toolbar, one of several new toolbars that you can place on screen. All told, DRAW offers you all these ways to zoom:

- Zoom In allows you to define a marquee around the area you want to magnify.

- Zoom Out moves out by a factor of two.

- Actual Size lets you display your drawing at the same size at which it will print.

- Zoom On Selected brings selected objects into the closest possible view.

- Fit In Window brings all objects in a drawing into the closest possible view.

- Show Page displays the entire page.

Hotkeys: F2 for triggering Zoom In mode, F3 for Zoom Out, Shift+F2 for Zoom On Selected, F4 for Fit In Window, and Shift+F4 for Show Page.

The Pencil Tool

 If the Pick tool is the essential editing tool, then the Pencil is the essential creation tool. It is the electronic equivalent of the artist's sketching pencil. The Pencil's primary missions are to support *freehand drawing* and *Bézier drawing*.

Freehand drawing really is like working with a pencil: To draw, you hold the mouse button down and move around the page. If you remember the old Etch-a-Sketch contraptions, you can get a good idea of the type of free-form (and sometimes dreadful) work this tool is capable of.

Bézier drawing creates the smooth curves required by fine art and illustration. When drawing in Bézier mode, you do not hold down the mouse button to create curves. Rather, you click once to define a starting point and then click again to define an ending point. The path that connects the two is treated as a curve or a line whose shape and position can be readily changed. Most of the attractive work you see produced with DRAW makes extensive use of Bézier curves.

Hotkey: F5.

The Dimension Tools

 With this set of six tools, you can create three things:

- Lines that automatically calculate their distances and (new to version 6.0) their angles; Figure 2.7 shows several of these

- Captions that have lines connected to them

■ Lines that will connect and stay connected to two objects (also new to version 6.0), for the purpose of creating flowcharts and organization charts

The Dimension tools are live and dynamic as you move them on screen. Notice the Dimension flyout; as of **DRAW 6**, it can be torn right off the Toolbar and placed on screen.

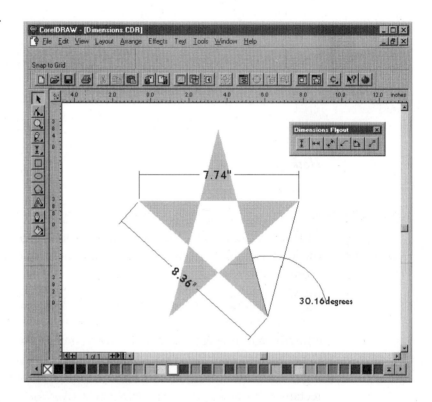

The Rectangle and Ellipse Tools

The first tools most new users reach for—the simple Rectangle and Ellipse tools—produce their respective shapes with simple click-and-drag maneuvers. Once created, these shapes inherit the default outlines and fills that are in effect during the DRAW session.

With both the Rectangle and Ellipse tools, if you hold the Shift key while dragging, the object draws from the center out. If you hold the Ctrl key while dragging, you can create squares and perfect circles.

Hotkeys: F6 for Rectangle, and F7 for Ellipse.

The Polygon Tool

This exciting, powerful (and potentially dangerous) new tool does more than just create stars. It creates dynamic objects with multiple sides, all of which move as you move just one of them. Hidden in the Polygon tool are two other tools, one for making spirals and another for making grids.

Hotkey: None.

The Text Tool

This tool brings the written word to your drawings. By clicking once on the Text icon and then once on the page, you can create *artistic text,* the more versatile of the two text types. This text can be enhanced with all the special effects DRAW has to offer, such as extrusions, blends, and fitting to a path.

When you click and hold the Text tool, you get a *flyout menu* displaying the other text choice—*paragraph text.* You create paragraph text by clicking on its tool and then clicking and dragging on the page to create a rectangular frame into which you type text.

Artistic text is designed for headlines and small strings of text; paragraph text is for larger blocks of copy.

Hotkeys: F8 for artistic text, and Shift+F8 for paragraph text.

The Outline Tool

The Outline tool and the Fill tool (described just below) are an order of magnitude more involved than the tools examined so far. The Outline tool is the one-stop shop for assigning outline colors and widths to any selected objects, be they curves, rectangles, ellipses, or text characters. You can choose from five preset outline thicknesses, and seven percentages of black. Or you can access the Outline Pen dialog or roll-up and treat yourself to a bevy of controls. Clicking on the × button removes any outline from a selected object (just like the × on the color palette at the bottom).

If you use the Outline tool without first selecting an object, DRAW informs you that you are about to change the default, which will affect subsequently drawn objects.

Hotkeys: F12 to reach the Outline Pen dialog, and Shift+F12 for the Outline Color dialog.

The Fill Tool

 Perhaps the richest of all the tools, the Fill tool is the gateway to some simple chores, such as assigning a pure color to an object. It's also what you use for more exotic tasks such as creating a fountain or textured fill. (For simple color fills, you might prefer to use the on-screen color palette.)

When you assign a fill, it affects only the selected object, like the Outline tool (above). If no object is selected, the change is made to the default, filling all subsequent objects. And you can access other dialogs and roll-ups that bring the full power of this tool to your fingertips, just as you can with the Outline tool.

Hotkeys: F11 to reach the Fountain Fill dialog box, and Shift+F11 for the Uniform Fill dialog box.

Figure 2.8 shows one of DRAW's textured fill patterns. Your artistically challenged lead author produced this picture in about 15 minutes. Here are the steps he undertook:

1. Showing incredible cunning and guile, he calmly retrieved DSPSAT.CMX from the clip art supplied with the DRAW software.

2. Then he drew a big rectangle and placed it behind the satellite with Arrange / Order / To Back.

2.8

Fifteen minutes of fame: DRAW's automated features and clip art library make it easy to produce attractive art.

3. Next he clicked on the Fill tool and chose the icon for the Texture Fill dialog (the fifth one on the top row).

4. From Texture Fill he chose the pattern labeled Sky 5 Colors and clicked OK.

5. Last, he saved, printed, and promptly proclaimed it his finest work ever.

You'll find this drawing in the PICTURE directory on the Companion CD of this book, as well as in the Color Gallery as Illustration 1. This is not because your lead author thinks it is actually worthy of admiration, but because we want to show you how quickly and easily you can bring a few elements together into a simple, attractive piece.

Browsing the Menus

As we said earlier, it's possible to produce several simple drawings without having to access the needed functions from DRAW's pull-down menus—especially if you make a habit of using hotkeys such as Ctrl+S (Save) and Ctrl+P (Print). Whether you're a hotkey kind of person or not, though, it's important for you to understand how the menus are laid out and what kind of logical (and in some cases, illogical!) groupings the program employs for its commands.

The File Menu

This menu is DRAW's Grand Central Station, where all files enter and exit. This is the menu from which you open files, save files, import files, export files, and print files (just as it is in practically all Windows pro-

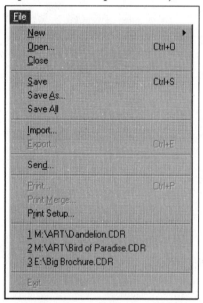

grams). Veteran users will notice something new: the Send command, providing mail and fax capability, via Microsoft Exchange, directly from the File menu.

Note the underlines sprinkled throughout this menu indicating the keyboard alternatives for invoking commands and dialogs, as well as the plethora of hotkeys (Ctrl and Alt key-combinations).

Also, do you notice that the Export command is dimmed? This is DRAW's way of telling you that the command is unavailable. In this instance, you can't use the Export command because there are no objects in this new drawing—nothing created, nothing to export.

The three drawings listed at the bottom of the menu are the most recently opened files. If you wanted to reopen one of them, you could click there, instead of having to choose File / Open and then go find it.

Finally, the … (ellipsis) that follows many of the commands is there to tell you that a dialog or roll-up is lurking underneath. By contrast, commands that perform their entire functions as soon as you activate them—such as Save and Exit—don't have the ellipsis.

The Edit Menu

This menu is in charge of changes, duplications, copying, deleting, cloning, undoing, redoing, and repeating all of the above. As it does in all OLE-compliant programs (that is, programs that support Windows Object Linking and Embedding), the Edit menu acts as the headquarters for all Clipboard activity coming from and going to other programs.

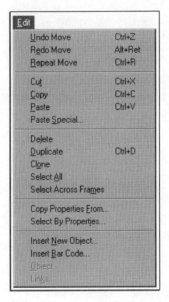

New players on the Edit Menu include the Select By Properties roll-up, which allows you to find, say, all objects that have purple fills. This has been a long-awaited and often-requested feature, but Corel has met its users only halfway (details in the next chapter).

On this menu, the Paste and Paste Special commands are available, indicating that there is an object on the Clipboard, placed there by DRAW or another program.

The View Menu

The View menu takes charge of almost all on-screen activities. These controls let you specify which parts of the DRAW interface you want to make visible or keep hidden, as well as how much detail of your drawing's components you want displayed.

The Layout Menu

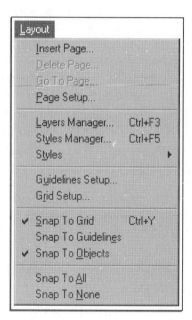

The Layout menu offers controls that address fundamental drawing issues such as page size and number of pages, and the minutiae of laying down the little blue dots that act as guides. Grid, Guideline, and Page setups all reside here, as do the roll-ups for Layers and Styles.

Note the new Snap To All and Snap To None commands, which replace the tedious maneuver of having to toggle three separate snaps.

The Arrange Menu

If it needs to be ordered, layered, aligned, collected, skewed, stretched, moved, taken apart, or put back together again, it's a job for the Arrange menu. Here you can insist that two objects be moved and sized together, with the Group, Combine, or Weld commands, or coupled more exotically with the Intersection and Trim commands.

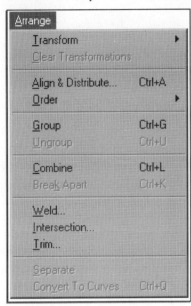

The Order flyout has the commands for moving objects to the front and back and for moving forward and back one place. Like many seasoned DRAW users, you will want to commit to memory the keyboard shortcuts for these commands, because they are nested somewhat inconveniently a level below the other functions in the Order flyout. You'll find the key assignments displayed on the flyout itself.

New to the Arrange menu is Distribute, which lets you ensure that selected objects have the same amount of space separating them.

The Effects Menu

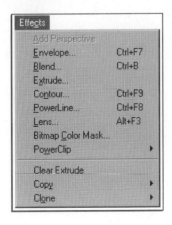

This is DRAW's most happening place, and houses a very lively set of functions. The Effects menu contains the commands that define DRAW's outgoing personality—the blending, extruding, enveloping, masking, and clipping. Here you'll find an utterly absurd assortment of hotkeys. Ctrl+B and Ctrl+E, both inherited from version 3.0, make nice mnemonic sense, but the others are a complete jumble. (Alt+F3 for Lens? Yeah, right.)

This menu is unchanged from DRAW 5, except for the addition of the Bitmap Color Mask roll-up, and the relocation of Transform and Clear Transformations to the Arrange menu.

The Text Menu

The Text menu is your supermarket for text formatting and editing, and a wide assortment of powerful tools can be found here. The Fit Text To Path command is perhaps the most widely used special effect in all of DRAW history.

On the other hand, Proofreading and Thesaurus might be the two least-used commands. As DRAW continues to increase its support for text-heavy documents, these word processing features might see more action; as of now, however, they lie almost dormant. At least, so say our demographic studies across thousands of DRAW 4 and 5 users.

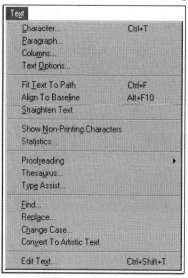

We wrote last year that the new 5.0 feature, Type Assist, would vie for rookie-of-the-year honors. We were wrong. This year, we'll go out on another limb and predict that the Convert To Artistic/Paragraph Text commands, which automatically convert text between the two formats, will share the rookie honors in the Text division.

The Tools Menu

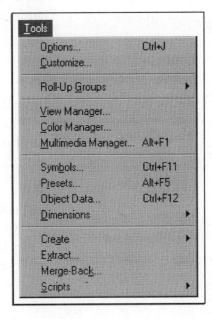

Brand-new to DRAW 6.0, the Tools menu is the electronic equivalent of the tool shed you may have out back, or the large peg board hanging in your garage. Before embarking on a big project, make a stop here and pull down the various tools that you will need along the way. With a few notable exceptions covered in Chapter 3, most of these tools existed in previous versions but were scattered across various menus.

Also on this menu is the nifty Customize dialog, which allows you to decide what goes where, how, when, and why. (Well, okay, maybe not why.)

The Window Menu

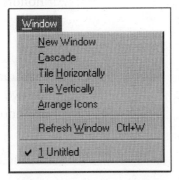

This new menu reflects DRAW 6.0's support for the Multiple Document Interface (MDI). You can now open up more than one drawing at a time, and this menu helps you manage them by giving you a better view and letting you switch among windows. Most regular Windows users have encountered this menu in their other applications.

Perhaps the most overlooked and underrated member of this support team is the Ctrl+W hotkey, which redraws the screen for you—a frequent requirement when you're working with complex and overlapping elements.

♣

Now that you've had a taste of DRAW's tools and menus new and old, you're probably ready to take a closer look at all that is new in DRAW 6.0. Chapter 3 has all the details.

What's New in CorelDRAW 6

This is the third consecutive edition of *Mastering CorelDRAW* in which we are including this chapter—a comprehensive overview of the new features and additions in the latest version of CorelDRAW. We first decided to write this chapter because Corel itself decided not to. In its user guides for DRAW 4 and 5—two robust upgrades—the documentation team devoted no space at all to new features. But we did, and Chapter 3 became immediately popular with our readership.

Corel's online help includes a good overview of the new features of version 6.0, and we are happy to see that. But we are including our What's New chapter, anyway. After all, we started it...

We make two assumptions in this chapter. The first is that practically all of you are new to the operating system, and many Windows 95 issues are salient to DRAW users. (Our definition of adventure: acting as a beta tester for pre-release software, running on a pre-release version of the operating system!) We include several of these issues here in this chapter and will point you to more extensive discussions in later chapters.

Our second assumption is that users most interested in the new features are those that know the old ones. We hope that all DRAW users will find value in Chapter 3, but it is directed primarily to experienced users, ones who have some knowledge of and familiarity with the program.

Finally, we offer our standard qualification from the previous two editions: Don't expect this chapter to be a dry and even-handed recounting of new features. We intend for this chapter—actually, the entire book— to reflect our role as users of the software. So we don't hesitate to add our own commentary, and we won't waste your time with phrases like "in our opinion" and "if you ask us." We know that you didn't ask us, and you might not give a hoot about our opinions. But you did buy our book, so now you're stuck with us, bias and all.

AUTHOR'S NOTE

This chapter focuses on changes to the DRAW module. Part VIII, "The Supporting Cast," describes the program's other modules.

Have It Your Way

DRAW 6.0 has some nice new features, no question. But we start here with what promises to be front-page news for advanced users, and a significant development for all who expect to use the program regularly. We refer to DRAW's new interface. It provides a level of flexibility never before seen in any Corel product. Part IV of this book gives you the details on these exciting new interface additions, but this chapter lets experienced users get their feet wet right away.

For starters, if you don't like one of DRAW's keyboard shortcuts or you wish a particular function had one, wish no longer. Instead, go to Tools / Customize and change or add that shortcut. Every command in DRAW's menus is available for key assignment or reassignment, from an easy-to-use menu. For instance, we export drawings far more often than we extrude objects, and so would prefer to have Ctrl+E trigger File / Export instead of Effects / Extrude. Figure 3.1 shows how easy it is to make this change.

As you can see from Figure 3.1, your ability to customize commands goes far beyond keyboard shortcuts. You can also rearrange menus and add items to them, determine how roll-ups behave, and edit existing toolbars or create your own. As we mentioned in Chapter 2, we like DRAW 6.0's Standard Toolbar (formerly called the ribbon bar)—now that we can tailor it to suit our own needs. We don't need icons for Save

3.1

DRAW's new Customize dialog gives you uncommon control over the interface.

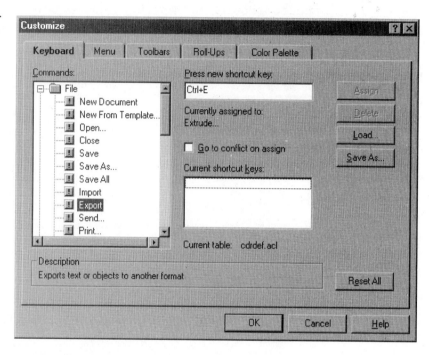

and Print, because Ctrl+S and Ctrl+P are just as easy. But we do want icons for invoking the Import dialog, for getting to Print Setup, and for several other out-of-the-way commands that we use frequently.

We also found several commands that existed nowhere *except* in the Customize dialog. For instance, we aren't too thrilled with the new combined Intersection/Trim/Weld roll-up, which requires too much futzing around when all you want is a quick trim or weld between two selected objects. Then guess what we found in the list of commands under Customize: Quick Intersection, Quick Trim, and Quick Weld. By adding them to the Arrange menu, we can now use those three commands in the way we prefer—the way they functioned in version 5.

Figure 3.2 shows a version of the Toolbar we have just finished designing to better suit our needs. The commands we chose are (from left to right) Import, Export, Print Setup, Select All, Character Attributes, Paragraph Attributes, the Symbols roll-up, four different pattern fills, the Save Style command, Multimedia Manager (formerly Mosaic), regular Help, and context-sensitive Help.

3.2

Now *here's* a useful Toolbar, with commands that otherwise require multiple clicks to access.

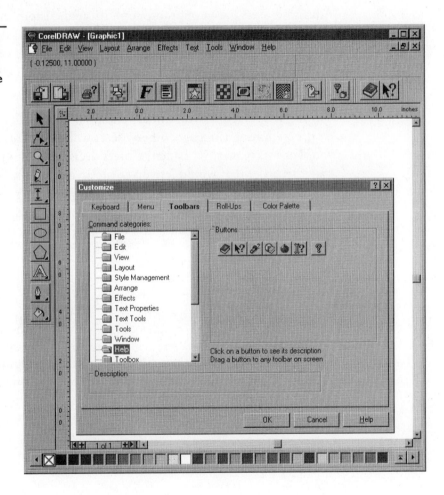

AUTHOR'S NOTE

In Chapter 15, we will do this toolbar customization step-by-step, as well as examine some advanced customization options.

Write Your Own Scripts

Advanced users have even more sophisticated customization tools, via the new Script and Dialog editors. With these powerful applications, you can develop strings of commands—like, say, invoke Export, choose .EPS format, specify IMAGE.EPS as the file name, include an 8-bit image header, use 128 fountain stripes, and go.

Writing scripts requires an understanding of Visual Basic or some similar programming language; otherwise, it will seem like rocket science to you. For this reason, we lament Corel's decision not to include an automatic recorder that would let you create scripts simply by going through the motions (like DRAW's Preset function). Without this, the Script Editor remains very much a tool for the privileged. Figure 3.3 shows what the code looks like for a task even as relatively simple as creating the Corel logo.

The fruits of your labor will ripen when you take your scripts, turn them into icons, and place them directly on toolbars. This is the zenith of customization. (Well, okay, the true zenith is being able to invoke a command by thinking of it; this is close.)

We suspect Corel wants to include a recorder, but couldn't implement it by DRAW 6.0's original release date. Look for it in one of the maintenance updates.

3.3

Writing scripts with Corel's new editor is not exactly an intuitive procedure.

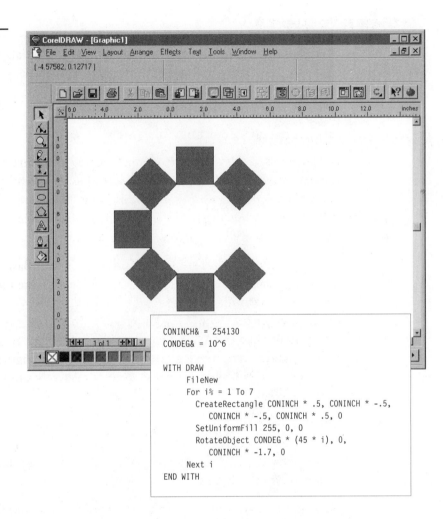

```
CONINCH& = 254130
CONDEG& = 10^6

WITH DRAW
    FileNew
    For i% = 1 To 7
        CreateRectangle CONINCH * .5, CONINCH * -.5,
            CONINCH * -.5, CONINCH * .5, 0
        SetUniformFill 255, 0, 0
        RotateObject CONDEG * (45 * i), 0,
            CONINCH * -1.7, 0
    Next i
END WITH
```

Move Anything Anywhere

Another indication that DRAW 6.0 is quite different from previous releases is the fact that no part of the interface (except the menus) any longer has roots. Default positions, yes; roots, no. You can pick up any tool and reposition it, change the location of the status bar, move the Color Palette, and—most intriguing—create your own little toolboxes by "tearing off" icons from other tools.

In Figure 3.2, you saw the Customize dialog in action creating a toolbar. Now take a look at Figure 3.4, where we created all sorts of toolbars, just by tearing off other tools' flyouts. The Toolbox, Standard Toolbar, and Color Palette are all floating, along with several other toolbars that were torn from other places. The observant reader will note that we even created a brand new toolbar, called Crazy.

3.4

The sky (or at least the screen size) is the limit when it comes to the number and type of toolbars that you can create.

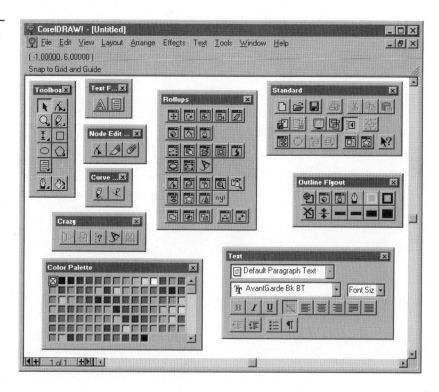

The point of all of this is not to clutter up your screen as much as we have done. On the contrary, it is to give you more control over your workspace. We're in the conference and seminar business, and one of our most significant constraints is that of presenting CorelDRAW on a 640×480 display (the maximum resolution allowed by most projectors). So we need all the vertical space that we can muster.

3.5

With the movable parts placed along the sides, a standard portrait page can be displayed at closer range.

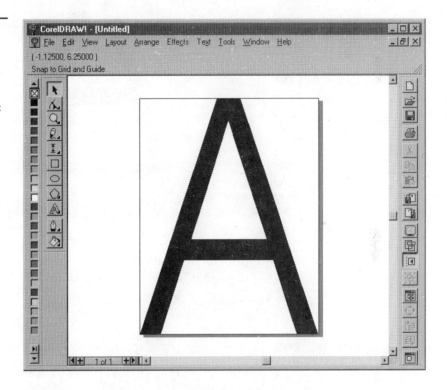

We suspect that Figure 3.5 will represent the default environment for our presentation computers using DRAW 6.0. Notice how much extra space we have acquired by moving the Standard Toolbar and Color Palette to the sides. For comparison, Figure 3.6 shows the traditional workspace. You can see that the full-page character on the screen is much larger in Figure 3.5.

3.6

This traditionally arranged DRAW screen has much less vertical space than our customized one.

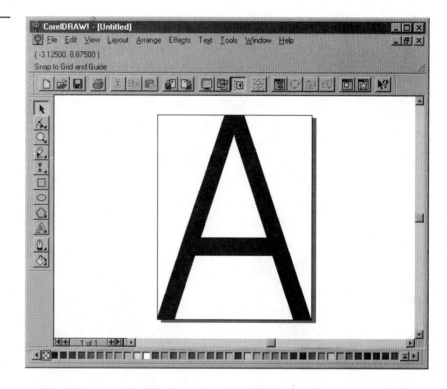

If you work mostly in landscape, you would want to do just the opposite and move the Toolbox along the top or bottom. And that's exactly the point: You now have the freedom to do so.

Get Lots of Status

DRAW's status bar has always offered lots of information in its six panels. It, too, can be customized in DRAW 6.0. Right-click on any panel of the status bar and then decide for yourself what type of information to display in that panel, as well as what size it will be. You can choose between one column or two and between two rows (DRAW calls them "panels") and six. As in previous versions, you can decide to have the status bar at the top of the screen or at the bottom (the default), though we have yet to meet a user who leaves it at the bottom once they know they can move it to the top.

Right-Click 'til You Drop

The third significant interface feature involves the previously underused Button 2 on the mouse (the right button for most users, and hence the term "right-click"). With Windows 95, Microsoft has promoted right-clicking in a big way, and Corel has followed suit. The secondary mouse button *always* brings up a context-sensitive menu of functions and commands.

Our advice to you is simple: Right-click on everything! We suspect there must be an underlying scheme to Corel's implementation of right-clicking, but it defies description and is impossible to remember. So instead, just right-click on every possible screen element, every object, tool, and icon, and take note of all the options that present themselves.

AUTHOR'S NOTE

When we give instructions throughout the book, most of the time we will stick to the old-fashioned way of invoking commands: pulling down menus and choosing items from there (or from established hotkeys). You are free to take other routes as you like, such as right-clicking, going to a custom toolbar, or a script.

Oh No! What About My Shortcuts?   Like us, you may be accustomed to assigning a global shortcut to Button 2 on your mouse—say, for access to Node Edit or Full Screen Preview, perhaps. If so, you may be upset by the new Windows 95 role for the secondary mouse button. But don't despair—you can still select one of your traditional shortcuts to appear as the first item on all of the pop-up menus. You'll find the list of available choices under Tools / Options / Advanced / PopUp Menu Customization / First Menu Item.

Functionality Loves Company

Functionally speaking, the big events in DRAW 6.0 are about roll-ups and multiple windows.

Roll-up Families

Roll-ups can now be coupled with other roll-ups, which promises to make life a bit easier on screens with limited resolution. Figure 3.7 shows two of DRAW's roll-ups, Symbols and Presets, merged into one group. We did this by holding Ctrl while dragging one title bar over another. Then we clicked on the generic name New Group 1 and renamed it Automatic Objects.

3.7

By grouping roll-ups, you can save screen real estate and couple similar functions.

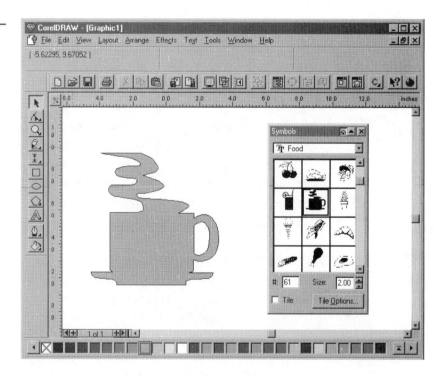

Roll-ups have a new element—the push pin. You can see it on the title bar of the roll-up in Figure 3.7. (We think it looks more like a mushroom cloud than a push pin.) Click it and it pops up; until you tell it otherwise, that roll-up will function as a dialog, going away after you use it. This has been a long-standing complaint about many roll-ups that served one-time needs. Now you can decide which roll-ups will be "modal," and which ones "modeless."

Have Seconds…and Then Thirds

DRAW now supports the Multiple Document Interface (MDI). In DRAW 6.0 you can open several drawings within the same session and, equally handy, multiple windows of the same drawing. You can work at close range in one window while another window shows the entire drawing.

Is 32-Bit Better?

Most of us watching the coming of the Age of Windows 95 have associated "32-bit processing" with "faster computing." By and large, this is true; it is also only half the story. We heard early complaints by users that "DRAW 6.0 isn't faster than DRAW 5—in fact, it's slower." But when we inquired further, these users all acknowledged that they were using as their yardstick everybody's favorite barometer of performance: How fast does it load?

As with every version before it, DRAW 6.0 loses out in the race from the Desktop icon double-click to the appearance of page borders on screen. DRAW 6.0 loads considerably more code than its predecessors, and our stopwatch reports that DRAW 5 loads in 15 seconds on a 486DX2, while DRAW 6.0 needs 20 seconds.

Performance in the Clutch

Okay, fine—now let's get to the stuff that matters. DRAW 6.0 clocked in faster than DRAW 5, sometimes significantly so, in virtually all of our tests. See Table 3.1.

And now—the rest of the story…

Huge Numbers, Tiny Numbers

Indeed, 32-bit processing brings more than just speed. In DRAW, it brings greater precision and larger capacity for text characters and grouped elements.

Table 3.1:   Our Performance Tests for DRAW 6.0

TASK	DRAW 5	DRAW 6.0
Load a 1.4MB TIFF file	15.23	10.46
Redraw the 1.4MB TIFF file	5.09	1.11
Contour a capital S	2.10.00	1.20.00
Create a shaded extrusion	20.53	12.78
A 360-step blend	7.34	6.13
A 64-step blend between fountain-filled objects	15.62	6.37

AUTHOR'S NOTE

We think it's safe to say that no output device in the world is capable of resolution better than .001 mm, so those two additional decimal places are, shall we say, phony precision. Sure, it's good that DRAW uses the maximum available precision internally, to avoid errors in rounding off and in unit conversion. But we doubt you'll have much legitimate use for those two additional decimal places, except maybe in very large scale drawings.

Object controls that used to be precise only out to one or two decimals are now precise out to five decimals. If you want to move a rectangle .00001 millimeters from its current position, now you can do it. Same with rotation, scaling, and all of the other controls in the Transform roll-up.

And if it's big you want, you have come to the right place. Sign makers won't have to resort to go-between software for printing banners larger than 30". Now you can print up to about 176 feet, and a string or frame of text can hold (gulp) 32,000 characters.

Most of this is made possible by the move to 32-bit computing.

New Features

What would a new version of DRAW be without new features? As if a revamped interface and migration to a brand-new operating system isn't enough, DRAW 6.0 sports several additional tools—enough to justify this upgrade on their own merits. Here is a browse through DRAW 6.0's new players.

Erasing and Cutting

As extensions to node editing, with DRAW 6.0 you can cut with a knife and remove with an eraser. Instead of taking up residence in the Arrange menu where you will find similar tools, Knife and Eraser live in the Shape tool flyout.

Knife is a quick-and-dirty version of Trim. With Trim you create an object that becomes the trimming tool, and as such, you have the opportunity for extraordinary precision. By contrast, Knife lets you trim on the fly, simply by clicking on the periphery of an object.

Eraser works just like the one on your pencil; you drag it around an object to eliminate the parts.

For both Knife and Eraser, behind the scenes DRAW converts the object to curves (if necessary), adds nodes along the cutting or erasing path, and removes them or fuses others together. Neither tool does anything that you couldn't do with the Shape tool and the Node Edit rollup, but Knife and Eraser do it much faster.

These tools work on individual objects, not groups, and will work on objects that are filled or hollow.

Figure 3.8 shows the result of taking Knife and Eraser to a simple circle.

3.8

Knife and Eraser doing their things to a circle

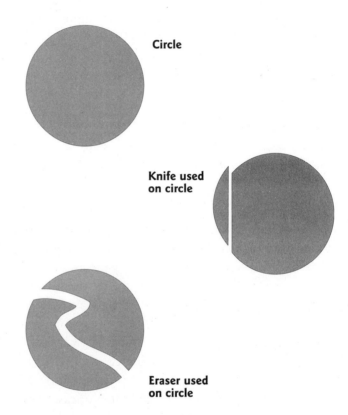

Circle

Knife used on circle

Eraser used on circle

The Search for Missing Paths

Conventional node editing, as well, has received a face-lift in DRAW 6.0, although early reports are mixed as to whether it is a turn for the better or worse.

The Add Line Segment command will be quite helpful in tracking down open paths. In Figure 3.9, for instance, the object looks to be completely closed, yet it won't take a fill pattern—a sure-fire indication that the path is actually open. Upon close inspection, you'll find that one corner, which looks closed, is actually two nodes only a few pixels apart.

3.9

Searching for open paths is no longer needed, thanks to Add Line Segment.

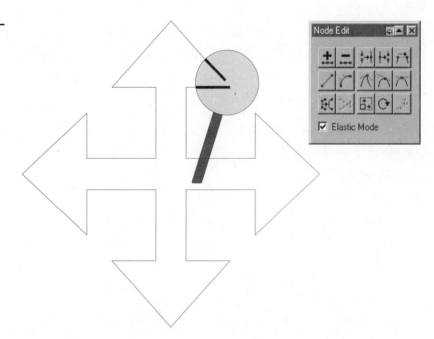

Finding these open paths can sometimes be difficult, and so DRAW 6.0 supplies a detective in the Node Edit roll-up. Select the nodes of an object and click on Add Line Segment (the top-right icon), and DRAW automatically finds the area(s) where the curve's path needs to be closed, and adds a line between the two nodes.

Why are early reviews mixed? Take a look at the roll-up in Figure 3.9 and you'll see that Corel has gone icon-happy. Beta testers wondered why buttons that simply displayed "Line," "Curve," and "Auto-Reduce" were replaced with all these icons, most of which are too similar in appearance to be useful. Early users have resorted to just remembering them by position. Fortunately, you can also right-click on a node to reach many of the node-editing functions.

Nodes? On Bitmaps??

No, the last we knew, nodes were reserved for vector-based objects. Corel's creative developers, however, have turned the Shape tool into a free-form cropping tool for use with bitmap images. Node editing of bitmaps and curves is performed the same way, but as Figure 3.10 shows, the results can be striking. In this bitmapped image, you can see the control points emanating from the selected nodes along the lower-right portion.

New Objects

DRAW 6.0 sports one new addition to its Toolbox—a flyout that offers three new shapes: polygons, spirals, and grids. Spirals are kind of cool, and grids are nothing more than a bunch of grouped rectangles. But the polygon tool is noteworthy for its symmetrical action. Once you have the polygon created, select a node with the Shape tool and move it; all similar nodes respond in kind. Corel calls this *mirror editing,* and it definitely simplifies the creation of custom stars and other multisided objects.

Making Arrangements

In addition to the standard set of layering choices, DRAW 6.0 offers two more: In Front Of and Behind. With these new options, you can specify that one object be placed right behind or in front of another object, without having to fuss with sending one all the way to the back or trying to go one object at a time. When you invoke either function, DRAW displays a pointer to identify the second object.

3.10

Fancy cropping comes to DRAW 6.0.

The Distribute command makes its debut with DRAW 6.0 after many requests. Figure 3.11 shows the kind of quick work Distribute can make of positioning a group of objects that need equal spacing among them. The objects in the column on the left are placed haphazardly, and in previous versions of DRAW you would have needed a careful and trying session with grid snaps or guidelines to space the objects evenly. The column on the right shows the same objects, after Distribute has done its work.

The only drawback to Distribute is the company it keeps. It has been housed with the familiar Align functions, and although this makes a certain logical sense, it reveals more icon-happiness on the part of Corel. Those who used Align regularly in DRAW 4 and 5 knew the shortcuts

3.11

The Distribute command makes quick work out of "equidistance."

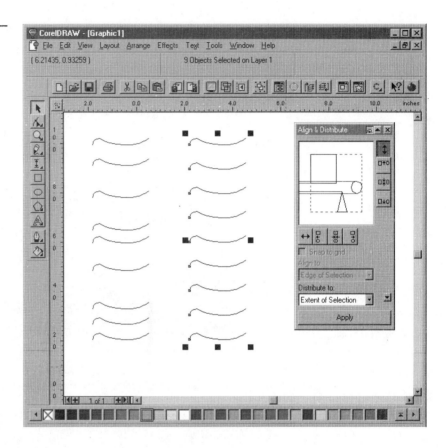

by heart; unfortunately, they're all gone in DRAW 6.0. Using Distribute and Align is now a mouse-only proposition. Gone are the good old days when a quick Ctrl+A, C, Enter was enough to place two objects one on top of the other.

One more item on the subject of arranging objects: The ever-valuable guidelines just got more valuable. Now you can create them at any angle you wish.

And finally, you'll find two other new additions to help you when working with objects. Treat All Objects As Filled makes it easier to select and move objects that have no fill. To turn this on, right-click on the Pick tool and choose Properties. Then you can click on the interior, even if it is hollow. The second addition is "marquee-select by touching." (We made that up; the feature doesn't seem to have a name.) This very handy maneuver lets you press Alt while dragging a marquee around objects and be spared having to completely surround each object. Just touch the object or group with the marquee and it becomes selected.

New Special Effects

There are two noteworthy additions to the Effects menu. First, Bitmap Color Mask enables you to identify certain colors in an imported bitmap image and assign varying degrees of transparency to them. Figure 3.12 shows a nice picture of a butterfly (original, top-left) and three radical variations of it, with certain colors being set to transparent.

3.12

Bitmap Color Mask can cut holes in pictures at particular colors.

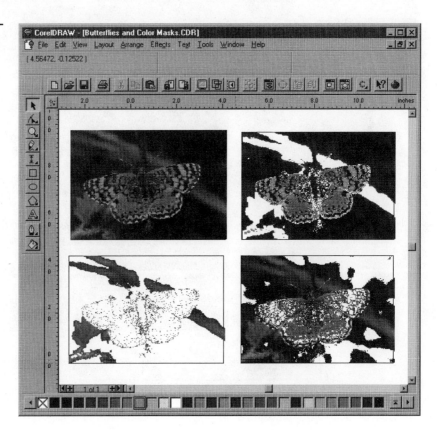

The Lens roll-up, as well, has seen significant work. It now sports several new perspectives on life as DRAW knows it. To the existing eight lenses, DRAW 6.0 offers a Custom Color Map lens, handy for creating negatives of images; a Wireframe lens; and a Fish Eye lens. Figure 3.13 demonstrates two of these new lenses.

AUTHOR'S NOTE

You can read all about DRAW's lens effects, new and old, in Chapter 22.

3.13

Two of DRAW's three new lenses—Custom Color Map (the left oval) and Wireframe

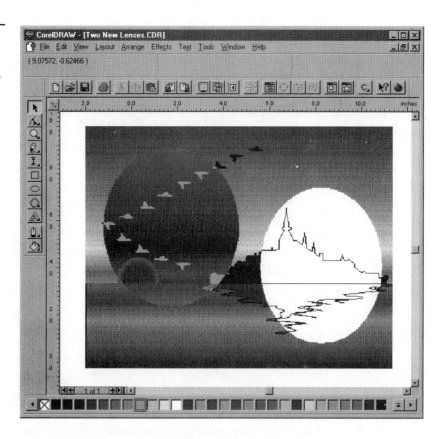

Furthermore, Corel has taken the camera analogy an extra step, adding the capability of taking snapshots through the lenses and moving the resulting picture to another place in your drawing. When you click the Frozen button, the image showing through the lens becomes permanent and no longer requires the originating object. Also, with the Edit Viewpoint controls you can move your "camera" to a different angle and take the picture from there.

Finally in the area of Effects, you might find it interesting (well, moderately interesting…okay, so it's trivial) to learn that PowerLines have some added functionality. Once drawn, you can convert a PowerLine to curves, delete the original line, and reduce nodes all in one step. It's this last part, the auto-reduce, that will be the most welcome, because the one big knock on PowerLine has been its propensity for creating dozens, in some cases hundreds, of excess nodes.

New Viewing Tools

The method for viewing a drawing has undergone evolution as well as revolution. Zooming is now a "tool," which means it behaves like the other objects that are now called tools. You probably couldn't care less about whether it's called a tool or a function or a game of checkers, but Corel has chosen to adopt the Windows 95 conventions for how tools behave. (In fact, many of DRAW's beta testers believe Corel didn't know where to stop. The Zoom tools are at the center of this little controversy.)

First off, the Zoom icon in the Toolbox now provides only two functions—marquee-zooming and, new to DRAW 6.0, a Panning function for quick movement to other parts of the screen. In order to get at the other zooming functions, you must double-click the Zoom icon to invoke the View Manager, or activate the Zoom Toolbar.

This has frustrated users in the early going. When you reach for the Zoom tool, it's with the intent of moving in or out for a different look, right? Chances are good that you want to do this once and then be done with it. But a Windows 95 tool stays around until you explicitly tell it to leave, and because the Zoom Manager roll-up and the Zoom flyout are "tools," they hang around long after you need them. You can use the push pin to make the Zoom Manager be "modal," but this is still a much more unwieldy arrangement than in version 5.

Here are three ways you can respond to these changes:

- If you normally use the hotkeys for zooming (F2, F3, F4, Shift+F2, and Shift+F4), then your work habits won't change at all, because all of the hotkeys have been maintained.

- You can take the Zoom Toolbar and permanently attach it to the Toolbox or the Toolbar. Then you end up with better access than you had in DRAW 5, since all of the Zoom tools are one click away instead of nested within a flyout.

- Click once on the Zoom icon and then right-click on the page. All of your zooming options will be at your mouse tips. After your zoom, press Spacebar to return to the previous tool.

The new Zoom Manager might be overkill for a simple zoom in to or out from an object, but it is a very handy tool for projects with well-defined zoom requirements, perhaps even spanning across several pages. Each time you zoom in or out, you can add that zoom state to the View Manager, not unlike a preset. For each zoom preset, DRAW remembers the page, the area on the page, and the magnification. To move from one zoom preset to another, you just double-click in the View Manager.

AUTHOR'S NOTE

We predict that View Manager will go from unheralded to most valuable player status through the life of version 6.0.

This will prove an awesome tool for those who work with complex drawings and are saddled with long redraw times. View Manager lets you whisk yourself from a close-up view of one object to a close-up of another, without having to first zoom out and then zoom back in or, worse, scroll over.

Finally, the Panning tool allows you to scroll without using the scroll bars. This is significant because scroll bar action is strictly vertical and horizontal; the Panning tool can move in any direction. It takes a bit of practice at first, but you'll catch on quickly. Typical of us, we wish that Panning had a hotkey—especially since Shift+F3 is just sitting there in the midst of two other zoom functions, just waiting for action. So we took it, thanks to the Customize Keyboard services.

New Text Handling

Once again, changes to the interface steal the headlines. DRAW has thrown out the Text roll-up, replacing it with a Toolbar that can float on or be anchored to the screen. The Text Toolbar provides access to all of the commonly-used text formatting tools, including the font preview window.

The other notable addition to the typesetting arsenal is support for line breaks within paragraphs of copy. Removal of this long-standing thorn in the sides of users will be welcomed everywhere. It means we can finally break a line of copy or set multideck headlines without having to worry about spacing between paragraphs getting in the way. Shift+Enter inserts a line break, as it does in most other programs that you work with.

Other changes to text handling include the following:

- Kerning for selected text.
- An impressive Proofreading engine that checks spelling, grammar, and syntax.
- Force-justification of paragraph text.
- Leader tabs.
- Added controls for underline, overscore, and strikethrough.
- A Change Case command.
- Ability to break apart text. Arrange / Break Apart works with both artistic and paragraph text, separating it first into separate lines and then—in the case of artistic text—into separate words.

- On-screen editing of text along a path, instead of having to go to the Edit Text window.

- An automatic converter between artistic and paragraph text.

These text enhancements aren't blockbuster improvements, and that is either good news or bad, depending upon your point of view. If you belong to the "ain't broke, don't fix it" school, you don't mind DRAW's text-handling methods. You appreciate not being force-fed a bunch of new features and are happy with increased convenience and a few well-conceived additions.

On the other hand, we have been listening to the loud collective voice of typesetting purists asking for more and smarter typesetting controls, for the last three versions of the program. This group is still waiting for

- Hyphenation support that includes manual control, a library of exceptions, and a limit on successive hyphenations.

- Justification that supports minimum and maximum word spacing and more flexibility in letter spacing.

- Interactive text kerning with keyboard controls.

- Character width control, to support condensed and expanded variations of a typeface.

From this group comes the annual battle cry: "Maybe next year…"

A DRAW 6.0 Potpourri

Here is a sampling of various little fixes, tweaks, and featurettes in this new release, including Windows 95-related items.

CorelDRAW Stuff

Let's begin with the application itself.

Better Typeface Names   It took years of clamoring, but users finally succeeded in convincing Corel to change the names of the typeface files. Since version 3.0 we have been saddled with such unintelligible, unintuitive file names as C031016T.TTF for the typeface Castle-Bold.

Changing the typeface file name in no way upsets your typeface configuration. A drawing that requires, say, Brittanic Light will be able to find it in your system regardless of Brittanic Light's file name.

Large Color Swatches   If you are using a custom palette with few colors, you can ask for color swatches larger than the normal tiny square. To do this, right-click on the Color Palette, select Customize, and turn on Large Swatches.

Better PostScript Textures   We know that many DRAW users haven't taken the time to learn the PostScript texture patterns, given that they are complex and ungraphical (that is, you couldn't see what you were choosing until you printed it). But now PostScript textures are visible in a preview window and they will print to non-PostScript printers (though they still do not display on the page).

Better Presets   Version 6.0 has added several new features to Presets, all with an eye toward better usability and portability:

- *Merge Presets:* Presets from another file can be merged with the current presets. This way, when your colleague has produced a cool preset and wants to share it with you, he or she can do so without overwriting all of yours.

- *Alternate Presets:* Presets from another file can replace without eliminating the current presets.

- *Edit Colors:* You can modify a preset to change the fill or outline color that was recorded when the preset was originally created.

- *Change Thumbnail:* You can modify, add, or delete the thumbnail associated with a preset.

No More Stupid Styles   Yay! Corel has maintained the intelligence of styles, but eliminated the stupidity of templates. Now when you save styles, DRAW no longer incessantly asks you about saving the template.

The styles are stored with the .CDR file, as always, and are only incorporated into the current template if you explicitly save it.

Printing Improvements   The Clone Frame feature introduced in the version 5 print engine was an impressive feature for those who wanted two-up or three-up print jobs. Version 6.0 does that one better for printing on labels: There is direct support for label printing all the way down to product ID numbers from standard suppliers, such as Ace and Avery. When you choose Label as the page size in Page Setup, DRAW offers several hundred label types and creates a page that is the size of one label. When you go to print, DRAW programs the Clone Frame button to exactly match the page specs for that label.

Another key printing improvement is the Auto-Increase Fountain Steps feature, which calculates the optimum Steps setting for fountain fills, based on resolution and line screen settings.

The enhancements to the print engine are significant and many—too numerous to detail here. We refer you to the "Print, Darn You!" chapter for specifics on all of DRAW's new printing features.

Connector Lines   An extension of DRAW's dimension lines, connector lines create a live link between two objects, for use in projects such as org charts. Connector lines cannot themselves be moved; you must move the objects they are connected to.

In a related development, the new callout lines are much better than the Caption tool that was part of dimension lines in version 5.

Mega Groups   The maximum number of groups that could be nested below another group used to be 10. Now you can create groups that contain up to 99 subgroups.

Select By Properties   This command allows you to search for specific object characteristics. For example, you can search for all ellipses or rectangles with blue outlines or particular fountain fills, or for all text strings.

This new feature would have received much better billing—perhaps top billing—if it had lived up to its initial promise of being a search-and-replace engine. (A search engine isn't much good if you can't act upon the objects that are found.) Corel was unable to provide this long-requested item in a fully functioning form, and is hoping that you'll find some uses for it as is. We're not so sure...

Smarter Saves   DRAW 6.0 offers what it calls a *persistent thumbnail,* which saves time when you're making small changes to large drawings. In the Save As dialog, by choosing Current in the Thumbnail drop-down box you tell DRAW to save the changes but not to update the thumbnail. (Oftentimes, the little bitmap thumbnail takes longer to update than the actual code in the drawing.)

Windows 95 Stuff

As most of us begin to get up to speed with Windows 95, it is likely we will find elements that we love and others that we don't. You have probably already discovered that the Desktop can house pretty much anything imaginable, and not just icons or groups (now called folders). You might have already taken a liking to the Start button, programmable with any type of hierarchy you might want, including folders of DRAW templates or other frequently opened files.

Following are some of the notable Windows 95 elements that have implications for DRAW users. You'll find more extensive discussions of these topics in Appendix C, our traditional "Junk & Miscellany."

Longer File Names   File names under Windows 95 have broken out of the 8.3 constraint that has defined them since the beginning of time (1981), and can now be practically any length at all.

Auto-Loading of CDs   Windows 95 has built-in support for CDs to automatically start themselves when inserted into the drive. The CorelDRAW CD automatically runs Setup when you insert the disk. This proved to be a very controversial issue during beta testing, and we'll be more candid with our feelings about it in the Junk & Miscellany appendix.

The Desktop   The Windows 95 Desktop can wind up looking a lot like your actual desktop if you're not careful, because you can store any amount of junk there that you want. This includes scraps of drawings that you want to stash somewhere for the time being. Just drag them from DRAW onto the Desktop, and Windows will automatically create icons for them. When you want to use one of them, just drag it back to DRAW.

Font Management   Windows 95 has revamped its scheme for managing installed fonts, and though it might be transparent to the casual user, it will be profoundly different for curious users who explore under the hood. See Appendix A for more on this.

Uninstall   Windows 95 applications that are installed can also be uninstalled. Go to Control Panel / Add/Remove Programs for a list of all programs that can be safely removed; DRAW 6.0 should be on the list.

Document-centricity   What does that mouthful mean? Simply that Microsoft wants you to have the opportunity to view your document, not the application, as the central player in your game. Instead of launching an application and then opening a file, Windows 95 makes it easier for you to simply "launch a file." Do you organize your drawings into directories or folders based on their projects? By adding a shortcut to one of those folders to your Desktop, you are only two double-clicks away from any document (one double-click on the shortcut, another on the document). By leaving the current project folder open on the Desktop, one double-click gets you the document you want.

Looking Back...

We note with interest and optimism that many of the elements we cited as missing in the last version have made it into DRAW 6.0. Our list of 1994 wishes in *Mastering CorelDRAW 5* was compiled mostly from users from whom we heard throughout the year. Judging from that list, Corel did a pretty good job of playing Santa. Here is a summary:

■ **Multiple Document Architecture:** Users wanted it in 1994; Corel added it in 1995.

- **Uninstall:** With Windows 95 supporting an uninstall procedure at the OS level, this was easy for Corel to include.

- **Keystroke access in roll-ups:** Still no luck. Roll-ups are largely a mouse-only activity. But now you can make them go away after each use.

- **Smart Save:** Still no luck, although this might be added in a maintenance release.

- **Quick replacement of colors:** Corel flirted with search and replace but gave us only search. There still is no way to find all instances of one color and replace them with another.

- **Distribute:** In there.

- **Controls for underlining:** In there.

- **Forced justification:** In there.

- **Condensed and expanded type:** Still absent.

- **Forced line breaks:** In there.

In our next chapter, we dive into the CorelDRAW gene pool and look at The Miracle of the Curve.

The Miracle of the Click

e mentioned it in Chapter 2 and it bears repeating here: The
manual skills required to operate DRAW are not hard to acquire. They consist mostly of clicking, double-clicking, and
a bit of dragging. Don't misconstrue this to mean that producing beautiful work in DRAW is easy; manual skills and design expertise are two
entirely different things. Only a little can we help you with the latter,
but we can get you up and running nicely with the former, and that's
what this chapter is all about.

Working with Objects

There are five ways to place an object into a DRAW file: You can create
it yourself; you can import a piece of clip art; you can paste it from another program across the Clipboard; you can drag artwork from another
application and drop it into DRAW; or you can get it from DRAW's online Symbols library. Regardless of their origin, all these objects behave
the same once they arrive. They are all subject to (drumroll, please)
Altman's Laws of DRAW.

Altman's Laws of DRAW proclaim the following rules for objects:

- Thou shalt be selectable by the mouse.
- Thou shalt be at liberty to move about the page.
- Thou shalt be free to be resized, reshaped, and rotated.
- Thou shalt include an outline, which can be colored and
  thickened.

■ If thou art a closed object, thou shalt accept an internal color, tint, or pattern.

■ Thou shalt be disconnectable.

Only one type of object is exempt from these laws: bitmap images that are imported or pasted into DRAW (discussed later in the chapter). Bitmap images cannot be filled, outlined, or taken apart, but they can be sized, shaped, and rotated. All the rest (all vector objects) follow the CorelDRAW fold.

Creating, Moving, and Changing Objects

If you have used Windows applications at all, you already know how to create an object, and as we said earlier in the book, you could probably get behind DRAW's steering wheel and create an ellipse or a rectangle on your first try. The simple *click-and-drag* maneuver is all that's required. Creating lines and Bezier curves is a bit more involved than ellipses and rectangles, and that technique will get a starring role in the next two chapters.

To get started with objects in DRAW, the only other things you need to know are how the click and double-click work: One click selects objects on the page or colors from the on-screen palette; and two quick clicks selects files from various dialogs (Open, Import, Save, Export, and so forth). You'll always know when an object in a drawing is selected, because it grows little black handles around its periphery.

INSIDE INFO

Not quite getting the hang of the double-click? Maybe it's your mouse that needs a bit of taming. From the Windows 95 Start menu, choose Settings / Control Panel, and then Mouse / Buttons / Double-Click Speed. By moving the slider in the "Slower" direction, you can personalize double-clicking to the slower speed you need.

The click-and-drag is indeed the handiest maneuver of all. It is responsible for accomplishing many tasks in DRAW:

- To move a selected object that is filled with a color or shade, click anywhere inside the object, keep the button down, and drag the object to where you want it. You can do this to unfilled objects also, if you go to the Pick tool Properties and activate Treat All Objects As Filled. Otherwise...

- To move an unfilled object, click anywhere on its outline, hold the button down, and drag the object to where you want it.

- To change the shape of an object, click on one of its handles, hold the button down, and drag the handle to another position.

- To rotate or skew an object, select it, click again, and then click and drag on one of the arrows, as shown in Figure 4.1.

There are several other handy controls for moving objects. One is the Position command from Arrange / Transform, whose controls enable you to move an object within tolerances of .001 pt. Another is to use the Ctrl key while dragging an object. By holding Ctrl as you drag, an object is constrained to move either up and down or side to side, but nothing in between.

The Ctrl key might become your best friend in DRAW, because it provides precision in many different situations. For instance:

- Hold Ctrl while rotating an object, and rotation is constrained to 15° increments.

- Hold Ctrl while sizing an object, and sizing is constrained to whole increments. You can double the size of the object, or triple it, and so on, but nothing in between.

- Hold Ctrl while working the preview in Fountain Fill, and you constrain the fill angles to 15°.

4.1

The click-and-drag technique is responsible for many feats within DRAW, including the rotation of this suave gentleman.

AUTHOR'S NOTE

In DRAW, think of CONtrol as an abbreviation for CONstrain.

You've probably already realized it: DRAW can't do diddly to an object on the page until you first select it. That's how you call the object to DRAW's attention. When you have a few simple objects on a page, selecting the objects is easy; but as your drawing board becomes more crowded, selecting will become more challenging.

For Teeny-Weeny Motion, Be a Nudge

There is some debate as to how this feature is pronounced. Most DRAW users go with *nudj*, rhyming with *fudge*. Those of you influenced by a bit of Hebrew or Yiddish (or a New York state of mind) will prefer *noodge*. However you say it, the definition is the same: to poke or prod along. Nudge is one of DRAW's handiest features, allowing you to move objects with exceptional precision using your arrow keys. Through Tools / Options / General / Nudge, you establish the amount of motion, as big or small as you want. Then when you move your arrow keys up, down, left, or right, the object moves in that direction, by that amount— the ultimate in control. This is an excellent tool for when two objects need to be touching and there is no snap point available: Zoom way in, set a Nudge factor for half a point or even less, and then press the appropriate arrow key until the object is just right.

One often overlooked fact is that you can nudge nodes with the Shape tool, as well as entire objects with the Pick tool.

The beauty of Nudge is how it constrains you to move in only one direction, greatly facilitating the challenging task of placing objects precisely.

Importing Objects

When it comes to incorporating files from other programs, DRAW will digest almost anything you throw at it. DRAW can accept text files from word processors, tables of numbers from spreadsheets, image files from paint programs, vector art from itself, and even drawings from competing programs. The key requirement is that you either tell DRAW what type of file it is, or give DRAW the opportunity to figure it out for itself. But if you try to import a .PCX file while telling DRAW to expect a Word for Windows file, you're asking for trouble.

The gateway to all importing is the File / Import dialog shown in Figure 4.2. In this instance, DRAW has its sights set on importing a .CMX file from one of the clip art directories that come with the program. Like most programs, DRAW expects certain formats to have particular file name extensions, and it behooves you to follow standard naming conventions when you create your files. We suggest you try importing one of these files now yourself from CorelDRAW CD No. 2.

4.2

DRAW's Import dialog has the new Windows 95 look and feel.

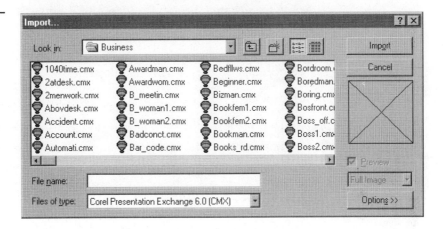

Some Things to Remember About Our Exercises A couple of the instructions in the following exercise will appear a lot throughout this book.

- In step 2 we tell you to use the Look In drop-down list to find a directory. That list functions as a window to your entire system, including local and network drives and all items on your Desktop. You can click on any one of your drive letters or on My Computer, and the directories for the selected drive appear automatically in the large window.

- When we tell you to "OK the box" (see step 4), remember that when you're choosing files from a list, there are three ways to OK your choice: Highlight the file and click the OK button, or highlight the file and press Enter, or double-click on the file. All of DRAW's dialogs that involve choosing files work this way.

Now here are the steps for importing a file:

1. In the Import dialog, at the Files of Type box, choose All Files.

2. Using the Look In drop-down list, navigate your way to the PRACTICE subdirectory on the Companion CD.

AUTHOR'S NOTE

Whenever an exercise in this book requires a piece of clip art, we have made sure that it is either available in Corel's clip art library, or included on the Companion CD bound with this book.

3. Choose one of the files in the File window.

4. OK the box.

Most of the time, DRAW does a pretty good job of figuring out the format of a file, meaning that you could keep the Files of Type field set to All Files. If DRAW tells you that a certain file you have tried to import is corrupted, don't believe it blindly. Try importing it again, but this time set the file type explicitly (for instance, set it to TIFF bitmap for a .TIF file).

Pasting Objects

DRAW's support for the Clipboard has always been robust, and version 6.0 continues the tradition. Just about anything that you place on the Clipboard can be brought into DRAW. Try the following exercise using PHOTO-PAINT or some other paint program that reads .TIF files:

1. Open PHOTO-PAINT or another paint program.

2. From the PRACTICE subdirectory on the Companion CD, select UFO.TIF and OK the box.

3. Using the selection tool of your paint program (PHOTO-PAINT calls it the Rectangular Mask tool), select all or part of the image.

4. Choose Edit / Copy.

5. Switch back to DRAW (or open it if it's not already running).

6. Choose Edit / Paste. On the DRAW screen you will see the image, much like Figure 4.3.

4.3

This Unidentified Flying Object just flew through your Windows Clipboard.

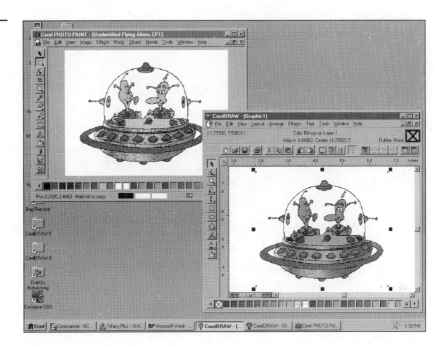

Dragging and Dropping Objects

Here is another way to get your alien friends into DRAW.

1. Open the Windows Explorer. (*Note:* In Windows 95, Explorer is the successor to File Manager.)

2. Navigate your way to the Companion CD and into the PRACTICE directory.

3. Find UFO.TIF.

4. Open or switch to DRAW and position its window so that you can see both DRAW and Explorer.

5. Now drag UFO.TIF into DRAW and drop it there.

Behind the scenes, the maneuver in this exercise is essentially the same as using the Copy / Paste procedure of the Clipboard, but it's more fun. And in the right situation, it's very useful. For more Clipboard discussion and a look at DRAW's support for Object Linking and Embedding (OLE), check out the chapters on importing and exporting in Part VII.

N E W   F O R   6

Unlike the Windows 3.1 File Manager, the Windows 95 Explorer provides access to the Clipboard; this lets you copy graphics and paste them into DRAW more easily. For instance, if DRAW were not running and you wanted to drag and drop a graphic from Explorer, you could find the graphic, right-click, and choose Copy. Then you would start DRAW, open a new drawing, and choose Edit / Paste.

Using the Symbols Library

For an easy starting point to creating a simple drawing, nothing beats DRAW's online Symbols library. To access it, choose Tools / Symbols, or press Ctrl+F11. From there you can browse through several categories of symbols. When you find one that you like, just drag it out of the roll-up and drop it on the page.

By clicking on the Tile button in the roll-up, you can create a mass of symbols, like the army of smiling faces shown in Figure 4.4. When you tile symbols, the one at the top-left is the master, and all others are clones of it. Any change you make to the master will also change all the others.

4.4

Have a **VERY** nice day... This horde of smiling faces was created in one operation: by choosing and tiling a symbol from the roll-up.

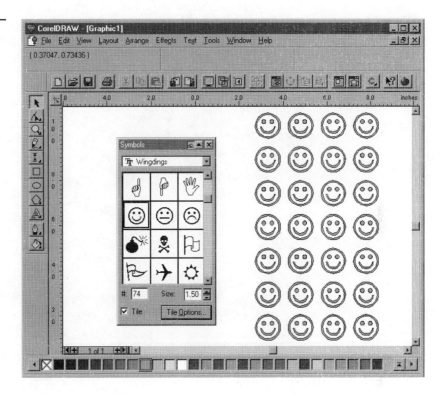

Using Fills and Outlines

One of the first things that new DRAW users do to selected objects is apply fills and outlines, undoubtedly because the controls of the on-screen Color Palette are right there in front of their noses. Although the Outline and Fill dialogs and roll-ups have considerable depth, it's easy (as usual) to perform the basic moves. To apply a fill to a selected object, try this:

1. Open Funny Face.CDR from the PRACTICE directory of the Companion CD. (Remember, in Windows 95, file names can be longer and can include spaces.)

2. Zoom in on and then select the nose of this funny face.

3. Find red on the color palette at the bottom of the screen, and click it with Button 1 (see Figure 4.5). Voilà!

4.5

Once an object is selected (note the handles), changing its appearance is easy with the on-screen palette.

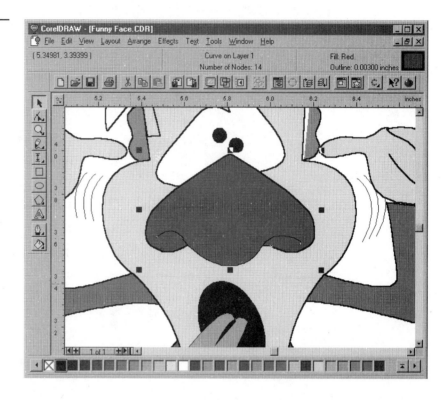

4. To create a red outline around the nose, click red on the palette, using Button 2.

Any object can be outlined, but only objects that are *closed* can be filled. A closed object is one that is fully self-contained, such as a circle or a rectangle. Chapters 8 and 9 offer considerable detail on outlining and filling.

To explore beyond the colors and fills available in the on-screen palette, experiment with the dialogs and roll-ups found under the Outline and Fill tools.

Selecting Multiple Objects

DRAW allows you to select literally thousands of objects at one time, for the purposes of grouping, moving, duplicating, deleting, or mass editing of fills and/or outlines.

If the objects are in close proximity and well defined, you can drag a *marquee* around them to select them. (Marquees are explained later in this chapter.) If you need to pick and choose certain objects to select amid others that you don't want to select, the trick is to use the Shift key, like this:

1. Select the first object.

2. Hold down the Shift key.

3. Click on another object. Now both objects are selected.

4. While still holding Shift, click to select as many more objects as you want. As long as you continue to hold Shift, previously se-lected objects will remain selected. If you click on a selected ob-ject while holding Shift, you deselect that object.

The one caveat to the above technique is this: If an object does not have a fill, then you will have to click on its outline to select or deselect it, or make sure to activate Treat All Objects As Filled from the Pick tool properties.

Once you have succeeded in selecting the desired objects, consider grouping them (discussed next), even temporarily. It's easy to ungroup them later, but not as easy to reselect all of them should they become deselected.

If an object is completely surrounded by a larger object, you might want to take a quick trip into Wireframe view, where only outlines are displayed, no fills. (You toggle Wireframe with View / Wireframe.) Figure 4.6 shows two renditions of the same butterfly (thanks to DRAW 6.0's new ability to show two simultaneous views of the same drawing). Notice that it is easier to pick out the individual objects that make up this but-terfly when it is displayed in Wireframe. In Wireframe, you need not be concerned with objects that are on top of others—clicking on any part of its outline will select the object.

Of course, if you want to select all of the objects in your drawing, you can forget about marquees or Shift+clicks or any of that nonsense and head straight for the Edit / Select All command.

4.6

Using Wireframe view is often the answer to picking out small pieces of a drawing.

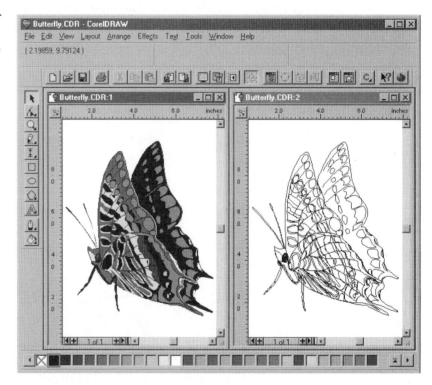

Turning Many Objects into One

DRAW offers three commands that, in some fashion or another, take multiple objects and lump them together so you can work with them all at once. When used correctly, each of these commands are enormously helpful in organizing the various elements contained in drawings. The three commands—Group, Combine, and Weld—are found on the Arrange menu.

Grouping Objects

The most straightforward of the three "lump together" functions, Group uses an imaginary paper clip or rubber band to collect a set of objects. In other words, the objects are completely independent of one another; they are just being held together so you can move, size, or

color them as one object. Grouped objects can always be ungrouped—
each maintains almost complete autonomy from the other members of
its group. Figure 4.7 includes a set of grouped objects (top left); notice
how the members of this group appear the most autonomous of the
three sets.

4.7

**The three com-
mands that join
objects can pro-
duce startlingly
different results.**

If you apply a fill or an outline to a group, all the objects in the group
will receive that fill or outline (unless one of the elements is not closed,
in which case it will not be filled).

It's a good idea to get into the habit of grouping objects *after* their spatial relationship to one another has been established. You can always make individual changes later, but to make sure the objects stay put in relation to one another, group them. The two hotkeys for grouping and ungrouping, Ctrl+G and Ctrl+U, will come in handy.

INSIDE INFO

You can select an individual object within a group by holding Ctrl and clicking on the desired object. You'll know when you did it right when you see round handles (instead of rectangular ones) around the object.

Combining Objects

Combining gives you a less flexible set of objects than does grouping. First, the objects that are combined lose their individual identities; in other words, rectangles, ellipses, and text characters become generic "curves" after being combined. The individual components still have their shape and their properties, but they have become attached.

Since combined objects represent a single curve element, they have only one outline and one fill. Of all the objects in the combined set, the one selected last will determine the outline and fill. Where areas overlap, a hole is created. With the circles in Figure 4.7, there are many overlapping areas, and therefore the result of combining them (see center image) creates a striking mosaic of filled and hollow areas.

You can break apart an arrangement of combined objects, and Arrange / Break Apart is in fact the name of the command that does this. But don't expect them to remember how they used to be! Objects you break apart are just curves, and they each inherit the outline and fill of the combined object before it was broken apart. It's not terribly significant that a rectangle becomes a curve, because it still looks and acts the same. However, when *text* is combined with other objects and then broken apart, it loses all of its text properties. It may still look like text because even text characters are actually a collection of curves, but it can never be edited as text again.

Welding Objects

You can take the Weld command literally: It takes separate objects and melts them together. In welding, as in combining, the last selected object determines the outline and fill for the new object. Weld, however, unlike Combine, couldn't care less about the points at which welded objects intersect; Weld removes all overlapping areas. No holes are created, and overlapping objects lose their individual shapes entirely. As the lower-right image in Figure 4.7 shows, Weld is determined to turn all selected objects into one big blob, and in so doing, removes the parts of objects that overlap others. When you use Weld, you do radical surgery.

The Undo command will reverse the Weld effect altogether. Other than that, there is only one way that a Weld can be taken apart, and that is if the welded objects do not touch at all. In that case, Weld is the same as Combine, and the objects can be uncombined. But if they touch at all, welded objects become permanently fused and cannot be taken apart. They truly become one object.

Other Points of Interest

As you take your first few tours of DRAW, there are several other stops you will want to make. The following tasks are easily learned and performed, like all the other commands and functions discussed in this chapter.

Saving and Opening Files

Saving your work is arguably your most important task in DRAW, without which nothing would be permanent. We won't insult your intelligence by explaining how to do it. (The only time we have ever actually done that in a book or magazine article was in 1986, when we attempted to show how to save changes in EDLIN. And no, we don't remember how to do it…)

The key to effective saving is to first establish an organized directory structure. DRAW remembers the directories you last chose for saving and opening files. So if you are consistent with your use of files and directories, you will have far less navigating to do in DRAW's file windows.

Our only other advice: Remember the hotkey Ctrl+S; it makes saving as automatic as a Michael Jordan jumpshot used to be, and still is once again.

Zooming

The easiest way to zoom in on an object is to press F4. This hotkey takes into account all the objects in your drawing and chooses the magnification that will allow you to see them all.

If you need to zoom in on just a piece of your drawing, you've got two choices: To zoom in on objects that are selected, click the Zoom tool, move out to the page, right-click, and choose Zoom To Selected from the flyout. (Or just use the hotkey Shift+F2.) To zoom in on a particular collection of objects that may or may not be selected, click the Zoom tool and move out to the page. Now any marquee you create on your drawing becomes the zoom area, and DRAW will automatically calculate the magnification.

AUTHOR'S NOTE

And you thought a marquee was just for displaying movie titles! In DRAWspeak, you create a marquee around objects when you click and drag diagonally from one corner to the opposite corner, covering the objects entirely. You'll hear the term often, as in "drag a marquee" or "marquee-select an object."

With DRAW's support for multiple drawings and multiple windows, you can open the same drawing in two different windows, keeping one of the windows zoomed out on the whole while the other window is zoomed way in on a particular area. To open a drawing in a second window, go to Window / New Window. Then use one of the Tiling commands, if you want, to arrange the windows.

Arranging Elements

When two or more objects are selected, the Align command becomes available for duty. With it you can reposition selected objects so that they line up precisely along their tops, bottoms, or sides.

Align can be used even on a single object. When a single object is selected, Align can position the object with respect to the page. In the last edition, we prepared two pages of examples demonstrating how objects can be aligned to one another (we used a basketball and a backboard). But in DRAW 6.0, the new Align roll-up has very nice visuals that show exactly how each option will act upon selected objects. Though we object to the sudden absence of hotkeys for aligning, we acknowledge that this new roll-up will be easier for new users to pilot.

Also, be sure to experiment with the ordering commands of To Front, To Back, Forward One, Back One, Reverse Order, and (new to 6.0) In Front of Object and Behind Object.

Using Undo

DRAW's Undo command has a very good memory, and you can make it even better. In Tools / Options / General, you can set the number of *levels* for Undo. Let's say you do the following to a circle: 1) change its color, 2) move it two inches away, 3) make it larger, and 4) delete it. You can undo each of those actions, starting with the most recent and working back in time. Each action is called a level, and the default number of levels for Undo is four. If you have enough computer memory, you can create a much larger safety net that will remember a few dozen of your last actions.

Be aware, however, that you cannot pick and choose the actions that you want to undo; they must be undone in order. For instance, in the example above, you cannot undo the color change without first undoing the move and the resize.

There are four actions that cannot be undone with Undo:

■ Changes to View settings

■ File operations such as Save, Import, and Export (although DRAW does save backup files, so in the case of Save, you can retrieve previous versions stored in .BAK files)

■ Selection of objects

■ Printing (obviously)

Finally, when you save a drawing, DRAW forgets all past actions, regardless of how many Undo levels you have set.

Copying Attributes

With two or more objects in a file, you can take the properties of one object and assign them to another using the Copy Properties From command on the Edit menu. To copy attributes:

1. Select the object(s) you want to format with the attributes of another object.

2. To invoke the Copy Attributes dialog, select Edit / Copy Properties From. Choose the particular component(s) you want to apply—an outline thickness, outline color, fill pattern, or text attribute.

3. When DRAW changes its cursor to an arrow, point to and click on the object that *already has* the attributes. The selected objects change immediately.

Using the Repeat Command

In conjunction with tedious tasks such as applying special fill patterns or outlines to many objects, or even just careful placement of objects, nothing beats the Edit / Repeat command and its Ctrl+R hotkey. Here is a good use for Repeat:

1. Create a small object.

2. Drag the object a short distance away, and click on Button 2 before releasing Button 1. This creates a duplicate.

3. Press Ctrl+R to repeat the action in step 2 over and over again.

Drag and Dupe

We teased this technique in the preceding exercise. Its official name is Leave Original, but we prefer our own Drag and Dupe. It refers to the extraordinarily popular technique of making a copy of an object while moving or reshaping it. Let's see how this works.

When you move, rotate, skew, or distort an object, it involves the following four basic steps:

1. Select the object.

2. Click and hold Button 1.

3. Perform the move/rotate/skew/distort action.

4. Let go of Button 1.

To do a Drag and Dupe, tap Button 2 *before you let go of Button 1,* anytime between steps 2 and 4. This automatically creates a copy of the object and applies the effect you are creating—to the copy, not to the original. Try this:

1. Create a long, thin ellipse.

2. Change to the Pick tool, and click once on the ellipse to get the rotation handles.

3. Click on one of the corner rotation handles and rotate the ellipse by about 10°.

4. While still holding down Button 1, tap Button 2.

5. Now release Button 1. See what Drag and Dupe does? It leaves behind the original object (hence the official term Leave Original).

Don't stop now: Because steps 2–5 were actually all one maneuver, they can be repeated all at once with Ctrl+R.

6. Press Ctrl+R…a bunch of times.

7. Now for the pièce de résistance. Select all the ellipses.

8. Go to Arrange / Combine.

9. Fill the object with a fountain or fractal fill of your choice.

You'll find this 30-second masterpiece (Figure 4.8) in the PICTURES directory and in the Color Gallery as Illustration 2. The miracle of this one is in its use of the tools, just as it was for the illustration created by your design-impaired lead author in Chapter 2. It demonstrates that you can turn an impossibly tedious project into a 30-second task when you know how and when to use each tool and command.

♣

In the next chapter we'll give you some quickies. Now, now, no jokes, please. It's actually a series of short drawings for you to tackle, each one with a different theme.

4.8

**A 30-second drag-
and-dupe
masterpiece**

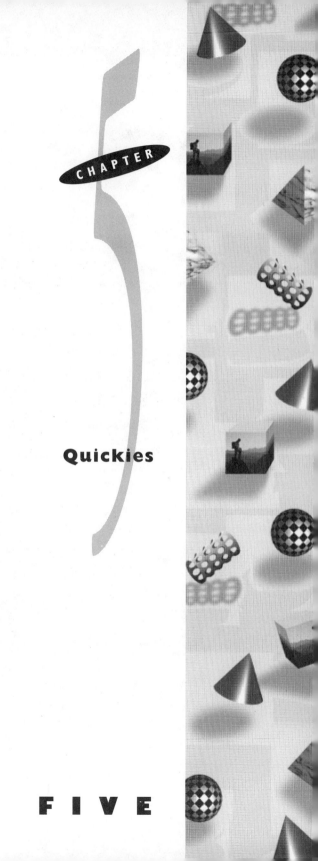

CHAPTER

5

Quickies

FIVE

This from Terrance Whitmore, a reader of our previous edition: "Thanks a lot for including the chapter in the book where you have us create an illustration all by ourselves. It was enjoyable, educational, and exhausting. I stayed up until 4:00 in the morning completing it!"

We appreciate the compliment but feel a bit guilty about depriving Mr. Whitmore of his sleep. (After all, his own CorelDRAW projects are perfectly capable of doing that.) And so we present in this chapter three small projects guaranteed *not* to keep you up past 4:00 a.m.—provided you start them before 3:30 a.m. Should you *want* to pull a Corel-style all-nighter, there's always Chapter 6.

These exercises run the gamut not only of subjects but also of techniques used. If you are a beginning user, you'll be able to start each one without any trouble, but you might not be able to finish them without first learning a bit more about a particular tool or effect. We suggest you use this chapter as a road map; if you get lost, look for further discussion of all these topics throughout the book.

If you are an experienced DRAW user, try browsing these exercises and predicting the techniques we have employed.

Creating a Logo

If there is one graphics project that defines the essence of what Corel-DRAW can do, it is the logo. A good logo is the cornerstone of an entire corporate image or business personality, and as such could represent the role of the CorelDRAW user's most important project.

A logo doesn't have to be complicated or elaborate—quite the opposite, in fact. Some of the finest and most memorable logos ever created came from very simple images. Nobody won an award for a single-color drawing of an apple with a bite taken out of it—you could create it in DRAW in about five minutes—but Apple Computer has made it the heart and soul of its identity for over a decade.

Figure 5.1 shows a logo for the fictitious Silent Oaks Tennis Club, and the following steps will take you through its creation. In this and the other two quickies in this chapter, we don't always take the most direct route to completion if we think that a detour might be educational for you. And we guarantee you'll pick up some advanced alternatives and shortcuts before you're done.

5 . 1

This logo emphasizes the importance of placing objects precisely.

The tennis logo consists of four parts: a circle that defines the shape of the logo; four enclosures; the initials of the club; and the tennis ball in place of the letter O. In our view, the two challenges to producing this logo are

- Ensuring proper alignment between elements
- Producing the four enclosures

We can easily dispose of the first challenge by correct use of the Align command. The second challenge requires a bit more thought, and it also gives us our first opportunity for a detour. Here we go, via an intentionally circuitous route (pun intended, as you'll soon see).

1. In an untitled drawing (which DRAW 6.0 calls "Graphic 1") choose File / Save As. Name your new drawing TENNIS CLUB.CDR (or any name that you choose).

2. From the rulers, drag one vertical guideline and one horizontal guideline onto the page, so that they intersect near the middle of the page.

3. Go to Layout / Snap To Guidelines and make sure that the snap is on. (If it's not checked, check it.)

4. Click on the Ellipse tool in the Toolbox (or press F7) and place your cursor at the intersection of the two guidelines.

5. Hold down Shift and Ctrl, and create the circle with a click-and-drag. Your screen should look like Figure 5.2.

6. Press F12 to quickly reach the Outline Pen dialog. Set the Width of the outline to half a point. You will probably have to change the unit of measure first, using the drop-down window nearby.

Once you have dragged the guidelines onto the page, the Snap To Guidelines setting ensures that you can start your circle in the exact intersection of the guidelines. Holding Ctrl constrains the Ellipse tool to drawing a perfect circle, and holding Shift forces the tool to draw from the center out (instead of from one side to another). Experiment on your own by drawing ellipses without holding down Ctrl and/or Shift.

Creating the Four Sections

The crucial part of the project is precisely lining up the four sections that make up the inside of the logo. Later we'll discuss the advanced maneuver for this task—using the PowerClip command—but first, you have to pay your dues by learning to create these shapes manually. To do that, you'll use a handy feature of the Ellipse tool.

5.2

A perfect circle,
brought to you by
your neighborhood
guidelines and con-
strain keys

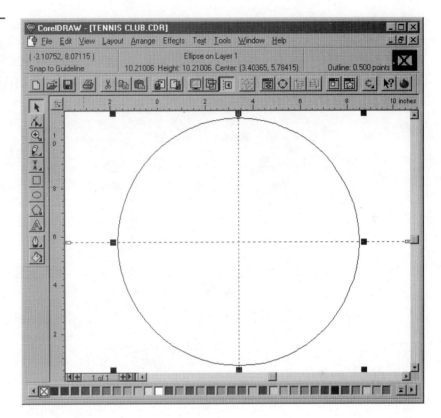

1. Select your circle and press Ctrl+C to put a copy of it in the Clipboard. With the copy safely tucked away, you can work with the circle on your screen, secure in the knowledge that you can fix any mistakes by just pasting the original back in.

2. With the circle still selected, click on the Shape tool or press F10. You'll see a small node at the top of the circle (there are actually two, one on top of the other).

3. With the cursor *inside the circle,* click and drag the node counterclockwise, releasing the mouse when the node snaps at the horizontal guideline, 90° from the top. You have now created a perfect quarter-slice of pie.

INSIDE INFO

What happens if you don't keep your cursor inside the circle? Instead of creating a pie, you create a semicircle. This is not a bug— it's a feature. The Shape tool lets you modify circles into pie slices and semicircles, and DRAW gets its cue from the position of the cursor while you drag. Drag along the inside and you make pie slices; drag along the outside and you get semicircles.

4. Color this slice black, using the on-screen palette.

5. Press Ctrl+V to paste the original circle back onto the page. Make sure the Shape tool is still active.

6. This time, drag one node 180° to the bottom, and the other node 90° counterclockwise.

7. Color this slice solid white. Your screen should look like Figure 5.3.

8. Press Ctrl+V and create the third slice, by dragging one node 90° clockwise (snapping on the horizontal guideline) and the other node 180° to the bottom. Color this third slice solid black.

9. Paste the circle back to the page one more time.

INSIDE INFO

Although using guidelines is an excellent habit to develop, these four slices could have been created just as precisely without guidelines. To constrain the angle of the slice to 15° increments, you'd hold Ctrl while dragging the nodes. (You could even go to Special / Options / Constrain Angle and set the value to 90°.) With this constraint in place, you wouldn't need the guidelines.

5.3

These two pie slices are perfectly aligned, thanks to the Snap To Guidelines setting.

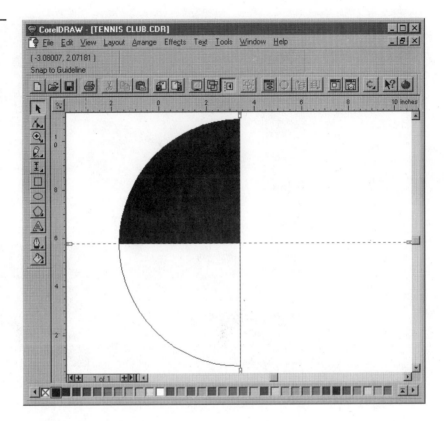

10. The last slice is a bit tricky. Make sure the Shape tool is still active, and drag the first node a few degrees clockwise and then the second node 90° clockwise. Then drag the first node back to its origin. Color this pie slice white and see if your screen doesn't look like Figure 5.4.

Creating the Initials

Creating the initials of the logo is fun and easy, the only challenge being the proper alignment of each letter. Our examples use the Geometric Heavy face from Corel's typeface collection, but you can use any typeface you want.

5.4

The completed
slices, all created
from ellipses

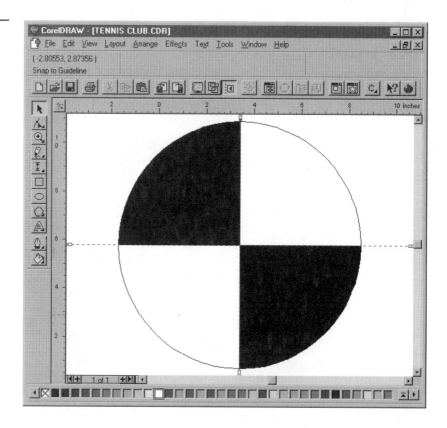

1. Activate the Text tool, from the Toolbar or by pressing F8. Click once on the page, and type a capital S.

2. Press Ctrl+Spacebar to return to the Pick tool. Stretch one of the corner handles to size the text so that it will fit into one of the slices. You can fine-tune it later.

3. Go to Text / Character and choose the desired typeface.

4. Use the on-screen Color Palette to color the text solid white.

5. Drag the S into the first pie slice and position and size it so it looks to be about right. Zoomed in tight, your screen should look something like Figure 5.5.

5.5

The first letter of the logo will determine the placement of the other two letters and the tennis ball.

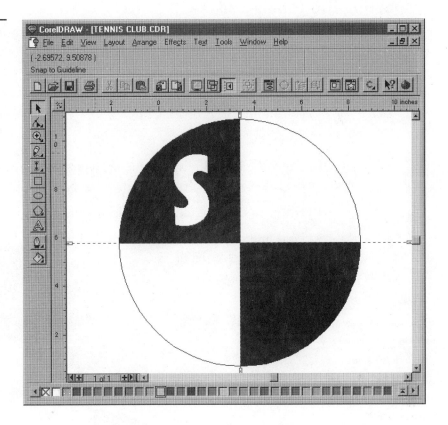

A good rule of thumb for most DRAW projects is to create the elements first and worry about their exact positions later. Following this guideline, create the other club initials now and just eyeball their positions. You can concentrate on getting them perfect afterward.

6. Using the drag-and-dupe technique discussed in Chapter 4, click and drag the S to the bottom-right pie slice, and tap button 2 before releasing button 1. Now you've got another S.

7. Repeat step 6 to place a letter in the lower-left slice, too. Fill that one with black so you can see it.

8. Select the lower-left S, press F8 to get an editing cursor, and replace the S with the T. Repeat this for the lower-right S and turn it into a C.

Importing the Tennis Ball

If you have never before imported artwork into a drawing, then take note: The following procedure is the standard, plain-vanilla form of importing a file. Here goes.

1. Look in the PRACTICE directory of the Companion CD, and you'll find TENSBALL.CDR.

2. Go to File / Import.

3. Using the Look In list and the file window, navigate your way to the PRACTICE directory of the Companion CD.

4. Find TENSBALL.CDR and click Open.

5. Drag and size the tennis ball so it is in its pie slice. Your screen should look like Figure 5.6.

5.6

The four initials of the logo. Notice that they're not yet aligned but are just placed in appropriate positions.

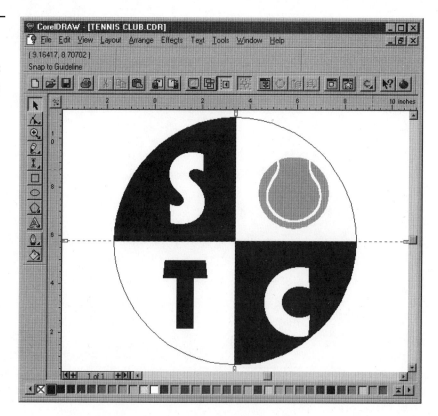

Aligning the Letters

Once again we call upon guidelines and snaps, coupled with the Align command, to bring precision placement to the drawing. The S will serve as our anchor.

1. Drag horizontal guidelines onto the page at the very top and bottom of the S. Figure 5.7 shows this in action. Note two things about this figure: We are zoomed way in for extra precision; and we have switched to Wireframe view (Shift+F9) so that the guidelines are more visible.

2. With Snap To Guidelines turned on, size and position the ball so that it fits precisely within the top and bottom guidelines.

5.7

Guidelines on the top and bottom of the S will help position the tennis ball.

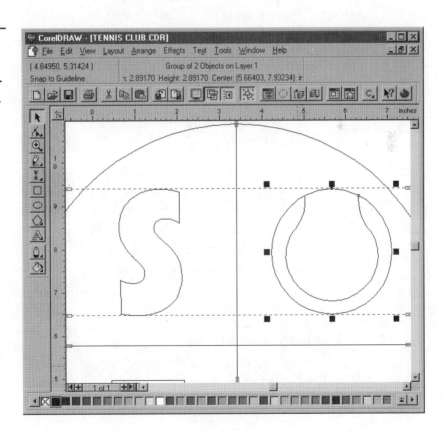

3. Using the Nudge keys (Left Arrow and Right Arrow), nudge the tennis ball left or right until its lateral position is just right.

4. Select the T at the bottom-left. Again, use Nudge (this time the Up Arrow and Down Arrow) to position the T vertically in the pie slice.

5. While the T is still selected, hold Shift and select the S also.

6. Press Ctrl+A to invoke the Align & Distribute roll-up. Click on the Vertical Center icon (the one with a line going down the middle of the rectangle and ellipse).

7. Click on Apply and watch the T become centered automatically to the S. (If you're wondering why the T aligned with the S and not vice-versa, it's because you selected the T first. The object most recently selected determines the position of the two aligned objects.)

8. Select the C and then Shift+select the tennis ball. Repeat the Align command operation from steps 5 and 6. (If it was the last move you made, you could press Ctrl+R to literally repeat it.)

9. Click away from all objects to deselect them. Then select the C and Shift+select the T.

10. To bottom-align these two letters, click again on the Vertical Center button to release it. Along the right side, click on the button with the line below the objects (representing horizontal bottom alignment).

11. Click Apply, press Shift+F9 to leave Wireframe view, and see if your screen doesn't look like Figure 5.8.

Extra Credit: Creating the Background Using PowerClip

There is another, perhaps easier, way to produce the background of this logo, thanks to the PowerClip command introduced in version 5.0. The top part of Figure 5.9 shows four squares and a circle (the circle is outlined in gray for clarity). This is not the way the logo is supposed to

5.8

The finished logo

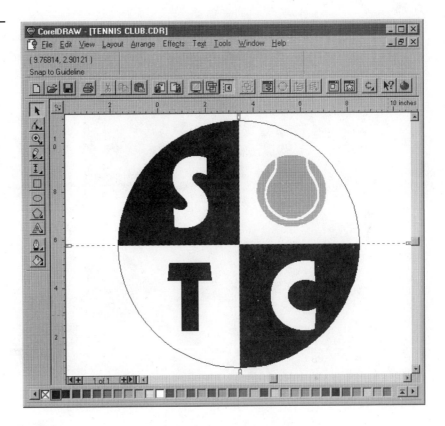

look, but it is the perfect starting point for PowerClip. The bottom image in the figure—the way the logo is to appear—was produced in three easy steps:

AUTHOR'S NOTE

To read all about working with PowerClips, see Chapter 21.

1. We selected all four squares.

2. We invoked Effects / PowerClip / Place Inside Container.

3. When prompted, we clicked once on the circle.

Once the background is done, the four initials can be added just as you did before.

5.9

The PowerClip command is perfect for creating the background of this logo.

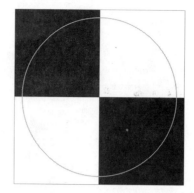

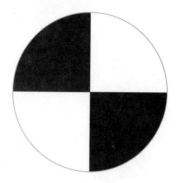

A Three-Dimensional Cube

Perspective and depth as handled by DRAW make for fascinating study, because true three-dimensional space only exists in the real world, not the simulated world of computer graphics. DRAW works in only two dimensions: height and width. To show the illusion of depth, you'd have to create…well, an illusion. This next simple exercise introduces you to that.

The cube shown in Figure 5.10 is made up of three rectangles and three letters. The sense of perspective in this drawing is produced by distorting the rectangles and the letters.

5.10

**Does this cube
really have depth
and dimension,
or is DRAW just
fooling us?**

Creating the Frame

You wouldn't build a house without first building the frame, and the same principle holds for little cubes. Once you have the frame, you can literally "snap" the objects onto it. Get ready for some more dragging and duping.

1. In an untitled drawing, drag one vertical guideline onto the page by clicking and dragging on the vertical ruler. Save the drawing and call it CUBE.CDR.

2. From Layout, verify that Snap To Guidelines is activated.

3. With the rectangle tool, create a perfect square by holding Ctrl while dragging. Position the square so that its right side is touching the guideline, as shown in Figure 5.11.

5.11

With Snap To Guidelines on, it's easy to line up this square right where you want it.

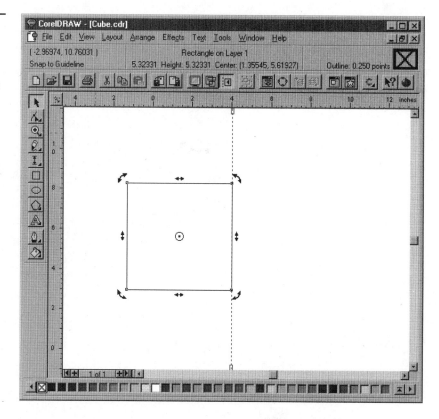

4. Click a second time on the square to get the rotation handles that you see in Figure 5.11. When you select an object and click it again, DRAW takes you into a "rotation mode" in which you can rotate or skew an object by dragging the handles that are around the periphery.

5. Click on the middle-left rotation handle (the vertical arrows) and drag up approximately 20°. Notice that as you drag, the status bar reports on the amount of skew you have imposed.

You have now created one side of the cube, and though this wasn't too difficult to do, there's no reason why you should have to duplicate those efforts. For the sake of both efficiency and precision, we'll use the first side of the cube as the basis for creating the other two sides. Here goes:

6. Click again on the square (it's now actually a parallelogram); the regular selection handles return.

7. Click on the same middle-left handle, hold Ctrl, and drag the square across the guideline to the other side.

8. While still holding down Button 1, tap Button 2 once.

9. Now release Button 1.

What you've just done is just like drag-and-dupe, with two differences: Instead of moving the object, you sized it (by dragging the selection handle). And, by holding Ctrl, you forced DRAW to size the object in 100% increments. We like to call this variation "flop-and-dupe." Anchored by the right side, the duplicated square flopped right over across the original, leaving two perfectly symmetrical squares, as shown in Figure 5.12.

Next, to create the top side, you will follow the contours of the first two sides, and that means you need another type of snap: Snap To Objects.

1. Go to Layout / Snap To Objects and click on it if it is not already activated.

2. Click on the Pencil tool in the Toolbox (or press F5) and place your cursor near the top-left corner of the left parallelogram. Because of Snap To Objects, all you have to do is get close.

3. Click once and follow the side to the top-right corner of the same parallelogram. As you move nearer, your cursor should snap to the corner. When it does, release the mouse.

4. Click on the Pick tool (or press Spacebar) to select your new line segment. Because it follows precisely the contour of the square, you'll only see the line's selection handles, not the line itself.

5. Perform another flop-and-dupe: Hold Ctrl, drag the middle-left handle to the right across the guideline, tap Button 2, and release. Again, you won't be able to see the line segment, but the appearance of the selection handles tells you that you did it right.

5.12

Thanks to a variation of drag-and-dupe, one square creates two perfectly symmetrical parallelograms.

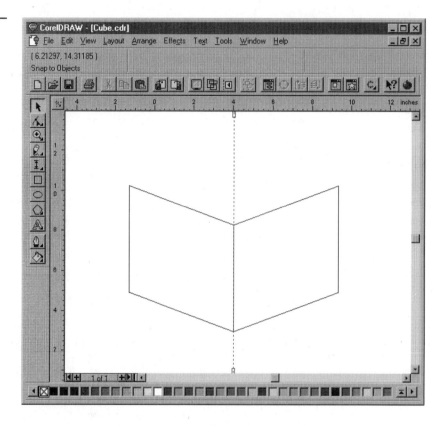

6. On that same line segment, perform another flop-and-dupe, but this time send the bottom-middle handle up over the top.

7. Select the original line segment on the left side of the guideline, and repeat that last step with Ctrl+R. Your screen should look like Figure 5.13. Almost done.

8. Drag a marquee across the entire cube and go to Arrange / Combine to turn them all into one curve.

Creating the Cubes

The three sides to the cube are nothing more than squares with letters inside of them, and you may not need to be led step-by-step through

5.13

You know that this cube is proportionally correct, because the second and third faces were created from the shape of the first face. Drag-and-dupe and flop-and-dupe were the featured performers.

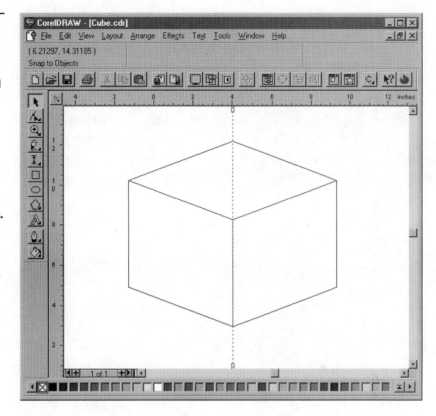

this part. Create the first one (hold Ctrl to ensure that it is a perfect square), assign a color to it, and remove the outline. Now use drag-and-dupe to create a second, and Repeat (Ctrl+R) to make a third. Don't worry about their positions; any empty part of the screen will do. Finally, make each square a different color.

Next, create three separate text strings, each with one letter. (We used A-B-C and chose three totally different typefaces.) Size each letter so that it fills out the square, and then follow these steps to start assembling the cube:

1. Select the first letter and the first square.

2. Go to Arrange / Align & Distribute and choose the center icons for each direction. Click Apply.

3. Select the second letter and the second square, and press Ctrl+R to repeat the Align command.

4. Ditto for the third letter and third square.

5. To select the first square and its letter, drag a marquee around the square. Then press Ctrl+G to group them together.

6. Repeat this for the second and third squares. Now each side of the cube is grouped with its respective letter, and the sides are ready to be shaped to the frame of the cube. Your screen should look something like Figure 5.14. (We have removed the guideline, as it is no longer needed.)

5.14

The three sides are ready to get warped.

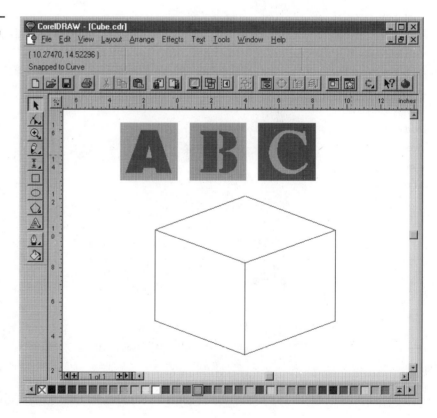

7. Make sure that Snap To Objects is still activated. Then bring the first side of the cube next to the frame, and go to Effects / Add Perspective. When you do, the selection handles around the square will give way to four nodes, one at each corner.

8. Take one of the nodes and drag it until it snaps to the corresponding corner of the frame. As you do, the square and letter will distort severely, as shown in Figure 5.15. That's okay. Do this with the other three nodes, until all four sides are molded onto the face of the cube.

5.15

We have ways of making you talk… This poor square and letter appear to be getting tortured, but when the other three nodes are in place, everything will fit nicely on that side of the cube.

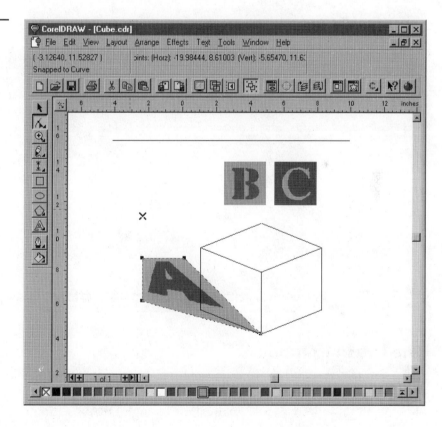

9. Repeat step 7 for the other two squares. Figure 5.16 shows the second square in mid-warp.

10. When you are done, you may want to delete the frame or change its outline to a light shade of gray or another color.

5.16

Now I lay me down to rest: This square has two of its nodes fitted and looks ready to go down for a nap.

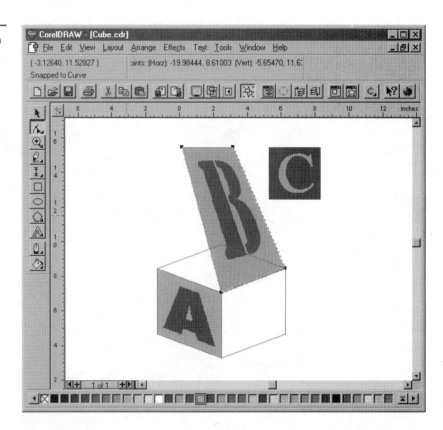

The Extrude Option

As you can tell from the first two quickies, we are quite, ahem, attached to DRAW's snap-to functions. We are also great believers in learning DRAW's tools "manually." Though DRAW's automated features are terrific aids and time-savers, we think you have learned more by creating this cube from scratch than you would have by pushing an electronic button and creating one out of thin air. Nonetheless, you have will soon see that DRAW's Extrude tool is designed to create shape and dimension from flat objects, and you could have added an extrusion to a square to create an effect similar to what you just did. Figure 5.17 shows an extruded square. For the full story about Extrude, consult Chapter 20.

5.17

Nothing beats the precision of a carefully created cube, but DRAW's Extrude command can quickly give the feeling of dimension to an otherwise flat object.

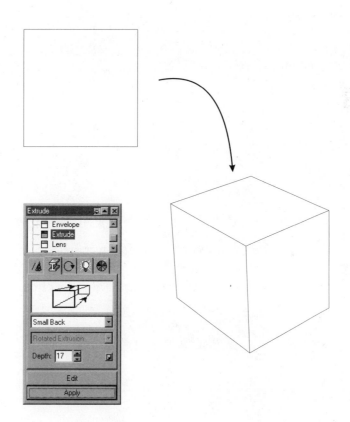

Creating a Key

In the last of our three quickies, we examine the ways in which objects can be combined to form new and different objects. The key that you see in Figure 5.18 started out as nothing more than two rectangles, a circle, and a squiggle. But with each transformation—a weld here, a trim there, and a combine—the whole became greater than the sum of its parts.

5.18

**This key might
look intricate, but
its raw materials
are very simple.**

We've saved the key for the last because we think it will be the most fun.

1. Let's start with two simple rectangles. Create them as shown just below. Use the Align & Distribute roll-up to ensure that the top rectangle is centered above the lower one.

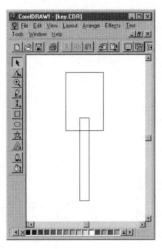

2. Select the top rectangle and switch to the Shape tool. If this were a plain old curve, the Shape tool would allow you to make fundamental changes to its shape. With rectangles and ellipses, on the other hand, DRAW makes you first convert them to curves before you can radically reshape them. (Remember how the Shape tool created pie slices with the circles of the logo?)

3. Choose any node and move it. You will see instantly how the Shape tool behaves when applied to a rectangle. Note that all four corners become rounded.

4. Repeat step 3 for the longer, thinner rectangle.

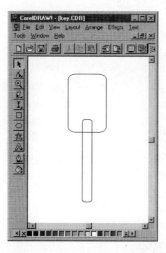

5. Return to the Pick tool and, with the bottom rectangle still selected, open the Weld roll-up (Arrange / Weld). Click the Weld To button and, with the bold black pointer that appears, click on the upper rectangle. This is a very powerful command that finds and eliminates the areas where objects overlap, essentially fusing multiple objects into one. Incidentally, the two rectangles have now lost their special status as protected objects and are subject to radical surgery by the Shape tool.

Creating a Jagged Edge

Before DRAW 5.0, making a jagged edge like the notches of our key was an annoying task, requiring a tedious session with the Shape tool, the Node Edit roll-up, and the mouse. Then along came the Trim command to make quick work of such tasks. For the key, you are going to make what amounts to a cookie cutter, and use it to slice into the key as if it were cookie dough. First you'll use the Pencil tool to create a shape with many jagged corners.

The first time you picked up the Pencil tool, you probably went right out to the page and did a click-and-drag, making a curve that resembled something out of your old Etch-a-Sketch contraption. The right way to create line segments, however, is not click and drag. It's best instead to click once, move to the next point, double-click, move to the next point, double-click again, move to the next point, and so on. At each double-click, the first click places a node at your cursor position and the second click tells DRAW to attach another line segment at that node.

1. Switch to the Pencil tool and create a shape similar to the one shown below. It is important that your jagged shape be a closed object, so make sure of two things: that your very last click is right on top of your first click, and that the very last click is just one click and not a double-click.

2. Make sure your "cookie cutter" is selected.

3. Return to the roll-up, click Trim from the list of functions, and make sure that both of the boxes below Leave Original are unchecked. This tells DRAW you don't want to work on a copy of the key, you want to modify the key itself. And since you aren't interested in the modifier (the cookie cutter) after this operation is done, DRAW will delete it.

4. Click Trim. When prompted with the arrow ("Okay, Trim what?"), say "Trim this" by clicking on the key image.

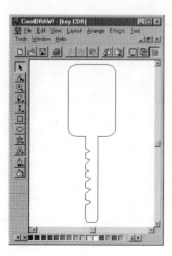

Bear in mind that this key is one object, even though you have used three objects to make it. When you welded the two rectangles, they became one, and your cookie cutter took a bite out of the key object. DRAW reports, nevertheless, that your key is one curve with about 30 to 40 nodes.

Filling the Key

How does light bounce off a key? In all different directions and intensities, that's for sure. You can add this effect with DRAW's Fountain Fill dialog, which gives you plenty of opportunity to be the hero...or the goat. We asked our resident expert on realistic lighting, Byron Canfield, to approach the coloring of a key scientifically. He pointed out that with so many edges on the key and so many possible light sources (in the car, a parking lot, on the nightstand, hanging on the key ring, or lost between the couch cushions), there would be no hard and fast rules on how the light might be reflected.

In Figure 5.19 you see what Byron calls "anybody's best guess" as to how a key might look in front of a light source. As you can see in the dialog box he has really gone to town with intermediate colors (indicated by all the little triangles on the color bar).

For your own experiment with filling the key, we suggest that you press F11 to reach the Fountain Fill dialog, click on Custom, and have at it. Any time you double-click on the color bar, you create a point on which you can change the key's fill pattern. Byron used various tones of gold, by varying the percentages of yellow, magenta, and black, to create the gradient look. To study the key now, complete with fill and in its finished form, open FINALKEY.CDR in the PRACTICE directory.

Finishing Touches

Have you ever met a key without a hole in it? We haven't, so let's get busy and poke a hole in our key now.

1. Using the Ellipse tool and holding Ctrl, create a small circle. Approximate its size relative to the key.

5.19

**DRAW's custom
Fountain Fill tool
is perfect for
capturing the ran-
domness of light.**

2. Give the circle a color—any one will do. Then drag the hole
   into position, using your eye and the Nudge keys to position the
   circle horizontally as well as vertically.

3. With the circle still selected, Shift+select the key. Be sure you select
   the circle and then the key, in that order (more on this shortly).

4. With both objects selected, go to Arrange / Combine and compare your key with the one in Figure 5.20.

Combining these two objects has effectively cut a hole in the key, similar to the way that Trim works. When one object completely surrounds
another, Combine and Trim work the same, although Combine is faster.

Selecting the hole first and then the key told DRAW to use the key's fill
pattern after doing the Combine command. You'll find this principle to
be a recurring theme with DRAW—that the last thing selected determines something important. So far, you've seen it in action with Trim,
Align, and Combine.

5.20

The Combine command has used the small circle to cut a hole in the key.

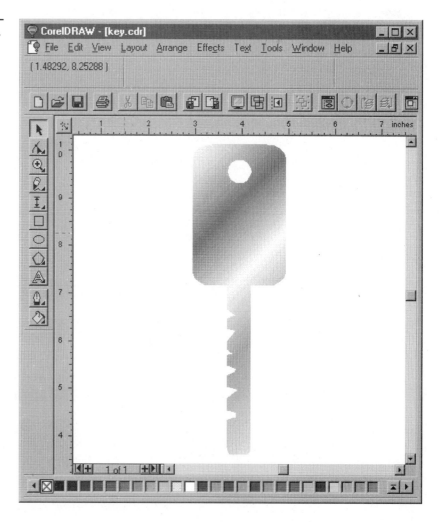

Let's take stock now: How many objects have contributed to this key?

- One large rectangle
- One small, thin rectangle
- One squiggle
- One circle

Those four objects came together to make one self-contained curve. Our key is a model of simplicity in form, and DRAW's ability to create simple objects from complex ones is one of its most enduring virtues. All that's left for you to do is make the rounded rectangle that creates a ridge for the upper half of the key. For that, we don't think you'll need our help. Figure 5.21 shows the key in its finished form, including a few effects that we have not covered here.

5.21

The finished key, with depth, shadows, contours, and beveled edges

As stated earlier, we're going to return to this key in the exercises of later chapters, so you can use it as a barometer for your developing skills. We suspect that what appears scary to you now won't after you explore the program a bit more.

♣

In the next chapter, you'll tackle a more elaborate CorelDRAW project.

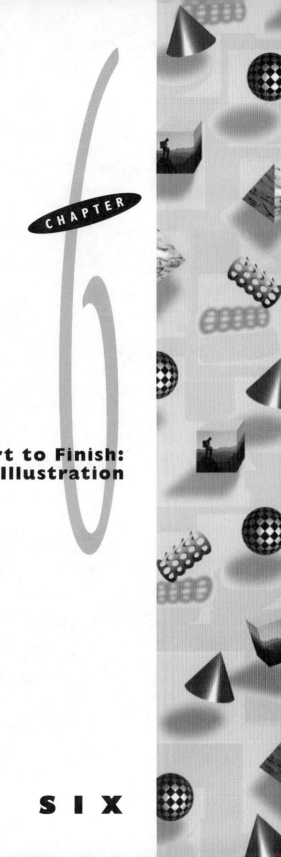

CHAPTER

6

From Start to Finish:
Creating an Illustration

SIX

This chapter continues to promote the theory that the only way to really learn is to do. Here is your opportunity to witness or participate in the creation of an entire illustration, from setup through completion. Figure 6.1 shows the finished piece. You'll also find a print of it in the Color Gallery, and the finished .CDR file as SUNSET.CDR in the PRACTICE directory of the Companion CD.

If you are a new user and this task intimidates you a little bit, well, good—we're counting on that. We want this project to appear somewhat daunting at first glance. But you're about to see how a systematic approach and attention to the drawing's individual parts can make any project go more smoothly.

The View from the Top

Your sunset project will expose you to many of DRAW's tools and functions. To complete the drawing, you will

- Create precise fountain fills
- Blend two objects
- Create objects with the Pencil tool
- Duplicate and resize objects
- Import a scanned image and trace it
- Edit curves with the Shape tool
- Apply an envelope to a shape
- Blend between compound objects
- Create, format, and apply a lens effect to text

6.1

If you think you could never produce a piece like this, think again... and then do it.

Like the accomplished artist that you are (or aspire to be), you'll produce the general background elements first, and then the more detailed parts, in this order:

- The ocean and the skyline
- The setting sun
- Birds
- The city skyline silhouette
- Reflections on the water
- The text in the sky

Getting Started

Two of the most important ingredients of a successful illustration, as in all projects, are the approach you take and the work habits you adopt.

So before you take your first step, get oriented by asking yourself the following questions:

■ **What Size?** Your illustration will be printed on a standard letter-sized page, in landscape orientation. Tell that to DRAW right now by going to Layout / Page Setup, choosing Letter for your paper size and clicking on Landscape. While you're there, make sure that Show Page Border is checked.

■ **What Name?** This is arbitrary, of course—and in Windows 95 you can call your drawing something as elaborate as "My Very First Picture of Birds, Sun, and Water.CDR" if you want to. We have gone the conservative route and named it simply SUNSET.CDR.

■ **Where?** If you haven't already done so, you should establish a network of subdirectories to house your DRAW files. Something as simple as a single directory called ART will do just fine for now. Then, once it's created, save your fledgling drawing. The Ctrl+S hotkey will work (if you issue the Save command with an untitled drawing, DRAW treats it as a Save As command). Navigate your way to the directory of your choice, enter a file name, and save the drawing.

Finally, in accomplishing this project, you will be frequently moving in and out of Wireframe view, so you'll want to memorize the Shift+F9 hotkey that toggles you back and forth.

The Backdrop

Your first order of business in this project is to determine the horizon. This is where the ocean will meet the sky, where the sun will set, and where the silhouette of the city will begin. We decided that it should be one-third of the way up the drawing, and so we placed a guideline 17 picas up from the bottom. To do this, follow these steps:

1. Go to Layout / Grid and Ruler Setup.

2. On the Ruler page, set the Horizontal and Vertical units to picas, points. Be sure the Origin is set to 0,0 for both Horizontal and Vertical.

3. On the Grid page, set Frequency to 1.00 per pica, Horizontal and Vertical. Make sure that the Snap To Grid box is checked. (You can also toggle Snap To Grid from the Layout menu or with the hotkey of Ctrl+Y.)

4. OK the dialog. When you return to the page, you should find the origin of your rulers set for the lower-left corner of the page.

5. Drag a horizontal guideline down from the top ruler and place it at 17 picas. Your screen should look like Figure 6.2.

6. Go to Layout and make sure Snap To Guidelines is checked. (If it isn't, click it once to toggle it on.) By snapping to guidelines and to the 1-pica grid that you have established, you'll find it an easy task to create two rectangles in the space defined by the page and the guideline.

7. Using the Rectangle tool, create one large rectangle in the space above the guideline, and one smaller rectangle in the space below. If you did it right, your screen should look...well, not much different than before. The two rectangles should be right on top of the page border and the guideline.

Coloring the Sky

In the bad old days, creating a mosaic of changing colors representing a skyline and ocean horizon at dusk would have involved an intricate network of closely linked rectangles, each containing a fountain fill. Together, they would produce a continuum of color—provided they were created, aligned, and positioned just right.

Since DRAW 5.0, the custom fountain fill option gives us a much better means to this end. For the sky, for instance, you will use just the top rectangle rather than several small ones to create the changing pattern of colors produced by the setting sun. You'll use the bottom rectangle for the water. (You could actually do the whole thing—sky and water—with just one rectangle; but two is easier as you'll soon see.)

6.2

This guideline
sets the horizon,
which is one of
the anchor points
of this drawing.

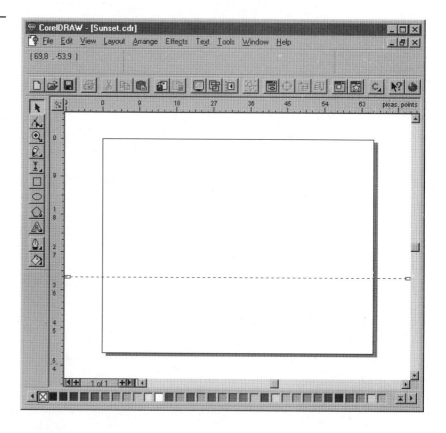

1. Your default rectangle probably has an outline and no fill—precisely the opposite of what you want. So, to remove the outline (if there is one), select each rectangle in turn and click with Button 2 on the × icon in the on-screen color palette. With their outlines removed, you can't select these rectangles with the mouse (no outline or fill, so nothing to click on). You could go to Wireframe, where all object outlines become visible, but it's easier to just use Tab to select each object.

2. Open the Fountain Fill dialog—either press the F11 hotkey, or click on the Fill tool and then the first icon, bottom row of the flyout.

Let's take a moment to lay some groundwork for using the custom fountain fill option. You probably know that a conventional fountain fill involves a gradual change from one color to another. The custom option allows you to gradually change from one color to another…and then to another, and another, and another, and so on. We think this option should have been named multiple instead of custom, but by any name it is a powerful tool, and the perfect one for producing both the sky and water.

We asked our resident expert in matters of realistic lighting, Byron Canfield, to devise a color scheme that would accurately represent the gradual transitions of dusk sunlight. He came up with the following, listed here as percentages of the four process colors, cyan, magenta, yellow, and black:

Red horizon	0C-50M-25Y-12K
Shift to orange	0C-60M-100Y-0K
Light yellow, up high	0C-0M-40Y-0K
Gradual turn to dark	40C-50M-0Y-0K
Night sky	100C-70M-0Y-25K

Equal in importance to the radiant colors of the sky at dusk are the locations where these colors begin to change from one to another, and there Byron admits to having little science to draw from. "You could look at a thousand sunsets and you might never see the same one twice," he says, sounding like the consummate artist, "so a lot of it is feel and instinct."

Now let's create this custom fountain fill:

3. Under Color Blend, click on Custom and then click on the small square at the left end of the color bar.

4. Click on Current and then Others to reach the standard Fill dialog. You should now have two dialogs open, one on top of the other, each labeled Fountain Fill. (We think there was probably a better way to design this, but at least you're not likely to forget that you are in the middle of a fountain fill operation.)

5. Enter the four values for the red horizon (0C-50M-25Y-12K), and OK this dialog.

6. Click on the small square at the end of the color bar and follow the same steps to enter the values for the top of the sky (100C-70M-0Y-25K).

7. Finally, under Options, set the Angle to 90°. OK the dialog, and your screen should look like Figure 6.3.

6.3

The fountain fill is responsible for smooth transitions between colors, like this one between the horizon and the nighttime sky.

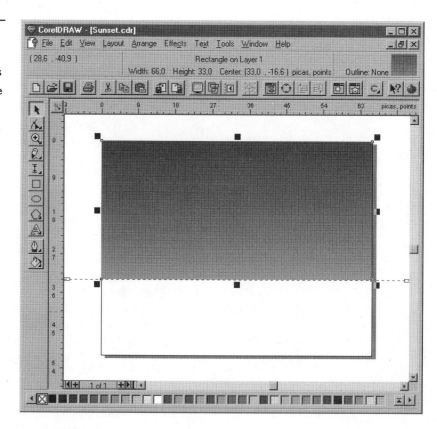

You have defined the starting color and the ending color for this rectangle. Rather than blending from the first color to the second in one step, your goal is to make intermediate stops at different colors. You first need to define the three intermediate colors.

8. Return to Custom Fountain Fill, and double-click on the color bar, close to the left end, to add an intermediate color to your fountain. Enter **6** in the Position window to place the new color exactly at 6%.

9. Set this color to orange. You might be able to pick out orange from the custom palette, but if not, click on Current and mix it yourself (0C-60M-100Y-0K).

10. Double-click again on the color bar, and enter a position of 20%.

11. Set this color to 0C-0M-40Y-0K.

12. Repeat this process to define the third intermediate color, located at 42% and set to 40C-50M-0Y-0K.

13. OK the dialog, and your screen should look like Figure 6.4 (where we have inset the completed Fountain Fill dialog at lower-right).

Coloring the Water

Now that you're an expert on custom fountain fills, do the water on your own. Use the same technique you just employed for defining starting, ending, and intermediate colors. The following table provides the essential information:

Drawing Element	Location	Color Values
Dark water		100C-70M-0Y-50K
Not-so-dark water	25%	42C-55M-0Y-25K
Light streak	54%	0C-0M-40Y-25K
Deep red	75%	0C-60C-100M-20K
Horizon		0C-49C-25M-25K

6.4

The many patterns
of an evening sky,
brought to you
by the custom
fountain fill

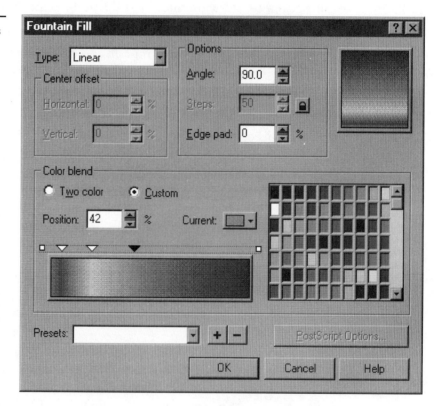

When you have finished the water, your screen should look like Figure 6.5. The foreground and background are now complete. We mentioned in passing that you could have produced both of these elements with one rectangle, and from what you know of the custom fountain fill, it should be clear that one object could indeed contain the dark water as one start point, the dark sky as the other, and all eight intermediate colors. However, it is important to know exactly where the horizon is, and by separating the backdrop into two distinct objects—each snapped to the same guideline—you now have a distinct location around which all horizon objects can be anchored.

**The completed sky
and its reflection
on the water**

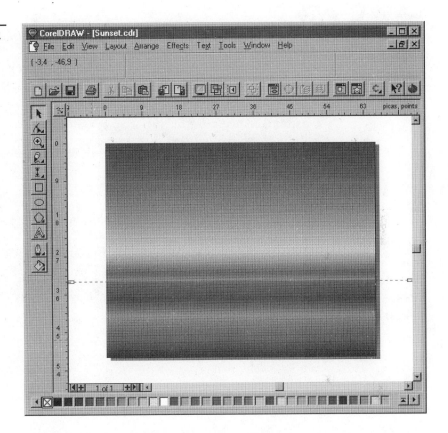

The Setting Sun

You could draw the sun in one of two ways: either with an ellipse containing a radial fountain fill—in which the color transition goes from the inside to the outside—or with a blend between two ellipses. For the sake of variety and to accommodate an advanced maneuver that comes later, you're going to create the sun with a blend between two ellipses.

1. Draw an ellipse in the approximate size, shape, and location shown in Figure 6.6. (Notice that Figure 6.6 depicts the drawing in Wireframe view, because those fancy fountain fills that you created previously now serve as a distraction.) Your circle doesn't have to be perfect—usually a setting sun isn't. The amount of the ellipse that you place under the horizon level is up to you.

WATCH OUT!

With Snap to Guidelines turned on, it might be difficult to extend the sun across the guideline. Anytime you go near the guideline, your cursor will snap to it. You should either nudge the ellipse with your keyboard arrow keys to move it into position, or just turn off the snap temporarily.

6.6

Creating the sun and positioning it properly is more easily done in Wireframe view (Shift+F9).

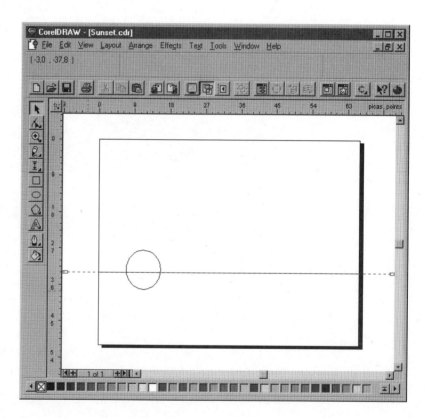

The ellipse you've drawn represents the sun's outer circumference. In order to create a blend, you need another ellipse inside—a perfect job for size and dupe. Recall what you learned in the Quickies chapter: that holding Shift forces all sizing and shaping operations to be performed from the center, and tapping Button 2 leaves behind the original object and creates a copy.

2. Select the ellipse; then press and hold Shift.

3. Shrink the ellipse to about one-quarter of the way to the center.

4. Tap Button 2 once and then release Button 1.

5. Switch out of Wireframe view.

6. Fill the inner ellipse solid yellow and the outer ellipse solid red. (Both colors can probably be picked from the on-screen Color Palette.)

7. Remove the outline from both ellipses (using Button 2 and the × icon on the on-screen palette), and see if your screen doesn't look like Figure 6.7.

6.7

These two ellipses form the basis for a nice sunny blend.

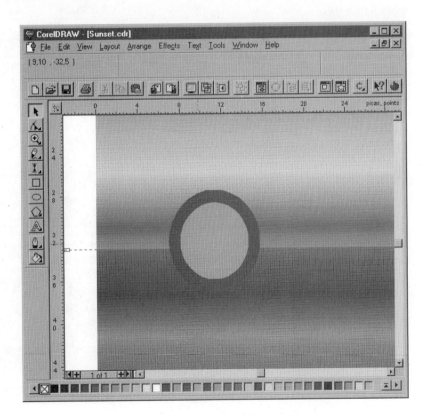

Blending the Sun

Blending objects can be surprisingly simple or alarmingly complex, but happily this is an example of the former. A blend between two objects is like a morph—intermediate objects are automatically created, which represent the transition. Blending between a big circle and a little one is very simple. You only need to decide what number of intermediate steps you want.

1. Select the inner ellipse and then Shift+select the outer ellipse.

2. Go to Effects / Blend to invoke the roll-up.

3. Set the Steps to 32 (a standard number for blends between small objects like these) and click Apply. You'll get 32 ellipses, each one with a gradual shift from yellow to red, between the two original ellipses. See Figure 6.8.

6.8

Your finished sun, magically positioned in front of the horizon. If only real life could be so interesting.

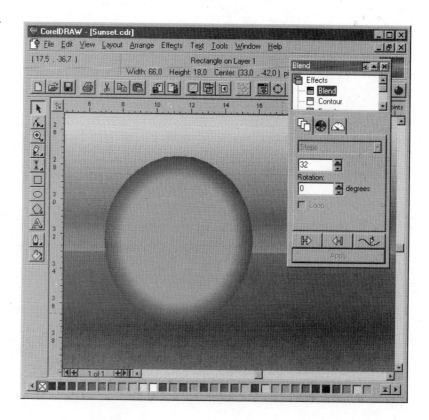

What's wrong with this picture? Well, when the sun really sets, part of it is invisible below the horizon. Granted, there is some reflection in the water, and we'll get to that later. But for now, the part of the sun that is below the horizon should not be showing. This is a simple matter of layering objects—in this case, moving the water in front of the sun.

4. Select the lower rectangle, and press Shift+PgUp to move it to the top of the stack of objects. Now that's more like it, as the printout in Figure 6.9 shows.

6.9

Now this sun is really setting.

The Flock of Birds

This illustration won't win awards for its realistic depiction of a flock of birds, nor is that its goal. In fact, we would argue that using true-to-life birds would detract from the overall piece. These simple five-node objects don't offer any detail, but we guarantee that nobody will take them for anything other than birds.

These birds have a simple design, but their creation is quite inventive. Figure 6.10 shows you the process, and we invite you to follow along

6.10

The process of creating a flock of birds

Phase 1: Connect five lines in a rough shape

Phase 2: Convert to curves and shape paths

Phase 3: Fill with black and flip, flop, and flutter

Phase 4: Duplicate and arrange in a dynamic pattern

and create your own birds. You'll read in Chapter 7 that creating an object often begins with straight lines, even if the object is to be curved. These birds each began as five straight lines. Using straight lines helps to ensure against your using too many nodes.

To convert each five-line segment to curves, activate the Shape tool and marquee-select one of the birds; be sure to select all five nodes. Hold Button 2 for a moment and click on To Curve. Then shape each node or path to taste.

Once you have one bird, creating the others is easy. You can perform a series of drag-and-dupe operations and then modify each copy, flipping it vertically, reducing or enlarging it slightly, or skewing it slightly. When you have your flock, position them in a V shape, marquee-select them all, and group them together with Ctrl+G. Figure 6.11 shows the final product—a nice flock of birds against the evening sky.

WATCH OUT!

> When you marquee-select a group of objects, make sure to start with your cursor *outside of* any object; otherwise, you might ina$vertently move it. For the flock of birds, begin the marquee outside of the rectangle representing the sky. Try doing it the right way, outside the rectangle, and then start the marquee inside the rectangle. You'll quickly see the reason for this warning.

The Skyline Silhouette

Creating the shadow view of the city landscape makes for a fascinating study in node editing. (Consider this a crash course; our full discussion of node editing appears in Chapter 7.)

There are four ways to include a shape like this cityscape in your drawing:

- Use your mouse or drawing tablet and try your best to draw around the entire shape, all the while praying for a miracle that it comes out okay.

6.11

Nothing fancy about these birds, but the route that you took to creating them was a model of efficiency.

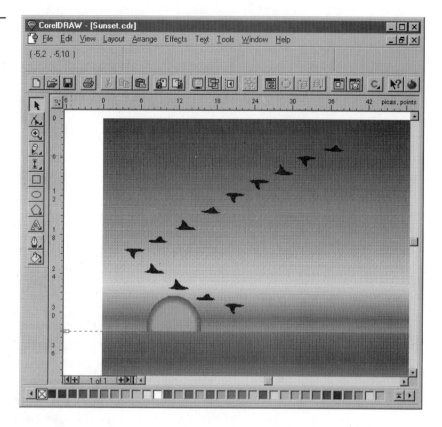

- Scan an existing printed image and use CorelTRACE to convert it to a curve.

- Scan the existing image, bring it into DRAW, and then clean it up with the Shape tool.

- Scan the image, save it as a TIFF file, import the file into DRAW, and leave it alone.

As you can guess, we're not too wild about the first idea, because computer input tools are not nearly precise enough for that kind of drawing.

The last option is okay if you have a good scanner, but you will be hard pressed to produce the reflections in the water (coming up shortly). We think that the cityscape needs to be a group of vector curves, not a bit-map image, so we are recommending a combination of the second and third strategies: Scan the image, trace it, and then bring it into DRAW for clean-up.

In the PRACTICE directory of the Companion CD you will find three different skyline files to work with. Decide which file to use based on the phase at which you want to enter this task:

- SKYLINE.TIF is a scanned image that we created from an original printed image. If you are familiar with TRACE and you want to try your hand at creating a TRACE file from this .TIF file, have at it.

- SKYLINE.EPS is an already-traced version of the scanned image, which you can import directly into DRAW (using the CorelTRACE file type) and begin to refine.

- SKYLINE.CMX is a finished version of the skyline—scanned, traced, cleaned up in DRAW, and ready for use.

Figure 6.12 illustrates all the phases of creating the skyline, from scan through clean-up. Although you can always fall back on the finished version, SKYLINE.CMX, it wouldn't hurt for you to try a bit of node editing. (If you're new to this territory, Chapter 7 cites chapter and verse about paths, lines, curves, cusps, and other node-editing arcana.) Figure 6.12 shows the images rendered in a light gray, but when you import either SKYLINE.TIF or SKYLINE.EPS to work on, they arrive in solid black. It's easy to change the fill patterns, and we recommend you do so, as node editing is easier to perform that way. You can change SKY-LINE.EPS the standard way—by using Button 1 and the on-screen palette—but you'll need to change SKYLINE.TIF with Button 2 (Button 1 would add a fill to the background).

6.12

From dots to curves: This skyline gets ready for prime time.

Phase 1:
Scan image and save as SKYLINE.TIF

Phase 2:
Send bitmap to TRACE, save as SKYLINE.EPS, import to DRAW, fill at 20% Black.

Phase 3:
Choose Shape tool, select all nodes, and click Auto-Reduce. Nodes trimmed from 367 to 131.

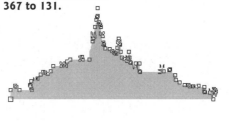

Phase 4:
Remove fill from drawing, apply light shade to bitmap, align on top of each other and look for areas that need smoothing.

Phase 5:
Delete bitmap, remove outline from drawing, set fill to black, and position on the horizon in SUNSET.CDR.

When you are finished creating the skyline, verify that Snap To Guidelines is on and move the skyline to the horizon. It should be (warning: bad pun alert) a snap.

Figure 6.13 shows the pieces of the drawing so far, and as you can see, we already have a credible picture. In the upcoming two sections you'll add realistic shadows and reflections, so get ready to switch into a higher gear. If you are unable to perform all of the maneuvers and techniques, fear not—we have lots of pictures and ready-made files for you to take apart and examine (and we'll point you to them throughout this chapter). We suggest you use the rest of this chapter as a barometer for your CorelDRAW skills; if you can't do it now, come back and try again after you've finished this book. You might surprise yourself.

6.13

This drawing is looking pretty good. Now it needs a bit more realism.

Earthly Reflections

Your drawing so far is a credible rendition of an oceanside sunset, clear at first glance to anyone who looks at it. That is certainly a significant achievement. But to take the drawing to another level of expression, you need to add other elements. For instance, the water shows no effects from wind or waves. We can see no reflections on the water of the cityscape or of the sun.

Adding these effects with DRAW's tools is both a trick and a treat: The good news is that you don't have to re-create from scratch the objects you want to use to depict the reflections. The bad news is that the technique for accomplishing this is somewhat advanced.

Reflecting the City

To make a reflection of the city, you might as well start with the city, right? So follow these steps to create a copy of the city in the right position for the reflection:

1. Switch to Wireframe view and select the cityscape.

2. Drag the top-middle handle below the horizon, until the mirrored image is about three-quarters the size of the original.

3. Click Button 2 once and then release Button 1. Your screen should look like Figure 6.14.

4. Switch out of Wireframe view now, and you'll see the reflection in the water. If this were a small pond on a very still night, you might be convinced that the reflection could be this perfect. But to be more believable it needs to shimmer on the water, so you need to warp the image a bit—and DRAWspeak for warp is Envelope.

5. Zoom in on the left side of the mirrored image. The best way to do that is to press F2 and then marquee-select the area to zoom.

6. With the image selected, go to Effects / Envelope and click on Add New.

6.14

The reflection of the city is anchored at the horizon, because you dragged the top-middle handle down but didn't touch any other handles.

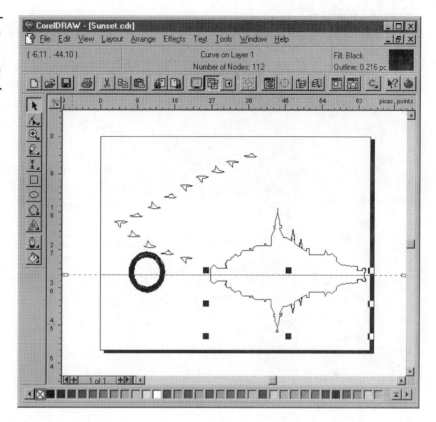

7. Marquee-select the top-left node and the one below it.

8. Press the + key on the numeric keypad three times, or until you have 16 nodes running up and down that left edge. Your screen should look like Figure 6.15.

9. Click away from the nodes to deselect them.

10. Click on the path between the top two nodes and drag it to the right (toward the inside of the reflection).

11. Click on the next path and drag it to the left.

6.15

These 16 nodes will allow you to distort the drawing in small sections.

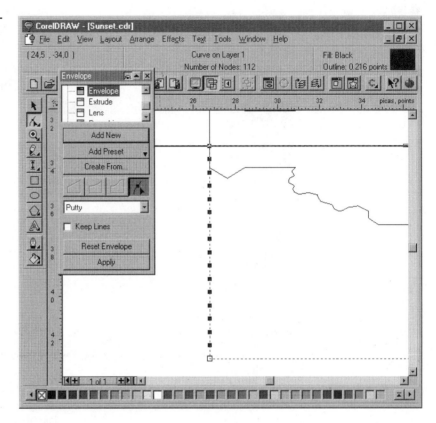

12. Click the next path and drag it to the right, and so forth, continuing until your screen looks like Figure 6.16. These nodes, and the curves you have added to the paths, define the warp.

Let's stop for a moment. We want you to notice two things about Figure 6.16. First, we did not try to stretch each path equally. The physics controlling water reflections are not for us mortals to know, and virtually any type of distortion will look credible. Second, the image doesn't look any different yet, despite all the strange things you've done to the nodes around it. Though you have defined the type of envelope, until you click Apply nothing will happen.

6.16

You have defined the warp. Now you just have to apply it.

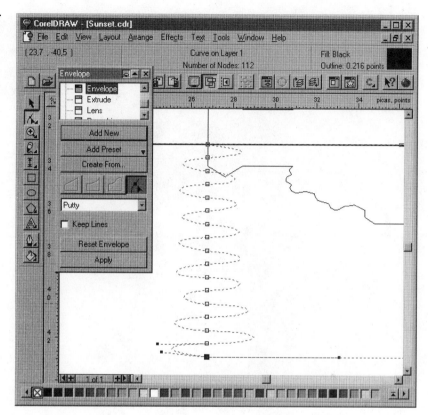

13. Click Apply and you'll have something much like Figure 6.17.

14. Now you need to repeat this process on the other side of the image. As you do, pay attention to three things:

   - Don't click on Add New to begin the other side. If you do, DRAW resets the envelope to its original position and you'll create an envelope on top of an envelope. Instead, stay with the Shape tool and continue node editing.

   - To create the 16 nodes, marquee-select the lower-right and middle nodes (not the top and middle ones).

   - If you want to reshape any part of the envelope, grab the Shape tool and go—just as if this were a regular curve. Remember to click Apply to execute the change.

6.17

Now the reflection looks warbled and warped, just as it would in a large body of water.

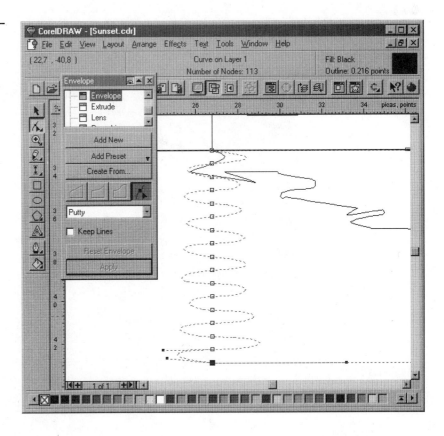

15. Switch out of Wireframe view, and your screen will look like Figure 6.18.

Reflecting the Sun

We thought we would take the same approach to warping and node-editing the shape of the sun "sitting" on the water—to reflect the sun in the ocean. But when we studied several pictures of sunsets, we noticed three different effects: In windy, choppy conditions, we saw a diffuse scattering of light on the water; in calmer conditions, we observed

6.18

The envelope gives the impression that the water is moving.

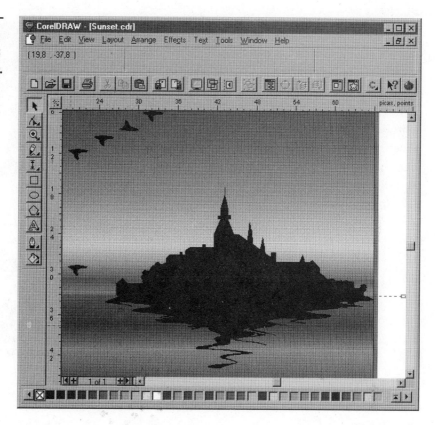

several flattened reflections of the sun; and in very calm conditions, there was just one unbroken, severely warped image of the sun near the horizon. We want our sunset to be calm and serene, so we chose between the latter two effects, both shown in Figure 6.19. We decided to produce the one on the right.

The reflection on the left is created by converting two ellipses to curves, adding nodes, warping each one, and then blending them. The one on the right is a drag-and-dupe operation, one that is considerably more involved than what you did with the key in Chapter 5.

6.19

The sun can be reflected in the water many different ways. Very calm water reflects the single, unbroken image on left; water with more ripples produces the multiple reflections on the right.

WATCH OUT!

Selecting an entire blend isn't as easy as you might think. Click on the interior and you get the control curve; click near the end and you might get the other control curve. Your objective is to have the status bar read "Blend Group." Often, the safest route is to drag a marquee across the entire object.

1. Start by selecting the sun and making a quick copy of it with the + key on the numeric keypad.

2. Bring the new sun to the front with Shift+PgUp. Press Ctrl and drag it below the horizon level. (Ctrl means your drag will be straight down.)

3. Flatten the sun reflection like a pancake, by pinching together the top- and bottom-middle handles and by stretching out the side handles. Hold Shift while stretching outward, and your stretched sun will stay centered beneath the real sun. See Figure 6.20 for the desired results.

6.20

By dragging side handles, you can distort any object, including a blended one.

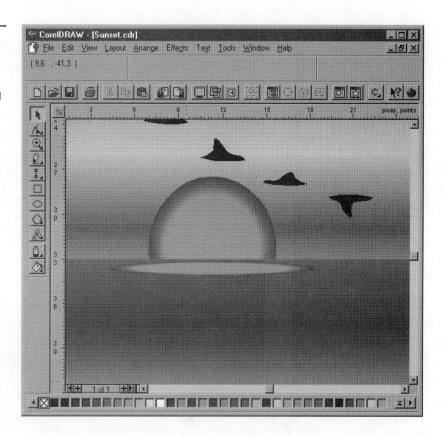

4. Use drag-and-dupe to create a second reflection below the first one.

5. Use the side handles to make this reflection smaller and narrower.

6. Select the yellow control curve. Then press Shift+F11 and back off on the yellow, to about 40%.

7. Select the red control curve, using your status bar to verify you have selected the correct object. Tint both the yellow and magenta back to 40%. Your screen should look like Figure 6.21.

6.21

By defining the outside reflection and the inside reflection, you can use Blend to fill in the middle.

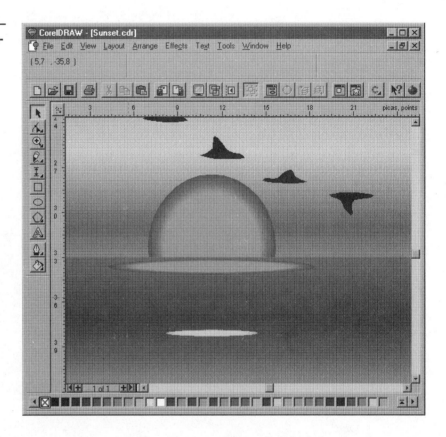

Blending Between Blends Just as you did to create the intermediate ellipses in the sun, you can use Blend to blend between other blends. Got that? If that's not confusing enough for you, note that in order to blend a blend, you first have to group it so that it becomes a group and not a Blend group. We'll have a quiz on this tomorrow, so follow these steps:

1. Select one of your flattened suns, making sure the status bar reads "Blend Group." Then press Ctrl+G to convert the blend into a conventional group.

2. Repeat this for the other flattened sun.

3. Select both newly grouped suns, and invoke the Blend roll-up with Ctrl+B. Set the Steps to 2.

4. Click Apply, and check your screen against Figure 6.22.

6.22

These reflections on the water are typical of a sunset on a mildly breezy day.

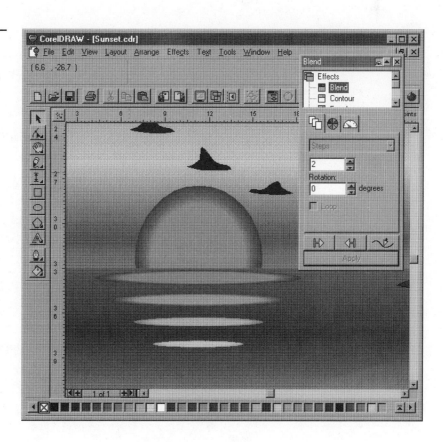

Are you wondering why all the shenanigans with grouping blends were necessary? You'd have to ask the Corel engineers to be sure; all we can tell you is that DRAW can blend between two single objects and it can blend between two groups. But it cannot blend between two objects that are themselves blends. So when you select a blend and issue the Group command, you essentially turn the object into a group of curves, without regard for which ones are the original control objects and which ones are the results of the blend.

Don't try too hard to figure this one out—it's not worth it. Just remember that DRAW does not allow you to create a blend between two objects that are already blends. Instead, you must "convert" the blend to a conventional group.

The Type in the Sky

You're almost done, and the hardest part is behind you. Setting the text in the sky is a matter of installing the right typeface and playing a bit with transparencies and highlights.

In choosing the appropriate typeface, we sought the advice of Daniel Will-Harris, one of the CorelDRAW community's bona fide typeface gurus. Here is his response to us:

If you want to show transparency and you want it to be casual, friendly, warm, and bold enough so that you can easily see the transparency in action, you might try one of these:

- Kaufmann: a Miami deco-like look
- Cancun: informal and beachy
- Oz Handicraft: so narrow you can make it very tall; also soft and warm
- Skidoos: looks kind of like it's melted—very bold and unusual
- Lithograph: always popular with a very heavy bold
- Neuland: bold and natural looking
- Letraset Harlow: might be great, might be awful

From Daniel's list we chose Oz Handicraft, which is indeed a narrow and very distinctive face. It's in Corel's library of typefaces, and installing it into Windows 95 is quite simple; you don't even need any of the fine after-market font installation tools that are available. Just follow these steps:

1. Click on your Windows 95 Start Button and go to Settings / Control Panel.

2. If you're not sure whether Oz Handicraft is currently installed, check for it now. Double-click the Fonts icon to see all the typefaces that are installed on your system.

3. Place CorelDRAW CD No. 1 in your drive. (Hold Shift while closing the door to prevent that infernal automatic menu from appearing, or press Cancel if it does anyway.)

4. From the Fonts folder, go to File / Install New Font, and navigate your way to the Corel CD. Continue down through the Fonts directory, the TTF subdirectory, and finally to the O subdirectory.

5. Find Oz Handicraft at the bottom of the list, OK the dialog, and close Control Panel. You should be able to begin setting type with Oz immediately, even if DRAW is already running.

6. Create the word **SUNSET** in the top-right portion of the drawing, and stretch it out so that it fills the entire open space. Fill it with white for the time being so you can see it against the dark sky. Check your screen with Figure 6.23, and notice how the word is sized and positioned so that one of the birds is obscured—this is intentional.

See-Through Letters

At this point, we have to throw realism out the window, because there are no norms or standards governing how letters should look when they are floating in the sky. We'll start by making the letters transparent—easily done with DRAW's Lens tool.

1. Press Ctrl+C to place a copy of the text in the Clipboard (we'll use it later).

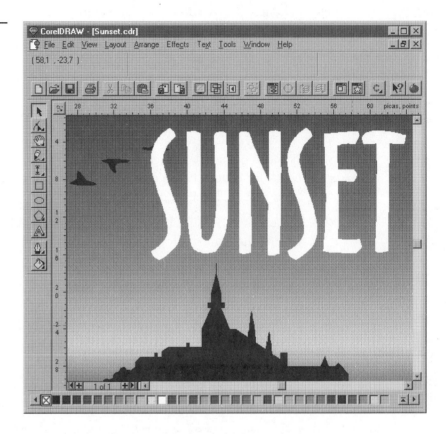

2. With the text selected, go to Effects / Lens Roll-up.

3. From the list of lens effects, choose Transparency (it is probably already chosen) and set Amount to 65%.

4. Click Apply and your screen should look like Figure 6.24. Notice how the bird that you obscured is now visible, and the gradual shift in the darkening sky can be observed beneath the letters.

Finishing Touches

We could probably call it a day (or a dusk) at this point, but we can't resist wondering how the sun would be reflected in this text that is

6.24

With the transparent lens, this text appears to be etched out of the sky.

magically floating in the sky. So if you want a bit of extra credit, try the following exercise:

1. Press Ctrl+V to paste in the copy of the text that you stashed in the Clipboard.

2. Use the Uniform Fill dialog to set the color to 0C-12M-75Y-0K.

3. Set your Nudge value to 1 point. Then nudge the new text string to the left once and downward once.

4. Press Tab one time to select the original text in the back.

5. Go to the Arrange / Trim roll-up. In the Leave Original section, make sure that Target Object is unchecked and Other Object(s) is c(ecked. This tells DRAW to let the object that is going to be your cookie-cutter (the modifier) remain in the drawing after the trim, but to remove the stuff that you cut away (the target).

6. Click Trim. When prompted with the arrow, click on the new text string. DRAW studies the areas of these two text strings and removes any part of the new text that overlaps the original text. The result, shown in Figure 6.25, provides a glint of sunlight reflecting in the surfaces of the text facing the sun as it sets.

Thanks once again go to our own Byron Canfield for coming up with this clever technique.

6.25

We imagine that if text could float in the sky, it would reflect sunlight.

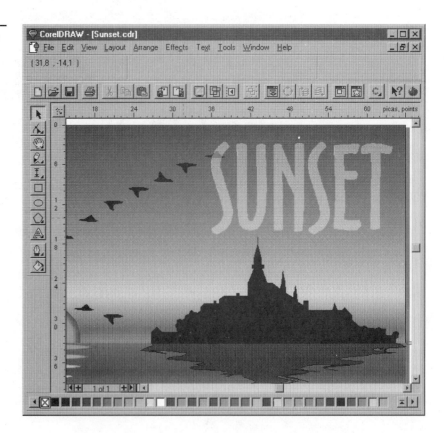

One Last Effect

There is one additional place in this drawing where you could try your hand at a transparent lens: the cityscape's reflection. With all of that light bouncing around from the setting sun and the water, the reflection wouldn't be a uniform color. If you apply a transparent lens at a rate of about 50%, the changing color of the water underneath will show through ever so slightly. Experiment with this on your own.

We want to encourage you not only to try and put this drawing together, but also to take it apart. "Reverse engineering" is one of the best learning tools around, and you can use it to take our sunset apart by retrieving SUNSET.CDR from the PRACTICE directory of the Companion CD.

As we conclude this chapter, we are done with what we consider your introduction to DRAW. In Part II, we will examine more closely some of the functions that really make the program tick.

PART II

LIFE IN AN
OBJECT-ORIENTED WORLD

If you worked through the exercises in the last two chapters, you survived (we hope) a trial by fire. Hands-on experience is always the best way to learn a subject—whether it's computer software or a game of croquet—and don't let any book author tell you otherwise. The next three chapters fill in any blanks left by Chapters 5 and 6. They also serve as a reference for new users who have just finished creating the projects in the preceding two chapters. And experienced users will find Part II helpful as a source of new insight on the use of the program's tools.

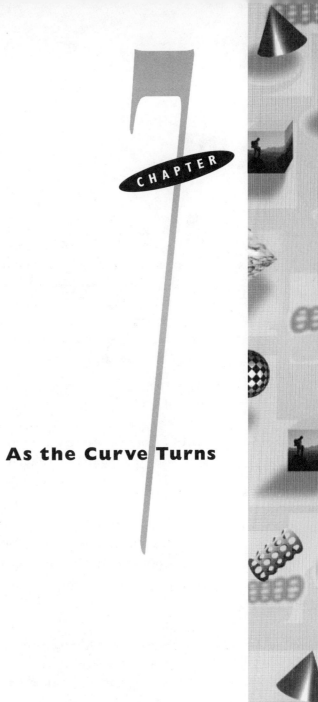

CHAPTER

7

As the Curve Turns

SEVEN

f you read Chapter 1, you know our belief that the curve is the key to everything in DRAW. Even objects that are called something else—like rectangles or ellipses—are really curves in disguise, and you could argue that text characters and even straight lines are seen by DRAW as curves. Maybe we are painting with a rather broad brush in this theory, but we want to make an important point: DRAW treats all of its vector-based objects in essentially the same manner. (Imported bit-maps are different.)

Vector-based objects all have exterior outlines that define their shape, as well as interiors that, if closed, can be filled with colors or shades. And—of particular relevance to this chapter—all objects created in DRAW contain two components: *paths* and *nodes*. We hate burdening you with these terms (especially path, which has dozens of different meanings throughout the computing industry), but here is how DRAW defines them:

■ In DRAWspeak, a *path* represents the distance from a start point to an end point. With a rectangle, for instance, any side would be a path; same for a triangle. With an ellipse, the entire shape is one path. The letter *D*, for instance, contains two paths, one straight and one curved. A crooked line drawn with the Freehand Drawing tool might consist of many paths.

■ Paths are defined by their start and end points, and those little points are called *nodes*. A rectangle has four nodes; a circle has two, one on top of another; your crooked freehand line might have a dozen. Every object you create in DRAW contains these two basic elements—paths and nodes—and in all cases, DRAW provides access to them for editing and reshaping at the most fundamental level.

When you draw with the Pencil tool, you are automatically creating lines or curves. End of discussion. But when you use the other four tools—Ellipse, Rectangle, Polygon, and Text—you create objects that DRAW treats with a bit more reverence. Ellipses, for instance, always have one continuous circumference; rectangles always have four sides; polygons maintain their symmetry; and text carries with it a host of special attributes such as typeface, style, spacing, and size.

Until you say otherwise, DRAW identifies these objects as having special properties. When you do say otherwise—that is, once you use DRAW's Convert to Curves command—then DRAW strips those objects of their special status; they are just curves. You are then free to add a fifth side to a rectangle, turn circles into odd shapes, and commit all sorts of unspeakable crimes on text characters.

Let's start by looking at curves and lines; we'll cover ellipses, rectangles, polygons, and text characters later in the chapter.

Creating Curves and Lines

If you worked through Chapters 5 and 6, you created and edited curves when you made the trimming tool for the key and when you created your flock of birds. To further explore the dynamics of curves, grab the Pencil tool, choose the freehand drawing mode, and draw a curve on screen. Any curve will do, like the one in Figure 7.1.

Click on the Shape tool, and count for yourself the number of nodes and paths that make up the curve. In Figure 7.1, 14 nodes were required, including the first and last ones, to represent the 13 paths of the curve.

Because you used the Pencil tool to draw the curve on your screen, your object is already a curve and is subject to immediate editing. Any node or path can be altered, provided you first activate the Shape tool from the Toolbar. Click and drag any curved path now to change it; click or marquee-select any node to show its control points and drag them in any manner. This clicking and dragging has immediate on-screen consequences, and you'll notice that all the nodes don't behave the same.

This thing may not look like much, but it can teach you quite a bit about how DRAW views nodes and paths.

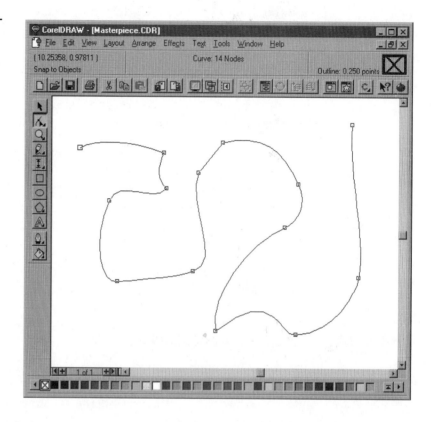

Watch your status line as you select various nodes, and you'll note that DRAW refers to them as either *smooth* nodes or *cusp* nodes. As you drew your masterpiece, DRAW made on-the-fly decisions as to which type of node to employ at each turn.

DRAW uses smooth nodes where it finds a gradual transition from one path to the other, cusp nodes to make sharper turns, and lines when it senses that you have laid down two nodes in a straight path. Figure 7.2 zeroes in on one of the cusp nodes. Notice how the curve makes a sharp turn; this is a job for a cusp, and so DRAW automatically uses it.

Our curve also contains a straight line, between the seventh and eighth nodes (counting from the left end of the curve). We didn't draw the line intentionally, but DRAW sensed that the path was close to a straight line and so it forced it to be one.

7.2

**DRAW sees you
turning a sharp
corner here, so it
automatically uses
a cusp node.**

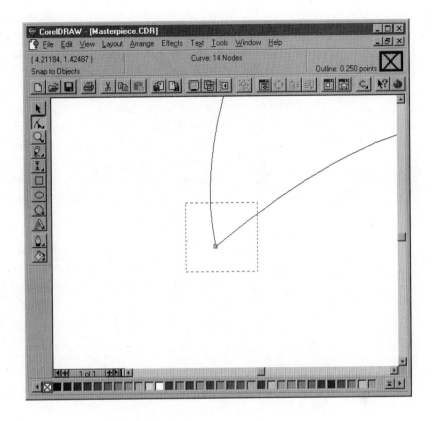

Now here is a closer look at the four types of nodes: lines, cusps,
smooth nodes, and symmetrical nodes.

What Are These Nodes?

The node—the simplest of CorelDRAW elements—is in some ways the
most difficult to define. It's easy to describe the behavior of a node and
it's easy to identify one on screen. But defining a node is kind of like defining the word *the*. You know how to use it and you know what it
does, but it's so elementary that it practically defies definition. We may
fail to come up with an actual definition of nodes, but we'll at least give
you every opportunity to experiment with them yourself.

With your curve still in memory, open a new drawing with File / New / Document. (Remember, in DRAW 6.0, you can have more than one drawing open at once.) Create a large rectangle of any shape and fill it with any light color or shade. Recall from Chapter 5 that using the Shape tool on a rectangle rounds its corners, but nothing else. To really get at the nodes of a rectangle, you must tell DRAW to stop thinking of it as a rectangle and consider it a plain old curve, instead. Go to Arrange / Convert To Curves to do that. Then select each node in turn and watch your status bar. For the top-left node, it reports "First Node of a Closed Curve." For the other three nodes, it reports "Line Cusp." This rectangle started with four lines; therefore, its paths are all straight lines and its nodes all line cusps. Now do the following:

1. Select the lower-right node and press Ctrl+F10 to invoke the Node Edit roll-up. (You can also double-click on the node to get the roll-up, but we recommend against it. When you double-click on nodes, you tax your patience, strain your wrist and finger, and run the risk of inadvertently moving the node in the process.)

Let's stop here for a moment, because we have to make allowances for Corel's icon-happiness. Corel decided to "fix" the Node Edit roll-up even though it wasn't broken, and now this roll-up consists of 15 tiny icons with lines, curves, and arrows. Two of them are obvious, six of them could probably be guessed with a bit of scrutiny, and the other seven are hopelessly vague. (We wonder to whom this new roll-up is supposed to be more user-friendly. We doubt if it's the users, and know for sure that it's not book authors…) So for the remainder of this chapter, when we direct you to an icon from the Node Edit roll-up, we'll call it by name and by the number that we have assigned to it, as shown here:

2. On the roll-up, click the To Curve icon (no. 7), which converts the node from a straight line to a curve. If you did it right, the appearance of the line running down the right side will change slightly, and you'll be able to drag it into a different shape in step 3.

3. Click and drag the path on the right and watch this former rectangle change shape drastically. Drag to the inside and your screen will look something like Figure 7.3. Notice that the status bar now calls the node a "Curve Cusp."

4. Instead of moving the path, click on the node and move it. Note the effect this has.

5. Now click and drag the control points that emanate from the selected nodes, and watch what happens.

7.3

By changing a node from a line to a curve, you can dramatically reshape this rectangle.

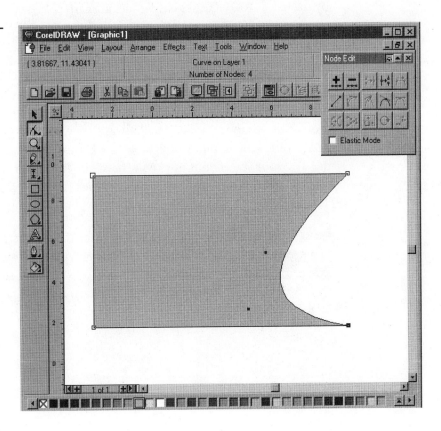

INSIDE INFO

Remember how Ctrl equals CONstrain? In this exercise, too, it will constrain your node editing. When holding Ctrl, any dragging that you do to a node, a path, or a control point is constrained to purely vertical or purely horizontal movement. Try it for yourself.

What would happen if you were to turn this node back into a line segment? As you can probably guess, the curve that you created would instantly convert back to a straight line. Go ahead and do it if you want to see for yourself, but then press Ctrl+Z to undo, because now we're moving on.

Smooth Operators   The curved path that you just created turns a very sharp corner because the other side of the node is still a straight line. By default, DRAW creates cusp nodes at sharp corners. You can probably guess what would happen if you converted that lower-right node to a smooth node. The Smooth icon is no. 9, and Figure 7.4 shows the result.

You can really see the smooth node in action if you select the lower-left node and convert it to a curve. Do that now, and then reshape the path running along the bottom; notice that the path along the right changes, too. With a smooth node, you'll always see a smooth curve through that node. Your screen might now look like Figure 7.5—but even if it doesn't, your screen and ours will share one important element: The control points emanating from the smooth node form a straight line. This is by definition, and we'll talk more about that in the next section.

Node Symmetry   Many DRAW users misunderstand the dynamic of a symmetrical node. They think symmetry means any shape on one side of the node must be the exact same on the other side. But the best way to think of symmetrical nodes is to imagine yourself exercising. If you're on a rowing machine, for example, when you pull your arms toward you,

7.4

As a smooth node, the paths on either side become, well, smooth.

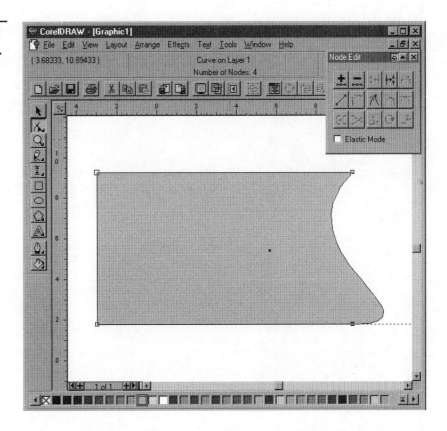

your legs thrust away from you. These actions are not identical, but they are symmetrical. When you're swimming, every stroke of your hand in one direction propels your body in the other direction. This is symmetry of motion, and symmetrical nodes work much the same way.

Select the lower-right node of the rectangle, and use the Symmetrical icon (no. 10 in the roll-up) to turn it into a symmetrical node. Study the behavior of the node. Think of any movement as energy, and re-member back to that axiom you learned in high school physics about every action having an equal and opposite reaction.

7.5

With both sides
of the path being
curves, you can
really see the
qualities of a
smooth node.

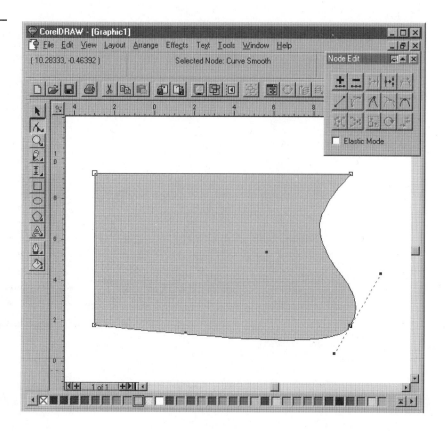

Which Kind Is It?

To review, the path of a curve can either be a straight line or a curve. If it's a curve, the nodes that control the path can be one of three types: symmetrical nodes, smooth nodes, or cusp nodes. DRAW has fairly strict rules for the behavior of its curve nodes, as follows:

When Do You Know It's a Symmetrical Node?

When the node's control points always form a straight line *and* remain equidistant from the node, it's a symmetrical node. Figure 7.6 illustrates this: In the top image, the lower control point for the selected node is about to be dragged downward. Because this is a symmetrical node, the upper control point moves away equally. The result, shown in the lower image, is a curve that behaves symmetrically with respect to the node.

7.6

Any change made on one side of a symmetrical node will cause an equal and opposite change on the other.

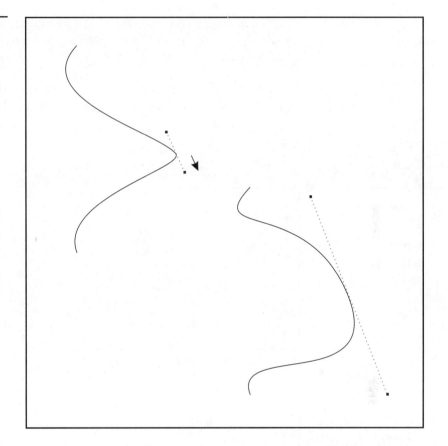

Symmetrical nodes can be very useful but exasperating, because they change the shape of the adjacent path whether you want them to or not.

When Do You Know It's a Smooth Node?   When the node's control points always form a straight line but do not need to remain equidistant from the node, it's a smooth node. Like symmetrical nodes, smooth nodes ensure a gradual transition from one side of the node to the other, but they do not require equal and opposite movement on the opposite side. Figure 7.7 illustrates the dynamics of a smooth node. As the control point is extended downward and at an angle, the opposite control point adjusts only its angle, to maintain the straight line; however, this control point does not extend in the opposite direction. The curve adjusts to remain smooth (hence the node's name), but there is no symmetrical action.

Smooth nodes are useful in a variety of circumstances, but be aware that they, too, will change the shape of the path on both sides of the node.

7.7

This smooth node reacts smoothly but not equally and in reverse on the other side.

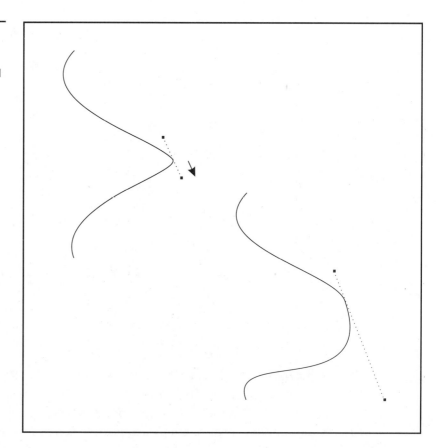

When Do You Know It's a Cusp Node?   When a node has totally different paths on either side of it, it's a cusp node. This is the don't-mess-with-me type of node. Cusp nodes do not allow movement on one side to affect the other side. The two control points do not have to form a straight line with the node, and they can move with complete independence. As Figure 7.8 illustrates, the upper control point doesn't react at all when the lower one is extended out and at a different angle. If you want a high degree of control over the paths of a curve, cusp nodes are the best choice.

7.8

Cusp nodes feature pairs of control points that don't give a hoot about what the other one is doing.

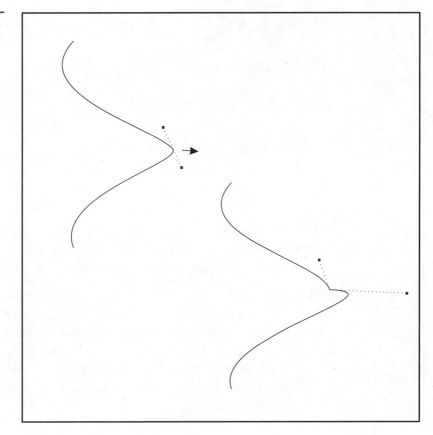

More Practice   At this point, we suggest you return to the free-form curve you created (which you can do from Window / Masterpiece or by pressing Ctrl+F6). Play with the different nodes: Change the curves to lines, change them from cusps to smooth nodes and from smooth to symmetrical nodes. Drag nodes, drag paths, and drag control points.

While you're playing, click on the other icons in the Node Edit roll-up.

In particular, note the following:

- You can select two nodes at a time by selecting one and then Shift+selecting the other, or by marquee-selecting one, holding Shift and marquee-selecting the next one. We prefer the latter because marquee-selecting is easier on your hand and carries little risk of inadvertently moving the node when you click on it.

- If you select the two end nodes, you can automatically connect them by clicking the new Add Line Segment icon (no. 5), or merge them into one with the Join icon (no. 3).

- You can split any node into two—using the Break icon (no. 4). When you do this, you create two *subpaths* within the one curve, and if the object was closed previously, it's now open. Switch over to the other window with the converted rectangle and try this; you'll see that when you break a node, the object will instantly lose its interior fill because it is no longer a closed object.

- Try creating new nodes. Click once on a path and you'll see a small dot appear. Click on the + icon (no. 1, or press the gray + key on the numeric keypad) to create a new node at that spot. You can also create nodes by selecting an existing one and clicking the + icon (or pressing the gray + key on the numeric keypad). The new node will be precisely halfway between the selected node and the one next to it.

- If you select more than one node, you can rotate or align them with the icons of the same name (no. 14 and 15).

Draw Straight, Curve Later

Your curve was created by selecting the Pencil tool and clicking and dragging, but it will be easier for you—and ultimately better for your reputation as a desktop designer—if you learn the value of drawing straight lines. Instead of holding the mouse button and dragging through the entire curve, you leapfrog from one point to another to draw straight lines. You don't double-click, but you do click twice in a row (there is a difference). Here are the actions of a DRAW user creating a series of straight lines:

Click to define start point.

Move the mouse.

Click once to define the end point for the path.

Click at the same place to define new start point.

Move the mouse.

Click to define end.

Click again at the same place to define new start.

Continue.

Figure 7.9 shows, in rather dramatic fashion, the value of creating straight lines and the folly of not. The top image shows the ease with which you can create a simple outline like this building with just a few clicks. On the other hand, as the lower image illustrates quite splendidly, it's not so easy to draw the building freehand. And this is not just another example of our lead author's undeveloped drawing skills—the most accomplished CorelDRAW artist couldn't do much better with instruments as clumsy as the Freehand Drawing tool and a mouse. Drawing tables would yield somewhat better results, but that is largely irrelevant because that's not what DRAW is all about. When you work in a vector-based application, you are not a painter and your physical drawing skills are secondary. Success in DRAW is determined in large part by your skill at playing leapfrog and hopping from one point to the next.

7.9

DRAW's tools reward you for taking the most efficient route from one point to the next.

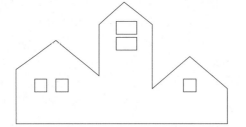

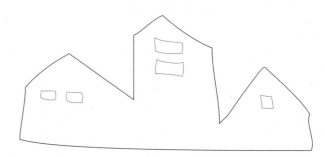

Setting Thresholds

DRAW makes decisions about cusps and straight lines based on settings that you control from the Tool Properties dialog. Click once on the Pencil tool; then right-click and choose Properties. There, you can set various *thresholds* that determine DRAW's tendency to use cusp nodes when turning corners, and straight lines when going from node to node. The lower the number you enter for the Corner threshold, the greater DRAW's tendency will be toward creating cusps. The lower the number you enter for the Straight Line threshold, the greater DRAW's tendency will be toward drawing curves.

The other fields in this dialog affect drawing, also. Press F1 from within the dialog to get descriptions of each field.

Drawing in Bézier Mode

Creating curves with the Freehand Drawing tool is easy, if inelegant. As we mentioned in an earlier chapter, it's not unlike using an Etch-a-Sketch, with which you move haphazardly from one point to another. Creating curves with the Bézier drawing tool is a truly different experience, both in the way the tool operates and in the results.

We have read all of the books, scoured the CorelDRAW User's Manual, sifted through all of the magazine articles, and taken copious notes at CorelDRAW seminars—and we have reached an inescapable conclusion: *It is impossible to teach anyone the Bézier drawing tool.* Drawing in Bézier mode is like sculpting with warm Jell-O. Every action has an opposite reaction, and you'll gain little understanding of how the tool works by reading someone else's prose. Nonetheless, we press on, and our stiff-upper-lip advice follows.

The Bézier tool doesn't follow every bump and jiggle of your mouse through a path. It looks for a beginning point and an end point, and then connects them with one curve. When creating Bézier curves, you do not click and drag across the entire path; rather, you click at the start and end points and drag *once* to shape the curve between the two points.

However—and this is one of several confusing aspects—you can choose *when* to perform the drag. You can either

- Drag after laying down the start point, and then click once on the end point. Or,

- Click once to create the start point, and then click and drag on the end point.

We warned you: This stuff is impossible unless you put hand to mouse. So open a new window and try the following two maneuvers:

1. From the Pencil tool flyout, choose the Bézier tool (the second one from the left).

2. Click once anywhere on the page.

3. Move the mouse elsewhere.

4. Click and drag. As you drag, you will be creating a smooth curve.

Press the Spacebar twice to disconnect from the curve you just drew. Then try it this way:

1. This time, you will define the curve *as* you lay down the start point. Start by clicking anywhere on the page; then drag the mouse away from that point.

2. Release the mouse and move it elsewhere.

3. Click once. The path between the two points is automatically a curve.

You can also use Bézier mode to create a series of straight lines, by clicking from one point to the next. This is easier than the Freehand Drawing tool because you don't have to click twice in a row; on the down side, however, you don't see the path of the line until you click on the end point. In our travels, we have found that most users stick with the Freehand tool—and frankly, we don't expect many of you will appreciate or excel at the Bézier tool. We'd be happy to help you with the finer points of warm-Jell-O sculpting, but for the majority of DRAW users, the intricacies of the Bézier tool are not worth mastering.

This is not to say that you can't use Bézier curves effectively—quite the contrary. In the next section, we recommend a particular strategy for creating simple and effective curves, and it doesn't require mastery of the Bézier tool.

Painless Drawing

The most important lesson you learn about the Shape tool may turn out to be this: *You don't need to make a curve perfect the first time!* Nodes and paths are forever editable and changeable and can always be reshaped later. It is often better to rough out a general shape without regard for accuracy, and then go back and clean it up. Trying to make it perfect the first time will likely take you much longer than it will to make two passes.

At this point, we want to remind you of the mission of this book: It's not to make you a master illustrator, but rather to help you add confidence and skill to your existing sense of design. After watching both new and experienced users fumble with node editing and Bézier curve drawing, we have settled on what we think is the best procedure. Here it is:

- Lay down the basic shape of the curve as simply as you can.
- Draw lines first; convert them to curves later.

Imagine an artist formulating an idea for a painting or a sketch. How fastidious do you think he or she would be at this early stage? Many of our colleagues use the back of an envelope and the margins of the daily newspaper to sketch out their ideas. When starting out, the artist wants merely to collect thoughts, dump ideas, and "catch the muse." Making the work perfect comes later. And so should it be with you, the DRAW user—even more so, in fact, as today's electronic tools make it easier than ever to change your mind and fiddle with elements.

The following sections define our best advice for drawing curves and creating shapes.

Step 1: Define the Basic Shape

Figure 7.10 is a simple drawing of a spade, the kind found on playing cards. Whether you are drawing this from scratch or tracing around an image already scanned into DRAW, your first objective should be to define the rough shape with as few nodes as possible. If you would like to follow along, this image is SPADE.CDR in the PRACTICE directory of the Companion CD.

Switch to the Pencil tool and start at the top. To produce the shape with the fewest number of nodes, look for the *points of inflection*—the points on which a curve turns from one direction to another—and click on them. If you do nothing else other than just click, you are well on your way to producing the intended shape. Figure 7.11 demonstrates this process. All paths are created with straight lines. (The final image is in the background in light gray to provide you with a comparison.)

This first sketch is both perfect and grossly inaccurate—inaccurate because it obviously doesn't follow the contours of the spade; perfect in that it uses the minimum number of nodes, and the nodes are all in just the right places. For instance, as you can see in Figure 7.11, the first path down from the top in either direction is a straight line. That path needs a node on both ends. Then the spade curves all the way around to the underside. Then there is a sharp turn back out to the base, a straight line to the other side of the base, and identical curves on the other side.

7.10

This simple shape
is good practice for
drawing and shap-
ing curves.

7.11

Using straight lines
and seven nodes to
define a basic shape

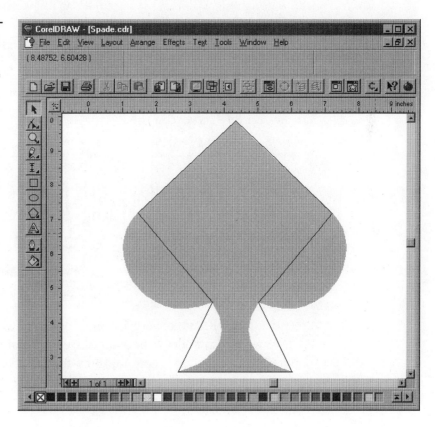

It is important that you not click and drag to create any portion of this drawing, as that would create many nodes. Instead, you want to leapfrog from one point to the next, creating nodes and straight lines that define the places where the spade changes direction.

Note: So that the upcoming instructions for creating the curve will work correctly, start at the top and work clockwise around the figure. Make sure to complete the spade by making your final click right on top of your initial start point; otherwise, your curve won't be closed, and you won't be able to fill it.

Step 2: Create the Curves

Because you played leapfrog from one point to the next, every path you created is a straight line. Starting from the top and working down the left side, you don't need to do anything to the first path because it's a straight line right where there should be one. But then you need to create a curve between the next two nodes.

1. Select the curve and choose the Shape tool.

2. Select the second node from the top, moving counterclockwise.

3. Click on the Curve icon (no. 7).

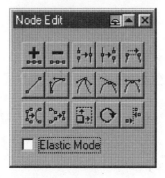 

4. By default, DRAW converts the line "before" this node into a curve with cusp nodes at both ends. But you want a smooth node at the upper end, because you want to make sure that the transition from straight line to curve is as subtle as possible. Find the Smooth icon (no. 9) and click it.

5. Shape the curve to fit the spade, using the path and the control points. Don't move the nodes themselves, unless you find that one of them is not in the right place. When you're done, your screen should look like Figure 7.12.

6. The next curve dives sharply in the other direction and therefore needs a cusp node to anchor it. Select the node at the other end of the curve (the third from the top along the left side), and click the cusp icon.

7. Click and drag the path itself to contour it to the shape. You'll find this one much easier to do than the first one. (Incidentally, if you want to really see the difference between a cusp node and a smooth node, change that third node from a cusp to a smooth node and see what kind of havoc it wreaks on your little drawing.)

7.12

By converting that straight line to a curve, re-creating the shape of the spade is easy.

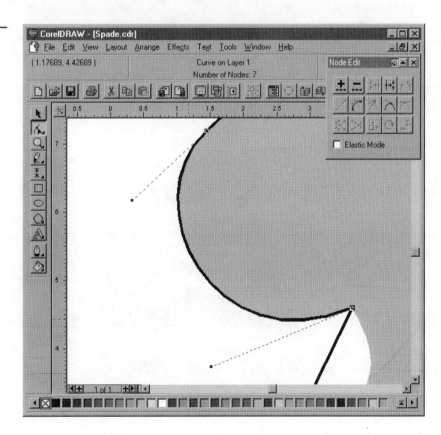

8. Now do the right half on your own, changing and shaping nodes as needed. Remember to think about which node to select for converting a given line to a curve. Your choice will be different on the right side because it was drawn top to bottom; the left side was drawn bottom to top.

9. Color the spade white and move it away from the original to check your work. If you were successful, your screen will look like Figure 7.13.

7.13

Dead ringers: Seven nodes, three line segments, and four curves make up this perfect copy of the spade.

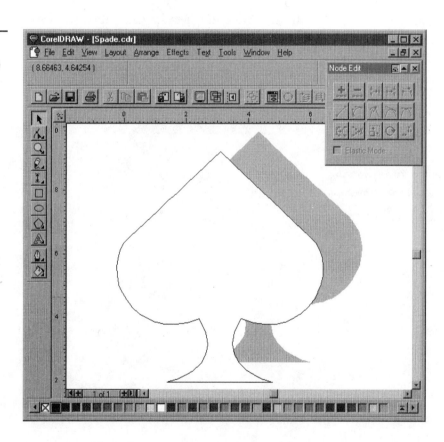

Tracing and Reducing

You might be wondering why we didn't advise you to use TRACE to make a duplicate of the spade. TRACE is the automated utility included with CorelDRAW that studies scanned images and converts them to vector-based art. Some would say it's easier to use TRACE than to manually trace around an object, as you just did with the spade.

If you were to poll our team of writers and artists, you would hear different opinions about whether to use TRACE or to create curves manually. Some believe that TRACE is an excellent starting point; others don't trust it. Regardless of our collective or individual dispositions about TRACE, however, we don't think it's wise to depend on TRACE for node editing and curve creation. Learning these skills—the building blocks of all DRAW's work—is in our view a necessary fundamental.

TRACE seems to us to be the microwave oven of vector-based projects. The microwave is wonderfully convenient and great for simple chores. But to make your meals a success, you must use other utensils and appliances, as well—the stove and the regular oven, a cutting board, mixing bowls, and so forth.

Furthermore, TRACE cannot be considered a viable tool unless it is used in tandem with a conscientious clean-up session in DRAW. Figure 7.14 compares two close-ups of the spade—the one we just did by hand, and one we asked TRACE to create from a scanned image of the spade. Study the two curves, and you'll see several imperfections in the lower image; the top one is much more refined.

Upon further examination, it is easy to see why the TRACE rendition of the spade is inferior—it has dozens of unnecessary nodes. Figure 7.15 shows the spade we drew by hand on the left, with seven nodes; that's the minimum required to create the various shapes. Each node serves a precise purpose, and nothing whatsoever would be gained by adding more. On the other hand, the version created by TRACE has 54 nodes strewn throughout, and each unnecessary node adds a bump to the curve.

7.14

The top image, drawn by hand, is noticeably superior to the unedited TRACE image, below.

Spade created manually

Spade created with TRACE

Auto-Reduce to the Rescue

One reason TRACE remains a workable source for object creation is the handy Auto-Reduce feature. Auto-Reduce studies a curve and sniffs out unnecessary nodes. It not only cleans up drawings and improves their fidelity, but is also helpful with very complex drawings that have pushed your printer beyond its limits. By reducing the number of nodes, you reduce the complexity of a drawing.

The simplest way to use Auto-Reduce is to switch to the Shape tool, drag a marquee around the entire figure, and choose Auto-Reduce (icon no. 11 in the Node Edit roll-up). Now, can you trust Auto-Reduce to maintain the fidelity of your image as it eliminates nodes? Not completely. You can, however, tell DRAW how restrictive you want this crash diet to be. Just choose a value in the Auto-Reduce field of the Node Edit Tool Properties dialog (reached by clicking on the Shape tool, then right-clicking, and choosing Properties).

7.15

The hand-drawn image on the left is the very picture of simplicity, the other one a study in overproduction.

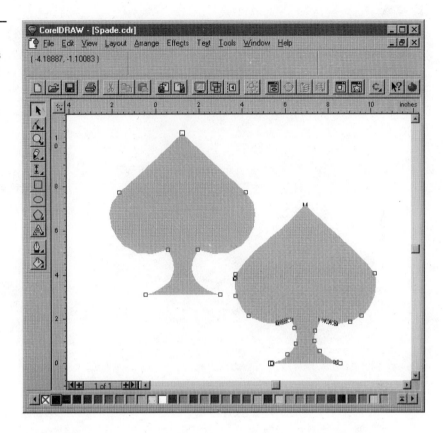

Figure 7.16 shows the consequences, both good and bad, of Auto-Reduce. With Auto-Reduce at moderate settings, unnecessary nodes are removed and the image quality is not decreased. With higher values, however, image quality degrades as nodes crucial to the image's shapes are removed. Experiment with different values on your own to get a feel for this tool.

We must also point out that this spade requires three times as many nodes as the spade we drew by hand, despite the efforts of Auto-Reduce. It's not enough just to take out unnecessary nodes; the nodes must be in the proper place and of the correct type to begin with. TRACE didn't do that, and all the auto-reducing in the world won't matter. In the end, even with Auto-Reduce, art that comes from TRACE is likely to require work on your part.

7.16

Auto-Reduce is a powerful and helpful tool, but use it with caution.

Original Image from TRACE
Nodes: 54

Auto-Reduce at .2 points
Nodes: 23

Auto-Reduce at .5 points
Nodes: 15

Auto-Reduce at 1 point
Nodes: 11

Auto-Reduce at 2 points
Nodes: 8

Auto-Reduce at 4 points
Nodes: 6

Node Miscellany

The following sections cover a host of other items relevant to node editing and curve shaping.

AUTHOR'S NOTE

Don't forget that you can always invoke the Node Edit roll-up with the hotkey Ctrl+F10.

Joining and Breaking Paths

So far, you have worked with connected paths, each node being one of a continuous train. DRAW's tools enable you to disconnect paths into *subpaths*, and to join two open paths into one. To break a path, select a node or nodes and click on the Break icon (no. 4).

The two disconnected subpaths remain parts of the same curve; however, as soon as you break the node, a closed shape becomes open and instantly loses its interior fill pattern.

Joining nodes is just as easy as separating them. To join any two nodes that are in separated subpaths, select the nodes and click on Join (icon no. 3). To join nodes from two separate curves, you must first use Combine to integrate them into one curve. Remember, though—as soon as you do this, the newly combined object gets only one outline and one fill. Once combined into a curve, you can select any two nodes and join them.

Rotate

Rotate brings the capabilities of object rotation to selected nodes; it is available when two or more nodes are selected. The Rotate icon (no. 14) presents you with the familiar arrows that appear around selected objects when you click them a second time. You can then rotate or skew the orientation of two nodes just by clicking and dragging.

Stretch

The Stretch icon (no. 13) helps you to size selected paths of a curve. It works identically to the interactive stretching you can apply on screen to a selected object by dragging its handles, except that this stretching is performed only on two or more selected nodes instead of on the entire curve.

Align

Selected nodes can be aligned along a straight horizontal line, a vertical line, or right on top of one another. The Align icon (no. 15) invokes a small dialog in which you choose your alignment specifications.

Elastic Mode

By enabling Elastic Mode, you can change the motion of two or more selected nodes when they are moved. Instead of the spacing between the nodes being preserved, the nodes move in direct proportion to the one actually being dragged. Think of it this way: With Elastic Mode on and two or more nodes selected, the node that you choose to drag will move faster and farther than the other selected nodes. If it's pursuing the others, it will appear to chase and almost overtake them; if the node is ahead of the others, it will pull away. It's best to see this one in action, so let's try it:

1. Create a curve with multiple nodes, and switch to the Shape tool.

2. Select two or more nodes.

3. Drag one of the selected nodes, and observe how all selected nodes move away an equal distance.

4. Open the Node Edit roll-up and check the Elastic Mode box.

5. Drag one of the selected nodes. This time, watch how the relational motion is different. The node you are dragging moves faster than the others.

Mirror Editing

Node editing of polygons is especially engaging, because every side of the polygon will react to the editing you do to any one side. Figure 7.17 shows the phases that a polygon undergoes with less than one minute spent with the Shape tool.

In the original image (a), we switched to the Shape tool, selected one of the nodes along the straight line (that is, not at a corner), and moved it away from the center. As we did, the nodes on each of the other four lines moved away also, resulting in a star shape (b). Then we chose one node (it could be any node), changed it from a straight line to a curve, and moved it back toward the center, resulting in object (c). Finally, we added a node to one side—which, again, was mirrored on the other sides—and moved it around a bit to produce object (d).

On-Screen Identification

Here are several visual cues that will help you identify and select nodes when you are working with them on screen.

- The first node in a curve is larger than all the others, and you can quickly select it by pressing Home.

- To select the last node in a curve, press End.

- To select all nodes, use Ctrl+Home or Ctrl+End.

- Line segments can be recognized by their distinctive hollow nodes, which are slightly larger when selected.

When a Curve Isn't a Curve (Yet)

Though it's true that all objects created in DRAW have paths and nodes, not all objects behave the same. As we told you at the beginning of the chapter, ellipses, rectangles, polygons, and text strings are given special status. They have properties that DRAW considers sacred.

7.17

Symmetry is the Polygon tool's middle name.

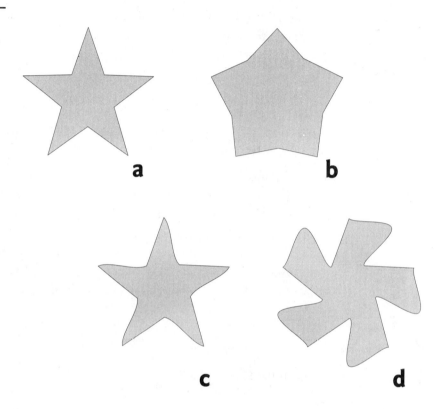

Draw a rectangle on your screen, and you'll notice a few things. First, in the status bar DRAW calls it a rectangle, not just a curve. Practically everything is considered by DRAW to be a curve (or a line, which is really a curve in disguise), but this rectangle object has special status. Second, although this rectangle clearly contains four nodes, the Node Edit roll-up is not interested. All of the options are unavailable. *This rectangle cannot be shaped or node-edited.* With the exception of its corners, which can be rounded, the rectangle's shape is sacred.

Ellipses have the same restrictions. The Shape tool cannot be used for node editing, but by clicking on the node in an ellipse and dragging it around the circumference, you can create pie slices and semicircles (as you did in Chapter 5).

And, as mentioned earlier, when you node-edit a polygon you'll find total symmetry across all of its sides. Move a node, and the others move, too; add a node, and another is automatically added to each side. (You can create some nice effects by selecting nodes of a polygon and spinning them.)

Remember: The essential properties of ellipses, rectangles, and polygons remain intact when you use the Shape tool.

Node editing in text strings is somewhat more involved, but the techniques follow the same limited dynamic as for ellipses, rectangles, and polygons. Node-editing a character or group of characters is akin to local text formatting: You can adjust letter spacing, control baseline shift, and work with basic formatting such as typeface, style, and size.

In Figure 7.18, the last few characters are crying out to be shifted to the left—a perfect job for the Shape tool. The figure shows that the string "erned!" is already selected, and a simple drag or nudge to the left will close the gap between letters.

In none of these sacred objects can you add a node, shape the path between nodes, or change the basic properties of the object. Rectangles must have four corners, ellipses must have a single path, and text strings must have a full character set and typeface formatting.

INSIDE INFO

If ever there's a time to use **Nudge** or the **Ctrl+drag** combination to constrain movement, it's when you're kerning characters. For instance, when moving the text string in Figure 7.18 closer to the other characters, it is of paramount importance that you keep it aligned on the baseline. You can ensure this by holding Ctrl while you drag the characters to the left. If you forget to use the Ctrl key and you suspect that the selected characters have wandered off the baseline, make repairs using the **Align To Baseline** command from the Text menu (hotkey **Alt+F10**).

7.18

When used with text, node editing can kern and format selected characters.

Converting Objects to Curves

But my, how quickly the mighty can fall from grace. It takes but two mouse clicks or one hotkey to knock these privileged classes down a peg. The command responsible for the demotion is Arrange / Convert To Curves. Apply this command to a selected rectangle, and you reduce it to a plain old curve. Haunt a circle with it, and you can then add a dozen nodes and disfigure the circle for life. Impose it upon a string of text, and you'll never again be able to edit the text.

WATCH OUT!

Before you convert a text string into a collection of curves, make sure the text says what you want it to say. Once converted, there is no turning back (except with Undo).

In each of these events, the object (or string of text characters) becomes a collection of paths and nodes. As Figure 7.19 shows, former text characters get no respect. Once you use Convert To Curves, their basic shapes and outlines can be freely altered.

7.19

This text is no longer text—it's a curve, with nodes that can be freely moved to other places.

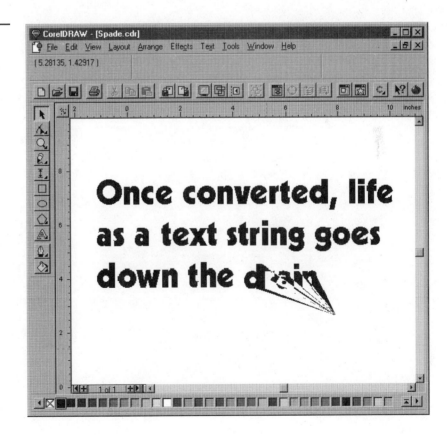

♣

In Chapter 8, you will return to the object level and work with whole entities again. But remember what you have read here, because this chapter is analogous to the quantum mechanics of DRAW illustrations. Paths and nodes are the essential building blocks of all objects that can be created with DRAW.

Understanding Outlines

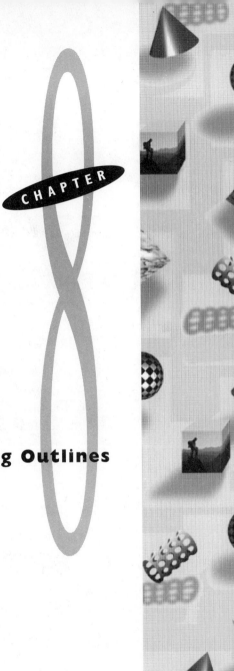

EIGHT

We are covering outlines before fill patterns, but not because we think outlining is more important, or because its tool happens to come first in the Toolbox. Compared to DRAW's fill tools, the outlining feature is a second-class citizen, and truth be told, we intend to make quick work of it here before going on to the more dramatic fill effects. But to be fair, it's *only* when they're compared to fill patterns that outlines seem unspectacular.

If you have read or browsed Part I of this book, you already have had exposure to DRAW's Outline Pen, particularly in Chapter 2, "A Tour of the Tools," and Chapter 6, "From Start to Finish: Creating an Illustration." Here in this chapter, we will assume you are familiar with the fundamentals of outlining, and will explore in somewhat more depth the tools and features that lie below the surface.

Working with Outlines

First, let's define a few terms. Every object created in DRAW has an outer perimeter, but it does not necessarily have an "outline." In DRAWspeak, an *outline* is a *visible line* that follows the perimeter of an object, and the Outline Pen is the tool used to create or modify visible outlines.

According to DRAW, when you "add an Outline Pen" to an object, you are giving it an outline. If an object's outline is not visible (that is, when the Outline Pen has no width), then the object is regarded as simply not having an outline at all.

And now, on to the outlining tools.

AUTHOR'S NOTE

A line or shape with no outline or fill? What for? you may ask. Though not a visible part of the drawing, this type of object can still sometimes be very useful. For instance, you might use an invisible rectangle to set the exact boundaries of a graphic whose elements must remain a particular size when they're imported or linked into another document. As you'll see in Chapter 12, invisible lines or objects are often used to fit text to a path. And when you're enveloping and doing PowerClips (Part V), the possibilities become endless.

Accessing DRAW's Outline Tools

Figure 8.1 shows you DRAW's collection of outlining tools. The numbers next to the Outline flyout at the top match the larger numbers next to the corresponding dialog or roll-up. Outline attributes are controlled by the Outline Pen dialog (no. 4 in the figure) and the Outline Color dialog (no. 1). You can access these dialogs through both the Outline tool flyout and the Pen roll-up (no. 3 in the figure).

The Pen roll-up and the Color roll-up (no. 2 in the figure) both provide subsets of functions from the corresponding dialogs. (For reasons known only to Corel, the Color roll-up does not allow access to the full Outline Color dialog.)

As our Figure 8.1 overview shows, you can get to the Outline Pen dialog by

- Clicking icon no. 4 in the Outline tool flyout
- Clicking the Edit button on the Pen roll-up
- Pressing the hotkey F12

8.1

A tour of the outline tools

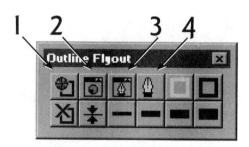

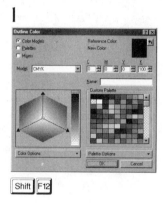

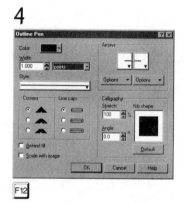

You can reach the Outline Color dialog by

- Clicking icon no. 1 on the Outline flyout
- Clicking the Color button on the Pen roll-up (the black bar)
- Clicking the Color button in the Outline Pen dialog
- Pressing the hotkey Shift+F12

NEW FOR 6

One of the biggest changes in DRAW 6.0 is the extent to which the user interface can now be customized, and the Outline and Fill flyouts are no exceptions. You can leave them connected to the Toolbar, or you can detach, reshape, or move them into any desired position on the screen.

The Outline flyout—in addition to being the gateway to both dialogs and roll-ups—has six preset outline widths, including no outline at all (represented by the × in a box). It also has presets for setting the outline color to solid white or black.

DRAW 6.0's new Color roll-up allows quick selection of a limited range of outline or fill colors. Remember that you can also set the color of the Outline Pen for any selected object by using the on-screen palette and Button 2 on your mouse.

The last item in this collection of outline tools is the Pen roll-up. It offers direct access to the most frequently used features of the Outline Pen and Outline Color dialogs, including a variety of line and arrow styles, as well as preset choices for outline color and thickness. As with DRAW's other roll-ups, your rule of thumb for choosing between the Pen roll-up and a dialog that includes these same functions should be based on a question of repetition. If you expect to be tweaking an Outline Pen or color more than a few times, then the roll-up's persistent on-screen presence pays off. If you need to make a one-time change to an outline, the most direct route to the dialogs would be the flyout menu, or better still, the hotkeys.

A New Wrinkle: The Windows 95 Way

Windows 95's use of context-sensitive pop-up menus provides yet another way to access the Outline Pen and Outline Color dialogs from a selected object:

1. Click on the object with Button 2 (that is, right-click on it).

2. Choose Properties from the pop-up menu; then choose Outline from the Object Properties dialog (shown in Figure 8.2).

AUTHOR'S NOTE

One of our long-standing pieces of advice to DRAW users is to explore the menus and try out every option you see. In DRAW 6.0 we now add the following suggestion: Right-click on everything in sight! You'll be amazed at what appears.

8.2

Taking the pop-up menu route to the Object Properties dialog

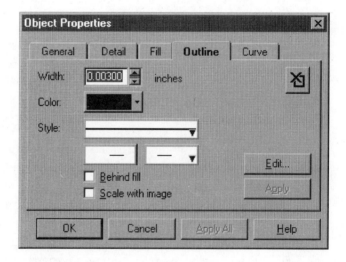

From this Outline page you can make changes to outline thickness, apply line and arrow styles, and select a color from the current custom palette. If you need to access the full Outline Pen dialog from here, click on the Edit button. If you need the full Outline Color dialog, open the Color drop-down box and click on More.

The Many Roads to Outlines and Fills

Life used to be so simple...DRAW had an Outline tool and a Fill tool, and each of them had a flyout. From the Outline flyout (or using the Shift+F7 keyboard shortcut), you could call up the Pen roll-up, which offered basic outlining functions and provided access to the full Outline Pen and Outline Color dialogs. From the Fill flyout (or using Shift+F6) you could access the Fill roll-up, with basic functions for all fill types except PostScript textures. Selecting any fill type and clicking on Edit always took you to its full dialog.

DRAW 6 still has an Outline tool and a Fill tool, but the distinction between them is no longer as clear. There are now two roll-ups on the Outline and Fill flyouts, and they handle a combination of fill and outline functions. The Color roll-up, selectable from both flyouts, helps you select and apply either outline or uniform fill colors. Unlike DRAW 5's Fill roll-up, however, it does not provide access to the full Outline Color/Uniform Fill dialog; nor can you update your choice from a selected object.

On the Outline flyout, you'll also find an icon for the Pen roll-up (identical to the Pen roll-up in DRAW 5). From the Fill roll-up, you can call up Special Fill, which is similar to DRAW 5's Fill roll-up, except for the omission of Uniform fills.

The Many Roads to Outlines and Fills (continued)

DRAW 6.0 has combined the Pen and Special Fill roll-ups into an Attributes roll-up group, which means once you have invoked the Pen roll-up, it's easy to switch to Special Fill or vice versa. But this may be more confusing than helpful, for two reasons. First, we think it seems logical to also include the Color roll-up in an Attributes roll-up group, but Corel has not done this. And second, we don't see the logic of accessing Special Fills from the Outline tool or the Pen roll-up from the Fill tool. To confuse matters even more, Shift+F7 (the old Pen roll-up shortcut) still brings up the Pen roll-up, but Shift+F6 (the old Fill roll-up shortcut) is no longer functional at all.

You can change the default roll-up groupings, and this will probably be the second thing many users do. (If you're at all like us, the *first* thing you'll do is to rename Windows 95's My Computer.) But if you prefer to stay with DRAW's default setup, our advice is to simply forego these somewhat confusing roll-ups. When you need a subset of DRAW's fill or outlining functions, use the Fill or Outline pane of the Object Properties dialog, where the choices for fills and outlines are much more clearly delineated and you always have a direct route to the full dialogs. Or just cut to the quick and go straight to the dialogs themselves—either from the fly-outs or by using shortcut keys.

The Outline Pen Dialog

The Outline Pen dialog is the more heavily traveled of the two menus, because most users need to adjust the width or style of an object's outline more often than its color. (In fact, many DRAW users have yet to work in color at all.) What's more, this dialog offers another path to the Outline Color dialog. For that reason, it's wise to consider Outline Pen the headquarters for outlining; when in doubt, you can always press F12 and you'll be on the right track.

Through the five presets on the flyout menu, you can set outline widths in the following point sizes: 0.2 (hairline), 2, 8, 16, and the rather grotesque 24 points. Any other width must be entered from the roll-up, the Object Properties / Outline page, or the full Outline Pen dialog. The Pen roll-up is more flexible than the flyout but is equally arbitrary in its set of choices, only offering widths in fixed increments. The Object Properties / Outline page allows you to enter any value, but you can't change the units of measurement. So for DRAW 6.0, as for previous versions, we draw the same conclusion: If you really want control over outlining, reach for the Outline Pen dialog.

Here is a rundown of the settings available to you from Outline Pen, in order of approximate frequency of use.

Outline Width

The Width settings give you total control over the thickness of an object's outline. You can designate anything from an impossibly thin one-tenth of a point to an almost absurd four inches, using any of DRAW's six standard measuring units—inches, millimeters, picas and points, points, ciceros and didots, or didots.

You can either dial up the numbers on the little "spin buttons" next to the Width field, or place your cursor in the box and type the value yourself. Here's the fastest way:

1. Select an object and press F12 to invoke the Outline Pen dialog.

2. Tab once to select the Width field and highlight the current value.

3. Type in a new value.

4. Press Enter to OK the dialog.

Regardless of the route you choose to get there and the way you enter the values, the Width field provides the most flexibility for setting Outline Pen widths.

Arrows

The two Arrows boxes provide access to several dozen arrow styles (see Figure 8.3), ranging from a variety of normal-looking arrows to airplanes, a writing hand, and a starburst.

Do you see an arrow style here that you *almost* like? Maybe it would be just perfect if it were a little larger, or more elongated, or pointed in the opposite direction? It's easy to create simple variations on arrow designs with the built-in Arrowhead Editor.

AUTHOR'S NOTE

DRAW stores all the arrowhead style definitions in a file called CORELDRW.END located in the CUSTOM subdirectory. Before editing any of the default arrow styles, you may want to make a backup copy of this file.

For example, DRAW doesn't offer long and thin or short and squat arrows like the ones shown in Figure 8.4. But, using the Arrowhead Editor, you can create either of these arrows from an existing one. Just pick the arrow you'd like to use as your starting point, click on the Options button under the corresponding arrow selection box, and choose Edit. DRAW will bring up the Arrowhead Editor screen, where you can resize and reshape your arrowhead, and reposition it in relation to the end of the line.

You needn't concern yourself with keeping the arrow precisely in the center of its line—that's what the Center on X and Center on Y controls are for. (Remember your geometry? The x-axis runs along the horizontal, and the y-axis along the vertical.) The Reflect buttons mirror the arrow along each axis. The Reflect in Y button actually turns the arrow completely around, so it faces the line, when you want to point to where you've been rather than where you're going.

8.3

**DRAW offers a
variety of line and
arrow styles.**

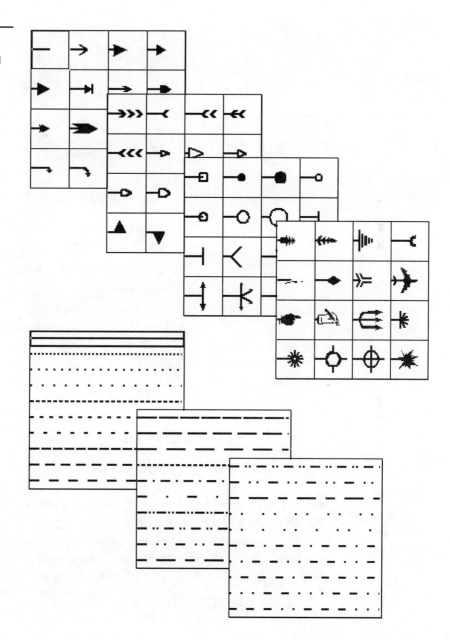

8.4

The Arrowhead Editor is responsible for custom arrows like the ones shown here.

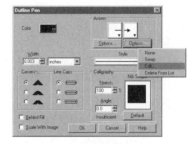

Theme...   ...and Variations

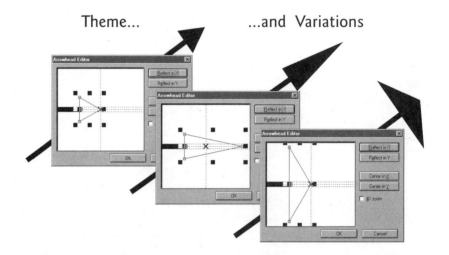

WATCH OUT!

Unfortunately, it is impossible to duplicate an existing arrowhead style and then edit the copy so that you end up with both the original and the variation available to choose from. Instead, the edited version simply replaces the original on the drop-down list.

Finally, if you want a truly exotic arrow, there is nothing stopping you from rolling your own. For instance, Figure 8.5 shows how easy it is to design a custom arrow with a musical flair. Here are the steps:

1. Create or import an object—any single-curved object will do. We've used the Symbols roll-up (no. 1 in Figure 8.5), and dragged and dropped a French horn (no. 2) on the page.

2. Use the Tools / Create / Arrow command (no. 3 in the figure) to add the object to DRAW's collection of arrows.

8.5

An arrow with a musical theme, compliments of the Create Arrow command

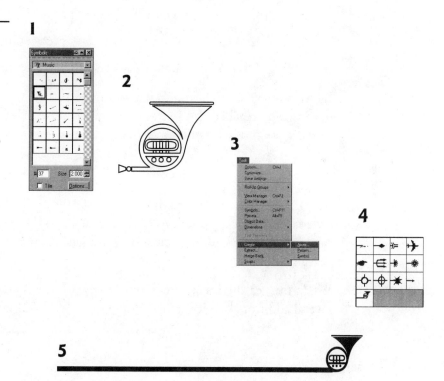

NEW FOR 6

In previous versions of DRAW, the Create Arrow command was located on the catch-all Special menu. This menu has been eliminated in DRAW 6.0; most of its entries are now in the Tools menu. The new path to Create Arrow is Tools / Create / Arrow. Note that the Arrow option is grayed out until you first select an object.

3. Browse the list of arrows and find the new one at the end of the list (no. 4 in the figure). You can do this from the Pen roll-up, the Outline Pen dialog, or the Object Properties / Outline page.

4. Edit your creation to adjust its size and proportions, if necessary.

5. Apply your newly created arrow to a selected line, and voilà (no. 5).

By the way, DRAW permits a maximum of 100 arrowhead styles. If you have already reached this limit and want to create new arrows, you must delete some of the existing ones first.

Line Style

This drop-down list offers you a choice of solid lines plus 26 other line styles. They are combinations of dots, spaces, and dashes. To use one of them, simply click on it. Your selected object will automatically inherit that line style.

When this feature is used in conjunction with the Line Caps settings, several additional useful styles of dotted and dashed lines can be created.

INSIDE INFO

DRAW's line styles are stored in an ASCII file, CORELDRW.DOT, through which you can control the size of the dash, the pattern of dots and dashes, and the space between elements. You are allowed to define up to 40 different line styles. The syntax for customizing lines is not for the neophyte, but the ambitious DRAW user willing to experiment can create custom styles and apply them to any objects with outlines. Brief instructions are embedded in the file. Look for CORELDRW.DOT in the CUSTOM subdirectory under your main CorelDRAW directory. As always, create a backup of your file before you do any editing. You must restart DRAW before any changes to CORELDRW.DOT can take effect.

Color

Your handy entrance to all of the Outline Color controls is the Color drop-down box in the Outline Pen dialog. Here you can choose among all the colors in the current palette. If that's not enough, click on More to reach the Outline Color dialog. From there, you can change palettes, choose spot colors, search for names of PANTONE colors, and mix your own CMYK, RGB, or HSB values. (For more on the foreign language of color models and palettes, see Chapter 28.) We will revisit this dialog shortly.

Corners

Here are three choices for controlling how outlines are drawn on objects with sharp corners. As Figure 8.6 demonstrates, these controls operate very intuitively.

8.6

Changing corners
on corners is as
easy as a click.

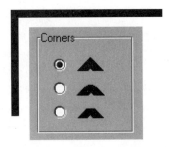

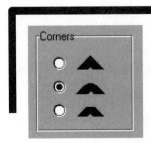

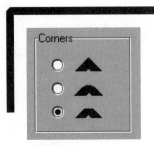

Line Caps

These three options determine how the ends of lines are rendered. The first choice (the default) cuts the line off right at the end. The middle option draws round caps that extend beyond the end of the line, and the third control draws square caps that extend beyond the end of the line.

Figure 8.7 shows how your choice of line cap can affect lines that almost join. Notice that with the default line cap (the first one), there is an obvious gap between the two lines, while the other two choices both produce the illusion that the lines meet.

8.7

**The influence of
Line Caps on lines
that almost meet**

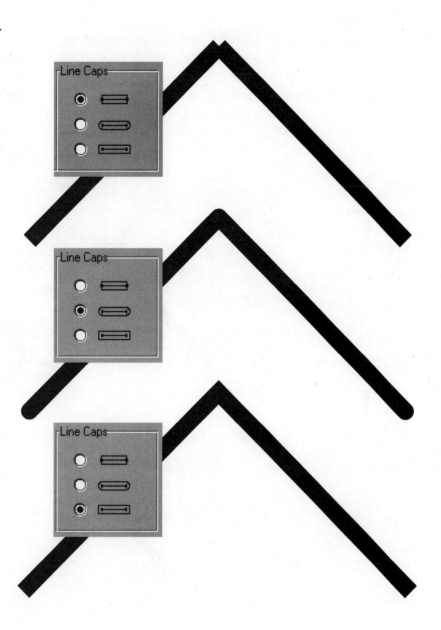

Calligraphy

Using these settings to control the shape and orientation of the Outline Pen is not unlike working with a pressure- and orientation-sensitive ink pen. By adjusting the size and angle of the pen, you can create realistic calligraphic effects. Figure 8.8 shows two such examples with their settings, along with an example of what is produced by the default settings (100% Stretch and 0° Angle).

8.8

Results of various Outline Pen Calligraphy settings

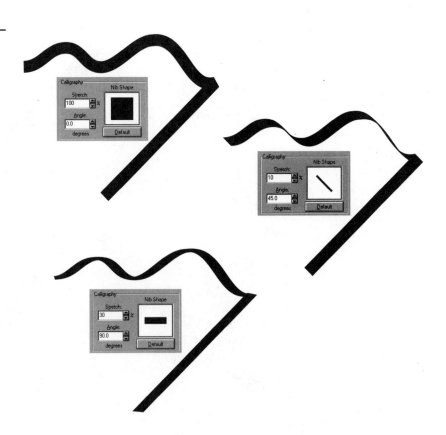

Behind Fill

This option determines the position of the Outline Pen, either in front of a fill pattern (the default) or behind it. When an object has no fill, this control is of no consequence. When there is a fill, however, and this option has been checked, the outline is placed behind the fill. Since outlines are centered on the object's perimeter, placing an outline behind the fill means only half of the outline is visible. Figure 8.9 demonstrates an opportunity for using this control. When text characters are kerned tightly so that they appear melted together, turning on Behind Fill keeps the outline from ruining the effect.

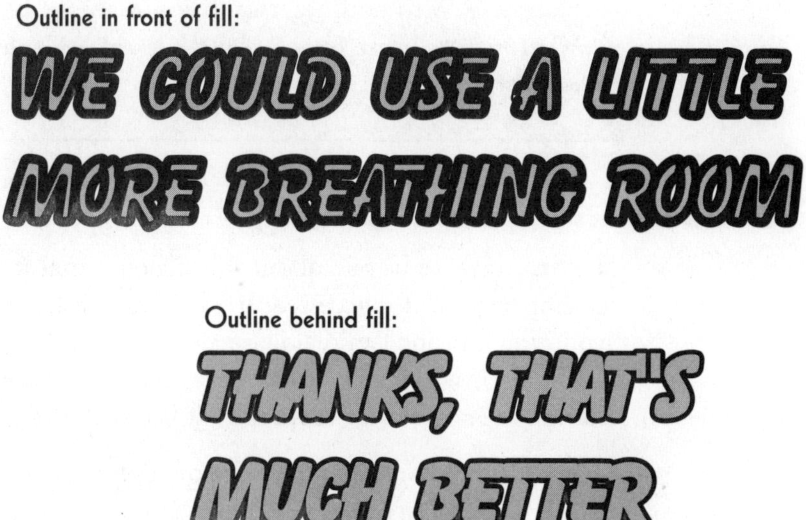

8.9

With the outline *behind* the fill, severely kerned text takes on a whole new look—and a much more readable one.

Outline in front of fill:

WE COULD USE A LITTLE
MORE BREATHING ROOM

Outline behind fill:

THANKS, THAT'S
MUCH BETTER

Scale With Image

One problem with an outline is that, by default, its thickness does not change as the object is enlarged or reduced. Though this is sometimes desirable, many times it is not.

Let's say you create a rectangle and apply an outline to it. If you then scale the rectangle up by 200% or reduce it by 50%, the width of the outline will stay the same. You may end up with a very small outline that seems out of place once the rectangle is enlarged, or a large outline that is unattractive when the rectangle is reduced. In either case, you can turn on the Scale With Image option. This ensures that the Outline Pen remains proportionally correct to the rectangle, regardless of the rectangle's size.

AUTHOR'S NOTE

When you scale arrowheads, they exhibit behavior similar but opposite to scaled outlines—that is, the size of the arrowhead always increases or decreases as the thickness of the line changes. As with outlines, this may not always be what you want; unfortunately, there is no way to override this default condition with arrowheads.

The Outline Color Dialog

The first thing to be said about this dialog is that its name changes depending on how it is accessed: If you invoke it from the Outline tool flyout, the Outline Pen dialog, or the Shift+F12 hotkey, it is called Outline Color. If you invoke it from the color bar in the Pen roll-up or the Outline page of Object Properties, it is called Select Color.

Except for the advanced technique of applying color trapping for offset color printing (discussed in Chapter 29), this dialog doesn't see a lot of action in its role as Outline Color. For most users, there is only so much you can do to a line around an object. This dialog becomes more vital when used to change an object's fill color, when it takes on yet a third name: Uniform Fill. All the controls that make this such a robust dialog— choices of palettes, color models, percentages of color values, and custom names—are in fact applicable to outlines as well as fills, but we'll postpone a full discussion of them to Chapter 9.

Setting the Outline Pen Defaults

With its factory settings, DRAW creates black outlines with a width of .2 point for all graphics objects, and no outlines for text. Although it's rare that you'll want outlines around text characters, you might very well want a different default condition for outlines around graphic objects such as ellipses, rectangles, and curves.

To change one of DRAW's default outlines for the current drawing, proceed as though you are changing an existing object—just don't select one. Whenever DRAW senses that you have invoked an outline command without selecting an object first, you are asked one of the questions shown in Figure 8.10. You can change the outline default settings for three different sets of elements: graphic objects, artistic text, or paragraph text. If you want to apply the same new default to all three types of elements, check all three boxes before continuing.

8.10

You can change
pen defaults simply
by *not* selecting
an object before
invoking one of
the outline tools.

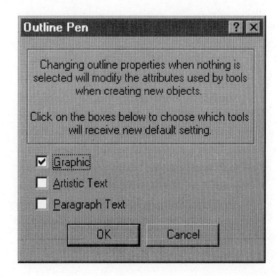

NEW FOR 6

In all previous versions of DRAW, changes made in this way were applied permanently to the default text or graphic styles, and affected every subsequent document created. So if your chosen default for graphic objects was a 5-point purple outline, that's what you would get for every ellipse, rectangle, and curve that you drew until the end of time or until you again changed the defaults, whichever came first. In DRAW 6.0, these changes only apply to the current document, and you must use the Styles Manager roll-up to make permanent changes to the default styles.

For more insight into establishing and controlling default settings, check out Chapter 14, where we will discuss some of the exciting changes in DRAW's styles and templates.

And now...on to the superstar fill tools.

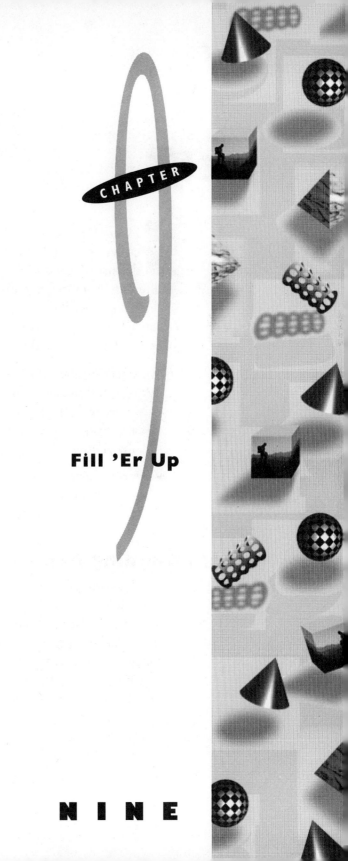

CHAPTER

9

Fill 'Er Up

NINE

If CorelDRAW were a football team, the nodes and paths we discussed in several of the earlier chapters would be our offensive and defensive ends and linebackers—the backbone of the team, though often unrecognized and unloved by the fans. Continuing the analogy, in this chapter we'll look at DRAW's marquee players, the team's superstars. They may not always be the most valuable performers, but they consistently capture the spotlight with their glamour and charisma.

We're talking about DRAW's wildly popular tools for filling objects. It's not that outlines aren't important, and we don't deny that nodes and curves are truly the foundation upon which everything else stands. But fills are always in the public eye, grabbing the headlines and capturing the imagination of the public.

As in the previous chapter on outlining, here, too, we assume you have a modest familiarity with the fundamentals of filling objects, as introduced in Part I. This chapter picks up from there.

Understanding Fills

There's nothing very complicated about the concept of applying fill patterns. Just as an outline is the visible perimeter of an object, a fill is whatever is placed inside that perimeter. Any color, shade, or pattern that is inside an object is considered a fill. The sole requirement is that the selected object must be completely closed before it can accept a fill, which makes sense when you think about it—how else could DRAW identify the boundaries of the area to be filled? (See Figure 9.1.)

9.1

Any closed curve
can contain a fill.

These objects have defined closed areas

These objects do not—how would DRAW know what to fill?

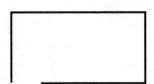  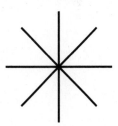

When a vector graphic is closed, you can treat whatever is inside as a single entity. If the area contains a fill and you enlarge or reduce the object, the fill follows suit. It's all part of the "intelligence" we discussed in Chapter 1—the result of creating objects from mathematical descriptions rather than individual pixels on the screen or dots on the paper. (Although, as you'll see later, bitmapped patterns can be used as fills.)

Figure 9.2 is an overview of DRAW's fill tools. The relationships between the Fill flyout, roll-ups, and dialogs are similar to those for outlines—the flyout's icons offer access to the two roll-ups (no. 2 and 3 in Figure 9.2); to all the dialogs (nos. 1 and 4–9); and to a few preset values. The roll-ups give a more extensive selection of values, plus access to most of the full dialogs.

9.2

The Fill flyout and roll-ups are your gateways to a myriad of tools and functions.

1 2 3

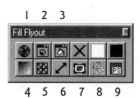

4 5 6 7 8 9

5

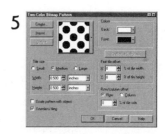

I

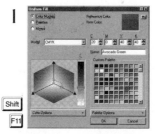

Shift

F11

6

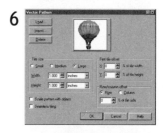

2

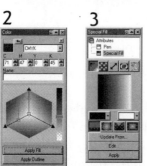

3

7

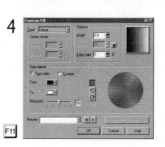

8

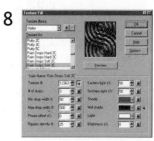

4

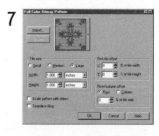

F11

9

But this bird's-eye view, complex as it appears, is only a surface view. Underneath is a labyrinth of interrelated functions and dialogs, up to three levels deep. At the risk of oversimplifying, we group DRAW's fill capabilities into four categories:

- **Uniform fills,** in which a single color or shade covers the entire selected object.

- **Fountain fills,** in which colors or shades gradually change as they traverse the object. There are four types of fountains: *linear, radial, conical,* and *square.*

- **Patterns,** in which a repeating pattern covers the object. There are four types of patterns: *two-color bitmap patterns, full-color bitmap patterns, full-color vector patterns,* and *PostScript textures.*

- **Texture fills,** in which an artistic blend of bitmap images is poured into the object. This feature was shown off in Chapter 2.

Applying Fills

The Fill flyout is your gateway to the Color and Special Fill roll-ups and all of the Fill dialogs.

We already introduced the Color roll-up (no. 2 in Figure 9.2) to you in Chapter 8. It provides quick access to solid colors that can be applied as either uniform fills or outlines. The Special Fill roll-up (no. 3) takes you to fountain fills (dialog 4), two-color bitmap patterns (dialog 5), full-color vector and bitmap patterns (dialogs 6 and 7), and texture fills (dialog 8). Just click one of the roll-up's icons to get the basic functions for that fill type. Click the Edit button, and you get the full dialog, with all the bells and whistles.

The × icon on the Fill flyout lets you remove all fills from an object. To the right of the × are icons for applying white and 100% black.

Like the Pen roll-up, the Fill roll-up is most handy for quick, frequent changes, where you want the controls right at your mousetips. Otherwise, you may prefer heading straight to the dialogs. F11 and Shift+F11 give you immediate access to the Fountain and Uniform Fill dialogs, for working with the most spectacular and most popular, respectively, of DRAW's fill types.

There is some overlap between the topics in this chapter on fill patterns and the subjects covered in Chapter 28, "Color for the Color Blind." Most of the intricate color issues will be examined in Chapter 28. Here in this chapter we focus more on the *implementation* of color than on the theory of color, but these subjects cannot be completely separated and we don't try.

Uniform Fills

If the Fountain Fill is perhaps DRAW's most spectacular fill tool, the workhorse Uniform Fill is undoubtedly the most widely used. Uniform Fill's basic function is, as its name implies, to fill an object (technically, any closed curve) uniformly with a single color, tint, or shade of gray.

As with outline colors, you can select any color from your on-screen palette to fill a selected object, by simply clicking on that color with Button 1. But that's just the beginning of the possibilities.

Color Options Galore

The Uniform Fill dialog probably looks familiar to you. Except for the name on the menu bar, this dialog box is exactly the same as the Outline Color dialog you met in Chapter 8. Here the basic function is helping you choose a specific color, tint, or gray shade to apply to a selected object, and Uniform Fill does this with complete thoroughness. It offers seven different industry-standard models for defining colors, and an option to use custom palettes with specific color mixtures or names. Of equal (or greater) importance: You can choose shades of gray in increments of less than 1%, and set precise line screens in projects destined for high-resolution output.

Every film buff knows the classic, *The Three Faces of Eve,* the title of which springs from its heroine's multiple personalities. Well, the Uniform Fill dialog now has three faces, too. DRAW 5's Uniform Fill dialog was divided into three sections devoted to Color Models, Custom Palettes, and Mixers. But in DRAW 6.0, you choose instead among three different displays, shown in Figure 9.3. Click one of the radio buttons in the upper-left of the dialog, and here's what you see:

- Click on the Color Models radio button, and you get a drop-down box of ten different selections, with a three-dimensional representation of the color space for the model you choose.

- When you select Palettes, the drop-down list contains choices for Uniform Colors, FOCOLTONE, PANTONE (spot or process), TruMatch, SpectraMaster, TOYO, and DIC colors. The area just below displays the palette selected.

- Choose Mixers, and you get a workspace for mixing and blending colors that can replace or be added to colors on your working palette.

That's all well and good, but just what do those three terms mean?

Color Models View It's important to distinguish between color models and color palettes, and we'll get to palettes in the upcoming section. A color *model* is a standardized system for describing colors, using measurable, repeatable formulas to specify hues, tints, and shades.

DRAW supports seven different color models: CMY, CMYK, RGB, HSB, HLS, L*a*b*, and YIQ (CMY and L*a*b* are new to DRAW 6.0). In addition, there is a grayscale "color model" that is really more of a palette, containing 255 levels of gray. CMYK is the model you're most likely to use for any work destined for the printed page, since it defines all colors in terms of the four process-color printing inks. Color Models are discussed later in this chapter, and in more detail in Chapter 28.

9.3

**The three faces of
the Uniform Fill
dialog**

That was then...

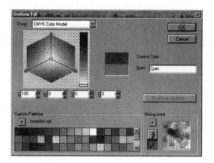

...And this is now

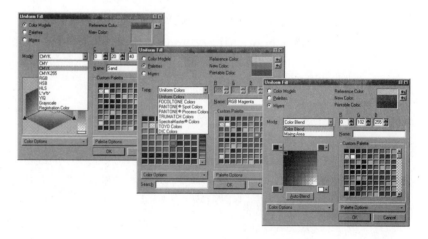

Color Palettes View   Think of these just as you do an artist's palette—a selection of colors you have available to paint with (in this case, to draw with). DRAW supplies several process color palettes, as well as RGB Uniform Colors and PANTONE spot colors.

Colors selected from one of these palettes are always based on the same color model, using the same proportions of the components of that model, and are identified by industry-standard names or numbers. Although colors such as "sky blue" and "forest green" might be subject to personal interpretation, the spot color PANTONE Reflex Blue is *always* produced with exactly the same color of ink, and the process color Tru-Match 22-A7 is *always* printed with 65% cyan, 0% yellow, 50% magenta, and 42% black.

Your current default palette is always displayed in the lower-left quadrant of the Uniform Fill dialog and (unless you choose to hide it) at the bottom of the screen.

Mixers View   Like any good artist, you may sometimes want to change one of the colors on your working palette, or mix a new color and add it to your palette. The Mixers option in the Uniform Fill dialog provides two ways for you to do this: You can create a blend from a combination of four selected colors, as illustrated in Figure 8.3, or use the brush and eyedropper tools available in the Mixing Area mode. You can "pick up" colors for your mixing area from either an existing palette or an imported bitmap.

Name That Color

The Uniform Fill dialog as pictured in Figure 9.2 (dialog 1) is considered the standard configuration: showing colors by the CMYK model. Practically any color imaginable can be created by mixing percentages of cyan, magenta, yellow, and black. If you are producing four-color work and want direct control over the percentages of those four colors, this is the color model you would use.

However, you can easily switch to a different method of specifying colors. Suppose, for instance, your new CEO is partial to fire-engine red and you are under corporate orders to henceforth set all headlines for the company newsletter in PANTONE 179 (one of over 700 spot colors defined by the PANTONE Matching System). Simply click on the

Palettes button, open the drop-down list, and choose PANTONE Spot Colors. Now select Show Color Names under Color Options, enter **179** in the Search field, and before you know it, your screen will offer you the list illustrated in Figure 9.4.

Use this same technique to select an industry-standard color from any of the process-color palettes.

You can also select other color models and dial up Red/Green/Blue percentages, spin the Hue/Saturation/Brightness wheel, or explore the possibilities of HLS, YIQ, and L*a*b*. Chapter 28 includes a comprehensive discussion of the differences between spot and process colors.

9.4

Choosing a PANTONE spot color is as easy as asking for its name.

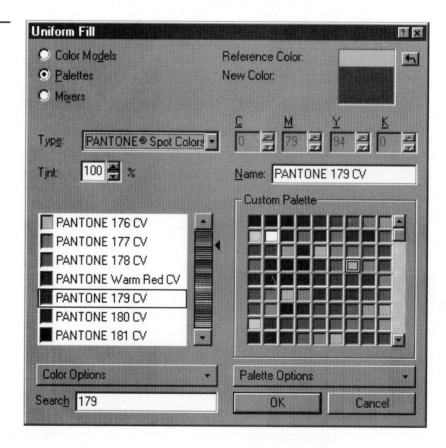

WATCH OUT!

When you're working with color, if you trust your monitor's representation of the color that you'll get on the final printout, you'll be in for a rude and potentially costly surprise. To put it plainly, monitors lie. Certainly they do the best they can, but they emit light and display color very differently from a printing press that's applying ink to paper. DRAW has built-in features to compensate for monitor distortion; but during crunch time, when your color projects are on the line, it's best to trust those handy color swatch books from **PANTONE** and TruMatch. Both will show you exactly what a color will look like when printed. Remember, if you choose colors by looking at your monitor and saying, "Gee, that one looks nice—I think I'll use it," you're asking for trouble. More on this in Chapter 28.

The Power of CMYK

CMYK may not be much in the acronym department, but the CMYK model for choosing colors is perhaps the most popular of all. An exhaustive range of colors can be created by mixing the right percentage of the four colors Cyan, Magenta, Yellow, and Black. *K* is for black rather than *B*, so that it's not confused with blue (which is actually not a primary color but rather a mixture of cyan and magenta). CORELDRW.CPL, CorelDRAW's default color palette, is a CMYK palette.

The CMYK color model (see Figure 9.5) provides you with the conveniences described in the following sections.

Precision   If you know the precise percentages of the four colors in your fill, you can enter them directly in the boxes provided for each color. But don't bother with the little spin-box arrows; try it this way, instead:

1. Highlight the number currently entered in the field for Cyan.

2. Type the new value desired.

3. Press Tab to instantly jump to the Magenta field.

9.5

Setting colors using the CMYK color model

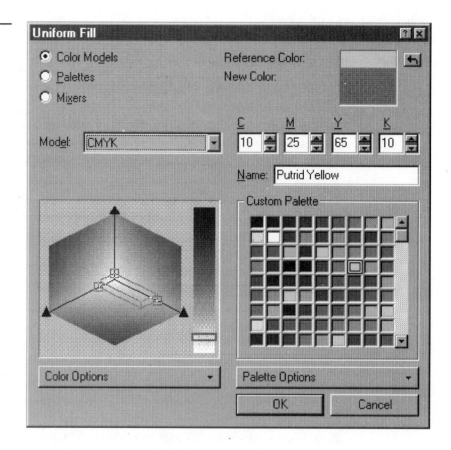

4. Enter the desired value and press Tab again.

5. Continue through the four color fields, and OK the dialog when you're done.

Flexibility   When you're looking for a color for an on-screen presentation, you may not much care about its specific composition—you just want it to look good. This is a job for the Uniform Fill dialog's visual selector (at bottom-left in the Color Models view), or the color palette (at lower-right in all views), or the mixing area (available in the Mixers view). With all three of these tools, you can browse across the entire spectrum of available colors. The preview box in the upper-right of the dialog shows you the current color for the selected object, and the new one you have chosen or mixed.

NEW FOR 6

As you can see in some of this chapter's figures, DRAW 6.0 sometimes adds a third section to the preview box, labeled Printable Color. This display is part of the Color Correction system; it warns you when the color you see on screen does not accurately reflect the color you will get from the printer. The warning only appears with certain colors, although we think it should be issued for all colors, all of the time.

DRAW 6.0 has the same three-dimensional CMYK visual selector introduced in version 5, with axes for cyan, magenta, and yellow. Dragging a corner of the center rectangle along any of the axes adjusts the amount of that particular color. The slider next to the cube is for independent adjustment of the amount of black to be added.

All views of the Uniform Fill dialog include a visible color palette, matching the currently selected on-screen palette, from which you can select, add, and reorder the placement of colors.

Notice in Figure 9.5 that DRAW permits you to assign your own names to colors. You can choose a technical name that describes the composition of the color, such as "4Magenta/85Yellow"; or one that is more descriptive of the color's use; or even, as we have done in the figure, one that reflects your opinion of it. Whatever you choose, your name for the color is what will appear in the preview box on DRAW's status bar when you select an object that uses that color.

NEW FOR 6

> In previous versions of DRAW, the status bar always contained preview boxes showing the outline and fill of a selected object. In DRAW 6.0, these are optional. You can customize the status bar (like just about everything else in the program's interface) to suit your tastes or needs. Two of the choices for display are large and small color swatches for the fill and outline color of selected objects. Fill color names are displayed on the status bar if you choose a large swatch; they are not displayed with small swatches.

Gray Shades   You can assign shades of gray while you are working in CMYK, by entering a percentage of less than 100 for Black and setting the other three colors to 0%. For even greater control over grayscale gradations, choose the CMYK255 model, which allows you to enter values between 0 and 255 for each color.

However, accurate reproduction of black-and-white drawings requires more than just selecting the correct shades of gray, and the subject of black-and-white printing can become complex in a hurry. In order to get high-quality output in black and white, you need to know something about how PostScript imagesetters render percentages of black. Chapter 29, "Turning Gray with Dignity," explores this topic. Whether you are sending your work to a 300-dpi laser printer or a high-resolution imagesetter or film recorder, you have to know how to tell DRAW what to do with all those dots.

RGB and HSB

These two color models are based on the theory that a color can be defined in terms of the percentages of red, green, and blue (RGB) that the color contains, as well as by the Hue, Saturation, and Brightness (HSB). The RGB and HSB models are less precise than CMYK, and because DRAW converts colors to CMYK values for color-separation work anyway, you might as well start with CMYK if you are doing separations.

For printing to an in-house color printer or creating color for on-screen work, RGB and HSB work as well as CMYK; just choose the one of the three that seems the most intuitive.

DRAW's Uniform Colors palette is an RGB palette. For more information on the RGB and HSB color models, consult the CorelDRAW User's Manual or online Help.

The Other Models

DRAW also includes three other specialized color models, designed for use in specific industries or applications rather than commercial printing.

- HLS, a variation on HSB, is based on Hue, Lightness (the perceived intensity of a reflecting object), and Saturation.

- YIQ is the color model used in North American television broadcast systems. The Y component contains luminance (black and white) information; color information is encoded into the I and Q components. The HLS and YIQ color models were first introduced in version 5 of DRAW and PhotoPAINT.

- New to DRAW 6.0 is the L*a*b* model, a device-independent model that encompasses all the colors that can be specified in both the CMYK and RGB models. L*a*b* is primarily used in industrial applications.

Using Custom Palettes

Although most users rarely change from the default palette (CORELDRW.CPL), the program ships with several other palettes. To use a different palette as your default, click on the Palette Options bar from any view of the Uniform Fill dialog, choose Open Palette, and navigate to the location of the palette you wish to use. CORELDRW.CPL is in the \CUSTOM directory, and DRAW'S other process-color palettes are in \PROGRAMS\DATA. It's always a good idea, before modifying any industry-standard palette, to save it under a different name. You can store custom palettes that you create or acquire in any convenient location on your hard disk.

You'll notice that the Open Palette dialog has a drop-down list where you can select between Custom (.CPL), Spot (.IPL), and Process (.PAL) palettes. If you're only using palettes from DRAW 5 and 6.0, all palette file names end in .CPL. Prior to version 5, DRAW's process-color palettes were .PAL files; spot color palettes were .IPL files. These older palettes can still be opened and used in DRAW 5 and 6.0, but any modifications will be saved in a .CPL file.

Creating Your Own Palettes

DRAW allows you to create custom palettes as well as modify existing ones. It supplies palettes based on several different color models, but you can mix additional colors and add them to a palette, rename or change the definitions of existing colors, or create whole new palettes.

Working with custom palettes is the first of several potentially confusing topics when you're learning to use DRAW's color engine. "As if this CMYK, RGB, PANTONE business weren't enough, you say I can create my own colors, too??" Well, not quite, and herein lies the confusion.

It helps to think of a palette in the literal sense. Imagine you are a painter working on a portrait. You probably have enough paint in your studio to create just about any color you might want, but as you approach a particular project, you choose a few in particular. You dab them on your palette and wield your brush. The palette is designed to make accessible to you *the specific colors you have chosen for this painting*. You know you can go get others, but on the palette are the ones you expect to use now. This analogy holds true in your electronic studio, as well. DRAW enables you to mix or pick out particular colors and add them to a fresh palette. And you can assign your own names to these colors, too, just as you can in existing palettes.

Let's say you are in charge of newsletters for three different divisions of a large company. The corporate publishing department has established an official color that you are required to use for the logo and certain other elements. Beyond that, you have established a few other color standards of your own: a yellow tint for frames around text and captions, and a shade of gray for bullets and drop caps. The only other color you expect to use in the three newsletters is black for the text.

This is a job for a custom palette. Here is how you would go about creating it:

1. Open the Uniform Fill dialog box. (Select or create an object first, so DRAW won't think you are trying to change the default fill pattern.)

2. At Palette Options, click New Palette on the flyout menu list.

3. Enter a filename for your new palette and select the directory in which you wish to save it. We'll take advantage of Windows 95's long file names and call this one Newsletter. DRAW automatically adds the .CPL extension.

4. Click on Save to return to the Uniform Fill dialog. Your screen will look like Figure 9.6. Notice that all the colors in the default palette have vanished.

5. You know the specific CMYK color composition of the predefined logo, as well as for the yellow tint you are using for text boxes. So, if CMYK is not already selected, choose it from the Model drop-down list.

6. Enter **70%** for Cyan, **80%** for Magenta, and **0%** for Yellow and Black.

7. In the Name text box, type **Corporate Logo**.

8. Click the Color Options button and choose Add Color To Palette. The new color will promptly appear in the first box on the on-screen palette.

9. Click the Palette Options button, and choose Save Palette.

9.6

A fresh palette, just
waiting to have some
colors added to it

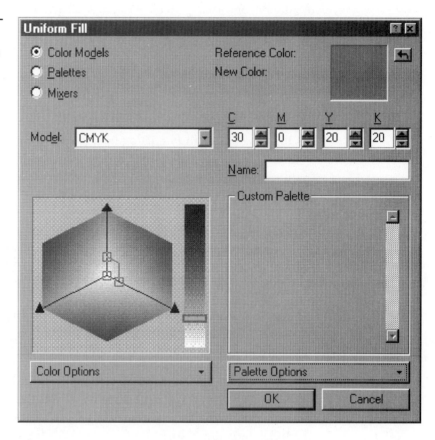

You haven't just "invented" this color. That's not what we mean when
we say "creating a custom color"; chances are pretty good that someone,
somewhere, has already used 70 Cyan/80 Magenta. But by adding the
color and its name, Corporate Logo, to your new palette, you have
made it your own and can now easily apply it to elements in your
newsletters.

To create the yellow tint for text boxes, follow the steps above, this time
setting the color to 0% Cyan, 0% Magenta, 70% Yellow, and 0%
Black. Let's call this color Yellow Screens. The bullets are 50% Black

with all other colors at 0%; you will probably want both a solid white and black in your palette, also. And don't forget our CEO's favorite—PANTONE 179 from the PANTONE spot color palette. Because this is a named color in a standard palette, PANTONE 179 CV will automatically appear in the Name field. You'll have no problem whatsoever mixing colors from different color models in the same palette. Remember, all you are doing is making these colors more accessible to you. Any color that you can identify in DRAW can be added to a custom palette.

When you're done, your Uniform Fill dialog will look like Figure 9.7; to keep this palette for later experimentation, choose Save Palette from the Palette Options drop-down list.

9.7

Your completed color palette

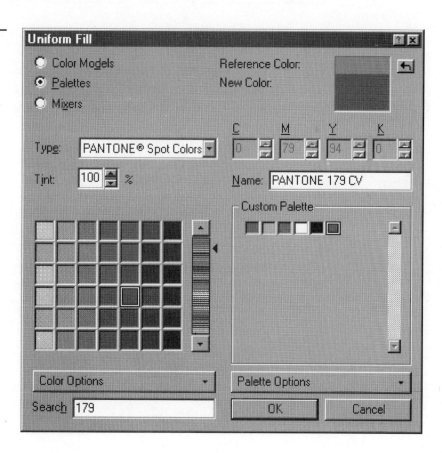

INSIDE INFO

A Tip for Locating Colors: If you are using one of the color palettes that represent an established collection of colors—such as PANTONE or TruMatch—you could spend quite a long time searching for a color that you know is buried in there somewhere… Try this: Get a list of the specific names assigned to the colors, by clicking Palette Options and selecting Show Color Names. Then use the Search box to locate the color by name. For instance, typing in 586 with the PANTONE spot palette selected will retrieve PANTONE 586 CV, a shade of yellow with a bit of cyan mixed in.

Keep It Simple   Restricting yourself to a palette with a limited number of colors that complement each other is often the best way to produce visually effective documents. This "enforced discipline" is the idea behind the color palettes used in the templates of most presentation programs, including Corel PRESENTS. And, as you'll see in Chapter 13, this same kind of restraint is the key to effective typography. Using ten different fonts in a document won't necessarily make it five times better than using two; however, it might make it five times worse. The same caution applies to color.

At first, you may feel hemmed in by such a small assortment of color choices, especially if you have grown accustomed to seeing an entire row of colors on your working palette. But remember, you can always use other colors, even if they are *not* on your palette. Just return to Uniform Fill and dial up any CMYK, RGB, or other values you want. Whenever a color isn't named in your custom palette, DRAW will refer to it on the status bar as "unnamed color." Name or no, DRAW will honor the specific mix of colors you have designated for it.

We have discussed using custom colors in the Uniform Fill dialog—but what about the Color Palette? It's easy. If you want to see your custom colors on your palette, just choose View / Color Palette / Custom Colors. However, many DRAW users prefer to keep their palettes set for a particular color model, such as PANTONE or TruMatch.

♣

Before you begin the next section and wade into the treacherous waters of fountain fills, it is a good idea to return your palette and color model selection to their original defaults. Set your color model to CMYK and use the Palette Options button in the Uniform Fill dialog to reopen CORELDRW.CPL.

Fountain Fills

Of the two stars in the DRAW show—Uniform Fill and Fountain Fill—the fountain is the superstar with the flamboyant personality. It goes to only the most exclusive clubs, stays out late dancing every night, and always seems to be embroiled in some public controversy or another. Not surprisingly, fountain fills are responsible for some of the most fabulous work ever done with DRAW, as well as some of the most fantastic disasters.

Also known as a *gradient fill,* a fountain fill is most often used to render an object in a constantly changing light. The rendezvous of sky and water at a horizon serves as the classic opportunity to use a fountain fill. When commanded, DRAW starts at one side of the object with one shade or color, and gradually changes it into another color or shade at the other side. You tell DRAW what the starting and ending colors are, how abruptly or gradually to make the transition, and where to begin making the transition.

Fountain fills have been available in DRAW since the early days, but version 4.0 brought many new features to fountains—the most noteworthy being the ability to change from one color to another and then to a third, fourth, fifth, and so on, within the fill. This capability made the fountain fill that much more powerful…and that much more dangerous. Here, we'll discuss not only how to use fountains, but also when and when *not* to use them.

To create your first fountain fill, follow these steps:

1. Draw a large rectangle and make sure it is selected.

2. Open the Fountain Fill dialog. You can do this from the Fill fly-out menu, with the hotkey F11, or from the Special Fill roll-up.

3. OK the dialog as is; click Apply if you used the roll-up.

That's it—you have created a fountain, as shown in Figure 9.8. Both the dialog and the roll-up will default to a fountain going from white on top to black on the bottom.

9.8

DRAW's default fountain fill—from white all the way to black

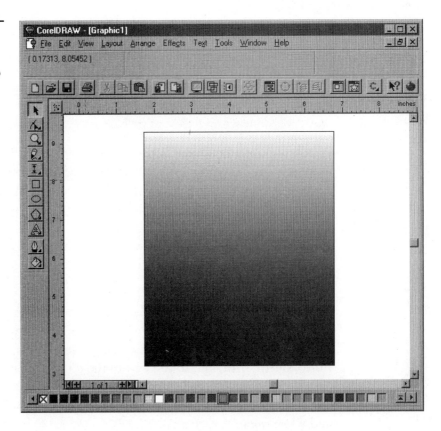

AUTHOR'S NOTE

If you try the fountain in Figure 9.8 on your system, it may look
different. That's because rendering fountain fills is a very taxing
proposition for video cards. Don't worry if your fountain fills
don't look as smooth as the ones shown here; on-screen
representation has no impact on printing. You can still get the
highest-quality output.

Lines, Rads, Squares, and Cones

Figure 9.9 shows the Fountain Fill dialog, with the Type drop-down list
displaying the four types of fountains that you can apply to a closed object.

9.9

**The foot of the
fountain**

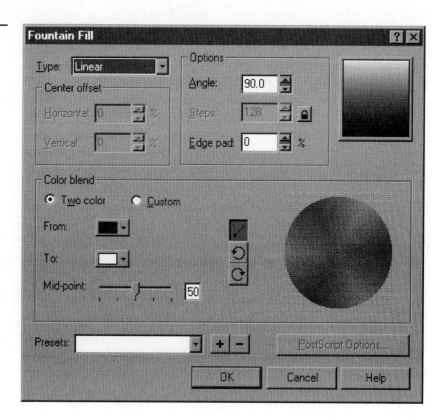

The default fountain is a *linear* fountain fill—one that flows evenly from one side of the object to the other. *Radial* fills travel in concentric circles from the inside to the outside of the object. In a *conical* fill, each band of color extends from the center to the edge of the object. In DRAW's *square* fountain fill, the gradations of color are produced by small rectangles that work their way from the outside to the center. All four types are illustrated in Figure 9.10.

9.10

DRAW can create four types of fountain fills—linear, radial, conical, and square.

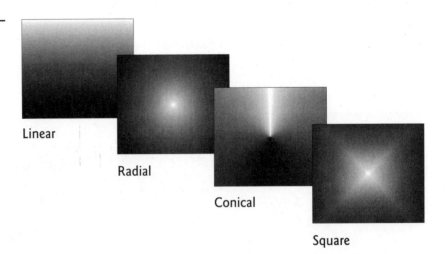

Linear

Radial

Conical

Square

If you haven't noticed already, you soon will: DRAW takes longer to draw fountains to the screen than it does uniform fills. Sometimes a *lot* longer—especially with the radial and conical fountains. If these delays are unacceptable, you have three choices:

- Switch to Wireframe view, where the fountains won't show.

- Move the filled objects to another layer and hide the layer.

- Reduce the value for Steps. You can do this either from the Options box of the Fountain Fill dialog, or from the Preview Fountain Steps box in Tools / Options / Display / Preview Fountain Steps. Reducing the Steps instructs DRAW to transition more bluntly and less often.

Try the last alternative first. If you keep the Steps number at 20, your fountains will draw much faster. As Figure 9.11 shows, they won't look as good, but at least you'll be able to see them; the other strategies require that you hide them altogether. For the best output, increase the value when you're ready to print. We'll talk more about Steps later in the chapter.

9.11

If fountains become a drag on your system, tell DRAW not to show you so much detail. These 20-step fountains required less than one second to draw; the ones in Figure 9.10 needed almost five seconds.

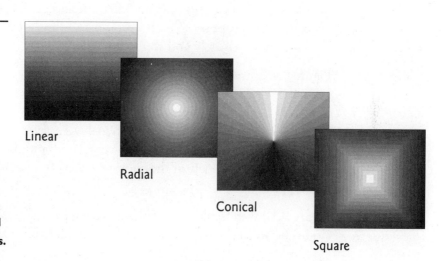

Linear

Radial

Conical

Square

With all four fountain types, the preview box in the dialog gives you a fair approximation of the fill's appearance—at least, of how it would look in a rectangle. Of course, you can apply a fountain fill to any object or collection of curves, as long as they contain closed shapes.

Choosing Colors

Perhaps the most important factor in a fountain fill is your choice of colors or shades, and DRAW doesn't make the choice easy, throwing lots of variables at you. The From and To color buttons display drop-down boxes containing all the colors in the currently active palette, so you can determine the start and finish colors for the fountain. If you need more precise control over colors, you can click Others from the drop-down list and reach the Uniform Fill dialog. (Its title bar will say Fountain Fill, however, so you know you are choosing the color for one side of the fountain. Nevertheless, it is identical in every way to the Uniform Fill dialog discussed earlier in the chapter.)

Creating the Right Blend

Once you have chosen the start and finish colors, you can then choose how DRAW will transition from one to the other. The default setting takes the shortest possible path from start to finish, but you can also choose a more leisurely and scenic route.

Figure 9.12 shows two different fountain fills, both changing from pale green to red. The top example is a direct blend, and the diagonal black line on the color wheel verifies the quick route from one color to the other. The lower example, a counterclockwise blend in which DRAW spirals around the color wheel, involves a larger number of colors. The three buttons to the left of the color wheel allow you to choose the blend path.

Figure 9.12 is incapable of truly illustrating the difference in color transitions between the two, so we suggest the following study aids:

■ Notice how the line for the direct fountain passes near the center of the color wheel where all the colors combine—we like to refer to the colors in this area as "yuck." But the rainbow fountain around the perimeter passes through colors that are purer and more defined.

■ Open 09-12.CDR from the PRACTICE directory of the Companion CD. On screen, you can really see the difference between the two.

Now try creating a rainbow fountain fill, by following these steps:

1. Draw a rectangle or ellipse of any shape, select it, and press F11 to access Fountain Fill.

2. For Color Blend, choose Two Color, and click on the clockwise rotation icon.

9.12

The lines on the color wheels show us the path these fountain fills will follow.

 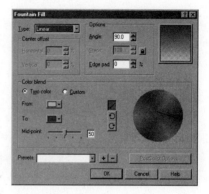

 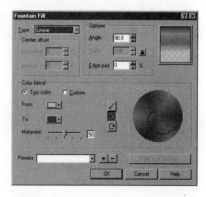

3. Set the From color to blue. You can probably pick it out of the drop-down color palette next to From; if not, click More and enter **100%** Cyan and **100%** Magenta, leaving the other two colors at **0%**.

4. Set the To color to cyan, using either the palette or the Fill dialog.

5. OK your way back out to the page, and notice the fountain fill applied to the object.

6. Use drag and dupe (see Chapter 4) to place a copy of the object near the original.

7. Press F11 to reach Fountain Fill. Leave the Blend set to Two Color, but now select the counterclockwise rotation icon.

8. OK back to the page and notice the dramatic difference.

Once again, our black-and-white rendition in Figure 9.13 doesn't do justice, but you can still get a sense of how many more colors are traversed from start to finish in the lower oval. You will find Figure 9.13 in the PRACTICE directory of the Companion CD as 09-13.CDR.

NEW FOR 6

By default, the midpoint of the transition between the From and To colors or shades of a fountain fill occurs at the exact center of the object being filled. DRAW 6.0 allows you to move the position of this midpoint closer toward the start or end of any linear or rainbow fill, using the Midpoint slider control located below the From and To color selection boxes. Figure 9.14 illustrates the effect of changing the midpoint of a linear fountain fill.

Creating Custom Fountains

Custom fountains let you create fountain fills that have a starting color, one or more middle colors, and a finish color. Simply choose Custom under Color Blend, and then designate the intermediate colors. Beware: The technical limit of intermediate colors—almost 100 colors!—far exceeds the limits of good taste.

9.13

Rainbow fountain fills can include dramatic shifts in color.

Try creating a linear fountain that goes from yellow at the bottom to blue in the middle to white at the top:

1. Create an object on the page and invoke Fountain Fill. We chose a balloon from the clip art library, but any object will do.

2. Set the angle of the fill to 90°.

3. Click the Custom button under Color Blend, and note that the small square on the left end of the color bar is darkened, indicating that it is the current color.

4. Click on yellow in the palette; or click on the color square next to Current to reach the Fountain Fill dialog, and set the color to a pleasing shade of yellow. The left side of the bar turns yellow.

Midpoint = 50

Midpoint = 25

Midpoint = 75

5. Double-click on the small black square; it turns white to indicate it is no longer the current color, and a black downward-
pointing triangle appears next to it. Drag the triangle into the
middle of the color bar. (To place it *exactly* in the middle, enter
50 in the Position box.)

6. Set the color for the middle to blue, from either the palette or the Fill dialog.

7. Click on the square on the right end of the color bar and set its color to white. Your screen should look like Figure 9.15.

9.15

You can define up to 99 intermediate steps in a custom fountain.

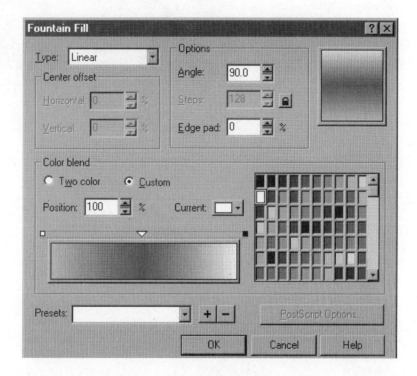

8. OK your way back out to the page, where your selected object will have a fill like the one in Figure 9.16, which is also included in the PRACTICE directory of the Companion CD.

By the way, the above steps are what we did to apply the fancy fountain fill to the key in Chapter 5.

9.16

A three-way foun-
tain, from yellow
(bottom) through
blue (middle) to
white (top). We'll
leave it to you to
improve on our ren-
dition of the Corel
balloon.

A Word About Choosing Colors

Nothing is more fun and exciting than mixing many colors
to produce rainbows and fountains on color displays. Printing them, however, is an entirely different matter, and mistakes can be costly. Before you go wild with fountain fills,
you should know both your target output device and your
budgetary constraints.

Printing to a Color Desktop Printer: In this case you can go
wild. Color laser printers, thermal transfer printers, and ink-
based printers can create virtually any color. Limit yourself only
by your own imagination and (please!) your own good taste.

A Word About Choosing Colors (continued)

Creating Four-Color Separations: If you plan to create four negatives, one for each of the CMYK colors, then you can once again spread your wings. You can be confident that whatever colors DRAW uses as it traverses the rainbow, your four pieces of film negative will be able to represent them. Just remember that the printed colors will bear only a general resemblance to what your display shows.

Creating Spot-Color Separations: Here you must proceed with caution. Covered in detail in Chapter 28, spot-color printing is the method by which you can add just one color to a project, not four. Instead of using the CMYK model, requiring four separate pieces of film, you designate a single color—the spot color—and your print house makes two print runs (black and the spot color), not four.

With spot-color work, you must be careful not to create fountain fills that overstep your bounds. The safest route is to create fountain fills that vary the same spot color. This is easily done:

1. Define the From color. Click the From button, then Others, then Palettes, and choose PANTONE Spot Colors from the drop-down list. Let's say you choose Blue 072.

2. Use the same Blue 072 for the To color, but assign a different tint to it, say 30%. You can set a tint to any spot color, as shown in Figure 9.17.

This gives you a nice fountain, staying entirely within your spot color, Blue 072. The transition will be from 100% to 30%. If you want fancier fountains, you'll have to spring for extra colors, and you know what? They won't necessarily look as good.

9.17

To create a fountain that varies the intensity of one spot color, use a tint of less than 100% for one side of the color. Here, the To color is defined as a 30% tint of PANTONE Blue 072.

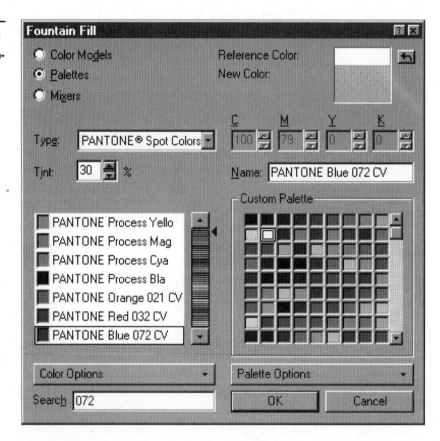

Other Fountain Options

Once you have defined the colors, you still have a treasure chest of toys to play with, all available in the Fountain Fill dialog. As with all of DRAW's tools, it's easy to get carried away, but you can also produce some very attractive and interesting effects. The following options let you determine various elements of how a fountain is displayed and printed.

Angle

When creating any fountains except radial, you can change the angle of the fountain, by either entering a different value for Angle in the Options box or directly manipulating the preview box. To do the latter, click and drag in the box, using Button 2. As you do this, the value in the Angle field automatically adjusts. Conical and square fountains will spin the start point around the center axis as the angle changes; linear fountains simply change the angle of the fill pattern. Radial fountains do not use the Angle field.

INSIDE INFO

> The Ctrl key constrains mouse movements in the preview box, just as it does on the page. If you hold Ctrl while changing the *offset* of a radial, conical, or square fountain, the incremental change is constrained to 10%. If you hold Ctrl while interactively changing the *angle* of a linear or conical fountain, you will notice the angle snapping to even increments. The amount of constraint—15° by default—can be changed in Tools / Options / General / Constrain Angle.

Center Offset

This set of controls affects the center point around which radial, conical, and square fountains are built. Negative values shift the center down and to the left; positive values shift the center up and to the right. As with the Angle option, you can either type values directly into the Horizontal and Vertical fields, or you can move your mouse into the preview box and directly manipulate the center offset. Click and drag with Button 1, and watch the center move and the corresponding Horizontal and Vertical values adjust.

Steps

The Steps field (under Options) controls the number of *bands* used to display and print a fountain. Fountain fills change from one color or shade to another; the number of gradations in the change is determined by the Steps value.

This can get confusing, because there are two other places in the program where you can effect this change, and the three controls interact.

If you keep the Steps field in its *locked* position (notice the little padlock to its right), then the number of steps displayed on screen defaults to the value set under Tools / Options / Display / Preview Fountain Steps (the "PFS setting"). Locked, therefore, means the value is locked to the *variable* value of the PFS setting. That setting is dynamic and global; change the PFS, and the display of all existing objects with fountain fills will adjust, as long as they were created with the Steps value locked.

If you unlock the Steps field in Fountain Fill and enter a value, you are establishing a permanent and fixed number of fountain steps for both displaying and printing that object. In other words, you are unlocking it from its dependence on the PFS setting for display, and the Fountain Steps settings in the Print or EPS Export dialogs.

Which leads us to the third place you can control the number of steps in a fountain fill: the Print or EPS Export dialog. If you change the Fountain Steps setting during printing or EPS exporting, you override the PFS setting for that particular print/export job. However, if you have manually entered a Steps value into Fountain Fill, that value cannot be overridden.

A Strategy for Steps   You're probably a little lost right about now, so here is our recommended strategy for Steps:

- Keep the Steps value in Fountain Fill locked, except when you want a particular fill to have a specific number of visible and printed steps.

- Keep the PFS setting in Tools / Options / Display set to 20, or some other number that gives you a realistic on-screen impression of the fill pattern without degrading performance.

- During printing and exporting, adjust the Fountain Steps setting as needed.

This strategy has three advantages. It lets you have fast screen response as the norm (with Fountain Steps of only 20); you can increase them all at once for better screen accuracy, just by increasing PFS; and you have complete control over steps during printing or exporting.

NEW FOR 6

> **DRAW 6.0 has added a fourth ingredient to the steps stew: an Auto Increase Fountain Steps option for PostScript printing and EPS exports. When this box is checked, the optimum number of steps is calculated at printing time based on the resolution and screen frequency of the output device, and each fountain fill (or pair of colors in a custom fill) that has been set to a lower value is increased to use that number of steps. The opposite side of the coin is Optimize Fountain Fills, which reduces the number of steps to the maximum number that can be printed by the device, for faster output.**

Figure 9.18 shows a few of the effects possible by adjusting the Offset, Angle, and Steps values for a fountain fill.

Edge Pad

This Options setting determines the level of the start and end colors for the fountain. At its default setting of 0%, the transition from one color to the next is smooth and consistent, and this is fine for most objects. But if you have created a curve that, say, comes to a sharp point at one end, the finish color at that end might not be visible. By adding an Edge Pad value, you tell DRAW to provide more room for the start and finish colors.

Figure 9.19 is an example of a simple shape that needs an edge pad in order for the entire color span to be displayed. Each of the three stars has the same linear fountain fill from dark to light, headed diagonally upward. The image on the top has no edge padding and, as you can see, the finish color of white is not present. DRAW starts at one edge of the selected object and goes to the other—but what we want to point out is that DRAW starts the fill at the very lower-left of the graphic, *where the selection handle is*, and goes all the way to the handle on the opposite corner. Because there is no part of the image in that top-right corner,

9.18

You can change
more than just a
fountain fill's colors.

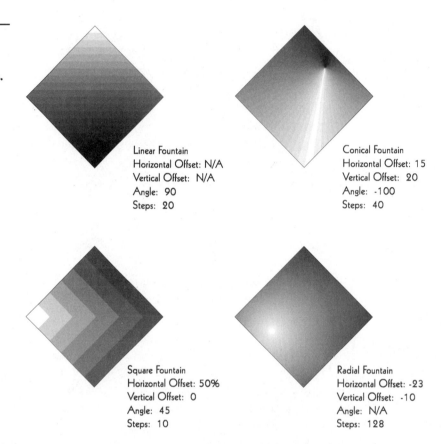

Linear Fountain
Horizontal Offset: N/A
Vertical Offset: N/A
Angle: 90
Steps: 20

Conical Fountain
Horizontal Offset: 15
Vertical Offset: 20
Angle: -100
Steps: 40

Square Fountain
Horizontal Offset: 50%
Vertical Offset: 0
Angle: 45
Steps: 10

Radial Fountain
Horizontal Offset: -23
Vertical Offset: -10
Angle: N/A
Steps: 128

the finish color is not represented. The bottom images in Figure 9.19
have edge pads of 15% and 25%, effectively bringing the white color
farther into the fountain fill.

One-Sided Edge Pads   Bear in mind, also, that Edge Pad works on
both sides of the fill, which may not always be necessary or desirable.
Notice there is extra black on the lower-left side of Figure 9.19's two
padded images. If you only want an edge pad on one side of the fill,
then you need to take a different approach: Create a custom fountain
fill, following the steps presented in the section just above. Designate an
intermediate color for your fountain fill, but *keep it the same as the ending color.* In effect, you will be creating your own edge pad, but just for
one side of the object.

9.19

In the two stars at the bottom, adding an edge pad allows the fountain fill to run its complete course.

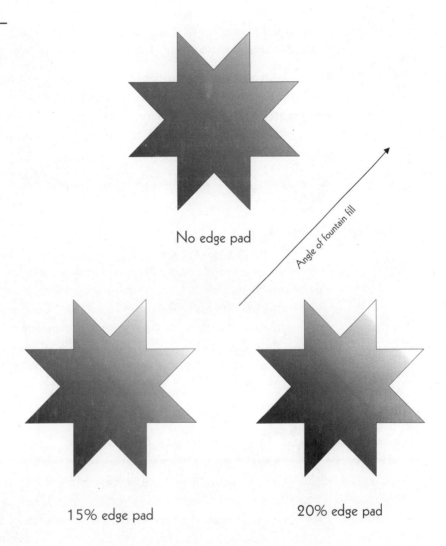

No edge pad

Angle of fountain fill

15% edge pad

20% edge pad

Presets

If you create a certain fountain fill over and over again, you can capture its settings as *presets* and easily apply them to other objects. This was a very tedious chore prior to DRAW 4.0, requiring you to find the object (usually in a different file), copy it to the Clipboard, open the file that has the object you want to fill, paste the object in from the Clipboard, copy its attributes, and then delete the pasted object. Whew!

Fortunately, those days are in the past. If you use a particular fountain fill repeatedly, in DRAW 4 and later you get to store all of the settings in a preset *and instantly apply those settings to other objects.*

To do this, you simply create the fountain fill, type a name in the Presets field, and save it by clicking on the + button at the right. Your new settings are then available to any closed object within any .CDR file. This holds true until you delete the preset (by selecting it in the Presets drop-down and clicking on the – button).

We'll explore Presets in greater detail in Chapter 14.

PostScript Options

This is the place to go for specifying halftone screens and overprint options when a job is destined for high-resolution film and/or color separations. If you work mostly with laser printers color or black-and-white—this may be unfamiliar terrain for you. But for those of you working regularly with an outside service bureau (or if you *are* a service bureau), then the settings in this relatively advanced dialog are crucial. These options are relevant only if you have installed a PostScript printer driver in Windows.

Chapters 27 and 29 contain in-depth discussions of the PostScript Options dialog.

The Last Word on Fountain Fills

Here is our parting thought concerning fountain fills: When in doubt, *don't use them!* We're not kidding. If you are undecided about whether the use of a fountain fill will add any value to your drawing, then it probably won't. In fact, it might detract.

We're prepared to be even more direct on this subject: If you output your final work on a 300×300-dpi printer, then you should *never* use fine fountain fills, which aim to show a smooth transition from one color to another. Your laser simply can't handle this; even its best effort will portray you as an amateur designer who tried for too much. The only fountain fills

The Last Word on Fountain Fills (continued)

you should attempt in this case are ones with low Steps values, designed to have blunt transitions, or ones with very coarse dot patterns. The 600×600 laser printers can produce credible results, provided you keep the From and To colors close together—for instance, from 15% to 45%.

Perhaps we have done you a disservice by showing you in this chapter the screen images that fountain fills can produce with a true-color 24-bit video adapter; you'll be hard-pressed to re-create them even on higher-resolution printers. If you expect to use fountain fills regularly for projects destined for film, you should read the discussions about setting Post-Script halftone screens in Chapters 27 and 29.

When desktop publishing first struck big, we could spot an amateur job from across the building: It had large Helvetica type inside a rounded rectangle with a gray background. Today, the dead giveaway of a bush-league electronic illustration is the misplaced fountain fill. If you want to help rescue the community of electronic designers from this collective notoriety, you'll approach fountain fills with caution and restraint.

Pattern Fills

Would you believe us if we said that you're only two-sevenths of the way through DRAW's fill tools? There are five more to go, but rest assured you've covered the two most important ones. The next four—the ones that produce patterns—constitute the frills, and in fact these patterns often go largely unused, even by very talented and skilled DRAW users.

Here is a brief run-through of the four tools that produce patterns for your objects.

Two-Color Patterns

Great for simple backgrounds, the Two-Color Bitmap Pattern dialog (no. 5 in Figure 9.2) comes packed with a few dozen patterns that can be quickly applied to selected objects. You don't need to know anything special to start using these patterns, except how to work a DRAW dialog. Try it:

1. Create a closed object and make sure it is selected.

2. Click the checkerboard icon on either the Fill flyout or the Special Fill roll-up. If you use the roll-up, clicking on Edit takes you to the full Two-Color Bitmap Pattern dialog. (When you invoke the dialog from the flyout, the bottom half of the dialog will be hidden. To see it, click the Tiling button.)

3. Click once on the pattern preview box to see all of the preset choices.

4. Find one you like and select it.

5. Click OK (then Apply, if you used the roll-up) to apply the pattern to the selected object.

Figure 9.20 shows a Two-Color Bitmap Pattern dialog, along with a representation of the pattern chosen in the dialog.

All of this dialog's controls invite experimentation. The Colors buttons work just as they do in the Fountain Fill dialog, and the Tile Size and Offset controls change the pattern's size and placement. Notice the Post-Script Options button is here again; we still owe you that discussion on advanced halftone settings, and you'll find it in Chapter 29.

AUTHOR'S NOTE

Most Transformations applied to objects with two-color bitmap pattern fills do not affect the pattern. For example, if you mirror or rotate the object, the orientation of the pattern remains constant. The same is true for full-color bitmaps, vector patterns, and texture fills. However, there is a Scale Pattern With Object option for two-color or full-color bitmaps and vector patterns.

Creating Your Own Patterns If you can't find the pattern you want, you can always make your own. Any objects you create, paste,

9.20

**One of dozens of
two-color patterns
for you to use**

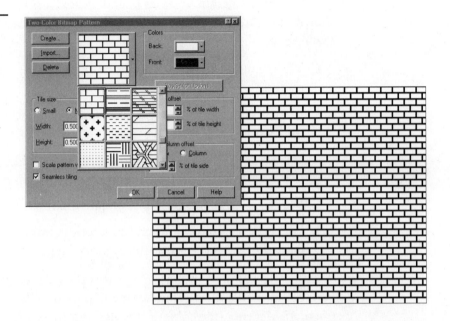

or import into DRAW can be turned into two-color bitmap patterns with the Tools / Create / Pattern command. You are asked to drag a marquee around the area, and then DRAW does the rest, creating a pattern from your objects and making it available in the pattern preview box.

You can also

- Import a file—any file, any format—directly into the pattern preview box.

- Create your own pattern from scratch with DRAW's built-in pattern editor, operating at the pixel level. To access the pattern editor, just click on the Create button in the Two-Color Bitmap Pattern dialog.

Clearly, the extent of DRAW's capabilities in this area make it possible to exceed the bounds of good taste. Remember that these patterns render only two colors, and you can't expect that any old image is going to make for a good pattern. At the very least, however, patterns are fun. We certainly enjoyed ourselves when we went back to SUNSET, the drawing you created in Chapter 6, and created a storm of birds, as shown in Figure 9.21. This was pretty easy to do, as described in the following general steps:

1. We opened SUNSET.CDR and removed the text and the flock of birds.

2. After selecting the rectangle that represents the sky, we opened the Two-Color Pattern dialog.

3. We imported EAGLE.CDR from the PRACTICE directory on the Companion CD.

4. We chose Large for the Tile Size, and offset the rows by 20%.

5. We chose a color other than black for the front (or foreground), clicked OK, and watched the eagle storm gather.

Adding a background to the eagles wasn't possible, because that would have constituted a third color. We could have used Black and 50 Cyan/25 Magenta (the color of the sky), but then the white part of the eagles would have also been the sky color. To provide a background for this picture, we would have to turn to...

Full-Color Patterns

Because full-color images use the entire CMYK spectrum of colors, virtually any color can be represented in a full-color pattern. DRAW 6.0 lets you choose from two types: full-color bitmaps and vector images.

Full-Color Bitmap Patterns   Full-color bitmap patterns are new to DRAW 6.0. They are implemented in essentially the same way as two-color bitmap patterns, and from a nearly identical dialog (no. 7 in Figure 9.2). However, each pixel in a two-color bitmap is limited to one of two colors you define; full-color bitmaps may contain any number of colors.

9.21

**Alfred Hitchcock
plays with
CorelDRAW.**

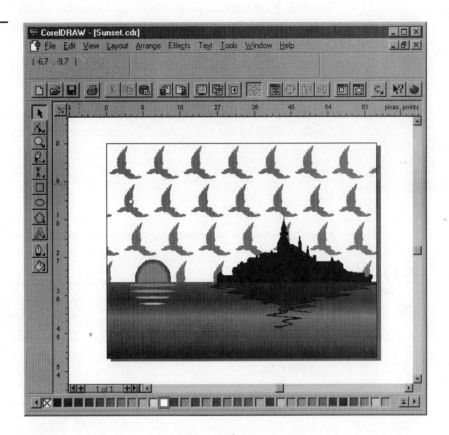

You cannot create full-color bitmap patterns from selected objects, but you can import existing bitmap files. When you import a color bitmap file, the resulting fill pattern will retain all of the colors in the source file.

Although any external bitmap can be imported to use as a full-color fill, remember that all of DRAW's supplied fills are designed to create a seamless effect when tiled. So if the design of your imported file is not symmetrical, it probably will not produce an attractive fill pattern.

Vector Patterns Full-color vector patterns are saved as DRAW files, but with .PAT instead of .CDR file name extensions. You can open and edit these files as you would any other DRAW file, or use any other existing DRAW file for a vector fill. The vector fill patterns supplied with DRAW are located in the \CUSTOM\PATTERNS directory.

To create a new vector fill, use the Tools / Create / Pattern command in the same way as for two-color fills, but choose the Full Color option from the Create Pattern dialog before you marquee-select the area to be used for the pattern.

You cannot change any of the colors in a vector pattern from the Vector Fill dialog (no. 6 in Figure 9.2). When making your own full-color patterns, you need to define all of your colors before you create the pattern.

INSIDE INFO

If you want your new vector pattern to be available in the Vector Fill dialog's drop-down list, be sure to save it in the \CUSTOM\PATTERNS subdirectory. Deleting a vector pattern from the drop-down list will also delete the corresponding file from your hard disk.

Here's what we did to create the eagle storm against a blue sky:

1. In an untitled file, we drew a small rectangle. Then we imported the eagle from the Companion CD.

2. We colored the rectangle 50 Cyan/25 Magenta (the same color as the sky) and positioned the eagle in front of the rectangle.

3. In Tools / Create / Pattern, we chose Full Color and drew a marquee around the two objects. Then we saved the pattern as EAGLE.PAT. As Figure 9.22 shows, we were careful to draw the marquee *inside* of the rectangle, so no seams would show in the pattern.

9.22

**Defining the area
that constitutes
the pattern**

4. We opened SUNSET.CDR, removed the existing background and text elements, and drew a rectangle behind the other elements. With the hotkey Shift+PgDn, we made sure the rectangle was in the back.

5. We invoked the Full Color Bitmap Pattern dialog and continued with the procedure of picking the pattern and adjusting it into place.

Figure 9.23 shows the new eagle storm with a more plausible sky color. As you can see from Figures 9.21 and 23, these patterns look more like wallpaper than realistic objects in a drawing. We suggest you think of them that way, too.

PostScript Patterns

These sophisticated fill patterns are, in essence, little programs written in the PostScript page-description language, and digestible only by Post-Script printers or other PostScript interpreters. Though you cannot add your own patterns to the ones supplied here, you can alter them significantly using various controls provided in the PostScript Texture dialog (Figure 9.24). The parameters available to you in this dialog will depend on the texture selected.

9.23

These lucky eagles now get to fly in a sky instead of in a white hole.

9.24

Creating sophisti-
cated PostScript
still takes some trial
and error, but the re-
sults are worth it for
those seeking elabo-
rate fill patterns.

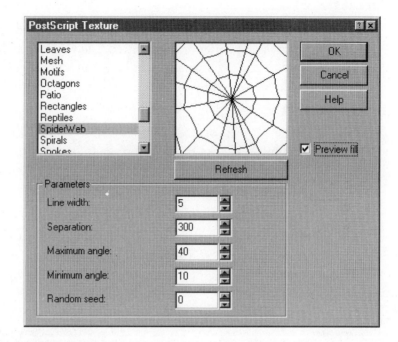

NEW FOR 6

Until now, you couldn't tell what your fill looked like without
printing it to a PostScript printer. This was tedious at best, and
made it virtually impossible for users without PostScript
printers to incorporate PostScript fill patterns in drawings that
would ultimately be output on a PostScript device. The good
news for DRAW 6.0 users is that, using a built-in PostScript
interpreter, you *can* now preview PostScript patterns on screen.
This is a tremendous time-saver, especially for anyone who
customizes PostScript patterns. And that's not all: You can also
output them to *any* printer, PostScript or non-PostScript.

Texture Fills

Texture fills are bitmap images that will display on any screen and print to any laser printer or imagesetter. Still the new darling of DRAW's fill family, texture fill patterns are based on a library of bitmap images, all produced according to an engine that allows for individual aspects to be adjusted with breathtaking precision.

Figure 9.25 shows one of the more elaborate textures, a five-color mineral fractal fill. Ten individual properties make up this texture, and each component can be separately adjusted. The color selection buttons are gateways to the now-familiar Select Color dialog.

There are different images for each texture—lots of them. In the case of the five-color mineral fractal, for instance, you can browse among (ready for this?) 32,768 different variations.

9.25

If you can get past how much fun they are to play with, you might actually create some nice work with **DRAW**'s texture fills.

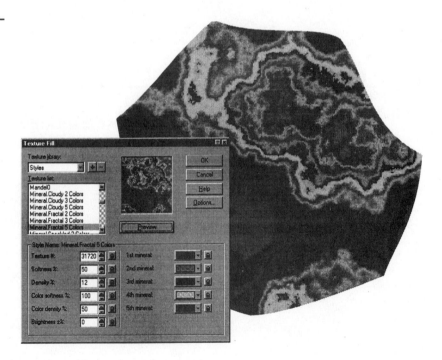

Each of this dialog's controls has a lock icon next to it, and this takes a bit of explaining. Texture fills have a decidedly video-game nature, and the preview button is intended for you to use as a random generator of different textures. When you click Preview, every element that is not locked will change randomly. The Softness % value might change from 83 to 17, the Brightness % from −22 to 60, the Texture # from 5742 to 28475, and the colors to just about anything in the spectrum.

If you have locked all elements, then you can use the Preview button to change one particular aspect: Make the change you want, and click Preview to see your change in the Preview window before activating it. In other words, locking any element will prevent it from being randomly changed, but you can always change an element manually, locked or not.

A word of caution: These elaborate textures can devour memory, hard drive space, and printer resources. If you apply them to large objects, or put many of them on a page, be prepared for some backtalk from your hardware. We created a rectangle and filled it two ways, with a simple fill pattern and with a texture. Here are the essential statistics of the two operations:

Fill Type	Size of File	Code Sent to Printer	Time to Print
Uniform	10K	31K	6 seconds
Texture	156K	130K	21 seconds

We would invite you to browse these textures for yourself, but please don't take us too literally. If you were to view every possible permutation of one of the simpler ones—say Aerial Photography, which has controls for just Texture #, Softness %, Brightness ± %, Background and Foreground colors. Let's see…32,768 textures, 0 to 100% for Softness, Brightness settings ranging from −100 to +100…and millions of possible values for the foreground and background colors—well, we estimate you would have 11,892,928,546,860,000,000,000,000,000 variations to look at for just Aerial Photography. And between DRAW's three texture libraries, there are nearly 200 different texture fills to choose from, most of which have far more permutations than this one. Aren't you glad that you can't add your own…

♣

In the next chapter, we switch gears completely and begin Part III of this book. Get ready to explore the depth, breadth, wonder, and mystery of creating, formatting, and editing text in DRAW.

WORKING
WITH TEXT

Let's start with what Part III isn't. It isn't a lengthy dissertation on typography, and you won't find pages upon pages discussing ascenders, x-heights, splines, and a host of other topics that make up the specialized field of typography. To take absolutely nothing away from the art of typography, this part of the book is more interested in the science and the mechanics of text. To pretend that any book can teach fine typography is an affront to the field's professionals—just as it is to claim that illustration and design themselves can be learned by reading the pages of a book.

Instead we will focus on down-to-earth text issues—matters of technique, strategy, and performance. Many thousands of CorelDRAW users buy the package just to set type. Nodes, curves, and fountain fills? They could hardly care less—just give them those 1,000 or so typefaces, the Text and Effects menus, and they're set for life. In these four chapters, we offer insight into why DRAW's text handling is so popular. And—what's fair is fair—we'll also look closely at the areas that have earned the most criticism.

Love it or hate it, DRAW's text handling is an awesome force to reckon with, responsible for the livelihood of a great many artists, illustrators, T-shirt makers, sign and banner manufacturers, and a host of other DRAW users who take very seriously the business of putting letters down on printed pages.

10

Working with Text

TEN

We expect this chapter to be shorter than it was in the previous three editions of this book, and that is good news. Until now we have had to invest a fair amount of space discussing how and why DRAW handles type differently from most other Windows programs. Thankfully, as of version 6.0, that has changed to a significant degree.

Of DRAW's two distinct reputations in the electronic publishing and graphics community, one of them is now a distant memory. Still appropriate is the title of Typeface Giant, thanks to the always huge library of typefaces that ships with the program, but DRAW is starting to live down the rap that it is plagued with imprecision and poorly crafted typefaces. DRAW's typefaces will now hold their own against all but the most finely crafted electronic typefaces in the industry. Though its text-handling support is not quite in the Ventura or QuarkXpress league, DRAW is now well above average.

DRAW 6 Is Kosher for Windows

Just about all that's needed to get you started with text handling in DRAW 6.0 is to show you Figure 10.1. If you use Word for Windows, Ami Pro, or Word Perfect, we hardly have to do more than tell you to use DRAW 6.0's new Text Toolbar. End of discussion, end of chapter. Like today's word processors, DRAW's Text Toolbar provides access to styles, typefaces, sizes, weights, positioning, and alignment.

Watch Your Language!

Rarely are phrases mangled and misused more than the ones that describe type. We have been on our high horse many times concerning the distinction between a *type family* (a collection of typefaces with a unifying design, such as Helvetica), a *typeface* (one in a collection, such as Helvetica Medium or Helvetica Bold), and a *font* (a typeface set in a specific size, such as 9-point Helvetica Italic). Software manufacturers often misuse the terminology, referring to type families as typefaces and to typefaces as fonts. It is therefore sometimes difficult for us to be typographically correct in our prose, so no letters, please.

10.1

If you set a lot of text in DRAW, you'll welcome the new Text Toolbar.

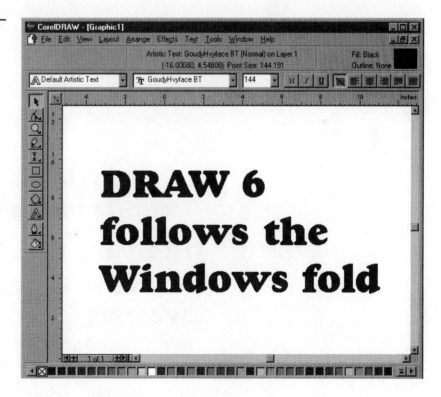

NEW FOR 6

To activate DRAW 6.0's Text Toolbar, go to View / Toolbars and check the box next to Text. You can also click Button 2 on the Toolbox to quickly activate any flyout or toolbar. For more details, consult Chapter 15.

We won't insult your intelligence by providing tutorials on this toolbar—just select the text and go to the toolbar. Put your cursor over a button, and a pop-up will tell you what the button does. Any questions?

What *is* worth discussing is this toolbar's flexibility, like that of all DRAW 6.0's new toolbars. If you are tight on screen space—and who isn't—you'll appreciate being able to move the toolbar into any position and virtually any shape you want to. Figure 10.2 is a composite image of several placements for the Text Toolbar, including outside of the DRAW window altogether.

10.2

A few of the many different profiles of the Text Toolbar

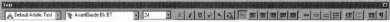

To float the Text Toolbar, double-click on it or drag it down from its standard position. To return it, do the opposite. And to reshape it, just start dragging its edges.

Setting Type with DRAW: Paragraph and Artistic

DRAW offers two avenues for creating and manipulating text: *artistic text* and *paragraph text*. Artistic text is created by selecting the Text icon from the Toolbox and then clicking once on the page to place the cursor. Paragraph text is created by clicking and holding on the Text icon, choosing the Paragraph icon from the flyout, and then either clicking once on the page or creating a marquee on the page. You can also use the handy new Text flyout, as shown in Figure 10.3, but our favorite

10.3

Many of the tools in DRAW's Toolbox can be pulled off and placed in convenient locations on the screen.

method of access continues to be the F8 and Shift+F8 hotkeys for artistic and paragraph text.

DRAW refers to a unit of artistic text as a *string* of text, and a unit of paragraph text as a *frame* of text. We will, too, and in Chapter 11 we'll explore the differences between text strings and text frames. First, however, we'll look at the similarities. Regardless of how you create text in DRAW, artistic or paragraph, you can do the following things to it.

Change Its Size

You can set type as small as .001 point for the really fine, fine print of a contract, or up to 3,000 points for the Goodyear blimp (at 72 points to an inch, we're talking 30" tall letters). You can resize text characters from the Text Toolbar, or from the Character dialog, shown in Figure 10.4. Here are your choices for reaching the Character dialog:

- By going to Text / Character

- By pressing the hotkey Ctrl+T

- By right-clicking and choosing Character from the pop-up, if you have assigned it to Character in Options

- By clicking on Character in the Edit Text dialog (discussed shortly)

N E W F O R 6

The Character dialog gets a Windows 95 facelift: All of the positioning controls are now in the Alignment page. There's a new setting for kerning; and Edit buttons next to Underline, Overline, and Strikeout lead to a variety of custom controls. Be sure to experiment with the new Force Justify command and its effect on paragraph text.

10.4

The venerable
Character dialog,
with a few new
elements

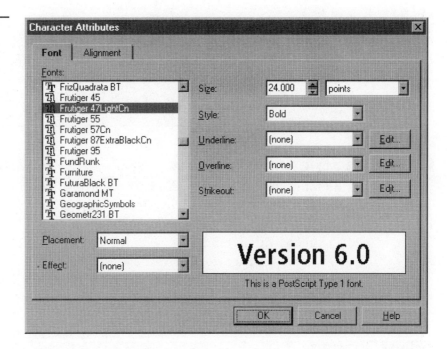

Change the Size of Strings, Too   You can also size strings of artistic text simply by clicking and dragging the corner selection handles.

We wondered in our last book if the Edit Text dialog would be relegated to second-class citizenry because the Character dialog took over the coveted Ctrl+T position. With on-screen editing much faster now than in earlier versions, an editing window is not as important as it once was, and in our travels we don't encounter many users who regularly turn to this dialog anymore. Nonetheless, when you're working with large blocks of copy, a quick Ctrl+Shift+T will take you to the Edit Text dialog and offer you easier and faster editing—especially if your text frame is large enough to require a lot of scrolling for on-screen editing.

While the Edit Text dialog suffers a demotion in DRAW 6.0, the Text roll-up is an outright casualty, being eliminated altogether in favor of the Text Toolbar.

INSIDE INFO

> If you still use the Edit Text dialog and have spent the last 12 months mourning the loss of Ctrl+T as its shortcut, now you have recourse. Go to Tools / Customize / Keyboard, and reassign Ctrl+T to Edit Text. (For explicit instructions on this process, see Chapter 15.)

Change Its Style and Alignment

Both the Toolbar and the Character dialog provide full control of typeface selection, style (bold, italic, and so on), size, and alignment (left, center, right, and justified). With the toolbar, you can change font and alignment with just one click; with the Character dialog, you must burrow down one page. Keyboard-aholics will be interested to note that Ctrl+Tab will quickly take them to the Alignment page of the Character dialog, shown in Figure 10.5.

Adjust Spacing

With DRAW's spacing tools, you can adjust the space between characters, between words, and between lines of type. You can do this from the Paragraph dialog (reached via Text / Paragraph) or you can quickly set single-, one-and-a-half- and double-spacing from the toolbar. And even though the dialog is titled Paragraph, its controls work for both artistic and paragraph text.

Line spacing (known in the industry as *leading*) can be set in exact measurements of points or by percentages of the text. The latter method is handy if you are resizing text with the on-screen handles and you want line spacing to adjust accordingly.

Figure 10.6 shows text set with various amounts of leading. You would think that 9-point text set with 10 points of lead would correspond to a percentage of *over* 100%, not *under* (97%). But in determining the percentage, DRAW uses the distance from the top of the *tallest character* to the bottom of the *longest descender,* rather than the actual point size.

10.5

The new Alignment page is just a Ctrl+Tab away.

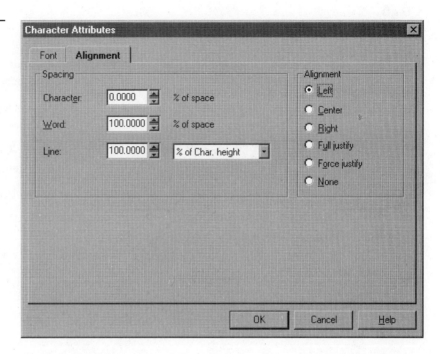

There is actually more to the story than what we have shown in Figure 10.6, because DRAW supports three different measuring systems for determining line spacing:

- *Fixed Points:* The traditional and largely preferred way to measure space between lines of type is in the fixed units of measurement that you know as points. If you have set a string of text in 11 points, you can establish the line spacing at precisely 13 points.

- *Percentage of Point Size:* The old DRAW 3.0 measuring system, in which 11-point text set at 100% spacing would result in line spacing of 11 points (considered by most to be too tight).

- *Percentage of Character Height:* The third option, shown in Figure 10.6, measures the spacing as a percentage of the character height—from the highest ascender to the lowest descender. Text set in 11 points and 100% character-height spacing would result in line spacing of almost 14 points.

10.6

DRAW can set text spacing in fixed points, or as a percentage of the type size.

This is 9-point text
with 10-point spacing

This is 9-point text
with 11-point spacing

This is 9-point text
with 12-point spacing

This is 9-point text
with 13-point spacing

This is 9-point text
with 97% spacing

This is 9-point text
with 106.8% spacing

This is 9-point text
with 116% spacing

This is 9-point text
with 126.3% spacing

We don't mind having three different types of controls, but we do mind having to go to two different places to change size and leading. With line spacing options placed on the Alignment page of the Character dialog, we suspect that more and more DRAW users will take the easy way out by setting line spacing as a percentage of their type, allowing it to adjust automatically. Unfortunately, in the process they will lose a critical element of precision in their work.

Kern Individual Characters

Lateral adjustment of characters is called *kerning;* the term is also used as a verb—*to kern* characters means to remove space from between the characters. Capital letters, like the ones in Figure 10.7, often need manual kerning to look good. The sample at the top of the figure shows proper kerning for capital letters.

In artistic text you can take any character in a string and move it left, right, up, or down. To do this, choose the Shape tool, not the Pick tool. The Shape tool treats each character in a text string as a node (you'll actually see a node on screen in front of each character). Select the node and you can drag a character in any direction; or better yet, set a Nudge value and use your keyboard arrow keys. As Figure 10.7 illustrates, this can be put to good use or to positively hilarious use. You can also kern an entire string of text, a frame of text, or a selection of text with the Kerning control in the Character dialog.

10.7

Character kerning is especially helpful with text set in all caps.

NOT SO BAD

AVOID AWFUL KERNING

BAD

AVOID AWFUL KERNING

WORSE

AVOID AWFUL KERNING

RIDICULOUS

AVOID AWFUL KERNING

INSIDE INFO

In addition to the Character dialog, DRAW offers on-screen support for character and line spacing. Select the text, artistic or paragraph; then choose the Shape tool and look for the strange-looking arrows at the bottom of the text, one pointing down and one pointing to the right. These allow you to interactively change the line spacing (arrow pointing down) and the character spacing (arrow pointing right). If you do not have a specific number in mind for line and character spacing and are working on the basis of look and feel, you will save a lot of time and mouse activity by using these handy arrow controls.

Like most good typefaces, the ones in DRAW ship with built-in intelligence about which character combinations need more or less space between them—this is referred to as *kerning pairs.* Invariably, however, text set at large sizes or in all caps needs to be scrutinized for proper kerning.

Format Individual Characters

In addition to character kerning, DRAW supports character reformatting. To do this, you can reach for the Shape tool again and select the node in front of the character, or choose the Text tool and select characters by dragging across them. Either way, the Text Toolbar and the Character dialog are the gateways for reformatting characters.

The Text tool is more intuitive, providing a standard text cursor for selecting text, but the Shape tool has the advantage of allowing you to select noncontiguous characters. Select one character, hold Shift, and then select others anywhere in the string.

WATCH OUT!

Individual character formatting is overridden by changes made to a text string's size or style. In other words, if you format characters using the Shape tool and then format the entire string in the conventional manner, your custom formatting will be lost. Changing the typeface, style, or size after individual formatting spells trouble. Rule of thumb: Format the entire string first, and then format the individual characters.

10.8

Extortion notices, thanks to DRAW's character formatting

Figure 10.8 shows how we encourage DRAW users to attend our annual conference.

Check for Spelling and Synonyms

DRAW's online proofreading tools and Thesaurus will improve your spelling, vocabulary, and grammar throughout a DRAW document.

■ To check spelling, select a string or frame of text and choose Text / Proofreading / Spelling. You can spell-check an entire string or frame, or any portion of text that you have selected (using the Text cursor).

■ To use the Thesaurus, select a word within a string or frame and choose Text / Thesaurus.

Even if you have ignored these two functions, the new Proofreading command might make it more attractive to turn to DRAW for text-heavy projects. As Figure 10.9 shows, you can get help with copy editing without having to send the text out to a word processor. DRAW's spelling and synonym dictionaries rival those of major word processors. (Although…regarding the previous sentence, the Proofreading feature said we should avoid the use of all caps, as in DRAW, and instead use Draw. Perhaps Corel's copyright attorney needs to get involved in product development…)

1 0.9

Now you can check spelling, synonyms, and grammar in DRAW.

Full Proof Reading - Informal

Check range: Selected Text

Sentence:

And our prediction is that DRAW users will be pleasantly surprised by the breadth of the program's dictionaries.

Change to: (No Alternatives)

Error description:

Informal. It is preferable to avoid beginning a sentence with 'And'.

Next Sentence

Ignore

Ignore All

Change

Change All

Add word   Options   Close

Creating Artistic Text

Most DRAW users create text in the standard form, artistic text. This is the most intuitive method. You click once on the Text tool (or press F8), move out to the page, and type away. Press Enter when you want a new line. When you're done typing, you decide on the typeface, style, size, and alignment. Select a string of artistic text, and you can size, stretch, skew, and rotate it by tugging on its selection handles.

Artistic text is eligible for all of the cool special effects found in the DRAW's Effects menu, like the extrusion shown in Figure 10.10. For a close look at the Effects menu, see Part V.

10.10

All of DRAW's effects, including Extrude, can be applied to artistic text.

Fills and outlines, as well, can be applied to text as freely as you would any other object. As Figure 10.11 demonstrates, you can produce many different effects just by varying fill patterns. The background is a large block of lightly filled text sitting on a gradually shifting background.

The text on top is a pattern fill with a contour behind it. The text in the middle has an angled shadow with a transparent lens applied to it. Next is simply a string of text with no fill whatsoever and a thin outline. And finally, at the bottom, is text that appears to be embossed, thanks to a trick that we'll uncover in Chapter 17.

10.11

When it comes to applying fills and outlines, DRAW treats text like any other object.

Artistic text also has its limitations. Compared to paragraph text, artistic text is slower to render when changed. It does not support tabs or indents. Nor can it do "authentic" justification, because it has no word wrap (it just extends every line of text out to an arbitrary ending point). You will want to avoid using artistic text for setting large blocks of copy, turning instead to paragraph text, the focus of the next chapter.

11

Understanding Paragraph Text

It is one of computing life's little tragedies that so many DRAW users remain oblivious to "that other way to create text." Paragraph text became a legitimate tool in version 4, and in version 5 started to steal users away from competing applications. We have met a few hundred users who were accustomed to creating art in DRAW and assembling the pieces of a brochure or an advertising layout in PageMaker. Now they do the whole thing in DRAW, thanks to the program's beefed-up support for setting, formatting, and editing large blocks of copy.

You create paragraph text inside a text frame, instead of directly on the page as you do artistic text. A subtle distinction, perhaps—since you click on the page in either case—but paragraph text has a different personality. Paragraph text uses *soft returns*, just like the documents you create in your word processor, to create text that flows freely from one line to the next. The shape of the text flow is determined by the frame, which you establish either when you first create it or when you reshape it later. Figure 11.1 shows three renditions of the same paragraph of text, each one shaped differently.

The Purpose of the Paragraph

The chief limitation of paragraph text is its indifference to most of DRAW's special effects. You cannot distort, skew, extrude, or do any of the other gee-whiz things to paragraph text. In reality, though, this is more of a safety measure than a flaw, because if you are trying to apply a special effect to a frame of text, one of two things is probably taking place:

- You are using a small amount of copy, so you can convert it to artistic text and have your special effects.

- You are trying to apply a special effect to too large a block of copy, the results of which will probably be an aesthetic disaster.

11.1

Dragging the selection handles of paragraph text affects the flow, not the size, of the text.

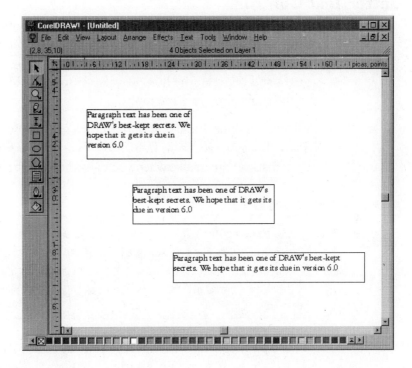

No, the purpose of paragraph text is to allow you to set a lot of copy, not a lot of way-cool copy. To this end, you'll find a treasure of features hidden within paragraph text, as described in the paragraphs that follow.

Faster Redraw

Paragraph text is much faster on the redraw than artistic text. When you change typeface, style, or size, paragraph text adjusts almost instantaneously, while artistic text has to think about it for several seconds.

Much Larger Capacity

In DRAW 6, artistic text and paragraph text both share the huge capacity of 32,000 characters. This capacity is almost obscene as applied to paragraph text, for you can also set 32,000 paragraphs within one frame of text. In other words, there are no practical limits on the amount of text you can set with DRAW's paragraph text.

Better Text Control

Paragraph text offers the kinds of controls you would expect to find in a program that supports large quantities of text. You can set tabs and indents; create left and right margins; set space above and below a paragraph and between the lines of a paragraph; and attach bullet characters to the beginnings of paragraphs.

All of this is done through the tabbed Paragraph dialog shown in Figure 11.2. These dialogs are accessible from Text / Paragraph, or from the Properties sheet that you can invoke when you right-click on a frame of text.

AUTHOR'S NOTE

The Paragraph dialog is not accessible when artistic text is selected, even though some of the Paragraph functions are appropriate to artistic text. Corel gets around this by duplicating these functions on the Alignment page of the Character dialog.

The Spacing Page   This page provides controls for space between characters, words, and lines within a paragraph (leading). You can also designate space above and below paragraphs (remember, you can have many paragraphs within one frame of text). Alignment controls and hyphenation are here, as well.

NEW FOR 6

Hurray! DRAW users can finally insert line breaks into paragraphs—hard returns that do not signify the end of the paragraph. Unlike paragraph breaks, DRAW does not add any space above or below a line break. It simply drops down to the next line without waiting for the text to wrap at the end. You insert these line breaks with Shift+Enter.

11.2

The pages of the Paragraph dialog, for controlling paragraph text

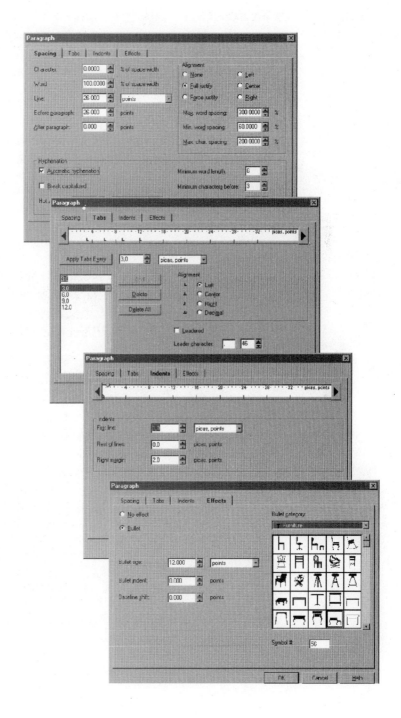

The Tabs Page   These controls work like every other tab function known to computingkind. New to 6.0 are leadered tabs. These are tabs of little dots, or any other character you choose. (Smiley faces, maybe? Okay, maybe not.)

The Indents Page   Cleaned up considerably from DRAW 5, this dialog controls indents. Gone is the control for Left Margin, which seemed to do nothing but confuse people because the Rest of Lines control does the same thing. Now this dialog behaves more intuitively.

Figure 11.3 shows three of the most common Indent settings, along with their results. The shaded rectangles behind the text indicate the boundary of the text frame.

The Effects Page   This set of controls enables you to precede any paragraph with a bullet. Any typeface that is identified as a "symbol" face (a property given to a typeface by its developer) will show up here in the list of available faces. This means you can go way beyond the bounds of good taste when setting bullets, as clearly demonstrated by Figure 11.4.

Curiously, one command has been left out of the Paragraph dialog and banished to a separate, lonely dialog. To set the number of columns in a frame and the space in between, you have to go to Text / Columns. (We couldn't get a particularly noteworthy explanation from Corel about this.) The good news, however, is that the controls for setting columns are much smarter. In DRAW 5, if you set a 3" wide frame in two columns, DRAW would create two columns, each 3" wide! Now, it more sensibly creates two columns, including the desired space in between, all within the 3" width.

11.3

Controlling margins and indents is easy with paragraph text.

Paragraph text has been one of DRAW's best-kept secrets. We hope that it gets its due in version 6.0 with the addition of smarter controls, better performance, and more flexibility.

First Line: 2 picas

Paragraph text has been one of DRAW's best-kept secrets. We hope that it gets its due in version 6.0 with the addition of smarter controls, better performance, and more flexibility.

First Line: 0
Rest of Lines: 2 picas

Paragraph text has been one of DRAW's best-kept secrets. We hope that it gets its due in version 6.0 with the addition of smarter controls, better performance, and more flexibility.

First Line: 2 picas
Rest of Lines: 2 picas
Right Margin: 2 picas

11.4

There could come a time when Frosty the Snowman or a Big Mac would be suitable as a bullet character. Then again, maybe not.

 There is only one thing that can stop you from using really stupid bullets in your text: your own good taste.

 There is only one thing that can stop you from using really stupid bullets in your text: your own good taste.

Irregular Text Wrapping

The one special effect that can be applied to paragraph text is the irregular text wrap. This is done with the Envelope command, the results of which essentially allow you to node-edit a text frame as if it were a curve. Figure 11.5 shows the result of enveloping text within and outside of an object. We'll cover this in detail in Chapter 12.

11.5

With the Envelope tool, you can wrap text around and inside an object.

Lorum ipsum dolor sit amet, con; minimum venami quis nostrud laboris nisi ut aliquip ex ea com color in reprehenderit in voluptate nonumy. Lorum ipsum dolor sit amet, con; minimum venami quis nostrud laboris nisi ut aliquip ex ea com color in reprehenderit in voluptate nonumy. Minimum veniami ex ea con dolor in reprehenderit in voluptate nonumy. Lorum ipsum dolor sit amet, con; minimum venami quis nostrud laboris nisi ut aliquip ex ea com color in reprehenderit in ate nonumy. Lorum ipsum dolor sit amet, venami quis nostrud laboris nisi ut aliquip ex ea com color in repre henderit in voluptate nonumy. Lorum ipsum dolor sit amet, con; minimum

Lor um ipsum dolor sit amet, con; mini mum venami quis nostrud laboris nisi ut aliquip ex ea com color in reprehenderit in voluptate nonumy. Lorum ipsum dolor sit amet, con; minimum venami quis nostrud laboris nisi ut aliquip ex ea com color in reprehenderit in voluptate nonumy. Mini mum veniami ex ea con do lor in reprehenderit in volup tate nonumy. Lorum ipsum do lor sit amet, con; mini- volupt mum con; minimum

Navigating Your Way

We remember a time when the only thing you could do in DRAW while your cursor was in a line of text was type. With version 6.0, you can practically use DRAW as your word processor. Here are some of the reasons why.

On-Screen Controls

Not too long ago DRAW didn't even have tabs. Now there is an almost full-featured Text dialog, and fast and friendly on-screen controls in the ruler. As shown in Figure 11.6, when your cursor is in a frame of paragraph text, you can change tabs (using the marks in the ruler), indents (using the small triangular pointers), and margins (using the indicators on each side of the text). Just drag any of these symbols to a different position to change the setting. Tabs, margins, and indents are only relevant for paragraph text.

11.6

On-screen controls make paragraph formatting much easier.

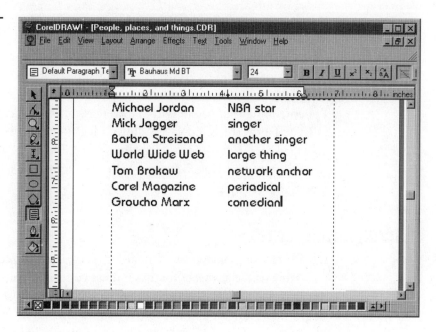

Proofreading

We used to laugh at DRAW's spell-checking engine; now we actually use it. Figure 11.7 shows its friendly interface in the process of catching a typo. DRAW's spell checking is part of a new network of Proofreading tools that include grammar and syntax checking. The Proofreader caught the misspelling of the word *periodical,* and we note with interest that it suggested a more conventional spelling of Barbra Streisand's first name.

11.7

The more you use **DRAW** for text, the more you will take advantage of its new proofreading tools.

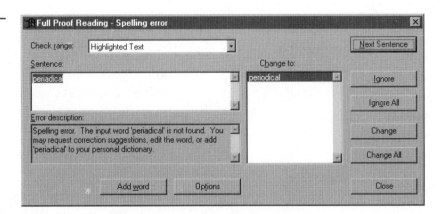

DRAW's proofreading tools purport to spot more than just spelling errors, and on that we found mixed performance. When we set the text of a poem, a line that began with a lowercase letter was called an error by DRAW. Figure 11.8, however, shows a less-than-succinct paragraph that managed to slip through—even though we told DRAW, through Advanced Options / Rule Manager / Wordy Expressions, to watch out for excessive wordiness.

Full Alignment of Text

DRAW has long offered the standard choices (left/right/center/justify/none) for setting text alignment. You reach those controls from Text / Character / Alignment, or Text / Paragraph. A sixth choice, Force Justify, determines the length of the longest line and forces all other lines in the text to extend to that point. As Figure 11.9 illustrates, you must use Force Justify with care.

11.8

This screen shot seems to indicate that DRAW's advanced proof-reading skills are "something less than completely accurate" in spotting errors and making judgments about the volume of words that is "appropriate" to represent a particular thought.

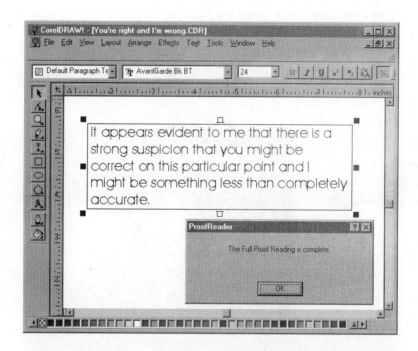

11.9

Forced justification of paragraph text must be used with considerable caution.

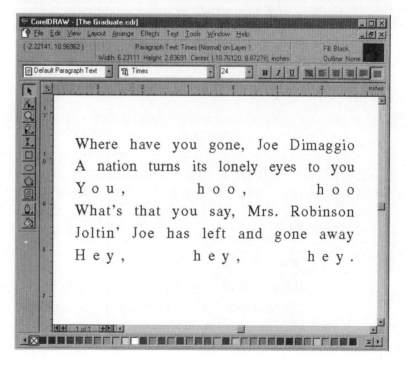

Also important is the fact that you can force-justify artistic text, as well. This brings together the flexibility of working with an easily adjustable string of text plus the ability to control line endings. We put this to use each year when conference season rolls around, as shown in Figure 11.10.

Where might you use Force Justify? Good question—and Figures 11.9 and 10 illustrate that *use* and *misuse* are first cousins. The key to appropriate deployment of Force Justify is using lines of text that are similar in length to begin with.

Editing Controls

There was no real value to having powerful editing controls in the early versions of DRAW because, most of the time, you weren't able to create text quickly enough or in sufficient volume to take advantage of them. Text rendering in DRAW 6.0 is much faster, so it will pay off for you to practice some of the in-line editing commands that DRAW offers. Odds are, though, you already know them from the time you have put in with your word processor. Here is a summary:

What You Do	What DRAW 6.0 Does
Double-click	Selects the current word
Shift+click	Selects from the insertion point to the cursor

What You Do	What DRAW 6.0 Does
Ctrl+click	Selects the current line or sentence
Ctrl+Right Arrow	Jumps one word to the right
Ctrl+Left Arrow	Jumps one word to the left
Home	Jumps to the beginning of the line
End	Jumps to the end of the line
Ctrl+Home	Jumps to the beginning of the text string or frame
Ctrl+End	Jumps to the end of the text string or frame
Shift+Right Arrow	Selects to the right of the cursor, character by character
Shift+Left	Selects to the left of the cursor, character by character
Shift+Home	Selects all text from cursor to beginning of line
Shift+End	Selects all text from cursor to end of line
Ctrl+Shift+Right	Selects to the right of the cursor, word by word
Ctrl+Shift+Left Arrow	Selects to the left of the cursor, word by word
Ctrl+Shift+Home	Selects all text from the cursor to the beginning of text string or frame
Ctrl+Shift+End	Selects all text from the cursor to the end of text string or frame

Instant Editing

You can set Button 2 of your mouse to provide a shortcut to the Character or the Edit Text dialog, using Tools / Options / Advanced / PopUp Menu Customization.

If you choose Character for the first menu item, then clicking Button 2 places Character at the very top of the context-sensitive menu. This is different from previous DRAW versions and not quite as immediate as before, but arguably more refined. Before, you had to know whether to click quickly or whether to click and hold for a moment to access either the shortcut or the context-sensitive menu. Now you know that any type of right-click is going to get you the context menu, with the command of your choice appearing first.

Choosing Between Artistic and Paragraph Text

In some cases, it doesn't matter whether you choose artistic or paragraph text to set type. A standard headline of three or four words at the top of a newsletter is going to look the same regardless of which mode you use to create it. Other times, however, your decision will be crucial to your work flow. Here are our rules of thumb.

When Is Artistic Text the Best Choice?

Use artistic text in the following situations:

- *When you resize, stretch, and skew.* Artistic text can easily be scaled and stretched—you just tug at the selection handles. (Paragraph text can only be resized from the Text Toolbar or Character dialog, and cannot be stretched or skewed at all.)

- *When you mirror, extrude, envelope, or change perspective.* These are effects that can be applied to artistic text only. The Envelope function can be applied to paragraph text, as we did in Figure 11.5, but when used with artistic text, Envelope and the other special effects actually bend the characters.

- *For editing character shapes.* If you want to change the very shape of text characters by converting them to curves and then editing the nodes, you must use artistic text. If you try to choose Arrange / Convert to Curves when working with paragraph text, DRAW just ignores you. In Chapter 12, we will take apart some characters and edit their shapes.

When Is Paragraph Text the Best Choice?

Use paragraph text in the following situations:

- *To set large blocks of copy.* As appropriate as artistic text is for the headline of an article, so is paragraph text perfect for the article itself. Paragraph text can accommodate thousands of characters and thousands of individual paragraphs, and you can create pages and pages of text.

- *To control text flow.* Paragraph text can flow from frame to frame and from page to page. Also, you can easily change the length of each line in paragraph text, thanks to the soft returns it employs. (The only way to end a line of artistic text is to use a hard return.)

- *To control the baselines of text.* A handy use for paragraph text is when you want to set text along an angle, and we'll discuss this in the upcoming section.

NEW FOR 6

We're astonished and delighted to report that DRAW 6's artistic text is no longer so far below paragraph text in terms of performance. And there is no longer a severe penalty for using PostScript typefaces. The sample data that we used in Figure 11.11 is a chart from our last book, showing the time required in DRAW 5 to reformat on screen a block of text set in various typefaces. In artistic text, TrueType performed faster than PostScript faces; but paragraph text was much faster than artistic regardless of the face. In DRAW 6, the differences in performance are all within one second. Not even worth making a chart!

Baseline Control Figure 11.11 shows an example of using paragraph text for baseline control in what would otherwise be a tedious job of text alignment. To produce the text along the bottom axis of this graph, we set it as right-aligned paragraph text. Then we rotated the entire frame of text 90° counterclockwise, so the text was appearing to hang down from the top of the frame. Then we invoked the Precision

Skew roll-up (inset into the figure) and skewed the frame by −30°, quickly and neatly angling all of the text.

Had this been artistic text, the characters themselves would have bent backwards, and that is a fundamental distinction between the two types of text. When you select a string of text, DRAW applies the chosen effect to the characters themselves; when you select a frame of paragraph text, DRAW applies the effect to the frame. In Figure 11.11, DRAW skewed the baseline of text, not the text itself. (P.S. You could also skew this frame interactively by holding Ctrl and taking advantage of DRAW's Constrain angle of 15°.)

I I . I I

Precision baseline alignment is easily produced with paragraph text and DRAW's skewing commands.

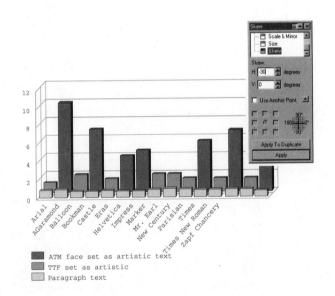

Switching from One to the Other

What happens when you create text in one form and discover that you really need it to be in the other? In past editions of this book, we heaved a sigh of frustration and showed you the multistep process for cutting text to the Clipboard from one format and pasting it back as another.

We get to save a bit of ink in this edition (he says, as he adds yet another page to his 1,000-page book…) because DRAW 6.0 now offers a handy conversion option. If you select a string of artistic text, the Text menu displays the option Convert to Paragraph Text; if you select a frame of paragraph text, the option reads Convert to Artistic Text.

Remember the Hotkeys

The hotkey shortcuts can make text creation tasks much easier:

- Press F8 and click once to create artistic text.

- Press Shift+F8 and click once to create paragraph text. You don't have to drag a marquee to create paragraph text—if you have a shape in mind for your paragraph, then go ahead and create the marquee. If not, just click once and let DRAW create a default rectangular shape. You can always change it later.

INSIDE INFO

If you have text currently selected, you can press the appropriate hotkey—F8 for artistic, Shift+F8 for paragraph—and immediately get a text cursor at the end of the line. This is undoubtedly the easiest way to edit text. With one hand on the mouse and the other on the keyboard, select the text, press the hotkey, and you're ready to type. If the text is one of few objects on the page, you don't need the mouse at all: Press Tab until the text is selected, press the hotkey, and start typing.

♣

Follow the simplest of strategies—to use artistic text for display type, and paragraph text for body copy—and you will probably be correct 90% of the time. In the next chapter, we'll let artistic and paragraph text run wild. Please wear your seat belts.

Advanced Text Handling

T W E L V E

If you are hoping for one unifying theme to bring together all of the topics in this chapter, we should warn you that the chapter's title is as close as you'll get. As we once again open our overstuffed file folder entitled "Miscellaneous Text Stuff," we predict that this chapter will wander from one idea to the next, as it has in previous editions. It has always been one of our more enjoyable chapters, and we hope it will be one of yours, too…

Shaping Text Around Objects

One of the litmus tests for graphics software today is its ability to wrap text around and inside of an object. (Before Corel added support for this in version 4, DRAW was widely regarded as "nice software, but it can't wrap text.") DRAW provides this capability by extending its node-editing functionality to include frames of paragraph text.

In the following examples, you can watch or follow along as a piece of text is shaped around a curve in one of three ways:

- By controlling the shape of paragraph text in a frame
- By warping a string of artistic text
- By fitting text to a path.

You can follow along with us by opening WRAPTXT1.CDR from the Practice directory of the Companion CD, or you can study the finished effect by opening up WRAPTXT2.CDR.

Wrapping Paragraph Text: Three Examples

As you can see in our first example, Figure 12.1, we have intentionally used a very simple curve to demonstrate wrapping paragraph text, so as not to distract from the effect we are concentrating on. The following paragraphs recount how we produced this drawing.

1. First, we created the curve, mustering all of our creative strength and resources. Then we used GREEK.EXE, the text greeking program found on the Companion CD, to create a frame of dummy text. (Once we created the text, we simply imported it, using the ASCII import filter.) We set the text in 9/11 Goudy OldStyle and designated a hyphenation hot zone of .25″ (meaning that any text coming within .25″ of the right margin is eligible for hyphenation). *Hint:* The more hyphenation, the better the fit of the text around the curve. As shown in Figure 12.2, we sized the frame so that its bottom margin was aligned with the bottom of the curve.

1 2 . 1

Wrapping text around objects is a matter of knowing your nodes.

Lorem ipsum dolor sit amet, con; minimum venami quis nostrud laboris nisi ut aliquip ex ea com color in reprehenderit in voluptate nonumy. Lorem ipsum dolor sit amet, con; minimum venami quis nostrud laboris nisi ut aliquip ex ea com color in reprehenderit in voluptate nonumy. Minimum veniami ex ea con dolor in reprehenderit in voluptate nonumy. Lorem ipsum dolor sit amet, con; minimum venami quis nostrud laboris nisi ut aliquip ex ea com color in reprehenderit in voluptate nonumy.

Lorem ipsum dolor sit amet, con; minimum venami quis nostrud laboris nisi ut aliquip ex ea com color in reprehenderit in voluptate nonumy. Lorem ipsum dolor sit amet, con; minimum venami quis nostrud laboris nisi ut aliquip ex ea com color in reprehenderit in voluptate nonumy.

Lorem ipsum dolor sit amet, con; minimum venami quis nostrud laboris nisi ut aliquip ex ea com color in reprehenderit in voluptate nonumy.

Lorem ipsum dolor sit amet, con; minimum venami quis nostrud laboris nisi ut aliquip ex ea com color in reprehenderit in voluptate nonumy. Lorem ipsum dolor sit amet, con; minimum venami quis nostrud laboris nisi ut aliquip ex ea com color in repre henderit in voluptate nonuy. Mini- mum vex ea con do- lor in reprehen- derit in volup- tate nonmy. Lorem ipsum dolor sit

12.2

The two elements are in place—let the enveloping begin.

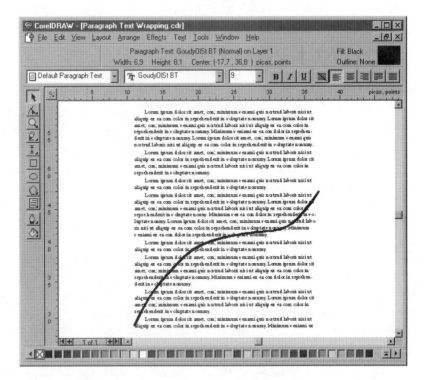

2. In studying the contour of the curve, we found only one change in direction: a subtle shift in the angle of inflection, highlighted in Figure 12.3. That is the only point along the curve where we needed to place a node.

3. We invoked the Envelope roll-up and clicked on Add New. Of the four icons in the middle, we chose the one on the right, for flexible node-editing. Enveloping is covered in detail in Chapter 18; but for now, when in doubt choose the node-edit mode, as it provides the most flexibility in shaping an object. In this enveloping mode, you can adjust nodes in any fashion, add new ones, and change them to and from lines and curves.

4. While holding Ctrl, we dragged the middle-right node to a point just above where the curve ends. Then we deleted the lower-right node and moved the node at the bottom up to the point of inflection highlighted in Figure 12.3. At this point, we are concerned with only three nodes: Node 1 at the lower-left, Node 2 in the middle, and Node 3 at the top-right of the curve.

1 2 . 3

**The highlight
shows the one spot
where the curve
changes direction.
That's where the
node goes.**

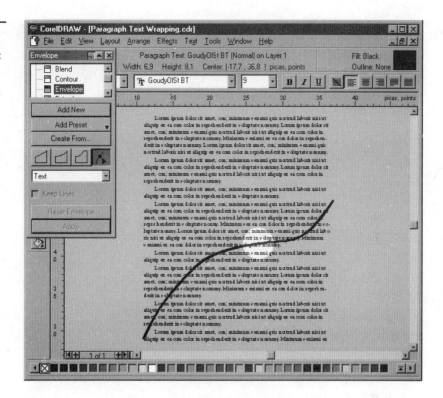

5. We invoked the Node Edit roll-up and changed Node 3 to a cusp.
That way, it could support the straight line above it and the curve that
defines the path below it.

6. We tugged and pulled on the various control points, nudged here
and there, and gradually succeeded in fitting the frame around the
curve. Precision wasn't important at this stage because, even if the text
were set justified, it wouldn't go right up to the edge of the frame. Since
we were working with left-aligned text, all we had to do was get close to
the shape of the curve. Our screen at this point looked like Figure 12.4,
and when we clicked Apply, it looked like Figure 12.5.

12.4

This text frame has been note-edited to fit the path of the curve...

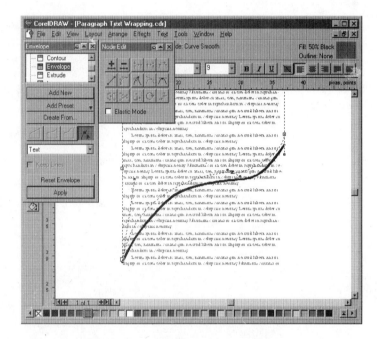

12.5

...and by clicking Apply, the envelope is imposed upon the text.

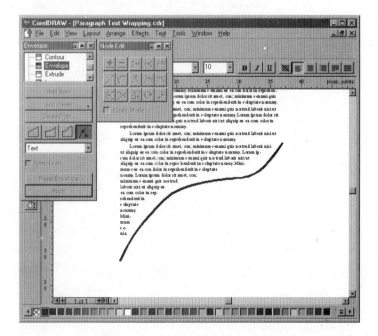

Example 2   Figure 12.6 shows another example of text wrap, this one featuring a two-column frame and a dark background. We want to show you this drawing for two reasons. First, the ability to wrap frames that have more than one column is more than just a nicety—it's a necessity. Imagine how difficult it would be to read the text in Figure 12.6 if it were one long column, especially as you get down near the bottom. Breaking the frame into two columns (done with Text / Columns) is not just showing off; it is imperative.

The second point we want to make about this drawing is that producing this text wrap virtually requires the use of Wireframe view. As Figure 12.7 shows, trying to find a dark control handle in a nighttime sky is next to impossible; in Wireframe view, the handle shows up much better.

WATCH OUT

We can well advise you against the following mistake, for we have made it many times: If you want to go back and fine-tune the shape of an enveloped frame, do *not* click on Add New (which is the conventional way of accessing the nodes before creating an envelope). That action will return the frame to its original shape (DRAW thinks you want to start over). The right thing to do is change to the Shape tool, just as if you were editing an existing curve. Remember, once a frame is enveloped, DRAW thinks of it as just another curve. Only when you are done with node editing should you reach for the Envelope roll-up, and then only to click Apply.

Example 3   Figure 12.8 shows two more envelopes—one around, and one inside of, an object. The envelope around the French horn is nothing new; you node-edit the frame, as we just did above. But the one below uses the Create From option on the Envelope roll-up. You select the text frame, click on Create From, and then click on an existing object that is of the desired shape. Instantly, the frame of text assumes the shape of the model object. Click Apply, and the text *automatically* reflows into the new shape. Then you can align the object with the text to give the appearance of the text flowing within the object.

12.6

You can create wraps with frames of multicolumn paragraph text. In fact, in cases like this one it is a practical requirement that you do so.

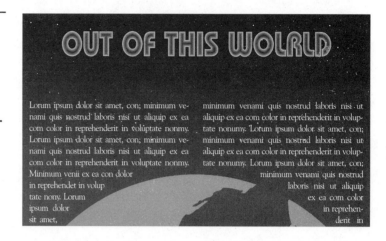

12.7

Don't hesitate for a second to switch to Wireframe when you are enveloping text against a dark background.

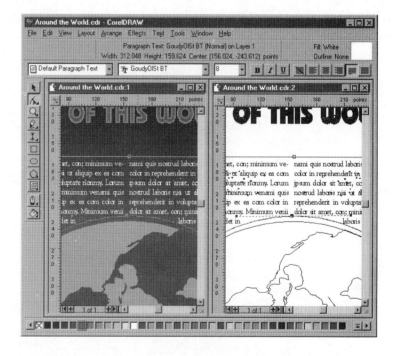

There is a fundamental drawback to Corel's engineering of this Create From command: It is not a dynamic effect, like Blend or Extrude. For example, if we were to reshape or resize the piano in Figure 12.8, the text would not automatically change. For that we would have to repeat the steps of enveloping, using the Create From option. Our best advice about Create From is to wait until late in the game before using it.

12.8

Making text flow inside of an object is even easier than wrapping it around the outside.

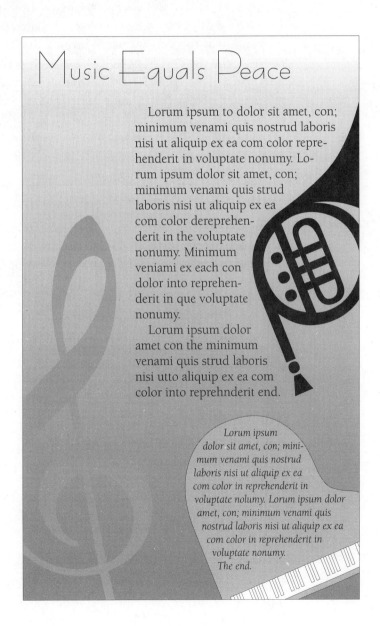

NEW FOR 6

> The Create From option—DRAW's new automatic text-wrapping feature—is similar to auto-tracing, in that DRAW studies the shape of an object and automatically creates and positions nodes. In the case of automatic text wrap, the automation is in the enveloping of the text frame. To wrap an object around a text frame, right-click on it, go to General, and check **Wrap Paragraph Text.** We are intrigued by the technology but underwhelmed by the results of this feature. It's not nearly as intelligent as you are when you're wielding the Envelope roll-up and the Shape Tool. We recommend you view automatic text wrap as a curiosity and a work in progress.

Wrapping Artistic Text

When you apply the Envelope tool to a string of artistic text, you end up with a drastically different effect than with paragraph text. Instead of just bending the frame in which the paragraph text flows, the Envelope tool actually bends the characters of artistic text. Figure 12.9 shows the result of enveloping artistic text around our sample curve. Though the effect is quite different from paragraph text, the same basic steps were used:

- Size the text to fit the object.

- Invoke the Envelope roll-up and click on Add New.

- Choose the node-editing icon.

- Shape the text as if it were a curve, shaping paths and tweaking and adding nodes as necessary.

- Click Apply.

Fitting Text to a Curve

There is yet a third way to alter text with respect to a curve—the Fit Text To Path command. To use it, you must select a curve and a string

12.9

The effects of wrapping artistic text and wrapping paragraph text are worlds apart.

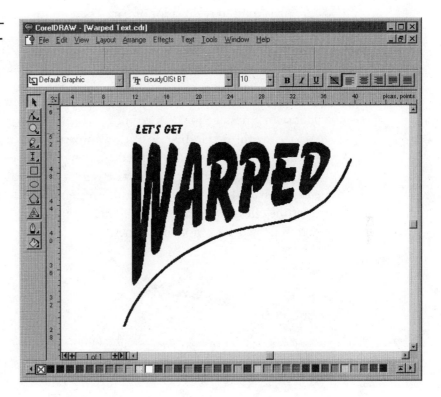

of artistic text together. Then the tool studies the contour of the curve and automatically adjusts the baseline so that the characters follow the curve's path.

We have reached a definite conclusion concerning Fit Text To Path: Practically nobody knows by heart how to use it. There are many highly skilled DRAW users who produce brilliant work with it, but if you were to listen closely as they fine-tune fitted text, you'd probably hear something like this: "Okay, to move the text under the curve instead of over... Let's see, I think it's this one... No, how about this one... Well, maybe I should click here and then here... No, how about that one... Maybe I need to hum my mantra, too... There, got it!" And just when you think you understand the interplay between the controls in the roll-up, DRAW turns your text inside-out or upside-down.

We're not going to waste a lot of paper describing every turn taken by the Fit Text To Path command—this is one set of controls that must be used to be learned. On the other hand, we do offer a few rules of thumb, and some good and bad examples of well-executed text fit to a path.

Choose Your Curve Wisely   Above all, text must be readable. If you lose the message in the medium, you've lost everything. A sure way to do that with the Fit Text To Path command is to choose the wrong path. If your path has sharp corners, the only way the Fit Text effect will work is if the text turns the corner between two words. As you can see here, however, the result is harsh and unfriendly, and you run a high risk of the effect overshadowing the message. Moral: When in doubt, use rounded corners, not sharp ones.

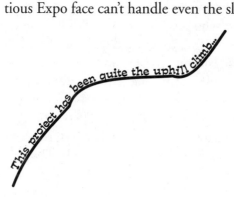

Choose Your Typeface Wisely   If you are pushing text along the contour of a crooked path, you need to choose a typeface with good shock absorbers. In our second effort at fitting text to a curve, the curve is much smoother than the previous one. But notice that the ostentatious Expo face can't handle even the slightest bump.

In our third try, we solved these two problems by switching to a more nimble typeface (BakerSignet) and by smoothing out the curve even more. It was easy: With the Shape tool, we selected each of the two sharply turning nodes, right-clicked, and chose Smooth from the flyout menu.

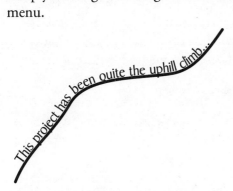

Keep Your Distance   What else is wrong with our fitted text? The text is sitting right on top of the curve—very distracting. Either the text needs to be lifted off the curve, or the curve needs to be removed altogether. (In the latter case, the text *becomes* the curve, not needing any other object to represent the intended shape.)

So here's what we did for Take 4: We set the horizontal alignment control to the one shown here (this roll-up is the hardest one of all to describe in words), with the text appearing to jiggle up and down. Then we clicked the Edit button and set the Distance From Path just enough to raise the descenders up off the curve.

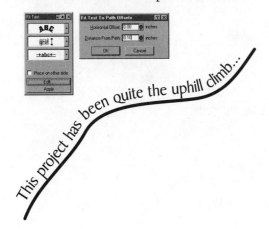

Incidentally, this little exercise pretty well typifies how we use Fit Text to Path: we fiddle, we fumble, we flounder, we futz, and eventually we get where we want to be. We never get what we want on the first try.

We considered removing the outline altogether. (Not the curve, but just its outline. The curve must remain in order for the effect to stay dynamic.) But we decided instead to scale it back somewhat. So we reduced its thickness from 4 points to 2, and tinted it back from solid black to 50% black.

This project has been quite the uphill climb...

Our final tweak—and you judge for yourself whether you prefer it or not—came at the hands of the text orientation control, the top one on the Fit Text To Path roll-up. The vertical skew and the slight upward rotation give the impression that the letters are actually climbing up the curve. We have included the roll-up in the accompanying graphic because, again, it's practically impossible for us to show or describe this text orientation control. But seeing how you asked: "You know the first drop-down box with the fat *ABC* letters? Click it and choose the second set of fat letters." There.

We carefully chose the foregoing example of text fitting, picking something that started out with big problems in order to show you the pitfalls. Figure 12.10 is an example that has no problems. Corel's Technical typeface is perfect for text fitting because its letterforms are friendly and appear to be walking an uneven path, anyway. Also, the tree branch in this figure is an ideal path, with smooth and friendly curves. Finally, the text is comfortably positioned off the path, preserving the integration of the two elements while avoiding overcrowding.

12.10

This fitted text is an unqualified success.

Creating Embossed Text: Theme and Variation

Practically every CorelDRAW book on the market includes a tutorial on producing *embossed text*—the effect shown in Figure 12.11. Embossed text appears to be raised up from, or chiseled into, the page. This year, we present "theme and variation."

We didn't invent this technique, and we suspect you have seen it elsewhere and perhaps even produced it. The first part of this exercise (the theme) is great practice for using hotkeys. In fact, we would argue that

12.11

Creating embossed text involves knowing your hotkeys.

producing this embossed text is easy when you know your way around the keyboard, but close to impossible when you don't. We offer the second part (the variation) as a demonstration of one of DRAW's most popular features: Trim, introduced in version 5.

Theme: The Conventional Embossing Technique

To follow along with this next exercise, open EMBOSS.CDR from the PRACTICE directory on the Companion CD. Figure 12.12 shows your starting point. We chose the typeface Geometric Heavy and stretched the characters vertically. Though not essential to the task, we also converted the text to curves so that your screen will look similar to ours, and you won't have to bother with installing a typeface you might not have.

Two actions are crucial to this procedure: Nudge and the Tab key. As objects overlap (which they soon will), the only way you will be able to pick out individual ones will be with the Tab key, and the only way to reliably move them is with Nudge.

12.12

The four main in-
gredients for
creating embossed
text

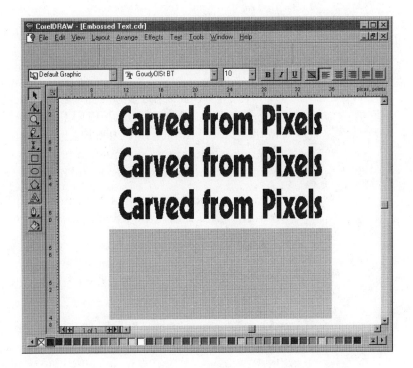

AUTHOR'S NOTE

We suggest that before you start this activity, you go to Tools /
Options / General / Undo Levels and set an Undo level of about 8.
That way, it will be easy for you to retrace and repeat your steps
with Ctrl+Z. Then, to analyze a particular action, you can do it,
undo it with Ctrl+Z, redo it with File / Redo, and keep rocking
back and forth until you understand the dynamics of each move.
Corel eliminated the hotkey of Alt+Enter for Redo in DRAW 6.0,
but you can resurrect it with the Tools / Customize dialog and
the instructions in Chapter 15.

Here are the essential steps for creating the embossed text sample:

1. Open EMBOSS.CDR, and make sure that your status bar is visible (View / Status Bar).

2. Select the top "Carved from Pixels" text string and change its color to 20% black, the same color as the background rectangle. If you are using the default CORELDRW.PAL palette, you should be able to pick out 20% black from the Color Palette. Otherwise, you can go to Uniform Fill, or use the Copy Attributes From command to grab the fill of the rectangle.

3. Leave the middle text string black, and change the bottom one to white, using either the palette or the Fill flyout.

4. Drag a marquee across all three text strings. (Even though the third one is invisible against the white page, you can still select it. Your selection handles and the status line will confirm that you have selected all three.)

5. Choose Arrange / Align & Distribute. In the roll-up, click the icons for horizontal and vertical alignment, and click Apply. Press F4 to zoom, and your screen will look like Figure 12.13.

6. With the three text strings still selected, hold Shift and select the rectangle, too.

7. With all four objects selected, repeat the horizontal and vertical alignment. (If you haven't issued any other commands since Step 5, you can just press Ctrl+R to instantly repeat the center alignment.

At this point, your text will be completely invisible—the 20% black rectangle covers the 20% black text, which in turn covers the other text strings. If it weren't for the Tab key, it would be virtually impossible to individually select the text strings; but with Tab, it's easy. Try it now: Press Tab several times, and watch how your screen reacts. Your visual cue is the right side of the status line (assuming it is still in its default configuration), which flashes the color of the selected object; that will be your guide as you complete this job.

12.13

Three strings of text rolled into one

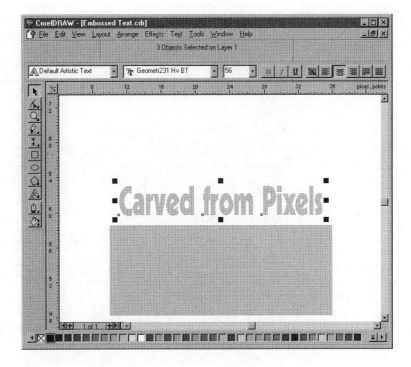

8. Go to Tools / Options / General / Nudge and set the Nudge value to .5 point.

9. Press Tab until the status line indicates that you have selected the black string of text. This is the text that should be moved up and to the left.

10. Press the Up Arrow once and Left Arrow once. Thanks to Nudge, you are insured against any extraneous motion—just a half-point up and a half-point to the left. Zoom in even closer; your screen should look like Figure 12.14.

11. Press Tab until you have selected the white string of text.

12. Nudge that text once to the right and once downward.

I 2.14

The shadow of the text takes shape...

13. Press Esc to clear the selection, Ctrl+W to redraw the screen (if necessary), F4 to zoom out, and you're done—does your screen look like Figure 12.15?

Does the text appear raised or depressed to you? This is similar to one of those cubic illusions that changes every time you blink. Our surveys indicate that, for most people, when the shadow is top-left and light is bottom-right, the letters look carved out of the background; when the shadow is lower-right and light top-left, the characters look raised. Your own mileage may differ, so you should experiment with all variations.

To repeat, we do not consider embossed text to be an advanced or complicated procedure for DRAW users, but we want to reemphasize how

12.15

Now the text appears carved out of the background.

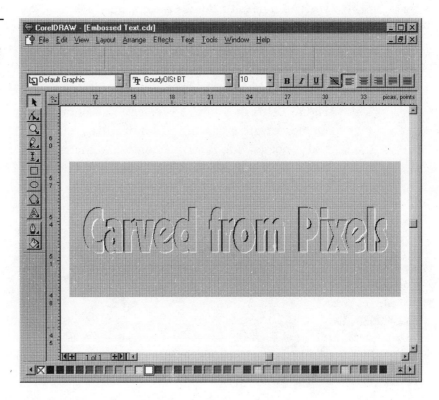

difficult it would be to produce this effect without the Nudge feature and the Tab key. Imagine selecting individual strings of the overlapping text with the mouse! And once you do manage to select a string, think about having to move it in tiny but precise increments. Without the keyboard, these tasks would probably earn you a case of arthritis…not to mention teach you a few choice words.

The Trim Variation

Let's suppose you want to show some embossed text carved out of a background that is not uniform. No problem, you say, you'll change the background to a fountain fill or perhaps even a fractal fill. Of course, you'll also need to change the text string that sits on top—because the whole illusion is that the text on top is not really there, but only represents the effect of chiseling into or raising above the background. Piece of cake, you think, you'll just apply the same effect to the top string of text as you did to the background.

Figure 12.16 shows the on-screen result of doing this. Though the Drapes texture is engaging, it's not what we intended. The span of the text is not as wide as the rectangle, and therefore the pattern of the texture is different. The text looks cool, but it does not appear chiseled or embossed.

12.16

A variable background adds a challenge to creating an embossed effect.

Instead of having a string of text on top, what we really want is *no text on top*, so the background can show through. Of course, we'll need to magically trim away all three strings of text, not just the one on top. The solution? The magical Trim tool. Try this:

1. Zoom way in on the characters, as close as you can go.

2. Select the top string of text (the gray text; use the status bar as your guide).

3. Go to Arrange / Trim. Under Leave Original, make sure Other Object(s) is checked and Target Object is not checked. (These are the defaults, if you haven't changed them.)

4. Click Trim, and use the bold black pointer that appears to select the object to be trimmed (the white text string).

5. Repeat steps 2 and 3, this time trimming the black text.

What exactly are you trimming, and how come your screen doesn't look much different? Remembering back to Chapter 5, the first object you select is the cookie cutter, and the object you select with the special Trim pointer is the cookie dough. Therefore, you just used the Trim tool to trim away all of the white and black text that was being covered by the textured text on top. And your screen doesn't look any different because, before the trim, that portion of the text was covered; now it's simply gone.

AUTHOR'S NOTE

This is not the most intuitive maneuver ever devised. So if you're having trouble visualizing the effect, undo it, then switch to Wireframe, you will actually see the part of the text that is being trimmed away.

6. Select the text on top and delete it. Your screen should look like Figure 12.17.

1 2 . 1 7

This text looks like the background because it *is* the background.

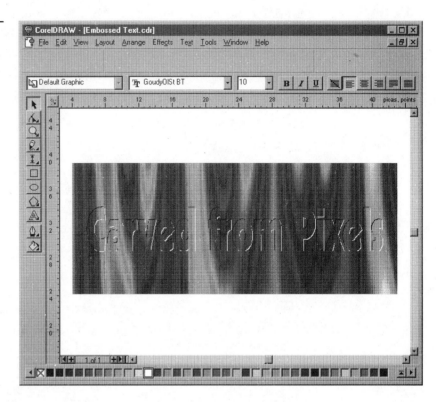

Instead of three strings of text, this embossed-text-on-a-variable-background technique is being produced with two slivers that represent the text shadows and highlights. The text in front no longer exists—the pattern is defined by the background, and the shape of the words is defined by the two slivers that survived the Trim command.

The CorelDRAW Squeeze Play

Here is another technique guaranteed to make your time in front of the computer marginally more amusing. Figure 12.18 shows the intended effect: The characters of the text appear to melt together. As with embossed text, this is not difficult to re-create, as long as you know to employ one important but infrequently used function of DRAW.

12.18

This effect requires one little command. Do you know which one?

First, set up a line of artistic text, and choose a nice fat typeface. (We picked Balloon ExtraBold from Corel's library.) Enlarge it to about 100 points, choose a light color or shade of gray for the interior, and then add a very thick Outline Pen, say 12 points. We chose to shade the outline 50% black; you can use any dark color, including solid black. The Uniform Fill (Shift+F11) and Outline Pen (F12) dialogs are the places to go for these tasks. At this point, your text will look rather unattractive, as demonstrated in Figure 12.19.

Now you're going to make the text look even worse by smashing all of the letters together. To do this, change to the Shape tool and move the funny-looking arrow at the end of the text to the left. Keep going until every character overlaps its neighbor (Figure 12.20).

By the way, you could also do this by entering a value in the Characters field on the Alignment page of the Character dialog. With our 100-point type, we arrived at a Character value of −28.

However atrocious your screen might look, DRAW is behaving normally, placing outlines in front of fill patterns by default. However, as long as the large outline sits on top of the text, the result is never going to look good. Your task is to place the outline *behind* the fill, and that is precisely the name of the command that you will use. Return to the Pick tool and reselect the text. Then press F12 to open the Outline Pen dialog, and check the box that says Behind Fill. What a difference! Now the outline draws first and the fill draws afterward, producing the look that you're after.

12.19

This text won't
win any awards
for elegance...

12.20

...and now it's even
worse.

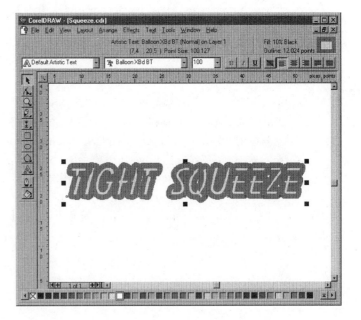

All that's left for you to do is make sure that each letter touches the one to its right. Use the Shape tool and kern the characters until they all touch; when you're done, your screen should look like Figure 12.21.

12.21

With the outline behind the fill and certain characters kerned, this text just melts together.

Creating a Text Mask

One of the more striking effects that you can create with text in DRAW is that of looking through one object to see another object behind it. The technical term for this is *masking*, and DRAW has an automatic way of doing it. In the following exercises, you will create a mask.

But first let's talk about this word, *mask*. We suspect that accomplished artists use the term when they want to intimidate us amateurs. "*Oh, we'll just mask off that image, cut an overlay, and do a burn on the plates.*" Yeah, right—and then we'll go up on the Internet and discuss new radiation therapy with the Stanford Medical Center.

To understand masking, think of it literally, like a Halloween mask—an object with holes, through which elements behind the mask are visible (such as the eyes of the person wearing the mask). It has become an annual tradition that the lead author's daughter, now almost three years old, makes her appearance in these pages. This year, Figure 12.22 shows how we applied text masking to a photo of her.

12.22

Three-year-old Erica Altman, clipped inside of her own name

Hiding Erica Behind Her Name

In this case, the letters that spell Erica's name constitute the mask, or *clipping path*, and the photo of her is the object behind the mask. For good measure, we applied a gray outline to the lettering and then dropped a second copy of her name behind the image, to act as a shadow.

Open ERICA1.CDR from the PRACTICE directory of the Companion CD and you'll see the starting point that we have provided for you: Erica's photo, scanned into PhotoPAINT and then imported into DRAW, and the string of text. We have taken the liberty of preparing the text for you already, set in Balloon ExtraBold and positioned so that the letters move downward and overlap slightly. Then we converted them to curves (so you don't need to install the typeface just for this exercise).

Your objective is not just to place the text in front of Erica, but actually to hide her behind it so that she is peeking through. First, you need to weld together the five letters in the name:

1. Select the letters in Erica's name.

2. Go to Arrange / Weld and click Weld To. When prompted with the pointer, click on any one of the characters. The letters should appear melted together at the points where they previously overlapped.

3. Now that you have your mask, you must position it correctly. Move Erica's name (which is now one single curve) over her photo.

4. Position it so that the text covers both of her eyes and fits within the photo. Resize and reshape if necessary.

At this stage your screen should look similar to Figure 12.23. Now you have to think in reverse: The only parts of the photo that will be visible when you're done are the parts that are now obscured. With this point of view, you can see that both of her eyes and most of her nose and mouth will show.

5. With the text still selected, press Ctrl+C to store a copy of it in the Clipboard (explanation forthcoming).

6. Press Ctrl+J. Make sure the item called Automatically Center New PowerClip Contents is unchecked.

7. Select the photo, and go to Effects / PowerClip / Place Inside Container.

8. Move the arrow to the text and click once. Does your screen look like Figure 12.24?

12.23

The text mask is now in position.

12.24

The PowerClip command took the object that you selected first and stuffed it into the object that you clicked on second. Whatever fits remains visible; whatever doesn't is hidden.

WATCH OUT!

In step 6, we asked you to go to Options and turn off the curiously named Automatically Center New PowerClip Contents check box. When that option is on, DRAW automatically centers the image in the container. If you hadn't turned it off, DRAW would have automatically repositioned Erica's photo, spoiling all your careful alignment of text with photo. Corel engineers chose to have this automatic centering option on by default, but we have concluded that almost all DRAW users prefer to keep it off, for precisely the same reasons that you needed to here.

Finishing Touches

In Step 5 above, we asked you to copy the text to the Clipboard. This was necessary to create the shadow behind the mask. Here are the steps:

1. Press Ctrl+V to paste the text back onto the screen. It should return right on top of the clipped photo.

2. Nudge it slightly down and to the right.

3. Fill it with 5% black and remove the outline (if there is one).

4. Send it to the back with Shift+PgDn.

5. Go to Effects / Contour.

6. From the first page of controls (the one with the concentric squares), set the direction of the contour to Inside, the Offset to .1 point (or .00"), and the Steps to 30. Translated, this means duplicate the selected object 30 times, each one gradually getting smaller and moving toward the center in .1-point increments.

7. From the second page (the one with the color wheel), set the fill color to 50% black. This will gradually shift the color from the object's original shade of 5% gray to 50% gray.

8. Click Apply and check your screen against ours in Figure 12.25.

12.25

Contour is a great tool for creating re-alistic shadows.

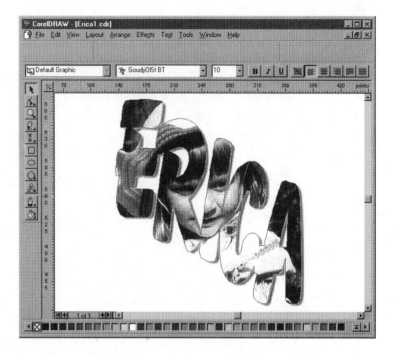

We've thrown a lot at you in these last eight steps. To read more about the Contour tool, see Chapter 19.

Creating Transparent Text

Creating the effect of see-through text used to be very difficult, if not impossible. Now it's easy, thanks to the Lens tool introduced in version 5.0. We'll cover lenses thoroughly in Chapter 22, but as a sneak pre-view, here is how we set a bit of transparent text over Erica's photo.

First, we imported Erica2.TIF into DRAW from the PRACTICE direc-tory of the Companion CD. This is the same photo used in the mask-ing exercise, but there we cropped it tightly; here we are using the entire image. We set Erica's name in the Brody script typeface. Using the Shape tool and Nudge, we positioned the letters on a sloping baseline. Then we set the text to white and gave it a thin gray outline. In the Lens roll-up, we asked for a Brighten lens at a rate of 50%, clicked Apply, and we were done. (Why Brighten instead of Transparency? Frankly, we didn't plan on it, but in our experiments, Brighten simply looked better.) Figure 12.26 shows the result of our efforts.

12.26

This transparent text allows the photo underneath to show through.

Working with "Untext"

What do we mean by *untext*? It's text that is no longer text, stripped of its special status by the Arrange / Convert To Curves command. When you convert text to curves, you gain access to all of its nodes and paths, just like any other type of curve. This opens the door to many fascinating effects, with which you can personalize your text to a level beyond just what the typeface offers.

Unfortunately, whenever this feature is shown off in public at user group meetings or trade shows, the result always seems to look something like Figure 12.27. A guest at one of our recent seminars stood up and asked if we could show her how to use the "Text Uglifier tool"—so closely identified is this tool with its potentially hideous results.

12.27

Yes, but is it art?

In many ways, working with converted text requires even more care than working with abstract objects, because readers know how a text character is supposed to look. If you distort a character too much, you can offend your readers' sensibilities; and if you don't change it enough, they might not notice the effect at all and decide instead that you are just using poorly crafted typefaces.

Figure 12.28 shows a couple of simple yet effective examples of text effects. What began as a string of Futura Black became four characters that stayed out in the sun too long. Erie Black was the source for this creative logo that connects two letters together.

12.28

When you convert text to curves, don't think you have to do something dramatic. Usually, simpler really is better.

Futura Black Before:

After:

Erie Black Before:

After:

This chapter began on the technical side and ended on the aesthetic side. We'll continue with this somewhat softer theme in Chapter 13 as we discuss avoiding some of the potential disastrous results of working with text in DRAW.

Avoiding Text Disasters

THIRTEEN

CHAPTER 13

For a third consecutive edition of this book, we are including this chapter. It's written for and by the CorelDRAW user without a professional background in typesetting or illustration who must create and format lots of text. And because that description doesn't apply to several members of our writing team, this chapter comes to you in first person voice—that of your lead author.

My writing teammates might share my views on this subject, but not my *point of view,* because many of them don't have the same perspective as I do—that of an amateur, to be blunt. I lack the skills, the vision, and probably the judgment required to produce consistently professional artwork with CorelDRAW, but this is certainly not true of some of the award-winning illustrators on my team. Perhaps one of the smartest things I have done as a desktop publisher is to acknowledge my amateur status every single day I go to work.

This chapter delivers one prevailing message:

> CorelDRAW's job is to assist imagination and creativity in becoming reality. It is *not* CorelDRAW's job to *replace* imagination and creativity.

There are no shortcuts to good design. It takes years of training, experience, and practice; yet many amateurs believe the marketing hype that says "yes—you, too, can produce professional work if you buy CorelDRAW and products like it." If you absorb nothing else from this chapter, remember this: Becoming proficient with CorelDRAW does not make you a good designer—only a prolific one. And I'm sorry to say that I know plenty of prolific bad designers.

I named this chapter carefully; it won't pretend to teach you how to produce beautiful text-based illustrations, but rather how to avoid bad ones. I won't burden you with long dissertations about how to think like a designer. I won't foist upon you a bunch of makeovers, where you are shown a page that you don't think is all that bad in the first place, and then you see it transformed into some ultra-modern, techno-crazed production that leaves you entirely unsure whether "after" is better than "before." And let's remember one thing: I'm a writer. I believe in the power of the word. I remain unconvinced that one of Item A is really equal to 1,000 of Item B.

One other thing: Good design is timeless and versionless. It transcends software releases, operating systems, varieties of computers, and computers themselves. Though I routinely freshen up the examples and develop new exercises for the other chapters in this book, here in this chapter about design principles many of the anecdotes and much of the advice are unchanged from when I originally published them in the late 1980s.

The Look at Me! Syndrome

I have a friend who works at a photocopy store that recently added a color publishing department, and he now produces fliers, prints photos, and creates color brochures for drop-in customers. He acknowledges that he doesn't know the first thing about publishing in color, but his customers are usually so tickled by getting something back in a color other than black that they leave happy. "Colors!" he exclaims. "That's all they care about." He also laser-prints dozens of projects that come in with clip art, dingbats, big fat borders, extruded characters, rainbow ornaments, and text fitted to a path…effects used for no other reason except that they are made possible by today's software.

My friend's customers have been seduced by the Look at Me! approach to design, in which the appearance of a printed piece takes on an artificially inflated significance. The Look at Me! syndrome is characterized by the designer's (perpetrator's?) tendency to utilize in one project every single effect offered within a software program, regardless of whether it is appropriate to the task. Look at Me! is one of the major contributors to "laser sludge," which is what traditional designers like to call the less-than-brilliant efforts from today's desktop publishing community.

It's only natural that desktop design would spawn such a syndrome; after all, its primary focus is the *presentation* of ideas rather than the ideas themselves. You can see examples of Look at Me! everywhere. A product's order form used to have a bit of bold in it, maybe a few hairlines. Now it has rounded rectangles, gray shading everywhere, bold and italic all over the place, fancy borders, and little hands pointing to all the important things. The only embellishments in yesteryear's newsletters were page numbers; now they have little clip-art people holding signs with the page numbers on them. Technical manuals had bold headlines, maybe set a few points larger than the body text; now they have drop caps, small caps, and white type in black boxes—*all at the same time.*

The well-intentioned author of the piece in Figure 13.1 became so infatuated with his work that he actually submitted it to Corel's Annual Design Contest. Unfortunately, the only distinction this drawing is eligible for is the Look at Me! Award. Do you have any idea what to read first in this flier? Granted, the large, overblown extrusion hits you like a ton of bricks, but too many other elements are competing for your attention. This flier is the electronic equivalent of sitting in a Silicon Valley traffic jam with the radio blaring and two kids screaming from the back seat.

Diagnosing and Treating Look at Me!

Do you suffer from Look at Me! syndrome? Take the following quiz and find out:

- Do you routinely set headlines in sizes above 36-point? Above 48-point?

- If a headline can't be read from across the room, does that mean it isn't big enough?

- Do you use color in documents just because it looks good on your new monitor?

- If one typeface looks good, does that mean two will look better? How about three? How about 40?

- If bold isn't strong enough, would all caps and bold be better?

13.1

"Look at Me!"
shouts this flier.

- Is an underline better than no underline?
- Is a double-underline twice as good as a single underline?
- Do you ever add fountain fill backgrounds to your text just because you feel like it?

■ Do you set white type on a black background to make it more dramatic?

And the special bonus question:

■ Do you ever start producing a brochure or a flier before you have determined what you want to say?

If you answered Yes to more than a couple of these questions, you might be suffering from Look at Me! It means you make a habit of overembellishing your work—even if it's just a study on the refrigerator life of a box of baking soda. It means you look for ways to grab your readers before they read the first sentence. You try to make your documents say, "Look at Me!"

Figure 13.2 is not a makeover of 13.1; it's a tear-down. Instead of six typefaces (including—alas!—Avant Garde *and* Arial), there are two. Instead of an ostentatious extrusion, there is a drop shadow. Instead of the sophomoric script face, there is italic; and instead of the cartoonish clip art, there is nothing. I kept the lightning bolts because, when seen above the visual noise, they actually imply a sense of speed and quickness.

Before this piece can be made over, it must be torn down. In fact, I contend that if all you do is the tear-down and you don't get around to the makeover, or are incapable of it, that's okay. At least, the tear-down version won't become known for its arbitrary use of DRAW's special effects. Someone looking at it might decide that Herman's Courier Service is actually worth trying.

Clean, simple design has rewards beyond the aesthetic. The torn-down version of Herman's flier is not only more relaxed visually, but it proved much easier to open, save, print, and export. For Figure 13.1 with its two rainbow extrusions, the .CDR file required 30 seconds to open or save, and over 7 minutes to spool to the printer or export to a file, and then another 4 minutes to print. But Figure 13.2 opens and saves in 5 seconds, and prints or exports in less than a minute.

13.2

Here is the same flier, torn down to its essential message.

Tired of using conventional courier services?
Next time, call on

Herman's Courier Service

⚡ **Competitive prices:** Our prices are typically 35–50% below the competition.

⚡ **Trained staff:** Our workers are thorough professionals who have all undergone extensive training at our academy.

⚡ **Satisfaction guaranteed:** If your package does not reach its destination on time or you are not satisfied, your money will be refunded. No questions asked.

Call 800-1-ONTIME

You can cure yourself of the Look at Me! syndrome by remembering that it's not necessarily the *design* of your work that needs to say "look at me," it's the *ideas.* If only I had a nickel for every time I have proclaimed in seminars or consulting sessions: Let the content determine the form. Only use the big headline when the idea merits it. Don't italicize a passage unless it is truly significant. When you highlight too many passages of text, you don't present a clear sense of priority to your readers, and they have little motivation to continue reading. In short, when you make everything bold, you make nothing bold.

Those of you suffering from Look at Me! syndrome should ponder the following arguments.

The Message Is Everything!

If you spend 10 minutes making a headline look fancy, spend 20 minutes making sure it says the perfect thing. It's so easy to get carried away formatting text in DRAW, because so many elements can be attached: space above, below, to the left and to the right; rules, bullets, and boxes; shading, dingbats, and all of the special effects discussed in Part IV. You have many, many opportunities to louse up a perfectly good line of text, so at the very least, make sure its message is strong enough to survive if you do overdesign. My rule of thumb: For every minute spent using the Pick or Shape tool and the Effects menu, spend two with the Text cursor. Make sure your text conveys the precise message you intend.

Bigger Is Not Better

If a headline stands out sufficiently when set in 24-point, don't set it larger "just to be sure." I still remember a client of mine in 1989 who had been using her trusty HP LaserJet II printer, the one for which font support generally consisted of about two or three sizes and weights of Dutch and Swiss. Then she added to her printer a PostScript interpreter, providing lots of typefaces and built-in scaleable fonts. The laser sludge she began cranking out was proof positive of her new love for the technology.

"What size is that headline?" I asked.

"Forty-five points."

"How'd you arrive at that figure?"

"Forty-four didn't quite fill the entire column."

Looking at her work, I always had the feeling she'd produced it while at a Rolling Stones concert.

Then one day, a miracle occurred: The PostScript board in her printer went out and she was forced to use it as a plain old HP LaserJet. It was the most important step she ever took toward capable design. Instead of automatically making her headlines huge to compulsively fill the space, she began manipulating the space around her heads. She complained the whole way about not having all the choices with which she had become so infatuated, but having her choices limited was a positive constraint on her projects' appearance.

You can see a modern-day example of this same dynamic when you browse the World Wide Web on the Internet. Many of the Web browsers allow only simple font changes, but others have lots of bells and whistles…just waiting to entrap the innocent user. Figure 13.3 demonstrates how too much power can be hazardous to your health. These polka dots do nothing to further any cause; they are likely here because the author discovered that it was possible to create a tiled background for a Web page.

Those of you with a bit of exposure to HTML authoring know that you have more formatting capabilities if you use Netscape Extensions to create your pages. Two such extensions are the ability to include background images and use large font sizes. This extra capability did not help the Figure 13.3 Web site in the least. Figure 13.4, though, shows how the same page looks from the Mosaic browser, which doesn't support the Netscape Extensions. It's plainer, less creative, and about a million times better looking.

Easy on the Attributes

Don't apply text attributes to more than one passage of text per column or page. You've all seen those "YOU MAY HAVE ALREADY WON…" sweepstakes letters, usually with Ed McMahon's face on the envelope, that pile up in your mailbox. Open one, and you have no idea what to read first. Wait, I'd better take that back… Your name is set red in 128-point Garamond Ultra, so you probably read that first. After that, every

13.3

Felony on the Internet! Just because some Web browsers allow you to create pages like this, does that mean you have to do so?

third paragraph is either bold, italic, underlined, or maybe all three. This isn't even laser sludge; it's generally produced on a high-resolution imagesetter. That, of course, doesn't save it from the Desktop Publishing Hall of Shame.

As I said earlier, when you highlight everything, you highlight nothing. Your readers don't know where to begin, and if they somehow make it through the rough terrain of your artwork, their psychological reaction to its look will probably overshadow any ideas you intended to convey.

13.4

This Web browser is akin to the 1989 HP LaserJet printer—plain, simple, and perfectly capable of producing good clean results.

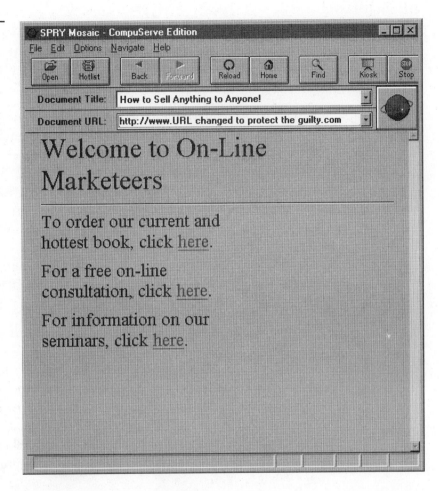

The next time you want to highlight a passage, try just using white space

like this.

It will be easier on your readers' eyes, it will accomplish the same purpose, and it will demonstrate both your sense of design and your sensibilities in general. It will probably be easier to produce, too.

Be Brilliant!

Write something that's so good, it truly merits special attention. I have no magic strategies here, except to say that writers struggle with the same tendency toward overproduction that illustrators do (you should have seen this manuscript before three editors pared it down).

For example, suppose you lead off your advertisement with the words, *Finally, the product you've been waiting for!* It's an attention-grabber all right, and if you set it in a 48-point bold typeface with an extrusion behind it, whammo—instant laser sludge. Or you could begin with two simple words: *It's here.* (No exclamation mark.) Now your headline conveys a clarity of thought and purpose, and if you can't resist setting it in big type, it won't look so bad because it's only two words. It may take you hours to hone your prose down to its simplest, most effective form, but it will be worth it. Good writing is only part art and inspiration; it's also craft and perspiration.

Figure 13.5, though it may not look like it at first glance, is actually quite carefully prepared. The image on the left, which we'll call "Ugly," is taken straight from one of the back pages of a general-interest magazine (except for the name of the product and its description, which I sort of made up). The rounded rectangles, the ultrabold headline, the boldface letters, the tight margins, the exclamation marks—they all contribute to make this a shining example of desktop design at its worst. (I can't say for sure that this was produced on the desktop, but the rounded rectangles and the Helvetica text push that probability to about 95%.)

The image on the right, deemed "Not So Ugly," has only one objective: to deliver its message. I forced myself to produce it in less than ten minutes and limited myself to nothing fancier than the single gray bar at the bottom. The white space around the entire piece makes it much more inviting than its counterpart, and the white space around the essential message ("Stop smoking, eat good foods…") calls it gently to your attention. I was tempted to set it in italic, but resisted. I did allow the move from Brittanic Light to Medium.

13.5

Form vs. content:
Ugly vs. Not So
Ugly

The Miracle That You Have Been Waiting For!!

Yes, you, for a limited time only, can finally unlock the key to longevity. For the first time ever in the Western World come the deep, dark secrets of the **WALA WALA PLANT**, featuring a special, scientifically tested and certified herb that actually *slows down the aging process.*

And it can be yours for the low, low price of $39.95 per month. But wait—there's more! The price drops to $37.95 once you pass your 80th birthday, and then drops by a dollar every five years after that!

Operators are standing by, so pick up the phone and order your lifetime supply of the WALA WALA ageless wonder. Not available in any stores!!

The Secret is out

For centuries, humans have searched for magical potions that will increase their life spans—the mythical fountains of youth. Silver-haired Americans have spent an estimated $13 billion on various "if you act now" schemes that claim never-ending youth.

But now the secret is out.

If you want to live longer, you don't need to pay anyone, eat exotic herbs, or chant unrecognizable hymns. If you want to live longer, do this:

Stop smoking, eat good foods,
and exercise regularly.

That's the secret. That will be $150, please...

Not So Ugly has one sustaining virtue: It is not so ugly (this is a teardown, not a makeover). It does not detract from its message, nor does it try to be more than it should be. An accomplished artist might take Not So Ugly and produce wonderful things with it. Could you? If not, perhaps you shouldn't try.

Small Is Beautiful

A first cousin to the Look at Me! syndrome is Pompousitis—the uncontrollable compulsion to use graphic and text elements—and we've already touched on some of its symptoms in the previous sections. Look at Me! usually has a purpose: to call attention. Pompousitis, on the other hand, is an aimless attempt to cram as many elements onto an electronic page as possible. It's kind of like eating potato chips in front of the television—you do it because they're there and because you want to.

The suggestions in the following paragraphs might not be appropriate for every DRAW project, but the minimalist approach is a good, safe starting point for many illustrations. Not only will it yield cleaner-looking work, it will be easier on your schedule: Bad design usually takes longer to produce than good, simple design.

Diagnosing and Treating Pompousitis

Let's find out if you have Pompousitis.

- If everything on your page is in regular type, do you feel compelled to italicize something?

- Do you create headlines that are mostly boldface *and* italic? How about boldface, italic, and all caps?

- If a section of your page is empty, does that mean that you've done something wrong?

In your next project, try subscribing to the belief that Small is Beautiful, and Less is More. Consider the suggestions in the following sections.

No Lines Allowed

Create a document with no rules, hairlines, or underlines at all. When I lecture before Ventura Publisher or PageMaker users, I approach the subject of ruling lines with great trepidation, because I know they are going to be abused—especially shaded lines, which never look as good when laser-printed as they do on your screen. When I see newsletters or technical manuals with lines running in all directions, I am reminded of childhood summer vacations: We would go to the park and throw tanbark at one another because we couldn't think of anything better to do. I think many desktop publishers use ruling lines the way I used to use tanbark. Take those ruling lines out, and don't feel compelled to replace them with anything.

Take the Two-Typeface Challenge

For one entire project, try using only one or two type families. Here again, you can find very attractive text-based work coming from the old HP LaserJets, which didn't give their owners 35 different typefaces with which to hang themselves. There is nothing wrong with mixing, say, a sans serif headline with serif body text, but many desktop publishers don't know where to draw the line. It's far better to use too few faces than too many.

Somebody forgot to tell that to the well-intentioned designer of the Sunday supplement advertisement shown in Figure 13.6. It seems pretty clear that the perpetrator of this ad owns CorelDRAW and is luxuriating in all of its typefaces. We stopped counting after 16. This is the classic case of Pompousitis—use of typefaces as determined by possession. You have 'em, so you use 'em.

It's best to pick just one or two type families for a complete job. Figure 13.7 shows the same ad, but with two typefaces instead of two dozen. I chose ITC Eras and American Garamond, both from Corel's collection. This tear-down, I'm afraid, took much longer than ten minutes, even though I did not overhaul the piece. I was careful about what I changed, removing a few lines and boxes but keeping the same basic layout. I even decided to leave in those hideous round boxes with prices in them.

This is as much an exercise in willpower as it is sound typographic advice. Do you know why professional typographers have type libraries consisting of thousands of faces? It's not so they can use them all for all of their projects; it's so they can pick the right *one or two* for a given project. Once they make those choices, they leave the rest for another day.

Most well-conceived DRAW projects use one or two type families with various weights, styles, and sizes. Some skilled illustrators may be able to use more typefaces with deft discretion, but most of us would benefit from taking the Two-Typeface Test when we produce work in and out of DRAW. We should force ourselves to make do with just two and maybe even one typeface (or type families, to be precise) for an entire project.

Use White Space

It's usually a good decision to create an illustration that has more white space than text. When I was the editor of *Inside Tennis* magazine several

13.6

**Oh, god of fonts,
how do I love thee?
Let me count the
ways**…

years ago, I found art director Thomas Burns to be a master of white space. The magazine was a jam-packed tabloid, and Thomas was usually shackled with far too many elements for each article. But every so often he would be given a bit of breathing room, and beautiful things would

1 3 . 7

This advertisement, redone with only two typefaces, is far less likely to offend your eyes or your sensibilities.

Authorized Reseller Since 1987

Optimum Computers

15555 State St., Elkwood, KS 66205
Phone (913) 555-0880   Fax (913) 555-0881
Hours: Mon – Fri, 9:30 – 6:30
Major credit cards accepted

486SX-33 $1,249
486DX-40 $1,429
486DX2-66 $1,599
486DX-33 $1,395
486DX-50 $1,549

- 128K External Cache
- 4MB Ram
- 250 MB Hard Drive
- 1.2 & 1.44 MB Floppy Drives
- 101 Key Keyboard

- 2 Serial, 1 Printer, 1 Game Port
- Hi-Color 1MB Video Card
- SVGA Color Monitor
- 2 Year Parts & 5 yr. Labor

CUSTOM CONFIGURATIONS AVAILABLE

Networks

Novell Authorized Reseller Since 1987

**Novell, MS-Workgroup & Lantastic
Installation and Support
Large Selection Network Accessories**

3COM, Novel, Intel, SMC, Lantastic, David System
16Bit NE2000 Comp. Combo $79
10-BaseT & Coax

Upgrade your old Motherboard

486SX-25	VESA Local Bus	$189
486DX-33/40	VESA Local Bus	$395
486DX-66	VESA Local Bus	$595

Hard Drives and Memory

170MB IDE $189	250MB IDE $229
340MB IDE $289	540MB IDE $599
1.2GB SCSI $999	1MB SIMM $49

Conner, Maxtor, Western Digital, etc.

Multimedia

Creative Labs Multimedia CD - 16 Kit
Double-Speed CD-ROM Drive
Multi-Session Photo CD Compatible
MPC Level 2 Compliant
320ms access, 300 KB/Sec data transfer
Sound Blaster PRO 16, Stereo Speakers
Aldus Photostyler LE, Multimedia Encyclopedia

$469

Miscellaneous

9824 S/R Fax Modem	$59
14.4 USRobotics Modem	$169
WordPerfect 6.0 Educational	$199

All prices in this advertisement subject to change

PENTIUM SUPER SYSTEM

- Intel PENTIUM 60 mhz Processor
- True Pentium Local Bus Motherboard
- 8 MB 60ns RAM
- 340 MB IDE Hard Drive
- VLB Drive Controller
- Diamond Speedstar PRO VLB Card
- 15" Flat Screen SVGA Monitor
- Full Tower Case w/8 Drive Bays
- 101 Keyboard 2 Serial, 1 Parallel, 1 Game Port

$3695

Options
17" MAG 1280 x1024	$595
17" ViewSonic 1600 x1280	$795
Diamond Viper VLB 2 MB	$299
2 MB VLB Caching Controller	$269

GRAPHICS POWER SYSTEM

- Intel 486 Processor
- 2 Slot VESA Local Bus Motherboard
- 8 MB 60ns Ram
- 340 MB IDE Hard Drive
- VLB Drive Controller
- Diamond Speedstar PRO VLB Card
- 15" Flat Screen SVGA Monitor
- Full Tower Case w/ 8 Drive Bays
- 101 Keyboard 2 Serial, 1 Parallel, 1 Game Port

486/DX-33	$2179
486/DX-50	$2299
486/DX2-66	$2359

Options
17" MAG Monitor 1280 x 1024	$595
17" ViewSonic 1600 x 1280	$795
Diamond Viper VLB 2 MB	$299
2 MB VLB Caching Controller	$269

Optimum 486/66 Special

486-66 CPU & Motherboard • 4 MB Ram • 210 MB Hard Drive • 1.2 or 1.44 MB Floppy Drive • 2 Serial, 1 Parallel Port • 14" SVGA Color Monitor .28 DP • 101 Key Keyboard • CPU Cooling Fan • DOS 5.0

$1,299

happen. For instance, he might leave the top two-thirds of a page completely blank, save for the headline. Once, he threw the headline out entirely, opting for a very large drop cap to bring the page into focus. Everything he tried worked with such elegant simplicity (this despite the fact that he didn't know beans about tennis).

Try creating a drawing where the white space prevails. Then try incorporating entire columns of white space, or large top and bottom margins. As you experiment, make sure to print many samples, or at least toggle into full-screen preview often. It is often difficult to visualize white space on the screen, what with DRAW's page border, rulers, guidelines, and grid points taking up space.

Relax Your Posture

Many desktop designers exhibit a knee-jerk reaction to setting type: They justify all text, whether or not there is a legitimate reason for it. There are times when the formality of a document makes justified type appropriate, but all too often it just makes your work look rigid and boxy. Also, though centered headlines are often effective, they can become dreadfully boring if you employ them all the time.

If you're in the centered headline/justified text rut, break out of it by left-aligning everything and avoiding hyphenation, especially if you are producing documents with wider columns (narrow, multicolumn pages might need to be hyphenated). At first, this new practice may seem odd. Give it a chance, though; it will grow on you. Did you notice that the Not So Ugly rendition of Figure 13.5 included a right-aligned headline? It's subtle enough to elude the attention of many.

"Borrow" Good Design

Imitation is not only the highest form of flattery; it is often good business. No, I'm not suggesting that you republish the January issue of *Rolling Stone,* articles and all—just that you keep an eye out for advertisements, articles, newsletters, and graphics that you think are presented well.

The next time you pick up a magazine, skim it for more than just a good article to read. And when you find a well-presented piece, there is hardly better practice than to try re-creating it in DRAW or your preferred page-layout program. Use a bit of dummy text and a few fake headlines, and try to recapture the style and the design. Notice the following:

- The use of call-out text
- The size of subheads
- The use of white space around headlines
- How drop shadows are created
- The colors used for spot elements
- How photos are integrated into the layout
- How backgrounds are created
- The use of illustrations to communicate

Don't look just at the desktop publishing magazines—they usually try too hard to be noticed. Choose an established, national monthly magazine whose priority is a particular message, not the medium for delivering that message.

This "borrowing" is completely legal; you can't get sued for look-and-feel infringement on a publication's design. Good design belongs to the public domain. There is nothing wrong with adapting an existing design that you find appealing, as long as you don't clone a trademarked logo or copyrighted slogan.

I recently had occasion to borrow. I needed to prepare a full-page advertisement for the International CorelDRAW User Conference but had only 24 hours in which to do it. While browsing Corel's *ArtShow,* a compendium of entries in Corel's annual World Design Contest, I came upon a piece I especially liked. Shown in Figure 13.8, this piece by well-known CorelDRAW artist Chris Purcell touts a technical support system for COMPAQ computers, highlighting four of the system's features. I had intended to concentrate on four features of the Conference, as well, so I decided that Chris's basic design would be a good starting point.

13.8

Chris Purcell's QuickSource illustration was a good candidate to "borrow" from.

I didn't dare try to incorporate the flair of Chris's piece—I'd surely fall on my face—but Figure 13.9 is my honest effort to imitate it, and Illustration No. 6 in the Color Gallery shows it in color. I stole the background of the double-fountain-fills going in opposite directions, but didn't try the extra shadowing or the squiggles employed in Chris's design. My four squares use the same technique of type angled at 90°, and

13.9

The result of
your lead author's
thievery

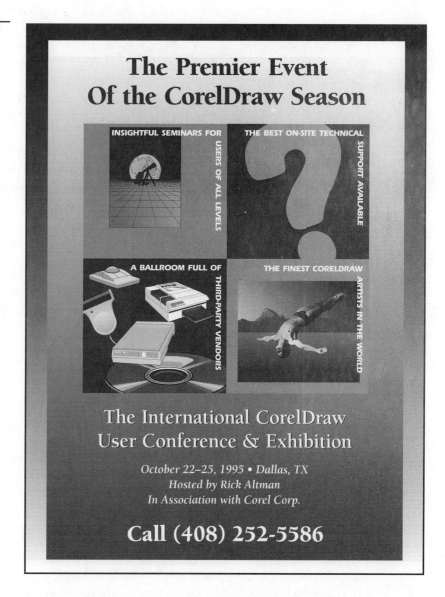

the large question mark was just right for advertising our own technical
support.

I knew that the dark type at the top would have good contrast against the light portion of the inner rectangle. On the other hand, I had no idea whether the white type near the middle ("The International CorelDraw...") would show up against the medium-colored part of the fountain. With no time to make an accurate color proof, I took the easy way out and placed a black shadow behind the type. One of those type strings, the white one or the black one, would surely show.

Chris likely created all of his elements from scratch or from raw materials such as clip-art shapes. I, on the other hand, used complete pictures from other sources, including the star gazer in the top-left square, the computer components at lower-left, and David Brickley's famous *The Diver* at lower-right. Chris won an award for his work; mine claims only that it succeeds in advertising the main features of the Conference and achieves an absence of ugliness.

Trying to replicate well-designed work is an excellent way to practice with DRAW's tools and develop your own sense of design.

Steal from Yourself, Too

While you're at it, don't forget to borrow from yourself. If you've done something that works, do it again. All successful designers do this. Think of two or three publications that you find to be particularly well designed, perhaps *Newsweek, Life, The Atlantic Monthly,* or *Sports Illustrated.* As you visualize them, certain characteristics will come to mind—such as *Life*'s use of large type, *Sports Illustrated*'s catchy headlines burned into full-page photos, and *Newsweek*'s section heads of white type on red bars.

These magazines are all well-designed, not because they do something fabulously different every month, but because they do the same good things over and over again. They all have found a design that works, and have stayed with it for years at a time. That is what makes them distinctive, and it will work for you, too. Every one of your projects need not be a perfect original—even the most skilled designers and illustrators don't try to achieve that. Once you produce a nice logo, a cover page for a brochure, or some other work you particularly like, "bottle" it—create a template from it and use it for your next similar project. You'll surely decide to vary the theme, but you can at least start with a well-tested design. When something works, *get as much mileage out of it as you can.*

Have a Plan

I promised no dissertations, so I'll make this short. Everybody has a plan when starting a project, right? Would that it were true! All too often, amateur designers sit down in front of the CorelDRAW controls with no idea at all of where they want to go. "If I play around long enough, something will come to me," is how one client of mine described this phenomenon. There is absolutely nothing wrong with that—it's the electronic equivalent of doodling on a cocktail napkin— but it's the *first* step in design, not the final one.

When you embark on a task—any task—first you decide what it is you want to do, then you determine how you are going to do it, and then you do it. That's a tried-and-true method in real life. Unfortunately, I encounter many CorelDRAW users who do it backwards. They sit in front of the computer, place their hand on the mouse, and start creating objects, hoping that a finished drawing will spontaneously occur. In no other aspect of their lives do they expect to achieve success in this manner, but they hold exempt from natural laws their relationship with CorelDRAW.

What it all boils down to is a question of process, of how you approach a publishing project. Humor aside, here is an effective plan of attack:

1. Decide what you want to do.

2. Do it.

This may sound trite, but again, you'd be surprised by how many inexperienced DRAW users do *the exact opposite.* They become enamored with the tools, they start to play around, they begin to build, and build, and build, and then, "*Oh…what was it that I wanted to say in all of this?*" They lose sight of their message; suddenly, their objective has been reduced to visual razzle-dazzle.

I see it over and over again. And you might argue that we public figures in the CorelDRAW community are the culprits, authoring books like this one, writing magazine articles, and giving seminars—all devoted to the use of this software. Indeed, I hold myself accountable for the unusual attention given here to the creative process. If you read only Part V of this book, about DRAW's special effects, you might walk away believing that those fancy effects are a substitute for sound judgment in design, technical skills, and a trained eye. However, until DRAW offers a command called "Paste Brilliant Design Idea," nothing could be further from the truth.

Here is how I see the possible outcomes of form versus content:

Best Case:	Your use of fancy graphics fits the message
Still Okay:	Graphics are weak, but message is strong
In Trouble:	Graphics and message are both weak
Worst Case:	Fancy graphics with weak message

If you have succumbed to the Worst Case scenario, you are the electronic equivalent of the stereotypical dumb blonde, essentially telling your readers: "I don't have anything to say, but I'm nice to look at."

You can't just live the Nike commercial; you can't "Just do it." You must first decide what you want to do. Then you can go do it.

♣

We now move from the aesthetic to the pragmatic, as Part IV features strategies and techniques for customizing CorelDRAW.

HAVE IT
YOUR WAY

We wanted to include this part in the last edition of this book but couldn't because the tools were not evolved enough. This year, it's a different story. With DRAW's styles finding new maturity, with presets a bit smarter, and most of all, with the rollout of a totally customizable interface, advanced and ambitious users can have a field day. Opportunities now abound for tailoring the software to fit your needs and work habits.

These chapters in this part uncover the concealed jewel in the software: support for automating and customizing.

Understanding Styles and Presets

ime is a luxury those in the graphics business usually aren't allowed. When the big client says they want the slides done tomorrow, you order some take-out and settle in for a long night. As the clock ticks on, you can't afford to waste time repeating commands over and over while formatting text and graphics. CorelDRAW's styles and presets are the answer: You can store frequently used formatting attributes and access them later with a click of the mouse. Who knows—with a little help from styles and presets you might be able to catch your favorite late-night talk show after all.

This chapter is divided into three sections. First, we focus on creating and applying text and graphic styles. The second section discusses templates, which store styles and other page layout information. The last section examines presets, with which you can capture a sequence of commands and play them back quickly.

What Is a Style?

A *style* is a collection of formatting attributes, such as color and font, which can be applied to text and graphic objects quickly and easily. Rather than assigning each of the attributes individually (selecting the color, choosing the font, adjusting the outline width, and so forth) you can apply a style in one quick step.

Styles are saved in the .CDR file and, if you choose, in a DRAW template file. Saving styles in a template allows you to use the styles with other documents. How styles and templates work together is discussed later in this section.

Desktop publishing and word processing applications have long been able to create text styles, and so can DRAW—but DRAW lets you create graphic styles as well. For instance, the attributes of a graphic style might be a texture fill with a 3-point outline. DRAW's text styles are separated into Artistic Text and Paragraph Text styles.

The power of styles goes beyond speed—styles also help you achieve consistency in design. They help guarantee that every title in a project uses the same font, style, and color, adding to overall appeal of your work. You can also establish a dynamic connection between all objects using a particular style. This connection allows you to change the attributes of the style—the fill color, for instance—and thus affect the fill color of every object that uses that style.

Suppose you are in charge of producing a weekly sales presentation. By creating styles for the presentation's graphic objects and for the title and body text, you're giving yourself a head start on building the next presentation. The styles are saved in a *template*, and the template is used to build the next presentation. (As you'll see, templates can even store objects such as the slide background and a company logo.) Say you get halfway through the project and realize the body text needs to be smaller. Simply change the body text style, and all text with that style also changes. Notice how that weekly job suddenly doesn't sound so bad after all?

The Copy Attributes From command is another way to apply formatting to several objects in a drawing. In this case, however, the objects are not linked, so changes made in one object do not affect other objects with the same formatting. When you use styles, any change to the styles affects all objects using that style.

Using the Styles Manager

True to its name, the Styles Manager helps you apply and manage styles. From the Layout menu, select Styles Manager or press Ctrl+F5. As you can see in Figure 14.1, the style's name and type—graphic, paragraph text, or artistic text—appear in the Manager window.

14.1

**Press Ctrl+F5 to
quickly display the
Styles Manager, for-
merly known as
the Styles roll-up.**

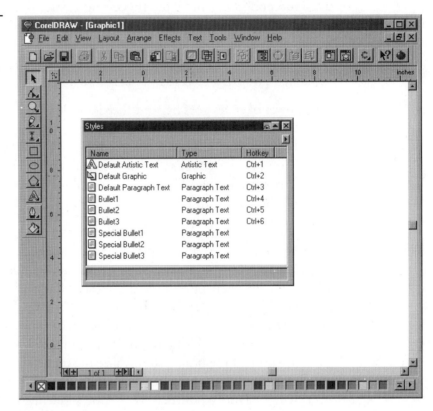

You can control how the styles are sorted in the Manager by clicking on
the Name, Type, and Hotkey buttons. For instance, click once on the
Type button to sort the styles by type in A–Z order. Click again to sort
the styles by type in Z–A order.

The Styles Manager has a flyout, containing many of the commands for
working with styles. To use it, click on the arrow button just above the
vertical scroll bar.

Unless you have loaded another template, the styles saved in DRAW's main template (CORELDRW.CDT) appear in the Styles Manager. There is a default style for graphics, artistic text, and paragraph text, as well as several paragraph text styles for creating bullets and subheads.

Adjusting the View

Icons at the left of each style name indicate the type of style. As you can see, the big *A* denotes an artistic text style; the tiny document means paragraph text style; and the little collage of shapes is the symbol for a graphic style.

You can adjust the size of the icon and the information displayed for each style by selecting View from the flyout. Choose Large Icons to get the display shown in Figure 14.2. The List and Small Icons views both show you a small icon and the style name. The Small Icons view, however, stacks the styles in columns, letting you see more styles in the Manager at one time. Choose Details to display a small icon, the style name, style type, and hotkey (keyboard shortcut) if there is one; this is the display used in Figure 14.1.

14.2

Use the View menu to adjust the display of the icons in the Styles Manager.

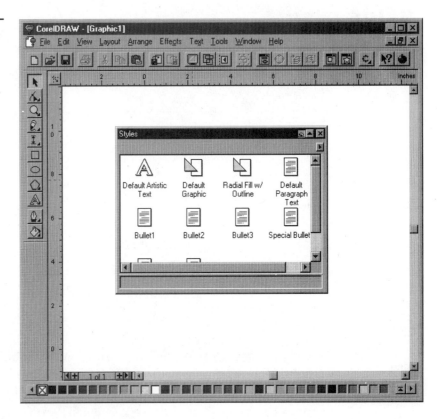

Displaying Style Types

DRAW lets you decide which types of styles are displayed in the Manager. By default, all style types are shown, but you can "hide" certain types to make the Manager more in tune with the current task. For instance, if you're working with text, you may want to hide the graphic styles.

To specify what style types you want displayed, open the flyout and select Show. Just click to remove the check mark from any style type you do not want displayed. Select the Auto-View option to see only styles for the type of object selected. For instance, when a string of artistic text is selected, only the artistic text styles are displayed in the Manager.

Creating and Applying Styles

The first step in creating a style is to build an object with the formatting attributes to be saved in the style. For instance, to create a text style, you would build a text string with the desired font and fill attributes. That formatted object becomes your "prototype" for creating the style. Don't worry if you're not absolutely sure about all the formatting—you can easily make changes and adjust the style later.

After the prototype is formatted, you're ready to save the style. Select Styles / Save Styles Properties from either the Layout or Object menu. The Save Style As dialog box appears, where you enter a style name and choose which attributes are to be part of the style. In Figure 14.3, both the fill and outline settings will be saved in the style. To add or remove a set of attributes, click to check or uncheck the folder.

14.3

The check marks by the Fill and Outline folders indicate these attributes will be saved as part of this graphic style.

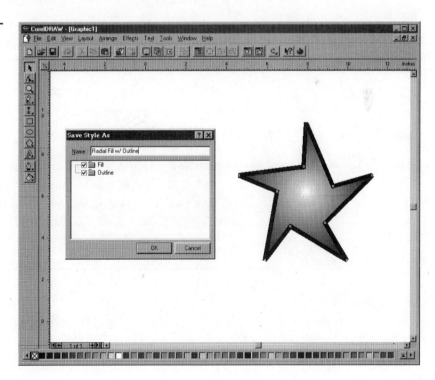

After entering a style name and designating the desired attributes, click OK to save the style. If the Styles Manager is displayed, you'll see the new style is added to the list.

As discussed later in this chapter, styles can be saved in templates, and we'll discuss the advantages of that strategy in a later section. If you don't save a new style in a template, DRAW stores it in the .CDR file and it will only be available in that document.

Here are some tips for working with styles and the Styles Manager:

- The Styles Manager takes up a lot of screen space—you may wish to roll it up or remove it from the screen before creating styles.

- Unless you enter a new style name, DRAW saves the formatting as a default style. Changing the default affects how graphics and text are formatted when you first draw or type them on the page.

- You can enter up to 32 characters for the style name. You'll want to keep it descriptive but short, however; long style names just take up more space in the Styles Manager.

AUTHOR'S NOTE

The process for creating graphic styles and text styles is basically the same. In the following sections, you'll find step-by-step instructions for creating graphic, artistic text, and paragraph text styles. Since the styles created in these instructions are used as examples as you work through the chapter, you may want to take a minute now and create them so you can follow along later.

Graphic Styles

Any attribute applied with the Fill or Outline tool can be saved in a graphic style. For instance, fountain fills, two-color pattern fills, arrowheads, and dashed lines all can be attributes in a graphic style.

WATCH OUT!

In DRAW 6.0, special effects such as perspective and extrusions can no longer be saved as part of a graphic style. Ouch!

Let's create a graphic style using a fountain fill and a thick outline.

1. Draw a square or any closed graphic object. Select the square and apply a conical fountain fill—you select the colors. If desired, offset the center of the fill slightly. For the outline attributes, apply a 6-point outline to the square.

2. Right-click on the square to bring up the Object pop-up. Select Styles / Save Style Properties to display the Save Style As dialog.

3. Enter **Fountain** for the style name. Make sure check marks appear in both the Fill and Outline folders.

4. Click OK. If the Styles Manager is open, you can see the new Fountain style in the list.

Graphic styles are useful when all graphics in a project need to use a specific spot color. For instance, suppose you're creating a piece using black and PANTONE 192 Red. When it comes time to output color separations to film, it can be a real mess if some objects use PANTONE 192 Red and others use PANTONE 185 Red (you'd get a separation for the 185 Red, also). Creating a graphic style with the desired PANTONE color guarantees you'll always apply the right one.

Artistic Text Styles

Text attributes, just like fills and outlines, can be saved in artistic text styles. You can include the following text attributes:

- *Font:* Typeface, type size, and type styles such as bold and italic
- *Alignment:* Left, center, and right, plus full justification and forced justification
- *Spacing:* Between characters, words, and lines

388 CH. 14 USING STYLES AND PRESETS

- *Lines:* Underlines, overlines, and strikeout

- *Text effects:* Superscript, subscript, and capitalization

Now try creating an artistic text style using your choices of various text attributes and a texture fill.

1. Enter some text with the Text tool. Format the text to display in 100-point Impact with a single thin underline. Change the alignment to center. Apply a texture fill, and set the outline to None.

2. From the Layout menu, select Styles / Save Style Properties. Enter **Texture Text** for the style name.

3. Double-click on the Text folder to reveal additional folders for specific text attributes (see Figure 14.4).

4. Double-click on the Lines folder to reveal folders for Underline, Overline, and Strikeout. Remove the check mark by Underline so this attribute is not saved with this style. All other text attributes will be saved.

14.4

Building an artistic text style named Texture Text

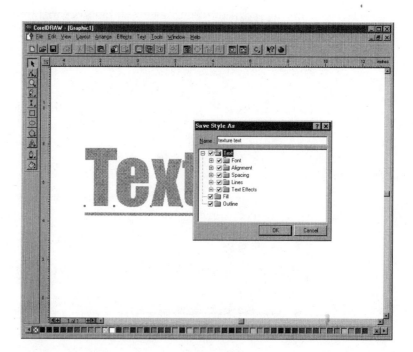

5. Click OK. If the Styles Manager is open, you will see the new style in the list.

Paragraph Text Styles

Attributes unique to paragraph text must be saved in paragraph text styles. For instance, bullets are only available with paragraph text, so any style with bullets will have to be a paragraph text style. You can also include tabs, indents, bullets, and hyphenation, in addition to all of the text attributes possible in an artistic text style.

Here are the steps to create a paragraph text style with bullets.

1. Enter three lines of paragraph text (click and hold on the Text tool and choose Paragraph from the flyout). Format the text to display in 24-point Arial. Apply bullets and a left indent to the text; Figure 14.5 shows an example of bulleted text. If desired, change the fill and outline attributes.

14.5

Bullets, indents, tabs, and hyphenation can be saved in paragraph text styles.

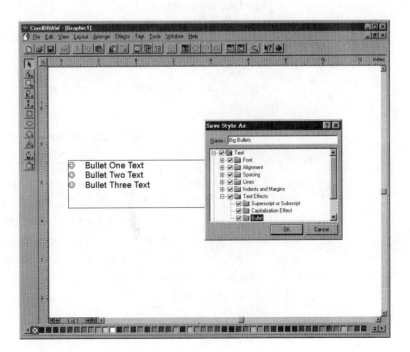

2. From the Object menu, select Styles / Save Style Properties. Enter Big Bullets for the style name.

3. Double-click on the Text folder. A folder for Indents and Margins appears when you're creating a paragraph text style.

4. Double-click on the Text Effects folder to view a folder for the Bullet attributes.

5. Click OK. If the Styles Manager is open, you will see the new style in the list.

Applying Styles

Applying a style is easy. First, select the text or graphic to which you want the style applied. Remember, to make sure it is a closed object if you want the fill attributes to take effect. Then:

- If the Styles Manager is open, click on the style name and choose Apply Style from the flyout. The Apply Style command can also be invoked from the pop-up menu displayed when you right-click on a style name.

- If the Styles Manager is not open, you can apply a style through the Layout or Object menu. From either menu, select Styles, click Apply and then the name of the desired style. For instance, in Figure 14.6 we're using the Object menu to apply the Texture Text style.

Instantly, the selected object takes on the attributes stored in the style.

In the case of a graphic style, the newly formatted object may not look identical to the original; if its essential shape is different from the object on which the style was based, the new object will remain different even when the style is applied. This is not a bug, it's a feature: An object's shape and position are not attributes of a style, nor should they be. The idea here is not to create duplicates (the Edit / Clone command does that), but rather to give you the power to take specific attributes and apply them to other objects.

The Object menu makes it easy to apply a style without opening the Styles Manager.

Graphic styles can be applied to text; and, likewise, text styles can be applied to graphics. The ability to apply a text style to graphics comes in handy. Suppose you want to use the same fountain fill on all the headings and graphics in a document. Rather than having to make both a graphic and a text style, you can just make a text style and then apply it to both text and graphics. One requirement: You must apply the style using the Styles Manager. The Layout and Object menus only offer styles for the type of object selected. For instance, when a graphic is selected, the menu only shows graphic styles.

Applying Styles with Hotkeys

As if there weren't already enough ways to apply styles, you can also set up hotkeys (keyboard shortcuts) to speed up the job. Actually, hotkeys might be the quickest method. It's certainly easier than working with the rather large Styles Manager.

To assign a hotkey to a style, highlight the style name in the Styles Manager, and select Edit Hotkey from the flyout or the pop-up. When the Customize dialog appears, enter a hotkey combination in the Press New Shortcut Key box—say, Alt+B as shown in Figure 14.7. You'll be alerted if this combination is already used for another command. If necessary, try another shortcut key; when you find the right combination, click on the Assign button.

Once the hotkey for a style is saved, you can apply that style by simply selecting the object and pressing the hotkeys. In our example, pressing Alt+B will format paragraph text in a bulleted list with large bullet characters.

14.7

In the Customize dialog, you can enter hotkey combinations to speed up the process of applying styles.

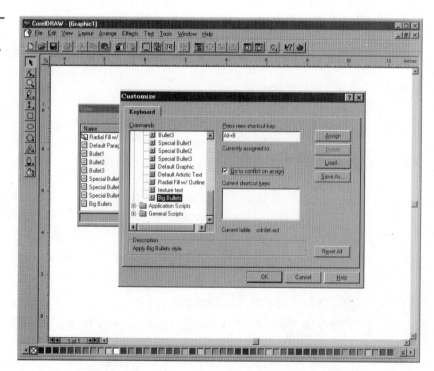

AUTHOR'S NOTE

In addition to Styles commands, hotkeys (or *accelerator* keys) provide quick access to other frequently used commands. Accelerator keys are stored in accelerator files. The first time you save a hotkey combination you will be asked to create an Accelerator (.ACL) file. For more information, refer to Chapter 15.

Changing Style Attributes

Applying styles is easy, and so is changing a style's attributes. Basically, you apply the style, make the desired changes, and then save the changes in the style. As an example, let's say you want to change the colors used in the style named Fountain. You apply that style to an object and then proceed as usual to change the fountain fill's colors. Then you select Styles / Save Style Properties from the Layout or Object menu. The dialog box that appears is just like the one used to create the style. Make sure Fountain appears at the top and click OK. As soon as you do, all objects using the Fountain style (except objects where attributes were applied individually, as we'll explain shortly) are automatically changed.

Using the Properties Command to Change Style Attributes

If you've ever created a style and then wished for a quick way to see the style attributes, you're in luck. Right-click the style in the Styles Manager, then choose Properties from the pop-up menu to display the Style Properties dialog. Tabbed pages will appear for each of the attributes in the style, as shown for the Texture Text style in Figure 14.8. Use the Style box at the top to check or change the properties of another style.

As you might guess, the Properties dialog can be used to make changes to a style. After making changes, click on the Apply All button to preview the new formatting on all objects using that style. When you're happy with it, click OK to save the changes in the style.

14.8

You can view and
edit styles with the
Properties com-
mand in the Styles
Manager.

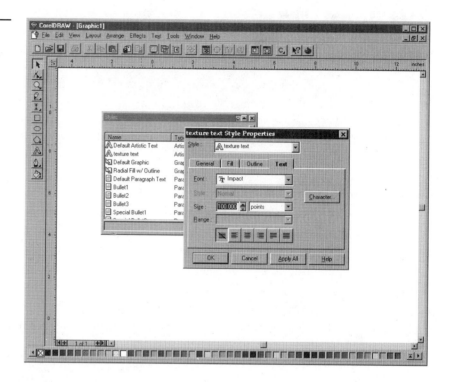

Changing the Default Styles

The three default styles for paragraph text, artistic text, and graphics control how objects are formatted when they are originally created on the page. These default styles can be modified using the same process used for changing other styles (see above). You can also change the default styles by accessing the Fill or Outline dialogs or flyout menus without first selecting an object. DRAW will ask you if you really mean to change the default, and will then record your changes as the new default style for whatever object types you select (graphic, artistic text, or paragraph text).

Modifying the default style is an alternative to creating a new style. For instance, if your brochure uses 48-point Impact in red for all headings, you could save these attributes in the default artistic text style. Bear in mind, however, that every time thereafter when you create artistic text, it will be automatically formatted to display in 48-point Impact.

Overriding Styles Attributes

The idea behind styles is, of course, to make your formatting tasks more efficient. Being able to apply consistent fill, outline, and font attributes to objects is an important element of that efficiency. Nevertheless, there will undoubtedly be times when you wish to format one object independently. Take a look at Figure 14.9. All of the stars in the figures use the Fountain graphic style, but the fill attributes of one star were changed to make it stand out from the rest.

14.9

"Local" formatting overrides formatting applied by a style.

The star with the different fill still uses the outline attributes set up in the Fountain style. However, when we applied a new fill to the star, this "local" formatting took precedence over the Fountain style's fill attributes. If we proceed to change the outline of the style, the outline of the special star *will* change. If we change the fill attributes of the style, the fill of the special star *will not* change. To sum up, the star retains its local formatting (in this case, the fill) until another style is applied or the original style is re-applied.

Managing Styles: Renaming, Deleting, and Finding

After creating a style, you can rename or delete it with the Styles Manager. You cannot rename or delete the default styles, however.

- To rename a style, select it in the Manager and choose Rename from the flyout or pop-up menu.

- To delete a style, select it and choose Delete from the flyout or pop-up menu.

After applying styles to the objects in a complex design, it can be tough to remember which style is applied to which object. The Find command in the Style Manager flyout lets you search for objects with a specific style.

For example, it's a good idea to find all objects using a particular style before making changes to that style. Finding the objects first will let you verify which objects will be affected by the change.

To find occurrences of a style, select the style in the Styles Manager and choose Find from the flyout or pop-up menu. DRAW will select the first object to which the style is applied. Select Find Next from the menu to select another object with the style, and keep going until you've located all the affected objects.

When and When Not to Use Styles

Styles are designed to save you time. Here are some tips for deciding if you need to create a style.

Use a style in these situations:

- When you want to link many objects together. A style's greatest value is the collective control it gives you over multiple objects. You never have to worry about one of them being wrong—they're either all correct or they're all wrong.

- When you have several attributes you want to apply at once. Simply make the changes to one object, save the changes, and all objects using that style will automatically display the new formatting.

- When you anticipate that you might be changing all instances of one color, fill, or outline in a complex drawing. With styles, tracking down all occurrences of a particular attribute and applying a different one gets done in one or two steps rather than ten or twenty or more.

- When you want to control elements across multiple pages or even multiple files. Styles are saved in templates (described in the upcoming section), so they can be used across long distances.

Sometimes, other tools will work better than styles. Here are situations where you may want to choose another strategy:

- You already have a custom palette created, and you want to quickly assign colors to objects. Though you could create several styles containing these colors, using a palette is a better method.

- You want one or more objects to look *exactly* like an original; this is a job for the Clone command. Clones don't need to be applied or updated; they automatically and instantly take on all the appearance attributes of the master object.

■ You want to borrow just one attribute of a formatted object and are not interested in a link to that object. Though you could apply the style and then strip off the attributes you don't want, it's wasted effort. A better way is to use either Edit / Copy Attributes From, or Effects / Copy. Both commands let you choose the particular attribute you want to copy from an existing object. This is better than using a style when all you want is a piece of the style.

And finally, some situations call for yet another DRAW efficiency expert: presets. We'll get to these later in the chapter.

Working with Templates

Templates help you organize and manage styles. You can store a group of styles in a template designed for a specific type of documents, such as a slide presentation or a sales brochure. Template files store more than just styles, though; they also save page layout information and text and graphic objects. A template for a slide presentation could include the page setup and the company logo, as well styles for bullets and titles. A template for sales brochures might contain the graphic elements that appear in every brochure.

In addition to the templates you create yourself, DRAW includes several predesigned templates for menus, invitations, and catalogs.

Templates are separate files with .CDT extensions. When you create a new document using a specific template, DRAW automatically loads the .CDT template when the .CDR file is opened. Until you load another template, DRAW uses the default template, CORELDRW.CDT, to preside over your global operations. We'll begin this section by examining the CORELDRW.CDT.

INSIDE INFO

> When you create styles, you don't have to save them in a template—DRAW stores them directly in the .CDR file. If you don't save the styles in a template, the styles are loaded in the Styles Manager when you open the .CDR file. The advantage to saving them in a template is that they are available in other DRAW documents, as well.

CORELDRW.CDT, the Default Template

The first time you start CorelDRAW, the default template (COREL-DRW.CDT) is opened. All new documents use this template unless you specifically load another one, using File / New / From Template.

The CORELDRW.CDT template includes default styles for graphics, artistic text, and paragraph text. You can modify this template by adding styles or changing the default styles, following the procedures already outlined in this chapter. After making style changes, if you want the changes to be available in future documents using this template, you must save it. If you don't, the new and modified styles are only saved in the .CDR file—they do not become part of the template.

To save changes to the default CORELDRW.CDT template, select Template / Save As Default For New Documents from the flyout in the Styles Manager. (Remember, you can display this same menu by right-clicking in the Styles Manager.)

The Template / Save As command is another way to save the COREL-DRW.CDT file. The Save Template dialog appears, with COREL-DRW.CDT as the file to be saved. Click OK to save changes to the default template.

WATCH OUT!

The engineers at Corel have fixed many of the problems and inconsistencies with styles and templates in previous versions of DRAW. One difference in DRAW 6.0 is that you are no longer prompted to save the template when you exit DRAW. Although you are no longer pestered by reminders to save changes as you were in DRAW 5, the pressure is now on you to remember to save the template if you want changes to become permanent.

CORELDRW.CDT is a plain old file, residing on your hard drive like all other files. Therefore, before you start any wild experiments with your default settings, you might want to back up this default template first. You'll find it in the COREL60\DRAW\TEMPLATE subdirectory.

Creating a New Template

Instead of filling up CORELDRW.CDT with all kinds of different styles, you may find it more effective to save particular groups of styles in individual templates. Then, when you're ready for a certain set of styles, you can just load the desired template. As mentioned earlier, DRAW's templates can contain more than just styles; they can contain any element that would normally go into a drawing. With templates, you can give yourself a major-league running start toward the completion of a repetitive project.

You can create the template before you've made style changes, set up the page layout, and added objects; or you can do it afterward. In fact, it's probably more practical to save the template after making these changes to a drawing, so you don't have to save it again to catch the latest changes.

WATCH OUT!

When saving the contents of a drawing to a template file, only objects on the first page will be saved.

You must use the Styles Manager (Ctrl+F5) to create templates, because the Object menu does not provide access to template creation (only style creation). So, to create a template, you select Template / Save As from the flyout in the Styles Manager, name the template, and turn on the With Contents option to save the page setup and any text and graphic objects. See Figure 14.10.

14.10

Use the Save Template dialog box to create a new template.

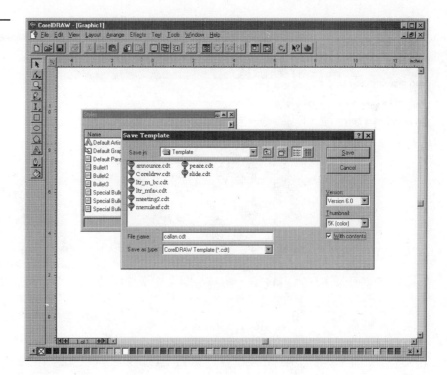

The following exercise steps you through the process of creating a template for a business card.

1. Start a new file, and adjust the page setup to be 3″ wide by 2″ tall.

2. For a logo, add a red circle and blue rectangle to the business card, along with text for your company name (see Figure 14.11).

3. Change the default artistic text style to Impact 36-point. Add a new artistic text style in Arial 24-point green.

4. Open the Styles Manager flyout and select Template / Save As.

5. Type in **business** as the file name. Turn on the With Contents option in the lower-right corner of the dialog.

14.11

Page layout information, text objects and graphic objects, as well as styles can be saved in a template file.

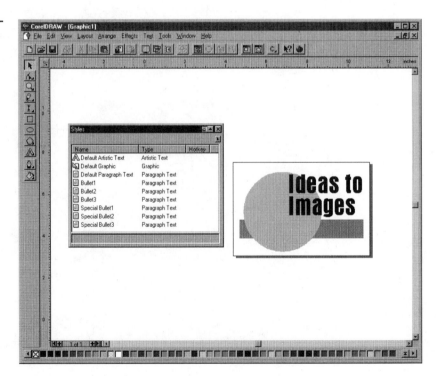

6. Store the file in the COREL60/DRAW/TEMPLATE subdirectory.

7. Click Save to save the new template.

If you make any additional changes, you will need to save the template again.

You can also create a template with the File / Save As command. Open the Save Type As drop-down list and choose CorelDRAW Template *.cdt to save a template file. When you save a template using this method, the With Contents check box is not available.

Using Your Templates

When you're ready to use the styles and objects stored in a template, you have two choices: Choose a template when you begin a new document, or load a template after the document has been created. We'll look at both methods here.

Creating a New Document from a Template   Selecting a template first, as you create a new document, quickly loads the styles, page layout information, and any text and graphic objects saved in the template. From the File menu, select New / From Template and find the template name in the file window. If you saved it in the COREL60\ DRAW\TEMPLATES subdirectory, you won't have to navigate to other directories. Select the template file, check With Contents, and click OK. DRAW places the entire template—text, lines, and all—on your page. This is a new file that you can name and save as you wish. You don't have to worry about altering the contents of the template or any existing file.

In addition to the templates you create, DRAW ships with several templates that will give you ideas for designing your own. Use the New / From Template command, and browse the .CDT files in the TEMPLATES directory.

WATCH OUT!

When you want to work with a template, make sure you use the New / From Template command and not the File / Open command. DRAW permits you to open templates just as you do regular files (you first have to change DRAW's file filter to show .CDT files), and any changes you then make are permanently recorded in the template. It's okay to do that conscientiously— that is, when you really want to change your starting point. Otherwise, however, make sure to use New / From Template when you want to create a new file from a template.

Loading Templates   To load a template after you've started a document, select Template / Load from the Styles Manager flyout. The With Contents option is not available when you are loading a template. Select the template file and click OK—the style names appear in the Styles Manager.

Succeeding with Styles and Templates

DRAW's styles can be enormously powerful when used to help you reach your productivity potential, so ask yourself some questions about your work: Do you regularly need to assign 2-point outlines with round caps? Create a style for them. How about a custom Calligraphic Pen? Create a style. And you can have all of these styles immediately accessible every time you start the program. Just park them right in CORELDRW.CDT.

To summarize, here are some important points to remember as you gain skill in the use of styles and templates:

- Keep the default styles simple. They won't be of much help if they give all objects a texture fill and a thick outline, or if they put all artistic text in 400-point Crazy Creatures. Save the fancy formatting in new, separate styles.

- All styles that you create are stored in the .CDR file itself. By saving styles in a template, you make it easier for new projects to use the same styles.

- Install the Avant Garde BT and Common Bullets typefaces. Many of DRAW's templates and sample files expect to find these two typefaces. Although you can use the PANOSE font substitution to make your own substitution, we have found that even ardently anti-TrueType users have capitulated and installed these two faces, just so they don't have to be bothered.

DRAW's Presets: Have It Your Way

Are you fond of red text in 100-point Futura, with drop shadow offset .15″ in 20% black? How about adding perspective and custom fountain fills to objects? Whatever your specialty, repeating the same steps over and over for your favorite effects can get monotonous. DRAW's handy presets enable you to record transactions and then play them back, to quickly format text and objects. Presets are similar to styles and to keyboard macros, but just different enough to have a special mark of distinction. Using presets is like plugging a very efficient tape recorder into your computer—a tape recorder that doesn't pay attention to the individual steps you took to perform a task, but records only what is essential to the result.

Working with Presets Files

DRAW includes several presets—in fact, you may find just the effect you are looking for has already been recorded as a preset. From the Tools menu, select Presets (Alt+F5) to display the Presets roll-up (Figure 14.12). A thumbnail of the effect appears at the top of the roll-up. Open the drop-down list of presets to reveal additional effects.

The presets included with DRAW are stored in the CORELDRW.PST file, and any new presets can be stored in this file. In addition, DRAW 6.0 lets you create additional .PST files for storing your presets. For example, you might create a file named POSTER.PST for storing presets used only with posters. We'll start by creating and opening preset files.

14.12

With the Presets roll-up you can record the steps for creating frequently used formatting attributes.

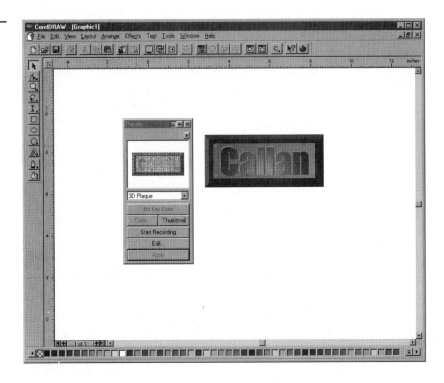

This way when you start creating new presets you can select which preset file you want to put them in.

AUTHOR'S NOTE

Presets are related to styles, in that both tools help you quickly apply formatting to a selected object. At the end of this chapter, we'll outline the essential differences between styles and presets and offer suggestions on usage.

Creating Preset Files When you want to store your own presets separately from DRAW's, create a new preset file. Making your own preset file also means you won't have to scroll through all those already stored in the CORELDRW.PST file.

To create a new preset file, click on the flyout arrow in the Presets roll-up, and choose New. In the New Presets File dialog (Figure 14.13), enter a name for your presets file and click Save. It's a good idea to store your preset file in the COREL60\DRAW directory with the CORELDRW.PST file.

Opening Preset Files   To open the default preset file, COREL-DRW.PST, or a previously created preset file, select Open from the Presets flyout. In the Open Presets File dialog, select the name of the file you want and click OK.

When you exit DRAW, it remembers the last preset file loaded, and loads it again the next time you start the program.

14.13

When you want to store new presets separately from DRAW's, use the New Presets File dialog to create a new preset file.

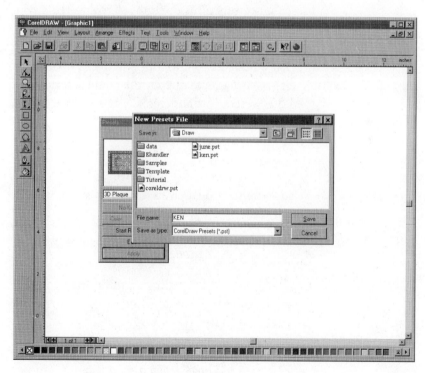

Merging Presets   New in DRAW 6.0 is the ability to merge presets from one .PST file to another. Keep in mind that DRAW merges all presets in the file—you do not get to pick and choose which presets are merged. To merge presets, open the .PST file where you want to add the presets. Select Merge With from the Presets flyout, choose the .PST file containing the presets you want to merge, and click OK. The presets are added to the current .PST file.

Creating a Preset

Imagine you want to apply a certain effect, perhaps a ten-step extrusion, to objects in several of your documents. This is a perfect time to create a preset, especially since extrusions cannot be stored in styles.

Start by selecting one object, called the *seed object*. When you play back a preset, all transactions operate relative to the size and location of the seed object. (The seed object cannot be a group.) For example, suppose the seed object is a 1″ square. The preset adds a fountain fill and enlarges the square 200%, to a 2″ square. When this preset is played back on a circle with a 3″ diameter, the circle is fountain-filled, too, and enlarged 200% to a 6″ diameter. Let's use this example to illustrate recording a preset.

1. Draw a 1″ square.

2. Open the Presets roll-up (with Tools / Presets or Alt+F5). Make sure the square is selected, and click on Start Recording in the roll-up.

3. Fill the square with a fountain fill. Using the Transform roll-up, enlarge the square 200%.

4. Click on Stop Recording in the Presets roll-up. In the Edit Preset dialog, supply a name and an optional description, as shown in Figure 14.14. Click OK.

A thumbnail of the new preset appears in the roll-up. If you entered a description, it will be displayed on a flyout window when you select this effect. The new preset is added to whatever .PST file was currently open.

14.14

After recording a
preset, you are
asked to enter
its name and
description.

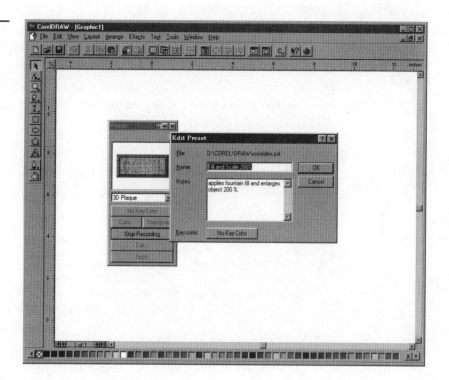

Applying a Preset

To apply a preset, select the text or graphic object you want to format.
Presets can only be applied to one object (not a group) at a time. They
can be applied to either text or graphic objects, regardless of what type
of object appears in the thumbnail.

Let's apply the fountain-fill-and-enlargement preset you just created to
another object.

1. Create a circle or some other object with a closed path.

2. With the new object selected, find the name of your preset in
   the Presets roll-up drop-down list, and click Apply.

Watch as DRAW goes through the motions of creating the preset effect.

Creating Objects During Recording

In the previous example, you created and applied a preset that filled and scaled any selected object. Suppose you want the preset to not only modify the selected object, but also add another object. For instance, say you want to add another object and then create a blend effect. In this case, the preset needs to record the creation of an object, as well as the blend.

DRAW allows the creation of rectangles, ellipses, and polygons during the recording of a preset. Presets cannot record the creation of grids and spirals.

This next preset, when applied, will automatically create the object and format it:

1. Click Start Recording in the Presets roll-up.

2. Create a rectangle, ellipse, or polygon. Use the Transform roll-up to set the object's exact size, position, and rotation/skew angle.

3. Apply whatever effect you want to the object.

4. Click on Stop Recording, and assign a name to the preset.

If other objects are created with the preset, they are stored in a group; you can ungroup this and edit if necessary.

INSIDE INFO

Before you can apply a preset to a grid created with the grid tool, you will need to ungroup it (Arrange / Ungroup). In addition, you will need to convert polygons to curves before applying a preset (Arrange / Convert to Curves).

Creating Text Presets

Presets for formatting text can be big time-savers. When you record a preset on artistic or paragraph text, DRAW tracks the font, its attributes (bold, italic), line attributes (underline, overline, and strikeout), placement (superscript and subscript), and spacing between characters, words, lines, and paragraphs.

Try the following exercise to create a preset for formatting text:

1. Create a line of artistic text, and select it.

2. Click Start Recording in the Presets roll-up.

3. Using the Text roll-up or the Character dialog, change the face, the style, and the size. It doesn't matter what you change them to, as long as you make some kind of change to all three.

4. Click OK or Apply, stop the recording, and assign a name to your preset.

Because you selected a new face, style, and size, this preset will apply those attributes to any string of artistic text. If you had only changed the point size, the preset records just that change. For example, suppose the text you are using to create the preset is in Avant Garde 24-point. While recording, you leave the face at Avant Garde but change the color to red and the size to 100 points. When this preset is applied to text in Century Gothic, the text will be sized to 100 points and filled with red, but the font will stay Century Gothic. Since you did not select a font while recording, it did not become part of the preset.

In other words, the preset recording function does not take note of the current dialog settings; it only pays attention to what you *specifically change*. For instance, if you want to create a preset that changes text to 14-point Century Italic, left-aligned, you'll have to make sure that none of those specs are current. You literally have to change the settings in order for the recorder to take note. This applies to graphic presets, as well. If you're creating a preset for a blue fill and a red outline, make sure you select the blue fill and red outline during recording. If you don't, those attributes are not stored in the preset.

Two other points concerning text and presets: First, you cannot apply a preset to paragraph text, only artistic text. You can use either type of text when recording the preset, but DRAW won't let you play back a preset to paragraph text. Second, you can only apply a preset to an entire string of text, not a few characters selected with the Text tool.

INSIDE INFO

If you need to apply a preset to text created with the paragraph text tool, you can convert it to artistic text and then apply the preset.

What You Can and Can't Do with Presets

Taking full advantage of presets requires that you know their limitations. DRAW has packed a wallop of power into them, but they are not allowed to tread in certain areas.

You *Can* Use Presets for These Tasks:

■ To create rectangles, ellipses, and polygons

■ To delete objects

■ To Copy Attributes From

■ To group, combine, weld, intersect, and trim

■ To change fills and outlines (except custom arrows)

■ To apply anything from the Transform roll-up

■ For duplicating and cloning

■ For converting to curves

■ To format text

■ To add perspectives

■ To add an extrusion

■ To create lenses

- To realign or reorder objects
- For blending two objects together

Let's take a closer look at the last two situations. As noted earlier, DRAW does not record in presets any functions that involve your selecting more than one object, unless you perform some other operation in the middle. For instance, DRAW would bark at you if you tried to record a preset that included creating a second object, selecting it and an existing object, and blending them together. On the other hand, if you were to merely nudge the first object by 1 point, then create the second object, select both, and then blend, DRAW would permit that preset.

So, to record a preset that aligns two objects together, you must take the following steps. Watch out—if you try this without step 2, it will fail.

1. Select one object and begin recording the preset.
2. Nudge the selected object in one direction and then back again.
3. Create a new object.
4. Select both objects and align them.
5. Turn off the Preset recorder.

You *Can't* Use Presets for These Tasks:

- To create lines, curves, grids, or spirals
- To compose or edit text
- When more than one object is selected initially
- To apply two- or full-color patterns
- To apply envelopes or PowerClips

Luckily, when you perform an operation that cannot be recorded in a preset, DRAW lets you know. You'll see a message that the last operation will not become part of the preset.

INSIDE INFO

> Presets have some odd behavior and restrictions. A preset can only be applied to an existing spiral; it can only be applied to a polygon if the polygon is first converted to curves. Also, you have to ungroup a grid before applying a preset to it. However, all three of these objects—spiral, polygon, and grid—can serve as a seed object when you start recording a preset.

What We *Wish* Presets *Could* Do:

- Control the interface. We'd like to set grids, change page size, control nudge and fountain stripes, and swap color palettes with presets.

- Perform file imports and exports

- Record and play back actual keystrokes

- And finally, we *really* wish we could assign hotkeys to presets, as we can to styles.

Choosing Between a Style and a Preset

In many instances, styles and presets will help you accomplish the same thing. Here are some tips for determining which tool is best for the task you need to get done.

Situations That Call for Styles

- *You have already created and formatted an object.* A style works better here, because it can be created from an existing object. With a preset you would have to repeat all of the formatting steps to record them.

■ *You want changes you've made to one object to affect other objects.* If you anticipate that additional formatting changes will be needed in the future, you're better off using a style. By changing one object and then updating the style, you automatically change the others. There is no such global link, however, with presets.

Situations That Call for Presets

■ *You want to transform an object.* Use a preset here. In a preset you can record all of the functions in the Transform roll-up. A style does not save these transformations.

■ *You want to convert an object to curves.* Again, this is recording an action taken on the object, rather than applying a format to it. Styles can't do that.

■ *You want to create objects automatically.* A preset can actually create a rectangle or an ellipse as part of its playback. A style cannot create objects.

■ *You want to record a blend between two objects.* Remember the curious requirement of nudging the original object first when recording the preset. After that, you can use the preset to create a quick blend between an object you select and the one you've recorded in the preset.

■ *You like to add descriptions of the effect.* The Presets roll-up allows you to store the name of the preset, a description up to nine lines long, and a visual thumbnail of the result. In contrast, the Object menu doesn't give you much opportunity to describe a style—about 30 characters on one line. If you find yourself forgetting what a style does and why you defined it in the first place, you might have better luck recording a preset.

♣

Styles and presets are powerful automation tools that let you customize the way you work with objects and formats. But for the ultimate in customization, you will definitely want to read the next chapter…

Your Very Own Interface

15

As authors, we have been waiting three years to write this chapter; as experienced DRAW users, we have been waiting three years to read it. This chapter won't teach you about any new special effects or drawing commands, and it won't show you how to wrap text around a graphic or create a parallel extrusion. In fact, this chapter doesn't contain any tips and tricks at all, at least in the conventional sense. We'll even go so far as to suggest that if you are satisfied with the way DRAW presents itself to you and with the overall design of the interface, you can skip this chapter and the next, and move on to special effects in Part V.

But if you're like us—if you've been patiently waiting for Corel to provide an interface that moves—you'll want to read every word of this chapter. Corel has given DRAW 6.0 an interface that is almost completely customizable, and it takes center stage here.

This chapter includes step-by-step instructions, and we do start with the basics. But the ramp is short and steep, because we know that most of you who want to customize the interface are already familiar with it in the first place.

Tool Terminology 101	This chapter will be easier to digest if you start by learning a few terms.
	Microsoft's definition of a *tool* is very specific, and Corel has done its best to comply. DRAW has always had a *Toolbox* (the one on the left of the work area), and all of the icons on it (Pick, Shape, Zoom, and so on) are referred to as

Tool Terminology 101 (continued)

tools. But what used to be known as the Ribbon Bar is now called the *Standard Toolbar*—although you'll discover in this chapter that there is nothing standard about it. Also at your command are the *Text Toolbar,* displayed prominently throughout the chapters in Part III, and various *other toolbars*—including ones that you can make up to suit yourself.

Flyouts also fall into the "toolbar" classification. These emanate from the eight Toolbox icons that have a small triangle in the lower-right corner. When you click and hold on one of these tools, several additional icons "fly out" from there. Flyouts can be the source of untold confusion because of their expanded role in DRAW 6.0: They can be separated from the Toolbox. When you do this, technically speaking the separated flyout becomes its own toolbar. At least, that's what one of Corel's engineers told us…another told us that they are still flyouts…but the Toolbar dialog includes them in its list of existing toolbars…but that dialog still calls them flyouts, not toolbars. So we're not really sure…maybe nobody really knows…y' know?

The *status bar* is still the status bar; ditto for the *Color Palette,* the *rulers,* and the *scroll bars.*

To best understand how DRAW has made itself over, you should try to keep the following straight in your mind:

- The Toolbox. Its default home has always been on the left of the screen.
- The Standard Toolbar. By default it lives above the horizontal ruler and contains the icons for the Open, Save, Print, Cut, Copy, Paste, and other fundamental commands.

Tool Terminology 101 (continued)

- Toolbars. Some of these ship with DRAW and others can be created by you from the commands you need most. Toolbars can float freely on the screen or be docked at any edge.
- Flyouts, which you display by clicking and holding on one of the eight Toolbox icons that have the triangle.

Use Figure 15.1 as your cheat sheet as needed throughout this chapter.

15.1

These are the featured players in the customization game.

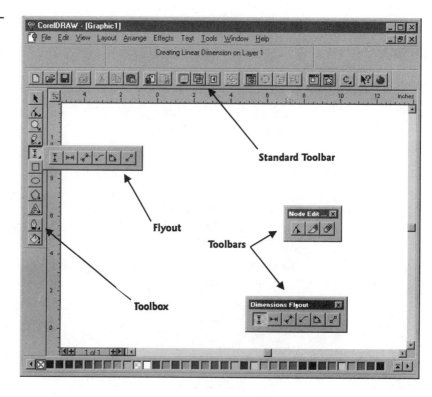

Flying Tools

Let's start with a basic technique that works with all of DRAW's tools (and we use that word in its official Windows 95 sense). Look closely at the Toolbox. You'll notice that it sits inside of a *region*—our term for this area defined by the edge of the screen on the left, the ruler on the right, and small lines at the top and bottom. Once you're aware of this region, you'll notice that the Standard Toolbar and the Color Palette both have defined regions, as well. Now do this:

1. Move your cursor anywhere in the empty space around the Toolbox, but still inside its region, as defined just above.

2. Now click and drag out to the page. If you did it right, the entire Toolbox will up and leave its home, and switch to a floating horizontal toolbar.

The Toolbox (or should we now call it the Toolbox Toolbar?) can be reshaped to be vertical or into a block, just by dragging its edges, and it can be moved anywhere on the Windows Desktop. This "floating" of the Toolbox is not new, and inquisitive users might have discovered this same capability in DRAW 5. But the way it is done—by clicking and dragging on the region that defines it—is a key characteristic of the DRAW 6.0 interface.

Playtime is not yet over; now try the following:

3. Drag the Toolbox to the right edge of the DRAW window. As you do, it should jump back to a vertical arrangement. Release the mouse, and it takes up residence (Corel calls this *docking*) on that edge, once again creating a little region for itself.

4. Drop the Toolbox on top of the color palette, and it docks itself and creates a region just above the palette.

5. Drop the Toolbox on top of the Standard Toolbar, and they appear to merge; then the Toolbox docks itself on the left or right side of the Toolbar.

This basic drag-and-drop maneuver can also be used on the Standard Toolbar and the Color Palette. You can pick them up, move them anywhere, and dock them on any of the four sides of the application. (The status bar can be moved to the top or the bottom of the screen, but not floated or docked on the sides.)

INSIDE INFO

Windows 95 sees a toolbar as a mini-application and gives it a title bar and a Close button. If you close a toolbar, you can reopen it by going to View / Toolbars and checking its check box. To restore the color palette, go to View / Color Palette and choose a particular palette to display.

Flying Flyouts

If you're a veteran DRAW user, flyouts are old friends; they emerge from many different tools on the Toolbox. But DRAW 6.0 adds a dimension to the behavior of flyouts.

Go to the Toolbox now, and click on the Fill tool and hold for a moment. As expected, the Fill flyout emerges. But study it closely and you'll see that it, too, like the Toolbox, has its own region. Pull the flyout away and, you guessed it, it becomes its own little toolbar.

All toolbars behave the same, so you can float this Fill flyout-turned-toolbar anywhere on your screen, or dock it to one side of the application. Guess what—that Fractal Fill dialog can now be one click away instead of two, for the first time in its three-year history. It can also be much closer to your cursor and the objects in your drawing. Those two qualities are the enduring virtues of floating toolbars. Icons that used to require two clicks can now be reached in one; icons that used to reside on the edge of the window can now be placed right next to your objects.

In Figure 15.2 we are using two windows, one to view an entire flower and another to zoom in on one of the flower's petals. We save a lot of time and mousing around by keeping the essential tools nearby.

15.2

In the window on the right, the new toolbars can be positioned right where the action is. No excess mousing required.

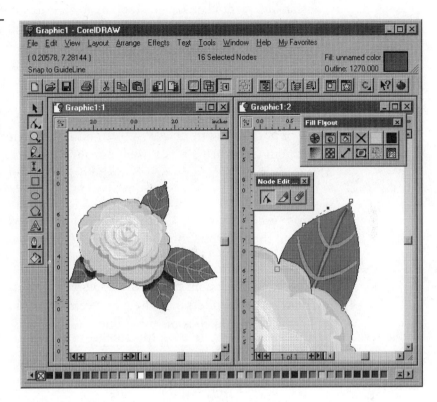

Calling All Toolbars

DRAW ships with 12 toolbars (in addition to the Standard Toolbar and the Toolbox), eight of which are accessible by tearing them off the Toolbox. The other four can be reached by going to View / Toolbars and checking off the ones you want to place on your screen. As an alternative, you can right-click on the Standard Toolbar or Toolbox and choose the desired toolbar from this pop-up menu:

You can also right-click on the Toolbox to activate a toolbar, but then you must be careful to click *outside of* the icon you want. Otherwise, you'll get a different pop-up menu—the Tool Properties menu, which provides controls and details about that particular tool.

Repairing DRAW 6.0's Zoom Services

Most of the changes in DRAW 6.0's interface are significant improvements, but Corel had a bit of trouble dealing with its Zoom tools. In this section we'll suggest some repairs to help clarify things.

By definition, tools are persistent—they stay on screen until you close them. But nobody wants a persistent zooming tool; you want to zoom once and then do something else. So the first zoom issue to be dealt with is that there is little to be gained by a floating Zoom Toolbar.

Furthermore, the Zoom tool in the Toolbox does not function as it used to. Now its flyout offers only the marquee zoom and the new Panning tool, and when you click on either one, the tool stays active until you change to another tool. This is especially aggravating when you have just marquee-zoomed and, expecting to be once again working with the Pick tool, you go to select an object...only to be surprised by zooming in on it even further. DRAW 4 and 5 were smart enough to revert immediately back to the Pick tool after a zoom, but in DRAW 6.0 that would be in violation of the properties for a tool as defined by Microsoft.

Further confusing matters is the curious fact that no less than *four* zooming controls are available to you. Oy vay...read 'em and weep.

- You can click on the Zoom tool in the Toolbox and tear it off, to get a little toolbar of just those two tools.

- You can right-click on the Zoom tool to bring up Tool Properties, and check Use Traditional Zoom Flyout to have Zoom function as it did in previous versions of DRAW.

- You can right-click the Standard Toolbar and choose Zoom to get a toolbar that consists of all zooming commands.

■ In Tools / View Manager you can turn on a full-featured roll-up
   for saving and retrieving zoom states in your drawing.

What to Do?   Here are our recommendations. First off, avoid the
Zoom tool in the Toolbox altogether—whether floating or docked. Unless you change its operation, via Tool Properties, it doesn't function the
way it used to, or the way that most want it to. Just ignore it.

Second, as we mentioned in Chapter 3, the best way to zoom continues
to be with your hotkeys:

■ F2 for marquee zoom

■ F3 for zoom out

■ F4 for zoom to all objects

■ Shift+F2 for zoom to selected objects

■ Shift+F4 for zoom to page

Pressing F2 to marquee-zoom is not like clicking on the Zoom tool and
you don't have the problem of it not going away after use. In fact, it
never gets activated in the first place, and whatever tool was active remains so. But if you have grown accustomed to using the icons for
zooming, we suggest that you try this:

1. Go to View / Toolbars (or right-click the Standard Toolbar) and
   choose Zoom.

2. With the Zoom Toolbar now active and floating on your screen,
   dock it on one of the edges of your window. On an 800 x 600
   display or higher, you have enough room to store it vertically underneath the Toolbox; if not, dock it on the right side.

Now you have a set of zoom controls that are better than the ones in
DRAW 5, because you can reach all of them with just one click instead
of two. They're better than the zoom tools in the Toolbox, too, because
they go away after each use. Figure 15.3 shows how it looks on our
screen, with the Zoom Toolbar comfortably docked below the Toolbox.

15.3

A Better Mouse-trap: With the Zoom Toolbar docked vertically below the Toolbox, zooming functions go from being worse than pre-vious versions to better.

Corel's engineers got themselves in a bit of a pickle with their strict adherence to Microsoft's specifications about tools. Luckily, because they have also given us such flexibility with the interface, we have the means to not only solve this interface problem, but design a better one.

And we haven't even gotten to the good stuff yet...

Build Your Own Bar

We hope you see the value in floating or docking various toolbars on your screen. For repeated use of a particular tool, there is nothing better than having it right next to your cursor. But the downside to this is the temptation to keep *all* of your tools close by. Give in to that, and before you know it your screen may look like Figure 15.4—and that's without any roll-ups!

15.4

Watch out—it's easy to go toolbar happy.

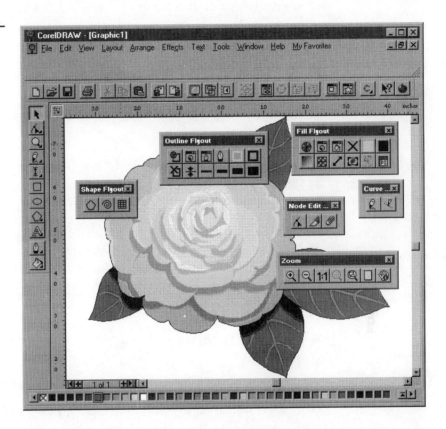

Clearly, another strategy is needed to keep a select set of tools within easy reach. DRAW 6.0 provides for that strategy. To best illustrate it, consider yourself hired as our new designer.

Special Tools for a Special Project

We have commissioned you to create a floor plan for our new editorial division, in which each member of our writing team will have an office.

We want the plan to be to correct scale, and it must have sufficient detail. We are paying you $335,000 for your efforts, so you'd better do a good job.

As a savvy DRAW 6.0 user, the first thing you do is think about what you will need for this project. You write down your tasks and the tools you will need for them:

- You'll need to import lots of objects from your personal home-furnishings library of clip art.

- The Clipboard will be kept very busy with frequent copying and pasting.

- You'll be creating lots of rectangles and free-form objects.

- The Copy Properties From command will be your faithful mule, helping you quickly take attributes from other finished pieces.

- You can already think of three layers that you'll need for the various objects.

- You'll have to set a grid, and will be regularly turning on and off Snap To Grid and Snap To Objects.

- You expect to be doing a lot of trimming and welding.

- The new View Manager, which can quickly zoom you into specific parts of the schematic, will be a welcome advantage.

- Your preliminary design reveals that certain shapes will need to be distinguished by black outlines, and others by 50% gray outlines.

With this list in hand, you float a few of the important toolbars on your page and quickly conclude that you have no room left to work. To correct this, you move all of these toolbars outside of the DRAW window and hover them over the Desktop. But now they are so far away from your cursor that reaching them via the menus would be easier.

Then you start to play with the Customize dialog, and you find DRAW 6.0's buried treasure. Here is what you do:

1. In Tools / Customize, you click on the Toolbars tab. There you find every tool, command, and roll-up that exists on the menus, in the Standard Toolbar, and in the Toolbox—and even a few tools that exist nowhere!

2. In the Command Categories list, you click on File. In the Buttons area, 12 icons appear, each one representing a command found in the File menu.

3. As you pass the cursor over each one, the pop-up help tells you which is which (because nobody actually identifies anything from those silly icons, do they?).

4. You find the button for Import and drag it from the dialog onto the page. As you do, DRAW automatically creates a toolbar to house it.

Figure 15.5 is our attempt to show action in a static medium. When you dragged from the Import icon onto the page, DRAW created a toolbar to house it. (It's a pretty small toolbar so far, only long enough to show the first letter.) Assuming this is your first custom toolbar, DRAW has called it Toolbar 1 (DRAW numbers them sequentially).

5. Referring to your list of tools and commands, you start moving through the menus in the Customize / Toolbars page. First, for the Edit menu, you decline the Clipboard commands because you can press Ctrl+C and Ctrl+V in your sleep. (Your sole criterion in selecting icons is ease of access, and you're a right-handed mouse user, so Ctrl+C is easier than clicking on an icon.) However, you do drag the Copy Properties tool to your new toolbar.

6. From the Layout menu, you take the Layers roll-up, Grid and Ruler Setup, and Snap To Objects. You don't need to take Snap To Grid because you've been pressing Ctrl+Y for that since version 2.0.

15.5

By dragging an icon from the Customize dialog onto the page, you have begun building your personal toolbar.

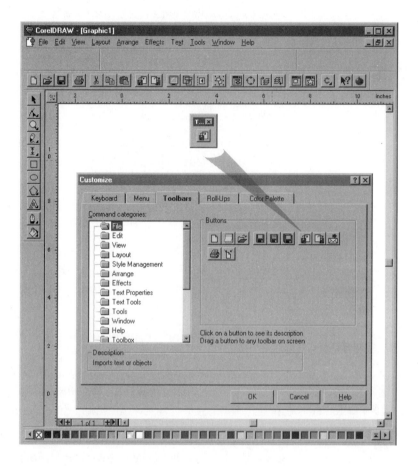

7. When you reach the Arrange menu, you notice three icons for welding, called Weld, Weld Target, and Weld Roll-up. Hmmm…what's this? you wonder. If you're like us, you're not too fond of the new grouped roll-ups for welding, trimming, and intersection. It's way too friendly, making you click on the first object and then the second object. You've already learned how to use Weld, and you've already selected the objects that you want welded. You recognize Weld Target from the roll-up, but wait—what is that icon named simply Weld? Aha! It's an automatic weld of the selected objects, just the way it was done in DRAW 5. You quickly drag that one to your toolbar.

8. You notice the same thing for Trim. "Yes!" you exclaim, and drag that one over, too.

9. From Tools, you take the View Manager roll-up, which is a tremendous help when zooming in and out of many different parts of a drawing.

10. Now you pause. "I'll probably want to add other tools and do more customizing later," you say to yourself. So you drag the Customize icon itself onto your personal toolbar.

11. Next, from Toolbox, you take the Freehand tool, because you can never remember the hotkey for it. You *do* remember, however, that F6 activates the Rectangle tool, so you decline that one.

12. Finally, under Outline, you choose the Black and 50% Black icons, and you're done choosing your icons.

13. One last thing: You discover that you can move the icons around on your toolbar, so you place Customize at the end and put the Pencil tool at the beginning. Your screen now looks like Figure 15.6 and you're psyched. You're ready to rock and roll.

INSIDE INFO

When you open the Customize dialog and click on Toolbars, you enter a special mode of operation in which any icon, anywhere on the interface, can be dragged and dropped to and from any other toolbar or the Toolbox. In other words, you can build your custom toolbar not only from the icons in the Customize dialog, but from any icons that are visible on the interface. And to remove any icon from any toolbar (except for the Toolbox), just drag it to Customize.

15.6

Your custom tool-
bar is ready for
action.

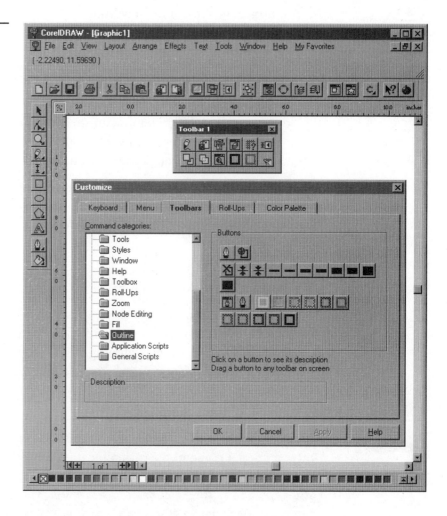

The only thing your special toolbar needs now is a name that's more interesting than Toolbar 1. So you close Customize, go to View / Toolbars, and find Toolbar 1 at the bottom of the list. Click on it a second
time to rename it. You decide on Special, and your screen now looks
like Figure 15.7.

The Toolbars dialog serves three important functions. It lets you make
visible or invisible all of the toolbars that are supplied with DRAW; it
lets you rename and delete custom toolbars; and it lets you reset the five

15.7

Your new, customized toolbar now gets a name apropos to its purpose.

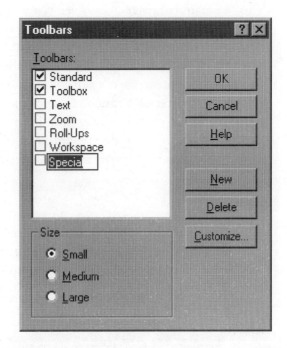

toolbars that DRAW permits you to alter—Standard, Text, Zoom, Roll-Ups, and Workspace—to their defaults.

Cleaning Up Your Environment

As you begin work on our editorial offices, you soon realize that, thanks to your Special Toolbar, you don't need much else on your screen. So, to get more work space, you remove the Standard Toolbar, the Color Palette, and the status bar. You'd like to remove the scroll bars, too, but DRAW won't let you. You decide to keep the Toolbox, also, just for good measure.

Occasionally as you work, you zoom way in on an object and find that your Special Toolbar is in the way. When you move it up and out of the way, it suddenly snaps into position above the rulers. "Of course," you realize, "I can just dock it where the Standard Toolbar used to be."

To maintain consistency between types of objects, you have created several styles. You've always disliked having to right-click or go to the Styles roll-up (called Styles Manager in DRAW 6.0) to apply styles, so you head back to Customize to see what it offers for Styles tasks. Under Style Management, there's a drop-down window that doesn't drop down, no matter how much you click on it. Then you realize that it, too, is an icon, and when you drop it onto your Special Toolbar, it becomes a working drop-down window showing you all of your styles. Figure 15.8 shows how easy it is in DRAW 6.0 to assign styles to objects.

Menu Mania

Toolbars aren't the only thing that you can rearrange in DRAW 6.0. Nothing is sacred anymore, including the menus that hold all of DRAW's commands, dialogs, and roll-ups.

15.8

No more navigating multiple flyouts to assign styles, thanks to the Styles list that you have added to your toolbar.

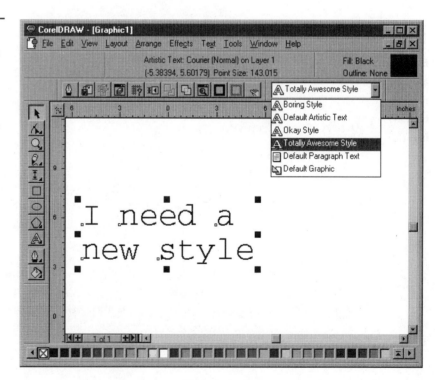

From the soon-to-be-famous Customize dialog, click the Menu tab. You arrive at the gateway to total control of the menus and their elements.

Adding and Removing Menu Items

Let's start this section with our favorite pet peeve about DRAW 6.0: the loss of functionality from Intersection, Trim, and Weld in the name of user-friendliness. Most advanced users already loathe this new combined roll-up because of the extra steps required to navigate it. But with Customize / Menu, "*We can rebuild it. We **have** the technology…*"

First, open Customize / Menu. This page of the dialog has two windows: The one on the left shows all available commands, whether or not they are currently assigned to a menu. The window on the right shows the current configuration of DRAW's menus. In the Menu window, double-click on Arrange, and your screen should look like Figure 15.9.

15.9

Every single menu and all its commands are subject to rearrangement from Customize.

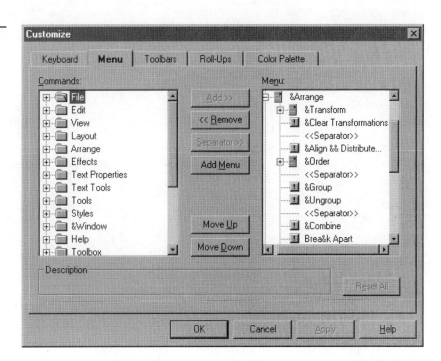

In the buttons next to the items in the Menu window, exclamation marks indicate commands. Plus signs and small right-pointing arrows indicate submenus that contain commands within (for example, the set of Order commands). You can either click on the plus button or double-click on the arrow to drill down to those commands. The <<Separators>> represent the dividing lines that appear in the menus. The & symbol designates the letter in the command that is displayed underlined, and which you can press to invoke the command.

The buttons between the two windows are the means for adding, removing, and rearranging of commands within the menus.

Figure 15.10 shows what the Arrange menu looks like in the Customize dialog and in actuality.

15.10

The menu tree on the left is responsible for the look of the menu on the right.

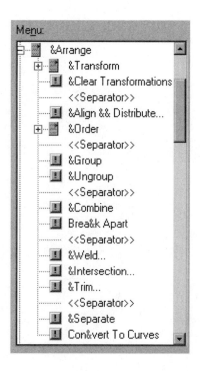

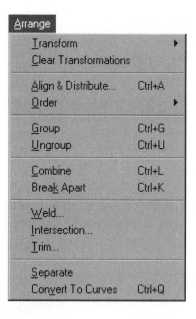

This...   **...Becomes This**

Those of you who dislike the combination Weld/Intersection/Trim roll-up as much as we do can follow these steps to return Weld, Intersection, and Trim to their DRAW 5 state in the Arrange menu:

1. In the Menu window under the Arrange group, find Weld and click the Remove button. Repeat for Intersection and Trim.

2. In the Commands window, find the Quick Weld, Quick Intersection, and Quick Trim commands. Click on the Add button to add them, one by one, to the Arrange menu on the right.

3. If necessary, position the <<Separator>> correctly in the Menu window, using the Move Up or Move Down buttons. Your screen should look like Figure 15.11.

15.11

We have removed the three commands that invoke the combo Weld/ Intersection/Trim roll-up, in favor of the traditional "quick" commands.

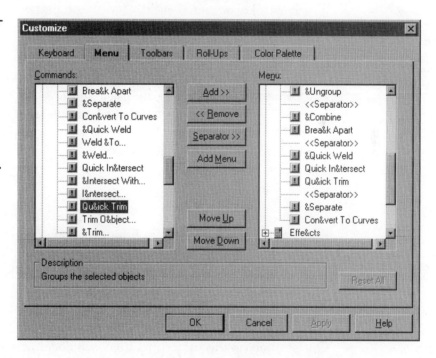

The only problem now is that keyboard users will encounter the wrong key assignments for the three new commands, but that is easily fixed: Click a second time on each menu item (just as you would in Explorer) to rename it or reposition the ampersand.

Creating New Menus

The handy Customize / Menu dialog goes beyond the rearranging of menu items—you can also add your own menus. Did you notice that all of the screen images in this chapter include an extra menu called My Favorites? (Ah, we can hear it now, the flutter of pages being flipped.) Here is how we did it.

1. In Customize / Menu, we clicked on the last item in the Menu window, &Help.

2. We clicked Add Menu and then typed **&My Favorites** in the box.

3. Then we browsed all of the menus looking for frequently used commands that would otherwise require more than one or two keystrokes or mouse clicks. When we found ones we wanted, we simply clicked Add. Then, if necessary, we renamed the added item and/or repositioned the $ and each <<Separator>>.

Figure 15.12 shows the My Favorites menu and its corresponding menu tree from the Customize / Menu page. Our favorites of these Favorites are the PowerClipping shortcuts, which save us from having to go Effects / PowerClip and then the particular command. Notice that we renamed Place Inside Container to PowerClip Now, and moved the ampersand so that PowerClip Now wouldn't have the same underlined letter as Pantone Spot Colors.

If you want to undo any changes that you have made to a menu, you can remove any particular item from a menu or the menu itself. Or click the Reset All button and restore the default configuration. (More on Reset All in the later section on managing the Killer Interface.)

The Keys to Happiness

Our position on this subject has been well documented over the years: In the choice between a mouse click and a keystroke, we'll take the keystroke just about every time. We have yearned for Corel to give us more

15.12

With menus that can be customized, you may never have to click through nested menu items again.

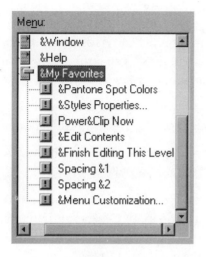

This...   **...Becomes This**

of them, even if the developers have to use some strange and bizarre ones (such as Ctrl+F9 for Contour and Alt+F3 for Lens). As of DRAW 6.0, however, we no longer have to accept either a shortage of hotkeys *or* weird key mnemonics. From Customize / Keyboard, we have total control.

Reassigning Keys

In Chapter 3 we shared with you our preference for Ctrl+E to access Export rather than Extrude. (Maybe every other or every third project might need an extrusion, but we turn to Export several times per project.) Making this change is easy, with the following steps:

1. Go to Tools / Customize / Keyboard. In the Commands window, double-click File (or click once on the plus sign to its left).

2. Click on Export, and then on the new and somewhat bizarre Ctrl+H under Current Shortcut Key. Click Delete to remove it, and place your cursor in the window labeled Press New Shortcut Key.

3. Press Ctrl+E. DRAW warns you that this keystroke is being used by another command. To reassign it anyway, you must check the Go To Conflict On Assign box. Then DRAW takes you to Extrude, where you can either remove the assignment to Extrude or assign another keystroke to it.

4. OK the dialog, at which point DRAW will ask you to name your new "accelerator file" (more on this shortly).

5. Try out your new keystroke. Notice that the File menu now shows the keystroke alongside Export.

We predict that most of you will waste no time creating hotkeys for Snap To Guidelines and Snap To Objects and other favorites.

Tips and Tricks for Key Assignments

If you have followed this chapter so far, you shouldn't have any trouble with keystroke assignments, because they follow the same basic implementation of toolbars and menus. However, here are a few hidden gems to keep in mind.

Anywhere on the Menus   DRAW will display all reassigned keystrokes in its traditional menus, and in any menus that you create. For instance, we added the Place Inside Container command (renamed to PowerClip Now) to the My Favorites menu, and then decided to give it a hotkey. So in Customize / Keyboard, we went to the Effects section of the Command window, found Place Inside Container, and assigned Ctrl+Shift+P to it. That keystroke then appeared on the My Favorites menu next to PowerClip Now.

Nowhere on the Menus   The Commands window in the Keyboard page is just like that of the Menu page: It includes every command defined by DRAW, whether the command appears directly on a menu or not. In other words, you can assign keystrokes to commands that are buried inside of dialogs, or even to commands that are found nowhere except in the Customize dialog.

Suppose, for instance, that you want to center a block of text. You can either go to Text / Character / Alignment and then click on the button for Center; or right-click on the text, go to Properties, and find the icon for centered text. But with Customize / Keyboard, you can find Center Justification [*sic*] under Text Properties, and assign Ctrl+Shift+C (or whatever) to it.

Some of the available commands in Customize—including Spacing 2, Increase/Decrease Indent, and the Quick Weld, Intersection, and Trim we spoke of earlier—do not exist in any of the menus or default toolbars.

Hot Tools   You can assign or reassign hotkeys to every tool and flyout in the Toolbox. In Chapter 3 we wondered why Corel didn't assign Shift+F3 to the Panning tool, because that keystroke is unassigned and sits between two other hotkeys for zooming. The question is now irrelevant, because we can do that ourselves. We can create a keystroke for the Bézier tool, the Knife tool, or the Slanted Dimension tool (should the mood strike us); and even for any particular fill type, such as Texture, PostScript, and even No Fill, which would otherwise require a trip to the × on the Color Palette.

Your lead author wasted little time swapping Uniform Fill with Fountain Fill—he has never understood why the busier Uniform Fill requires Shift+F11, while the more exotic Fountain Fill only needs F11. You might also be interested to know that all of the node-editing commands are assignable, such as Join, Break, Smooth, Cusp, and so on.

Something the developers omitted that might be asked for the most: hotkey controls for aligning objects. The new Align roll-up offers no keystroke access, while previous versions offered complete access.

Two Keystrokes, One Command   We're not sure why you would want to do it, but it's marginally worth noting (does that mean we should put it in the margin?) that you can assign more than one keystroke to a command. If you do this, the one you assigned first (or the original assignment that Corel made) shows on the menus.

Assign It and Bottle It   If your system serves multiple users, multiple projects, or just multiple personalities, you can save your keystroke definitions in a file. DRAW stores them in Accelerator Files with .ACL file name extensions. There are several advanced strategies that you can employ to manage these files, all of which are discussed in the final section of this chapter.

Roll-up Grouping for Roll-up Groupies

We find that user opinions about DRAW's roll-ups are considerably polarized. Almost everyone has an opinion on them, and they're either dearly loved or unduly loathed. If you love your roll-ups, you'll enjoy the DRAW 6.0 controls for managing them, the most noteworthy of which is the ability to group them together to save screen space.

Corel has already done a lot of roll-up management for you, supplying combined roll-ups for Effects, Shaping, Attributes, and others—but you can do it, too. The Tools / Customize / Roll-Ups page provides settings for this, but the easiest way to do it is back out on the page, where you can drag one roll-up and drop it on top of another.

1. With both roll-ups open, hold Ctrl while you drag one title bar to the other.

2. Let go of both the Ctrl key and mouse button, and the two roll-ups merge into one.

The new roll-up is given a generic name of New Group #, which you can change in the Customize / Roll-Ups page. If you need to ungroup a roll-up, just drag it back out of its group, and it will automatically separate itself. This holds true for all grouped roll-ups, whether you put them that way or Corel shipped them to you that way.

Note that working in grouped roll-ups requires more mouse clicking, not less, because you have to spend an extra click to choose the desired function inside the new roll-up. But if your priority is saving screen space, not mouse clicks, it's a good trade.

From Customize / Roll-Ups, you can also decide which roll-ups will open on the left side of the workspace and which on the right. You can also designate roll-ups to open automatically upon start-up of CorelDRAW.

A Kinder, Gentler Color Palette

The final page in the Customize dialog addresses the Color Palette, and for the most part, it's back-page news. This page lets you

- Opt for 3-D borders around each color swatch
- Show large swatches instead of small ones
- Designate the number of rows
- Choose whether or not to show empty wells for palettes that contain few colors

AUTHOR'S NOTE

Our interest was piqued initially when we saw the option for large swatches, but we were disappointed to learn that the swatches grow in both directions—tall as well as wide. We like the idea of larger color swatches on the palette, but not enough to give up vertical screen space and would have preferred a choice for wider but not taller swatches.

Creating and Managing the Killer Interface

If you are an advanced user who wants as much control over a program as possible, DRAW 6.0 might begin to appear in your happiest dreams. In addition to the interface improvements described so far in this chapter, there are a few back-door maneuvers available that can bring substantial power and swiftness to your daily DRAW activities. We warned you up front that the terrain in this chapter might get a bit steep; it's about to go vertical.

From the perspective of Corel's product support constituent, an obvious requirement for DRAW 6.0's flexible new interface was the means for its users to bring it back to its factory condition. You've no doubt noticed that the Keyboard, Menu, and Roll-Ups pages of the Customize dialog all contain a Reset All button, for returning settings to their defaults. And in the View / Toolbars dialog you can delete custom toolbars you may have created. Although it is comforting to know that we can return to some sort of ground zero, that's not what we're interested in; we're shooting for the stars. To do that, we need to study what DRAW does behind the scenes when we redefine menus, create toolbars, group roll-ups, and reassign keystrokes.

DRAW's Configuration Files

DRAW manages all of your customizations with configuration files that are kept in the DRAW subdirectory, one level below the directory in which the program was installed (typically COREL60). In that subdirectory, you will find four files:

CDRBARS.CFG

CDRMENU.CFG

CDRROLS.CFG

DEFAULT.ACL

INSIDE INFO

> You may see only three of the configuration files listed above, because DRAW only creates CDRMENU.CFG if a change has been made to the default menus. If CDRMENU.CFG isn't there, don't be alarmed—it just means you haven't yet customized any menus.

These files store all of the changes that you make in the Customize dialog (unless you conscientiously save your keystroke assignments to a different .ACL file). For instance, when you created the custom Special Toolbar earlier in this chapter and docked it on the top of the screen,

DRAW recorded all of that action into CDRBARS.CFG. Each time you launch DRAW, it looks in CDRBARS.CFG for instructions on how to configure its toolbars. If CDRBARS.CFG doesn't exist, DRAW uses its own factory settings and re-creates CDRBARS.CFG from those settings.

As a result, deleting .CFG files is never "fatal." You might lose whatever intelligence you programmed from the Customize dialog, but DRAW can always re-create the file and start up according to its factory defaults. The same is true for the keystroke (.ACL) files. If you delete DEFAULT.ACL, DRAW re-creates it; if you delete the .ACL file designated as active, DRAW reverts to DEFAULT.ACL.

Storing Your Preferences

We're not interested in deleting these configuration files, we're interested in *capturing* them. Because with these files, we know we can always restore DRAW to interface settings that we have chosen, not just the factory settings or the conditions in which the program was last left. To do that, prepare the interface as carefully and conscientiously as you can, using the Customize dialog to tweak all the controls to fit your needs just right. Then follow these steps:

1. *Be sure to exit DRAW first.*

2. Start Explorer or your preferred Windows or DOS shell, and go to the DRAW subdirectory under COREL60.

3. Find the four configuration files, and copy and rename them as follows, replacing the Xs in the new file names with letters you will recognize:

   CDRBARS.CFG to CDRBARS.XXX

   CDRMENU.CFG (if it's there) to CDRMENU.XXX

   CDRROLS.CFG to CDRROLS.XXX

   DEFAULT.ACL to XXXXXXX.ACL

For the file name extensions of the three .CFG files, use your initials or some other identifiable extension, and rename the copied .ACL file so that you'll recognize it. Though it's true that Explorer will let you give longer names to these files to better identify them—such as My Toolbar, My Menu, and so forth—then you would be limited to manipulating the files from within Windows 95, and not from DOS (where most of these automated techniques reside).

WATCH OUT!

Make sure that you quit DRAW before capturing or restoring configuration files. DRAW updates those files as it exits, not as you make the changes to the interface. So you must wait until DRAW exits before the .CFG files are written initially, or before you overwrite them with the ones you have stored. You won't crash or corrupt anything, but if you manipulate the files while DRAW is running, the program will simply ignore you.

With these four files safely copied, you know that no matter what you do to DRAW's interface, you'll always be able to get back to your preferred configuration. To do so, just do step 3 above in reverse—copy CDRBARS.XXX to CDRBARS.CFG, CDRMENU.XXX to CDRMENU.CFG, and so forth.

Copying configuration files is fine…if you like copying files. But the whole point to this process is automating these routines to save you time, not to make you manually copy files. Your task in interface management is to create work environments that are uniquely suited to particular projects or situations, and with a bit of DOS batch file know-how, you can create a sophisticated turnkey system for controlling DRAW's interface. In the remainder of this section, we'll study an example of such a system.

AUTHOR'S NOTE

Did you expect DOS and batch files to become dirty words in the Windows 95 age? Hardly. Not only are batch files still one of the most flexible tools for system configuration, they have become even more capable under Windows 95, because now you can execute both DOS and Windows commands from a batch file.

Setting the Scene for the Killer Interface

You run a small design firm—TipTop Desktop, Inc.—specializing in three areas: business stationery, corporate newsletters, and quarterly reports. Your long experience reveals that you have regularly turned to certain tools from DRAW's arsenal for projects in each of these areas. For instance, you make heavy use of grids and guidelines when creating business cards and letterheads, and you employ the Contour command regularly to drop shadows behind images that you place in newsletters. Meanwhile, quarterly reports include lots of charts and graphs that you often need to create from scratch, requiring quick access to several styles.

You begin work on stationery for a new client and decide to take full advantage of the Customize dialog. You want to create an environment that is perfectly suited for the task. You start by creating tools for the View Manager, all three snaps, and a few of your preferred roll-ups. Most of this client's work is in two-color, for which you trap colors yourself, so you are delighted to learn you can assign a hotkey to the Overprint Outline command (because you never quite got the hang of that right-click thing).

You finish the project in record time, your hands and the DRAW interface moving as one. You quit the program and you say to yourself, "Self, it would be nice to be able to retrieve this perfectly tuned environment the next time I have to do stationery. How do I keep from mucking things up in the meantime, as other types of projects come in?"

Ah, but you have already read this chapter that you are now reading, and so you already know what you're about to find out: That you *can* get back to this ideal performance state. So you do the following:

1. You remember to quit DRAW first.

2. You copy those key configuration files. In the new file names, you use the abbreviation STA to represent your stationery projects, as follows:

CDRBARS.CFG to CDRBARS.STA

CDRMENU.CFG to CDRMENU.STA

CDRROLS.CFG to CDRROLS.STA

DEFAULT.ACL to STA.ACL

CORELDRW.INI to CORELDRW.STA

The .INI file at the end, though not a configuration file per se, keeps track of many other settings of the current session—page and window sizes, nudge values, all directory pointers, and various other settings that tend to change from one session to another.

3. You open Notepad or some other editor that can create text files. You create the following batch file, making sure that the CD commands point to your actual CorelDRAW directory:

```
echo off
cd \corel60\draw
echo Restoring configuration files...
copy cdr*.sta cdr*.cfg
copy coreldrw.sta coreldrw.ini
copy sta.acl default.acl
echo Running DRAW...
cd \corel60\programs
start coreldrw.exe
```

4. You name this batch file STATONRY.BAT, or some other name (including a long name) that makes sense to you. By running this batch file, you ensure that DRAW will launch in exactly the conditions that you have set for your stationery projects.

Going Further

One week later, you start and complete one of your newsletters. In the process, you make wholesale changes to the interface to better reflect the needs and demands of these newsletters. When you're done and you've quit DRAW, you once again go to the DRAW subdirectory and copy the significant files, this time using NWS as the three-letter identifier.

One week later, you complete one of your quarterly reports, and capture the files yet again, using REP as the identifier for the files.

So now, the DRAW subdirectory has the following files:

```
CDRBARS.CFG
CDRMENU.CFG
CDRROLS.CFG (current files)
DEFAULT.ACL
CORELDRW.INI

CDRBARS.STA
CDRMENU.STA
CDRROLS.STA (files for stationery projects)
STA.ACL
CORELDRW.STA

CDRBARS.NWS
CDRMENU.NWS
CDRROLS.NWS (files for newsletter projects)
NWS.ACL
CORELDRW.NWS

CDRBARS.REP
CDRMENU.REP
CDRROLS.REP (files for report projects)
REP.ACL
CORELDRW.REP
```

Turning the Key

The secret to making this work? One good ol' batch file, with replaceable parameters. The STATONRY.BAT file we just described for you is a good start, but this next one must be able to service all three types of projects (and, for that matter, any others that you bring on line). The lines of code will look like this:

```
echo off
cd \corel60\draw
echo Restoring %1 configuration files...
copy cdrbars.%1 cdrbars.cfg
copy cdrmenu.%1 cdrmenu.cfg
copy cdrrols.%1 cdrrols.cfg
copy coreldrw.%1 coreldrw.ini
copy %1.acl default.acl
echo Running DRAW...
cd \corel60\programs
start coreldrw.exe
```

If you've read this far, you probably already know how the %1 works in this batch file: It represents whatever is typed along with the batch file name when the file is first executed. So if you name the batch file DRAW6.BAT and then type

```
DRAW6 REP
```

the batch file will substitute REP wherever it encounters the %1.

If this is all a bit too DOS-like for you, keep reading...

Adding the Pretty Face

You may think this batch-file business looks ugly on the inside, but it doesn't have to look that way on the outside. Just find some cute icon to represent it and place it into a pretty folder on your charming Desktop. Here's how:

1. Right-click on your Desktop, choose New / Folder, and name the folder **DRAW Projects** or some such.

2. Double-click to open the folder.

3. Once inside, right-click again, this time choosing New / Shortcut.

4. Enter the complete path to the DRAW6.BAT file you've created, or use the Browse button to find it. (As an alternative, you can also open Explorer or My Computer, find the batch file,

and right-click and drag to create a shortcut of it into this folder.)

5. Name your shortcut **Business Stationery.**

6. Select an icon for the batch file; we kind of liked the light bulb, representing brilliant ideas.

7. Click on the icon with Button 2, choose Properties, and go to the Program page.

8. To the end of the command line, add a space and the three letters **STA.**

9. Check the Close On Exit option.

10. Your project icon is ready to be tested; just double-click.

Once you have verified that this shortcut to the batch file works, make two copies of it (by Ctrl+dragging the icon). For each copy, go to File / Properties and change the three-character identifier at the end of the command line to whatever you have designated as your extensions for each configuration. Then rename the icon to reflect the project it represents, and optionally, change each icon to taste.

Figure 15.13 shows your new system in action. In this screen you have chosen Business Stationery. The DOS window in the foreground issues a confirming notice of the parameter you have chosen, showing the result of copying the files into place. The batch file has just reached the last command, that of starting DRAW, and therefore is about to go away (because you enabled the Close On Exit property). For reference, the batch file is open in Notepad.

There are lots of variations to this theme. For instance, you could use just one icon with a ? as the parameter instead of the three-character designator. That tells Windows to ask for input before executing the batch file. You could program the batch file to pass the parameter on, as you have done here, plus restore a standard default configuration if the batch file finds no parameter. As you store other groups of settings, you can call for them just as easily as these, as long as you name the files consistently.

15.13

Who would have thought that a batch file could be so useful? This one is responsible for our sample automated turnkey system.

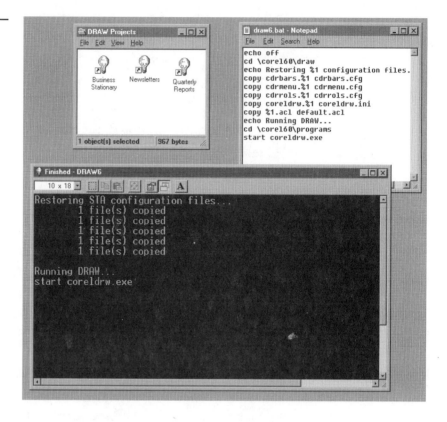

Finally, you can assign hotkeys to your batch file icons so you can invoke them from any point within Windows 95.

♣

We're not exaggerating when we say this is just a taste of what you can do to automate your CorelDRAW sessions. But our lead author is making us stop here, before you conclude that we're just a bunch of DOS-nerds. You're right—too late.

CHAPTER

16

CorelSCRIPT: A Work in Progress

SIXTEEN

This chapter might set a new record for Shortest Chapter Ever in a Software Book. We had very high hopes for Corel's scripting tool and for this chapter; in fact, we still do. But the module that was to take center stage here—CorelSCRIPT—simply isn't ready yet. Therefore, neither are we.

Corel did indeed package and include this partially baked module in the CorelDRAW 6.0 box—thus our obligation to say something about it. Based on the Visual Basic programming language, SCRIPT is a powerful and robust language that can send strings of commands to DRAW to automate repetitive tasks. These scripts are stored in .CSC files, a collection of which can be found in the DRAW and SCRIPTS subdirectories under the main CorelDRAW directory. The DRAW interface is designed to accommodate these scripts.

You can run a script in four ways:

- Go to Tools / Scripts / Run.

- Attach the script to a custom toolbar.

- Add the script to a menu.

- Assign a hotkey to the script.

With the Dialog Editor that's included in the CorelDRAW box, you can create mini-applications within DRAW 6.0 that prompt you for information and ask for specific values, colors, line widths, typefaces, and so forth. Everything is in place for this new application to become an immediate hit.

Well, almost everything. Corel left out one small thing: a recording module. To create a script for use in DRAW, you must build it yourself, line by line, or open an existing script and modify it. In either case, you need a good working knowledge of the programming language (a first cousin to Visual Basic). That eliminates about 99% of the CorelDRAW-using public.

Corel didn't do this on purpose; its engineers simply ran out of time. PhotoPAINT has a Command Recorder roll-up, and at the time of this writing, Ventura 6.0's list of features includes script recording. So we won't take Corel to task for omitting the recording module from SCRIPT when we know that the company intends to offer it. We do think, however, that if SCRIPT couldn't be delivered in its full form, it shouldn't have been included at all. This hurried version doesn't help Corel fight its reputation as a company with a penchant for releasing software too early.

Curious users can open scripts and run them directly from the DRAW interface. Those with programming experience can tinker with the code and build scripts, aided by the Script Editor's help file. The rest of us will have to wait for the recording module, slated for an upcoming maintenance release, or the next version of the program.

♣

On this less-than-stellar note, we close what has otherwise been an optimistic journey through CorelDRAW 6.0's advanced tools for automation and customization. We now switch gears in a big way and look at the superstars of the software: the special effects.

PART

EFFECTS AND AFFECTS

This part begins with a warning: CorelDRAW's special effects can be addicting, once you understand how they work. This is both wonderful and dangerous—you must beware the intoxicating power special effects give you. Use them, but don't overdose. More than a few layouts have been ruined by the abuse of special effects. You want proof? Browse through just about any computer magazine or the computer ads in your newspaper. You will see some great and some equally horrendous use of graphic special effects.

You've heard this from us before (fountain fills come to mind): It is not only our responsibility as computer journalists to communicate to you how the tools work; we must also advise you against overusing them. Nowhere else in the program—nowhere—is this more salient than with DRAW's corps of special effects.

Enjoy learning them, and please have fun with them. But always remember that you're carrying the electronic equivalent of a loaded gun and you are practicing your craft in public.

17

Appetizers

SEVENTEEN

Pâté…crostini…a glass of wine…and maybe some escargots. This chapter looks at the electronic equivalents of these hors d'oeuvre, all of which are found on the Arrange menu. The Arrange tools are not quite in the WOW! league of special effects, but they're close.

When we're done here, we'll move to the Effects menu and its more robust fare—from the simple entrées of enveloping, perspective, contours, and blends, to the chef's specials: lenses and PowerClips.

Transformations 101

If you want to move it, rotate it, size it, scale it, skew it, or raise its consciousness (okay, forget the last one), your first stop is the batch of Transform roll-ups under Arrange. Figure 17.1 shows all five of them, and their similarities in form and function should be apparent at first glance. You will also notice an almost absurd level of precision in the existing horizontal and vertical values. You have 32-bit processing to thank or blame for that; in many instances, the extra decimal places will just get in the way.

NEW FOR 6

If you find yourself using one of the Transform roll-ups more often than the others, there are now two things you can do to improve access. As in previous DRAW versions, the hotkeys Alt+F7 through Alt+F11 will get you to the respective roll-ups. In addition, as of DRAW 6.0 you can tear any one roll-up out of the grouped roll-up. Also, from Tools / Customization / Toolbar, you can attach one of these roll-ups to your Standard Toolbar or to any custom toolbar you may have created.

17.1

The five players in
the Transform
game

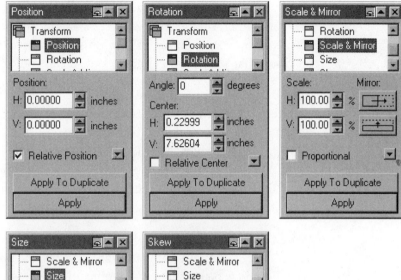

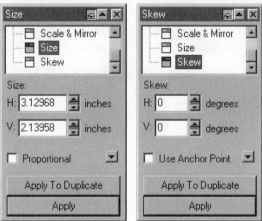

Working with the Transform Roll-ups

Working these roll-ups is easy, so instead of a tutorial, we offer a few
rules of thumb.

Select the Object First! If you don't have an object or a group selected, all five of these roll-ups will be dormant, grayed out, and otherwise asleep.

Apply to Duplicate   This button is essentially the same as the *blank*-and-dupes we have discussed in many earlier chapters. You fill in the blank: drag, rotate, scale, size, skew—they all can be done on screen with your mouse or through this group of roll-ups, the latter offering precision that your mouse, hands, and screen couldn't possibly approach.

The Button   Each of these roll-ups offers a check box that you can click to further define the operation. In three of them—Position, Rotation, and Skew—turning on this "clarification" option defines a relative position around which the selected object is moved, rotated, or skewed. In the Scale & Mirror and the Size roll-ups, you can provide for proportional operation, in which changing one direction (horizontal or vertical) will automatically cause the other to change by the same proportion.

What's the Difference?   "Couldn't Scale & Mirror and Size have been in the same roll-up?" you might ask. Yes, we might answer, the only difference being the way the object is sized—by percentage (for Scale & Mirror) or to an actual number (for Size). Corel might have included a % or # check box and rolled the two roll-ups into one, but keystrokers would lament the extra click that they don't presently have to do. The Mirror part of Scale & Mirror is the same as the flop-and-dupe that you have done with your mouse several times already in the exercises throughout this book.

By the way, the abbreviation for the Scale & Mirror roll-up is…uh, never mind.

Play Tic-Tac-Toe   On all of the Transform roll-ups, the little grid illustrated in Figure 17.2 allows you to quickly select one of the nine control points on the imaginary rectangle that encloses a selected object. The role of this grid varies slightly with the Transform mode you are using.

Figure 17.2 shows the result of using the Rotate roll-up, the tic-tac-toe grid, and the Apply To Duplicate button. Notice how the grid has changed the position *around which* the object rotates.

17.2

The Rotate roll-up, with the tic-tac-toe grid displayed

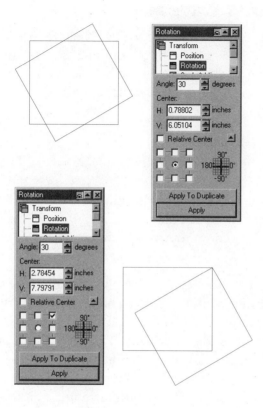

AUTHOR'S NOTE

Unfortunately, in DRAW 6.0 Corel has maintained the link between the units of measure in all of the Transform roll-ups and the Layout / Ruler setting. Because of this lamentable situation, whatever units you use for the rulers are the only units available in the Transform roll-up. In versions of DRAW prior to 5, you could select other units of measure from a drop-down list right in the roll-up. Now, to change the units for the Transform roll-ups, you must change the ruler settings or the page settings. This remains a major setback in productivity. To add insult to injury, other tools in the interface *do* offer flexible switching of units—Character Attributes, for instance, where you would almost never change from Points. Go figure…

Miscellaneous Caveats

Transformations can be tricky. Whenever you change an object from its original shape, you introduce some degree of risk that you will adversely affect it, or that you will not be able to put it back the way it was. Here are a couple of issues to watch out for.

Unfriendly Percentages

Want to louse up a perfectly level rectangle? Draw one and then open the Rotate or the Skew roll-up. Now apply the following degrees of change to it, one after the other: 17, –3, 38, 11, 16.6, –29, and 61. Okay, now return the rectangle to 0°, so it's level again. What happens? We don't know how to spell the sound of "Urrrghnt, Reject!" but that is the first thing that comes to mind.

Why can't you do it? Because DRAW does not keep track of the degree of change with respect to an object's original condition. There is no option to "remember original position," or any such safeguard. So each time you entered a percentage, DRAW added that change to the previous one. This is true of all five of the roll-ups—except the Position roll-up when the Relative Position check box option is off. In all other cases, the only way to return the object to its original position is to Undo like crazy, or manually reverse the operations by entering the negative value for every number entered, or have your calculator close by and ready to figure out the object's exact percentage or degree of change at any given point.

The safest solution: Store a copy of the object in the Clipboard before you begin. Then you can return the object to its original condition with Del followed by Ctrl+V.

The Curse of the Scaled Outline

When stretching objects that have visible outlines, there are two things that can happen to the outlines: absolutely nothing or bad distortion. What determines this fate is a control within the Outline Pen dialog, called Scale With Image.

If Scale With Image is off, the object's outline stays set at the original thickness, regardless of how much stretching, sizing, or skewing you do to the object. If you check Scale With Image, the outline scales with the image, *but only in the directions you stretch*. In other words, you could end up with a rectangle that looks like Figure 17.3, in which two of the sides have different outline thicknesses than the other two.

17.3

When Scale With Image is checked, distorting an object will also distort its outlines.

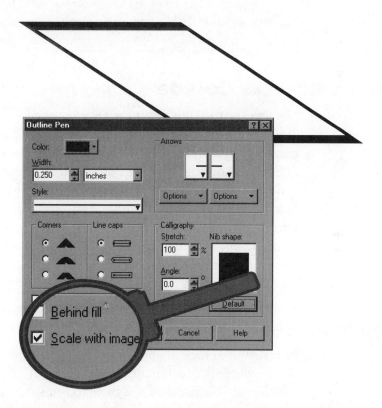

There are certainly appropriate times to turn this option on—for instance, when you want to render an object or an illustration at several different sizes. In that situation you would want proportionally correct outlines. That is, you would want your outlines to enlarge along with the other objects in the illustration. Use Scale With Image with care, however, when you know that you'll be performing any nonproportional sizing or scaling.

AUTHOR'S NOTE

> What an ideal opportunity for a script: toggling Scale With Image on and off. And you'll find just that, named **SCALEIMG.CSC** in the **PRACTICE\SCRIPTS** directory of the Companion CD. Copy it into the DRAW subdirectory. From there, you could run it by going Tools / Scripts / Run and picking it from the File list. Or, much better, use the Customize dialog to assign a hotkey to the script or place it directly on one of the menus.

When Objects Collide

No, we're not talking about the creation of a black hole or the crashing of your computer. (We're sure that Windows 95 and DRAW 6.0 *never* crash your system...) What we're referring to in this instance are the three most powerful functions on the Arrange menu—Intersect, Trim, and Weld. (Actually, the menu says "IntersecTION," but we think that's a typo because all the other Arrange commands are verbs.) Each of these commands studies the areas where objects overlap and then does something at that overlap. *What* each command does, however, is quite different from what its colleagues do. Together, the three make a very powerful team.

The Roles of the Shaping Triumverate

In DRAW 6.0 these shaping tools function quite differently from version 5, where they debuted, and we're already on record as preferring the old way. Nonetheless, the three roll-ups shown in Figure 17.4 are friendlier, especially Trim. The three tools share what we like to call the "Go Do It" button (Intersect With, Trim, and Weld To), as well as the two controls that determine the status of the so-called Target Object and Other Objects.

Let's begin by defining a few terms.

17.4

**The three roll-ups
in the Shaping
Triumverate**

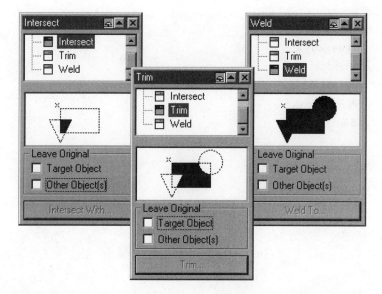

The Target Object   This is the object to which the effect gets applied. In other words, if you were to ask DRAW to find the intersection between the two ovals and the text shown in Figure 17.5, you would go to Arrange / Intersect, select two of the objects first, and then click on the Intersect With "Go Do It" button. Then you'd define the Target Object by clicking on it with the big fat arrow that DRAW presents you with.

In some cases, it's almost arbitrary what object you define as the target. As with so many other areas of this program, the object that you select *last*—the Target Object—is the one that determines the outline and fill for the new object created during the operation.

The Other Objects   As far as function naming goes, this is pretty lame. What the heck are *Other Objects??* Just think of them as the objects that you select first before clicking on the "Go Do It" button. That's really all you need to know: You select the Other Objects first (and don't try to make too much sense of that), click the "Go Do It" button, and then click on the Target Object.

17.5

These three objects will be our guinea pigs for studying the effects of Intersect, Trim, and Weld.

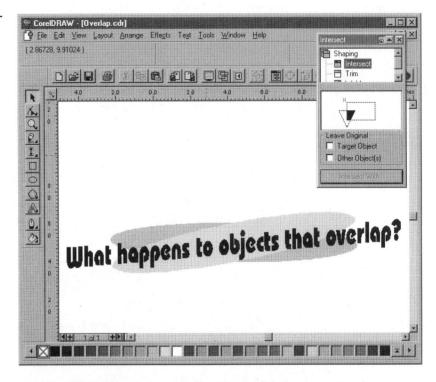

Leaving the Original It is not immediately obvious what happens when you check or uncheck the two Leave Original boxes, so we'll show you. Essentially, you can elect to use the objects just as a means for creating a new object (in which case you could ask DRAW to delete them when you're through), or keep the original objects on screen after you create your new object.

Finding the Intersection

Now that we have met the members of the Shaping Triumverate, we'll have our first audience with the Intersect function. Like Trim and Weld, Intersect studies the objects in question and determines the area where they overlap. It creates a new object that is contained within that overlap.

Go to the PRACTICE directory of the Companion CD and open OVERLAP.CDR. Your task here is to create a black object from the intersection of the two ovals and the text. You want to end up with just the intersection, not the original ovals. Here are the steps:

1. Select one oval and then Shift+select the other. These are the "Other Objects."

2. Make sure that both boxes in the Leave Original section of the roll-up are unchecked.

3. Click the Intersect With button, and then click on the text.

Your screen should now look similar to Figure 17.6. You'll notice in that figure (and the ones that follow) that we have taken the liberty of displaying in a light outline the objects that have been removed from the drawing. Also, the roll-up depicts the action you have requested. On your screen, you should see only the slice of black text (which is not text, but just a curve) that sits in that intersection. Why is the text black? Because the Target Object was. Had you selected the light oval and the text

17.6

This black slice of
text was created by
the Intersect tool.
The slice consists
of the area where
the three objects
overlap.

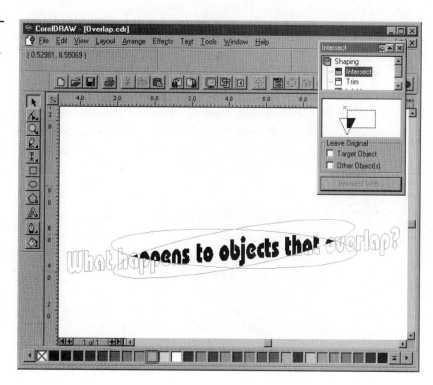

first as your Other Objects and then clicked on the darker oval, the resulting slice of text would be 20% Black, the shade of the darker oval.

The Intersect tool is always going to create the same object—there can be only one intersection between objects—but the effect will look different depending upon which object you choose as the target and which objects you leave in the drawing.

Figure 17.7 is a composite image of several intersection effects. In all cases, the text was the Target Object. For the image at the top, we asked that the Target Object be left on screen. Then we proceeded to apply a shade to the new object created by the intersection. Again, we have outlined the objects that were actually eliminated.

In the middle image, we designated that the Target Object be removed but not the Other Objects. And in the bottom image, we told all the objects to stick around. By shading the new object at the intersection, we produced the illusion that the ovals are semitransparent, allowing the text to show through, as though filtered.

Extra Credit

Study the bottom, "filtered" example in Figure 17.7 closely, and you might notice that something is not quite right. If the text is supposed to be sitting behind both of these two transparent ovals, how come some parts of the text don't appear filtered? Specifically, the only parts of the text filtered in Figure 17.7 are behind both ovals. In the real world, that wouldn't compute, so we need to change our technique to make this appear more plausible.

We need three intersections—one for each oval where it overlaps the text, and one for the places where both ovals overlap the text. Figure 17.8 shows the progression for accomplishing this. Starting with the original objects (top), we created an intersection between one oval and the text (shown in white for clarity in the second image). Next we made a second intersection using the second oval (third image down). Then we created a third intersection, using both ovals as the Other Objects. This third one is shown in black for clarity in the fourth image down.

17.7

The three faces of Intersect

What happens to objects that overlap?

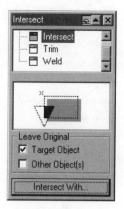

What happens to objects that overlap?

What happens to objects that overlap?

17.8

What looks like transparency is actually several objects stacked on top of one another, each one positioned exactly and in just the right shade.

Original objects

One intersection

Two intersections

Intersection of the intersection

Shading added

Let's imagine that the text really *is* behind two transparent ovals of different shades. The text would be filtered the least (i.e., would appear darkest) when behind the lighter oval; would be more filtered behind the darker oval; and filtered the most when behind both. We applied shades of 60%, 40%, and 20%, respectively, to those three areas, achieving a much more believable impression that the text sits behind two transparent ovals.

We have included the finished effect of Figure 17.7 in the PRACTICE directory as OVERLAP2.CDR.

Cookie Cutters and Cookie Dough

In many ways, Trim is the exact opposite of Intersect. Where Intersect finds an overlap and creates an object in that space, Trim find an overlap and carves a hole of that same size. Intersect adds; Trim removes.

The simplest way to view the Trim operation is to imagine yourself baking cookies of various shapes and sizes. You use cookie cutters to slice into the dough and create the shapes, trimming off the excess and eating it when nobody is looking. (Cathy of cartoon fame says those calories don't count because you weren't actually making cookies from that dough.)

This is exactly how Trim works, and Figure 17.9 illustrates this. The rabbit is the cookie cutter, and in the lower-left image he is pressing his way through the dough. The lower-right image shows the result—a hole cut out from the dough, in the precise shape as the rabbit.

17.9

The best way to think of Trim is to think of cutting a shape out of cookie dough.

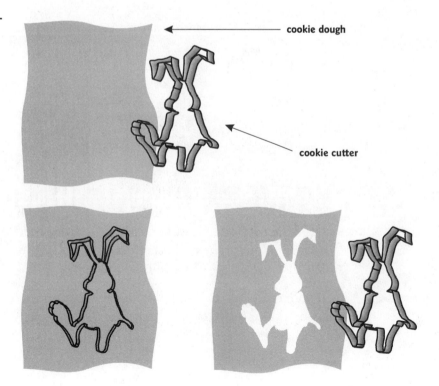

cookie dough

cookie cutter

With Trim, the Target Object is the cookie dough and the Other Object is the cookie cutter. And to continue the analogy, just as you could cut multiple shapes into the dough with different cookie cutters, so, too, could you use more than one object as Other Objects. That said, trimming is nevertheless more easily studied if there is just one object acting as cookie cutter, so the examples in Figure 17.10 show only one oval.

In the middle image, the oval is trimming the text; and in the lower image, the text has trimmed the oval. The only difference to you, the pilot of these controls, is which object you select first and then which object you click on with the big arrow.

17.10

Choosing the target can make a big difference when trimming.

What happens to objects that overlap?   Original objects

What happ~~~   ~~erlap?   Oval as cutter, text as dough

~~ppens to objects that ov~~   Text as cutter, oval as dough

Though it's quite easy for DRAW to carve a smooth path out of the text (as in the first example of Figure 17.10), it's far more difficult to carve each letter out of the oval (as in the second). That operation took over five times as long—11 seconds as opposed to 2.

If you read Chapter 5 and did our Quickies, you will remember how we used Trim to carve the notches out of the key.

Melting Objects Together

The third member of the Shaping Triumverate, Weld, has the most radical results. It finds the areas where objects overlap and obliterates all nodes and paths in that space. It reduces multiple objects to lifeless blobs that have nodes and paths only along the periphery, not the interior. With Weld, like Intersect, it doesn't really matter which object you select first and which one you call the target. The Target Object's only role, once again, is to determine the outline and fill color of the resulting blob.

Figure 17.11 shows the reign of terror that Weld imposes on unsuspecting objects. We selected the two ovals, clicked the Weld To button, and then chose the text. Weld hunted down and eliminated every node and path that was in the interior, leaving only the outline around the periphery. In both the Before and After, we have included a Wireframe version, because there the effects of Weld show up very clearly.

17.11

Weld is to electronic art as the sledge hammer is to a construction site.

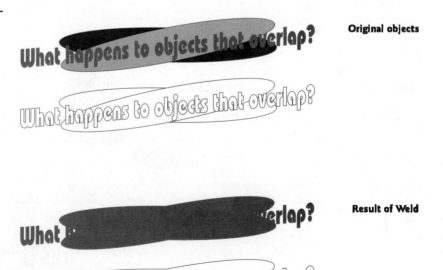

Original objects

Result of Weld

But Is It Art??

We doubt that Figure 17.11 will inspire anyone to use Weld if they don't already appreciate its value; Weld can turn a nice clean rendering into a shapeless mess. But it also simplifies objects by eliminating their interiors, and that can be very helpful in numerous situations. Here are just a few.

The Key Back in Chapter 5, we offered an ideal scenario for using Weld: when an intended shape, like that of the key, is most easily made by fusing together two Other Objects. Without Weld, you would have had to combine the two rectangles and then crawl down into the trenches with the Shape tool in order to break nodes, delete unwanted paths, rejoin paths, and so forth. Not anymore.

Creating Silhouettes If all you want is the form of an image but not the detail, Weld is your ticket. In Figure 17.12 you see how a picture of well-known relief pitcher Dennis Eckersley can be converted into a generic silhouette of an anonymous pitcher.

17.12

Weld maintains an object's form while sacrificing the detail.

Outlining Script Text   If you have occasion to create an outline around a string of fancy text, you might be frustrated to discover that many script typefaces don't truly connect their characters—understandable, given that they must be able to appear integrated with any other character in that face. This goes unnoticed with black text, but becomes quite annoying with text that has an outline color different from its fill.

Figure 17.13 illustrates this dilemma. In its unaltered state (top), characters set in Corel's Brody typeface (among many others) overlap where they connect, essentially prohibiting the setting of this text with an outline other than the text's fill color. But the bottom image has been welded. (You can weld a compound image, such as text, to itself by selecting it initially and then choosing it again for the Target Object). Notice how the overlaps are now clean.

17.13

Many script faces need to be Welded before they can be outlined.

Preparing for Sign Making   Printing your work on a laser printer is one thing; printing on a large sign-making device is quite another. If you print one object on top of another to your laser printer, you don't really care that both objects print, because one completely covers the other. On the other hand, when a vinyl cutter begins rendering an image, it will cut every location where it encounters a line. It can't go back and hide or uncut. So in the case of the script typeface, the cutter would render it quite poorly unless you modified the text first.

Weld has proven to be a great gift to DRAW users who send their work to vinyl cutters. Previously they had to manually remove all unwanted lines in the interior of an object. Now Weld does that automatically.

The Automated Option

The controls for the three Shaping tools worked quite differently in version 5, and we strongly suspect that experienced users will prefer the old way. Previously, you selected the first object, Shift+selected the target, and then simply went to Arrange and chose the desired command from the menu. You had already defined all objects as targets or "others," so all you had to do was say "Go Do It." This proves to be more productive for experienced users who don't need to be led step-by-step through the process.

The one possible exception is Trim, where users frequently want at least one of the original objects discarded, and that service is offered by DRAW 6.0's roll-up. But if you count yourself among the group that prefer the good old days, you can program DRAW to behave that way by following the discussion about it in Chapter 15.

♣

These are the tools that we consider the appetizers to DRAW's special effects course. In the next five chapters, we visit the Effects menu, where dining in earnest begins.

18

A Matter of Perspective

EIGHTEEN

18

This chapter looks at two effects that you have already flirted with in several chapters of this book—Perspective and Envelope. Each of them offers, in its own way, a different method of looking at an object or group of objects. When you created the cube in Chapter 5, you used Perspective to make the sides of the cube appear to be facing in different directions. To create the reflections on the water in Chapter 6, you used Envelope to distort the basic shape of the skyline and the sun.

Adding Perspective

The Add Perspective tool represents a transition between the simpler transformations described in Chapter 17, and the more complex effects coming up in subsequent chapters. Unlike blends and extrusions, which actually add new elements to your drawings, perspective is essentially a distortion of existing objects—similar to the Rotation, Skew, and Scale & Mirror functions of Transform. The difference is that Perspective is designed specifically to create a sense of depth or dimension relative to a particular viewpoint. This you cannot do with just the Transform tools.

To add a perspective, first select an object or group with the Pick tool. Then go to Effects / Add Perspective. At first it will look as though you have merely begun a node-editing session. In fact, the Shape tool becomes highlighted and you will see what appear to be nodes at the four corners of your selected object(s). These are actually the handles that you will drag to create the perspective effect.

Adding perspective to a drawing is quite easy. Follow these steps and see for yourself:

1. In a new drawing, create one straight vertical line, by using the Pencil tool and holding Ctrl while you draw. (You'll be using

Ctrl a lot in these steps, by the way.) Set the outline width to 2 or 3 points.

2. Drag and dupe a copy of the line just to the right of the original, holding Ctrl while dragging to make sure that the copy doesn't wander up or down.

3. Press Ctrl+R to make a third line.

4. Select the middle line, go to Outline Pen, and choose a dotted line as the style.

5. Select all three lines and group them with Ctrl+G.

6. Go to Effects / Add Perspective, hold Ctrl, and send the bottom-right handle way off to the right. Your screen should look like Figure 18.1.

Repeat the steps above, but at Step 6, drag the bottom-left handle off to the left and note the change. Then drag both bottom handles to the outside. Try it again, without holding Ctrl; try dragging the top handles, also. Try moving the "vanishing point"—the on-screen × that we'll explain shortly. Try everything.

WATCH OUT!

You cannot select several objects at once and apply a perspective to them. They must be grouped first.

One-Point Perspective

Our simple freeway in Figure 18.1 is an example of *one-point perspective*. One-point perspective gives the impression that the object is receding from view in a single direction. You create one-point perspective when you drag the perspective handles vertically *or* horizontally, but not both. In creating the freeway, we dragged all handles horizontally.

18.1

Thanks to Effects /
Add Perspective,
you are no longer
walking down the
middle of the road;
you are walking
along the left side.

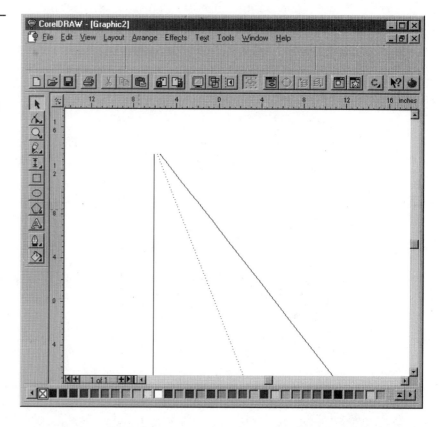

Not visible in Figure 18.1 is the hypothetical *vanishing point* that appears as an × on your screen while you are editing a perspective. Because this point represents the theoretical spot toward which the object is receding, it is normally very far away from the actual object. To see it, you might have to zoom out with F3 several times. Once it is visible, you will see the vanishing point move as you drag the handles. You can also move the vanishing point itself, as an alternative to moving the handles.

INSIDE INFO

To ensure that your drawings are constrained to one-point perspective, remember to use the Ctrl key. If you also hold Shift, the opposite handle will symmetrically mirror the movement of the handle you are dragging.

Two-Point Perspective

Remember that one-point perspective is maintained only if all handle-dragging is confined to either horizontal or vertical movements. You will still have a one-point perspective even if you move all four handles, *if they have all been moved along the same axis.* Two-point perspective involves motion along two planes, so objects appear to be receding in two directions at once. You can achieve this by dragging one handle up or down and another handle left or right, or by dragging one handle in a diagonal direction. Dragging toward the center of the object pushes the object into the screen, and dragging away from the center pulls the object toward you.

WATCH OUT!

Before you apply any perspectives, make sure your object is already shaped the way you want it. Once you apply a perspective to an object, you can't shape its nodes.

Imagine that you are playing a flight simulator game and you are a pilot coming in for a landing. Figure 18.2, with no perspective added, shows the view from straight overhead. When you miss your landing by this much, you'd better announce that you were doing a fly-by to survey the landing strip. Notice that the lines in the runway are evenly sized and spaced—there is no distortion in these objects.

18.2

This is the view from the Goodyear Blimp looking down at a plane hovering over the landing field.

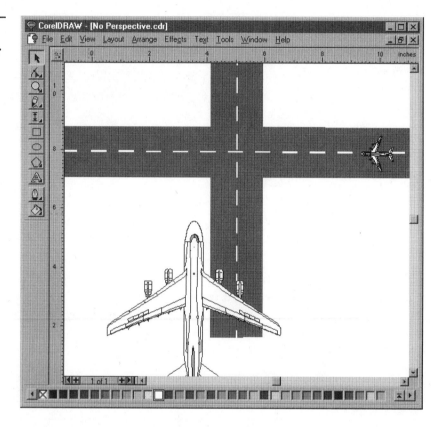

In Figure 18.3, we add one-point perspective: We group the landing strips and the small airplane on the ground, squeeze together the far handles, and spread out the near handles. Now our piloting skills are better represented. And from this perspective, it appears more likely that we will land our plane on the strip. Note how the lines on the runway, the runway itself, and even your own airplane all recede away.

In the side view in Figure 18.4, we're nailing this landing. This perspective was created by dragging the top-right handle in toward the middle, producing two-point perspective. Now, in addition to the original vanishing point off the top of the screen, there is a second vanishing point off to the right.

18.3

With one-point per-
spective added, this
view suggests a
more successful
landing.

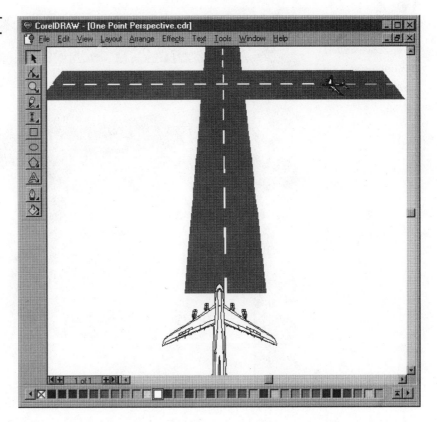

To drive home the difference between one- and two-point perspective,
imagine that you are working a camera on a movie set, on one of those
fancy cranes that allow you to move in all directions. If you swing
around the set in either purely horizontal or purely vertical motions,
your film will have a one-point perspective. But if you swing around
wildly, in all directions at once, you'll get a two-point perspective (along
with a queasy stomach).

18.4

With two-point perspective added, this becomes a side view.

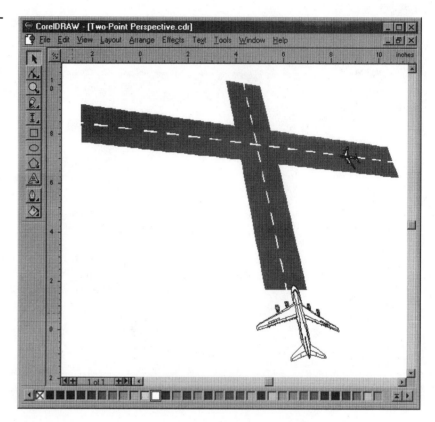

WATCH OUT!

Perspective can be a useful effect, but it has one important limitation: Applying perspective does not scale object outlines, even if you enable Scale With Image in the Outline Pen dialog. If you use a thick outline as a border on an object, don't expect it to scale realistically when you add perspective. Neither do pattern fills scale according to the perspective.

Copying Perspectives

Since version 2, DRAW has offered automatic copying of one object's perspective to another. Also since version 2, we have been searching for legitimate uses of this feature.

Copying a perspective sounds like a valuable operation, and you might expect that you could use it to create nice three-dimensional scenes. However, this command simply copies the same relative distortion from one object to another. It's quite unlike using true perspective lines in an original rendering, or the shared vanishing point that Extrude offers.

If you are trying to achieve depth and a sense of perspective for an entire scene, you will likely have to apply perspectives individually to objects, or reach for a different tool, as we have done with Figure 18.5. When we added perspective to the street, we figured it might be a simple matter to copy the same perspective to the street sign. No such luck—we destroyed the poor sign. But we spent about five seconds with the on-screen skewing controls and had much better luck.

INSIDE INFO

If you decide to apply perspective individually to various objects, you will probably want objects in the same plane to have the same vanishing point. You can achieve this by making note of the vanishing point coordinates shown on the status bar when you are editing a perspective. To re-edit an existing perspective, click on the object with the Shape tool.

Our Perspective on Perspectives

We have two final thoughts on perspectives. First, though it is possible to add perspective to a group or an object that already has a perspective, this isn't necessarily a good idea. You might end up creating a nice effect, but you lose control over it, because each perspective introduces a

18.5

Perhaps Copy Perspective should be renamed to Copy and Mangle...

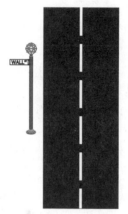

Original objects

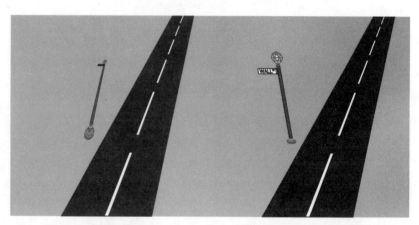

Hilarious: Perspective of road copied to street sign

Plausible: Street sign shifted with on-screen skewing

distortion on top of the previous distortion. So if your intention is to add a totally different perspective to an object, you're better off using Effects / Clear Perspective to clear the existing perspective and then adding a brand-new one. When your object has several perspectives on top of one another, Clear Perspective will clear them one by one, in the reverse order that you applied them.

The second thought is this: Add Perspective is good for applying simple visual effects to objects; don't expect more from it than it can deliver. When professional artists turn to DRAW to produce realistic work, they *don't* call on Add Perspective. A good case in point is the award-winner in Figure 18.6, authored by Antonio De Leo of Rome, Italy. This piece is dripping with realistic perspective, and you can bet that Antonio did not use the Add Perspective command to create it. Instead, he determined his own horizons in three-dimensional space, created his own vanishing points, and forced all of the components to conform to them. In fact, as Figure 18.7 shows, he probably spent more time creating his guidelines than most of us spend on an entire drawing.

18.6

This award-winning illustration by Antonio De Leo is a good example of an artist creating true perspective in a drawing.

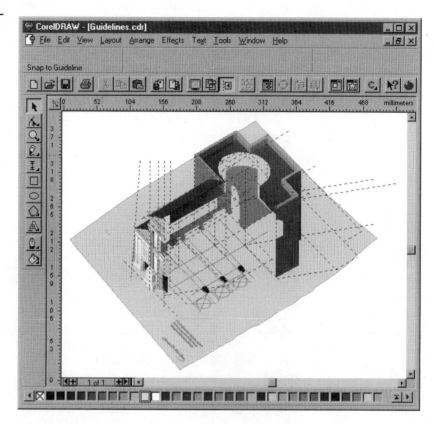

We simplified De Leo's drawing somewhat to show it here in black and white, but the full version—all 6MB of it—can be found in the Color Gallery, as well as in GALLRY05.CDR in the GALLERY directory of the Companion CD. We suggest that you open it just before heading out for lunch; it might be finished drawing by the time you return...

The Envelope, Please

Although DRAW's Envelope command is similar to Perspective, we think it is much more interesting and versatile. Like Perspective, Envelope reshapes objects without actually adding new elements to your drawing. When you apply an envelope to an object, the object becomes elastic. You can stretch it out so that it fills the perimeter of the envelope.

Envelopes can be applied to any object or group—even to open curves and text. Shaping text is probably one of the most common applications of envelopes, and you observed in Chapter 12 how both artistic and paragraph text can be enveloped, with strikingly different results.

Creating an Envelope

As with most of DRAW's tools, learning the mechanics of enveloping is not difficult; mastery of the tool is. Figure 18.8 shows the battlefield we

18.8

Can these simple objects show you everything there is to know about the Envelope tool? Stick around.

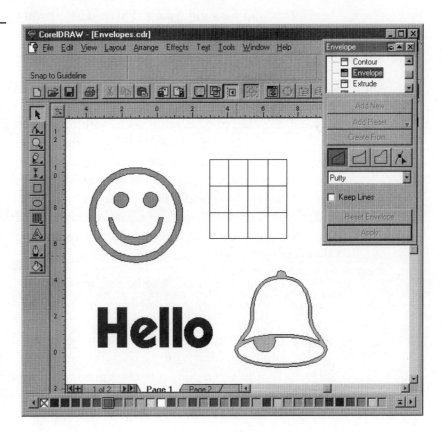

have built for exploring envelopes in this chapter. The first thing you must do to apply an envelope is select the object you want to envelope, or a group of objects (you can envelope multiple objects as long as they're grouped or combined). Then go to Effects / Envelope (or press Ctrl+F7) to invoke the roll-up shown in Figure 18.8.

Your creative options with Envelope are virtually unlimited, but your choice of controls is well defined. The four icons across the middle of the roll-up represent the envelope-editing modes. Just below the modes, the drop-down box and the Keep Lines check box both serve to further define the enveloping effect. Most users don't change the latter two controls very often, but the four modes get a lot of action. The first three—Straight Line, Single Arc, and Two Curves—allow you to change the shape of one side of an object or group. The fourth icon is a Shape tool look-alike, and for good reason: This mode lets you work an envelope as if it were a curve, shaping and adding nodes at will.

Enveloping Fundamentals

After you select a mode, click Add New to place an envelope outline around the selected object or group. Nothing has actually happened yet to the object; not even when you begin tugging and pulling on any of the eight nodes that appear around the object does anything happen. Not until you click Apply will the selected object conform to the envelope. This gives you plenty of opportunity to make numerous adjustments to the envelope, using the handles, before actually applying it to the object. You can even bail out and start over completely by clicking on Reset Envelope.

That is all you need to know to begin experimenting with Envelope. Each time you click Apply, any shifting of handles that you did takes effect. To return and re-edit an enveloped shape, select the object and activate the Shape tool. You will then be editing the envelope, instead of node-editing the object. And, as with Perspective, this is an additive procedure. That is, when you return to a previously enveloped shape, you will be applying another envelope, not replacing the one already in effect.

The Four Modes

Figure 18.9 shows the different effects of the first three enveloping modes. The original object, a grid of boxes, is shown at the top of the figure. In all cases, we took a very simple action: We took the right-middle node and we extended it to the right.

The fourth mode is so flexible that you could re-create any of these three shapes, or many others.

It will be helpful for you to think of the first three modes as "constrained" in some ways, and the fourth as completely unconstrained.

When you're shaping an envelope in the Straight Line, Single Arc, or Two Curves modes, you move the center handles either directly toward or away from the object's center. (These handles will not move laterally.) Corner handles can be moved either vertically or horizontally, and here it gets weird. You *can* move these handles diagonally; just not all at once. First you must move them up or down, then release the mouse, and then start dragging again, this time side to side.

The unconstrained mode, the rightmost icon of the group of four, provides the greatest versatility to envelopes. It allows you to shape the envelope using all the same techniques you would use to shape or node-edit objects. With this mode, you are quite literally node-editing an envelope; you can select and move several nodes at once, adjust control points to change the curvature of the nodes, and change the node type to be line or curve, cusp, smooth, or symmetric.

Keep in mind, though, the difference between shaping an envelope and directly shaping an object. In Figure 18.10, you can see the three steps that constitute node editing and envelope editing, respectively. The motions are the same—select a handle, drag the handle, and release—but the effect is considerably different. With node editing, you change one node; end of story. With envelope editing, you change the shape of the container that houses the object, which in turn changes the shape of the entire object.

18.9

The different effects of the three "constrained" modes

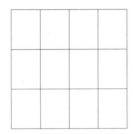

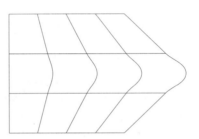

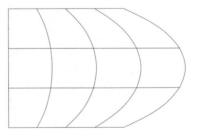

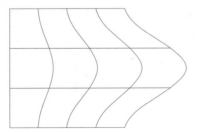

18.10

Node editing and envelope editing are two very different operations.

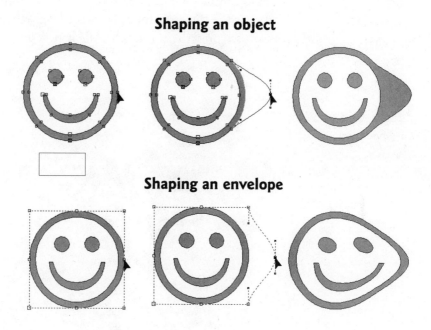

All About Mapping Options

Envelope mapping is one of the most arcane operations done in DRAW, and this is what you'll find in the way of explanation of it in the CorelDRAW User's Manual:

"   ."

We wouldn't be surprised if the reason for this glaring omission is that nobody at Corel truly understands envelope mapping; we don't either.

In rough terms, the mapping options control the way a selected object is shaped to fit into the envelope. There, don't you feel better? Figure 18.11 shows you what we and Corel can't really explain. In the top image, the Putty map stretches the objects uniformly, as if they were made of putty and you grabbed them and yanked them up and over to the right. In the middle image, the Vertical map, the objects appear to be folded down one side, right at the point where the right-side handles were originally located. And in the

Horizontal map (the coolest one, in our humble opinion), the objects are folded over the top—again, right at the original position of the handles. You can see how the top-left handle is functioning as an anchor for the shape.

18.11

Envelope mapping in action

Putty

Vertical

Horizontal

There is a fourth, seldom-used, mapping option, called Original. It maps the corner handles of the bounding box of the selected object or group to the bounding box of the envelope, so that...oh, never mind.

Just follow these rules of thumb and forget about all of the gibberish:

- If an object doesn't conform well to an envelope you are trying to apply, you will usually need to clear the envelope, strategically place some handles that can act as hinges, and try again.

- For artistic text, vertical mapping usually produces a result that is more readable and less distracting.

- If you plan to envelope multiple lines of text, create them as separate strings with an envelope applied to each, rather than a single envelope applied to one multiple-line string.

Keeping Lines as Lines

When you envelope an object, you are asking an otherwise orderly shape to radically distort itself to fit into another shape. Usually, this involves some intense curvatures of the original elements. You can disallow this, however. DRAW offers (we can't resist) a "line-item veto" for enveloping shapes. When you check the Keep Lines option, you tell DRAW to go ahead and distort any shape that is a curve, but keep as a line any part of an object that is a straight line.

Figure 18.12 illustrates this quite vividly with the letters in *Hello* that have straight lines. In the top image, all of the characters are flopping around inside of this crazy envelope. The bottom envelope is just as crazy, but the *H*, the two *L*s, and parts of the *e* are maintained as straight lines, producing a more jagged look.

If you're looking for a study in futility, try this: Create a rectangle, open the Envelope roll-up, enable Keep Lines, and then drag one of the center handles...well, anywhere you want to. You will get no result, because you're actually issuing two conflicting commands—one that says "try to bend this rectangle," and another that says "okay, fine, but don't bend any of the straight lines."

18.12

Lines will be lines...as long as you say so in the Envelope roll-up.

INSIDE INFO

If you convert to curves an object that already has an envelope, its shape is retained, but the Shape tool reverts to normal node-editing, as if an envelope had never been applied.

Automatic Envelopes

DRAW offers four ways to automate the creation of envelopes, including copying and cloning other shapes. In many cases, the easiest way to create an envelope is to go the prefab route.

Add Preset   Like so many other parts of DRAW, the Envelope tool includes several ready-made shapes for your enveloping pleasure. To use one of them, select an object, click on Add Preset, and choose the shape from the drop-down list. Your selected object will instantly inherit that shape as its envelope; then you can set it into effect with Apply, or manually edit it before applying it. Figure 18.13 shows a perfectly fine string of text getting manhandled by a preset.

18.13

Quick-and-dirty envelopes from Add Preset

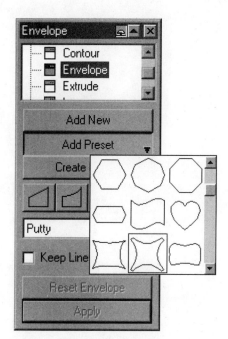

Create From   If you're looking for a particular envelope shape, you don't need to confine yourself to the shapes in the Add Preset list. The Create From button allows you to use any existing shape as the basis for creating an envelope. In Figure 18.14, we have used the inside of a bell to shape a string of text. Then we enlisted the Align & Distribute roll-up to place the enveloped text inside the bell. This took all of three minutes.

18.14

The Create From button is the fastest way to create envelopes.

1. Selecting This...

2. And clicking here...

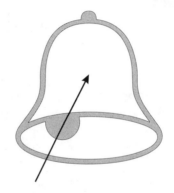

3. And then on this...

4. Creates this...

5. Which then makes this.

WATCH OUT!

> The object you select as the model for an envelope must be a single shape. It cannot be part of a group or a combined object. If, for example, you want to use a compound letter (such as a *B*) as an envelope, you must convert it to curves, break it apart, and select the object that represents the perimeter of the letter. That can serve as the model for your envelope.

Copying Envelopes   If you have an existing envelope and you want to use that envelope for another object, you can simply copy it by choosing Effects / Copy / Envelope From and then clicking on the enveloped object. Note the difference between this and Create From: Create From creates an envelope from an unenveloped object; Copy Envelope duplicates an existing envelope.

Keyboard Constraints   As you would expect, Ctrl and Shift provide several quick ways to constrain envelopes. Ctrl forces equivalent action on the side opposite to the one you are shaping; Shift forces symmetrical action; and the two together make all sides act in concert. Figure 18.15 illustrates this.

Envelopes and Paragraph Text

We'll send you back to Chapter 12 for a complete discussion and tutorial on applying envelopes to paragraph text. If you have already worked through that section, the discussion here is meant to drive the point home: Enveloping paragraph text works the same as enveloping artistic text or any other object. But you are not actually modifying the letterforms; you are modifying the frame in which the text flows.

When you select a frame of paragraph text, the mapping option in the Envelope roll-up automatically changes to Text, the only mapping option available. You can use any of the techniques already described (the three standard envelope modes; the "unconstrained" mode; Add Preset; and Create From). However, you can't apply more than one envelope to paragraph

18.15

The various effects
of Ctrl and Shift on
envelopes

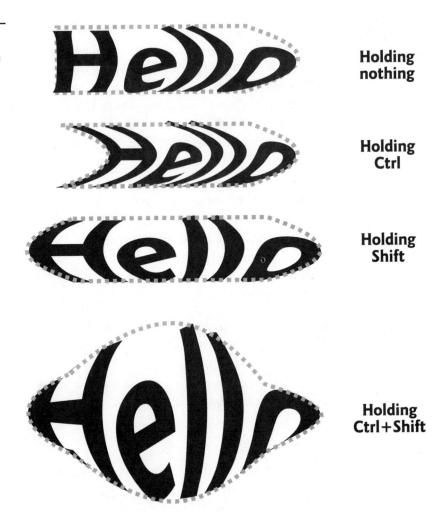

**Holding
nothing**

**Holding
Ctrl**

**Holding
Shift**

**Holding
Ctrl+Shift**

text as you can to other objects. If you apply a new envelope, it replaces the old one, rather than compounding the effect of the first envelope.

♣

The next chapter features two summary icon commands, Blend and Contour, that do more than merely warp and twist selected objects. Each adds different elements to your artwork, to enhance its appearance.

Metamorphosis

In the movie industry, one of the hot new special effects is *morphing*, thanks largely to modern computing and Arnold Schwartzenegger films. To morph means to change from one shape to another. CorelDRAW has its own set of tools for metamorphoses, and though they might not be quite worthy of Arnold and the Big Screen, they can produce stunning effects on your computer display. This chapter focuses on two of DRAW's tools—Blend and Contour—that take one object and turn it into many objects.

Blending Objects

Blending is suspiciously easy to both explain and visualize. You take a vector element, be it a single object or a group of objects. Then you take another element. Then you tell DRAW to go from one to the other. Then you tell DRAW how quickly it should make this transformation. Then you click Apply. Okay, our next topic is...

Well, perhaps it's not quite *that* simple, but like so many of DRAW's tools, the mechanics of blending are easily understood. And unlike some of the other effects, there are very few restrictions imposed on blending. You can blend between nearly any two objects, including grouped objects and complex curves (text being a good example). The only objects that cannot be blended are paragraph text, extrusions, contour groups, pattern fills, and of course, imported bitmap images.

A blend starts with two *control objects,* which DRAW refers to as the *start* and *end objects.* When you ask DRAW to create a blend between the two control objects, it produces a series of intermediate objects, or *steps,* that represent the transformation from the start object to the end object.

The transformation involves every component of the two control objects—their shape, fill, and outline—as each of these components is modified by a certain percentage in each step of the blend. If you ask for a few steps, the amount of change within each step is significant. With more steps, the amount of change is smaller, usually resulting in a smoother, less obvious transition (and a more complex drawing).

For the simplest of all blends, as shown in Figure 19.1, do this:

1. Create a rectangle at the top of the page, choose a light fill or shade, and remove the outline.

2. Use drag-and-dupe to create a copy of the rectangle at the bottom of the page. Color it dark.

3. Select both rectangles. Then go to Effects / Blend or use Ctrl+B. (Gasp! A hotkey that makes mnemonic sense!)

4. Set the Steps to 5 and click Apply.

The Anatomy of a Blend

If you followed the four steps above, your status bar should now read "Blend Group on Layer 1." This is obviously a group of objects, but not in the conventional sense (as if you had selected them and pressed Ctrl+G). The two control objects remain semi-independent from the blend group.

We say "semi-independent" because you can move the blend group as one, size it, rotate it, skew it, copy it, and so on, and the entire group adjusts. But you can also select the control objects and change them. Press Tab repeatedly and you'll see that you can bounce between the two control rectangles, and the status bar will verify that. Move one of the controls, and the blend adjusts. Refill it, rotate it, skew it, resize it...in all cases, the blend adjusts dynamically.

Sometimes it's difficult to pick out and select the control objects or the overall group. If you can click on an intermediate object, you can select the blend. Often, however, the objects are so close together (or even

19.1

The simplest of all blends: from a light rectangle to a dark one

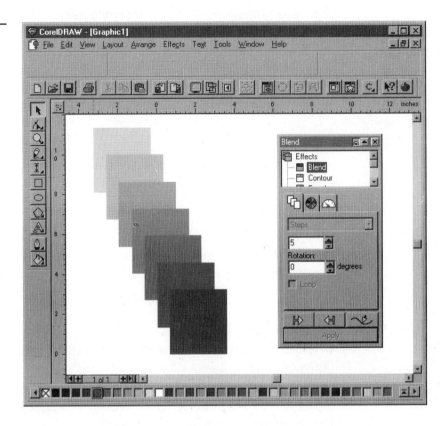

overlapping completely) that this is impossible. Here is a two-step process that will always work for selecting groups or control objects:

- To select the blend group, draw a marquee around the entire group.

- From there, press Shift+Tab and Tab to alternate between the controls.

A blend stays alive until you kill it, and you do that with the Arrange / Separate command. Once separated, a blend becomes three separate objects—the two controls and a group of objects that make up the intermediate steps. You can go on to ungroup the intermediate steps, but either way, these objects are now just a collection of no-longer-related elements.

Blending can be performed between two objects that are quite dissimilar. For example, an object with no outline and a fountain fill can be blended with an object that has an outline and a uniform fill. But beware—there are almost no limits to the types of objects that can be blended, and you can create hideous mutations if you're not careful.

Figure 19.2 shows several different blends, including a few techniques yet to be discussed. The first six are all relatively credible efforts: the letter that mirrors itself, the happy-to-sad face, the neon circle turning into a square, the double-blended squiggle, the polygon shuffle, and the square that inherits three extra sides. Then there is the mutant: the skeleton morphed into a bomb.

Regardless of your opinion of the first five, they all share the same correct strategy; that is, they are blends between objects that have the same number of nodes. The last two morphs violate this principle, however. In the weird square-to-polygon transformation, DRAW gets a bit confused in the middle trying to give the objects extra sides en route to becoming a heptagon. But because these shapes are not too dissimilar, the effect isn't too bad. The last one, however, speaks for itself. The disfigurement of the skull and crossbones is the result of DRAW not knowing what to do with nodes that have no counterpart on the other side of the blend. There is probably some formula that determines where those soon-to-be-orphaned nodes are placed, but you can be sure it has nothing to do with art.

Blending is possibly the single most important tool in DRAW's arsenal for creating realistic effects. It is no coincidence that, year after year, the award-winning illustrations that garner the most attention make constant use of blended objects. We'll show you some before this chapter is out.

The Blend Roll-Up

Your most valuable knowledge of blending will come from experimentation, but in the interest of our keeping our jobs, following is a tour of

19.2

The first five blends share "node agreement," but the last two do not.

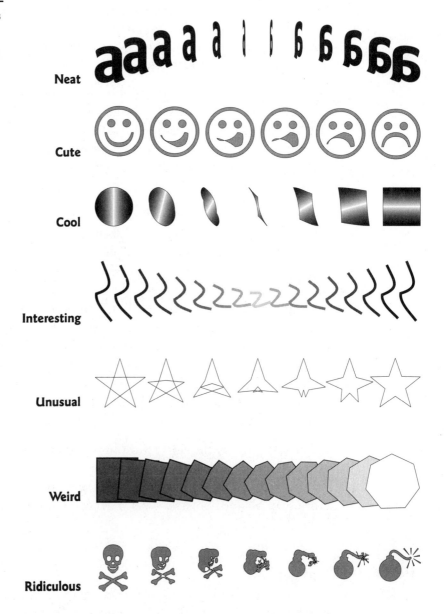

Neat

Cute

Cool

Interesting

Unusual

Weird

Ridiculous

the controls in the roll-up. It has three pages, identified by the three buttons across the top. The button with the tiled rectangles selects the default mode, which controls the geometry or layout of a blend, letting you specify steps, spacing, and rotations. The next button, the color wheel, opens options for applying color to intermediate steps in a blend. The little speedometer button contains a potpourri of controls to modify standard blends. The four buttons at the bottom, described later, are always visible, regardless of what mode is active.

Controlling the Controls

The first page of the Blend roll-up provides tools for manipulating the control objects. The most commonly used tool is the one for choosing the number of steps in the blend, and the other options on this page can produce striking effects when used appropriately. Here they are:

Rotation   Set to 0° by default, the value in this box determines the degree of rotation applied to the intermediate steps of the blend. In Figure 19.3, the top image is a standard, seven-step blend. The middle image includes a 35° rotation. Notice that the intermediate rectangles begin a counterclockwise turn, with the last one reaching the designated 35°. For clockwise rotations, enter a negative value.

The Loop check box becomes available when a Rotation value is entered. This option forces the rotation to be applied not to the objects along the blend path, but rather to the path itself. The third image in Figure 19.3 shows this quite clearly. Here the intermediate rectangles are all upright, but the path they follow to reach the other side is curved along a 35° path. Again, if the value were set to −35°, the loop would be up instead of down.

Incidentally, notice in Figure 19.3 that the fill patterns are blending from light to dark (moving left to right), while the outlines are blending from dark to light.

Starting Points   Usually, when you create a blend you know what to use as the two control objects. If you change your mind and want to use

a different object to start or end, you can substitute either one using the two arrows above the Apply button. The right-pointing arrow is for designating a new start object; the left-pointing one is for a new end object. Click on the arrow, choose New Start from the pop-up menu, and then click on the object that you want as your new start object. These arrow buttons can also be used to show you the current start and end objects.

WATCH OUT!

> DRAW has strict rules about substituting start and end objects. The replacement start object must be in front of the existing one, and the new end object must be behind your current one. If DRAW complains about your choice, you can get around it simply by reordering your objects—sending the object to front or to back as required. We wish, however, that DRAW would do this for us.

New Paths   The coolest of all the controls, New Path (the button with the curved line), lets you set your blend to a path, the same way that Fit Text To Path works on artistic text. The only extra ingredient needed for a pathed blend is a third object, the one that determines the new path. Once you have designated your control objects, click on the New Path button, choose New Path, and click on the object on screen. When you Apply this, the blend will follow the contour of the path. This next exercise takes you through the options and the nuances of this nice tool.

1. In a new drawing, create a circle; hold Ctrl while dragging to keep it perfect.

2. Fill this circle with the Satellite Photography texture fill.

3. Open the Symbols roll-up, and choose the first item in Animals1, a man. Color and size him to your taste. (But don't size him to proportion, please, or you'll have a small problem of scale vis-à-vis the planet Earth.)

4. Make a copy of the man and place him anywhere. Your screen should look like Figure 19.4.

5. Select the two men, click the New Path button, choose New Path from the flyout, and click once on the Earth.

19.4

For this blend, the two men are the control objects and the Earth will be the path.

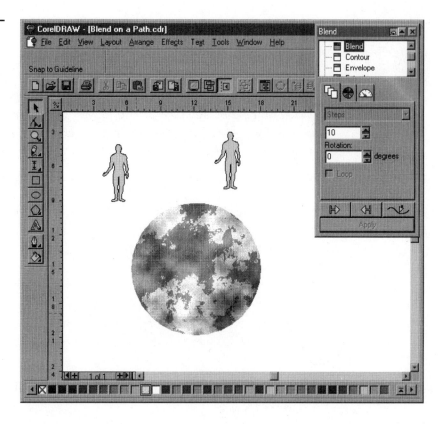

6. Set Steps to 10 and click Apply. Your screen should look like Figure 19.5.

If you're like most who use or study this tool for the first time, this is not the effect you had expected. Nonetheless, the command performed exactly according to your direction: It sent the men along the new path, setting them *the same distance apart as they originally were.* The two control objects were close together before they were blended, and so the 12 men are also bunched together. You can select either control man and move him around the path to space them all out—try that now before you move on.

19.5

These 12 men (2 control men and 10 intermediate ones) are making their way around this new path.

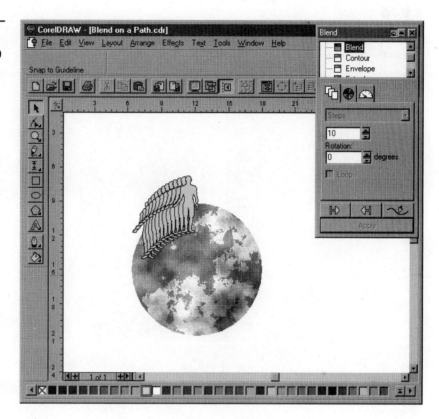

There is a more automatic way to space these men out, and we'll do that now:

7. With the blend group selected (status bar says "Blend on a Path Group on Layer 1"), click on Full Path. Apply that, and the men should be placed evenly around the Earth, as in Figure 19.6.

8. Click on Rotate All, and your 12 men will all be pointing out from the center, as in Figure 19.7. (You might need to manually rotate the control men a bit to get the proper angle. Experiment for yourself.)

19.6

Using the Full Path option for blending to a path

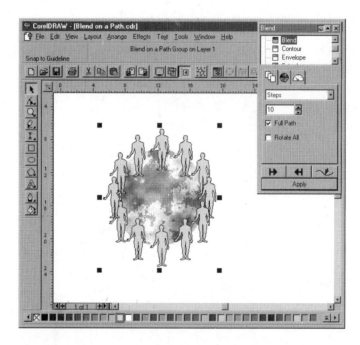

19.7

Using the Rotate All option

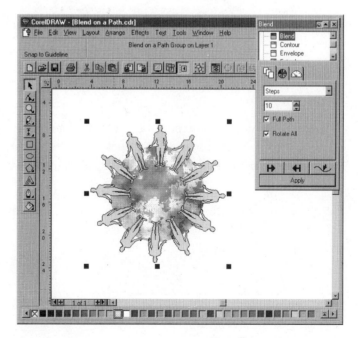

It's possible that you're still not seeing the effect you first visualized, and you could make a good case for enhancing this image if the men were actually standing with their feet on the surface of the Earth, not halfway inside. When DRAW rotates objects along a path, it uses as its anchor the center of rotation assigned to every vector object (by default, the center of the object). You can change this with the rotation pin that emerges when you click a second time on an object. Try this:

9. Press Tab until one of your control men is selected. Click a second time to display the on-screen rotation controls.

10. Move the rotation pin from the center of his body down below his two feet.

11. Repeat for the second control man. Now your screen should look like Figure 19.8.

19.8

Now your men are on top of the world.

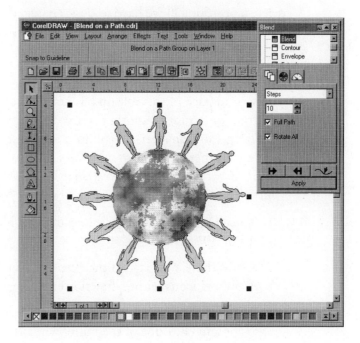

Only when you blend to a path does the drop-down box at the top of the Steps page become active. The other choice in this box, besides Steps, is Spacing. It allows you to adjust a blend along a path by determining the space in between each object rather than the total number of steps. We don't much like its operation, however. First off, to use Spacing you must turn off Full Path; otherwise, DRAW doesn't know which control to listen to. Second, the Spacing option tends to leave at least one object out of alignment. If you have better luck with this, please let us know.

Pathed Blends: Not Just for Artists   Most DRAW users wouldn't think of reaching for the blend-to-path technique for such pedestrian projects as an organization chart, yet Figure 19.9 was created in about 10 minutes, using a total of 15 steps. We created the drop shadows as clones of the foreground boxes, so they move when and where the others do. All of the boxes are tied to the lines. Not only is this org chart quick to create, but it is even quicker to modify. If we need to add or delete a position, all we have to do is change the Steps value for that blend, and the cloned drop shadow will follow suit.

Spinning Colors

The second page in this roll-up has just one job: determining the transition from one color to another across a blend. Just as in the Fountain Fill dialog, you can steer a blend into the most direct route from one color to another, or you can take the scenic route. If we were to try to show this without color, all we'd offer is mud, but you can see it for yourself very easily, as follows:

1. Create two squares, one yellow and one blue, and blend them in 15 or 20 steps.

2. Go to the Color page of the Blend roll-up, click on one of the Rainbow icons (either direction) and Apply.

3. For the widest color transition, set both controls to the same color and click one of the rainbow icons.

19.9

This org chart uses
the blend-to-path
technique for the ul-
timate in flexibility.

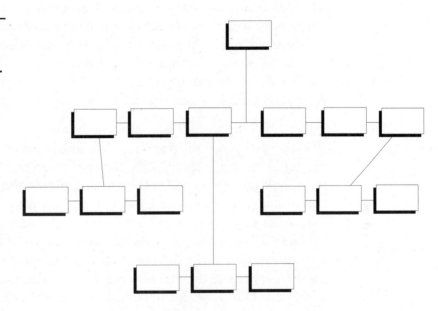

This page of controls is so brief because you make most of your color and fill designations directly to the control objects, using your on-screen tools. You set the fill or shade of the control objects yourself, and then DRAW creates the intermediate objects automatically. It only needs to know how leisurely you want it to switch from one color to the next.

Mapping Blends

In contrast to the Color page, the Mapping controls are far from elementary. There is nothing simple about DRAW's controls for breaking apart, reorganizing, and putting back together the elements of a blend. This page does a lot, and we'll start at the top.

Mapping Nodes   As it moves through a blend, DRAW "anticipates" which nodes it will transform into which. DRAW's standard operating procedure is to look for the first node of the start object (the one created first) and "map" it to the first node of the end object. (This is why objects that have unequal numbers of nodes don't make for good blending partners.)

The Map Nodes tool lets you deviate from DRAW's "plan," and over the years we have seen wonderful as well as awful results from this. Using the tool is easy: When you click on Map Nodes, all of the start object's nodes become visible and your cursor becomes a large arrow. Click on a node, and the end object lights up. Click on one of its nodes, then Apply, and DRAW recalculates the blend.

Figure 19.10 shows this node-mapping dynamic with simple objects. (We have designated the mappings with small squares on the mapped nodes.) In the top image, DRAW blends these rectangles according to the default plan—first node of one to first node of the other. In the middle image, we instructed DRAW to map the top-left node of the start object to the bottom-left node of the end object. Follow the top-left node, and you'll see that it gradually tumbles over to become the bottom-left node of the end object. The lower image is more curious; the top-left node of the start is mapped to the diagonally opposite node of the end. This causes the intermediate objects to collapse onto themselves as the blend essentially turns itself inside out.

19.10

Mapping nodes can make significant changes in your blends.

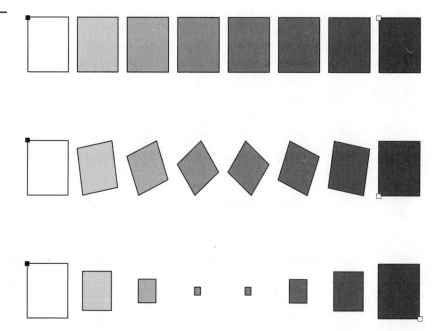

Splitting Blends   Split lets you create a fork in the road. With a blend selected, click on Split; and then click on one of the intermediate steps with the curly arrow. DRAW automatically splits the blend into two blends, turning the object you selected into an additional control object. Figure 19.11 shows this in action.

19.11

The Split tool creates a third control object across a single blend group.

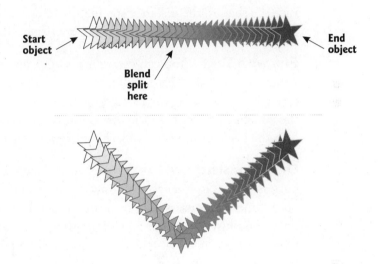

Start object

Blend split here

End object

Fusing Blends   Once you split a blend, you can fuse it back together by holding Ctrl, choosing a spot along the blend, and then clicking Fuse Start or Fuse End. We have yet to see any user or any .CDR file make use of this, so we won't bother you with it.

Blend Miscellany

Here are some random thoughts about blends.

Be Smart with Steps   The higher you set the Steps value, the smoother your blend will be...and the longer it will take to draw on screen. We recommend that you keep Steps to a minimum (under 20) as you are creating your drawing. When you are done and ready to make your final print or export, then increase it to the desired amount.

And what is that desired amount? That depends upon the range of colors, the distance spanned by the blend, and the final output device you have chosen. A 300-dpi laser printer can print relatively few shades of gray, so a blend of 100 steps would be a waste of time, except for admiring it on screen. Yet, when making film from a high-resolution imagesetter, you might need well over 100 steps—maybe over 200. If you can afford $15 or so for a piece of film, create several blends in which you vary the shades, the distance spanned, and the Steps. Create a print file, and see what you get back from your service bureau.

Fun with Text   You can create many nice text effects by blending strings of text with varying fill patterns, outline weights, and outline colors. We produced Figure 19.12 by just playing around a bit, without the benefit of a script. In the descriptions for each one, the start object is in the back and the end object is in front.

Drag Consistently   To ensure consistency—especially for blending purposes—get in the habit of drawing shapes in the same direction every time. Most users drag from the upper-left corner to the lower-right. And just a reminder: You'll get the best results when you blend objects that have an equal number of nodes. If you don't have an equal number, try adding nodes to one of the control objects until you do.

Blends within Blends   DRAW permits two kinds of nested blends. You can blend between two objects that contain fountain fills, or between two objects that are themselves blends. In either case, this creates a potentially fascinating mosaic of intermediate steps. Blending between fountain fills is easy—just create your control objects and go. Blending between blends involves one extra step: grouping. You may remember this curious gyration from Chapter 6.

If you created the drawing in Chapter 6, you made a blend-within-a-blend when you reflected the sun in the water. Each individual reflection was a blend, and you made two of them to act as control objects to create others. DRAW does not allow blends to be blended in their native state, but requires that you group them first. You have to select the blend group and press Ctrl+G to turn it into a regular group. The blend is still alive and well; it's just tucked inside of a group. This one

1 9 . 1 2

**Blending text
can create striking
effects.**

Only the Shadow Knows

Start Object:
  **No fill
  Thick black outline**

End Object:
  **No fill
  Thin white outline**

Only the Shadow Knows

Start Object:
  **30% black fill
  4pt 30% outline**

End Object:
  **30% black fill
  .5pt 30% outline**

ONLY THE SHADOW KNOWS

Start Object:
  **Black fill
  6pt white outline**

End Object:
  **Black fill
  .5pt black outline**

Only the Shadow Knows

Start Object:
  **No fill
  6pt white outline**

End Object:
  **Black fill
  1pt 30% outline
  set behind fill**

doesn't make too much sense, so you'll just have to memorize it: Blends
need to be grouped before they can be used as control objects in other
blends.

Blending Overlapping Objects   One of the most powerful techniques of all is the blending of objects that surround each other, though
using it might make you dizzy. We have two examples to show you.
First, Figure 19.13 shows the classic example of a ball being flooded
with light (we wonder if any CorelDRAW book in the history of

19.13

The classic ball-and-its-shadow illustrates a blend between one object and the larger one that surrounds it.

CorelDRAW books has not included this example). In the top figure, the Steps are set very low so you can clearly see the control objects. The ball is one blend, between a dark object and a white object, and the shadow is the same. (Incidentally, we created the shadow with a skew-and-dupe of the control object for the ball.)

The bottom figure is an exact duplicate of the top, with Steps increased from 6 to 100.

Figure 19.14 shows a much more sophisticated use of blend. This wonderful rendition of a pensive woman was a finalist in the People, Plants, and Animals category of Corel's 1995 World Design Contest. Her face, arm, and shirt are made up of numerous blends, most of which involve one control object inside of another. We have zeroed in on two particular blends on the shirt, and you can see from the Wireframe blow-up that, with each blend, one control curve is placed inside of another. This is the most common technique used by professional DRAW users to produce the appearance of shape, undulation, depth, and light variance.

And now, on to Blend's next of kin.

19.14

The blends on this woman's face, arm, and shirt provide a convincing sense of dimension and lighting.

Contours: The Lay of the Land

Contours are second cousins to blends and fountain fills, with similarities and dissimilarities to each. A contour begins as one object (unlike a blend) but involves gradual transitions from a start to a finish (like a blend and a fountain). Contours are a series of discrete steps, usually traversing a range of colors (like a blend). But the steps of a contour are based solely on a single start object (like a fountain), rather than a metamorphosis from one object to another. Each contour step maintains the same general shape as the start object. The steps get either larger or smaller by an amount you define, while maintaining the shape of the start object as closely as possible.

To see the dynamics of a contour, try this simple exercise:

1. In a new drawing, create a simple rectangle, shade it 20% black, and remove its outline.

2. Select the rectangle, invoke Contour (Ctrl+F9), choose Inside as the direction.

3. At Offset, enter a value of 0,6 picas, or .5 points, or approximately .05 inches.

4. Set Steps to 3.

5. Click on the Color wheel icon to move to the Color page.

6. Set the fill to a darker shade of gray, say 60%. Ignore the Outline Pen icon.

7. Here is the translation of these instructions so far: "Take three steps to the inside. Each step should be 0,6 picas, and the color should gradually change from 20% (the color of the original object) to 60% (the color set in the Contour roll-up)." Now click Apply, and your object should make the transition shown in the top row of Figure 19.15.

8. Make a copy of your contoured object (using the Clipboard, the gray + key, or drag-and-dupe).

9. On the copy, change the direction to Center. Apply, and the Steps field will gray out, because now your instructions are "Use 0,6 steps and move all the way to the center, using however many steps are required."

10. Make another copy of the first contour, and set its direction to Outside and Apply.

Figure 19.15 shows these three effects of Contour. The top contour heads inside by an amount determined by the Offset and the Steps. (If you do the math, you'll find the distance toward the center to be 1.5 picas.) The second contour heads inside with the same 0,6 pica, but you've sent orders for this one to go all the way in to the center, regardless of how many steps are required. The third contour heads to the outside.

If you set values that DRAW cannot abide by—for instance, 1 pica for Offset, 30 for Steps, to the inside of a 6-pica wide object—it will automatically reduce the Steps, not the Offset, until it finds a value that it can produce.

19.15

**The three faces of
Contour**

Like a blend, a contour is a dynamic group of objects. Sizing or positioning the control object will cause the contour to adjust; so will, of course, returning to the Contour roll-up and changing the settings.

Had the rectangle in this exercise included an outline, it would have become part of the contour, with the transition of outline color being controlled by the Outline Pen drop-down on the Color page. Figure 19.16 shows the same blend applied to another rectangle of the same size but with no fill and a gray outline.

As with other dynamic groups, you can use Arrange / Separate to break the contour group into unlinked components that can then be manipulated individually.

19.16

The same contours, applied to an object with an outline but no fill

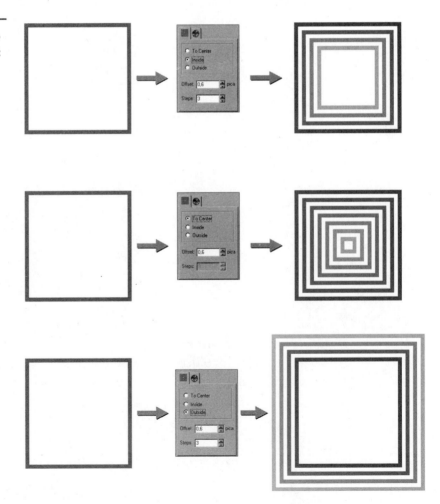

INSIDE INFO

You can use Effects / Clone to copy the contour settings from one object to another, just as you can use Effects / Copy for duplicating blends. Cloning a contour reproduces all the attributes set in the Contour roll-up and maintains a dynamic link to the original object. Update the original, and the clones come along for the ride. Lest you become overly enamored with this capability, please read "Be Smart with Steps," earlier in this chapter.

Shadowing with Contour

One of the simplest and cleanest uses for Contour is the creation of drop shadows for objects. Open SHADOW.CDR from the PRACTICE directory of the Companion CD and try the following steps:

1. Select the text, then the rectangle, and center-align them in both directions (press Ctrl+A to reach the Align roll-up quickly).

2. Drag-and-dupe the rectangle a bit down and to the right. Figure 9.17 shows what your screen would look like in mid-drag— or is that mid-dupe?

3. Send the new rectangle to the back with Shift+PgDn.

Let's take a minute to see what our goal is here. We want to produce the illusion that this announcement is raised above the surface and that light is casting a shadow on it. If there really were a light source, the darkest shadow would be directly under the object, with a gradual transition to white (or whatever the color is of the surface underneath). We intend to contour to the inside, so the object's original color would be the outside color, white. Here goes:

4. Set the rectangle's fill to white, using the on-screen Color Palette, and remove its outline.

5. From the Color page of the Contour roll-up, set the Fill color to a dark gray or black.

19.17

The duplicated rectangle will serve as the control object for the contouring operation.

6. Set the Offset to 1 point (or 0,1 pica or .01″).

7. Start with the Steps set to 20.

8. Apply. Your screen should look like Figure 19.18.

By setting Steps to 20, you force the Contour engine to switch from white to dark quite rapidly, creating a darker shadow. Adjust Steps to 50 and you'll notice a more gradual transition, resulting in a lighter shadow. The other adjustment you can make is the position of the contour group. By moving it further down and to the right, you make the announcement look raised even further off the page.

19.18

Contouring a rectangle is a quick and reliable way to create a realistic shadow.

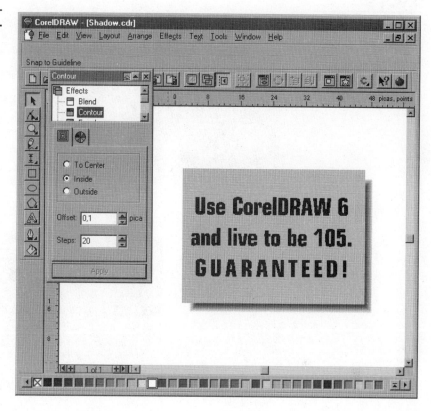

In Figure 19.19, four changes were made to the lower image to give it a softer shadow: (1) The contour was moved further away from the foreground object; (2) steps were increased from 64 to 125; (3) the End color was changed from solid black to 70% black; and (4) the corners of the control rectangle were rounded slightly.

Better Outlines with Contour

If precision is your game, forget about using standard outlines around objects. Why? Let's say you're creating a schematic according to some ultraprecise specifications. The plans call for an object 21mm by 33mm,

19.19

The top shadow is
sharper and darker,
while the lower
shadow is more
diffuse.

> Use CorelDRAW 6
> and live to be 105.
> GUARANTEED!

Offset: .25pt
Steps: 64
End Fill: Black

Offset: .25pt
Steps: 125
End Fill: 70% Black
Corners rounded

> Use CorelDRAW 6
> and live to be 105.
> GUARANTEED!

with a 4-point, 30% gray border placed precisely 16mm in from the schematic's left edge and 12mm from the top. Setting the page in millimeters is no problem, and establishing guidelines at 16mm and 12mm is cake. You can use the Transform roll-up to size your object to the precise spec, and you can snap it precisely in place along the 16mm guideline.

Calling for a 4-point border is no problem, either, right? So you use all of DRAW's precision controls, you place your object just so…and you are promptly fired from your job. Figure 19.20 shows the reason for your dismissal. By default, DRAW places half of an outline's thickness inside the object boundary and half on the outside. Therefore, 2 points of this object's outline are outside of the boundary.

19.20

Congratulations on creating a perfect rectangle with a 4-point outline. Now go clean out your desk and pick up your severance pay.

If you'd used Contour, you'd still be employed. Try it this way:

1. Create the rectangle without any outline, using the guidelines for precision placement and the Transform roll-up for precision sizing.

2. Fill the rectangle with 30% gray.

3. From the Contour roll-up, set the Offset to 4 points. (You'll need to momentarily change the unit of measure from milli-meters to points first, in Layout / Page Setup.)

4. Then set Steps to 1, the color to white, and Apply. Figure 19.21 shows the result, after having returned the global unit of measure to millimeters.

5. Ask for, and receive, a raise.

19.21

Because contouring doesn't need an outline, none of this object hangs over the boundary.

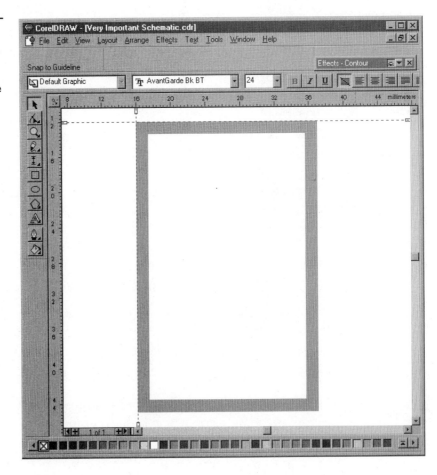

WATCH OUT!

There's no diplomatic way to say this: We hate having to fix the unit of measure in the Contour roll-up (and several other roll-ups, as well). The above exercise shows how awkward this can be when a page is set in one dimension and you need to manipulate objects on it using different units of measure. Corel has maintained this practice through two versions now, and we think it is one of the most egregious design errors across the entire suite of applications.

Open Contours

Although you cannot fill an open curve, you *can* apply a contour to it. This can give it a filled look, and an interesting one at that. When you select an open curve, Contour only allows you to step to the outside (there is no inside). After you apply the contour, set the outline to None, and experiment with the fill options. Your best bet is to fill the control curve with white, and then set the ending contour to another color. (If it doesn't make sense to be filling an open curve, trust us; it works.)

Figure 19.22 illustrates this technique. The top image is the original, drawn with straight lines; the bottom image is a ten-step contour of it. The initials of our lead author proved to be appropriate sample characters, because they could be created entirely with straight lines instead of curves. Why would we want to avoid curves? We're glad you asked...

Create a Contour, Take a Coffee Break

We've shown you the beauty of contouring; now we must present its dark side: Contouring simple objects like ovals and rectangles is quick and easy; objects that are more complex, however, can bring DRAW and even your system to its knees.

19.22

You can't fill an open path, but you can apply a contour to it.

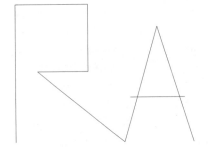

Figure 19.23 offers the chilling details. Each of the objects in the figure has had a 50-step contour applied to it. The first five objects, consisting of mostly straight lines, contour quickly. Even the letter *A*, a compound shape, takes the contour in short order because it is made up entirely of straight lines.

The big drop in performance comes with the letter *C*, composed entirely of curves. And then we sink into absurdity with the cloud (35 nodes), the gorilla (75 nodes), and the string of text. DRAW 6.0 doesn't show the hourglass flipping around as previous versions did; on the last contour we restarted our computer twice, so sure were we that the system had crashed.

19.23

Contouring simple objects is fast and easy; contouring complex objects is the computer equivalent of water torture.

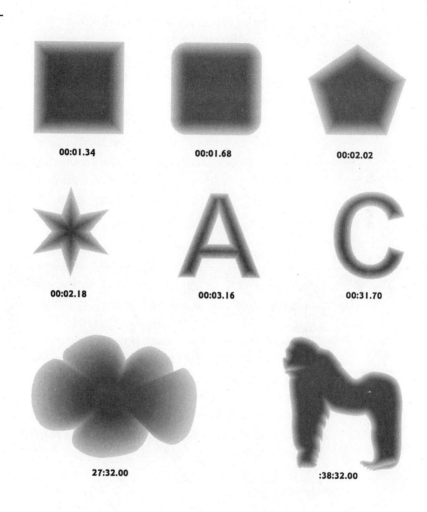

00:01.34

00:01.68

00:02.02

00:02.18

00:03.16

00:31.70

27:32.00

:38:32.00

1:52:44.00

When an object is a continuous curve, like the cloud and the gorilla, you can turn to Blend instead of Contour. For instance, we sized-and-duped the gorilla, creating a tiny duplicate inside of the original. Then we shaded it, selected both objects, and blended using 50 steps. Blend has the luxury of control objects on both sides, so its job is much easier than the Contour engine's, which must determine quite laboriously how each step is to be created.

On the other hand, with the "Supercalifragilistic" string, there is no way you can create a duplicate entirely within the original. So if you want to create this effect with a similar string of text, our best advice to you is, don't. (Patient: "Doctor, my head hurts when I bang it against the wall. What should I do?" Doctor: "I suggest that you not do that anymore.")

INSIDE INFO

Once you have an object contoured to your liking, group it. We acknowledge that it sounds unusual to group what is already a group, but it makes resizing much easier. When you resize a contour, DRAW notices that the control object has changed and then signals Contour to recalculate the object. But if you group it first, DRAW treats it differently. It becomes one grouped object that is simply being scaled, without need for any recalculation. The contour is still alive and well, and you can always ungroup it, or simply select the contour within the group and change it dynamically.

♣

Next up in our journey through DRAW's special effects: Extrusions.

20

Energizing with Extrude

The Extrude effect is one of our favorites. It is very powerful and, when used wisely, allows even the artistically inept to produce impressive art. We have to make a distinction here, however, between artistic ineptitude, as in "incapable of drawing straight lines and circles," and aesthetic insensitivity, as in "incapable of recognizing good art from bad art." If what you lack is good taste rather than a modest degree of skill, extrusions will only help you dig a deeper grave.

Extrusions Add Depth and Breadth

Extruding remains one of DRAW's most clever functions. With the Extrude feature you can select any simple object and easily turn it into something three-dimensional, as either a perspective drawing or an isometric drawing. In order to produce a 3-D appearance, Extrude creates new surfaces that are dynamically linked to the original object. It does this by projecting significant points of your control object and then connecting those points to form closed surfaces.

Both open and closed curves can be extruded, including multipath curves and text. Text that is extruded is still editable, and the extrusion will update automatically to reflect the edits. Similarly, other control objects can be stretched, skewed, rotated, and so forth, and the extrusion will be updated following the changes.

WATCH OUT!

> Be sure of your reasons for applying an extrusion. Don't apply one just for the sake of showing off your software. Unless a drawing is meant to be a three-dimensional rendered scene, you should usually limit the use of extrusions to one or two elements. This is especially true with text elements. Add too many, and the drawing loses its anchor; things appear to be floating randomly in space.

Perspective vs. Isometric Drawings

Figure 20.1 shows the difference between a perspective drawing and an isometric illustration. Basically, perspective drawings mimic the fact that large objects appear to get smaller the farther they get from the viewer, and isometric drawings do not. Perspective is largely an artistic effect used to make something appear more realistic. Isometric illustrations are primarily used for technical drawings, to allow the viewer to make accurate length measurements anywhere along the lines shown.

The Extrude Roll-up

As with most other special effects, Extrude has its own roll-up (see Figure 20.2). To access it, choose Effects / Extrude or press Ctrl+E (hooray, another one that's easy to memorize). In the figure, the roll-up is shown along with a large I-beam shape that is about to be extruded. You can see the outlines projecting out, showing how the shape will be extruded. Notice that the roll-up has icons across the top representing separate pages of controls.

In Figure 20.2, the Extrude roll-up is open to the Geometry page—the controls that let you govern the basic nature and shape of your extrusions. This page, accessed by the second icon from the left at the top of the roll-up, is the page you will probably use most frequently. Don't worry if, like us, you are lousy at geometry or have trouble visualizing

20.1

Will a perspective drawing or an isometric illustration better suit your needs?

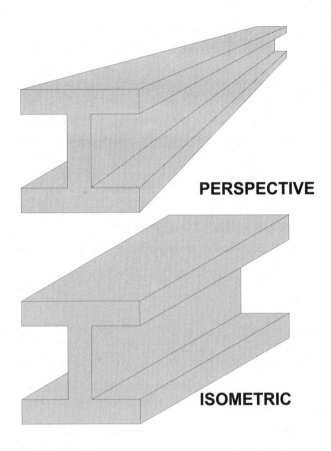

PERSPECTIVE

ISOMETRIC

spatial relationships. An extrusion is just another dynamically linked effect, so it is easy to edit until what you see is really what you want. All the settings on all the Extrusion pages can be adjusted before you actually apply the extrusion—or after, if you didn't like what you got the first time.

The small × in Figure 20.2 represents the hypothetical vanishing point of the object. If this screen shot showed the entire page, you would see that the × is in the center of the page, which is the vanishing point's default location when you first invoke the roll-up. You are free to move the vanishing point anywhere you like.

20.2

The Extrude roll-up, showing the page of geometry settings

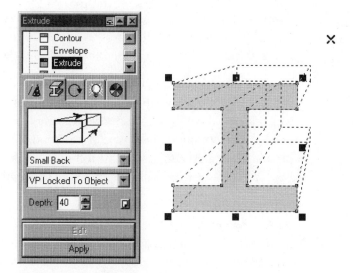

Backs, Fronts, and the Vanishing Point Just as with many effects, extrusions begin with a preset. We have four perspective forms:

- Small Back (the most commonly used)
- Small Front
- Big Back
- Big Front

and two isometric forms:

- Front Parallel
- Back Parallel

So what do they do, and how do you keep them straight? With the perspective forms you can think of it this way: Will the extrusion effect to be drawn be BIGger or SMALLer than the original shape, and will the effect be drawn in BACK of or in FRONT of the original? The isometrics work the same way: Is the effect to be drawn in BACK of or in FRONT of the original shape?

The Back extrusions place the perspective drawing behind your original shape, and extend away from the viewer. The Front extrusions seem to extend out of the paper toward the viewer, in front of the original shape, which makes the original invisible to the viewer.

In the drawing in Figure 20.2, notice the outlines indicating how the object will extrude. Sometimes these outlines are difficult to see and interpret, which is why the roll-up includes a little sample window to show you a graphic representation of the type of extrusion you have chosen. (The sample window is in the middle of the roll-up, directly above the drop-down list box.) You can see what will happen before you apply the extrusion.

Still wondering what the difference is between Big Front and Small Back? Look closely at the little graphics in the roll-up. The thicker outlines indicate where the control object is located, with the arrows showing the extrusion direction.

Perspective is the phenomenon that causes two or more parallel lines, when viewed from one end, to appear to converge. *Vanishing point* is an artist's term to describe the point on the horizon where two or more parallel lines viewed in perspective appear to meet. In CorelDRAW the extrusion effect builds a perspective drawing, and you can move the vanishing point, shown on the screen as an ×, to give the desired appearance. When you move the ×, you are moving the vanishing point in space. The depth of the extrusion is controlled with the depth box in the roll-up.

In an isometric form, the × has a slightly different function. You still manipulate it on screen with the mouse, but since isometrics don't "vanish," the × is used to determine the depth *and* angle of the extrusion. Wherever you place the × is where the *center* of the extruded object face will appear. For this reason, parallel extrusions have no numerical depth controls.

Figure 20.3 shows the I-beam ready to be extruded using Back Parallel. Notice that the × is in the center of the extruded I-beam shape.

20.3

The × offers direct
control of Parallel
extrusions.

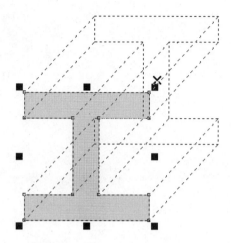

Getting Down to Business

We're sure you're getting anxious to start doing your own 3-D rendering. The next few exercises will take you on a tour of most of the options in the Extrude roll-up. At the same time, we will use a few features
introduced in earlier sections, and some hotkeys to get you accustomed
to the available shortcuts.

1. Create a new letter-size drawing, in landscape orientation.

2. Draw a light-colored square about 2" wide anywhere on the
   page. (Remember, holding Ctrl while dragging forces the shape
   to be square; watch the status line for size.) Apply a 2-point
   black outline to the square.

3. Draw another square (color doesn't matter) about 1" wide anywhere on the page.

4. With the Pick tool, select both rectangles. Press Ctrl+A (Arrange
   / Align), click Align to Center of Page, and then OK.

5. Rotate the smaller rectangle only, by 45°.

6. Reselect both rectangles, and press Ctrl+L (Arrange / Combine) to create an object with a hole in it.

7. Press Ctrl+E to invoke the Extrude roll-up, switch to the geometry settings (if necessary), and immediately click Apply. The results should look like Figure 20.4.

20.4

**Extruding a box
with a hole in it**

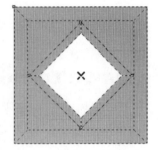

Not very exciting, is it? So far, you should have something that looks like a square with a diamond-shaped hole in it. The rather bland result of this extrusion is because the perspective (controlled by the vanishing point) is set as if you are looking at the object straight on, so not a lot of dimension is evident. (At least you can see the sides of the hole through the box.) This is due to the default settings in the Extrude roll-up. Notice that the standard extrusion is Small Back, with a depth of 20, and that the vanishing point is always placed at the center of the page when the roll-up is first invoked. That is why it shows up in the center of your object, since you centered the object on the page.

Okay, so you weren't impressed with your first extrusion. Let's make it more interesting. Notice that the roll-up and your object are still in Edit mode—the vanishing point is still visible and the Edit button is grayed out—so you can immediately start modifying the extrusion. (If you were to deselect this object and come back to it later, you would have to first select it and then click the Edit button in the roll-up.)

WATCH OUT!

When you reselect any dynamic linked groups such as extrusions, pay attention to the status line: It will tell you whether it's the group object or the control object that is selected. Although it doesn't matter which one you select when you are editing an extrusion via the roll-up or with most tools, it *does* matter when you're duplicating objects. For example, if you select only the control object of an extrusion and duplicate it, only that object is duplicated; it will not be part of any extrusion. If you select the extrude group, then the entire dynamic group gets duplicated. Also, in order to edit extruded *text*, you must select the control object only, not the entire extrude group.

8. Make sure the vanishing point is still visible. If not, click Edit in the Extrude roll-up. Then, click and drag the vanishing point diagonally up and to the right roughly 2", but don't click Apply yet.

9. Click the little paging icon in the lower-right corner of the roll-up, and choose the option Measured from Object Center. Adjust both values to read exactly 2". Now, click Apply.

10. Use the Fill tool flyout or Fill roll-up to apply a linear fountain fill of your choice to the control curve.

11. Click twice somewhere off the object, to deselect it.

Does that look better? You should now have a more distinctly three-dimensional object, as depicted in Figure 20.5. When you changed the fill of the control curve, the fill of the entire object changed accordingly. We had you choose a fountain fill just so you would be aware that you are not limited to solid-color fills for extrusions. You can fill them just about any way you wish.

20.5

This extruded box provides a feeling of depth.

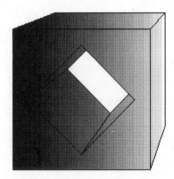

Editing the Vanishing Point

When you click on the paging icon in the lower-right corner of the Geometry page of the Extrude roll-up, the roll-up changes to display a set of options for precise positioning of the vanishing point. You can either drag the vanishing point and watch the values change in the boxes, or enter the exact values in the roll-up to reposition the vanishing point. You can position the vanishing point relative to either the *page origin*—usually its lower-left corner—or the *control object's center* (this was the option you chose in the foregoing exercise).

Color, Shading, and Lights

The default method of filling extruded surfaces, as you may have already figured out, is to match the fill of the control curve. If that changes, the rest of the object changes, without any further action required. But, are there alternative ways to fill the extruded faces?

Use Object Fill

Click on the color wheel icon at the top of the Extrude roll-up, and you switch to Extrude's Color settings page. There are three options for coloring. The default option is Use Object Fill. This means that whenever you select either the control object or the whole extrusion and assign any sort of fill, all faces in that extrusion will automatically change to the fill you selected. (The roll-up does not play a part in updating the color, once this option has been applied.)

NOTE

In the Extrude / Color settings, notice an option called Drape Fills. By default, it is turned on. Only applicable for the first fill option, Use Object Fill, the Drape Fills option treats the extrusion as a whole when filling it. In DRAW versions prior to 5, each surface of the extruded object was treated as a separate object when a fill was applied. This is irrelevant for solid color fills, but wasn't always satisfactory for fountain or textured fills. Take a look at Figure 20.6. Though the same linear fountain fill was applied to both objects, they look quite different. The block on the left has the Drape Fills option turned on; the block on the right does not. The default mode allows a quick and somewhat realistic shading pattern to be achieved. On the other hand, applying a draped fountain fill can come in very handy when a more uniform color graduation or pattern is desired to cover the entire extrusion.

20.6

Draped and undraped extrusion fills

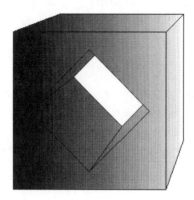 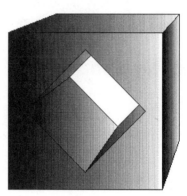

Solid Fills

Turning back to the Color settings, let's take a look at Color / Solid Fill. As its name implies, this option allows you to select a solid color from a flyout palette to apply to the extruded faces. Once it's chosen, the faces will retain that color, independent of how you choose to fill the control object.

The palette that appears always matches whatever custom palette you currently have loaded. You can click on the More button to mix or select any solid color from whatever color model you prefer.

Once Solid Fill has been chosen, if you need to change the extruded surfaces' fill, you must do it through the Extrude roll-up. If you select the extrude group and choose a fill the normal way, from the Fill dialogs or palettes, you will change only the control object's fill.

Adding Realism through Shading

Shade, the last Extrude / Color option, was designed to yield a more realistic shaded appearance to the surfaces of the extrusion. You can use Shade in that role—or you can ignore that and instead generate your own attention-grabbing color effects that have absolutely nothing to do with reality.

DRAW assumes that shading should naturally flow from the control object to the back—a reasonable assumption in most instances. You are free to change both the starting and ending colors of the shade. When you apply the Shade option, DRAW creates fountain fills for each extruded surface, based on the two colors you choose. Like Solid Fill, you get flyout palettes for selecting both start and end colors.

In the following exercise, you will create a simple shaded object.

1. Click on the object you created in the last exercise.

2. Click Edit on the Extrude roll-up.

3. Select White as the From color and Black as the To color.

4. Click Apply. You should now have something similar to Figure 20.7.

5. Try selecting some other From and To colors, and apply them to see the results.

6. With the object still selected, select another fill color for the control object. Note that the From color of the extruded faces now matches the front face's new fill.

You can change the colors used for shading the extruded parts, yet the dynamic link of an extrude group is still in effect.

INSIDE INFO

Because they are composed of fountain fills, shaded extrusions can take a fair amount of time to display. The more complex they are, the longer they will take. If you want to speed up redraws for any fountain fill, decrease the number of fountain steps displayed. This is done via Tools / Options / Display. Bear in mind that this setting does not affect how fountain fills are printed.

20.7

Color fills can be used to create realistic or surrealistic effects.

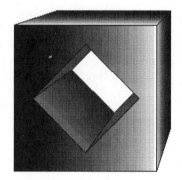

Lighting Effects

Shading can produce added realism in your objects, but it is not very flexible. The fourth page of the Extrude roll-up (its icon is a light bulb) gives you the Light Source controls. These settings allow you to simulate light falling on your extruded object from various directions (see Figure 20.8).

To select the origin and direction for a light source, click one of the three "light switches" on the left of the roll-up. As each switch is turned on, a numbered spot will appear at one of the 16 points on the grid at the right, surrounding a shaded sphere that represents your object. To change the position of any light source, you simply drag it to a different grid point.

The Intensity slider adjusts the currently selected light source (the numbered spot for the one that is selected will be black rather than gray). Thus, each source can be in one of 16 positions, and each can have its own intensity.

20.8

**Shedding more re-
alistic light on the
subject**

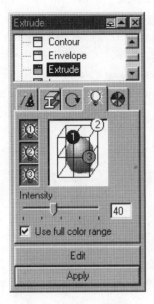

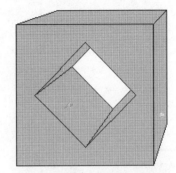

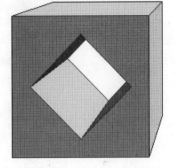

WATCH OUT!

> Be prepared to do a lot of experimentation with the Extrude / Light
> Source controls. You will soon discover that turning on the light
> will often darken object faces, unless the intensity is 100 and
> the light source is facing the surface directly. You may have to
> start with the object fill at a lighter color, in order to get the
> effect you ultimately want. You can also try adding another light
> at a lower intensity and an opposing position.

Applying a light source is fairly simple. Predicting the results is something of a hat trick. You'll want to experiment with the light sources on

your own. We've provided a few samples in Figure 20.9 to help you visualize the effects. In this figure are eight samples, each with different lighting effects. The center object is the original, with no lighting applied. For each sample, we have indicated the intensity of the light source by a number, and its origin by the number's position. The top row of samples all use a single light source; the two in the middle row use two; and the ones in the bottom row all use three.

20.9

The effects of various light-source combinations on an extrusion

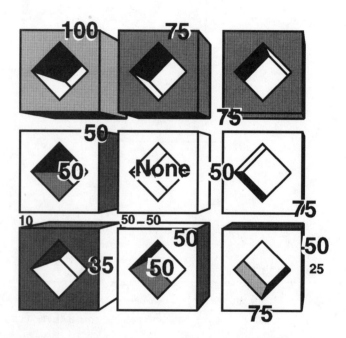

The light sources provided in DRAW 6.0 offer a good deal of flexibility. Still, as is evident in Figure 20.9, the effects are not very subtle when used with solid-filled objects. To get more impressive results, you can combine Extrude's Shade option with the light sources. In Figure 20.10 you'll find the same blocks from Figure 20.9, this time with Shade turned on for each one. (We've added our own special Earthquake Effect to them, as well. You'll learn how that was done shortly.)

20.10

A reprise of Figure
20.9—the same
light sources, but
with shading and
tremors added

Creating Cutaways, Explosions, and Other Tricks

Now we'll look at the possibilities of creating cutaway and exploded views. Version 4.0 introduced the technique of using the Ctrl key to select individual objects within groups. Once they're selected, you are free to move them, apply various fills and outlines, or even resize individual objects—without breaking the group apart. We used this capability to quickly create the cutaway in Figure 20.11.

We simply hold the Ctrl key down as we select the desired face. The status line reads "Child Curve," to which we assigned no fill, thus creating a transparent surface. Once one child curve is selected, you can press Ctrl+Tab to cycle through all the child curves of a group. This allows you to select surfaces that may not be fully visible. (This technique works for other dynamic groups, as well, such as compound blends.)

20.11

Exploded and cut-away effects can be created by manipulating child curves.

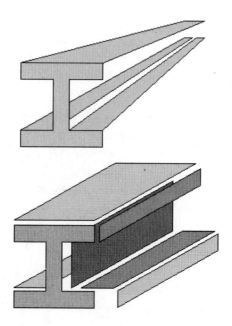

Bear in mind that any time you return to the Extrude roll-up to make a modification, you clear any modifications made to independent child curves. So if you are going to use this technique, make sure you have applied all desired roll-up settings first, before tweaking various child curves.

You can do almost anything you want to child curves, but there are several options that are not open. If you want to apply an effect that cannot be applied to a child curve, you need to separate the objects in the extrude group.

Beyond Extrude's Lighting Tools   Even combining Extrude's Light Source and Shade options may not give you the flexibility you would like for shading extrusions just so. As an alternative, you can select individual child curves and apply various fountain fills to them to get the shading you want. The top cube in Figure 20.10 was shaded using this technique. We think it's a more realistic-looking shaded object. Again, the only hazard with this technique is that updating any extrusion settings (or even the control curve's fill) will undo all your manual fills.

INSIDE INFO

If you've used the Shade option and you then apply a fountain fill to one or more child curves, changing the control curve's fill color will change the colors on the child curve as well, but the fill type (radial, conical, and so on) will be retained. We're not certain how useful this might be for you, but it was an interesting discovery.

Using the Separate Command If you want to manually fill an extrusion, and wish to make sure the changes are permanent to individual elements of an extruded object, you should separate and perhaps even ungroup the extrusion once you have it shaped the way you wish. It is then no longer a dynamic group, so all changes made to individual faces are independent of one another. The Arrange / Separate command can be used with any dynamic link group, to break the link. When applied to extrusions, the command breaks the extrusion into two objects: the original control object, and a conventional group made up of all the surfaces generated by the Extrude command. If you wish, you can further ungroup all the objects, so they are all directly selectable.

The downside of this is that you can no longer edit the object as an extrusion. So, before breaking the link, make sure it's the way you want it. If you use this technique, we suggest you ungroup the extrude surfaces, and regroup the entire set of objects. You can then select each child curve in the same way as usual (Ctrl+Click) to do your custom colorizing. Should you accidentally refill the entire group, Undo will recover what you had before. This way, you keep the geometric integrity of the extrusion and can still color it any way you want.

Rules of Thumb for Extruding

■ More often than not, the light sources and shading effects provided in the Extrude roll-up are too inflexible to get the proper lighting and/or shading on an extruded object. The light sources take time and experimentation to get suitable results. It is usually easier to reach for the Fill roll-up and apply fountain fills at various angles to child curves of the object.

■ If you decide to separate an extrusion, make a copy of it first, just in case you decide you want to modify the extrusion later.

Vanishing Points Revisited

Before we move on to the "Rotating Extrusions" section and look at how the tumbling blocks of Figure 20.10 were created, let's return to our old friend the vanishing point for a moment. Take another look back at Figure 20.9. Although lit differently, all the blocks have the proper spatial relationship. This was not a fortuitous accident; we accomplished it by making sure each object has the same vanishing point. DRAW 3 and 4 have indirect ways of accomplishing this, and in previous editions of this book we mentioned them as odds and ends. Since version 5, however, DRAW has had a better set of tools to offer you.

Apparently Corel realized that matching vanishing points was more than a cute parlor trick. DRAW 5 provided several new options for controlling relationships between the page, the extruded object, and its vanishing point. These benefits continue in version 6.0. Figure 20.12 shows the drop-down list of vanishing points.

Selecting the first option, VP Locked to Object, in the drop-down list of vanishing points is the same thing you would do to maintain vanishing points in versions 3 and 4. Once a vanishing point is set relative to the control face, it stays that way even if the extrusion is moved. In other words, the viewer's perspective changes with the object movement. With this option selected, if you copy an extrusion and move it to another part of the page, you will have two different vanishing points or two different viewer perspectives—not very realistic.

20.12

**Vanishing point
options**

By choosing the second option, VP Locked to Page, you can move the object around the page without changing the viewer perspective of the object. In this case, you could duplicate an object and move it to another portion of the page, and have a realistic-looking collection of objects. The Copy Extrude From and Clone Extrude From commands in the Effects menu work very well in tandem with this option. Creating objects this way ensures they all have the same vanishing point for realistic viewer perspective.

The third option, Copy VP From, is your afterthought option: It allows you to match vanishing points *after* extrude objects have already been created. It doesn't create any link between extruded objects, nor does it change any other Extrude options that are set. It simply causes the vanishing point of one extrusion to be matched to any other extrusion you select—similar to copying a fill outline from one object to another.

The last option, Shared Vanishing Point, creates a dynamic link of the vanishing points of two or more extrusions. With this option set, if you change the vanishing point of one object, all others that share that vanishing point are also automatically updated. This one is similar to a cloned extrusion. When you clone, you duplicate all extrusion settings, including depth and fill options. Shared Vanishing Point just ensures a common vanishing point.

Rules of Thumb for Vanishing Points

■ Cloning extrusions can be useful, but in very limited circumstances. Bear in mind that you cannot directly modify a cloned extrusion. Also, the difficulty of keeping track of the "master" extrusion makes extrusion cloning a dubious undertaking.

■ It is likely that you will be more interested in establishing common vanishing points (and other settings) among extrusions than in duplicating all the extrusion settings from one object to another. A more practical approach is to make use of the Shared Vanishing Point option and the Copy Extrude From command, because it leaves you the flexibility to modify specific settings (fills, depth, and so on) for each extrusion, while maintaining a common viewer perspective.

Rotating Extrusions

Now we'll show you how we created our tumbling blocks in Figure 20.10. The Extrude / Rotation settings (Figure 20.13) are accessed via the center icon, the one with an arrow circling clockwise. When this roll-up is on screen, clicking the paging icon in the lower-right corner displays the settings shown in Figure 20.14, allowing you to rotate by number instead of by sight, for greater precision when you want to borrow rotation settings from one object to apply to another. This type of rotation is entirely different from simply selecting the object and rotating it, as you would a two-dimensional object. The roll-up not only allows clockwise and counterclockwise rotations, which are the equivalents of simple object rotations, it also allows you to rotate in two other theoretical axes (horizontal and vertical). Further, you can combine rotations of varying degrees in all three axes.

20.13

Rotating by sight

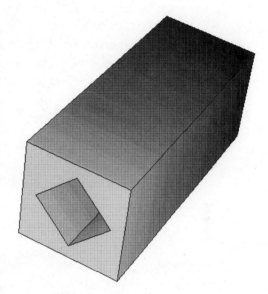

20.14

Rotating by the numbers

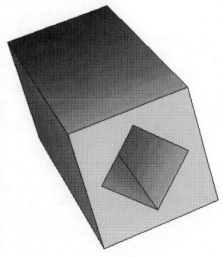

Version 5 used a visual rotation system that was far from intuitive. The new "trackball" system (shown in the form of a Corel logo) makes it much easier to visualize the effects of rotation. The extrusion can be clicked and dragged to any position, including fully reversed (indicated by blue facing), and the effects of the rotation will be shown in dotted lines on your extrusion. Clicking on the × button in the corner of the roll-up returns the extrusion (and the trackball) to its original position.

Figure 20.15 shows the way CorelDRAW 6.0 quantifies rotation in the numerical setting. Any rotations made in numerical mode will be retained and translated if you return to trackball mode, and vice versa.

20.15

Numerical rotation navigator

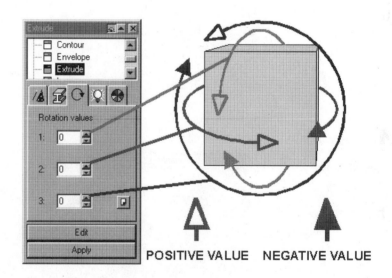

NEW FOR 6

Corel seems to have realized that the terms "horizontal" and "vertical" used in the numerical settings of version 5 were subjective and sometimes confusing. The new Rotation dialog has dropped these labels.

WATCH OUT!

You cannot use Extrude's Rotation controls unless you have selected Locked to Object as the type of vanishing point. Once you have applied a rotation, you cannot select the vanishing point and move it. If you try to grab it, you will be thrown out of Extrude's editing mode. When you *do* need to change the vanishing point, you must reset the rotations (use the center X button on the Visual Rotation page), adjust the vanishing point, and reapply the rotations.

Rules of Thumb for Rotating

- Make sure your vanishing point is set *before* you rotate.
- You can move a rotated extrusion, but its vanishing point will move with it (it's locked to the object).

Miscellany

Following are a few odds and ends concerning extruded objects.

The Extrude Roll-up Remembers

An important facet of the Extrude roll-up is that it retains the settings of the most recently applied extrusion. Along with all of Extrude's new copying, cloning, preset, and vanishing point matching capabilities, the roll-up's memory provides another means for quickly producing several related extrusions. If you created some extruded text, for example, with a depth of 15, shading, and a particular light source, the next extruded object you create will take on those same settings, unless you specifically change them.

Version 6.0 Continues Extrusion Presets

The next time you create some really fantastic extrusion and want to save its settings for posterity, you can do so through DRAW 6.0's Presets feature (as discussed in Chapters 9 and 14). Select the extrusion, click the first icon to switch to the Presets page of the Extrusion roll-up, and click on Save As. Name your preset (that is, name this group of settings), and you can apply it later to any extrudable object or even to an existing extrusion.

You can find your Extrusion presets listed in either the Extrude roll-up or the Presets roll-up (see Chapter 9).

When you apply a preset to an existing extrusion, the preset's settings supersede those of the existing extrusion—but there is nothing to stop you from going further and modifying an extrusion generated from a preset. Any or all of the predefined extrusion settings can be modified after you apply the preset. If you really like your modifications, you can save those as a preset, too, or use them to replace the old preset by saving them under the same name.

Experiment with creating and using presets. Even within a single project, a preset can be a valuable starting point for the creation of multiple extrusions. You can always delete the preset at the end of the session if you don't plan to use it in the future.

Taking Advantage of Common Vanishing Points

Figure 20.16 shows a trophy designed in the hopes that Corel would hold an Annual Virtual Tennis Tournament. This is an ideal example of how to utilize matching vanishing points. Each element is an extrusion that shares a common vanishing point, but with varied extrusion depths and fills employed.

For the base cube, we used a linear fountain fill. The larger cube and circular shape have conical fills. We weren't content with using the Shade feature, so we filled each child curve independently. The circular emblem was another story. Using the Shade feature produced a group

20.16

**Using common
vanishing points to
create complex
objects**

composed of 108 separate objects, which was a lot to deal with, so we gave the extrusion a solid fill, and the result was a group of just three objects. We were then able to use fountain fills to get the shading we wanted.

Getting the text to sit inside the circle shape required a few tricks. First we placed the text in front of the circular extrusion, and extruded the text itself using shaded fills and a shallower depth than the circular object. The result looked silly: On the left side, everything looked fine, but on the right the text solid sat in front of the circular solid (which was wrong). To fix this, we copied the control object of the circular extrude, and moved the duplicate curve to the front. The last step was to copy the control text, break it apart, and re-combine the *O* and the *R*, so that each letter was a single, separate curve. Then each separate letter could be filled with a custom conical fountain fill to get the metallic highlights.

Extrusions Don't Have to Be Fancy

Extrusions can be used in lots of ways that you might not ordinarily think of. Because open paths can be extruded, they can be used to build borders and other specialized effects and illustration tools. Because it is a dynamically linked group of objects, an extrusion can be used to build some objects faster than they could be rendered individually. The objects in the group can then be separated and used elsewhere. Figure 20.17 shows a fairly simple border made of pentagons that have been welded together into a single object.

20.17

Extrusions can make excellent components and borders.

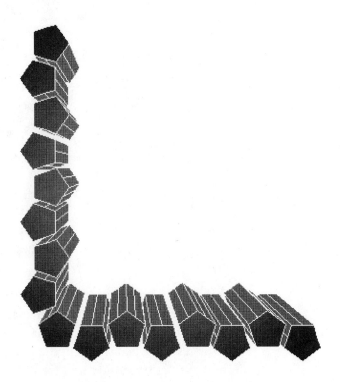

Finally, Figure 20.18 shows how an extrusion can breathe life into a simple figure such as this floor plan. Just because the tool is powerful doesn't mean you can't use it for simple stuff. The key to creating a floor plan is to make sure all elements composing the frame have no fill when you extrude them. You need it to be hollow; otherwise, you wouldn't be able to see inside. The walls derive their fill from the Extrude / Color / Shade setting.

20.18

An extrusion makes the floor plan come alive.

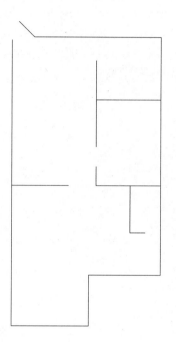

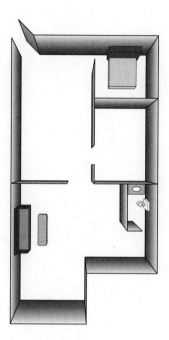

♣

This chapter focused on how the Extrude roll-up's controls can create depth from solid objects. In the next chapter, we'll look at how Power Lines can add depth to simple lines.

The Power of the Line

The standard knock against vector drawing programs, especially from users with a traditional arts background, is the distinctly computerish look of the artwork these programs produce. Even highly detailed work by top-notch computer artists usually has a certain geometric edge to it. Look at the various clip art images supplied with DRAW: As nice as they are, in most you can see their computer origins.

In traditional hand-drawn artwork, edges are usually much softer, and shading more subtle, because elements can be blurred or smudged together. Artists can affect the characteristics of curves by applying varying pressure with their drawing/painting tools. On the one hand, image-editing (bitmap-based) programs have been getting better at mimicking traditional artistic techniques. On the other hand, drawing (vector-based) programs have generally not evolved such techniques as smudging edges, applying transparent fills to objects, cropping portions of an image, and some of the other more "painterly" things that bitmap-based programs can do. In fact, in a previous version of this book, we said vector-based programs would never be able to do any of these things.

Well, we've learned never to say "never" (especially in print!). Power-Lines, introduced in DRAW 4, provided a significant though some-times awkward first step toward mimicking the traditional artist's pens, brushes, and pressure variations. DRAW 5 made them quite a bit more versatile, and DRAW 6.0 brings a few more improvements.

Making Heads or Tails of PowerLines

To both new and veteran DRAW users, PowerLines might be one of the more arcane and least intuitive tools in the program. If you read the User's Manual, you might assume PowerLines to be an extension of the Calligraphic Pen controls in the Outline Pen. Actually, PowerLines do

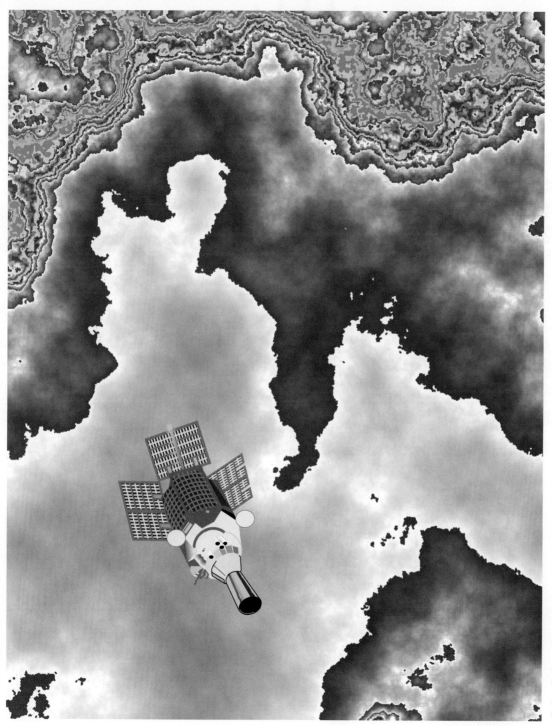

Color Gallery, Illustration 1

Instant art with CorelDRAW. This piece won't win any awards, but it shows how quickly elements can be integrated in CorelDRAW. We spent all of five minutes on it.

Color Gallery, Illustration 2

Another 30-second masterpiece, this one an example of the power of the tools.
Chapter 4 outlines the steps we took to create it.

Color Gallery, Illustration 3

This drawing is the star of Chapter 6, where you can follow along as it is created from start to finish.

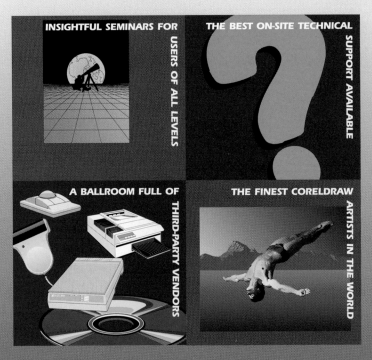

Color Gallery, Illustration 4

The fruits of your author's thievery. Inspired by a similar piece, Altman produced this advertisement for his annual CorelDRAW conference. Chapter 13 has the details.

Color Gallery, Illustration 5

This stunning example of lifelike perspective was created by Antonio De Leo of Italy. Chapter 18 includes a discussion of this piece, along with a picture of all of the guidelines he used to maintain accurate perspective.

Color Gallery, Illustration 6

Gary Priester's journey into elegance is chronicled in Chapter 23.

Color Gallery, Illustration 7

Simple shapes come together in ingenious ways to create this logo. Gary tells all in Chapter 24.

Color Gallery, Illustration 8

Matthew Lecher describes how he went from a novice to the creator of the award-winning Lighthouse in Chapter 26.

Color Gallery, Illustration 9

The stunning effects of DRAW's Lens tool are highlighted by the work that the Heat Map can do on black and white.

Color Gallery, Illustration 10

Georgina Curry has graced our pages with every edition. The pores of this woman's face are made up of tiny fountain-filled ellipses. As always, Georgina's work is not only a study in simple beauty, but also of patience!

Color Gallery, Illustration 11

Anyone for a game of Flight Simulator? John Morris of the United States captures stunning realism for the view of this cockpit. You can bet he didn't use the Add Perspective command to find his vanishing points. . .

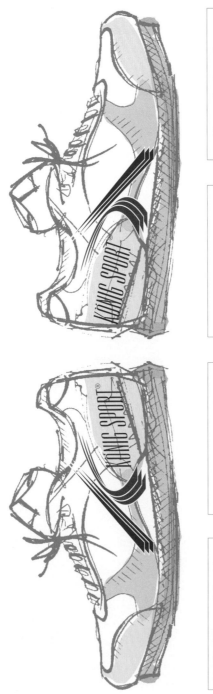

Color Gallery, Illustration 12

Who says that wonderful artwork has to be complex? Radim Mojzis from the Czech Republic virtually swept the awards at the 1995 World Design Contest, including some wonderfully intricate pieces. Nonetheless, we think one of his finest pieces is this simple logo for a sporting goods store.

Color Gallery, Illustration 13

What's a Color Gallery without an automobile? Amedeo Gigli of Italy mixes the traditional with the modern in his celebration of 50 years of automotive engineering.

Color Gallery, Illustration 14

Our lead author's favorite, this heavenly drawing by Silvio Martins Alegre of Brazil mixes sharp vector objects with soft bitmap images.

Color Gallery, Illustration 15

This is vintage Chris Purcell, the talented in-house artist for Compaq Computer Corp. He chooses and integrates colors into his work as good as any CorelDRAW artist we know.

THE COMPUTER DESIGN & ART EXHIBITION

DESIGN GROUP

Color Gallery, Illustration 16

Far out, Man! Piotr Lopatka from Poland put together this striking design for an art exhibition. Notice how the vertical lettering along the right appears to be raised off of the page.

extend the effects that users have tried to accomplish with Calligraphic Pen—but with a wholly different approach.

PowerLines are usually applied to open curves, but rather than changing only the outline shape, as Calligraphic Pen does, the PowerLine actually transforms the open curve into a closed curve with its own fill and outline. To further complicate matters, PowerLines can also be applied to closed (filled) objects and even multipath curves, such as text characters. However, this tool is primarily intended for use with open curves.

If this concept is confusing to you, recall that an open curve can also be extruded, and the resulting object always contains at least one closed filled curve. Think of a PowerLine as a shape that can be applied to a path.

The PowerLine roll-up, shown in Figure 21.1, is available from the Effects menu (surprise!) or by pressing Ctrl+F8. The roll-up contains several sets of controls, accessed via the icons at the top.

2 1 . 1

The PowerLine roll-up

The controls for PowerLines include a collection of presets, pressure and ink-flow settings, and the facility for creating and storing your own custom PowerLines. Below the drop-down list box is the Maximum Width setting, where you can dial or type in the maximum width for the Power-Line shape. The default Max Width setting, when the roll-up is first opened, is 0.50 inches. The Apply When Drawing Lines check box actually means "Apply When Drawing Any Freehand *Curves*," telling DRAW to create PowerLines as you draw a curve. This option is turned on by default, so a PowerLine is applied the minute you draw something with the Pencil tool. It won't automatically apply PowerLines to closed shapes, however. You must do that via the Apply button.

WATCH OUT!

Don't forget that Apply When Drawing Lines is on by default. You will usually want to turn this off, for two reasons. First, it's easier and faster to edit and shape a curve *before* a PowerLine has been applied to it. Second, PowerLines take some time to generate, and they will regenerate for *each and every change* you make to a curve, no matter how insignificant. If you have a slower computer, if you draw and shape fairly complex curves, or if you draw a lot of curves, be prepared to stare at the hourglass frequently unless you disable Apply When Drawing Lines.

An Exercise with PowerLines

This next exercise will give you a sense of the hows and whys of Power-Lines. You will first create four practice objects, as shown in Figure 21.2.

21.2

**Your PowerLine
practice objects**

1. Create a new, letter-size, landscape drawing.

2. Draw a single vertical line about 3 inches long, with a 2-point black outline.

3. Next to the vertical line, draw a dogleg composed of two straight lines, also with 2-point outlines. Don't try to use Ctrl to make the first line perfectly vertical. Just click, move down, and click to end the first line. Without moving the mouse, click again to start the second line, move diagonally, and click to end the line.

4. To verify that you have drawn the dogleg correctly as a single curve, select the object with the Pick tool; the selection box should enclose both line segments.

5. Further to the right, draw a light-blue rectangle, about 3 inches by 2 inches, with a 2-point black outline.

6. At the far right, create a capital letter using a simple block type-face, about 3 inches high, and with the same fill and outline as the rectangle. Convert the text to curves (Ctrl+Q). Your page should look something like Figure 21.2.

7. Invoke the PowerLine roll-up, via Effects / PowerLine or by pressing Ctrl+F8.

8. Select all the objects (Edit / Select All).

9. Select the first PowerLine preset, Wedge1, and click Apply.

You should now have something like Figure 21.3. Notice what a Power-Line looks like as applied to the various objects: open curves, a simple closed shape, and a shape with multiple subpaths.

21.3

The practice objects have been zapped with PowerLines.

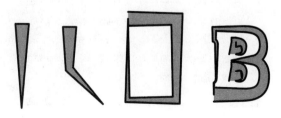

INSIDE INFO

It's important to remember that PowerLines can be applied to more than one object at a time. You can save a lot of time by applying the PowerLines as the final step to a collection of curves, rather than as you draw each individual element.

It is likely that the PowerLines you created from the two open curves had a different fill from the other objects, or possibly no fill at all. Ordinarily, you wouldn't think of applying a fill to an open curve, but DRAW keeps track of one anyway. When you initially draw an open curve, your default object fill is used. If your default is none, then no fill is applied.

10. Ensure that all four objects are still selected. Then drag the bottom-center sizing handle downward until the status line indicates about 150%, and release. (Be patient…unless you have a very fast computer, this will probably take a while. If you were applying PowerLines as you drew individual elements, and then modifying each of those objects, you would probably quickly lose patience.)

11. In the roll-up, change Maximum Width to .25 inch, and select the Trumpet3 PowerLine. Click Apply.

In addition to demonstrating another preset PowerLine and the effect of a different maximum width, the above exercise shows that you can change a PowerLine after one has already been applied. The new PowerLine replaces, rather than compounds, the original.

INSIDE INFO

When you have several changes planned for a curve that has been PowerLined, you will save a fair amount of time by clearing the PowerLine first, making all necessary curve modifications, and then reapplying the PowerLine.

Watch Those Nodes

Here is a simple exercise to show the consequences of creating Power-Lines with excess nodes in the original curve.

1. Create a new drawing, and invoke the PowerLine roll-up.

2. Change the preset to Teardrop2, but leave Maximum Width at 0.5 inches.

3. Make sure Apply When Drawing Lines is checked.

4. With the Pencil tool, draw an S-shape, roughly like the one at the far left in Figure 21.4.

21.4

A PowerLined S-curve, the hard way and the easy way

Drawn with freehand tool
(after two cups of coffee)

Drawn as straight lines and then
converted to curves and shaped

5. Now hold Ctrl and draw a strictly vertical line.

6. Choose the Shape tool, and double-click the line. On the Node Edit roll-up, select To Curve.

7. Using the control handles, shape the curve like the one at the far right in Figure 21.4.

You can see how long it took to generate the PowerLine, and how messy it looks. Drawing freehand inherently creates many nodes in a curve. The steadier your hand, the smoother the curve and fewer the nodes, but there are nevertheless usually far more nodes than necessary. Like other special effects, PowerLines take longer when there are more nodes. The curve on the right not only looks better, but the PowerLine was generated much more quickly. An alternative to drawing straight lines and converting to curves is to use the Bézier drawing mode. This will have the same advantages of fewer nodes and faster PowerLine creation.

Basic Rules for PowerLines

■ Regardless of your method for drawing curves, it is usually better to draw the curve *without* applying the PowerLine as you draw. Shape the curve, delete any unwanted nodes, and *then* apply the PowerLine. Remember, the PowerLine is regenerated for every little operation you do to the PowerLined curve.

■ Use "efficiency of scale." Draw and edit all curves that will share a common PowerLine *before* applying it. Select all the curves and apply the PowerLine to them all in one step. It will still take time to generate, but you have saved all the regeneration that would take place for each step along the way.

Pen Leakiness and Ink Spread

As in other roll-ups, the various PowerLine features are accessed by clicking on icons at the top of the roll-up. The CorelDRAW online help makes a game attempt at explaining the more sophisticated controls, but it probably won't make a lot of sense on your first, second, or even third reading. The results of using these controls are hard to pinpoint, because they vary with the type of curves drawn and the type of PowerLine chosen.

Figure 21.5 demonstrates how the Pen Leakiness (similar to Speed in version 5.0) and Ink Spread controls are used. (Both these controls are accessed via the ink bottle icon; see the roll-up below.) We drew a shape consisting of curved and straight lines that made some sharp turns (shape #1). Moving to shape #2, you see the same curve with a Wedge1 PowerLine applied. Notice how sharp the corners are.

In shape #3, we have added a Pen Leakiness setting of 100 and used the minimum Ink Spread setting of 1. The Pen Leakiness control has rounded the sharp turns of the PowerLine by adding extra width at the points where the line changes direction, but has also made the object somewhat lumpy. It has also flared the end of the PowerLine. This is where the Ink Spread control comes in. Shape #4 has a Pen Leakiness setting of 31 (to get rid of the end flare), and an Ink Spread of 10 (to provide continuity). This smooths out the unsightly lumps in the curve.

21.5

How to use Pen Leakiness and Ink Spread to get rid of unsightly lumps

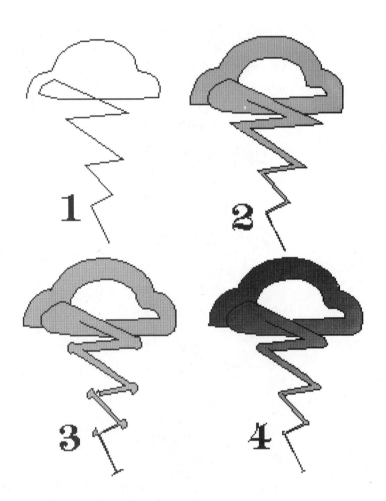

What's a Nib, Anyway?

In the PowerLines roll-up, the icon that looks like a fountain pen offers controls over the nib angle, ratio, and intensity. "Nib" is one of those state-of-the-art words that people started using about a thousand years ago. It really came into its own during the early part of the Industrial Age.

The nib is the part of a pen that makes contact with the paper. When pens were made from feathers (quills) and this was still something of an experimental art form, you would carve nibs in various shapes to get different effects: Broad, flat "chisel" points produced what we now call calligraphy. Sharp, narrow points were good for drawing.

Light industry brought the idea of a reusable pen "barrel" or handle with interchangeable metal nibs, and added variety that feathers didn't offer: round nibs, circular ones, square, flat, angled, or oddly shaped ones. Different writing styles were developed to take advantage of the diversity of nibs.

The ball-point pen did away with all that. Nibs are now the concern of only calligraphy pens, felt-tipped markers, and art pens...and computer graphics. The nib in CorelDRAW simulates the purpose of the physical nib—that is, to govern the way virtual ink hits the virtual paper.

The nib's behavior for PowerLines is similar to the Outline Pen's nib. Visualizing changes to the nib itself is easy. In Figure 21.6 you see both pages of controls for changing the nib; the paging icon toggles you between the two. You can adjust the nib numerically or by clicking and dragging it directly.

21.6

The nib controls

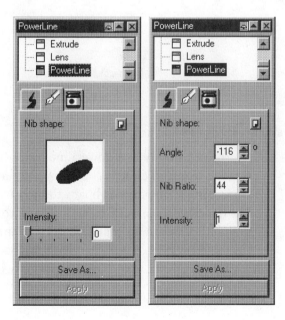

Rather than try to explain what the nib controls actually do, and instead of referring you to the online help for a generally unhelpful explanation, we offer you a few specific examples in Figure 21.7. We started with an ellipse and applied the Trumpet3 PowerLine. The next three objects are the same shape, with various nib adjustments added. Remember that nib changes, like any other changes, convert a preset PowerLine to a custom PowerLine.

21.7

Concept sketches for a Batman-type secret decoder ring

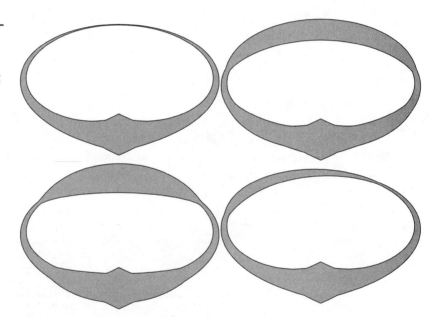

The Problem with Pressure

Pressure sensitivity in a PowerLine seems like a great concept: As you drag the mouse to create a curve, you can, in theory, press the Up Arrow or Down Arrow on your keyboard to increase or decrease the PowerLine width. Sounds wonderful, but it flies in the face of our advice to avoid freehand curve drawing at all costs (too many nodes, too little skill). Unfortunately, freehand drawing is the only way you can use pressure PowerLines; you cannot use this option with line-segment drawing.

Even if we were not predisposed to avoid freehand drawing, we find it next to impossible to synchronize the Up Arrow and Down Arrow keystrokes with a smoothly drawn curve. Perhaps with a pressure-sensitive stylus this option is more useful, but even in that case we think it easier to create a custom PowerLine using all the options discussed so far— plus one very powerful option that we'll introduce next.

Shaping PowerLines with Edit Width

We have already demonstrated that you can use the Shape tool (in the Node Edit roll-up) to modify a curve with a PowerLine applied. But there is an additional option available in the Node Edit roll-up when a power line is the subject: the Edit Width button (see Figure 21.8). This option allows you to customize a preset PowerLine, shaping it in almost any way you like. The following exercise shows you how.

21.8

The Edit Width button in the Node Edit roll-up can be used to shape PowerLines.

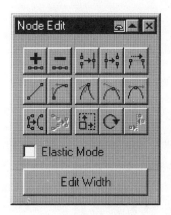

1. Start with a new drawing and, if it isn't already visible, invoke the PowerLine roll-up (Ctrl+F8).

2. Draw a vertical line about 6" long, with a 2-point outline.

3. From the PowerLine presets, choose Maximum Width. (This preset is probably the one you will use most frequently to create your own customized PowerLines.)

4. Set the Maximum Width value to **1.00** inch, and click Apply.

5. Apply a red fill to your PowerLine. You should now have what looks like a red rectangle with a black outline.

6. Select the Shape tool.

7. Double-click on of the nodes to bring up the Node Edit roll-up. Click the Edit Width button.

At this point you will see a rectangle with four flat little circles (or rounded squares, if you wish) at the corners, called *PowerLine nodes,* as shown in Figure 21.9. Each node in a curve will have two of these handles associated with it. These handles can be slid in or out along a path running perpendicular to the path of the curve. In your case, you have only two nodes at the moment, and hence four handles total. The next few steps show you how to manipulate the handles.

21.9

This "curve" can be fattened up or slimmed down, thanks to Edit Width.

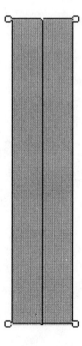

8. Click the top-left handle, and drag it about a half-inch to the left. Notice that the handle itself will only move on a perpendicular path to the curve (the rectangle, in this case). Press Ctrl+Z to undo the action.

9. Now marquee-select both top handles and repeat the move in step 8. Note that both sides of the PowerLine make the same move, in *opposite* directions. You can marquee-select handles vertically this way, as well.

10. Now point to a spot 1" below the top node on the center line and click. Just as in the regular Node Edit mode, this gives you the option of adding a node (or in this case, a set of PowerLine nodes) by clicking the + button in the Node Edit roll-up.

11. Repeat this once per inch until you have something like Figure 21.10, but without the highlighted handles.

21.10

Using Edit Width to get more handles on the situation

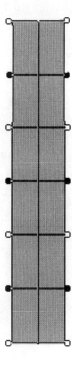

12. Now that you have more handles to work with you can do some interesting creating. Marquee-select the horizontal handle sets that are darker in Figure 21.10, one set at a time, and drag one of the handles about $1/2$ inch out.

13. From the Position page of the Transform roll-up, set Horizontal to +2.5". Click Apply To Duplicate. Then select the duplicate and make another duplicate from it. Repeat the process until you have four PowerLines all in a row.

14. Now return to Edit Width. Using the Shape tool, marquee-select all of the nodes in the first PowerLine.

15. Press Ctrl+F10 to get to the Node Edit roll-up and click the Edit Width button. The next roll-up offers a row of four buttons—To Line, To Curve, Convex, and Concave. Apply one to each of the four PowerLines.

16. Click somewhere off the PowerLine to deselect all handles.

At this point you should have four shapes like those shown in Figure 21.11.

2 1 . I I

**A mess of custom
PowerLines**

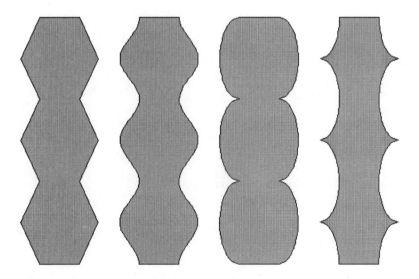

Congratulations! You have created four new PowerLines that can be saved and reused. Your next logical step would normally be to use the Save As button in the PowerLine roll-up so you could apply this shapely shape to other curves.

The real point behind this exercise was to introduce you to all the various options you can use in creating your own custom PowerLines. You are free to add as many handles as you like, modifying them singly or in groups, allowing you to create some substantially complex shapes. Generally, though, PowerLines are designed to be used with fairly simple forms for application to curves of various lengths and shapes.

Saving Your Own PowerLines

If you were to reproduce the foregoing examples yourself and then switch back to the main PowerLine controls, you would find the Maximum Width PowerLine gone. The list box would read "Custom." Once you modify a preset PowerLine in any way, it becomes a custom PowerLine. This brings us to the Save As button in the roll-up. When you create a custom PowerLine, you can give the settings a name and save them. Don't worry about overwriting the presets, because DRAW won't let you.

INSIDE INFO

If you save a custom PowerLine under an existing name, DRAW warns you. You can choose to overwrite the existing custom PowerLine, or enter a new name. Within the Save As options is a button for deleting unwanted custom PowerLines that you don't need anymore. But you don't have to save custom PowerLine settings to use them. Just keep the roll-up open, and continue applying the settings to new objects. Or you can copy the PowerLine attributes via the Effects menu.

In DRAW 6.0 you can copy PowerLines with the Copy flyout on the Effects menu or the Apply To Duplicate button in the Transform roll-up. You can also clone PowerLines, just as other effects can be cloned. Again, we recommend saving copying and cloning as a last step for a collection of curves, rather than applying as you go. The advantage: You can select the original, modify its PowerLine, and all clones will get updated in the same way, while copies or duplicates retain their characteristics. The problem: If you have more than a few curves, finding your original object can be tough.

What Cost, PowerLines?

If you work at all with complex shapes, you will discover that custom PowerLines take a long time to generate when applied to a curve, and they often do not give you the results you expect. For elaborate shapes, it is sometimes better to create them the old-fashioned way: by drawing closed freehand curves and shaping them.

In addition to the time they take to generate, PowerLines create complex objects with far too many nodes. Consider the Teardrop1 Power-Line applied to a straight line; re-create it in freehand drawing mode, and you'll see the equivalent could be done with a curve having just two nodes. Break a PowerLine down into curves, using the Arrange / Separate command; you will end up with the original control curve and not one, but at least *two* other curves. Select one of these curves with the Shape tool, and you will find it may have upwards of 100 nodes! Having all those nodes means more complex files and longer print times.

This is not meant to deter you from creating your own custom Power-Lines. Just don't be taken in by the glitter of PowerLines without being aware of the consequences of using them. PowerLines are excellent for developing simple shapes to be used over and over to give the impression of something, such as tall grass or the shaded pleats of a dress.

More Basic Rules for PowerLines

■ If you're only going to use a shape a few times in a drawing, it's better to create it the old-fashioned way, drawing closed curves with the freehand drawing tools.

■ Use PowerLines when you have many similar, simple shapes to create, such as leaves of grass or the strands of a horse's mane.

■ Beware of overly complex custom PowerLines. For each node on the control curve, there are many more on the PowerLine.

♣

In our final chapter on special effects, we will go Through the Looking Glass, focusing on PowerClips and Lenses, two of DRAW's stellar performers.

Through the Looking Glass

TWENTY-TWO

The final stop on our tour through DRAW's special effects might be the highlight of the trip for you. It features two of DRAW's superstar performers: PowerClips and Lens. They have played to rave reviews since DRAW 5, and in DRAW 6.0 the Lens roll-up has acquired a bit of new talent. Also covered in this chapter is the Bitmap Color Mask, new in DRAW 6.0.

If you think we're taking on too much by covering all three of these effects in one chapter, fear not—all three are quite easy to use. We see a common thread between PowerClip and Lens; both tools are concerned with how objects appear, not how they are shaped. Neither PowerClip nor Lens changes an object, as the Knife tool, Trim, Weld and others do. Instead, they determine how we *see* an object. The same goes for the Bitmap Color Mask roll-up, which allows you to change the appearance of imported bitmap images.

PowerClips

If you followed along with Chapter 12, you saw a good example of PowerClipping in action, where a picture of three-year-old Erica Altman was placed inside the letters that make up her name. You might think of PowerClip as the "stuff it inside" command; the job of this feature is to take one object and place it inside of another—but with no distortion. (Have you seen the Pepsi commercial, where the boy on the beach draws so hard on the straw that he sucks himself entirely into the bottle? That is *not* how PowerClip works.) PowerClip effectively trims the object to fit within a shape. Anything that falls outside the boundaries of the PowerClip *container* is simply hidden from view. (We'll explain containers shortly.)

Free-form cropping has long been a feature of painting and image-editing programs such as PhotoPAINT, but bringing this operation into DRAW was not so easy. With PAINT, it's simple to create a "mask" and simply erase all pixels that fall outside of the mask. But in a vector drawing program such as DRAW, in which drawings are composed of myriad separate objects, each one defined mathematically and consisting of curves, the program can't simply erase pixels. And if you have ever tried to use the node-editing tools to manually trim even a simple element so it will fit inside another object, you can appreciate how complex the programming is for a cropping operation.

Furthermore, unlike a paint program or a manual trim job—both of which delete the portion that is outside of the desired area—PowerClip maintains the integrity of the original object. The remainder isn't trimmed, but is hidden, instead. If you decide to undo a PowerClip, just extract the contents—it's as if nothing had ever happened to them. Try doing *that* with a paint program…

PowerClip Basics

Creating a PowerClip is simple: Select one or more objects to be clipped, go to Effects / PowerClip / Place Inside Container, and then click on the container object. The objects to be clipped can be literally anything, even an imported bitmap as you saw in Chapter 12. The container can be anything created in DRAW. That rules out bitmaps, but as far as we can tell, anything else is eligible, including multipathed objects, groups, text, envelopes, extrusions, even another PowerClip.

Try this exercise on for size:

1. In a new drawing, go to the Symbols roll-up. From Plants, drag the palm tree (symbol #33) onto the page. From Animals1, drag in an elephant (symbol #52).

2. Shade the palm tree dark and the elephant light, and then select and group them.

3. Draw a circle around the group, using the Ctrl key to make it a perfect circle. Remove the fill and then position and size the circle so parts of both the palm tree and the elephant are outside, as shown in Figure 22.1.

4. Reselect the group, and go Effects / PowerClip / Place Inside Container.

5. When the large arrow cursor appears, click on the circle to select it as your container (make sure to click right on the outline of the circle, not just somewhere inside it).

22.1

The raw materials for a PowerClip

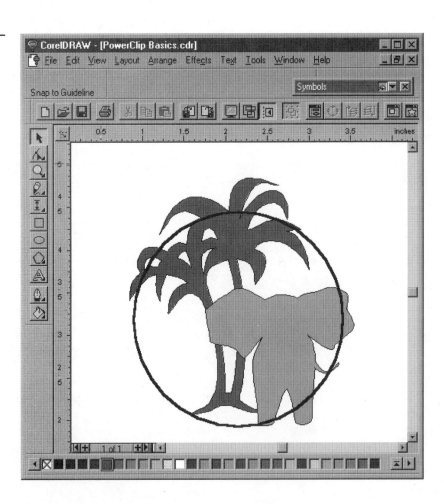

From such a simple set of commands comes such an impressive effect! Notice what the status line calls this new object, and of course, see what DRAW has done: It has automatically cropped the palm tree and the elephant according to the perimeter of the circle.

In Chapter 12, we discussed the similarities between using a PowerClip and using the Combine command to produce a hollow mask around a drawing. Prior to DRAW 5, the only way to produce this effect would have been to combine the circle with a large white rectangle. This mask would then be placed on top of the elephant and palm tree to crop them. No contest—this is a much easier task with PowerClip.

By the way, the circle used as the container in Figure 22.1 is hollow, but it could also be filled. The fill color would act as the background for the clipped objects.

Editing PowerClips

Your palm tree/elephant group probably wasn't positioned within the PowerClip exactly as ours was in Figure 22.1, but adjusting that would be easy. You have lots of ways to modify PowerClips after the fact. The simplest way is to select the PowerClip and select Effects / PowerClip / Edit Contents. DRAW proceeds to show you only those objects inside the PowerClip, and allows you to edit them any way you like. When you are done, reach for the Finish Editing This Level command. (It's so named because DRAW allows you to nest PowerClips within other PowerClips, and if you were editing a nested PowerClip, you would be modifying just that level.)

Following are some things to keep in mind as you edit PowerClips.

Avoid Auto-Centering   We like PowerClip's clean and intuitive design…with one exception. In its factory condition, DRAW sets a default that automatically centers all objects within their container. Most DRAW users—including us—don't like this, for two reasons:

■ We rarely want our objects exactly centered in the container, so making the default *no* centering would make better sense. It is more typical and more logical to position the objects and then clip them.

- The control for turning centering on and off is out of place. You have to go to Tools / Options and look for the awkwardly named Automatically Center New PowerClip Contents check box.

We suggest that you find this check box, uncheck it, and leave it that way. If you ever do want to center objects within a container, you can turn it back on for the moment—better yet, just use the Align roll-up before you start your PowerClipping.

Use the Lock Contents Option   The Lock Contents to Power-Clip option is somewhat hidden, yet is far more useful than the auto-center option. With this option on, when you create a PowerClip the contents are initially locked to the container, so that the whole Power-Clip is treated as a single object. That means the contents move, rotate, and scale along with the container. Most of the time you will want to keep this lock on, but sometimes you'll need to change the relative positions of the container and the clipped objects. You can always do this with the Edit Contents command on the PowerClip menu, but that is cumbersome for simple adjustments. That's when the time is right to unlock the contents. You do this by right-clicking on the PowerClip and unchecking the Lock Contents to PowerClip option. The container then acts as a movable window, letting you view different parts of the objects inside. When you are done repositioning everything, relock the contents to ensure that the PowerClip again moves as a unit.

Group While Editing   In the simple exercise earlier in this chapter, you grouped the palm tree and elephant before placing them in the PowerClip container. You could have just as easily marquee-selected the two objects and PowerClipped without grouping, but we wanted you to see that grouping simplifies your PowerClipping tasks.

There is nothing to stop you from ungrouping, regrouping, combining, and deleting elements, or changing fills, or doing anything else to the contents of a PowerClip. When you use PowerClip / Edit Contents, think of the contents as a separate drawing that will eventually be cropped by the container outline. Nearly anything you would normally do to objects in a drawing can be done at this point. Then, when you select Finish Editing This Level from the flyout, the PowerClip is re-applied to the contents. The one thing you cannot do with the Edit Contents command is reposition the container itself, but that is easily done before you create the PowerClip (by simply editing it) or afterward (by unlocking the contents).

Extrusions as PowerClips

Figure 22.2 shows another example of a PowerClip, this time using an extrusion as the container. At the top you see the elements that were placed inside the PowerClip, and on the bottom is the end result. Here are the steps for creating this mock-up of a product package:

1. In a new drawing, create a yellow rectangle about 5″ wide by 6″ tall, with a black outline of 0.5 point.

2. Create a small circle and a rectangle, and weld them together to form the slot from which this product could hang on a rack in the store. Place the slot near the top of the large rectangle, Shift+select the rectangle, and then press Ctrl+L to combine the two together.

3. Extrude the shape using Small Back and a depth setting of 5. Fill it with either a solid color or shading (but *don't* select Use Object Fill on the Color tab of Extrude).

WATCH OUT!

The Use Object Fill option does not work properly with extrusions as PowerClips, because the entire extrusion gets treated as the PowerClip, not just the control object. This would be an interesting feature if the contents would bend around the corners of an extrusion, but they don't, so it's not. Instead you end up with a visually confusing object.

22.2

Extrusions, too, can be PowerClip containers.

4. Drag a 5″ or so elephant (#52 in the Animals1 section of the Symbols library) anywhere on the page, and fill it 30% gray with no outline.

5. Create the words **L.E. Fonts** as shown; use two centered lines and about 150-point type in any font you wish. For now, don't worry about rotating or placement.

6. Select both the text and the elephant, and choose Effects / Power-Clip / Place Inside Container. Choose the extrusion as the container.

7. You now need to edit the contents of the PowerClip. Place the elephant approximately as shown in the bottom image of Figure 22.2. Rotate the text about 30°, and place it as shown in the

figure. If you like, change the color of the text and add an outline. Then select Finish Editing This Level.

Besides demonstrating how extrusions can be used as PowerClip containers, the foregoing exercise reinforces a point made earlier about the Edit Contents command: The sequence followed in the exercise left most of the object editing to be done *after* you placed the objects in the container. Remember that you can scale, shape, rotate, fill, and even blend objects either before clipping them or after. DRAW doesn't care.

We didn't include this in the exercise, but to spice up our design, we created a 20-step blend from a black elephant shape that we had distorted with an envelope, to a 30% gray elephant shape slightly reduced in scale.

Making PowerClips Jump through Hoops

If you're still not impressed with PowerClip, take a look at Figure 22.3. Here we used a PowerClip to create an image that would be very difficult to create otherwise: a dolphin jumping through a hoop. In the two-dimensional world of graphics software, this image simply cannot be created without some sort of illusion. PowerClip provides the illusion.

22.3

Can you make a dolphin jump through a hoop? It's not so easy...unless you turn to PowerClip.

Figure 22.4 shows the steps we took. We found the dolphin in Corel's clip art library. We drew a circle, extruded it, and shaded it to create the hoop. The top image in Figure 22.4 shows that simple starting point;

22.4

The four steps we took to make this dolphin jump through the hoop. A second dolphin is placed in front of the hoop and clipped into an invisible rectangle.

notice that the hoop is in front of the dolphin. In the second image, we selected the dolphin and made a quick copy using the + key, and then we moved it in front of the other two objects. Our choice of duplicating methods (Quick Copy, not Duplicate or Drag and Dupe) was important because the new dolphin had to be directly on top of the old one.

The third image shows the rectangle that we drew to act as the container. It encloses the part of the dolphin that will appear to be already through the hoop. We took the duplicated dolphin and PowerClipped it into this rectangle, so we had a dolphin behind the hoop (the original one) and half of a dolphin in front of the hoop (the PowerClipped one). As the last image shows, once we removed the fill and outline from the PowerClip rectangle, the two dolphins appeared to be just one that was halfway through the hoop.

PowerClips and Bitmaps

One area where PowerClips can dramatically improve functionality is when you're incorporating a bitmap into a drawing. DRAW has always allowed bitmaps to be placed in a drawing, but prior to PowerClip you had to work with a rectangular image. Even if you created an elliptical portrait by cropping the image in an image editor, the imported image would still be bound by a rectangular area, and that area would be solid white, not hollow. Yes, you can crop images with the Shape tool, and in 6.0 you can even crop them in a freeform pattern. Nevertheless, PowerClip still offers the ultimate in control over the cropping of a bitmap.

Prior to DRAW 5, the solution to bitmap cropping was to create a mask and place it in front of the bitmap, but assembling other elements in relation to the bitmap proved to be a major headache. It's better since DRAW 5. Figure 22.5, a postcard mailer for a fictitious athletic gym, demonstrates how a bitmap can be placed in a PowerClip, as well as how one PowerClip can be placed inside of another.

22.5

The body of the illustration is PowerClipped within the outer rectangle, and the picture of the tiger is PowerClipped within that.

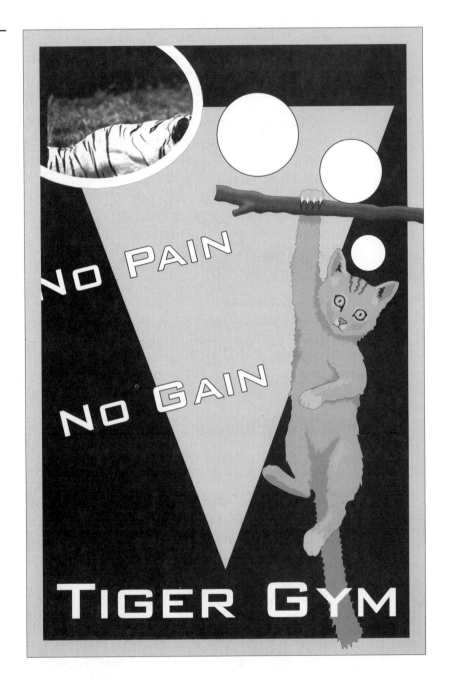

AUTHOR'S NOTE

The tiger we used for Figure 22.5 is from the Wild Animals volume of Corel's Photo CD library. We imported it directly into DRAW as a PhotoCD (.PCD) image, and then selected color depth and resolution.

After the tiger image was imported, we drew a hollow ellipse over it. Then we created a duplicate of the ellipse and sized it by adding .2″ both vertically and horizontally, to serve as a white backdrop. Then we PowerClipped the bitmap to the hollow ellipse.

What Cost, Clipped Pictures?

PowerClipping bitmap images is an exceptionally powerful technique, but it is not without its price—especially as you become more creative with your effects. We'll share with you one of our recent little disasters using the same tiger that we used in Figure 22.5.

When imported to DRAW and printed, the tiger created 3MB of print data—not bad for a detailed photograph at moderate resolution. When clipped into a simple container, like the ellipse in Figure 22.5, there was virtually no increase in code sent to the printer. But then we began to experiment…

We wanted to see how much harder DRAW would have to work in order to clip the tiger into a more elaborate container. So we created a series of squares and grouped them as shown in the top half of Figure 22.6. We then used the group of rectangles as the container and clipped the tiger inside of it. The result was striking, as shown in the lower half of the figure. But then we made the mistake of trying to print it. We produced over 36MB of print data! Why the gigantic increase? Placing an object into 40 little boxes isn't too difficult, in and of itself, but DRAW has to allow for the possibility that you might want to *un*group the 40 boxes that make up the group. (Indeed, if you were to take apart the

PowerClipped tiger, you would end up with 40 boxed, PowerClipped tigers.) We created some impressive effects, but we paid dearly in terms of hard drive space (when creating an .EPS file) and/or print times.

22.6

This PowerClipped effect is very cool, but we aren't sure it was worth the cost in disk space and print time.

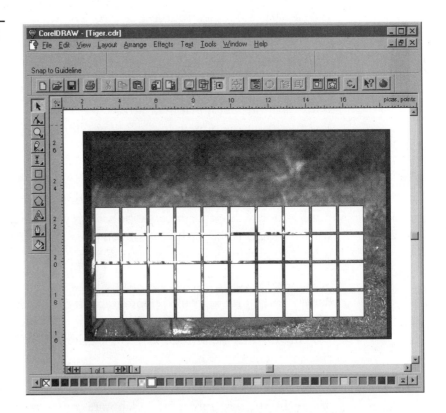

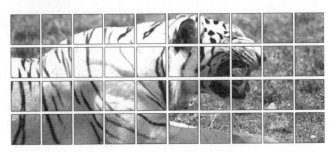

AUTHOR'S NOTE

Interestingly, DRAW 5 was smarter with this PowerClipped tiger. In earlier editions of this book, we reported a print file that was not significantly larger—about 3.2MB. It would have shot up into the stratosphere only if we had ungrouped the PowerClip group or began modifying one of the squares in the group (by selecting it with the Ctrl key). That's really the cue that you're going to require one tiger per square; until then, it's still a single image with a single defined container. DRAW 5 understands this; DRAW 6 does not. Guess we won't be clipping too many pictures into little boxes anymore...

New Lenses on Life

DRAW's lenses are probably responsible for more oohs and aahs at trade shows and product demonstrations than any other feature of Corel-DRAW, and DRAW 6.0 furthers this claim to fame. The Lens roll-up provides access to 11 different cameralike lenses that can be applied to an object. When you apply a lens, the object *becomes* the lens, filtering your view of all objects that are behind it. Thus lenses allow objects to become, in essence, transparent—an effect that was impossible prior to the debut of lenses in DRAW 5.

For an object to be a lens, it must meet two criteria:

- It must be a "single" element. It can have multiple paths and be a combination of objects, even ones that are not touching, but DRAW must view it as a single curve. An artistic text string is considered a single element, so it qualifies.

- It must be a closed object, capable of holding a fill.

Open LENSTOUR.CDR from the PRACTICE directory of the Companion CD, and you'll find a good practice file for learning about lenses. We prepared several rectangles with different fill types and patterns, and then a simple ellipse placed on top. The bars on the left are created from a rainbow blend, and the four rectangles on the right are (from top to bottom) a fountain fill, a two-color pattern fill, a full-color bitmap fill, and a fractal fill. Figure 22.7 shows the effect of one of the standard lenses—a 50% transparency. In other words, the ellipse in front is set to allow half of the color intensities from the objects underneath to show through. Meanwhile, the ellipse itself is filled with 50% black. You can re-create Figure 22.7 by following these steps:

1. Open LENSTOUR.CDR and select the ellipse.

2. Invoke the Lens roll-up (Effects / Lens or Alt+F3).

3. In the nameless drop-down window in the middle of the roll-up, choose Transparency as the type of lens.

4. Set the Rate to 50%.

5. Set the Color to 50% black, or some other medium shade.

6. Click Apply.

With LENSTOUR.CDR, you can experiment with all of the different lens effects. Try applying each style of lens. If you need to, refer to the descriptions in the following sections. When a particular lens has additional settings for rate, color, and so on, try varying them over a wide range to see the result.

In the PICTURES directory, we have provided a file called PHOTOS.CDR that demonstrates the application of all of DRAW's lenses. Notice the subtle differences between how a color image and a grayscale image are influenced by the same lens.

CorelDRAW's Lenses

Here are descriptions of the lenses.

Transparency   Likely to be the most used of the bunch, Transparency causes the colors of the objects under the lens to mix with the lens object's color, creating the illusion that you've placed a piece of transparent film over the object. In the Rate box, you enter a transparency rate

22.7

The effect of a 50% transparency lens on a host of different patterns

from 1% to 100%. The greater this value, the more transparent the lens object; at 100%, the lens essentially disappears.

Magnify This lens causes the objects under the lens to be magnified by the factor you specify in the Amount box, so it looks like you've placed a magnifying glass over the drawing. The maximum magnification factor is 10. Be careful when using this lens with bitmaps; at twice or three times the magnification, most bitmaps will look very jagged. However, with a vector object, like the coin in Figure 22.8, the effect is useful and realistic.

22.8

Creating a magnifying glass is easy with a Magnify lens.

Brighten This lens brightens the colors under it by the factor you specify in the Rate box, between−100% and 100%. At 100%, the colors are nearly white; at 0%, the lens has no effect at all; and at −100%, the colors approach black. This lens is similar to the Transparency lens, and in fact, you could create the same effect with either one.

Invert   With Invert you can switch the colors under the lens to their complementary colors, based on the CMYK color wheel. For example, red becomes cyan, green becomes magenta, and yellow becomes blue. In Figure 22.9, we converted a rectangle to a curve, made one of the sides wavy, and used that object as an inverted lens. The result might work well as the front of a contemporary music CD.

22.9

The Invert lens is definitely "out there."

AUTHOR'S NOTE

We have included Figure 22.9 in the **PRACTICE** directory of the Companion CD as **LENSTEST.CDR.** We suggest that you open it and apply the various lenses to it as they are introduced in this discussion.

Color Limit Color Limit works much like a color filter on a camera, filtering out all colors under the lens except the one you specify in the Color box. For example, if you place a green lens over an object, all colors except green will be filtered out within the lens area. You can also control the strength of the filter by specifying a value in the Rate box. For the green filter, a rate of 100% will allow only green to show through; a lower setting will allow other colors to show through.

Color Add The Color Add lens mixes the colors of overlapping objects. This lens has no effect where it overlays white objects, because white already contains 100% of every color.

INSIDE INFO

Once a lens is applied, you can select colors from the on-screen color palette or the Fill roll-up to change the lens tint. This may not seem to be a big deal, but when you're experimenting with lenses on a drawing, it does save having to constantly access the Lens roll-up and the Apply button.

Tinted Grayscale Objects under this lens appear to have had a tonal scale setting applied. Colors under the lens are mapped from the lens color to an equivalent tone of the color of that lens. For example, a blue lens over a light-colored object creates light blue; the same lens over a dark-colored object creates dark blue. This lens is very handy for decolorizing a drawing or imported bitmap, for proofing or for actual printing. To do this, simply cover the entire object with a rectangle or other closed curve, choose Tinted Grayscale, and set the color to Black.

Heat Map This lens is DRAW's contribution to the electronic psychedelic community. It maps colors to other colors in a predefined palette, creating a *heat map* or infrared look. Bright (or hot) colors are mapped to other hot colors (yellow, orange, and so on), and dark (or cool) colors are mapped to cooler colors (blue, cyan, and purple). The palette Rotation value determines where the color mapping begins. For example, a value of 0% or 100% causes mapping to begin at the start of the palette (at white) and move to the right (through cyan, blue, and so on). A value of 50% causes mapping to begin halfway through the palette (at red) and move to the right, and then go back to the start of the palette.

Custom Color Map   This new lens maps colors using a range that you define. The controls are similar to fountain fills—you choose From and To colors, and specify the direction that the mapping should take. You can map directly between the two specified colors; or start with the From color and go through the colors of the rainbow, forward or backward, to the To color.

Wireframe   This clever new lens is like switching to Wireframe view, but for just a portion of your screen. Try it on LENSTEST.CDR and you'll see instantly how it works. All objects are reduced down to one fill and one outline color, both of which you designate from the Lens roll-up.

Fish Eye   Just like the camera lens of the same name, this new lens magnifies and distorts the objects behind the lens. Figure 22.10 shows the process of creating a fish-eye effect.

None   Selecting None removes the lens from the selected object and returns the object to its normal state.

Frozen Lenses

Another new and remarkable addition to DRAW 6.0's lens arsenal is the ability to freeze and even extract a lens effect. Figure 22.11 is a continuation of Figure 22.10, where we created the fish-eye effect. After creating the lens, we froze it, by checking the Frozen option on the roll-up. Then the image that is seen through the lens no longer needs the object behind it. You can see in no. 6 in the figure that removing the grid behind the ellipse has no effect on the fish-eyed circle in the lens.

Frozen lenses work with bitmaps, as well.

22.10

Better vision through electronics—and DRAW's new Fish Eye lens.

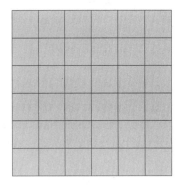

1. Grid created using the new Graph Paper tool.

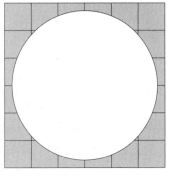

2. Circle drawn and placed in middle of grid.

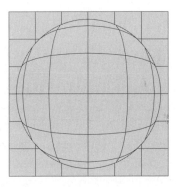

3. Fish Eye lens applied to circle.

22.11

Thanks to the Frozen option, a lens can stand on its own, without the aid of the background object that gave it its appearance.

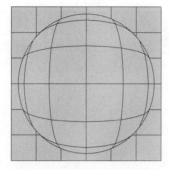

4. Fish Eye lens applied to circle.

5. Fish Eye lens frozen in place.

6. Lens no longer needs the underneath object. Removing it does not effect lens.

7. Lens now just a group of objects that can be edited (or destroyed), just like any other group.

INSIDE INFO

DRAW 6.0 has effectively given us one more way to crop objects and images, with or without a lens effect. For instance, a Brighten lens at a rate of 0% is the same as no lens at all. Freeze this do-nothing lens, and you have essentially cropped the object or image behind it.

Changing Your Point of View

The final enhancement of DRAW 6.0 lenses enables you to change the viewing angle through a lens. When you click on the Viewpoint check box and then the Edit button, an X appears on screen, similar to the one that you adjust to change the perspective of an extrusion. This X allows you to choose an area or object to be visible in the lens, other than whatever is directly behind the lens.

Figure 22.12 shows this in action. On top, a simple lens is placed over a portion of the drawing, brightened by 50%. But by activating the Viewpoint check box and designating another part of the drawing (middle), a different view is seen through the lens (below). This is a great tool for those who need to create blow-ups of an illustration to show detail.

Combining Lenses

As you experimented with DRAW's lenses, you may have noticed for yourself that you can overlay one lens on another. For example, you might want to both magnify and brighten an object underneath a lens. When you apply a new lens, you replace any existing lens; they are not added together. However, you can *stack* lens objects on top of one another. Make a quick copy of a lens object, which effectively duplicates the lens effect. Then change to a different lens effect, and you create a compound lens effect.

22.12

The Viewpoint option offers a whole new lease on lenses.

1. Normal Brighten lens applied to circle in front of cityscape.

2. Viewpoint activated. X dragged to the top of the building on left.

3. When applied, the lens shows the desired area, and will continue to until the Viewpoint is edited again or disabled.

In Figure 22.13 we have stacked two lenses to demonstrate a compound lens. The lens that angles left is a Transparency lens; the other one is a Heat Map lens.

22.13

When you place one lens on top of another, you double your viewing pleasure.

WATCH OUT!

Like PowerClips, lens effects move into the high rent district in a hurry. Draw creates lenses by duplicating the objects that are underneath. Thus a compound lens effect requires the *quadrupling* of objects, and in the case of the Full-Color Bitmap pattern in Figure 22.13, that results in no small amount of data. To give you an idea, Figure 22.7 was a single lens on top of the various bars and boxes; an .EPS file for this requires 1.8MB of storage. In contrast, Figure 22.13 with its double-lens effect needs almost 4MB.

Learning to Use the Lenses

Having experimented with the effects produced by each lens type, you've probably already thought of a number of uses for Transparency and Magnify. Here are a few handy uses for the others.

Tinted Grayscale for Cheap Color   If you want to add a bit of color or take away color, the Tinted Grayscale lens is your answer. We mentioned earlier that you can import a full-color photograph or drawing and apply a Tinted Grayscale lens to it, to convert it to grayscale. You can also colorize a black-and-white image by adding a Tinted Grayscale lens. Despite this lens's name, you can choose any color for it, making it easy and affordable to add some color to a project.

Heat Map   Like Tinted Grayscale, Heat Map is most effective when used with grayscale photographs. Try importing a photo and applying this lens. The result is an effect that has become very popular in Generation X publications. If you are planning to publish a magazine dedicated to heavy-metal music, this is definitely the lens for you. Figure 22.14 and Illustration No. 9 in the Color Gallery shows how dramatically the Heat Map lens can change a black-and-white image.

22.14

Even in black and white, you can see how wild and crazy the Heat Map lens can be.

Using Brighten to Create Text Backdrops   Another popular technique used in many publications is to brighten or "wash out" part of an image in order to place text over it. The Brighten lens makes it easy to accomplish this, as Figure 22.15 shows.

Masking Bitmaps

New to version 6.0, there is yet another way to manipulate bitmaps in DRAW without actually changing them. With the Bitmap Color Mask,

22.15

By brightening this photograph, regular-size text can be placed in front and be easily read.

Metamorphosis

There can be little in life more lovely than a butterfly's rich and colorful expanse. Similarly, there can be little in life more dramatic than its journey from the unloved and unconsidered moth to the revered creature that it is.

you can designate colors in imported bitmap images and make them invisible. And by invisible we don't mean white—we mean transparent, see-through, invisible. This is a fascinating concept and a very interesting tool, but it isn't quite ready for prime time.

You use the Bitmap Color Mask roll-up on an imported bitmap. After selecting it and activating the controls on the roll-up, you click on a part of the image. That color is automatically rendered transparent. There is a tolerance control on the roll-up, which allows you to set a fudge factor to determine whether or not colors that are close to the selected one would also become transparent.

Our frustration with the tool is its limited benefit in DRAW. The classic use of this tool is for removing a background from a picture, but in order for this to work, the background has to be very flat and distinct from the foreground. Otherwise, parts of the foreground image that share that background color would also be rendered transparent.

This roll-up is also available in PhotoPAINT, and our advice is that you use it there. Color masking is very much in the image-editing domain, and including it in DRAW would have made sense if PAINT were not included in the box. In PAINT, you can create a mask around an *area* of an image without concern for inadvertently changing pixels outside that area. We think that approach is easier to learn and to use.

We'll continue to watch with interest how this tool evolves, but for now we don't see it as a must-have, can't-live-without feature.

Putting It All Together

As we complete our long journey through DRAW's special effects, it is our prerogative to produce one kitchen-sink drawing, incorporating many of the effects discussed in this chapter and others preceding it. Figure 22.16 offers a little bit of everything, including extensive use of PowerClipped bitmaps, enveloped text, and a brightened lens.

One Last Thought About Special Effects

Here is our last piece of advice for you, as you continue to develop your proficiency with special effects: Try and think a bit like an artist and a bit like a computer programmer. If you start as the artist, with as clear a vision as possible of what you want to achieve, ask your alter ego (the special effects expert) to seek out the best way to go about delivering your product. This will require imagination and inventiveness distinctly different from the versions of these qualities that you use as an artist. From our discussions with DRAW users, we have concluded that artists learning about computers often don't think enough about how the tools actually work, choosing tools and techniques that most closely mimic traditional artistic methods, even if there is another tool that would be a better choice.

Conversely, computer users learning about art have a tendency to make the method more important than the result. They pick an effect and then try to find an excuse to use it. Whatever type you are (and there is undoubtedly a little of both in all of us), we recommend this sequence

22. 16

Lenses and Power-Clips team up to help create this poster.

of events. First, allow your artistic side to define what is needed; then ask your technical side to help achieve it.

♣

And now, in Part V, we allow the artistic side of our award-winning designers to take center stage.

PART

DOING IT

This section of the book we turn over to those who really do CorelDRAW justice: the professional designers who have turned to DRAW for their serious illustration needs and won awards for their efforts.

We don't expect you to be sitting at your computer while you read these next four chapters. You may be more comfortable on the patio, in your living room, or perhaps another room in the house in which you often do your daily reading...

An Elegant Exploration

23

Gary Priester is half of an award-winning husband-and-wife design team from Sausalito, CA. Gary and his wife, Mary Carter, have won a handful of awards for work with CorelDRAW, and the pair have become regulars in the trade journals and the seminar circuit. In this and the next chapter, Gary takes you inside his head as he works through the ebb and flow of his creative process.

It's my experience that the best design rarely comes with the first exploration, and sometimes not even in the first ten. This is not to say that sometimes I don't get lucky and nail a design on my first attempt. But more often than not, one design leads to another, and another, until eventually you know you've got it and you can stop.

The other factor is time. It's no surprise anymore when a client says, "Oh, and by the way, is there any way we can see the designs by the end of the week? We're off to Aruba for a little snorkeling and want to approve them before we go. That way you'll have the finished art when we return." My response is, "No problem. Give us 5 minutes and we'll give you a design. Give us 15 minutes and we'll give you a better design." Clients really believe that because we work on computers, we can get anything and everything to them overnight. Oh well, this is my problem, not yours.

The point I'm trying to make is simply this: CorelDRAW places a ton of bells and whistles at your disposal, so why not use them to explore a range of design possibilities? The project I have chosen to illustrate this process is what we call a *page look*. A page look is an exploration of many design executions for establishing the look of an ad campaign, brochure, or other such use. The theme of this project is "Return to Classic Design." I come from the old school that believes life is not a contest to see how difficult we can make our type to read. When I see

type that has been so tortured it is virtually unreadable, it's like finger-
nails on a chalk board. So, with me in the role of color commentator
looking over my own shoulder, here is a play-by-play account of Return
to Classic Elegance.

Laying the Foundation

Even though CorelDRAW ships with hundreds of typefaces, I have
many other favorites, one of which is Adobe Poppl-Residenz Light. It's a
beautiful, classic script font and a perfect typographical complement to
the message itself. I begin by setting the phrase "Now is the time to return to the beauty of classic design" in 36 point. I create a large cap *N*
and group it with the smaller *ow*, and call upon the mysterious new
Align & Distribute roll-up. (I say "mysterious" because I find this new
roll-up baffling.) After several tries I manage to center the two grouped
elements on the page, as shown in Figure 23.1.

23.1

The raw materials

I pick a feather motif from another non-Corel source, Monotype's elegant Arabesque Ornaments collection, and center it under the type. To add the look of gold leaf, I give the feather a custom fountain fill of various yellows. Then I add some borders. Choosing colors from my Tru-Match swatch book ensures the colors that print will be the colors I want. The result, in Figure 23.2, is classic simplicity.

23.2

Here is the basic visual theme. Let the exploration begin.

Now that I have a basic composition established, I begin to explore. I add a series of thin white rules behind the type. For use as a drop shadow, I create a duplicate capital *N*, fill it with a medium tan, and move it back between the white lines and the pale tan background color. I use the Tab key to select the original *N* and Shift+PageUp to bring it to the front. At this point my screen looks like Figure 23.3.

2 3 . 3

**The white lines
bring visual variety
to the illustration.**

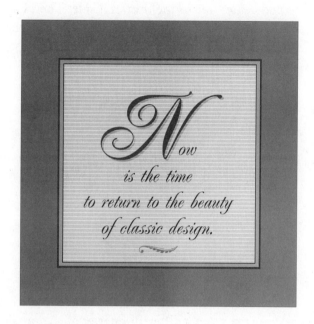

Patterns of Elegance

I love patterns, so I decide to create a repeating vector-fill pattern. I begin with a thistle symbol from Adobe Caslon Ornaments:

and then create four duplicate thistles, colored dark tan. Next I construct a square about twice the height of the thistle, fill it with light tan,

and center one of the thistles inside. Then I arrange the other four thistles, one on each corner, and align them so that each is half in and half
out of the square:

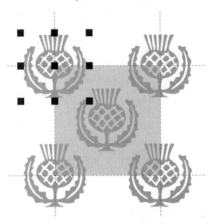

The square defines the pattern, or tile. Notice that the thistles on each
corner contain a different quarter of a complete thistle. When the pattern is tiled, it will appear seamless:

After some searching, I discover the Create Pattern function is now
called Create and has been moved from the Special menu into a new
menu called Tools. Create has a flyout with the choices I'm familiar
with, and I select Full Color. Then I use the crosshair cursor to drag a

rectangle to define my pattern. I save and name my pattern, which now looks like Figure 23.4.

23.4

Once saved as a pattern, this object can be used as a background or for other decorative purposes.

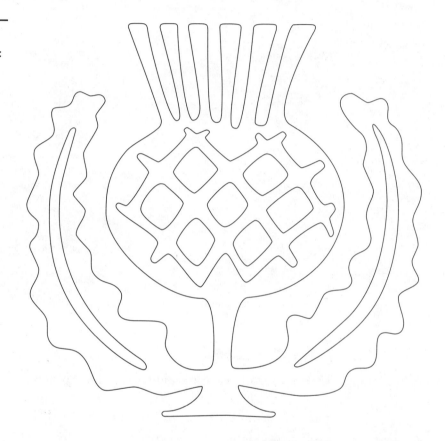

Next I select the outer border of my design, choose the Vector Fill option from the Fill tool menu, and select my newly created fill (see Figure 23.5). The results, shown in Figure 23.6, are quite pleasing and I'm tempted to stop here and call it a design. But then I remember my goal—explore!—and I press on.

23.5

The new vector pattern will be used to fill the background rectangle...

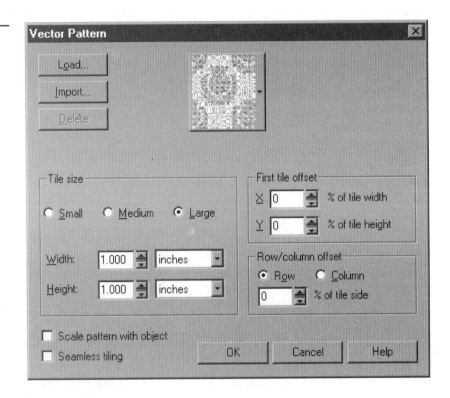

A New Lens on Life

One of the most exciting additions to DRAW 6 is full-color bitmap fills, and if I had to pick a favorite, it would be this marble paper pattern. These new pattern fills work the same way as the thistle fill I described just above: The design element is square, and clicking the Tiling button produces a seamless pattern (see Figure 23.7). I replace the thistle fill with the marble fill, and voilà, I love it!

23.6

...and the results
are a success.

23.7

The new full-color
bitmap fills offer a
new playground for
experimenters.

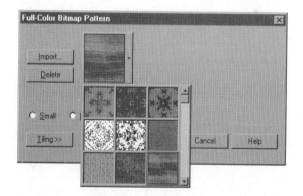

I combine the large *N* with the middle square. Selecting the filled letter
last produces a deep red rectangle with the N knocked out, to let the
marble paper show through (Figure 23.8). You'll read more about
knockouts in the "Color for the Color Blind" chapter, by the way.

**The marble paper
"frame" takes King
of the Hill honors.**

But I can't stop here. I call up the new Effects all-in-one roll-up and choose Lens. This is where the fun really begins. The first lens I audition is Brighten, set to 25%. This produces a "ghosted" version of the marble paper. I then add a very dark green—nice and subtle—to the type and outline. Actually, the Brighten lens is perfect for making portions of an image or photograph lighter so your type can be read easily, as demonstrated in Figure 23.9.

Moving on, I give the new Custom Color Map lens a workout. This is similar to the Tinted Grayscale lens, except in DRAW 6 you can use two colors to create a duotone effect. With the Forward or Backward Rainbow option, DRAW creates a rainbow between the two colors and then remaps the image to this new palette. (Forward and Backward refer to the direction—clockwise or counterclockwise—that is taken around the color wheel to create the rainbow.) When you're in non-rainbow mode, the little arrow button between the color buttons lets you toggle between the light color and the dark color. I hit upon Figure 23.10 and I like it, so I stop right there.

23.9

Better legibility, thanks to the Brighten lens

23.10

Striking effects from a new lens

Almost to Aruba

What? My lead author wants me to try one more approach? C'mon Rick, we've nailed it. Really, this is elegance personified! Oh, all right. What if I give the *N* my patented faux-gold fill? (This is a custom fountain fill that uses my secret blend of colors to create a convincing 24-karat gold look.) And just so you don't think I don't sweat the details, I'll add a thin white outline around the letter—not by adding an outline to the letter itself, by the way, because that would distort the letter inappropriately. Instead, I produce a duplicate letter with the + key, give it a 2.5-point white outline, press the Tab key to select the original letter, and then Shift+PageUp to bring the original to the front. Figure 23.11 shows my last gasp, er, my final effort.

23.11

The 11th time's the charm.

Hey Mr. Altman, will that do it for you? Great. Have a nice trip to Aruba; I'll have the finished art for you when you get back.

♣

You'll find a few of Gary's more colorful efforts represented in the Color Gallery, and in the GALLERY directory of the Companion CD, as files ELEGANT1.CDR through ELEGANT5.CDR.

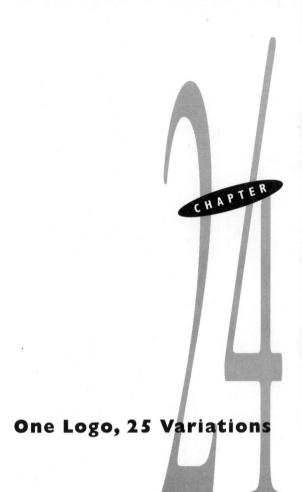

One Logo, 25 Variations

TWENTY-FOUR

This is the second of two chapters written by Gary Priester.
You design a logo. It's hot. You can't wait to get it printed on
your business cards, envelopes, letterhead, the side of your van,
the side of your house…heck, why not the side of Mt. Rushmore! Who
can blame you, but consider this: You're going to be living with that
logo for quite some time. When you look at it next week or next year,
are you going to hit yourself upside the head and mutter futile regrets
about using another typeface, background, or color palette?

When we design a logo, whether for ourselves or a client, we try to do
as many explorations as we have the time and energy to pursue. Explorations give us a chance to live and work with the logo for a while, as well
as for the logo's true personality to reveal itself. What follows is an exploration of a logo for Automated Money, Inc., a manufacturer and mar-
keter of ATM machines.

The Logo's Starting Point

We had produced several pages of preliminary sketches, and the one
that we preferred was a stylized ATM machine with keys and a screen.
The design featured a capital *A* for Automated; the hole in the *A* would
be the screen, and the legs of the *A* would work into the keypad. I was
reminded of a typeface I had seen someplace before. I typed in a capital
A, opened the Character Attributes dialog, and scrolled down the installed typefaces until—hello!—there it was: Orbit-B BT. I resized the *A*
until it was about 2″ square, as shown in Figure 24.1. Perfect! This
would save me a lot of drawing time—time I could spend doing logo
variations or playing on the Internet…

24.1

This elegant capital A proved a good starting point for an ATM logo.

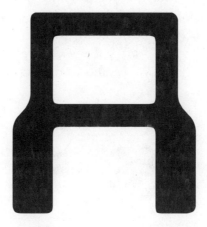

I made a small square and used the Shape tool to round off the corners, and then duplicated the square, making three rows of four squares. These would be used to represent ATM keys, as you can see in Figure 24.2.

24.2

The Rectangle and Shape tools make quick work of the ATM's keys.

Not wanting the design to resemble a computer, I decided to add a dollar sign. But which dollar sign? Corel has many to choose from. I needed something that was extended or wide—versus a condensed face—to conform to what would be the screen portion of the ATM. Figure 24.3 shows some of the finalists. From left to right, top to bottom, they are Cooper, Orbit-A, Bank Gothic, Stencil, Normandie, Pioneer, Tiffany Heavy, Umbra, and Compacta Black.

24.3

The finalists in the Mr. Dollar Contest

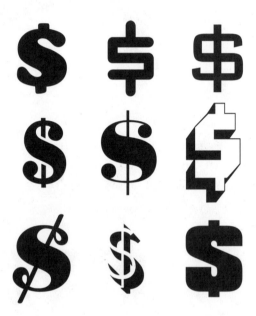

I liked Compacta Black but it was too condensed (why else would it be called Compacta?), so I stretched it in width about 200%. I don't generally like to do this because it greatly distorts, even disfigures the typeface. In this case, though, it seemed to work just fine. The Before and After are shown in Figure 24.4.

I positioned the dollar sign inside the screen, converted it to curves, and used the Shape tool to raise the top and bottom center bar to overlap the screen by about 1/16". Once I got the placement of the objects just right, I fused them permanently together with Weld. Then I added the company name, set in Kabel (pronounced Cobble) Medium, chosen for its formal yet friendly demeanor, as you can see in Figure 24.5.

24.4

And this fat dollar
is the winner.

24.5

Very simple shapes
combine to create
an effective logo.

Play Time

Logo exploration is the illustrator's version of free association, where we
allow one thing to lead to another until we find something we really
like, or someone comes in to drag us away kicking and screaming (or
both). Here we go with our ATM exploration:

Starting Slowly

The first attempt begins conservatively with a 20% gray fill on the *A*
portion of the logo. The keys are colored dark blue. I drop a yellow and

a red rectangle in back of the screen and make the "Automated Money, Inc." text green.

The worst thing you can do when you're working on this kind of exploration is to censor your own designs. Don't spend a lot of time on any one logo, and don't make any value judgments until you're finished. On my second attempt, I use a custom conical fountain fill going from orange to magenta to yellow, and offset the center 15° (DRAW uses 15%) vertically to hide the distracting bull's-eye center of the fill. Hmmmm...

Why not change the fill colors to chalk, gold, and pale yellow, I wonder. It works! I add an 8-point, dark-green (TruMatch 19-a7) outline to a duplicate logo and send it to the back (Shift+PgDn). I fill the text with the same TruMatch color.

For Take 4, I use a 3-point, purple outline with no fill. I apply the screen palette's green for the text because I know that it will print darker.

After a while you get to know how certain screen palette colors will print in CMYK and can feel confident in choosing them—although when you're short on experience, you should always, *always* use a swatch book to choose colors.

Picking Up Speed

To take the logo a step further, I give it a fountain fill angled at 95° going from white to 40% gray. Then I change the outline color to 70% gray and give the type a 60% gray fill. Next I make a duplicate, give it a 30% gray fill and outline, send it to the back, and nudge it two points down and to the left for a drop shadow. Now I'm liking this more...

Next, I remove the outlines from the original and the drop shadow, and color the text red.

This execution now has a nice subtlety about it, but I think it could be even more subtle. For my next try, I fill the logo with white, place a copy in the Clipboard (Ctrl+C), and delete the drop shadow. I give the logo on the screen a 10% gray fill and nudge it up and to the right 4 points. I paste a copy (Ctrl+V), fill the copy with 40% gray, and nudge it 4 points down and to the left. I paste in one more copy on top, and the result is a kind of embossed effect. I fountain-fill the text using red and green.

Automated Money, Inc.

Building on the embossed look, I add a rectangle, fill it 20% gray, send it to the back, and use the Shape tool to round the corners.

WATCH OUT!

If you intend to round the corners of a square or rectangle, make sure you size it properly when you draw it the first time. Resizing the rectangle before rounding the corners will cause the corners to distort, and they won't get 'round much anymore, cha cha cha....

I fill the rectangle with 20% gray and then place a copy of the logo in the Clipboard. Returning to the original, I nudge it up and left 2 points and fill it with 60% gray. I paste in a copy and nudge it down and right 2 points, adding a 5% gray fill. I paste another copy on top, this one with a 23% gray fill. Making it slightly darker gives it the appearance of being slightly lower or "debossed." I choose a light blue, TruMatch 31-c, for the text.

Going for the Gold

Golden time again. I repeat the same steps I just did for the last version, but this time I use a stylized gold fountain fill using a series of light yellows and gold. I reverse the light and dark so that the top logo is filled with chalk (a very light yellow) and the bottom logo is filled with brown. Now I have a raised, embossed look. I repeat the process for the text but in reverse order—dark copy on top, light copy on bottom—so the type will have the "debossed" look. At this point I can definitely see this logo on one of Automated's ATM machines.

In the next variation, I use red and blue instead of gray, and nudge up and left, down and right. I try a duplicate filled with white and placed on top to give the effect of red and blue outlines. This effect has worked well for me in the past. Unfortunately, not here. Move on.

Automated
Money, Inc.

I repeat the same steps as just above, this time giving the white logo a solid yellow fill. Better, but not by much. Keep moving.

Automated
Money, Inc.

Copies, Copies Everywhere

For my next variation, I place a copy of the logo in the Clipboard and give the logo on screen an 8-point red outline. I paste a copy on top and give it a 4-point white outline, then paste a final copy on top of the other two with a dark-blue fill and no outline. This combination of moves creates, in effect, a red-and-white outline.

Automated
Money, Inc.

Right about here in the exploration process I usually decide to try a realistic shadow. In this case, I use "size and dupe"—it's a variation of drag
and dupe, in which you drag one of the corner handles to size the object before right-clicking to leave behind the original. Then I click again
on the duplicate to get the rotation handles and skew it to the left. I add
a pale-purple fill; and for the front logo, a fountain fill from pale yellow
to yellow. Finally, I give the whole thing a pale purple outline, select the
shadow, and send it to the back.

Automated
Money, Inc.

I do another size-and-dupe to create a shadow copy, this time adding
perspective to the duplicate. Selecting the top-right control point on the
duplicate, I hold down Shift and Ctrl and pull to the right. This causes
the opposing corner to go in the opposite direction. I fountain-fill the
shadow from white (on top) to 50% gray.

Automated
Money, Inc.

As long as I was being tricky, I stretched the logo to the left about 20%
of the size of the original and clicked the right mouse button to place a
duplicate. I grabbed the right handle and moved it to the left, about in

line with the left edge of the original. I dragged a duplicate of this tall, skinny copy to the right side. After placing a copy of the main logo in the Clipboard, I fill the original with yellow, the truncated left logo with green, and the truncated right logo with red. Next I select the left and middle logo and create a 20-step blend, then select the center and right logo and repeat the blend. I use Tab to select the center control curve and bring it to the front. Last, I paste a copy on top and fill it with white. The effect is a glowing logo, so hot it's cool!

Automated
Money, Inc.

Reconstructive Surgery

While I'm in a blend mood I use the Shape tool to carefully separate the dollar sign from the *A* shape, by selecting the nodes, right-clicking, and choosing Break Apart. Once I have reconstructed the logo without the dollar sign, I drag a shorter duplicate of the dollar sign down to about 30% of the height of the original. The large dollar sign gets a light-green fill, the short duplicate a dark-green fill. I select both and add a 10-step blend. This is intended to give the impression of a dollar sign popping up like a cash register, but the jury is still out on this solution.

Automated
Money, Inc.

For the next version, I compress the logo by 50% in width and add perspective. Dragging the logo to the right about 1/4″, I click the right mouse button to drop a duplicate. Then I press Ctrl+R to repeat, adding another duplicate. The three logos get a red fill, a yellow fill, and a green fill, respectively.

Hmmm, I wonder, what would happen if I add perspective and then extrude the perspective logo in the other direction? I drag the vanishing point from the extrude to line up on the same horizon line as the perspective, and give the extrude a shade from purple to red. I add a gray rectangle to hold everything together and fill the text with a darker gray. Here's the result:

Home Stretch

I'm getting a little punchy at this point, so I decide to let auto-pilot take over. DRAW's Extrude roll-up offers several dozen predesigned settings called presets, which can be applied with one mouse click. With the

Extrude menu still open, I apply the Plastic Gold preset, but I shorten the depth from 45 to 25 to make the logo a bit more manageable.

Automated
Money, Inc.

Returning to the basic logo, I construct a rectangle from the center of the image to the left. I drag the rectangle's middle-left control handle over to the right, past the center, and while holding down Ctrl to constrain, I click the right mouse button, dropping an identical mirrored duplicate. (If you have friends who use a Mac, ask them if *they* can do any of this right-clicking stuff…heh, heh!) Where was I? Oh, right. I select the left rectangle and then the logo and use Intersect to create a new object spanning the area where the two original objects overlap. Intersect effectively slices the logo in half, producing a left-half logo. Now for the fills: red for the new half; green for the original (which is still there but one layer below the new half); light orange for the left rectangle; and yellow for the right rectangle.

Automated
Money, Inc.

There are certain things you just have to try because they're there. To start this rendition, I draw a circle around the logo. Another copy of the logo goes in the Clipboard (it's getting a workout!), and I fill the logo on the screen with olive. After bringing the circle to the front (Shift+PgUp), I apply a Magnify lens of 1.6x to get an interesting shape with a pale fill. I paste a copy in front, with a pale-yellow fill to stand out from the olive-green, magnified shape. The text gets an autumn-orange fill and a new position in front.

Things are rapidly getting out of control. I fill a rectangle with black marble from the wizzy new Full Color Bitmap fill tool. Now a Heat Map lens with a 60% rotation…far out!

Next I try a modified malachite texture, from the Samples list. (I call it "modified" because I know how elegant real malachite looks, and DRAW's texture fill is nowhere near.) Green screen colors are very deceptive and unpredictable, and this Banded Malachite prints out very dingy and gray. So I alter the texture fill and substitute TruMatch colors, saving it as CMYK Malachite Fill.

By the way, the burled-wood rectangle for the background is another one of the attractive full-color bitmap fills.

Now for dueling fountain fills: One rectangle is fountain-filled going from solid red to 10% gray. The logo and type are combined (Ctrl+L) and fountain-filled going from white to TruMatch 35-a blue. This one could actually work, I think.

Finally, for a background, I use a variation of a variation of one of DRAW's texture fills that resembles black marble (I've altered and renamed this fill so many times, I can't remember its original name). I revise the colors using 30% gray, 10% gray, and white to produce a white marble for my logo. (I could have used a Brighten Lens to produce the same effect.) And my secret gold fountain fill for the text adds a nice grace note.

♣

I could go on forever, but our lead author has given me a budget of only fifty cents per logo, not to exceed six bucks, and I'm already over budget. From this group of 25 logos, I'd probably select five that I could live with. At this point I'd make up some dummy printed samples and leave them lying around for a week or so, hoping that one would eventually win me over. Or, I could do 25 more—when do we start??

The Dragon Lord

This chapter and the next one feature two alumni, if you will, of the Mastering CorelDRAW series of books. Valorie Lennox is a 1995 Grand Prize winner for Dragon Lord, an animation she prepared entirely with MOVE; and Matt Lecher's The Lighthouse was a finalist in the Landscapes category. Both Valorie and Matt got their start with CorelDRAW by reading Mastering CorelDRAW 5. Perhaps we should have made an infomercial featuring these two artists, but we'll settle for having them tell you their stories on these pages, so you can benefit as well. We begin with Valorie Lennox's Dragon Lord.

♣

Early in 1995 I was reading the "Doing It" chapter in *Mastering CorelDRAW 5,* admiring from afar the work of the computer graphics artists featured there. I was fascinated by their explanations of the step-by-step processes they followed to create their winning entries in the Corel World Design Contest.

Until that point, I'd had no aspirations for the competition, beyond the free keychain I acquired for mailing in one of my modest scribbles-by-computer. After all, I'm not an artist, and I don't work in a graphics studio. Even with a ruler in hand, I have difficulty drawing straight lines. But the explanations in "Doing It" suggested that persistence also plays a significant role in creating award-winning entries. I know quite a bit about effort, and CorelDRAW certainly simplifies the creation of straight lines. "Give it a try," I told myself. "At the very least, you'll get a new keychain."

Enter the Dragon

Already underway on the computer was a MOVE project, the animation of a mock epic poem I had written several years earlier. (By entering something in the Animation category, I would not be eligible for Corel's Best of Show distinction, worth over $150,000. But I checked, and they were giving out the same keychain for the Animation category.)

Entitled *Dragon Lord,* my poem contained references to a fire-breathing dragon, some peasants and a hero, a battle scene, theft of cattle and crops from a village, lots of flame and smoke—all stuff I thought would look absolutely splendid on a computer screen.

I imagined my words fading on and off screen as if by magic, the flame-breathing dragon setting fire to a straw-thatched hut, the peasant rushing in to put the fire out. Ignorance was bliss. I had no idea how much actual work would be necessary for some of the scenes I wanted to create. (Several folks at Corel later told me they had never seen anything quite like *Dragon Lord* created with MOVE.) Perhaps because I worked backward—coming up with the ideas and then trying to figure out how to make the program create the effects I wanted—I ended up with a bag of tricks that are not part of MOVE's standard repertoire.

The Making of the Manuscript

I decided to create *Dragon Lord* as an animated, medieval manuscript. I had plenty of reference material readily available in my home library, and I thought the format of a manuscript would be especially suitable for a tale of Dragon versus Hero. Figure 25.1 shows the title page.

The electronic medium of MOVE proved to be ideal for creating an animation on my less-than-state-of-the-art home computer. In that environment, every "page" on screen is composed of smaller elements, each of which is animated to some degree. Instead of trying to fill an entire screen with a single moving image—which will appear jerky on all but the most powerful computers—I made almost all of the moving figures small. The result is much smoother animation because the computer is manipulating fewer pixels in each frame.

Calligraphy, borders, and fancy initial letters typical of a medieval manuscript are easily created in DRAW.

This format also works well within MOVE, which is a two-dimensional animation program. By putting the animation into a manuscript, which the viewer expects to see in two dimensions, I was able to minimize the lack of a third dimension.

For a manuscript, I needed vellum. Scraping and curing a sheepskin was out, so I settled for an electronic version. In DRAW, I drew a rectangle roughly the same size as the MOVE screen. Using the colors in a reproduced manuscript as a guide, I mixed two creamy shades in DRAW, one to match the darker outside edge of the vellum in my examples, and one similar to the lighter shade at the center of the page. I then used these two colors in a radial fountain fill inside the rectangle, offsetting the center slightly. Using an OLE link from MOVE to DRAW, I imported the rectangle as a prop that is displayed in the background throughout most of the animation.

I planned the animation for five pages. The first is the title page; the second is a page illustrated with a drawing of a "valley fair"; the third displays a dragon's cave; the fourth shows a village street; and the fifth features the flame-blowing dragon and lots of fire.

Setting up the text of the poem was easy. From several typefaces imitating black letter script, I chose GregorianFLF. (Corel's Fraktur, Fette Fraktur, or Cloister Black would have worked equally well.) I set all text originally in DRAW and then imported it into MOVE as either an actor or a prop, depending on how it would be animated in the scene (more on this later). I lifted decorative initial letters from Corel's selection of clip art and modified them, changing the colors from drab to bright.

Of Borders and Babewyns

Real manuscript pages tend to be heavily illuminated—with drawings all around the page, fancy initial letters, and small miniature scenes that are often surrounded with their own individual borders. Even the blank spaces at the ends of some lines are filled with illumination: small bars of color called *babewyns. Diapering* (small, repeated patterns) frequently fills the background of a border or scene.

Using DRAW, many of these detailed effects can be created with a few clicks of a mouse. For the first border on the title page, I drew a rectangle and used a Two-Color Pattern fill with a brown-and-gold basket-weave pattern. Layered on top are leaves that I found in Corel's clip art library. A blue outline completes the border.

With two exceptions, I took similar steps to create the other borders and babewyns scattered throughout the animation. The two exceptions are the tiny babewyn scene on page three, which I sketched in DRAW and stocked with cows from the Symbols library; and the wide border at the bottom of page 4, which I filled with duplicated copies of a clip-art pattern.

Bring on the Dragons

Having done the initial work on the pages, it was time to bring in the dragons and start creating some on-screen havoc. And havoc did happen, but not on screen. My old faithful—a 386DX/25 with 8MB, jerry-built to be a semi-486/30—crashed three times in 20 minutes when I tried to introduce my first animated effect. I bit the bullet…er, budget and purchased a 486/66 with 16MB of RAM.

I liked the advice that I read in the earlier *Mastering CorelDRAW* book about "working from a reference," but I couldn't find a live dragon willing to serve as a model. So I applied a knife, cardboard, and craft clay to a toy pterodactyl, creating a reasonable facsimile of a flying dragon. I then photographed the dragon from several different angles, traced these images, and scanned them into PhotoPAINT (using a grayscale, 4″ hand scanner). In PAINT they served as the basis for three of my dragon figures: the dragon on page 2, the flying dragon on page 3, and the fire-breathing flying dragon on page 4.

After studying illustrations of dragons and with much fumbling with a pencil and eraser, I managed to create two passable dragon images. These, too, I scanned into PAINT, for clean-up and eventual development as the fire-breathing dragons on pages 3 and 5 and the walking dragon on pages 1 and 2. Figure 25.2 shows how my dragon began.

Page by Page

Page 1 was straightforward—text and border.

On page 2, I wanted to have the dragon's shadow precede the dragon that flies into the page and over the text. I created a shadow using the Contour command in DRAW (contour fill to the inside, click on original contour and fill with white, then remove outline). Unfortunately, every attempt to use the shadow in MOVE crashed the computer, so I eventually gave up.

I created the first dragon figure in DRAW and filled the wings with a customized version of the "Leather" fractal fill. I saved this texture as "Dragon Skin" and used it on all subsequent dragons. Starting with a

This sketch, scanned into PhotoPAINT, was the basis for the flying dragon.

single dragon figure, I used DRAW's rotation commands to create changes in the dragon's direction of flight, and redrew the wings to suggest slow sweeps. I reduced the size of the dragon gradually and had the figure fly behind a mountain. Since MOVE does not allow an actor to go behind a prop but does allow an actor to go behind an actor, I redrew the mountain as an actor so the flying dragon could slip behind the cliff.

Next I drew the dragon that strolls out from the cave. I liked the figure so much I copied it, changed the color, and gave it more on-screen time on the title page.

Page 3 is my favorite. The miniature of the dragon cave was created in DRAW and includes a background blend; a gold Preset for the treasure pile; and tiny jewels, coins, and a bone (lifted from clip art) at the base of the dragon. Five little "sparkle" actors flash among the treasure when the animation is played. The whole drawing was then PowerClipped within a border adapted from Corel's clip art library.

In page 3, I abandoned the OLE link between MOVE and DRAW, because it became unstable as the size of the MOVE file increased. One of MOVE's other options is importing a series of sequentially named bitmap files to create an actor. So I started a crash course in PAINT…and I do mean *crash*. By the time the cels of the flame-breathing dragon were ready for import into MOVE, I had frozen and restarted my system more times than I could count. On the plus side, I learned to Save often.

The showy smoke-into-text effect on page 3 is a morph. There are three actors involved in the sequence. To create them, I saved text as an actor and gradually assembled morphing sequences. The first is the moving smoke that flows from the dragon's cave to the page. The second actor morphs from smoke into text and then back into smoke. The third actor morphs from smoke into text and then fades from the page.

All of the dissolves and fade-ins are also morphs. I took the object I wanted to dissolve, made a duplicate, and colored the duplicate as closely as I could to the background color of the page. Then I morphed from the original to the duplicate. When the morphed sequence is played, the original appears to fade from the screen. Reverse the order of the cels, and the original gradually appears on the screen.

It's All in the Timing

One of the delights in playing with the animation was creating illusions. On page 3, the dragon swooping onto the babewyn and stealing a cow from the field is an example. (If you haven't watched *Dragon Lord* from the CD-ROM, take a peek now before I ruin the fun by explaining how the "theft" is accomplished.)

In this sequence there are two dragon actors, one cow actor, and one prop. The babewyn at the bottom of the page appears to contain two similar cows in a field. But the cows are not the same: One is part of a prop and the other is an actor.

Partway through the animation, the motionless actor dragflt is replaced by dragon theft2, an 11-cel actor that flies down to steal the cow.

At frame 218 when the cow is taken, a number of things happen. The cow actor leaves the frame. Dragon theft2 is at cel 5, where the flying dragon is drawn for the first time with a cow between its claws. The cow is drawn in the dragon's claws from cels 5 to 11, and the cow in the field has vanished. The cow, therefore, appears to be carried off the page by the dragon, as shown in Figure 25.3.

25.3

Lunch to go—5 of the 11 cels that make up the thieving dragon illustrate how the cow is snatched.

The rest of *Dragon Lord* duplicates many of the techniques already described: morphing for dissolves, multicel actors to create movement and careful timing. Watch the folks in the bottom border on page 4—they look up when the dragon sets the hut on fire. On pages 4 and 5 I also used one animation from MOVE's library. The fire was too good to resist.

Roll Credits

Dragon Lord contains 39 actors and 22 props in 481 frames. When created in DRAW or PAINT, most were drawn larger than required and then reduced to fit the MOVE screen. Editing and fine-tuning of images were done pixel by pixel. Towards the end of the project, the file was larger than 7MB and became very unstable, so some changes to actors were made in a separate file and then imported back into the original file.

I initially hoped to enter the entire poem in Corel's competition, but when the deadline neared, I only had the first verse completed. I spent at least 100 hours—quite possibly more—on the project, and produced more crashes than a demolition derby.

The soundtrack is an ancient Celtic tune, "A Chomaraig Aoibhinn O." My friends Jo Lundstrom and Harry Warner dropped by and played a bodhan (Celtic drum) and penny whistle into a tape recorder. From that I made WAV files and edited the music into *Dragon Lord.*

The other credit at the end of *Dragon Lord* acknowledges friend and technical wizard Grant Eckberg, who assembled and kept a very cranky 486 computer limping through the project.

♣

You'll find *Dragon Lord* in the PRACTICE directory of the Companion CD as DRAGON.CMV. (Be forewarned—it's almost 6MB in size.) To access it, create a new file in PRESENTS and switch to Animation view. Import the CMV file, and in the Import Actor/Prop dialog choose Select All. The animation runs within a single PRESENTS slide; you may need to adjust the display time for the slide to allow the entire animation to run.

Oh yeah…I got my keychain.

The Lighthouse

CHAPTER 26

*F*or notes about Matt Lecher, creator of the piece described in this chapter, see the beginning of Chapter 25.

♣

" It's just a bunch of fountain fills." That's what I tell my friends who ask how I did *The Lighthouse* (see Figure 26.1). The next thing many people say is, "Well, it may have been easy to do, but I wouldn't have the patience." When I was thinking about entering Corel's Sixth Annual World Design Contest, the question I asked myself was exactly that: Did I have the time and the patience to produce a piece that had a fair chance of becoming a finalist in the contest? I hope the following story of self-inflicted, quick education will encourage anyone who is hesitant to dive in.

I work in Freeport, Maine, at DeLorme Mapping—a maker of fine-quality paper atlases, as well as some best-selling CD-ROM products. After working in DeLorme's production department for a couple of years, I wanted to become more "computer literate" and get more involved in the actual design work of our products. Unsure of what steps to take, I asked around and found out that Adobe Illustrator and Macromedia Freehand were the programs of choice at my firm. Oh, and there was also this program called CorelDRAW that was used occasionally for special projects.

AUTHOR'S NOTE

For a look at *The Lighthouse* in full color, see GALLERY8.CDR on the Companion CD.

26.1

The *Lighthouse*, designed by Matt Lecher, was a finalist in Corel's Annual Design Contest.

Over the next couple of months, I learned as much as I could about these three design programs, trying to decide which one I should adopt as my very own. Eventually, I decided on CorelDRAW. Quite simply, it seemed to be the biggest and best of the three. The box was bigger, the manuals were bigger…and there were oh, so many programs, bells, and whistles to choose from. Add to all this my slightly twisted tendency to want to master programs not everyone knew how to use, and my decision was made: Corel was the program for me.

I decided to enter Corel's World Design Contest when I read about it in December 1994, because I figured trying to create a decent entry would force me to learn the program quickly. At that point my only creations in Corel were a floor plan and a Darth Vader mask for a friend's birthday. So I decided to purchase a how-to book to help me learn the program fast. After days of searching through bookstores up and down the coast of Maine, I found exactly what I was looking for: Sybex's *Mastering CorelDRAW 5*. Its chapters describing the work of two past contest winners, David Brickley and Georgina Curry, were very helpful. I was especially pleased to learn that both of them had a background in fine arts, as I did.

Another useful section in the book was a walk-through of the steps to create an illustration of a snowboarder. *The Lighthouse* was done in much the same manner as the background of the snowboarder, but with a billion or so more shapes.

Getting Started

Choosing the subject for my design was easy. Coworkers have nick-named me The Lighthouse Painter because I can often be found spending breaks drawing pictures of a particular lighthouse in the Windows Paintbrush program. (A year ago, that was the only pseudo-graphics program I knew how to use!) Pemaquid Point Light of Bristol, Maine has long been a favorite spot of mine, so I decided to do the subject in Corel.

I had recently completed a colored-pencil drawing of the lighthouse, using two photographs I had taken, one of the lighthouse (Figure 26.2) and one of a sunset (Figure 26.3). Using pencil on tracing paper, I traced the outlines of the major elements—the cloud formations and the basic rock outlines—from my original pencil drawing. To get the form of the lighthouse, I traced the original photograph so that the proportions would be exact. (If you take some license when you draw a rock, who's going to know—or care, for that matter. But the lighthouse object was another matter; to be believable, its drawn dimensions had to match the actual structure.)

26.2

A photograph of a lighthouse served as a starting point for the drawing.

I then scanned the tracings and imported them into CorelDRAW (see Figure 26.4). Looking back, I suppose using CorelTRACE would have

26.3

The sunset photo-
graph was the
beginning of the sky.

26.4

The composite of
the major elements
combined with
tracing of the light-
house from the
photograph

been a good idea at this stage, because the imported scans took a long time to draw on the screen—especially when I zoomed in for the detail work.

Now I had a decision to make. Would this drawing be done in DRAW alone or as a combination DRAW and Photo-PAINT project? Though the subject lent itself well to the more rasterlike image possible in Photo-PAINT, I eventually decided to do the entire piece as vector art in DRAW, for several reasons. First, I had only two months to complete the project, and that didn't seem like enough time to learn both applications. Second, I thought I'd have a more promising candidate in the contest if my drawing had an obvious DRAW look to it. And, third, it would be a challenge.

The Underpainting

A painting instructor of mine once told me to start a painting by quickly filling the canvas with shapes of color that would serve as an underpainting. Hardly anything done in this starting step would be seen in the final product; it was simply a skeleton on which the painting could be built.

Using this technique, I quickly filled the screen with shapes of color using the Freehand Drawing tool. The polygon shapes were created using the imported tracings as a guide. Each shape or group of shapes was placed on different layers, representing a future rock, cloud, or whatever. My underpainting appears in Figure 26.5.

26.5

The underpainting
of *The Lighthouse*

This fundamental step took just a few hours. The remaining 100 or so hours spent on the drawing were used to repeat a cycle of adding and molding shapes, adjusting colors, and printing.

The Foreground

The rocky foreground shown in Figure 26.6 was probably the easiest group to construct, but it was also the most time-consuming part of the picture to complete. The rocks are quite literally just a bunch of fountain-filled shapes. I refilled the large, original shapes of the underpainting with dull, medium-tone colors such as brown, muddy red, and orange. I then created more defined shapes, one on top of another, to make the light-blue and orange highlights and the dark-brown shadows. Every section of rock, as well as all the shapes in the lighthouse made of curved lines, were created in the same manner.

26.6

A section of the
rocky foreground
of *The Lighthouse*,
showing build-up of
fountain-filled
shapes

I first drew the foreground shape roughly with straight lines using the Bézier drawing tool. Next, I selected all the nodes in the polygon, converted them to curves, and then cusped them. To refine the shapes, I moved the control points until I had what I wanted.

By the way, a friend at work recently explained the Bézier drawing click-and-drag method to me. If I ever do another drawing similar to this one, I will be sure to give this method a try. One thing I did try and use quite often when filling the rock polygons was the Copy Properties From command, which proved to be a very helpful time-saver. I then slightly adjusted the colors and fill angle, depending on what the new section of rock needed to look like.

The Lighthouse

The lighthouse itself took a relatively short time to complete. Its lightly colored base is just one fountain-filled shape (see Figure 26.7). The railings are two ellipses with outlines and no fills, duplicated in place many

26.7

The shapes used to construct the light-house structure

times. By reducing the outlines of these duplicates to small pieces and coloring each piece a slightly different shade of gray, I got the illusion of depth. Looking back, I suppose using PowerLines would have been an easier way to achieve this effect. The light itself consisted of blended, filled shapes, and the orange glow filling up the windows is a single radial-filled shape. The dark panels in the top section of the lighthouse are also simple, two-color, fountain-filled shapes.

The Sky and the Clouds

The last part of the painting to be done was the sky—and for good reason. I had no clue as to how to make a soft, cloudy sky using vector shapes. I tried out plenty of ideas with no success. Each and every one was just a bunch of rigid shapes trying to masquerade as a soft, cloudy sky…and failing miserably at it.

Eventually, I determined that a combination of two effects—contours and blends—was the best bet, and Figure 26.8 is the result. I started the sky by creating one giant rectangle with a fountain fill going from magenta and orange to off-white. This was the basic sunset. I then created the thin, lower clouds and filled them with two-colored fountain fills. Each one was then contoured a short distance to the approximate sunset colors behind them, to create a fading effect.

For the faint pink clouds drifting behind and above the lighthouse, I blended two sculpted shapes for each cloud. After creating the first initial cloud and filling it with the pinkish color, I duplicated it in place. I sent the duplicate back behind the original, switched to Wireframe, and moved each node of the duplicate out a ways from each corresponding node of the original cloud. The duplicate cloud was then filled with a color matching the sunset color behind it and blended to the original cloud, to once again create a soft, fading effect. Using blends instead of contours on these fluffier clouds gave me more control over where they faded.

The blue sky showing through the cracks in the clouds was created in much the same manner as the clouds, with one extra step at the end: duplicating in place the top shapes of the blue areas. These shapes were

26.8

The sky was created by placing smaller cloud shapes on a large rectangle filled with sunset colors.

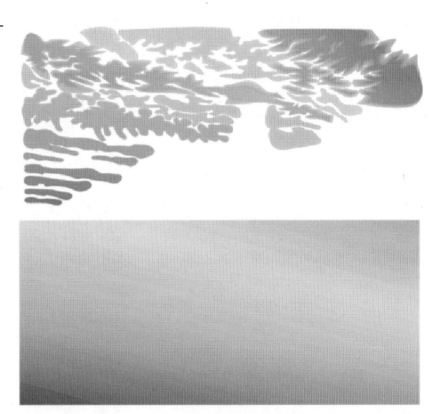

then combined and filled with a left-to-right fountain fill with slightly varying shades of blue, to create a little more depth in the sky.

Frequently it is more important to make a design that catches the eye rather than one that is perfectly accurate. When I showed the finished piece to a friend, he looked at the sky and asked if a sunset could really do that. "Do what?" I asked. He explained that the magenta section closest to where the sun would be was much darker than the off-white section behind the lighthouse. I suppose it is a little backwards, but I did it on purpose for the sake of effect. This way, the dark top of the lighthouse stands out more because the sky behind it is almost white.

By the time the drawing was finished, the sky looked nothing like the sky in my original photo. But, as they say in the upper realms of the modern world of fine art, "It works."

Some Final Thoughts

For *The Lighthouse* to win anything in the contest, I knew it would have to be pleasing to the eye. Technical difficulty was of secondary importance. I read somewhere that some of the best work ever done in DRAW was done by using simple filled shapes. So that's what I was shooting for—especially considering I didn't have time, anyway, to learn any of DRAW's fancy bells and whistles.

With the goal of eye appeal in mind, I knew I'd have to spend substantial time adjusting the colors within those "billions" of shapes. While working on one area of the picture, I'd realize the colors in another, supposedly finished area were no longer the correct hues to blend with the area I was currently working on. As I changed colors again and again, I added something to my CorelDRAW wish list: a way to select one or more objects and be able to adjust the darkness of the colors within these objects by simply moving a slide bar or typing in a percentage number. This command could be similar to Photo-PAINT's Brightness and Contrast commands.

This project was a great learning experience. I've heard many horror stories about fountain-filled designs that self-destructed when they were printed. I was pleased with *The Lighthouse,* and even more pleased when it was chosen as a finalist in the Design Contest. Ironically, Corel's prize package for finalists contained software and a printer. But I toiled over this drawing at my workplace during off-hours because I don't own a computer. Guess it's time to get one....

THE CORELDRAW
FREEWAY

Several members of this writing team live in the San Francisco and Los Angeles areas of California, where the jam-packed four-lane freeways are so crowded they reduce the term "freeway" to wishful thinking. You can have bumper-to-bumper traffic at midnight, and if someone so much as burps with the window down, there is likely to be a jam-up. Other writers on our team have fled to the Midwest and the Pacific Northwest, where it takes at least a loud honk to cause a back-up.

It's easy to imagine the Corel software being patterned after one of our freeways during a busy rush hour: used by dozens of different vehicles…lots of entrances and exits…rules that govern usage…lots of ways to break the rules…and, of course, a few disastrous crashes along the way…some of them fatal.

This part of the book looks at CorelDRAW as the giant freeway that it is. We explore how data comes and goes, how color and quality black-and-white images are produced, how professionals prepare for printing, how files are passed to and from, and how to choose the right fuel (spelled f-o-r-m-a-t) for the trip. We start with the largest artery of the Corel Freeway—the print engine—then move into color theory and on to importing and exporting.

Print, Darn You!

TWENTY-SEVEN

kay, you've created some great designs or a dynamite page layout in DRAW. Now what? Most likely, you want to print your handiwork. Even if you create art solely for placement in other applications, you are likely to want print proofs along the way.

DRAW—and many other applications—has a reputation for allowing users to create artwork that looks gorgeous on the screen but is too complex for various output devices. Workarounds have helped, but one goal in each DRAW upgrade has been to improve the print functions, minimizing the need for workarounds and troubleshooting.

So let's begin this chapter with a multiple-choice question: The Windows 95/DRAW 6.0 combination

(a) Gives you greater control over printing and is more foolproof than ever before.
(b) Makes printing more complex and confusing than ever.
(c) All of the above.
(d) None of the above.

The correct answer is (c). In both Windows 95 and DRAW 6.0, significant changes have been made to printer control. You get many new options and features designed to make printing more flexible and reduce the occurrence of failed or unacceptable pages. That's the good news. Unfortunately, more bells and whistles inevitably add up to increased complexity and potential confusion, and that's the bad news. On balance, though, we'd say that the improvements considerably outweigh the shortcomings.

Most of the print features in both Windows 95 and DRAW 6.0 are relatively easy to decipher—and most work as advertised. This chapter explores all that is both old and new in DRAW's print engine.

Printer Control in Windows 95

DRAW 6.0 is no different from its predecessors; much of your printer control needs can be accessed directly from within DRAW itself. Nevertheless, some tasks will lead you out to Windows 95's print controls—adding a new printer to your system, for instance. So, we'll begin by taking a look at how the Windows print controls have changed. Our coverage here is brief, and we encourage you to explore more fully on your own.

The Windows 95 Printers Folder

To access and control printers from Windows 95's desktop, click the Start button on the Taskbar. Then highlight Settings and click on Printers. Figure 27.1 shows the Printers folder, which displays icons for your installed printers as well as an Add Printer icon.

27.1

The Windows 95 Printers folder

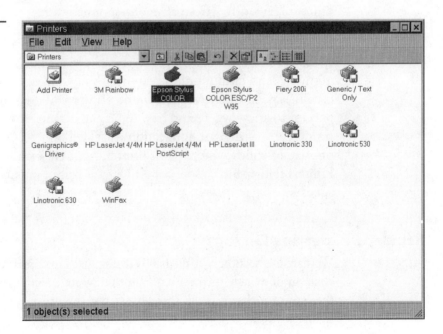

NEW FOR 6

> Well, actually, this is new for Windows 95, not DRAW 6.0. You can now change the name of any printer in the Printers folder, to something meaningful to you. Simply click on the name under the icon and edit it, just as you rename other files in Windows 95. More-descriptive names are especially helpful if you have similar printer driver names or happen to have several drivers for the same physical device. That's what we've done in Figure 27.1, to differentiate between the Epson Stylus driver from Epson and the one supplied by Microsoft.

Adding a Printer   Double-clicking on the Add Printer icon invokes one of Windows 95's omnipresent wizards. This will guide you through the process of installing a new printer, either picking from a list of printers that Windows 95 already recognizes with Microsoft-supplied drivers, or installing a driver from a vendor-supplied disk.

Designating the Default Printer   This folder is also where you specify your default printer—the one to which your applications will normally send output unless you specifically choose to do otherwise. It usually is good idea to set this to the printer you use most often. It is important to know where and how to set the default, particularly if you encounter any of the rare applications that will only print to the default printer. To choose your default printer, right-click on its icon in the Printers folder, and choose Set As Default from the pop-up menu that appears.

Printer Properties Dialogs

We start this section with a small warning. Our first instinct was to double-click on one of the printer icons in the Printers folder to gain access to the setup for that printer. Instead, we got the print queue for that particular printer.

In Windows 95, each printer now has its own separate job queue window and queue controls. To access each printer's settings, right-click on the icon for the specific printer and select Properties from the pop-up. (If you happen to open the queue first, you can click on the Printer menu and select Properties from there.)

The Properties dialog for each printer will vary, depending on what printer driver and what type of output destination has been chosen. In Figure 27.2 you see the Properties dialog for a Hewlett Packard 4M PostScript printer, which uses a Windows 95-supplied printer driver. All Properties dialogs have tabbed pages that contain various settings to control printed output. The options you have will depend on the printer. Initially, the General page of this dialog appears on top.

27.2

A Properties (setup) dialog for a LaserJet

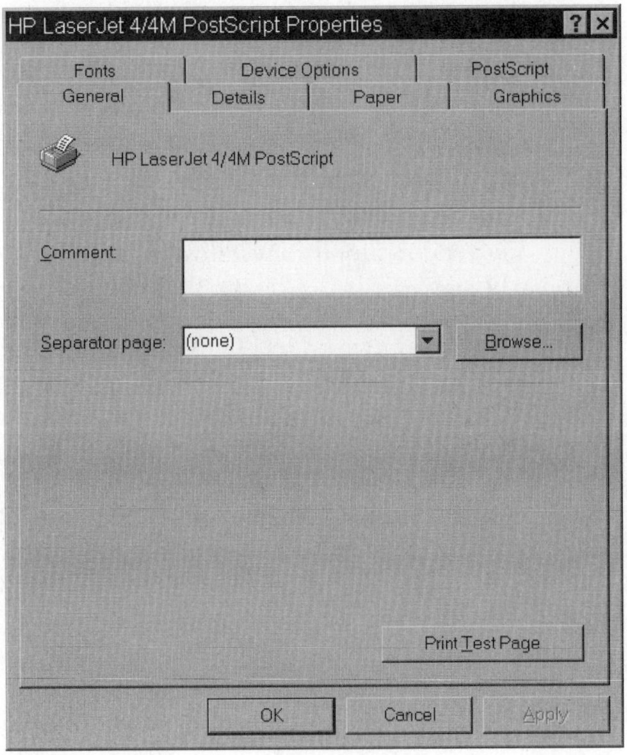

HP LaserJet 4/4M PostScript Properties

| Fonts | Device Options | PostScript |
| General | Details | Paper | Graphics |

HP LaserJet 4/4M PostScript

Comment:

Separator page: (none)   Browse...

Print Test Page

OK   Cancel   Apply

AUTHOR'S NOTE

> One nifty feature on the Properties General page, available for all installed printers, is the option to print a test page. This can be very helpful for troubleshooting. You can use this test page to quickly determine whether your printer is correctly installed and operational under Windows, or whether printing problems are application specific.

On the Paper page of the Properties dialog you'll find another feature common to Windows 95-supplied PostScript printer drivers. You can print multiple pages of a document, either two or four to a page, on a single sheet. This option works regardless of the application you are using. In general, you'll find more control available within the drivers than in prior Windows versions. They are worth taking some time to explore on your own.

Printers using older Win 3.*x* drivers will have fewer pages in their Properties dialog, and you can always find the Setup button on the Details page. This button takes you to the familiar Setup dialogs, containing more setup options specific to the printer driver. We haven't yet seen any vendor-supplied Windows 95 drivers, so we can't tell you what they will look like.

Before we move on to DRAW's printing controls, let's take a look at the progress Corel has made with DRAW 6.0's page setup mechanics.

A Word About PostScript Printers	Throughout this chapter we will refer frequently to *PostScript printers* and *non-PostScript printers*. PostScript is a very powerful page-description language developed by Adobe Systems Inc. A PostScript PRN file is simply a program for the PostScript printer—nothing more than a recording of the various commands that would normally be sent directly to the printer from the application.

A Word About PostScript Printers (continued)	One big plus for PostScript is that its command language is written as ASCII text. That means people knowledgeable in PostScript can find useful troubleshooting information in the file, should something fail to print correctly. And even we less savvy users can check this file to see that all fonts are properly downloaded. You would look for lines like the following:

```
%%BeginFont: AachenBT-Bold
%!PS-AdobeFont-1.0: AachenBT-Bold 003.001
```

Non-PostScript printers utilize a variety of command languages, typically Hewlett Packard's PCL (Printer Control Language). These languages have their own strengths but are generally less robust than PostScript. And many high-end output devices won't use anything but PostScript.

You Can't Print What You Can't Set Up

The Page Settings dialog in DRAW 6.0 (Figure 27.3) is a welcome improvement over version 5's. Instead of forcing you to go to three separate tabbed pages to complete a page setup, you can now accomplish all the same page setup functions tidily from a single screen. Access to this dialog is still found on the Layout menu.

DRAW Now Does "BIG"

One of the most significant changes to DRAW 6.0 is the increased maximum page size you can design and print. In prior versions, the maximum drawing page was 32" by 32". Now that DRAW 6.0 is running in the world of 32-bit software, that limit has been lifted. Oh, sure, there's still a limit, but it's now 150' by 150'! So feel free to design as large a page as you want. The bigger problem may be finding a device that can print it. Today's market, however, offers an increasing number of devices to handle large output, and later we'll show you how to print BIG using even your humble little desktop printer.

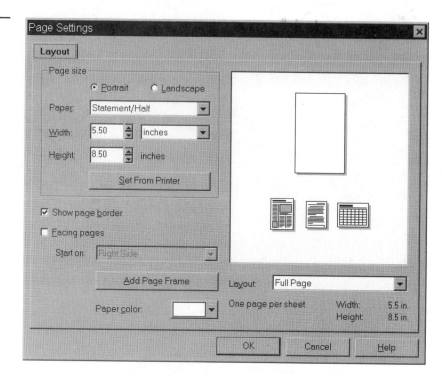

NEW FOR 6

Along with simplifying accessibility to page setup, the Page Settings dialog offers graphical representations of your choices, making them more comprehensible. For example, if you select landscape orientation, the picture of your page shown in the preview window at the right of the dialog rotates accordingly.

Page Setup: The Basics

In the following paragraphs we'll summarize the more fundamental steps of defining your document page.

Page Size Settings   Paper choice—size and orientation—is a fairly straightforward endeavor. (In a multipage file, all pages will be the same size and orientation.) The drop-down Papers list offers a variety of standard U.S. and international paper sizes. When you choose one, the Width and Height boxes are automatically updated to reflect the measurements of the page size chosen. You can change these measurements as needed.

NEW FOR 6

In DRAW 6.0, creating a custom page size is easier than in DRAW 5. Simply type new values in the boxes. The Paper description will automatically change to Custom.

It is important to understand that the Page Size settings determine the *drawing's* page size, and this may or may not be the same size as the paper or other media you print on. For example, perhaps you need to create a drawing page that is based on a newspaper ad specification: 27 picas, 6 points wide by 42 picas tall (about 4.6″ by 7″). You can easily specify this as a custom page by changing the units to picas, points, then typing in the values and setting the orientation to portrait. Now you can merrily lay out your ad, knowing exactly where to place objects in relation to the edges of the ad space.

If you sent this ad to a laser printer, you would likely print it on letter-size paper (A4 in Europe). From an imagesetter, it might be output on 12″-wide, continuous-length media, and perhaps even printed transversely (sideways) to save film, even though your original page orientation is portrait.

Add Page Frame   When you specify a page size, you are defining a nonprinting bounding box that indicates the edges of your drawing. A handy option in the Page Settings dialog—the Add Page Frame button—lets you create a printable frame the size of your document page.

It simply creates on your active drawing layer a rectangle that is exactly the size of the page you have defined. The rectangle will initially appear with whatever default fill and outline you have set for graphic objects. Because it's merely a rectangular object, you are free to change the fill and outline as you would for any other object.

INSIDE INFO

Another way to create a page frame—a page-size rectangle that is the bottommost object on the active layer—is to double-click on the rectangle tool. It does exactly the same thing as the Add Page Frame button in the Page Setup dialog.

Show Page Border   This option is on by default, and adds a non-printing frame for the page you have defined—which is quite different from adding a printable page frame as described above. This nonprinting border will not be visible if you switch to full-screen preview. You will normally want to keep Show Page Border turned on. In rare instances (when page size is irrelevant), you may benefit by turning it off to unclutter your work area.

Show Page Border does have a pronounced effect on two of DRAW's other features.

- When Show Page Border is on, the area outside the border serves as a virtual pasteboard, a special drawing layer called the Desktop (not to be confused with the Windows 95 desktop). In multipage documents, objects on this Desktop layer are always visible on all pages, and you can drag objects from one page to another. With Show Page Border turned off, you can still put objects on the Desktop layer, but it's more tedious. You must issue commands via the Layers Manager to accomplish it.

- When Show Page Border is turned off, the Fit To Page print option (covered later) will include all objects, since they are not automatically placed on the nonprinting Desktop layer.

Set From Printer   This button simply sets the page size to match the current paper size setting of the Windows 95 default printer.

Paper Color   The Paper Color drop-down palette is useful for visualizing your final product. Here you can choose a color that simulates your intended color media. (This choice has absolutely no effect on printing.)

There are some definite limitations to this feature. On screen, any white or lightly tinted objects will appear completely opaque against your Paper Color background. If you were actually to print these objects on colored stock, white objects would be invisible against the paper (unless, of course, you are using a spot white ink); and the paper color would leak through a lightly tinted object, changing the actual appearance of its color. Still, Paper Color lets you quickly and easily experiment with various color schemes without having to print samples.

INSIDE INFO

Imitating Textured Paper: **When you're using paper with a very defined pattern or texture, you can simulate it on your drawing screen—though it's a bit more complex than simply selecting Paper Color, and you need a scanner. Do a color scan of a small portion of the paper. Import this bitmap into DRAW; then use Tools / Create Pattern and create a full-color pattern from your bitmap. Create a page frame with Add Page Frame, and fill it with your new pattern. (To keep the page frame from printing, place it on a nonprinting layer.) Using a pattern instead of scanning the whole page keeps the file size down and gives you more versatility. Say you've got a project involving collateral material—stationery, business cards, envelopes, and so on. Use the pattern to simulate any page size you want; it will be a very good facsimile. If you don't have a scanner, try modifying one of DRAW's texture fills to simulate a particular paper.**

Most of the Page Settings options we've covered so far will be all the typical DRAW user needs. What follows is an exploration of the more specialized features found in this dialog.

Making Slides

One of the page sizes available in the Paper drop-down list is for creating slides. It generates a page size that has the same aspect ratio (height to width) of a standard 35mm slide, obviously not the physical size of the slide. (You could set up a page size identical to a slide's actual dimensions, but working at a normal page size is more convenient.) This way, settings for nudge and text sizes and so forth don't have to be altered. Once your slide is prepared, you use a special print driver to create a file to be used by a slide-imaging service bureau.

Layout Options

Regardless of the actual dimensions of the page size you define, more often than not you will work with a full-page layout. This is the default option in the Layout drop-down list. In Figure 27.4, you can see that other options are available, as well.

Each specialized layout has its own specific usage, but all share one common characteristic: Essentially, they subdivide the full page into a series of smaller frames. Choose Booklet, for instance, and the preview window shows you that layout, as depicted in Figure 27.4.

INSIDE INFO

A key to understanding how to use these layouts is to realize that each subdivision is represented as a separate document page in your file. For example, if you are making a side-fold card and want to print on all four panels, you must create four pages in the file. In this layout, each multiple of four pages in the file defines another card.

27.4

Optional page layouts

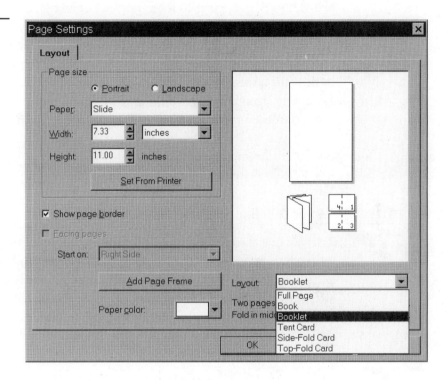

Card Layouts   The three card-style layouts—Tent Card, Side-Fold, and Top-Fold—can all be accomplished manually by subdividing a single full-page layout with guidelines, then rotating all elements in the upside-down panels 180°. By using one of the Layout options, though, you can more easily edit each individual panel because you can work right side up on all of them. Then, at print time, DRAW will do the thinking for you and make the appropriate rotations as it prints the full page.

Certainly it's easier to create cards this way, but it's also a bit more limiting than doing it manually. Let's assume you want to create a birthday card and you want some elements to span the front and back frames of the card. Easily done using the manual method, this is next to impossible using Layout's card options.

Books and Booklets   These two layouts look similar—both subdivide the full page into two halves—but they behave differently at print time. We're going to focus on the booklet layout, since we find it the more useful of the two. As with the other layouts already described, the booklet layout requires that you create pages in multiples of four in your file (minimum four pages for one booklet). You can edit each page in the normal sequence of the assembled booklet, and even flow paragraph text from one page to the next. At print time, the pages are printed in the proper imposition—for instance, in an 8-page booklet, pages 1 and 8, 2 and 7, 3 and 6, 4 and 5. You reproduce the pages as two-sided sheets, then fold and staple them to create completed booklets. (We'll return to this subject several times throughout the chapter.)

AUTHOR'S NOTE

Don't go searching for a way to print auto-generated page numbers in various locations on the pages of a booklet or other multipage document. This feature, common to most word processors, isn't available in DRAW. It's a significant oversight in an application that has long supported multipage files.

Facing Pages   We've saved the discussion of the Facing Pages check box until now, because of its handy application in a multipage document. Turning on Facing Pages allows you to view what would normally be the pages that face each other in a book or booklet.

INSIDE INFO

The Facing Pages option serves another very practical function in setting up books and booklets (see Figure 27.5). You can create objects that span two facing pages (known as a *spread*). When you print the book or booklet, these objects are split in half over the printed pages. In assembly, the two halves are reunited to a single object, just as you designed them with Facing Pages turned on. We'll discuss booklet printing a bit later in this chapter.

27.5

Creating, printing, and assembling booklets

How it appears on screen

1   2-3, 4-5, 6-7   8

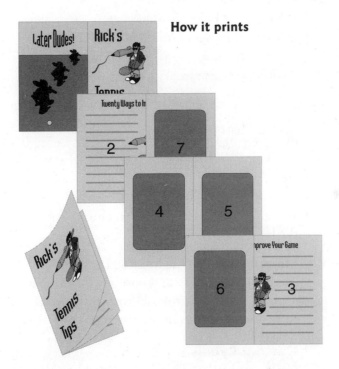

How it prints

Start On: (Right Or Left) One other Page Settings option used in conjunction with multipage files is the Start On: setting. Books and most other multipage files normally start on the right-hand (recto) page. Occasionally, however, the book's cover is produced elsewhere, or for some other reason the data in a file must start on the left-hand (verso) page. DRAW gives you the option to do so.

Unfortunately, this option is unavailable for booklets. If you are creating a booklet with preprinted covers and want printing to begin on the inside of the cover, create a blank first page to represent the cover and then feed the actual covers in at print time. This could get tricky, so it might make more sense to prepare separate files to use with the cover sheet, and create the rest of your booklet separately.

Labels

It has always been possible to construct a sheet of labels in DRAW—it just wasn't very easy. You had to do a good deal of measuring, calculating, and pasting, and you were limited to sheets of duplicate labels. But what if you want to print a series of labels to a single sheet?

DRAW 6.0 has taken label printing a step further, providing a Labels selection in the list of paper sizes. Choose Labels, and the Page Settings dialog changes considerably, as shown in Figure 27.6. Now you can specify a label by manufacturer and label type—no more having to measure your labels and manually create a label page. In the scrollable list, you can open a folder representing a label manufacturer and see the available label sizes. When you choose one, a graphic representation of the layout appears in the preview window.

More importantly, the information about the label is relayed to DRAW's Print setup and options, so you don't have to fiddle with those settings. It's not completely automatic, as we shall see shortly; but it's certainly easier than in prior versions of DRAW.

Custom Labels   In case the labels list doesn't have what you want, Corel provides the Customize Label button below the scrollable manufacturers list. Click this button and you see the dialog in Figure 27.7, in which you can arrange your own customized label layout.

As a starting point, this dialog will simply reflect the values for the last label you chose. Simply adjust the settings to completely customize a label layout. Click the big + button to save your layout settings as a

27.6

The Page Settings
dialog changes
when you choose
Labels for the pa-
per size.

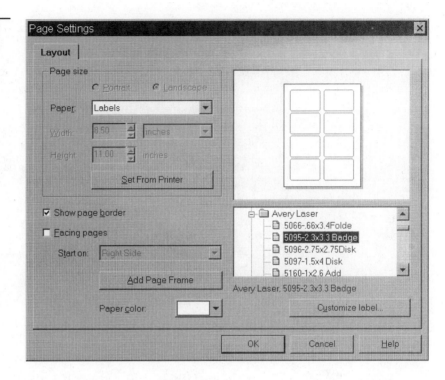

named label style. Next time you need this layout, you can select it from the User Defined folder in the scrollable manufacturers list. More on this later, in "Putting It All Together: Creating a Print Style."

As you can see in Figure 27.7, there are many options for positioning labels. Most are self-explanatory; but watch out for the Equal Margins check box. If you turn on this option and play with the top or left margin, it won't appear that anything new is happening. Equal Margins functions only in conjunction with the Auto Spacing check box in the Gutters section. Unless you tell DRAW to auto-space the labels based on your margins (equal or otherwise), then the top and left margins and the manually set gutter widths will define the resulting right margin; thus Equal Margins will have no effect. With *both* Equal Margins and Auto Space turned on, however, the net result is that the block of labels is distributed symmetrically on the page.

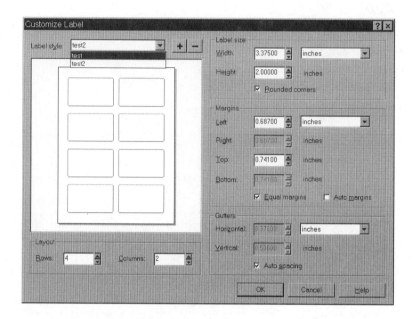

Printing ... **At Last!**

We've finally made it to the heart of the matter: actually printing your work. First up is the Print dialog.

The Print dialog, shown in Figure 27.8, tells you what printer is currently selected. Initially, this is your default printer. Selecting a different printer at this point is simply a matter of choosing one from the drop-down list.

WATCH OUT!

DRAW's new multiple-document capability allows each document to retain its own print settings. Generally, this is a good thing; it will reduce the required steps each time you print. You need to be careful, though, if you're working on several documents at once. If each document utilizes different page sizes, printers, and so forth, you may lose track of which file goes to what printer and with which settings. (We know this from hard experience!)

27.8

The Print dialog

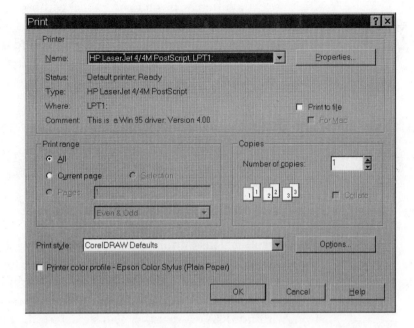

For many commonplace print jobs, all you'll need to do is make a few choices from this main page of the Print dialog. Often you'll do nothing more than click OK to produce your artwork. When you need them, the other frequently used print options are found on this page of the Print dialog. Following is a brief explanation of them.

Printer

This section of the dialog describes the currently selected printer.

Name   Initially, this is your Windows-designated default printer. From the drop-down list, you can select any other installed printer or output device (such as a fax/modem driver), and the other fields will change to reflect related settings. Most of this information is self-explanatory. The Status field is probably most useful in a shared-printer environment, when you need to know if the printer is available. The Where field is the output destination (either a port or a file name).

If you select a different printer and cancel without printing, your selection is promptly forgotten and the default printer is again selected. If you proceed and print a document, the printer and other options you choose are retained for subsequent printing of that document during the current session.

For the remainder of this chapter, the term *sticky* will be used to refer to options whose settings are retained for the duration of the session unless you change them.

Properties This button takes you to an abridged version of the dialog shown back in Figure 27.2. Here you can control many printer settings that would normally be accessed from the printer's Properties dialog in Windows. The main difference when you change the settings from within DRAW is that they will stick with the document for the duration of your session. Open another application or a new DRAW document, and everything reverts to the default printer and its settings.

Print to File

This sticky option allows you to create a file that can later be downloaded to the selected output device. You can install drivers for remote devices and record the printer command code in a print file (usually with a PRN file name extension) for later output. This option is especially useful for creating files destined for output at service bureaus. That means you don't need to own a $50,000 imagesetter, and the service bureau doesn't need to have CorelDRAW or your chosen fonts in their shop—or even a DOS/Windows computer, for that matter.

PRN files can be created for both PostScript and non-PostScript output devices. However, most devices found at service bureaus are PostScript.

Special Considerations for Mac Files This brings us to the For Mac check box. If you are preparing files for a Macintosh-based service bureau (and most of them are), you will want to select this option when you create a print file. It tells DRAW to strip out a start/end control character (Ctrl+D) from PostScript files. This character is informative to DOS-based printers, but it tends to choke Mac networks. The For Mac option is a sticky option.

NEW FOR 6

From the Advanced Options dialog of the PostScript page in your PostScript printer's Properties dialog (available only via the Windows 95 Printers folder), you can now tell Windows whether or not to include these control characters on a systemwide basis. You no longer have to worry about manually stripping these codes from documents generated by applications other than CorelDRAW.

Other Uses for Print To File

You may find the Print To File option useful even if you never use a service bureau. Use it whenever you need to print on a device not attached to your computer.

For example, perhaps you have a notebook computer that you take on the road, sans printer. You prepare some artwork for your office, which has a color printer. No one else in your firm uses DRAW (shame on them!), so it is installed only on your notebook, along with a driver for the office printer. You print to file, and at the office a quick DOS copy command:

```
copy filename.prn port /B
```

will produce your masterpiece! In this command, *port* refers to the port to which the printer is connected and typically will be either LPT1 or LPT2. The */B* tells the printer that

Other Uses for Print To File (continued)

you are sending binary information, so it won't treat the file as ASCII text.

Because Windows 95 is trying to wean us from the DOS prompt, we should probably look for other ways of downloading PRN files to a printer. Another way is to use a downloading utility (much like what the Mac service bureaus have always done), and we have included one on the companion CD (RAWPRINT.EXE). Once installed, it lets you select a PRN file and send it to the appropriate printer (PostScript or otherwise), without having to bring up the DOS prompt.

Print Range

With these options you tell DRAW what objects and/or pages you want printed.

- **All** prints everything on every page...almost. Specifically, it prints everything that falls within the document page borders— recall our discussion of the Desktop layer—and is on a printable layer. This doesn't include guidelines and the grid. Watch out: DRAW reverts back to All as the default setting after every printing. So pay attention and don't forget to reset the print range as needed each time you print.

- **Current Page** prints whatever page you are viewing when you invoke printing. This is useful when you're proofing multipage documents.

- **Selection** prints the objects you have selected with the Pick tool prior to printing, on the current page. A great productivity booster: You can print small sections of a complex drawing instead of the whole page. Also, you can force printing of objects on the Desktop layer (we'll explain this later).

■ **Pages** prints your specified range of pages—all even, all odd, specific pages, or a combination thereof—within a multipage document. You can, for example, combine choices to print only even pages in the range 4 –10. For a quick reference to the range options, click the big question mark at the top of the dialog and then click on Pages.

AUTHOR'S NOTE

DRAW tries to be helpful at every turn. One of the first things it does when you invoke printing is to find out if the orientation of your drawing page matches that of the printer page. If not, DRAW asks if you want it to change the printer page orientation. This will often be what you want, but not always. Let's say you've created an 11″×17″ landscape layout for a magazine's front and back covers. Since you don't have a tabloid-size printer, you need to print the cover objects to a letter-size sheet. Think you should select those objects and print them, using Selection in the Print Range section? Not so fast! DRAW will see your page setup as landscape and dutifully warn you that your printer orientation is wrong, offering to adjust it for you. But think first: Your default printer page was already set to letter/portrait. In this instance, that's really what you're after, so you'll want to refuse DRAW's offer of help.

Copies

This one's fairly obvious: It tells your printer how many copies of each page to print. Just remember to reset it for every print job; like Print Range, the number of copies always reverts to its default value (1).

PostScript printers and some non-PostScript printers can print multiple copies at the maximum rated speed of the printer, regardless of the complexity of the original image. (Typical ratings are 4, 8, or 12 pages per minute for laser printers.) The image is created in the printer's memory once, which may take a while, and then is duplicated as you've specified in Number of Copies. Other printers may require DRAW to regenerate the page for each printed copy and will be noticeably slower.

Collating The handy Collate option allows you to tell DRAW and your printer to produce collated sets from a multipage document. There's a disadvantage, though: You may lose the speed gain mentioned in the previous section. It depends on what type of printer you are using and the nature of the document. We did some informal speed tests on a Hewlett-Packard 4M printer. We printed three copies of a four-page file that included paragraph text on each page, along with some moderately complex graphic elements. The results are summarized below:

	POSTSCRIPT: NO COLLATE	**POSTSCRIPT: COLLATE**
First Page Out:	48 seconds	1 minute, 10 seconds
Last Page Out:	2 minutes, 58 seconds	5 minutes, 28 seconds

	PCL (NON-PS): NO COLLATE	**PCL (NON-PS): COLLATE**
First Page Out:	35 seconds	25 seconds
Last Page Out:	2 minutes, 8 seconds	2 minutes, 5 seconds

Whether you choose to collate or not will depend a lot on your printer and the nature of the job. If you're preparing 100 copies of a complex, two-page file using a PostScript printer, it might make more sense to print uncollated copies and manually assemble them.

So far we've covered nearly all the items in the Print dialog—except the Print Style drop-down list and the Printer Color Profile check box. We'll return to these options later in the chapter. Let's first look at the multitude of choices available to you by clicking the Options button in the Print dialog.

Not-So-Basic Printing: Consider Your Options

The Print dialog's opening page contains a button innocently titled Options. Click it, and you open up a labyrinth of tabbed pages, each with more options and more buttons leading to more pages, all chock full of yet more buttons and print options! Print options have become even more plentiful in DRAW 6.0, and you may find this maze intimidating at first. This section will make you more comfortable with what the various options do and how they interact.

The Layout Page

Thankfully, one thing is consistent when you enter the Print Options maze: Your first stop is always the Layout page (Figure 27.9).

The Preview Window   Here is your opportunity to, among many other things, preview what the printed page will look like. By default, the Preview Image check box always begins in the Off state; objects on the page are depicted in the preview window by a big rectangle with an × in the middle of it. This box represents the boundaries framing all printable objects on the page. The purpose of this presentation is, of course, to improve system productivity. Complex pages can take nearly as long to be rendered for preview as they do to actually print. Often, the bounding box is all you need to see the effects of various options and determine if your job will print successfully.

The printable area on the page is represented by dotted margin lines near the edge. If any objects in your document lie beyond those margins, they will be clipped on the actual printed version.

27.9

The Layout page of Print Options

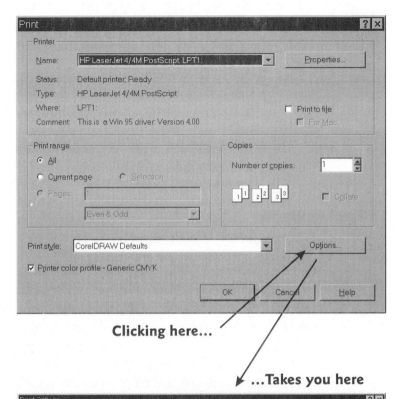

Clicking here...

...Takes you here

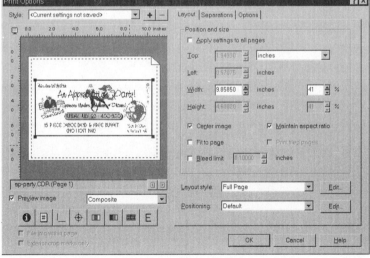

INSIDE INFO

For some devices, including imagesetters, you will not see any margins in the preview. The output media used with such devices is actually larger than the size of the declared print page; thus, the entire page area is printable.

The options in the Layout dialog are fairly self-explanatory, and we'll get to them in a moment. But what about those buttons under the preview window, with the fancy icons? Most of them are for use with commercial reproduction processes, and you'll read about them later in the chapter, in the section on color separations.

Position and Size Settings

Most of the settings in this section are easily understood. To begin, let's examine how they affect the printing of a simple, letter-size document that has a few objects on the page. In Figure 27.10 you see that document in the Preview window, which we got to by going File / Print, clicking Options, and turning on Preview Image.

In the representation of your page in the preview window, some objects extend beyond the printable area of the page. This is a bit difficult to see in Figure 27.10, and it may sometimes be equally difficult to see in your preview window. It's nice that DRAW depicts a truncated image, but that's not much use if you can't see the problem clearly. Fortunately, there is a solution...

NEW FOR 6

At the upper-left of the preview window is a small icon of a computer monitor. It's a toggle—click on it to see a full-screen representation of the preview window (Figure 27.11), and click again to return to the normal Layout dialog.

27.10

Default Layout settings for a simple test page

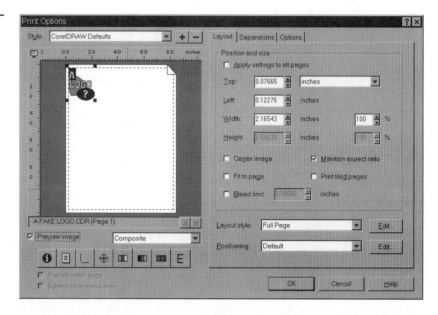

27.11

Full-screen print preview

From the full-screen preview in Figure 27.11, you can see that our logo is going to be clipped if we print it as is. So, what do we need to do? We could cancel printing, go back to the original art, and reposition it on the page. But maybe it's positioned there on purpose, perhaps for a final output device that doesn't have the same print margins as our proofing device. If you don't want to change the original artwork, you can do some adjustments from within the Layout page.

AUTHOR'S NOTE

In the discussion that follows, when we refer to size and position, we are referring to the collection of objects represented by the rectangle you see when Preview Image is turned off. This box represents the boundaries of all objects on the page, treated as a single entity.

There are two ways to adjust the position and size of what will be printed: You can do it numerically, with the settings on the Layout page; or you can do it visually in the preview window.

Let's look at the settings approach first. In the Position and Size area of the dialog, Top and Left indicate the position of the upper-left corner of the objects' bounding box. You can change the units in the drop-down list to whatever is appropriate for your project. Width and Height are the dimensions of the bounding box—the overall size of the objects—and are controlled by either typing in specific dimensions in the specified units you chose, or by selecting a scaling percentage.

Notice that Height is initially grayed out. This is because one of the other options, Maintain Aspect Ratio, is on by default. When this option is on, adjusting the width will automatically adjust the height to maintain the proper ratio.

Now for the visual sizing method. By the way, visual sizing is an improved implementation of a DRAW 4 feature that was dropped from DRAW 5. (Welcome Back!) You can adjust size and position visually in the preview window, in much the same way that you size and move objects on the drawing page.

Visual sizing can be done from either the small or full-page preview window. When you click on the image, you get sizing handles at the corner of the bounding box. You can click and drag these to resize the image, or you can click inside the box and drag to reposition it. Sizing will be proportionate, unless you first turn off the Maintain Aspect Ratio option.

Any changes you make visually are reflected in the numeric values at the right of the dialog page. Conversely, any changes you make numerically are reflected visually.

INSIDE INFO

Perhaps you've resized and repositioned, and then decide you don't like the results. How do you get back to the original settings? Simple! Click the Maintain Aspect Ratio option once, and it will reset all values. Watch out—if Maintain Aspect Ratio was already on when you used it to reset, you will likely need to turn it back on again before proceeding.

Center Image   This option centers the bounding box on the print page. It can be used with either visual or numeric resizing, but it locks the position. For example, in Figure 27.12 we have told DRAW to center our logo on the page and print it at 200% of actual size.

Fit To Page   This one's fairly obvious: Use it to print all the objects you've selected for printing. DRAW chooses whatever scaling factor is necessary to fit them within the print area, and automatically centers the result. This feature is particularly useful when designing large-format documents that need to be proofed on your desktop printer. It's also a quick way to scale up small objects, for proofing with better detail.

27.12

The original art, now scaled and centered

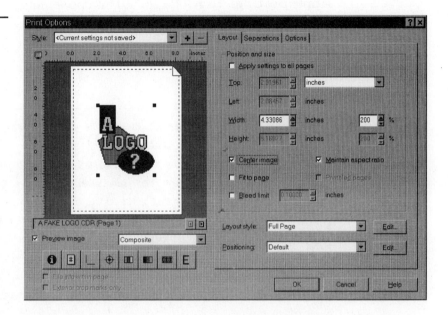

When your print range is a selection, Fit To Page force-fits all selected objects into the print area, even if some are way off the document page. This is the technique you would use to force objects on the desktop to print. Thus, to print all objects in and around your document, select them all, choose Selection for the print range, and turn on Fit To Page.

INSIDE INFO

In most cases, Fit To Page works correctly. With some printers, however, the assumed print margins do not quite match the actual unprintable area, and small portions of your image will get clipped. An easy solution: Turn on Fit To Page, note the resulting scale factor in the % box, and turn it off again; then select Center Image and manually enter a scale factor a few percent less than what was determined by Fit To Page.

Apply Settings To All Pages   This option, for use with multipage documents, takes whatever scaling and positioning values you've chosen and applies them to the collected objects on each page of the document. This is most often what you will want.

NEW FOR 6

> In DRAW 5, multipage documents were always treated as described just above. In DRAW 6.0, unless you turn on Apply Settings To All Pages, you are free to set scale and position values individually for each page. For instance, say you've designed a logo on page 1 and created a letterhead layout on page 2. You want an enlarged sample of the logo itself in order to proof the detail more clearly, but you still want to view the letterhead as it will actually print. By leaving this option turned off, you can set a large scaling factor for the logo page, leave default values for the letterhead page, and accomplish both goals in a single printing pass.

Bleed Limit   A *bleed* is a printing term that refers to extending large swatches of color, as in a rectangular background, past the physical borders of the document page. You do this so that the block of color will extend all the way to the edge when the page is printed and trimmed.

To create a bleed, remember that the document page must be smaller than the printer page in order to print the bleed. You then simply draw the objects so that they extend beyond the borders of the document page. The entire object will print, with a bleed margin for error.

Figure 27.13 shows a printed page with Bleed Limit off and with it on.

27.13

The effect of turning on Bleed Limit

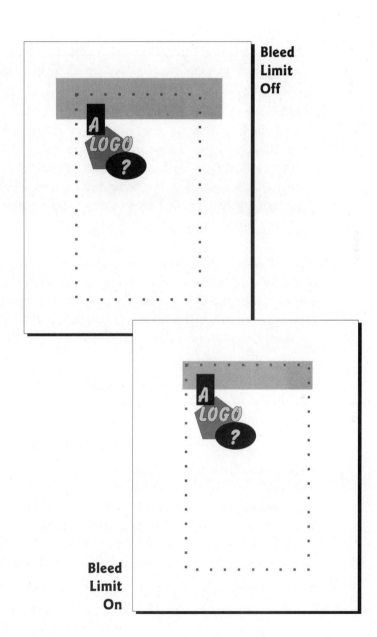

Bleed Limit Off

Bleed Limit On

Normally, a bleed extends as far off the page as you drew it (as long as the bleed fits within the print area). Sometimes you may not want this—for instance, when printing multiples of objects on a single printer page, as in label printing. Perhaps you drew the bleed so large that it overlaps into the next label. Bleed Limit lets you specify the maximum amount of bleed for the entire drawing. Unlike the other settings, this limit applies to all pages, whether the All Pages option is on or off.

Tiled Pages   We find the Print Tiled Pages option is consistently ignored by many DRAW users, despite its utility. This feature lets you print artwork that is larger than the printable page. Tiling is great for creating do-it-yourself posters and banners, and for proofing work destined for a large output device, at its full size. See the sidebar, "Budget Poster-Printing."

Exactly as its name implies, when you choose this option you get a series of printed tiles that, when trimmed and pasted together, form the full-size image. Tiling takes into account your printer's unprintable margins, by creating a certain amount of overlap on each tile.

Let's say you have an oversize document page to print. In the Layout page preview window, you'll see only a portion of your image, centered in the printer page. But click on Print Tiled Pages, and the preview window will automatically show you, using a grid, how many printer pages you'll need to print all the objects at full size. You can also take normal-size document pages and scale them up with this option.

Tiling has never been easier than in DRAW 6.0. Just use those sizing handles in the preview window to visually resize your image, with Print Tiled Pages turned on. When you resize, the number of tiles required to print at that size will change accordingly. So, you can adjust the image size to fit on a certain number of sheets.

You also now have the option of defining how much to overlap the images on each tile—handy for two reasons: (1) For those printers that don't quite accurately report the printable area to DRAW, when you need a larger overlap than the default to account for this. And (2) the process of trimming can be made easier if you use a standard overlap, such as a half-inch or one inch, instead of some oddball, hard-to-measure number.

Budget Poster-Printing

We created a 22″×28″ poster for a friend's 40th birthday. In Figure 27.14, you see how this would appear in the Layout preview if we tiled it on letter-size paper. There are several things you should notice. The tiling process works from a bounding box placed around the actual objects in the document, not the document page borders, and uses this box to position the tiled image. The upper-left corner of this box will be positioned in the upper-left corner of the tiled pages.

Now, notice that most of the Position and Size options (other than Width) are grayed out. This means we're stuck. We cannot center the image on the tiles. Worse, all the white framing space we intentionally created around the objects is now lost.

There is a way to solve our dilemma. If we first create a page frame for the poster, this will be included as an object in the bounding box. If this box is meant only to force the proper positioning of objects on the poster, we can apply no fill or outline to it so that it won't print. DRAW will still see our invisible rectangle when it positions objects for printing, even though there is nothing to print. In Figure 27.15 we've created a page frame (with a black outline for a trimming reference) and reproduced what the tiled page will now look like.

Notice that we set the Width to 99%, because 100% caused the image to spill slightly over into another column of tiles. This would have forced us to print twelve sheets for our poster. Matching the original drawing size exactly wasn't crucial, so we reduced the scale slightly and saved paper.

27.14

Tiling an oversize page

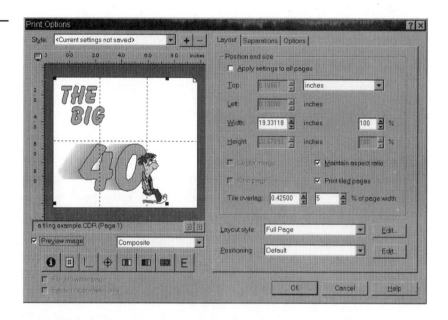

27.15

To control placement, use a page frame.

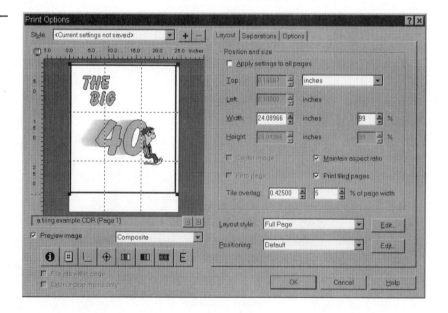

Predefined Card Styles

To this point, we've been discussing print options in terms of a full-page layout, with one or more pages. Things get a little more complex in printing the various other layouts described earlier in the sections on page setup. Figure 27.16 shows a four-page, side-fold card displayed in the Layout preview window. As you can see, the four pages will actually print on a single sheet, which you fold in the appropriate manner.

27.16

Print preview of a four-page, side-fold card

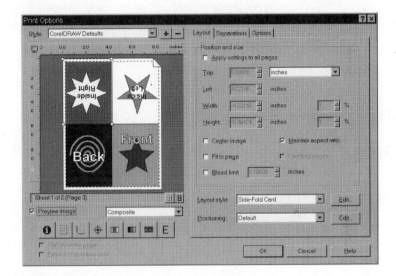

INSIDE INFO

When designing cards, keep in mind the nonprintable margins. If you want design elements to bleed off the page, you will have to size your card's overall document page smaller than the print page. You could set up an 8″×10″ custom page size, for example, define a side-fold layout to divide this into "pagelets," and print it to a standard letter-size sheet. After printing and folding the card, you would simply trim off the excess at the right and bottom edges.

If you create more than four pages in your file, you will generate multiple cards. For example, you might decide to prepare personalized holiday greeting cards for friends and family. You are likely to use certain graphic elements and text blocks repetitively throughout your card series, so this is a perfect opportunity to take advantage of the Desktop layer's pasteboard functionality. You might even make use of a Master layer (a printing layer that repeats on every page) for common elements.

Each set of four pages will be assembled at print time into a single card. Whenever more than four pages exist in your drawing file, DRAW reports the number of sheets (cards) you have and tells you which sheet you are looking at. In Figure 27.16 you can see this information in the status line beneath the preview window. You can scroll through and preview each sheet just as you do any multipage layout.

AUTHOR'S NOTE

Is this layout stuff beginning to get a little confusing? If so, we suggest you create a simple layout to play with, as we did to generate Figure 27.16. This is the best way to understand the interaction between various settings within your document and the Print options.

Book and Booklet Printing

Book and booklet printing is fairly straightforward and should not, in most cases, require twiddling any of the default settings in the Layout dialog. Some things get trickier when you choose a multipage booklet, however.

The first thing to realize is that you must leave the print range set to All to properly print the booklet. You will not get the proper page imposition if you choose to print only a range of pages. Because you must print all the pages at once, it might appear that you cannot accomplish the two-sided printing necessary for an assembled booklet, unless you happen to have a duplex printer. In version 5 this was exactly the case, greatly limiting the usefulness of this feature.

NEW FOR 6

DRAW 6.0 has a Manual Two-Sided Printing wizard. With this wizard you can self-publish multiple copies of a booklet on just about any desktop printer.

Using DRAW's Manual Two-Sided Printing Wizard   This wizard is automatically activated when

- You select a booklet or other two-sided layout

- You select an output device that is a nonduplexing desktop printer and not an imagesetter, or an output file other than a PRN file

- You are printing the booklet for the very first time to the selected device

The Manual Two-Sided Printing Wizard's steps help you (and DRAW) determine how to feed the stack of paper into your printer for the backs of the sheets, after the front sheets have been printed. Once the wizard is completed, the information is stored in the CORELPRN.INI file. Each time you print the booklets, all front sheets will be printed, along with an instruction sheet that directs how to place the stack back into the printer to properly print the backs.

The instructions within the wizard are fairly straightforward, but subject to possible misinterpretation. If you make wrong choices while completing the wizard, there is no option to go back and correct it. This should be fixed in future releases; fortunately, it is not too difficult to rectify such mistakes now. First, be sure to make a backup copy of the CORELPRN.INI file, found in the Corel60\Config folder (subdirectory). Then use a text editor to open the CORELPRN.INI file, and look for adjacent sections: PagePath Configuration and PagePath Section. Each section will contain one line for each configured printer, and these are the lines you need to delete if you have misconfigured your printer in the wizard. When you're done editing the INI file, run the wizard again to get the correct settings.

Printing Signatures

You may have noticed the Edit button next to the drop-down list of Layout styles. This button has two roles. One is to allow you to edit, if necessary, DRAW's predefined layout styles (cards, books, and booklets). This would need to be done only on the rarest of occasions.

The Edit Layout Style option's real worth, however, is in helping you to create custom page impositions, or *signatures*. Signatures are commonly used for high-volume book and magazine printing. Pages are ganged together on a single sheet—much like our side-fold cards, but the sheet is printed on both sides. After printing, the signature is folded and trimmed, producing a set of pages ready for binding in the book or magazine. Edit Layout Style would typically be used for production of camera-ready masters for output to an imagesetter, but you can use it with any output device. Thus, you might use a laser printer to proof signatures before sending the project to film.

You begin, as always, by defining the document page size. In the Page Setup dialog, the Layout selection will be Full Page, though the Page Size settings will normally represent a fractional portion of the signature size. Next, you create a multiple-page document. Printing signatures works something like creating a side-fold card. If you define a signature to have eight pages, for example, then each block of sixteen pages in the document will represent the front and back of a single signature sheet.

INSIDE INFO

Though you would normally define the document page to be the size of one signature panel, it is not absolutely necessary. DRAW will scale the panels to fit the resulting printer pages within your signature sheet. Be careful, though; when you let DRAW do the scaling for you, it does not account for any nonprinting margins.

Figure 27.17 demonstrates the process of defining a four-up, two-sided signature. Let's walk through it: Start by clicking on the Edit button next to the Layout Style drop-down list. You then see the Edit Layout Style dialog, shown at the top of the figure.

27.17

Creating a custom layout to print signatures

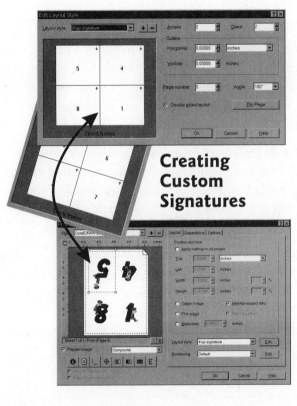

Creating Custom Signatures

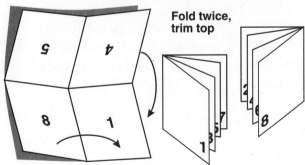

Fold twice, trim top

First you set the number of rows and columns for the signature, via the Across and Down boxes at the top; then set horizontal and vertical gutters, if any. Next, turn on Double-sided Layout if appropriate. (A signature usually would be double-sided; the Side-Fold Card layout in Figure 27.16 was not.) The preview window shows how the page will be subdivided, including a depiction of the gutter spacing.

Next, you click on one of the panels in the signature and assign it a page number via the Page Number box. With the panel still selected, you set the Angle for that panel to be either 0° or 180°. For a double-sided layout, you can click on Flip Page to complete the process for the back side of the signature.

Click OK to return to the Layout page, and the preview window shows the resulting front sheet of your custom layout. As with any layout, you can scroll through the fronts and backs of each sheet. (Remember, each panel on a sheet front or back represents one page of your document.)

NEW FOR 6

> Once you have completed your custom layout, you can save it as a named layout style for future use. Just click on the big + key next to the Layout Style drop-down list, and type in a name. Your layout style can be quickly recalled from the drop-down list in the main Print Options / Layout page or the Edit Layout Style dialog.

When printing a two-sided signature, the Manual Two-Sided Printing wizard will automatically kick in under the same conditions as it would for booklet printing. A 16-page file printed to the signature layout depicted in Figure 27.17 would print as two signature sheets.

WATCH OUT!

DRAW gets very confused if you try to print multiple copies of a two-sided signature. If you are proofing signatures on your desktop printer and need more than one set, you'll have to repeat the whole print process for each set.

What About Labels?

Perhaps you've wondered why, in all this coverage of fancy layouts, we haven't yet touched on printing labels. It's because DRAW considers label making to be a Positioning function rather than a layout style. (Why ask why?)

Okay, so you select a label layout from Page Settings, create the label, then confidently go to print it—and are you surprised when only a single label prints on your sheet! You click the Options button, turn on the preview image, and you find only a single label. Shouldn't there be a page full of this label? What happened?

To create a page of identical labels, you have to click the Edit button beside the Positioning drop-down, and turn on Clone Frame. This tells DRAW to repeat the document page the number of times dictated by the Rows and Columns settings in the Edit Positioning dialog (Figure 27.18).

Being an astute reader, you are probably already wondering, "If the Rows and Columns values are already set, based on my label customization in Page Settings / Layout, then why doesn't DRAW automatically clone the frame for printing?" Good question! The answer isn't immediately obvious.

Once you do a label customization, there is nothing to stop you from creating multiple pages in your document, each representing a different label. At print time, you have two choices. You can select Clone Frame in the Edit Positioning dialog, and you'll print one sheet of labels for

27.18

**The Edit Position-
ing dialog**

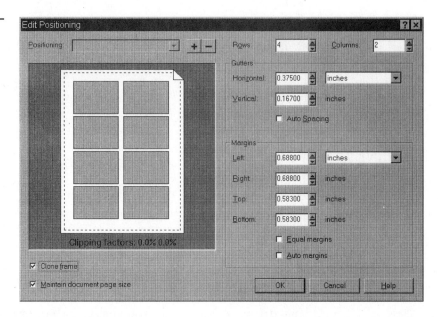

each page in your document. Leave Clone Frame off, and you get each page as a single label in sequence on the sheet. The layout shown in Figure 27.18 has six labels per sheet. Let's look at a couple of possibilities using this layout.

Assume you created ten pages (labels) in your document, each one unique with unique text. With Clone Frame off, the first six labels will print on sheet 1; the remaining four will print on sheet 2, leaving two labels blank. If you do turn on Clone Frame, you end up with ten sheets of labels, each with six copies of a given label. DRAW has no way of knowing ahead of time what you want to do, so the programmers chose a default that would conserve paper. (At least, that's what we'd like to believe was their reasoning…)

More on Positioning

In addition to rows and columns, you'll find controls for margins and gutters in the Edit Positioning dialog; they're virtually identical to the ones for customizing labels you saw in Figure 27.7. These options will help you work with more than just labels. Perhaps you have created a custom page and designed some business cards. Using the Edit Positioning dialog, you can construct a page of the business cards, similar to the page of labels described in the foregoing section.

Let's say you've started with a letter-size page and designated two rows and three columns in the Edit Positioning dialog. When DRAW creates the layout, the document pages will be scaled to fit within the resulting page frames. In this business card example, you want to fit as many as possible on the page, but you certainly don't want a standard business card to shrink as you increase the rows and columns. To force the page size to remain fixed, turn on Maintain Document Page Size. This way, you can experiment with increasing the number of rows and columns as well as adjusting margins and gutters, to determine the optimum layout. Just watch the preview window.

An example of this use is shown in Figure 27.19. At first glance, it might appear that we can fit three columns on the page with the margins and gutters we've defined. But look more closely at the preview window. The clipping factors at the bottom tell us what percent of our overall layout will be clipped in each direction if we print this layout. Notice that the first number (horizontal clipping) is small but definitely not zero. This tells us we need to adjust margins and/or gutters to actually fit the three columns to the page.

NEW FOR 6

Just like custom layout styles, your special Positioning settings can be named and saved for future use. Click the big + key next to the Positioning drop-down. More on this later, in "Putting It All Together: Creating a Print Style."

At this point, we've pretty well exhausted our coverage of DRAW's Page Settings / Layout and Print Options / Layout options. (If we've exhausted you as well, at least now you know how to make yourself a get-well card...) So, it's on to Color!

**Trial-and-error
positioning in the
preview window**

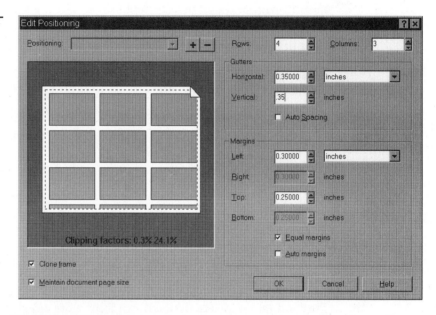

Color for the Masses

In previous versions of this book, discussion of color printing was confined almost solely to printing color separations—film destined for a commercial printing press. The last two years have seen great strides in other methods for achieving color output. Many service bureaus and quick-copy shops now offer high-end color copiers. Connected to a Fiery Rip (raster image processor), they can directly image your computer files in glorious, continuous-tone (photo-realistic) color.

Today's desktop color printers cost less and produce much higher quality work than their predecessors. Most are still being used for proofing purposes, but even some inexpensive models can now be used for certain commercial projects. We find ourselves scratching our head in wonder at how well photographs and complex DRAW objects reproduce on, say, a budget-priced Epson Color Stylus ink-jet printer.

Color output is a far more common goal today for average DRAW users. It's not only the graphics professionals who must confront the complex world of color. Which brings us to the issue of Corel's color management system—and in our minds, after much experimentation, it's still a big question indeed.

What Is Color Management and Why Should You Care?

The next chapter will discuss color theory and application in more detail, but let's start here with one problem that demonstrates the unavoidable need for color management in your work.

The custom DRAW palette has a color called, simply, Blue. As viewed on your monitor, Blue is an entirely apt name. Your monitor produces color by combining light from three light guns: red, green, and blue. Combine 100% of all three colors, and you see white. The color Blue is produced by firing the blue gun only, and it looks absolutely and undeniably Blue to all but the color-blind.

But what happens when this simple color is printed? Assuming you have no sort of color management/color correction mechanism, this Blue will invariably print as some sort of purple hue. Virtually all output devices use a mixture of either three or four inks to produce the illusion of all colors. This is just as true for commercial offset printing as it is for our humble Epson desktop printer. The inks used are cyan, magenta, yellow, and sometimes black (CMY or CMYK). Print 100% of C, M, and Y and you will see black. The so-called color Blue is produced by combining 100% cyan with 100% magenta, and unfortunately, this will always look purple.

To produce the illusion of various colors, a printer overlays semitransparent halftone dots of each primary print color. Each ink is printed at a different angle, so that the dots never sit precisely on top of one another. Each halftone ink dot can only be printed as 100% of one of the primary ink colors in use. Different hues and intensities of each primary color are produced by varying the size and spacing of the dots. The halftone dots are so small, your eye is tricked into perceiving a tint of the solid color, instead of a collection of dots. When these tints are overlaid, the illusion is a mixture of tints. Colors produced this way are called *process colors.* In commercial printing, film separations are used to produce four separate printing plates, one for each process ink used. The print job may also include additional plates for premixed inks called *spot colors,* such as those specified in the PANTONE Matching System.

On a desktop ink-jet printer, separate nozzles squirt the inks from their containers onto the page, simultaneously. Other desktop printers work somewhat differently, but the end result for all such printers is similar to commercial process printing. The colors are produced by varying halftone overlays of the primary printer inks. Desktop printers, however, having only process primary colors, can only simulate PANTONE spot colors, which require specially formulated, PANTONE-matched inks.

CorelDRAW automatically converts RGB screen color to CMYK color equivalents for printing, but they aren't always truly equivalent. Add to this the inherent difference in the physics of color production, plus variations among common devices (monitors and printers), and any attempt to reliably predict color in finished artwork becomes a task even Sisyphus might have shunned. You can see how there is a major disparity between how colors are produced on a monitor versus a printing device.

Corel's Color Manager

What can Corel's color manager do for you? Does it adjust the printer to match what you see on the monitor, adjust the monitor to approximate the printer, or a bit of both? Its philosophy is to adjust the monitor to more closely approximate what is normally printed, because the printer is the limiting factor. The CMY/CMYK print process cannot produce as wide a range of colors (the device's *color gamut*) as your monitor. So the emphasis is to tweak display colors to more closely represent what actually prints.

The color manager tries to normalize print devices to meet certain print standards. The printer profiles of some output devices get more adjustments than others. For example, it wouldn't make any sense to color-correct PANTONE spot colors when producing film separations on an imagesetter; PANTONE inks are already premixed and standardized. On the other hand, a desktop ink-jet printer might need a good deal of correction in this area, because it must use process inks to simulate PANTONE colors.

Corel's Color Management Wizard

The new, friendly Color Management wizard takes you step-by-step through development of a System Color Profile. Even if you find it necessary to customize the device profiles supplied, it's a more straightforward process than in prior versions of DRAW. How useful the results are is another question.

A System Color Profile comprises up to three device-specific components: a scanner profile, a monitor profile, and a printer profile. What your Profile contains and the complexity of creating it will both depend on your needs and system capabilities. At its simplest, you will choose predefined profiles for each of the three device types (Corel provides quite a few). You can take it further by beginning with an existing device profile and then using various built-in calibration options to adjust for the unique characteristics of your own equipment.

In fact, if you are going to create System Color Profiles at all, you will eventually need to do at least some calibration. This is because even devices from the same manufacturer have characteristics that vary from one unit to another and that may change over time, as well.

The Bad News and Good News on System Color Profiles

You are likely to need more than one System Color Profile. Let's say you always use a scanner and a particular monitor, but sometimes you print to a desktop color printer and sometimes to a PRN file for a Linotronic or Agfa imagesetter. You will need one System Color Profile for each combination of devices you use.

Profiles take a relatively short time to generate—if you stick to the standard device profiles and have a fast computer. On our Pentium 90, one such profile takes about five minutes. Expect to take substantially longer when you start to calibrate the settings for your own equipment. You'll need to do a good deal of adjusting and testing. This can be both time-consuming and expensive if you are trying to calibrate to a commercial printer's offset presses.

The good news is, once they're created, you can quickly select the appropriate device profile via the Tools menu in DRAW or PAINT, or by running the wizard as a stand-alone application (see Figure 27.20). Once chosen, the device profile is used by all applications in the CorelDRAW suite.

27.20

Pick your Profile from the Color Management wizard.

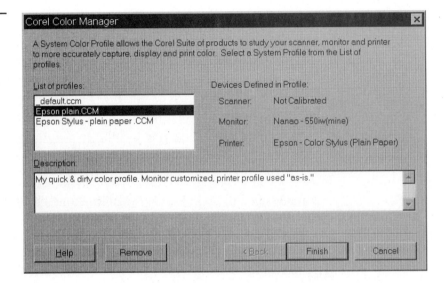

Once you create System Profiles, you can choose which profile to use at any given time, via the Tools / Color Manager / Select Color Profile option. Then you have a choice of how to employ the profile to color-correct your monitor. From the View menu, select one of the Color Correction options. Accurate / Simulate Printer usually gets results that most closely approximate what will be printed. You can select None to speed up screen redraws, but color accuracy will be lost. The Fast option is meant to be a compromise, but we found it far too inaccurate to be of any use. At print time, there is a check box in the main Print dialog, which determines whether the selected profile will be used to color adjust output.

Yeah, but Does It Work?

We're embarrassed to admit that we spent more time experimenting with the Color Manager than almost anything else discussed in this chapter. This was due, in part, to our being fascinated with our new color printer—but most of our time was spent largely on the inherently complex nature of color correction.

For all our efforts, our conclusion is (and here we'll quote from our lead author): "If you're going to be working with color, your best investment will be a set of PANTONE and TruMatch color swatch books. Never, ever trust what you see on your monitor." Though we were very careful in preparing our System Profile and spent hours experimenting, the results were far from completely accurate and reliable. They are, however, an improvement over no color correction at all.

In our testing, we ignored our scanner (since we weren't utilizing it with DRAW) and focused on the monitor and Epson Stylus color printer. We selected a monitor profile from the list of standard profiles and edited it using the Corel-supplied target photo for reference. The next task was choosing among three different printer profiles: for Epson Stylus-plain paper at 360 dpi, or Epson Stylus-special paper at 360 dpi, or Epson Stylus-special paper at 720 dpi. (Are you beginning to see how time-consuming this process can be?) In the interest of speed and expense, we chose the one with plain paper at 360 dpi for our tests, using the profile as is. (Calibrating a printer is more involved than calibrating your monitor.)

The printer driver for our Epson has its own built-in color correction, so we had something to compare against. We created a test file consisting of a series of swatches, filled with various uniform colors. We filled the first series with the primaries: cyan, magenta, yellow, red, green, and blue, respectively. Then we added 14 selected PANTONE spot colors, 13 TruMatch colors, and 5 levels of gray. (TruMatch is a series of standardized, numerically coded CMYK colors.)

We printed the test file four times, using each of the following settings: Epson's own color correction; Corel's device profile printed through the Epson print driver; Corel's profile printed through the Windows 95 print driver; and Corel's profile in combination with Epson's Ink Density Correction printed through the Epson print driver. (Still with us?) Then, using PANTONE and TruMatch swatch books as our standards, we rated the printed results. We decided on 1 for Good, 4 for Awful, with 2 and 3 being something in between. Sometimes one product was a 1 and the others were so bad they all got a 4. We applied only a single overall accuracy score for the gray swatches. Our results are in Table 27.1.

Table 27.1: Our Color Manager Test Results

	PRIMARIES	PANTONE	TRUMATCH	GRAYS	TOTAL
Corel Profile/ Win95 Driver	13	40	34	3	90
Corel Profile/ Epson Driver	9	36	30	3	78
Epson Correction/ Epson Driver	9	20	26	1	56
Corel Profile/ Epson Ink-Density Correction	9	18	21	2	50

What Did We Learn?   It was interesting to see that Corel's color correction, by itself, was not nearly as accurate overall as Epson's built-in system. Yet, when used in combination with just the Ink Density Correction portion of Epson's system, Corel's color manager yielded the best results. All combinations produced more accurate results than we expected, each having its own strengths.

- The Corel profile produced more-accurate reds.

- Epson correction seemed to handle blues, purples, and yellow-green tints better.

- None of them rendered basic magenta accurately at all. It looked way too purple in all tests.

■ Using the Windows 95 printer driver for the Epson produced a problem beyond color accuracy: poor-quality light tints. The halftone dots were far more obvious than when we used Epson's own driver.

Screen output with the calibrated monitor profile matched the Epson corrected output surprisingly well—a definite aid in predicting how selected colors will print. Blues were actually blue and purples were actually purple. Vivid reds, on the other hand, suffered in the translation. The screen-corrected reds looked duller than the printed ones; an uncorrected screen rendered truer reds. On balance, though, the montor/printer correlation was quite good.

Unfortunately, monitor/desktop printer correlation is not the litmus test for color management systems. It may suffice if you're only going to print color on desktop printers, but the true test for commercial printing is how well the monitor and the desktop proof conform to the end product. The results of our color management test were somewhat favorable, but we'll hang on to our swatch books, anyway, thank you very much.

After doing all our swatch comparisons, we ran a more subjective test with our color printer—we loaded and printed the digital photograph used as part of the monitor calibration process. A photographic print of the image is supplied in the DRAW package, so we had something to compare to. The monitor's rendering with Corel's color correction turned on was quite good, but some blues in the sky were a little off. When we printed, nothing produced quite what we hoped for.

■ The Corel profile used by itself produced horrid results.

■ The Epson corrected version was fairly accurate overall, more so than the Corel plus Epson Ink Density combination.

■ Corel plus Epson Ink Density produced hues that were less accurate. We did get greater intensity, however; by comparison, the Epson version looked very dull.

What this tells us is that (groan) we probably need to spend more time adjusting and testing with both correction systems, Corel and Epson. Eventually we should be able to find the optimum settings.

Despite the limitations, those of you doing a lot of commercial color work may find it advantageous to create and test color profiles for the imagesetters in the various print shops you use. A System Color Profile may help improve the design process…as long as you don't rely solely on your monitor screen for color choices.

Color Separations

It may seem obvious to some, but color separations themselves are not printed in color. Each separation is black and white, usually negative film, from which your printer burns a plate for the printing press. That's when the specified ink color for each plate is applied, resulting in the composite color product.

If you are serious about color work, sooner or later you will need to create color separations—usually image-set film destined for the commercial printer. You can also print color separations from a desktop laser printer, but the quality is not sufficient for commercially printed process color work. Silk-screeners sometimes use desktop printers for process separations, because they typically don't require high resolution and halftone frequencies (more on this later). Simple spot-color separations are not as demanding as process-color work and can often be handled by a good laser printer (as long as you avoid extensive use of subtle blends and fountain fills). But whenever you want commercially produced process-color printing, you are destined for a trip to a service bureau.

The Value of Postscript   Nearly all imagesetters are PostScript devices, as are many of the high-end color proofing devices. So if you are likely to be using service bureaus frequently, it's advisable to own a PostScript laser printer. At $10 or more per plate, mistakes at the imagesetter can be very costly. Proofing on a PostScript laser printer cannot eliminate all possible errors, but it can help minimize them. For instance, after we prepare a PRN file using a Linotronic print driver, we often copy the prepared file to our desktop laser printer, to verify the condition of all our plates. The pages we view are clipped and sometimes rather ugly, but at least we know all the pieces are there. Without a PostScript printer, we wouldn't be able to know this. We could print separations, but they would not be fully representative of the PRN file bound for the service bureau.

NEW FOR 6

> Speaking of viewing your separations, a long-desired capability has been added to the preview window in the Separations page of the Print Options dialog. A batch of options now drop down under the window: You can preview each individual plate, depicted in its intended color. If you've ever tried to figure out why you wound up with magenta and cyan plates in a PANTONE spot-color project, this feature is great news. Even if you are new to color separations and have never encountered this mystery, trust us, you will!

The Separations Page

The Separations page of the Print Options dialog contains the settings and options needed to print color separations.

To create separations, you simply check the Print Separations check box. When you issue it, a number of things immediately happen, and you will need to make some decisions.

As depicted in Figure 27.21, DRAW highlights the colors actually in use in your drawing, including any PANTONE colors. Normally you will print all separations at once, but you have the option of deselecting any colors you don't want printed. You can also tell DRAW to print a plate for every color, even if it is empty for a given page (using the Print Empty Plates option, discussed later).

Now, About Those
Buttons Under the Preview Window

The instant you select Print Separations, the first four buttons under the preview window turn on automatically. These buttons are used most frequently with color separations, although the first two are useful with

27.21

The Separations page of the Print Options dialog

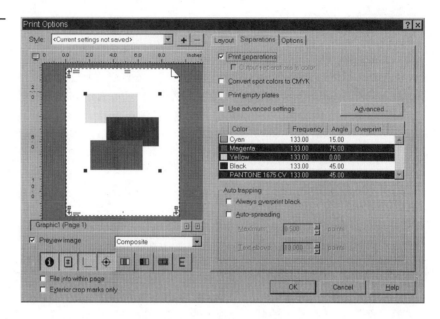

any file destined for commercial printing. So that you can better understand what these buttons do, in Figure 27.22 we've reproduced two of the four process plates for the graphic at the bottom. (We could only show you the resulting composite image in black and white, but you'll get the idea.)

Following are explanations of all eight buttons, in order from left to right.

File Information   This option prints information about the plate, at the top and bottom of the separations, near the left-hand crop marks. It identifies the plate's color; the System Color Profile used, if any; the halftone screen angle and frequency for that color; the file name; the date and time printed; and the plate number. Under the button is a check box option to force file information to be printed within the boundaries of the document page, so that you can print the information even when your printer page won't accommodate it.

27.22

Sample color
separations

Page Number   This is a new option in DRAW 6.0. This number
identifies an individual document page, as opposed to the plate number.
As we see it, the feature has little value. It functions only with the Full
Page and various label layouts and is thus no help in keeping booklet
and signature pages straight. And the numbers print outside the document page, so they're not a solution for printing page numbers within a
document.

WATCH OUT!

> Remember, these buttons turn on automatically when you print separations. And Page Number works for the label layouts. So if you're printing butt-cut business cards or a similar layout, with no gutters, remember to turn this button off. If you don't, the page number will print within your card.

Crop Marks   These are the vertical and horizontal lines that define the border of your document page, indicating where to trim or crop the finished piece. If you created a layout with multiple pages to a sheet, as in the business card example described earlier, this option will generate crop marks framing each document page.

NEW FOR 6

> For business cards and other similar layouts, printing crop marks can be trouble. This is especially true if you set the gutters to zero in order to butt-cut the cards at trim time. The internal crop marks would print right at the boundaries between cards, making it nearly impossible to trim the cards on that border with a single cut. In such a situation, check the Exterior Crop Marks Only option (under the preview window's row of icons).

Registration Marks   Registration marks are used solely for color separations, to ensure that the various color plates are *in register,* or aligned properly with one another. Without these little targets, it would be next to impossible to predict the press adjustment needed to bring the plates into register. You've undoubtedly seen examples of hideously blurred color pages, or pages with unsightly white gaps that result from mis-registration. We see at least one of these a week in our local newspaper.

Calibration Bars   This produces a series of rectangles, which in the primary print will display colors—cyan, yellow, magenta, black, red, green, and blue—on the plates. These are used to verify the accuracy of the inks coming off the press.

Densitometer Scale   This advanced feature is used with a *densitometer*, at either the service bureau or the printer, to verify that the film or printing plates were prepared within proper device calibration limits.

Print Negative   Turning this option on tells DRAW to output a negative image instead of a positive, and the preview window changes to indicate a negative will be printed. Surprisingly, you will not often use this feature when requesting negative film from a service bureau. Most bureaus have set up one or more imagesetters as dedicated negative film processors, with this option set. If you set this option in your file, too, you may ruin the file or, more likely, the ones that follow it in the queue. (Unfortunately, we've experienced this one firsthand. The imagesetter operator was rather irate!) Always check with your service bureau before turning on Print Negative.

Print Emulsion Side Down   When this button is enabled, the emulsion or light-sensitive coating on film will be on the bottom side of the film. This is the normal method for offset printing. Conversely, silkscreeners usually want film with emulsion side up—sometimes referred to as *wrong reading* vs. *right reading*. Like Print Negative, this option should usually be left unselected. Your service bureau will likely prefer to set that.

Options for Printing Separations

Under the Print Separations check box are three options for your separations job.

Output Separations in Color   Only available if your target printer is capable of printing color, this option prints each plate in its specified color. The value of this feature is for visualization and particularly useful if you print to transparencies. You can create a home-grown color key, wherein you overlay the transparencies to see how the composite image will look. This has limited usefulness compared with the professionally prepared color keys or matchprints provided by service bureaus, but it may help you catch certain glaring problems. If one color doesn't look right overprinting another, for example, it isn't likely to look right when printed commercially.

Convert Spot Colors to CMYK   This feature is specifically for use with the PANTONE Matching System of spot colors. Turning this option on tells DRAW that you do *not* want a separate plate for each spot color in the document. Instead, you want DRAW to approximate these colors with a CMYK equivalent. This can simplify the project and reduce printing costs. Be cautious, however. The degree of accuracy will vary among the PANTONE colors. This is not DRAW's fault; it derives from the nature of PANTONE's colors themselves.

INSIDE INFO

Even when DRAW's match to PANTONE's color is fairly accurate, make certain that a CMYK substitution is acceptable. When examined closely, packaging often reveals large patches of solid colors—cereal boxes are a good example. These patches are almost always spot-color inks, and for good reason. Using a PANTONE color often has nothing to do with achieving color accuracy. With a CMYK replacement, the hue might be correct, but the result will likely appear grainy when compared to a solid PANTONE print. Remember, to produce the equivalent color, the printer must overlay CMYK halftones. When a color has process components of less than 100% each, the halftone pattern is bound to be visible.

Print Empty Plates   Checking this option tells DRAW to print a plate for every color, even if it is empty for a given page, and is a means of minimizing confusion when a job is passed from you to service bureau to printer. This method of tracking can prevent the printer or someone else from erroneously thinking there are missing plates and holding up your job.

Using PANTONE Color in Fountain Fills

In prior versions of DRAW, an object with a fountain fill going from one PANTONE spot color to another would be automatically converted to CMYK color at print time. There was a workaround in DRAW 5, but it required editing the CORELPRN.INI file. Now DRAW 6.0 will normally separate such a fill to the appropriate PANTONE plates, as long as you don't turn on the Convert Spot Colors to CMYK option.

The same cannot be said for blends, however. When you blend two PANTONE-filled objects, you get intermediate objects that are filled with CMYK colors.

By the way, watch out—printing PANTONE fountain fills is risky business. Though we've occasionally done this successfully, muddy-looking fountain fills happen a lot. Best results come from using lighter PANTONE colors, or colors that are not too dissimilar. If you do attempt a PANTONE fountain fill, use two different halftone screen angles. A logical choice might be to use one of the CMYK standard angles (0°, 15°, 45°, or 75°) for each overlapping PANTONE color.

Bear in mind, however, that each plate imaged on film costs big bucks at the service bureau. A solution might be to supply a set of laser proofs that include empty plates for reference. Then prepare the film without the empty plates.

Auto-Trapping   Trapping itself will be discussed at length in Chapter 28, but let's take a look at the two auto-trapping functions here in the Separations page. They can help you in lieu of manually created color traps, for many situations.

Always Overprint Black does exactly what it says. It tells DRAW not to create knockouts where a black object sits on top of objects of other colors. (Knockouts are areas the shape of an overlying object that are "knocked out" of the underlying colors. The underlying color does not print in the knockouts, and thus does not cause a change in hue by mixing with the overlying color.)

Unless the colors over which black is printing are very dark, you can and should turn this feature on. Press operators get very upset when they are faced with the task of registering blocks of fine black text over a lightly tinted background that has been unnecessarily knocked out. Unless the registration is perfect, you get unsightly white gaps. So talk to your printer first about overprinting black, based on the specific project.

Auto-spreading creates a form of color trap, automatically. It takes an object that is *not* to be overprinted (knocked out, instead) and adds an outline of the same color that *does* overprint. This technique can work quite well but has limited application. The object in question must have a uniform fill, no outline of its own, and cannot already be designated as overprinting.

The Maximum value determines the largest spread, in points, for any object. The extent of trap is determined by the darkness of the object. Lighter-colored objects will have a larger spread because they cause less visible shift where colors overlap. And the Text Above value, new to DRAW 6.0, determines the minimum size of text to which auto-spreading is applied. Spreads applied to very small text cause blurring and illegibility.

Advanced Options for Separations

DRAW 6.0 has renamed its advanced settings dialog for color separations; now you click the Advanced (instead of Edit) button on the Separations page to get to them. More features have been added (see Figure 27.23), but all of them are for PostScript output devices only—yet another compelling reason to own a PostScript printer. Most users need never touch most of these complex options, and we'll get to that momentarily.

When you initially enter the Advanced Separations Settings dialog, the Screening Technology field is set to Standard Defaults. These are the normal halftone screen angles and frequencies for your output device. The angle settings have long been conventional in the preparation of

27.23

The Advanced Separations Settings dialog: for PostScript users only

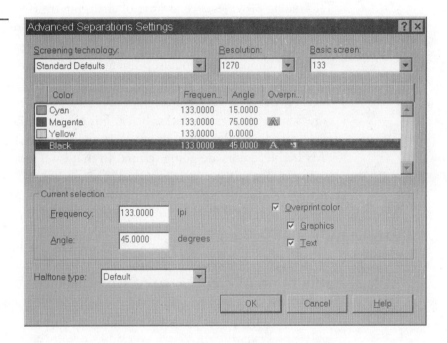

color separations: 0°, 15°, 45°, and 75° degrees, as you can see in Figure 27.23. They will be common to any output device you choose. The frequency defaults will vary depending on the output device and selected resolution.

AUTHOR'S NOTE

The concepts of screen angles and screen frequencies will be discussed in more detail in Chapters 28 and 29. For now, just be aware that most custom settings found today are designed to improve on traditional halftone techniques. They were developed to limit the occurrence of visible patterns—called moirés—that sometimes destroy the subtle illusion of continuous-tone color in a printed piece.

This dialog provides several ways of changing the default settings, though that will seldom be necessary. One way is to select a color and then type specific values in the Current Selection Frequency and Angle boxes. Or choose from the drop-down list of industry-standard screening technologies; these assign the values for all four CMYK plates at once. Any PANTONE color plates present will initially take on the same screen settings as process black. For most spot-color work, this is perfectly acceptable—though not if you have areas where tints of several PANTONE colors are going to mix. In that case, you can and should alter the angles.

A Word of Warning   If you prepare PRN files for high-resolution output at a service bureau, we urge you to talk to your service bureau before you venture into the Advanced Separations Settings dialog. One of the larger service bureaus in our area told us that typically, throughout the industry, virtually any angle and frequency choices you make in this dialog for CMYK plates will be ignored when the file is output. Although such screening technologies are used, the settings are made on the imagesetting system itself. When you submit your file and indicate the resolution and nominal screen frequency you want, the service bureau will set these values directly on their hardware, overriding the global settings in your file. One of Corel's engineers confirmed this and recommended the DRAW defaults. So, before you invest a lot of time experimenting with these settings, realize that in most instances they won't be used.

One scenario in which fiddling with the defaults might be useful is when you are outputting directly from DRAW to your own imagesetter or another device. Instead of constantly resetting your hardware, leave any custom screening turned off and simply set the desired frequency and angle values for each document as it is printed.

INSIDE INFO

> We asked our informative Corel engineer whether one might be able to use custom screening settings in a PRN file destined for a Brand X imagesetter that doesn't incorporate similar technology. The answer was no. Without the technology, the device can't produce the proper halftone dots required by the custom screen and frequency settings. So there would be no advantage over the standard screen settings.

Overprint Color This check box gives you the option of overprinting graphic objects, text, or both, that are filled with the color you select. This can be especially useful when working with PANTONE colors. It's much faster than having to overprint object-by-object (the tedious DRAW 5 way).

We've already mentioned that you can control the halftone settings individually for each color plate, including any PANTONE plates that will be made. (This, too, is new to DRAW 6.0—much easier than the tedious object-by-object procedure in version 5.) But, what happens if you have some areas filled with only a 15% tint of the dark PANTONE color? You certainly wouldn't want that to overprint. DRAW recognizes that, and has an inherent minimum tint of 95%, below which objects will not overprint.

Halftone Type The option to choose the halftone type is seldom used but can help you create some interesting special effects. Your choice determines the shape of the halftone object (usually a circular dot, but there are other choices available). You might, for example, choose to print a fairly coarse screen frequency for each color, while using a line or diamond halftone type to create an interesting texture.

Halftones for Skin Tones	Our Corel guru told us that selecting an elliptical halftone type can improve skin textures in photographs. Though mainly used in PAINT, the same technique is possible when printing photos in your DRAW files. It did, indeed, improve the skin tone in a photo printed to our HP 4M laser. Halftone types may adversely affect the vector objects in the artwork, so you'll need to experiment with specific choices for every project. For your own experiments with the halftone pattern on your laser printer, throw a Tinted Grayscale lens over full-color art before printing. Set the lens color to black. Then print your file, opening the Separations page and selecting Print Separations—but print only the black plate. (DRAW sometimes doesn't realize that this is the only plate with stuff to print.) You can then experiment with the angle, frequency, and halftone type settings on your composite image to see what interesting effects you get.

Some Tricks with Color Substitutions

Always keep in mind that separations are produced in black and white. The colors that actually get printed are determined solely by what color inks are used at print time. Armed with this knowledge and a little creative thinking, you can sometimes work around a few sticky situations, especially when working with spot colors.

We've often found it beneficial to use process color substitutes for preparing PANTONE spot-color print pieces. Say we're going for a final result printed in a specific PANTONE orange and pale green. Instead of designing with these two colors in DRAW, we use process black and process magenta to represent them. It's harder to visualize the finished artwork this way, but it opens a few doors for us.

For instance, blending objects with two different PANTONE fills always produces intermediate steps filled with CMYK color (see the sidebar, "Using PANTONE Colors in Fountain Fills"). When blending two PANTONE-filled objects is really your goal, this color substitution method is your answer. (But don't forget our caution about mixing PANTONE inks.) Blending process black to process magenta yields intermediate steps that have only black and magenta components. You can separate it to two plates, labeled Black and Magenta, and simply tell your printer which PANTONE colors to substitute at print time.

Here's another situation: You're confronted with a project for which only black-and-white or grayscale artwork is available, but you want to print it in a PANTONE color. Rather than attempting to recolor it, you simply let the black plate represent the actual printed PANTONE color. If the job requires its own separate black plate for text or other elements, you could create these in process magenta. This juggling of plate definitions won't harm your final product as long as your printer knows which ink to use with which plate.

Duotones offer another opportunity for color substitution. Duotones are black-and-white photographs enhanced by application of a single tint. If you're importing a photograph into a two-color layout and want to create a duotone out of it, the obvious choice would be to apply a Tinted Grayscale lens in one of the two spot colors. Though PANTONE colors can be selected for this lens effect, they're converted to CMYK at print time. Substitute a process primary as the lens color and for all other instances of that PANTONE color, and your problem is solved.

What, More Options?

We think the Options page of the Print Options dialog should have been named Even More Options, to distinguish it from the Options buttons you've encountered so far in this odyssey of printing. To add to the absurdity, notice in Figure 27.24 that this page contains a couple of buttons with names ending in the ellipsis, which means…you guessed it, more options! (And you thought printing was the simple part.)

Rest assured, for much of your day-to-day printing needs—especially if you rely mainly on a desktop laser or color printer—you may never

27.24

The Options page, with even more options...

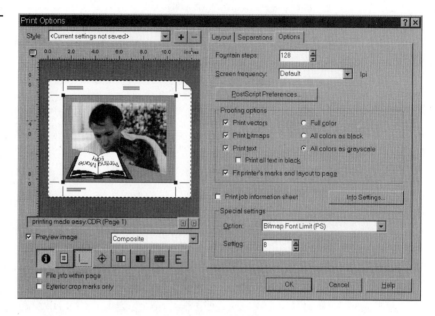

need to access this area. But there are some interesting and useful features here. You may need them in your work with color separations; some are only applicable when you print composite artwork.

Fountain Steps

When you create a fountain fill in a vector graphics program, it is displayed and printed as a series of discrete bands of color hues and shades. The more bands, the smoother the fountain fill appears, but the longer it takes to redisplay or print. How many bands your screen displays can be set in the Tools / Options / Display dialog. It has *no* bearing on how many steps are printed.

The value in the Fountain Steps box determines how many steps are printed, subject to two restrictions. First, the setting applies only to fountain fills that you left locked (the default) when creating them. As described in Chapter 9, you can unlock the steps setting for a particular fountain-filled object, and set a value independently for that object, which overrides what you set with this print option. Why set separate step values? Perhaps you're after an effect that requires a coarse fill and thus fewer bands. Or you may want a few objects to have more fill steps than others.

The other restriction has to do with the capabilities of the selected output device. A mathematical formula (discussed in Chapter 29) relates the number of gray shades (or shades of a separation primary color) that an output device can produce, to its output resolution. Basically, the higher the output resolution, the more gray levels are possible. Thus, you can set any value you want for Fountain Steps in this print options page, but it may not be achievable if the frequency is set too high for the output resolution. Instead, you may see (or, actually, may *not* see) many adjacent bands printed with the same shade of gray. You end up with banding, anyway. See Figure 27.25 for samples that demonstrate this problem. Given such a catch-22, there is no point in setting this value higher than what the device is capable of. It only increases processing time and the possibility of output failure.

27.25

At lower resolutions, higher halftone screen frequencies reduce the number of grays that can be printed.

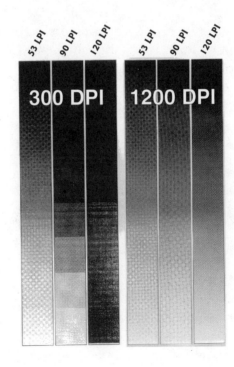

INSIDE INFO

There is an absolute limit to the number of gray levels that can be produced, regardless of output resolution. That number is 256 and is a by-product of the way grayscale information is stored digitally (8 bits per pixel = 256 possible grays). For a fill that only uses black or a single process color component, a value higher than this is meaningless. The number of possible color combinations that can be digitally represented increases geometrically from 256, to over 16 million! However, come print time, each separation plate will still max out at 256 steps in a fountain fill.

The initial value in the Fountain Steps box—the default step value—will vary depending on the selected printer. It is set to 128 for Post-Script devices and 64 for non-PostScript devices. Neither value is necessarily correct. The appropriate number depends on the resolution of the output device, the halftone frequency you choose, and the size of the filled objects. Happily, DRAW 6.0 has added some welcome new features to optimize the number of fountain steps, saving you from complex calculations.

WATCH OUT!

If you change the fountain step value, don't expect it to stick for subsequent printings. It reverts to the printer defaults every time you print.

Screen Frequency

We've already covered screen frequency as it applies to color separations. The value set in this box is an *overall* frequency setting. It is used for composite output, or as the default setting for separation plates unless you modify it in the Advanced Separations Settings dialog.

The Default setting for Screen Frequency uses the screen frequency for the device via the Windows 95 Printer settings. If you reset this value, it will stick throughout your session for subsequent printing of the document. This value is grayed out if you choose a non-PostScript printer.

Proofing Options

Before we move on to the options that come up when you click the PostScript Preferences button, let's take a look at the productivity-enhancing Proofing Options—all new to DRAW 6.0.

Three of these new options allow you to specify which general categories of objects you wish to print: vectors, bitmaps, and/or text. These can be useful when proofing complex layouts. You can also speed up the proofing process in general, by printing only those elements you are concerned about at any given time. Use these proofs to verify the integrity of each category of object, or help isolate troublesome objects.

When you print only the text from your drawing, you may find it necessary to use the *Print All Text In Black* option. In a layout that has white text on a black background, for instance, the white text would not be visible without its contrasting black background object. Printing in black would also be preferable when you have light-colored text that would ordinarily map to very light grays. If you needed to fax this to someone, the light text might not be legible.

The three options on the right side of the Proofing Options group are only applicable for work other than color separations, and only if you are printing to an appropriate device.

Full Color, for example, does nothing when printing to a standard laser printer. This monochrome printer will render your artwork in grayscale naturally, so the *All Colors As Grayscale* option would be pointless, as well. On the other hand, if your only printer is a desktop color model with a separate black ink cartridge, printing everything in grayscale could save costs if you only want to proof the layout for position and balance.

All Colors As Grayscale causes the preview window to display in grayscale rather than color. So, if your piece is bound for a laser printer, you might want to select this option to help you quickly determine whether the artwork has enough contrast to map effectively in grayscale when you do print it.

All Colors As Black might be useful to generate line art from color or grayscale documents—for faxing, perhaps.

INSIDE INFO

Here's a use of the All Colors As Grayscale option for something other than proofing: Suppose you are producing a brochure that will be printed using only black ink and one PANTONE spot color. You find a nice Corel clip-art piece that you want to place as a grayscale image on top of the PANTONE color background. To produce the two separations needed for this, you must have the clip art in shades of gray, but yours is in color. A Tinted Grayscale lens won't work, because it would influence the background color. So, with a PostScript print driver and All Colors As Grayscale turned on, print the clip art to a PRN file. Import it back into your layout, using the Interpreted PostScript import filter. Ta-da! You now have a grayscale version of your vector clip art. For complex clip art, this surely beats converting colors to gray object-by-object.

Finally, *Fit Printer's Marks and Layout To Page* is a welcome proofing option. Unlike the Fit To Page and scaling functions found on the Layout page, which only affect the artwork itself, this option scales everything that you've designated to print on the chosen page. Suppose your printer page is the same size or smaller than the document page; with Fit To Page you wouldn't see any printer's marks. When you have a large document that you need to proof on a laser printer, and you need to see everything that will ultimately appear on the film yet maintain the actual proportions of the document page, this is the option to choose.

Other Handy Options

You're ready for PostScript, you say? Hold on—we're almost there.

Special Settings   The settings in this drop-down list were formerly accessible only by editing the CORELPRN.INI file. Most of you won't need these advanced settings; they will be of interest mainly to service bureaus or anyone driving high-end output devices from CorelDRAW. DRAW's online help provides reasonable explanations.

Print Job Information Sheet   A fitting last stop (well, last before PostScript, anyway) on our tour of the Options page is this new-to-6.0 feature that lets you send an informational sheet to a selected printer, to a text file, or both. A sample is shown in Figure 27.26. This information will be useful for troubleshooting a problematic file, for job tracking, or for reproducing the same settings at a later date. Printing the information sheet is quite straightforward, and can be understood simply by studying the figure.

27.26

**Print job
information**

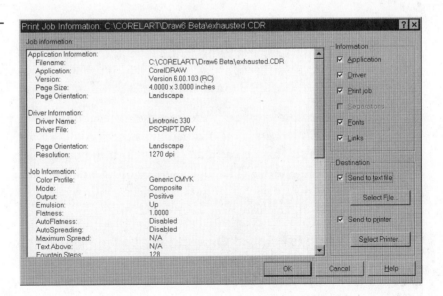

And now, on to PostScript.

PostScript Preferences

Clicking the PostScript Preferences button in the Options page of the Print Options dialog takes you to the dialog shown in Figure 27.27. Some of the features found here existed in DRAW 5, but some subtle yet important new tweaks have been added. Most are geared toward improving the appearance of your output and minimizing the risk of failed pages.

27.27

The PostScript Preferences dialog

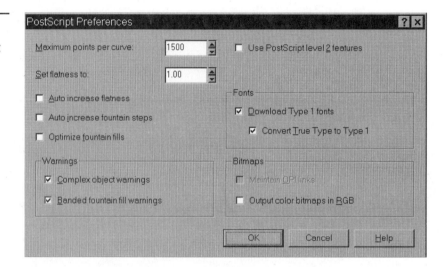

The PostScript error most frequently encountered by professional DRAW users is the dreaded Limitcheck error. This message essentially says you have created an object that is too complex to be handled by the output device. The total number of objects is not an issue, but rather the complexity of any single object. Unfortunately, if you hit one of these, the entire page fails to image.

But It Printed Okay on My Laser Printer!   You're far more likely to get a Limitcheck error on an imagesetter than on a desktop laser printer. Why? All else being equal, an imagesetter set to an output resolution of 2,540 dpi will require about 16 times as much dedicated memory to rasterize an object (that is, place the halftone dots) as would be needed to rasterize the same object on a 600-dpi desktop printer. Imagesetters seldom have this much dedicated imaging memory. Fortunately, you can make adjustments to avoid such Limitcheck errors.

NEW FOR 6

> *PostScript Level 2 Support* **is in both DRAW 6.0 and the Windows 95 PostScript driver. If you are printing to a PostScript printer that supports it, selecting the Use PostScript Level 2 Features option will probably mean fewer output failures for you. Level 2 PostScript is a rewrite of the PostScript page description language. It has new features and handles complex artwork more quickly and gracefully than Level 1. Many newer desktop printers, such as the HP4 PostScript printers, are manufactured with Level 2 support. And most service bureaus have updated their Rips to recognize Level 2 PostScript—but check first before you use the option.**

Maximum Points Per Curve

This option reduces the maximum number of "control points" PostScript uses to generate curves. Contrary to the implication, reducing control points is not at all like reducing nodes in an object. A processing function only, reducing control points will not degrade the quality of the output, but it may increase output time significantly. If you are getting Limitchecks, this is one option you can try. It is a sticky option that will remain set for each document during your DRAW session.

Another alternative, if you have an idea which objects are causing Limitcheck problems, is to simplify the objects. You might break apart complex elements into several less-complex components (converting stylized text to curves, for example). The advantage of this approach is in avoiding drastically increased print time. And it's permanent: You won't have to remember to set an option every time you open this drawing and print.

Set Flatness To, and Auto-Increase Flatness

Unlike setting Maximum Points Per Curve, adjusting flatness is a bit like removing nodes from an object. It simplifies printing but may also reduce printed quality. When a PostScript device creates a curve, it generates a series of small, connected line segments. (Using many small segments generates a smoother curve than using fewer large segments.) Keeping track of all these little lines also increases the demand on the output device's memory.

So, one way to simplify a drawing is to increase its flatness. Increasing flatness means producing fewer, larger line segments. You can do this up to certain levels with no noticeable degradation in quality. How much increase you can get away with will depend on the artwork in question and the results you want.

DRAW provides two ways to control flatness. One way is to type a specific value in the Set Flatness To box. This value will apply to all objects, and the default is 1.00. Figure 27.28 shows some reproduced samples that were originally printed on our laser printer. To make it easier for you to detect the change on the object, we've used some fairly extreme flatness values.

The other way to adjust flatness is with the Auto Increase Flatness check box. This option only kicks in when your output device encounters an object that will cause a Limitcheck error. PostScript then retries the object with flatness increased by 2. It continues increasing until the object prints successfully, or the flatness value reaches 10 over the Set Flatness To value. The advantage to this method is that it increases the likelihood of getting every object to print. The disadvantage is that the flatness value required to get past the error may produce unacceptable results.

27.28

The effects of flatness values

Flatness=1

Flatness=10

Flatness=100

INSIDE INFO

Here's how to determine if you are likely to encounter Limit check errors on an imagesetter, before you burn up expensive film: Set an artificially low flatness value and print to your desktop laser printer. How low? Divide your laser's resolution by the destination imagesetter's resolution, and use a setting slightly lower than the result. For example, divide a 600-dpi laser by a 2540-dpi imagesetter, for a resulting flatness value of 0.24. This method isn't foolproof, but if your artwork gets a Limitcheck on the laser printer, it almost certainly will on the imagesetter.

Smart Control of Fountain Steps

Determining exactly how many steps to use for optimum fountain fills is a difficult process. There's a lot of math involved, based on the output resolution, halftone frequency, range of color in the fill, and length of the filled object. You'll have to make trade-offs, and sometimes banding will be inevitable, depending on the selected halftone frequency and resolution. Once these two controlling parameters are chosen, DRAW 6.0 gives you a couple of options for avoiding the calculator and, hopefully, fountain-step banding, as well. These two new options can be used alone or in concert, and both options will stick for repeated printings.

Auto-Increase Fountain Steps looks at your output settings (resolution and halftone frequency) and determines the maximum number of steps that can be effectively reproduced. This may not eliminate banding, but it will give you the best possible results with the selected print settings. Note that this option will never reduce the number of steps. It can only increase them, and it will override any low values you may have chosen for an object in the Fill dialog.

Optimize Fountain Fills is the mirror opposite of the Auto-Increase option. It looks at your print settings and automatically reduces the number of steps for any fills that are set higher than the target printer can actually produce with those settings. Mirroring its counterpart's action, it will only reduce the number of steps, never increase them.

When you use both options in conjunction, all other settings for fountain steps will be overridden. This generates the best optimization of your printing, producing as many steps as necessary to minimize banding, while not creating more steps than are useful. Bear in mind that this will override any values you may have set via the Fill dialog.

DRAW's New Protective Warnings

The warnings section of the Postscript Preferences dialog contains exciting and helpful features that are new to DRAW 6.0. At the start of a DRAW session, both warnings are active by default. These alerts go a long way to reducing the number of failed or unacceptable pages you produce. We'll first discuss the warning about banded fountain fills, even though it's not the first one listed in the dialog.

Oh No! A Banded Fountain Fill!   This option issues a warning message, shown in Figure 27.29, that you are about to print a fountain fill that is likely to be banded. The alert is issued for each object encountered with a problem fill. We first tested this on a desktop laser printer, using default screen settings. The warning didn't seem very intelligent, cautioning us about each and every object on our test page. Actually, it was smarter than we thought! Banding is likely for most large objects, using the normal settings for a laser printer. Try experimenting with reduced screen frequencies and objects of varying size, and you will find that this feature does a pretty good job of detecting any problem children.

You can choose not to print that object and skip to another one, ignore the warning and continue, or cancel printing altogether. The advantage of skipping the object is that, when printing is completed, you'll be able to tell which object(s) are causing the problem.

27.29

Banded fountain fills at twelve o'clock!

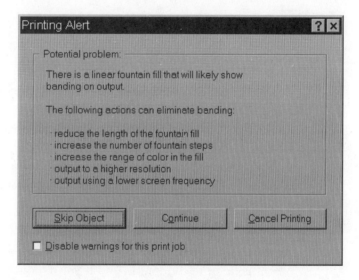

Your choice for this option will stick for repeated printings.

Danger: Complex Object Ahead   This alert is similar to the one for banded fountains; the warning box (Figure 27.30) just deals with a different—and often more significant—problem: Limitcheck errors. As mentioned earlier, just one of these errors can bring your entire print

27.30

Watch out for those complex objects.

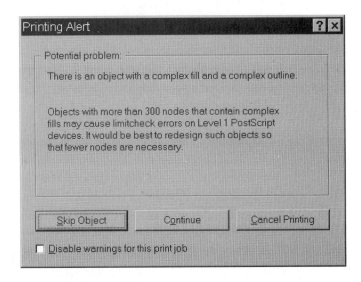

job to a screeching halt. For this type of problem, you'd be especially prudent to make use of the Skip Object button.

We've already discussed techniques for avoiding this problem in several parts of this section on PostScript. The first and best choice is to use Level 2 PostScript, if possible. Level 2 is far more adept at handling complex objects than was Level 1. When we chose to use PostScript Level 2 features, we were unable to create anything that would generate a warning. If Level 2 cannot be used or if you use it and you still have problems, you can either adjust the Maximum Points Per Curve setting, or manually simplify the object.

You may find these warnings annoying after a while, especially if your work has a lot of fountains. And if you're doing color separations, you'll be alerted for each and every problem it finds on each and every plate. So for eight problem objects, you could be alerted 32 times! There *are* two ways to kill the beast, if it is getting in the way. You can disable it entirely by simply turning off the check box. Or you can disable it after the first alert has appeared for a print job, using the check box in the alert box itself.

INSIDE INFO

When you're creating a PRN file destined for the service bureau, being alerted during preparation is helpful. Unfortunately, you won't know who the troublemakers are unless you actually image the file. Here's a solution: Use the appropriate imagesetter driver and create the PRN file, making use of the Skip Object button if you get the warning. Then copy the PRN file to your PostScript desktop laser. It may not look very pretty, but at least you can tell which hooligans would cause problems at the service bureau—they will be notable by their *absence* from the printout. If it is a large size layout, choose Letter as the paper size for your test file and turn on Fit To Page. Size has no bearing on this problem.

Font Handling

The first option, Download Type 1 fonts, tells DRAW to download either to the printer or to a PRN file any fonts required to reproduce the text in your document. With a PRN file, you don't have to worry about whether your service bureau has the right fonts. We prefer to work this way, even though an increasing number of service bureaus are accepting DRAW's CDR files.

Type 1 fonts are the only flavor that PostScript devices actually recognize. That's why Type 1 is the primary option in this dialog—and it's also why the second option, Convert TrueType to Type 1, exists. When Download Type 1 is on (which it is by default), the second option is also automatically turned on. This allows you to utilize either Type 1, TrueType, or both in your document and still have it print correctly on a PostScript printer.

You might be wondering what happens if you choose not to download fonts. Does your text not print? Does it print, but in the wrong font? Yes, the text prints correctly, but it is changed when it is reproduced. At print time, DRAW converts the text to graphic objects, either vector curves or (for smaller text) bitmaps. This works fine for small amounts of text but is highly inefficient for large text blocks, particularly paragraph text. Converting text to curves slows the printing process and can produce very large and unwieldy PRN files, and that can mean added expense at the service bureau.

When would you not use these options? Actually, there are situations where DRAW ignores font selection anyway. Any time you envelope artistic text, extrude it, or do some other artistic transformation, the text will be converted to curves at print time. And sometimes it's preferable to convert text to curves. In a page containing many short strings of artistic text using a large variety of fonts, the PRN file might be smaller if the text is converted, rather than downloading all the required fonts. Another reason to convert to curves: Too many different fonts can choke a PostScript device because only a limited portion of its memory is allocated to fonts. Most of the time, however, you will want to leave both these options on.

Type 1 vs. TrueType

The issue of which fonts are better is always a source of debate. Many service bureaus claim they always have difficulty with TrueType fonts, but there really is no inherent reason for their conversion and printing to cause trouble. Many DRAW users have been quite successful using TrueType fonts, and you will find font aficionados supporting both sides of the debate. TrueType fonts do account for more print problems, but they usually stem from the individual fonts, not the font format.

Most Type 1 fonts on the market have been carefully crafted by well-established digital font vendors. The same can be said for many but not all True Type fonts. Quite a few "cheapie" font packs exist, and they are almost always TrueType. Most shareware fonts, as well, are TrueType. Some obey the rules of font-mongering, others don't—and those are usually the ones causing print problems.

Type I vs.	Most of the fonts supplied with DRAW are properly crafted,
TrueType	and either format should work. We admit a bias toward
(continued)	Type 1 because it is the language spoken by PostScript devices. Why do a translation if you can supply the real thing?

Bitmap Options

DRAW 6.0 has introduced two new PostScript options for working with bitmaps, especially important to graphics professionals.

Maintain OPI Links   Certain bitmap formats—TIF, CPT, and others—can be used to create OPI (Open Prepress Interface) links. You can import one of these images into DRAW with the OPI option turned on, as explained in Chapter 30. If you do, you are telling DRAW that there is another, higher-quality version of this bitmap that your service bureau will substitute at print time. The obvious advantage here is that you can edit using a lower-resolution bitmap for your design and avoid the memory overhead of a high-resolution color bitmap. Such bitmaps can easily be larger than 20MB.

At print time, you have a choice. In the PostScript Preferences dialog, leave Maintain OPI Links checked (the default), and DRAW will place in the PRN file a reference to the path and name of the high-resolution version. For proof printing, you can turn off the check box and print the low-resolution bitmap instead.

Output Color Bitmaps in RGB   Normally, colors are either separated to CMYK plates or printed to a composite color device that uses CMYK colors. Some devices, such as slide makers, use RGB colors just as your monitor does. The Output Color Bitmaps in RGB option tells DRAW to store information in a PRN file or send it to an output device using the original RGB color component information, rather than converting it to CMYK components. This option can also be used with printers that lack black ink and use only the three primary colors, CMY, to produce composite color. Apparently, the translation from RGB to CMY is easier and more accurate than the reverse.

Putting It All Together: Creating a Print Style

In our earlier discussions about layout styles and positioning, we explained that you could save settings by name and recall them for use at a later date.

NEW FOR 6

You can take this concept a step further, by creating a master print style. Your style can include just about every option we have covered in this chapter—all but those choices you make from the main Print dialog, and halftone screen frequencies. (The latter always reverts to the selected printer's default value.)

The process of making a print style is quite simple. You select all the options needed to properly print your document. Then, before exiting back to the main Print dialog, you click the + key above the Print Options preview window. This opens the dialog shown in Figure 27.31.

27.31

Saving a print style

Save Print Style

Save print style as: my test

Settings to save in style

To change which settings will be stored in this style, click on the check boxes below. A shaded box means that only some settings in the category will be saved. To see what settings are included in a category, click on the +

- Pre-Press Settings
- Layout Settings
- Separations Settings
- Miscellaneous Settings
- Proofing and Color Settings
- PostScript Settings

OK

Cancel

Help

Certain settings, such as Layout style, are not automatically included in a Print style. It is a fairly simple matter to add the ones that aren't saved by default (or, for that matter, to remove some settings from the style). Simply open up the various category folders in the main window by clicking on the little + icon next to them, and select or deselect specific options. To include every possible setting, just click on each little checkbox icon until they are all checked and unshaded. Then you enter a name for your print style, and it is saved for posterity. You can also delete it by clicking the big – key at the top of the Print Options preview window.

Once you have a print style defined, its settings are there for you whenever you need them, at the click of the mouse. You can verify or change the settings as needed, by going through the Print Options dialog. When you want to use the style, just select it right from the main Print dialog, and all the options in the style are implemented automatically for that print job.

This will be a very popular feature with those who do a lot of repetitive printing. For example, a company that uses DRAW to design and produce packaging labels could make efficient use of print styles. Add in a Corel script, and the label project could be almost completely automated.

Tips for Reliable Printing

DRAW 6.0 has made significant progress toward making the print process as fail-safe as possible. Inevitably, however, problems will arise, some beyond DRAW's power to control. These will generally fall into two categories: hardware problems and poor design choices.

In the first category, you should realize that PostScript code and PostScript printers can be cantankerous beasts. If you are having trouble getting pages to print and no descriptive error messages are being produced, the first thing to do is turn your printer off, then back on again. You might want to clear the print queue as well, and start completely fresh. One bit of bad code can ruin a PostScript printer's whole day. This is the quickest and easiest way to set things right. And it can work for non-PostScript printers, too. They are less susceptible to the type of error that brings PostScript crashing down; but if you are having problems, try the same procedure. Clear the print queue, restart the printer, and try again.

The second issue—problematic designs—has been a recurring theme throughout this chapter. It's always possible to create stuff in DRAW that taxes or exceeds your printer's capabilities. In the first case, you may encounter very slow printing. In the second, you'll get a printed error sheet or, worse yet, nothing at all.

Following are other, more specific suggestions.

Simplifying Vector Objects

We've mentioned several ways to overcome Limitcheck errors produced by overly complex objects. You can either break the object up into smaller components, or try reducing the Maximum Points Per Curve in the PostScript Preferences dialog as a print option. Something else to try is increasing the flatness, also a PostScript Preferences setting.

You may find that an object cannot be broken into smaller components, yet it is still too complex. Try using the Auto-Reduce feature in the Node Edit roll-up to eliminate unnecessary nodes from the object. In many cases, the same curvature can be achieved with fewer nodes.

Handling Bitmaps

Since bitmaps are already simply a collection of dots or pixels, there is nothing particularly complex about them. However, the *number* of dots in a bitmap can run into the millions, and PostScript is not very efficient about handling them. Your biggest problem is likely to be speed, or rather the lack thereof (and potential surcharges at a service bureau).

Make the best of the situation by using every trick possible to minimize the amount of data in your bitmap that will still produce the results you are after.

Line Art, Grayscale, or Color? The first trick is to make sure you use the proper bitmap for the task. All else being equal, a grayscale (8-bit) image has eight times as much data as a comparably sized line-art (1-bit or black-and-white) image. Do you really need a grayscale image?

Color images can be 8-bit (256 colors) or 24-bit (16.7 million colors). It's nice to have that many colors available, but 24-bit image files can be huge. A 5″×7″ image with a pixel (ppi) resolution of 300 dpi will weigh in at a hefty 9.5MB! Will reducing the palette to 8-bit color suffice?

What About Size? More often than not, you really don't have much choice as to the type of bitmap to use. The next best alternative is to see about reducing the size (in pixels) of the image. The first tactic to employ is to consider the bitmap's final printed size as compared to its original size. If you're including a 300-dpi image in your artwork but plan to reduce it to half-size in the printed piece, you should scan it at 150 dpi.

Resolution is really a relative value for bitmaps. Though it's expressed as dpi (dots per inch), it's actually a measure of pixels per inch—something quite different from a printer's dot. We tend to think in terms of the resolution of a bitmap, since this defines the quality of output. But the absolute measure of a bitmap is how many pixels it contains. When we set a scanning resolution for a given size, we are in fact determining the number of pixels in the bitmap. For example, an image 500 pixels wide by 700 pixels tall contains 350,000 pixels. If it's an 8-bit image, the file size is about 350 kilobytes. If you size this image in DRAW to 5″×7″, it will have an output resolution of 100 dpi. The same image, when sized to 2.5″×3.5″, will be 200 dpi. Conversely, it would only be a 50-dpi image if sized to 10″×14″.

Output resolution should not be confused with *printer resolution*—they are two separate but related things. One is an expression of the image in pixels per inch (though we use the term dots per inch). The other is an indirect expression of the smallest size dot a printer can produce.

What Resolution Is Absolutely Necessary? So, what resolution do you need? For line art, it will depend on how free of jaggies you want it to be, and what the printer's resolution is. There is a direct mapping of pixels to printer dots, since no halftones are involved. If a printer can print 600 dpi, you could utilize an image with a resolution as high as 600 dpi. You probably won't need this in most cases, so use your best judgment.

For color and grayscale, the halftoning process changes the applicable rules. The rule of thumb is to make sure the bitmap's output resolution, expressed in dpi, is at least 1.4 but not over 2 times the intended halftone screen frequency, expressed in lpi. A common halftone frequency for Linotronic output is 133 lines per inch, for instance. At this value, there's no need to create any image with a resolution higher than 266 dpi, and you'll probably get acceptable results with as low as 186 dpi.

Optimizing the bitmap size can speed the printing process, liberate valuable disk space, and save bucks at the service bureau. Sometimes you really need a large, high-resolution image.

AUTHOR'S NOTE

Don't forget about using OPI links. (See the "Postscript Preferences" section.) This won't ease printing, but it will certainly speed your design process and save disk space, if the service bureau stores the image.

Fonts and Fills

There is really only one thing to say with regard to fonts: Try to limit the number of fonts used within a single document. This is important from a printing efficiency standpoint, but is also simply good design policy. As mentioned in the "Font Handling" section, if you must include a lot of fonts, with small bits of text set in each font, it might be preferable to let DRAW convert the text to curves at print time, instead of downloading the fonts.

From the same perspective, don't get carried away with special fills. Effective art makes judicious use of these—use too many, and they can lose their impact. Specialized fills also can affect print efficiency. They take longer to print than objects filled with uniform color, and some are worse than others.

Fountain fills print fairly fast. The only caution here is regarding quality. Are you seeing a lot of banding in the result? (Don't forget the optimization features; see "Smart Control of Fountain Steps.")

The various Pattern fills are quite another story. Whether they print quickly or really bog the printer down depends on various parameters. We printed a solid fill pentagon, created with the new Polygon tool, to our PostScript laser printer in about 9 seconds. Then we filled it with a simple two-color pattern set to a large tile size, and it took about 18 seconds. Next, we changed the tile size to small. Whoa! Print time shot all the way up to 1 minute, 43 seconds.

These tests were printed using PostScript. Using PCL (non-PostScript) mode instead, the large tile version was out in 1 minute, 20 seconds; the small tile took 1 minute, 50 seconds. Another significant difference between the two printing modes was that the computer used far less time to prepare the image for PostScript. We were returned to our drawing almost instantly.

Other Tips for Non-PostScript Printing

Bitmaps usually print trouble-free on most non-PostScript devices. Laser printers do have finite memory in which to image your work, so the foregoing advice to optimize the pixel size of bitmaps holds here, as well. If you find printing is frequently very slow or you often get messages such as "Print Overrun" or "Mem Overflow," you might need to invest in additional printer memory.

On some non-PostScript printers, notably laser printers that use or emulate HP's PCL language, fonts and vector objects can be handled in one of two ways. The printer can treat these objects as vectors and do its own rasterizing, or you can tell the computer to send a rasterized image to the printer. Using vectors is faster but can cause problems. If you get errors, try switching this option for your printer (look in the Properties / Graphics options).

♣

We started by saying that printing is usually a simple affair. You click Print, then OK, and away you go. So why are we just now, many pages later, ending our discourse? Printing is the ultimate payoff for all your hard work creating documents and artwork in the first place. It is fortunate that DRAW's printing options have evolved along with the program, and fortunate indeed that they work so well. Through both subtle and not-so-subtle enhancements, DRAW 6.0's print engine has become one of its strongest components.

CHAPTER

28

Color for the Color Blind

TWENTY-EIGHT

At our ongoing series of CorelDRAW seminars, we routinely ask the audience for a show of hands: "Do you think you have a good understanding of color publishing?" In a crowd of 100, it is unusual for more than a dozen to raise their hands. Despite the proliferation of color scanners and affordable desktop color printers, the realm of color publishing continues to give DRAW users a case of, to use the technical term, the heebie-jeebies.

Don't expect this chapter to be the ultimate treatise on working with color. Dozens of books dedicated to the subject are readily available to you from the usual sources. We want this chapter to serve as your launching pad. Once you've read it, we think you'll be able to recognize the terms, understand the concepts, and above all, be able to translate it all into effective use of DRAW as your front-end for color publishing projects.

Do You See the Light?

When creating the heaven and the earth in those first six days, God also created two ways that humans perceive light. We see light that is directly *transmitted* from a source (from the sun or a light bulb, for instance); and we see light that is *reflected* (from the moon, the clouds, the walls in your house, and the pages of this book). Why should you care about this self-evident fact? Because as a computer user, you deal with both types of light, so it's important to understand how they are different.

Like the sun and a light bulb, your computer monitor is a light source, and the light it uses to display images is transmitted directly to your eyes. On the other hand, your computer produces a printed piece that reflects light but does not transmit it. This is a very important point that we will return to throughout this chapter.

You have probably heard the terms before—RGB and CMYK. They are the color models that most distinctly represent these two kinds of light.

The ABCs of RGB

As we said, you've probably heard of RGB, and maybe you sort of know what it is—a way of defining colors—and that the initials stand for Red, Green, and Blue. (Maybe you've also heard the term "RGB monitor," which is a bit redundant, actually.) Although most light sources in the physical world emit white light, which is made up of all the colors of the rainbow, the human eye perceives only red, green, and blue light. In other words, all the colors that the human eye can perceive are registered by the eye as combinations and varying intensities of these three colors. That's why color monitors and TVs, which emit only red, green, and blue, can simulate the full spectrum. Call us closed-minded, but the only colors that we're interested in are the ones that we can see.

Figure 28.1 shows a woman looking at a computer monitor. In this black-and-white drawing you can't tell that she is seeing a monitor with a yellow screen, but she is. (And if you'll look for file 28-01.CDR in the COLOR directory of the Companion CD, you'll get the full-color version.) In this chapter, we'll ask you a lot of questions about things you usually take for granted, such as why does this woman see yellow? What forces are at work that cause "Yellow" to register in her brain?

AUTHOR'S NOTE

Here we are faced with our annual frustration: How to present a chapter on color publishing in a book printed in black and white. Thank goodness for our Companion CD—there you'll find all of the drawings in the **COLOR** subdirectory of the **PRACTICE** directory, named according to their figure numbers. For instance, Fig-ure 28.1 is file **28-01.CDR** on the CD.

Like all color monitors and TVs, this one emits RGB light, which means little rays of red, green, and blue light emanate from the monitor. In fact, if you were to hold a magnifying glass up to your own display, you would see hairline-thin lines of red, green, and blue. In Figure 28.1, the monitor is emitting red and green light, the two colors that combine to form yellow. Why, you ask? Because that's what red and green do. It would take too much time and ink to explain the science of RGB light, so let's just accept the fact that when red and green light are combined, they form yellow.

28.1

This monitor is transmitting red and green light, and those two colors combine to form the yellow screen seen by the woman.

RGB is the most straightforward of the various color models, not only because it depicts the behavior of light in the real world, but also because it is easy for humans to visualize. Imagine a bunch of red, green, and blue flashlights shining in various directions in a darkened room. When the rays of light overlap, they form other colors. By varying the intensities of the rays (pretend you have very sophisticated flashlights), you can create all the colors that the human eye can perceive.

When combined at full intensity, red, green, and blue form white, although you might have been tempted to guess the opposite, remembering your crayon-drawing days when using all of your crayons at once gave you a nice black mess. But black is actually the *absence* of light—a point that is obvious to anyone who has walked into the edge of the coffee table in the middle of the night. Speaking technically, black is actually the total *absorption* of light.

The RGB color model is considered an *additive model,* because those three primary colors combine together in various intensities to produce the spectrum of visible colors.

Reflections on CMYK

Most of you know that CMYK stands for Cyan, Magenta, Yellow, and Black (K for Black because B could also be for Blue). And you probably also know that those are the four ink colors used in conventional four-color printing. What you may *not* know is that CMYK is worlds apart from the RGB color model. RGB represents the *transmissions* of colors, but CMYK represents the *reflections* of colors.

The light you see from a printed piece is reflected light. This book, for instance, is not a light source (although we hope that it is illuminating); rather, the black ink on this page and the inks in the Color Gallery section absorb some light and reflects others, allowing you to see particular colors.

Figures 28.2 through 28.4 demonstrate the process of reflected light. In Figure 28.2, a man is looking down at a book and he sees red. Why? What forces are at work here that cause him to see red?

The page he is reading is not like a computer monitor—it transmits no light of its own. So to read the page, the first thing he needs is a light source. Like all light sources, this one emits red, green, and blue rays of light. In Figure 28.3 the desk lamp is flooding the book with RGB light.

28.2

This page is red, but in the CMYK world, what does that really mean?

28.3

Red, green, and blue rays of light are hitting this page. Why does this man see only the red?

The question now becomes this: If the light hitting this page is made up of the full spectrum of white light, how come the only light that bounces off the page is red? What ink colors are on the page that makes this so? Figure 28.4 has the answer: yellow and magenta (best seen in the CD's file). When the light hits this book, the yellow ink absorbs colors at the blue end of the spectrum. Why does this happen? Well, we could write another book entirely about that topic—it's called the "subtractive" theory of color. That's what yellow does—it absorbs blue light. And the magenta absorbs the green, because that's what magenta does. So with all of the blue and the green light absorbed by the ink on the page, the only color that reflects off the surface is the red.

28.4

The ink on the page absorbs most of the color spectrum, but allows the red to pass through and be reflected off the white paper.

This man sees red because the page contains yellow and magenta ink. Though you could say that yellow and magenta combine to make red, that's actually RGB-speak. Rather than combine, they each filter out one of the other two colors, resulting in red. This is fundamentally a semantic distinction, but it helps to better digest the whole color thing when you think of CMYK inks in terms of what they take away, not what they add.

You don't need to understand the intricacies of additive and subtractive color theories, but we do want you to grasp the moral of this story so far: Color from your monitor is totally different than color from a printed piece. We will return to that point throughout this chapter.

The Two Kinds of Ink

Now that we have distinguished between monitor colors and ink colors, let's focus on the difference between the two types of inks. The two primary methods of designating inks invoke names that are probably familiar to you: *spot color* and *process color.* There are many criteria for choosing one printing method over the other, not the least of which is the amount of money you are willing to spend. Here is a quick overview.

Spots of Paint

The simplest and most affordable way to introduce color into a drawing is to use black and one other color. This is called *spot color printing,* so named because you typically choose a few spots here and there to add the color. A drawing that uses black and one spot color will only require two passes through a conventional printing press; a full-color print job, using CMYK inks, requires four passes.

Spot colors are premixed, ready-made inks that you use when you want to introduce one or two colors into a drawing. Cornering the market of spot colors is PANTONE, whose PANTONE Matching System and corresponding color-swatch books show every color in a 1,000-plus palette. Once you find a color you want to use, you can ask for it by name in DRAW's Fill dialogs.

WATCH OUT!

> **Choosing a PANTONE color because it looks good on screen is a fatal accident waiting to happen. Choosing a PANTONE color because it looks good in your PANTONE Color Formula Guide is the way the professionals do it.**

You will pay less for a print job that is black and one spot color than four colors, but price is not the only consideration for using spot colors. Sometimes you must use a color that cannot be reproduced by process colors. The color range of CMYK is a subset of what the human eye can perceive, and it is possible to create a specialty color that cannot be reproduced with CMYK inks. If you've ever asked your neighborhood quick-copy store for a fast print job employing Reflex Blue, for instance, you used a color that has no CMYK equivalent. The classic example is the red—known only as Coca Cola Red—that The Coca Cola Company uses for its soda cans. No combination of cyan, magenta, and yellow can create it faithfully, and press runs for the Coca Cola Company typically include a pass across the press for this company's proprietary spot color.

Spot colors do not mix if you overlap them, and indeed, you are not supposed to. They are opaque. Think of them as paint: You dab them in specific places in your drawing, but you don't overlap them with other colors—unless you really do want to produce a color of mud.

The Process of Transparent Ink

The other printing method, process color, is very different from spot color. Just four distinct colors—the familiar cyan, magenta, yellow, and black—team up to produce all the colors and shades that you might want to have in a drawing. This requires four separate passes through the press, but in return you get printed pieces in full color.

But let's back up for a minute. We just got through telling you that you can't mix and overlap spot colors. Why can you do it with process colors? How come you can take cyan, magenta, and yellow and just throw them together to create other colors? How come they don't create mud?

The answer is in the ink. The inks for these colors is not like regular ink; they are like transparent gels. Light passes through them and is either absorbed or reflected off the surface. For the red page in Figure 28.4, it didn't matter which ink was laid down first, the yellow or the magenta. The yellow absorbs the blue and allows the red and green to pass through, and the magenta catches the green—regardless of which one receives the light first.

Separation Anxiety

This one word, *separation,* is responsible for a lot of gray hair among desktop designers, but it's a necessary evil for anyone who wants to print large projects in color. As many readers know, creating separations is how you prepare a drawing for color printing. You make separate pieces of paper or film, each one representing a specific color—spot or process—used in the drawing.

Figure 28.5 shows a simple drawing of a postage stamp, created in DRAW. It is made up entirely of the four process colors and, as such, is perfect for a color separation exercise. If you want to follow along, open STAMP.CDR from the PRACTICE directory of the Companion CD.

Making a Proof

First, you will create a proof for your desktop laser printer.

1. Open STAMP.CDR and go to File / Print.

2. Choose your desktop printer from the drop-down list of printers.

3. Click on Options, and then on the Separations tab.

28.5

All four of the process colors are used to create this postage stamp.

Element	C	M	Y	K
32¢	60	40	0	40
Left semi-circle	40	0	40	0
Middle	0	100	100	0
Right	20	60	0	20
US Postage	60	0	60	20
Border	30	20	15	40

4. Check Print Separations, and notice that all four colors in the colors window become highlighted. If this drawing used only three of the process colors, one of them wouldn't be highlighted. Similarly, if the stamp used a spot color, that color's name would be highlighted in this window.

5. Click on Preview Image under the preview window, and your screen should look like Figure 28.6.

6. Click OK and OK again to print. Your laser printer will deliver four pages that look a lot like Figure 28.7.

NEW FOR 6

To the right of the Preview Image button is a drop-down box (set to "Composite" by default). Here you can choose to preview your separations color by color. Cycle through the various colors in the box, and DRAW will preview each, one at a time.

28.6

With the settings in this dialog, you're going to get four separations—one laser-printed page for each of the colors used in the previewed stamp drawing.

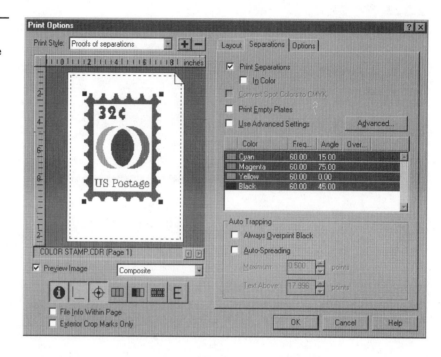

28.7

Together, these four printouts make the postage stamp.

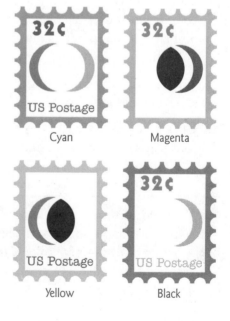

Cyan

Magenta

Yellow

Black

Making a Print File

When your proofs are satisfactory, you are ready to move from dress rehearsal to live performance: You are ready to create print files. The procedure is the same as the five steps above, but instead of printing to your laser printer, you ask for all print information to be stored in a file that you can transport to your service bureau (assuming you don't have one of those large and expensive imagesetters in your office). The details of creating print files are in Chapter 27.

If you have a color laser printer, you can check the In Color box below Print Separations. Each page will be printed in the actual color of ink to be used. This is handy for demonstration purposes—especially when you use transparencies—to create an actual color key; the printed pages, however, will bear little resemblance to what you will deliver to your print shop. Those folks aren't interested in color; that part comes when the ink is loaded onto the press. Your objective in the print file is to tell your print shop where the color goes, and that is done in good ol' black and white. The areas that are printed in full intensity indicate that the particular color is to be printed at 100%, and the areas that are tinted represent the corresponding tint of the color.

So to get this postage stamp printed in color, you would deliver to your print shop four pieces of film or paper that look like Figure 28.7, right? *Wrong!* As part of the process of making the metal plates that go onto the press, the operators at your print shop will need not positive images but negative ones, like the ones shown in Figure 28.8. They want film negatives, so that is what you ask for when you send the print files to your service bureau.

DRAW offers an option to create negative output on the Options page of its Print dialog, but most service bureaus would rather do it themselves. So check with your service bureau first. Chances are that you will be asked not to check the negative option, but instead give them a positive print file.

Unless you have a lot of experience studying film negatives, they are difficult to use as proofs because they are quite different from the image that you see on screen. That's why it's crucial to make proofs and trial separations on your laser printer. Don't worry if you don't own a color

28.8

Now we're getting somewhere. These negative images are just what your print shop wants as it prepares your work for press.

Cyan

Magenta

Yellow

Black

printer and can't proof in color. In some ways, it's better to proof in black and white, because that's how the film will be made. At the proof stage, your job is to make sure there are no copy errors (obviously) and that all the colors that you intend to use are correctly represented on the separated printouts.

How CorelDRAW Lies to You

If you were to take a color print of your postage stamp and hold it up next to STAMP.CDR on your display monitor, how would the two compare? Would they look

(a) The same?
(b) Close enough?
(c) Quite different?
(d) Ridiculously different?

If you did this comparison 100 times, it's likely that the result would be (a), the same, approximately 0% of the time; and it's equally likely that the answer would be (d), ridiculously different, more often than (b), close enough. In other words, *forget about accuracy when you're using your display monitor to view printed colors.* And now that you've read this far in the chapter, you know why that is: You can't expect an RGB device—one that's made for directly transmitting red, green, and blue rays of light—to be able to depict how light will reflect off a surface filled with cyan, magenta, and yellow inks.

A handful of programs are available that purport to help you with on-screen color management, and some of them are somewhat successful. Corel, too, has its own built-in Color Manager, which makes similar claims about more accurate representation of colors on screen.

We want to be as diplomatic as possible here, because we respect the efforts of companies like PANTONE, TruMatch, Candela, Eastman Kodak, and Corel, in offering their various color management tools. All their tools can help you, by making on-screen colors look more like the colors that you have already chosen for a project. But we choose our words very carefully here: *colors that you have already chosen.* We don't want to give you the impression that using Corel's built-in color correction makes it safe to pick colors based on how they look on screen. Don't *ever* choose colors from their on-screen appearances. That is a serious, potentially expensive, and embarrassing mistake.

The only reliable way to choose colors for a job is to pick from printed samples. Base your choices on jobs that you have already done; or use a swatch book, such as the PANTONE Color Formula Guide for spot colors or the TruMatch Colorfinder for process colors. Once you have chosen the colors and assigned them to parts of your drawing, then you can turn on Corel's color correction feature and hope that the colors' on-screen appearances will be more accurate. But if they are not—if your screen looks radically different from the printed color—take comfort in the fact that you have chosen your color scheme responsibly. You have picked colors from printed samples, not from your screen.

Only one situation is an exception to this rule, and that's when you're using DRAW to produce artwork for an on-screen slide show. In that case, your monitor *is* your final output device, and you can choose any color that strikes your fancy.

Trap Your Colors Before They Trap You

In the "Separation Anxiety" section we discussed the importance of proofing your color work before sending it off to your print shop, but one thing your proofs won't show you is whether you need to apply *trapping* to your work. This word typically strikes fear in the hearts of experienced, well-intentioned designers—we're even afraid of writing about it. Color trapping defies a simple definition, so bear with us here.

Print shops do their best to make sure that a sheet of paper running through a high-speed press will come out with all the layers of colored ink placed in exactly the right place. The degree of accuracy in this process is called *registration,* and one of the options when you print in DRAW is to enable registration marks—little bull's-eyes that print on every piece of film for a given project. Despite their best efforts, print shops can't align the paper perfectly on the press every time. Truth is, registration errors are common in color-printed work, but the degree to which they harm your finished work depends upon the nature of your drawing and the extent to which you can prepare for these errors. This section is a qualitative introduction to color trapping—why you need it, how you can apply it, and in some cases, how you can best avoid it.

INSIDE INFO

Color trapping is not required when printing to a desktop color printer, slide processor, or other single-pass output device. Trapping is only required for printing on a traditional printing press, where the various colors will be applied to the paper in separate passes.

Where Colors Touch

Figure 28.9, which is also available in the COLOR directory of the Companion CD, is a rendition of the cube that you created back in Chapter 5, along with the colors used throughout. If you were to print it in color, the cube would require three distinct pieces of film and three individual passes on the press (there is no black in this cube).

28.9

Can you find the places on this cube where color trapping is required?

Element	C	M	Y	K
Left face	0	0	100	0
Letter A	0	100	0	0
Right face	100	100	0	0
Letter C	100	0	0	0
Top face	0	20	0	0
Letter B	0	100	100	0

Understanding registration and trapping issues begins with an analysis of the areas in a drawing where colors meet, because that is where registration errors can hurt you. For instance, the top face of the cube is made up of 20% magenta, and the left face is 100% yellow. Let's assume that there is a registration error when printing the yellow; it is not lined up exactly where it is supposed to be. If this error causes the yellow to be placed too high (and in terms of registration errors, we're talking about errors of less than 1 point), then the yellow will bang into the magenta. By all accounts, this is a "friendly" error. A tiny bit of yellow overlapping the magenta will probably be unnoticeable. Even if you could see it, you wouldn't react negatively to it because your eye is expecting to see both yellow and magenta in that vicinity. There would be about a quarter-point of space where the magenta is a bit redder than it should be, and that's okay.

But what if the registration error is such that the yellow is placed too low, so that it doesn't actually reach the magenta? Again, we're talking about less than a quarter-point, but now instead of an overlap of colors, there would be a small area without any color. You'd see a streak of white (or whatever color the paper is) which, though tiny, would be both noticeable and objectionable.

There is no way for you to know whether a registration error is a friendly one or not, so you have to "trap" against all possibilities. (Hence the term, trapping, and this is about as close as we can get to a simple definition—although you will soon see how to actually apply trapping.)

Trapping will also be needed for the big *A* that is inside the yellow face. Here there is no possibility of a friendly registration error, because any error will result in a white streak somewhere. This becomes clearer if you stop and think about how this cube is actually printed. Figure 28.10 offers a depiction of the process. Notice how the yellow face has a large *A* cut out of it, right where the magenta *A* is to go. This is called a *knockout,* and it is necessary in process-color printing. If the *A* weren't knocked out of the yellow, then the two ink colors would overlap to form red (remember, process-color inks are transparent). The knocked-out area where the *A* is to fit must not have any ink color at all, except for the magenta, the intended color.

In Figure 28.10 we have tried to make it look like a jigsaw puzzle, which strikes us as a pretty good way to think of this knockout dynamic. You can see why it's so important for the registration to be accurate; the

28.10

The yellow face has
the outline of the *A*
"knocked out" to
accommodate the
magenta *A*.

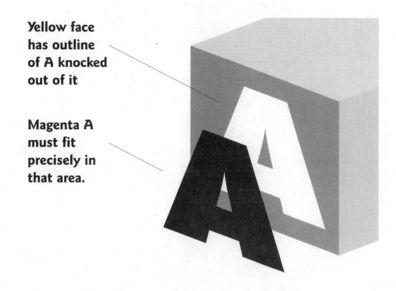

Yellow face
has outline
of A knocked
out of it

Magenta A
must fit
precisely in
that area.

magenta A needs to fit precisely into the hole in the yellow face. But
again, you can't always count on perfect accuracy, so you must take matters into your own hands.

Eight Ways to Deal with Trapping

Because registration issues have been around for as long as there have
been color presses, numerous strategies have evolved that you can adopt
to ensure good-quality color output. Here are the most common ones.

1. Use Trapping Software   These days you can choose from a collection of sophisticated software whose job is to study a PostScript print
file, determine the areas where colors butt against one another, and apply trap to those areas. The program will then create a modified version
of the PostScript print file, which you can in turn send to the imagesetters at your service bureau. The software that runs on PCs, called Trap-
Wise, is made by Adobe. This is not typical, run-of-the-mill software—
it costs nearly $4,000. Some businesses can justify that type of invest-
ment, but it's more likely you would seek out a service bureau that has
purchased TrapWise and can apply it to your work for a usage fee.

2. Find a Smart Imagesetter   Well-equipped service bureaus may use a special imagesetter made by Scitex. This machine reads composite print files (that is, ones that are not separated), separates the colors, and applies trap where needed. Then it sends output directly to a raster image processor that creates the film. Using the Scitex machine will cost close to twice the usual $12–$18 for a piece of film produced on a standard imagesetter.

3. Choose Common Colors   If your drawing's color scheme has any flexibility, you can avoid trapping errors by choosing your colors with that in mind. When two objects share at least 20% of the same color, then you have effectively eliminated the risk of registration errors.

For instance, let's say that the big *A* on our cube doesn't have to be pure magenta, but instead could have a slightly red tint of 100% magenta and 25% yellow. Now think about how the yellow ink would be laid down in that area: It would be at 100% intensity around the face of the cube and at 25% in the space where the *A* is to go.

Now when the *A* is laid down, it still needs to be placed in the knock-out area, but because that area already contains yellow ink, a registration error is not going to be unsightly. Remember, a bad registration error is one that produces white streaks where there is no ink present at all. In this case, though, the entire face has yellow ink, including the knockout area for the *A*. As you can see in Figure 28.11, the knocked-out area of the face has a small amount of ink coverage—enough to keep a registration error from being objectionable.

Incidentally, the top face of the cube and the red *B* need no trapping because they share a common color; the *B* has yellow and magenta, and the top face also contains magenta. The same is true for the right face and the *C*, which share cyan.

4. Overprint Small Objects   Applying trap to your drawings can be a daunting task, but there is one situation that is easy to handle. When you have small text or other objects on a colored background, the trapping strategy is simple.

28.11

This knockout area of the cube is effectively trapped by using a common color. The entire face of the cube has some amount of yellow, eliminating the possibility of the paper color showing through.

Face of cube is 100% yellow and outline of A is 25% yellow

Even if the A doesn't fit exactly, there is still ink coverage across the entire face.

Figure 28.12 shows a two-color drawing with black body copy placed on a colored background. The simplicity of this piece belies the trouble it will cause when it goes on the press, and Figure 28.13 shows why. By default, DRAW creates separations using knockouts, as described in the preceding section. Imagine the registration nightmares of printing this piece, what with all of those fine serifs and thin ascenders in the 9-point text. This job would be virtually impossible to register properly.

This project offers an ideal opportunity to use *overprinting* of your black text. Overprinting is the opposite of knocking out. Instead of creating white holes on the other color plates, you tell DRAW to ignore the black text on all other plates and pretend that it isn't there. Let's back up one step: Earlier in this chapter, we established that objects had to be knocked out of other objects. Otherwise the transparent inks will overlap, creating an unwanted color. But that doesn't apply to black, because it absorbs all light. When you mix black with another color, you get black. Therefore, you don't need to knock out small black text; you instead can ask for it to be overprinted.

28.12

What could possibly go wrong with printing this simple two-color job?

We remember it as if it were yesterday: the day that CorelDRAW was first released. Up until then, the closest thing to illustration software were unremarkable paint programs and non-graphical applications that required a degree in programming to run. CorelDRAW was one of the first Windows-based drawing programs to take hold.

Today, nearly ten years later, CorelDRAW is one of the giants of the industry, both in terms of its customer base, its stature, and the sheer volume of programs that are included in this one product.

It is no mystery to us why this is so. From its inception, CorelDRAW became known as the most approachable, the most inviting of the drawing and illustration programs, and its stable of users covers virtually all corners of the graphics community. Fine artists...illustrators...technical artists...freelance designers...logo creators...desktop publishers...book publishers...sign-makers... t-shirt designers...newsletter editors...converted secretaries...department managers...and even the lead author's three-year-old daughter. Becoming proficient with CorelDRAW might be a daunting task; however, hundreds of thousands of users will attest to the fact that playing around with, developing a feel for, and even getting the hang of the program is not difficult at all.

28.13

How would _you_ like to try to line up these two plates on the press?

We remember it as if it were yest released. Up until then, the closest markable paint programs and no gree in programming to run. Core drawing programs to take hold.

Today, nearly ten years later, C try, both in terms of its customer ba grams that are included in this one

It is no mystery to us why thi came known as the most approach illustration programs, and its stable graphics community. Fine artists...ill designers...logo creators...desktop t-shirt designers...newsletter editors managers...and even the lead autho ficient with CorelDRAW might be sands of users will attest to the fa for, and even getting the hang of

Color separation
with black text
knocked out

We remember it as if it were yest released. Up until then, the closest markable paint programs and no gree in programming to run. Core drawing programs to take hold.

Today, nearly ten years later, C try, both in terms of its customer ba grams that are included in this one

It is no mystery to us why this came known as the most approach illustration programs, and its stable graphics community. Fine artists...ill designers...logo creators...desktop t-shirt designers...newsletter editors managers...and even the lead autho ficient with CorelDRAW might be sands of users will attest to the fa for, and even getting the hang of

Black separation

You can ask for overprinting in DRAW two different ways.

- On an object-by-object basis, you can instruct that outlines or fills be overprinted by right-clicking on the object, choosing Overprint, and then Fill and/or Outline from the Overprint flyout.

- Globally, you can turn on the Always Overprint Black option in the Separations page of the Print Options dialog. With this option set, any object that contains at least 95% black will be set to overprint.

Figure 28.14 shows the effect of asking for text to be overprinted. By eliminating the knockout, you have also eliminated any registration issues.

28.14

Bye-bye, registration errors. With overprinted text (on the left), there are no fine serifs and other small objects to try to align.

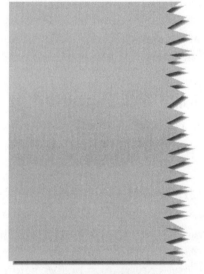

Color separation
with black text
overprinted

Black separation

We remember it as if it were yes... released. Up until then, the closest... markable paint programs and no... gree in programming to run. Core... drawing programs to take hold.

Today, nearly ten years later, C... try, both in terms of its customer ba... grams that are included in this on...

It is no mystery to us why this... came known as the most approach... illustration programs, and its stable... graphics community. Fine artists...ill... designers...logo creators...desktop p... t-shirt designers...newsletter editors... managers...and even the lead autho... ficient with CorelDRAW might be... sands of users will attest to the fac... for, and even getting the hang of t...

Purists argue that black overprinted on another ink color produces a different type of black—referred to by some as a "juicy black." Technically, they're right, but the point is not really worth arguing for any but the most demanding of print jobs. Certainly, if you ask for a 72-point headline to be overprinted, you're laying down a whole lot of black ink on top of other ink colors and that would be noticeable. This is why the Always Overprint Black option should be used carefully, and overprinting should only be used for small objects. Nevertheless, when you are working with smaller text, fine hairlines, rules around boxes, and other small black objects that are to be placed on top of other colors, overprinting is the answer to your trapping needs.

5. Let Your Print Shop Take Care of Trapping   The next option in the trapping gambit is to do what designers and publishers have been doing for as long as there have been color presses: Send your film to your print shop and ask them to trap your colors for you. The operators there will place your film under a powerful camera, study the areas where there might be problems due to misregistration, and apply tiny amounts of a common color to those areas. If your print shop employs skilled camera operators, this option is the friendliest of all…though not necessarily the cheapest. You'll be charged from $30 to $150 for this service.

6. Do Nothing   Believe it or not, thousands of professional DRAW users take this route. They decide that they don't want to be bothered with the specter of trapping, and they turn their film over to their print shops and hope that the job comes out okay.

7. Tell DRAW to Trap for You   Since version 4, DRAW has offered an option called Auto-Spreading, found in the Separations page of the Print Options dialog. This option will spread, or expand, certain objects by minuscule amounts, thus providing the tiny overlap needed to prevent registration errors. Three criteria must be met before Auto-Spreading can be applied to an object: (1) it must contain a uniform fill; (2) it must not be set to overprint via the pop-up menu; and (3) it cannot have an outline.

We're not wild about DRAW's Auto-Spreading feature. In theory, it's a credible tool, but we don't trust it in actual implementation—and you'll probably encounter many DRAW-using color professionals who agree with us.

8. Do It Yourself We've already discussed how you can trap black text by having it overprinted. With a bit of careful thought, you can use a technique based on the overprint strategy to trap all the objects in your drawing. This technique is called a *trapping outline*.

In our discussion of the cube, we established that the boundary between the yellow face and the magenta face is a danger zone in the event of a registration error. This is because there is a risk of a white streak appearing if the yellow face is placed too low. The same issue applies to the vertical boundary between the yellow and the blue face. A trapping outline applied to that area is the answer. This thin, yellow rule will nudge into and overprint on top of the magenta and blue faces. Here are the steps to make it happen.

1. Apply a half-point yellow outline to the yellow face. (Rule of thumb: When you have a choice, apply the trap to the lighter-colored object.)

2. Right-click on the face, and choose Overprint / Outline.

When you apply an outline to an object, half of its thickness is on the inside of the object, and half on the outside. In our example, therefore, a half-point outline will encroach upon the magenta face by a quarter of a point. With a normal outline, the yellow would merely begin knocking out the magenta a quarter point higher than otherwise, and you would have accomplished nothing. But in applying this trap, you set the outline to be overprinted, and that's the key to the entire puzzle. In that quarter-point space, the magenta will be laid down underneath the yellow, and both ink colors will be present in that area. Now if a registration error causes the yellow face to be placed too low, the magenta ink will still cover that area. You have set a trap against registration errors, thanks to one little overprinting outline.

WATCH OUT!

> One implication of the trapping outline: It has added one-quarter point of thickness to only one face of the cube. This will likely go unnoticed by many of your audience—but you'll know it's there. If it bothers you, you can add a corresponding half-point outline to the other two faces, in the name of consistency.

The other area in this drawing that needs to be trapped is the magenta *A* and the yellow face of the cube. Once again, a trapping outline is the solution, this time applied to the magenta A: Use the same color as the character itself, set it for a half-point thickness, and designate it to be overprinted. As Figure 28.15 shows, the outline will be placed on top of the yellow ink, ensuring ink coverage all the way around the *A*.

28.15

The trapping outline around this character prevents a white streak in the event of registration errors.

Outline around A spreads the character thickness by a quarter-point and will print over the yellow ink.

Incidentally, Figure 28.15 is heavily exaggerated. First of all, the outline color is supposed to be the same as the fill color (good for actual trapping, bad for demonstrating same). Second, the actual outline is supposed to be very small, not the bulky 3-point outline that we have applied here. When you trap for real, the outline won't be seen because all you are adding is a tiny outline colored the same as the object itself.

♣

In the next chapter, we turn off the color and examine the world of black-and-white printing, and the sometimes mysterious dynamics of printing gray tones.

CHAPTER

29

Turning Gray with Dignity

TWENTY-NINE

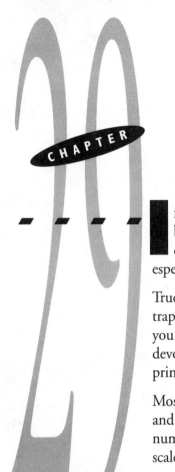

I f you think that working in color is complicated and working in black and white is simple, you're only half-right. Color *is* complicated. But so, too, is black and white, and everything in between—especially the in-between part, otherwise known as grays.

True, to understand grays you don't need to concern yourself with color trapping, PMS numbers, complementary colors, or CMYK values, but you must know your dots and lines, to which an entire special lingo is devoted. And if that weren't enough, to really master black-and-white printing, you need a refresher course in algebra and geometry.

Most of this chapter is light on the math, qualitative in its approach, and heavy on simple illustrations. It finishes, however, with a bit of number crunching, for those who need to know the intricacies of gray-scale printing.

Dots All, Folks

You probably already know about print resolution—that's the easy part. The *resolution* of your output device is a measure of how many dots it can squeeze into a small space. Standard laser printers can print 300 × 300 of them in a square inch, newer printers get 600 × 600 into that same inch, and the high-resolution imagesetters pack in 1,200 dots or more.

You don't need to know rocket science to figure out that in order to fit 1,200 dots across one inch, the dots must be considerably smaller than the ones that fit 300 to an inch. So if your dot is smaller, your blacks are blacker and your curves are curvier. Indeed, the smaller the dot, the finer the resolution, and the better the results of your design efforts. Figure 29.1 shows the bottom part of a lowercase italic *t*, printed at 300 dots per inch (dpi) and 1,200 dpi. At this magnification, the difference is obvious.

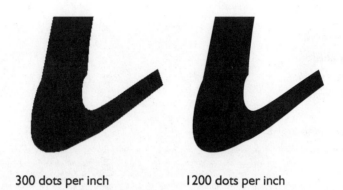

29.1

This blow-up of part of an italic serif t shows how dots at 1,200 dpi (on the right) turn corners better than dots at 300 dpi.

300 dots per inch   1200 dots per inch

When your task is simply to fill a space with black dots, the formula is simple: Cram in as many as you possibly can. But when you introduce the element of gray dots, the landscape changes significantly—primarily because *there is no such thing as a gray dot* in black-and-white printing. If you really do want a gray dot, then choose PANTONE Warm Gray 7, or perhaps Cool Gray 3. Ah, but now you're working with a second color, and that's cheating.

What's important to understand in all of this is how gray is created from black ink on a printing press. This is done by the not-so-simple process of printing small black dots in a regular pattern; the eye blends them into gray (if you don't look too closely). The array of dots is called a screen. This screen has nothing whatever to do with a video screen; in fact, it has more in common with your patio screen door. Usually, the dots are arranged in straight rows, and the fineness of the screen is indicated as the number of rows (or lines) of dots per inch. This may be stated, for example, as "85 lines per inch" or simply "an 85-line screen."

The number of lines per inch (lpi) only indicates the fineness of the screen, however, not how dark or light it appears. That is determined by the size of the dots. On a "10% screen," ten percent of the paper area is covered by ink, giving the appearance of a light gray. An "80% screen," on the other hand, is nearly black. Figure 29.2 is a simple illustration of this concept. In each of the 10 patterns (each with a portion magnified), the screens with smaller dots give the appearance of light gray, and the patterns with larger, overlapping dots produce the illusion of dark gray.

29.2

An enlarged view of the gray illusion. Smaller dots and more white space equal light gray; larger dots and less white space equal dark gray.

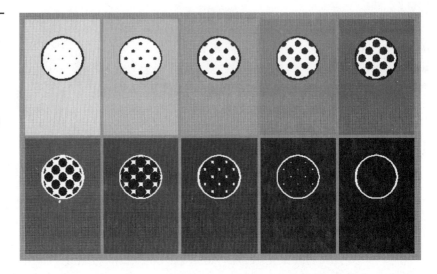

Now let's return to your laser printer: Another factor in the concept of grays is that the laser printer or imagesetter can produce dots of only one size. It cannot directly reproduce the various dot sizes used to create various shades of gray on a printing press. What the laser printer can (and does) do is create each dot of a screen as a group of the printer's own smaller dots. To avoid confusing these two types of dots, we will give them different names: screen dots (illustrated in Figure 29.2) and printer dots (the much smaller dots used by the laser printer to create both text and graphics).

Your printer creates screens by grouping its tiny printer dots to form the larger dots of the screen pattern. The smaller the dot your printer can create (that is, the higher its resolution), the more variety is possible in the pattern. You might think, then, that your goal would be to use as high a line screen as possible. Indeed, a higher frequency can produce finer grays and sharper images; unfortunately, it can also produce mud. You can only use a higher line screen if the printer dots are small enough; if you create a screen with too many lines per inch, you lose the ability to render gray.

When you print a scanned photograph containing 256 shades of gray, if the output device is of sufficiently high resolution, it produces 256 distinctly different screen patterns. Each dot pattern is slightly different, with dots and white space rearranged to produce varying illusions of gray. In order to render each shade of gray effectively, the output device needs to have sufficient elbow room—in other words, higher resolution.

Higher Isn't Always Better

This brings up an issue often misunderstood by many novice and not-so-novice users: Pushing a printer or a scanner to its maximum resolution won't by itself get you better gray tones. Higher resolution is of benefit only if you take advantage of it by using an effective arrangement of screen dots. It's not your job to tell the printer exactly how to create the matrix—the printer knows how to do that. It *is* your job, however, to ensure that the printer does *its* job, by knowing the resolution of your output device and checking the setting for line screen (discussed later in the chapter).

Getting Gray from the Grid

Standard laser printers produce larger dots than higher-resolution devices do. This does not mean that standard laser printers cannot produce gray tones, but there is a trade-off: You can get either higher resolution, or more gray tones, but not both. The smallest dot at 300 dpi is not small enough to give you the best of both worlds, leaving you with two choices. You can increase the line screen, which will improve detail but limit the number of gray tones rendered; or you can settle for a coarser line screen, which will sacrifice detail but increase the range of grays.

Let's quantify this. In order to get decent gray tones at 300 dpi, you will have to print with a line screen of about 60, as opposed to the 120- to 133-line screen supported by higher-resolution devices. If you tell DRAW to print to your 300-dpi laser printer with a very high line screen, you'll force the printer to use a smaller screen dot, thus providing fewer gray levels. The output samples later in the chapter illustrate this.

Figure 29.3 is the first in a series of various screen dot sizes. This 2 × 2 matrix provides just three gradations of gray (not counting solid black and solid white). With this pattern, you can produce 25%, 50%, and 75% gray images—that's all. Other patterns are possible, such as two vertical dots or a single dot on the lower-left, but then you are only changing the angle of the matrix, not the actual percentages of black and white. With only four printer dots per screen dot, there is very little opportunity for gray tones.

29.3

A 2 × 2 matrix of printer dots provides just three levels of gray.

Figure 29.4 shows the gray tones that can be achieved with a screen dot composed of a 3 × 3 matrix of printer dots. Figure 29.5 shows the grays possible with a 4 × 4 matrix; and Figure 29.6 shows the possibilities of a 5 × 5 matrix. You can achieve these tonal qualities at any resolution. You can get 24 shades of gray even from a 300-dpi laser printer, but that 5 × 5 matrix would require a low line-screen number (60 lines to an inch, to be precise).

29.4

A 3 × 3 matrix of printer dots gives 8 gradations of gray: 11%, 22%, 33%, 44%, 56%, 67%, 78%, and 89%, plus solid black.

29.5

A 4 × 4 matrix of printer dots gives 15 gradations of gray, from 6.67% through 93.33% in 6.67% increments, plus solid black and solid white.

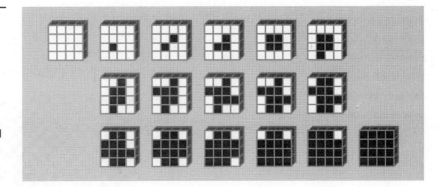

29.6

A 5 × 5 matrix of printer dots gives 24 gradations of gray, from 4% through 96% in 4% increments, plus solid black and solid white.

Think of it this way: You have a large sheet of graph paper, with squares that are 1/4" apart. Congratulations—you are the proud owner of a 4-dpi output device (4 squares to each inch). Your mission is to create the appearance of 50% gray, using only a felt pen. You are not allowed to write in between the squares; your only option is to fill in every other square in a checkerboard pattern, as shown in Figure 29.7. In this figure, the matrix is a group of 4 squares, with 2 dots on and 2 dots off.

29.7

**With squares of
1/4" and a 2-line-
per-inch screen,
this graph paper
can only produce
coarse gray tones.**

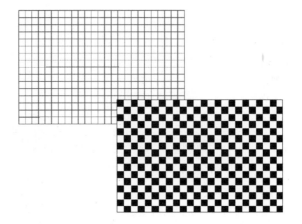

Figure 29.8 shows the same checkerboard pattern, but this time the squares on the graph paper are 1/8" apart. Ah, 8 dpi—you're moving up in the world. With the smaller matrix, this rendition of 50% gray looks more like gray (although, granted, these are very coarse resolutions). Compare a region of Figure 29.8 that is the same size as a matrix in Figure 29.7 (4 squares, 2 on and 2 off), and you'll see that there are many more dots in that area. The higher the resolution, the higher the frequency possible in the matrix—resulting in more gray tones.

29.8

**Better with a 1/8"
matrix**

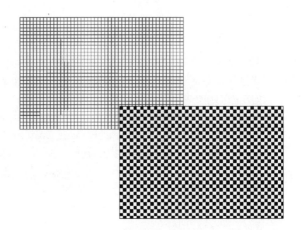

Figure 29.9, with its 16-dpi resolution, can produce a denser pattern. The graph paper gives you an idea of how the resolution affects your matrix, which in turn plays a vital role in the representation of gray.

29.9

Better still with a 1/16" matrix

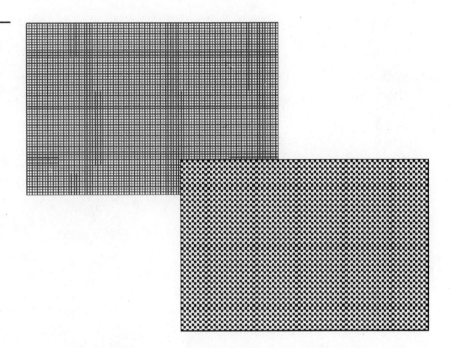

We've already fudged a little on our promise to keep the first part of this discussion qualitative and not too scientific (it gets much worse, you'll see). Unless you really need to know the inner workings of gray-scale theory, you'll get by if you just remember this: The illusion of gray is produced by the *pattern* between black dots and white space. If the pattern is too dense, the illusion of gray is lost. At lower resolutions, therefore, you need to use *fewer* dots, not more.

Figures 25.10, 25.11, and 25.12 illustrate the relationship between dots per inch (the size of the dot), and lines per inch (the frequency of the matrix). We use simple rectangles and text to show when clarity and readability are at their best and their worst.

29.10

300 dots per inch

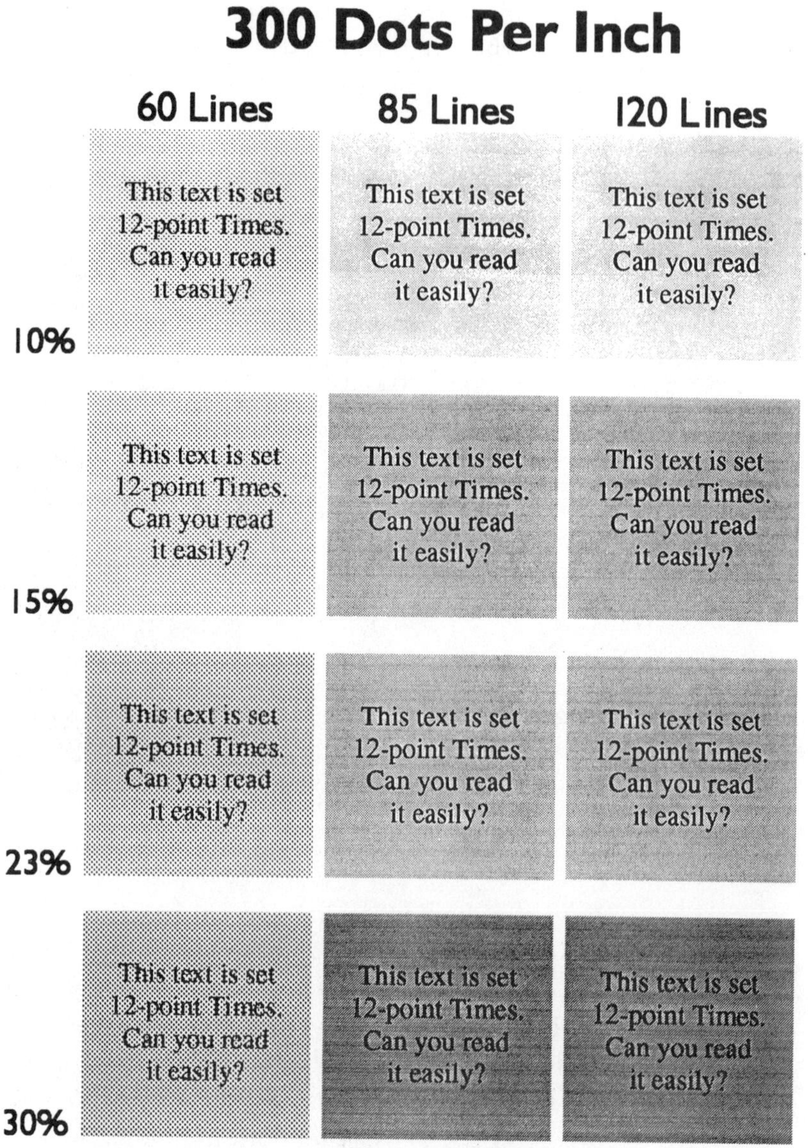

300 Dots Per Inch

	60 Lines	85 Lines	120 Lines
10%	This text is set 12-point Times. Can you read it easily?	This text is set 12-point Times. Can you read it easily?	This text is set 12-point Times. Can you read it easily?
15%	This text is set 12-point Times. Can you read it easily?	This text is set 12-point Times. Can you read it easily?	This text is set 12-point Times. Can you read it easily?
23%	This text is set 12-point Times. Can you read it easily?	This text is set 12-point Times. Can you read it easily?	This text is set 12-point Times. Can you read it easily?
30%	This text is set 12-point Times. Can you read it easily?	This text is set 12-point Times. Can you read it easily?	This text is set 12-point Times. Can you read it easily?

29.11

600 dots per inch

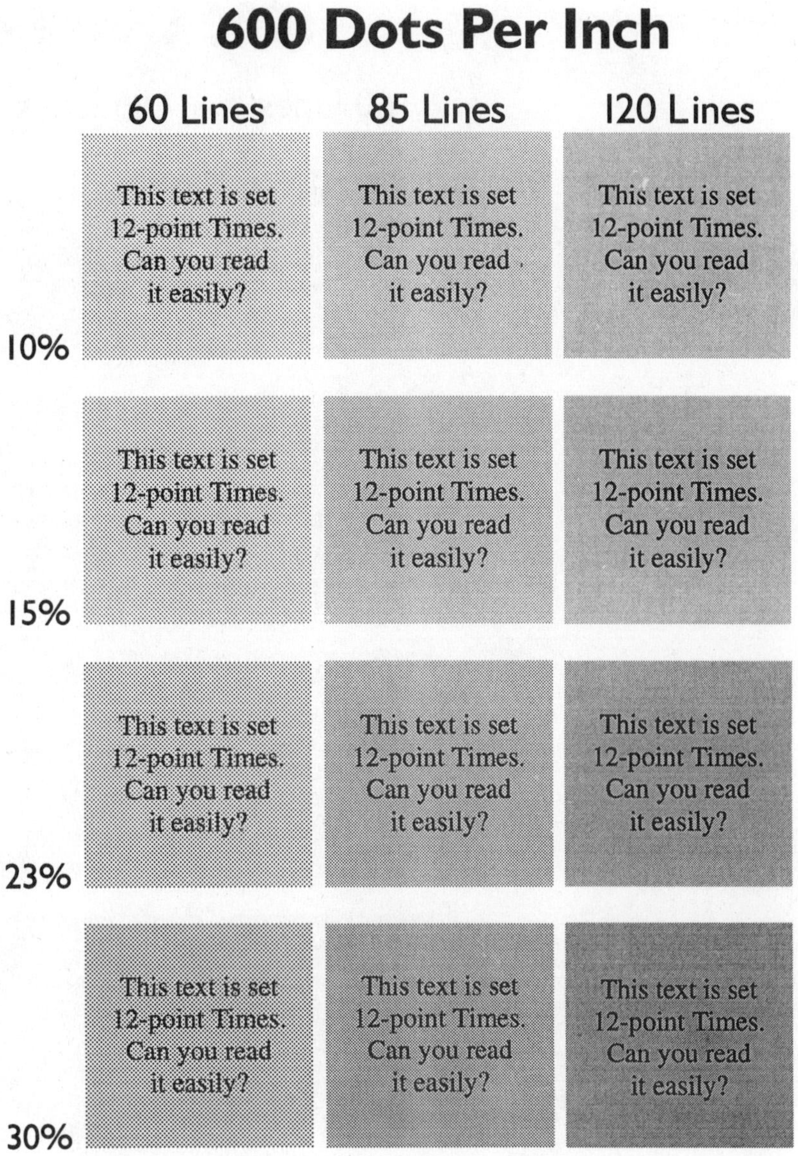

600 Dots Per Inch

	60 Lines	85 Lines	120 Lines
10%	This text is set 12-point Times. Can you read it easily?	This text is set 12-point Times. Can you read it easily?	This text is set 12-point Times. Can you read it easily?
15%	This text is set 12-point Times. Can you read it easily?	This text is set 12-point Times. Can you read it easily?	This text is set 12-point Times. Can you read it easily?
23%	This text is set 12-point Times. Can you read it easily?	This text is set 12-point Times. Can you read it easily?	This text is set 12-point Times. Can you read it easily?
30%	This text is set 12-point Times. Can you read it easily?	This text is set 12-point Times. Can you read it easily?	This text is set 12-point Times. Can you read it easily?

29.12

1,200 dots per inch

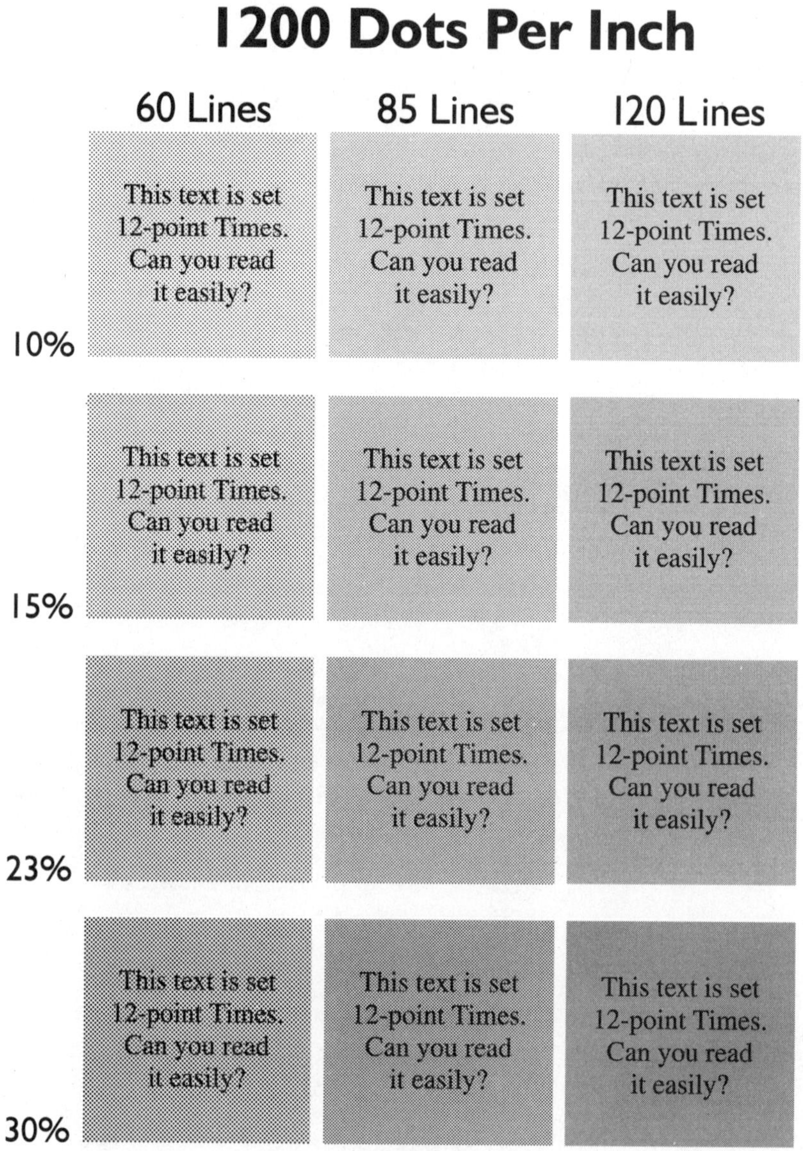

1200 Dots Per Inch

60 Lines	85 Lines	120 Lines

10%

This text is set 12-point Times. Can you read it easily?

This text is set 12-point Times. Can you read it easily?

This text is set 12-point Times. Can you read it easily?

15%

This text is set 12-point Times. Can you read it easily?

This text is set 12-point Times. Can you read it easily?

This text is set 12-point Times. Can you read it easily?

23%

This text is set 12-point Times. Can you read it easily?

This text is set 12-point Times. Can you read it easily?

This text is set 12-point Times. Can you read it easily?

30%

This text is set 12-point Times. Can you read it easily?

This text is set 12-point Times. Can you read it easily?

This text is set 12-point Times. Can you read it easily?

As Figure 29.10 shows, 300-dpi output cannot withstand much beyond a 60-line screen. If you have a new toner cartridge with even distribution, you can use denser patterns for boxes that don't have any text inside, provided that your laser printer output is intended to be the final product. If you take your laser originals to a photocopy center and ask them to reproduce your 85-line screen output, you'll get mud. Best to play it safe and stay at 60 lines for 300-dpi output.

According to Figure 29.11, 85 lines per inch looks ideal for 600-dpi output, as from an HP LaserJet 4M. And Figure 29.12 shows how the 1,200-dpi output can support an even higher density of lines. When ordering film at your service bureau, you can ask for 133-line screens, even 150 in some cases, if your print shop can handle such fine screens.

Setting Line Screens in DRAW

Whether or not you understand the intricacies of lines, dots, screen dots, and grays, you can still take measures to ensure good output with your black-and-white drawings. Using Figures 25.10 through 25.12 as your guide, you can establish proper settings for line screens and pass those settings on to DRAW.

The first thing to be said about this task is that line screens are a PostScript phenomenon, and only relevant when printing to a PostScript laser printer or creating print files to be taken to your service bureau. Other printers, such as non-PostScript HP LaserJets, have their own controls for adjusting dot patterns, accessible through the Windows Control Panel / Printers section.

Creating Print Files

Let's say that you are sending your work to your service bureau, and you determine that a screen of 120 lines will best produce the gray tones that you have incorporated into your work. Assuming that all of the objects are to be set at 120 lines, your course of action is clear and simple:

1. Select File / Print / Options.

2. In the Screen Frequency drop-down list on the Options page of the dialog, choose 120. ("Screen Frequency" means the same thing as line screen.)

3. OK this dialog and then OK the main Print dialog, and you're ready to issue the Print command.

Whether you are printing to a local printer or creating a PostScript print file (both of which are discussed in Chapter 25), all objects on the page will have a line screen of 120 lines. (This includes solid objects as well as gray tones, even though this setting doesn't matter with solids. When there is total coverage of dots in a given space, the screen density becomes irrelevant.)

INSIDE INFO

If you do not set the line screen before printing, you might still get the correct value. When Options / Screen Frequency is set to Default, DRAW consults the PostScript printer driver for the line screen value, using its current setting.

Creating Encapsulated PostScript Files

If your drawings are designed to be placed into another application, then you will want to create an *encapsulated PostScript* (.EPS) file, rather than a print file. DRAW's .EPS export command does not have controls for setting the screen density, but that doesn't mean you cannot control it. An .EPS file is designed to be incorporated into another document, perhaps one that has been created by a different program altogether. You set the screen when you print from that application. In PageMaker, for instance, you click the Color button on the Print dialog and then enter the value in the lpi box.

Many programs, including DRAW and PageMaker, have a control for the screen. Then again, many programs don't. However, practically every program provides access to the Windows PostScript printer driver, where you *can* adjust the line screen. To get there, use File / Print Setup, or click Setup from within the Print dialog (every Windows program offers one or both of these avenues). Then click Options, Advanced, and find the field called Halftone Frequency (yet another synonym for screen density).

One Print Job, Many Screens

The two methods for setting screens discussed above are global operations; they establish the screen that will prevail for all objects in a drawing. You can also set an individual line screen for a selected object in a drawing, as long as you observe one rule: You must be using a spot color model, not a process color model. Rather than dialing up the percentage of black and leaving the other three CMYK values at 0%, you would use a spot color model (such as PANTONE). From there, you would choose the color black and set a tint for it, as shown in the Uniform Fill dialog in Figure 29.13.

Once that's done, the PostScript Options choice within the Color Options button becomes available, and choosing it brings you to the dialog of settings shown on the right of Figure 29.13. For the Halftone Screen type, select Dot; then enter the desired screen density in the Frequency field. The value of 87 shown in the figure is a bit absurd (increments of 5 are barely noticeable at higher resolutions), but we wanted to show you that you can indeed dial up any value at all for the line screen.

By giving an object its own personalized line screen, you are overruling any line screen value you set for the whole image. If you set the Screen Frequency value in the DRAW Print dialogs to 100, it will prevail over all objects, *except* those to which you have assigned a custom line screen. The same thing applies to an .EPS file: When you place it in and print it from another document, the line screen settings when you print will act on all objects, except the ones to which you have manually assigned individual line screens.

29.13

Each object can
have its own line
screen setting.

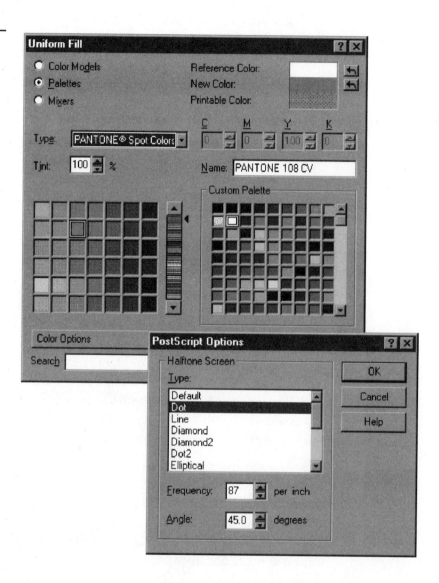

Creative Screens

Most users set screens by adjusting the frequency of the dot matrix, but
there are several other options that DRAW provides for you, with which

29.14

Who says fountain fills are only good at high resolution? Here are settings that produce effective patterns at 300 dpi.

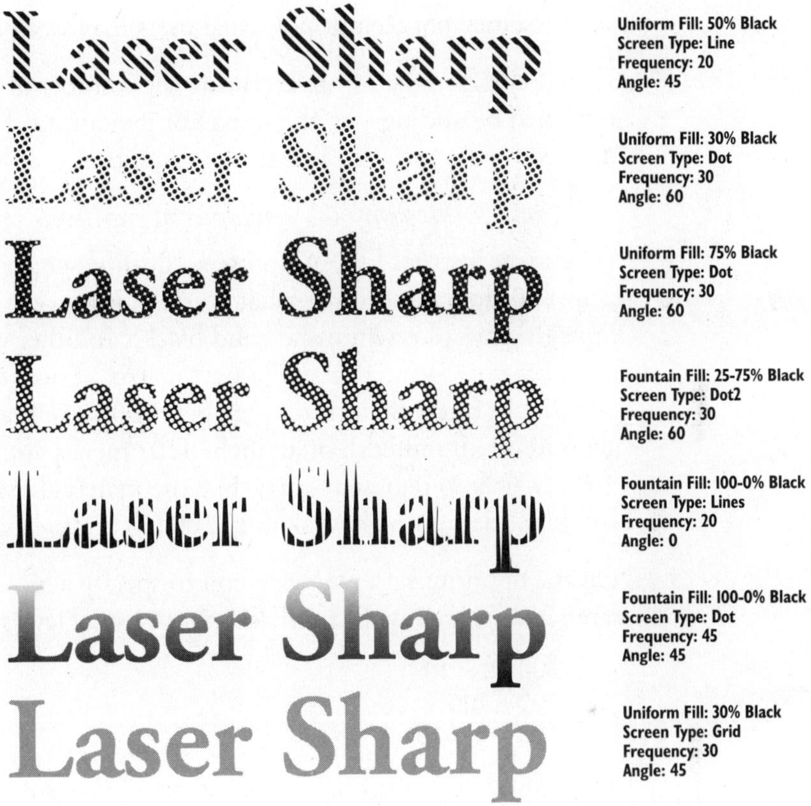

Laser Sharp

Uniform Fill: 50% Black
Screen Type: Line
Frequency: 20
Angle: 45

Laser Sharp

Uniform Fill: 30% Black
Screen Type: Dot
Frequency: 30
Angle: 60

Laser Sharp

Uniform Fill: 75% Black
Screen Type: Dot
Frequency: 30
Angle: 60

Laser Sharp

Fountain Fill: 25-75% Black
Screen Type: Dot2
Frequency: 30
Angle: 60

Laser Sharp

Fountain Fill: 100-0% Black
Screen Type: Lines
Frequency: 20
Angle: 0

Laser Sharp

Fountain Fill: 100-0% Black
Screen Type: Dot
Frequency: 45
Angle: 45

Laser Sharp

Uniform Fill: 30% Black
Screen Type: Grid
Frequency: 30
Angle: 45

you can create text effects that are particularly well suited for lower-resolution output. Figure 29.14 shows several of these, alongside the settings that produced them. These settings are all contained within the PostScript Options dialog available from any of the Fill dialogs. Remember, though, that these screens can only be seen when printed from a PostScript printer; they will not show on your screen.

By the Numbers (Ugh)

Just in case you haven't noticed the mathematical pattern emerging here, the number of gray levels can be figured by squaring the matrix size and adding 1. Say what? As we warned you, the following discussion is somewhat technical. Casual users may want to pass on this.

Here is the formula for determining the number of gray levels. It is determined by adding 1 to the square of the output device's resolution, divided by the specified line screen resolution.

$$(dpi\ /\ line\ screen)^2 + 1 = number\ of\ gray\ levels$$

When you instruct DRAW to use a 100-line screen for a gray tone on your 300-dpi laser printer, what you're going to get is 10 possible gradations (8 grays plus white and solid black). In other words, you're instructing your printer to start a new matrix of dots every one-hundredth of an inch. But if the printer only gets 300 dots in an inch, it can only get 3 in one-hundredth of an inch. That means your printer will use a 3×3 matrix to represent grays, like the matrix shown in Figure 29.4. So you get a relatively high resolution (100 lpi) at the expense of gradations.

On the opposite extreme, were you to specify a line screen of 30 on the same laser printer, you could achieve 101 gray levels:

```
300/30 = 10
10² = 100
100 + 1 = 101
```

This would give you a line screen of very low resolution, but many more gray levels—probably more than you would care to use.

When you print a fountain fill to a 300-dpi printer, in many cases you will get visible banding unless you use a line screen of very low resolution. What value you use depends greatly on the values of your fountain fill and the distance it will span. If the distance spanned by the gradient is small, the banding may not be noticeable. A gradient progressing from solid black to white across a 1/4-inch span, with a line screen of 60 on a 300-dpi printer, would create 26 bands—not distinguishable in that distance.

On the other hand, the same fountain settings to the same printer, but with a line screen of 75 spanning 17 inches, will be noticeably banded with 17 bands averaging about an inch wide. This gradient, output to a

Linotronic at 2,540 dpi, will provide a much nicer gradation, even at 100 lpi. This gradient provides 646 gray levels, which, divided into the 17-inch span, yield bands of approximately 2.5/100 inch.

♣

Next stop on the freeway: the on-ramps and off-ramps.

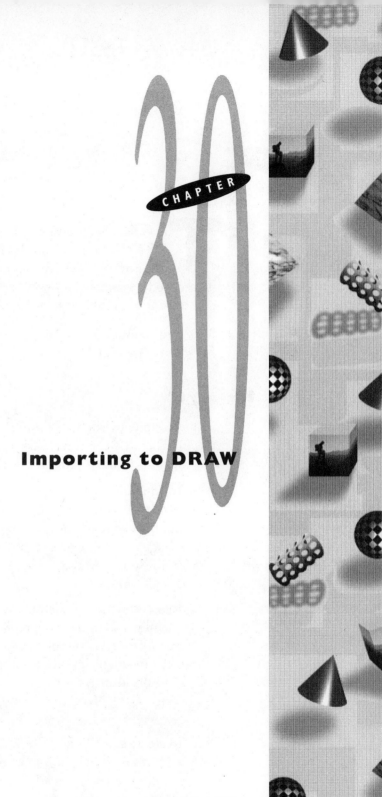

CHAPTER

30

Importing to DRAW

THIRTY

This brief chapter is not a tutorial on how to import files into DRAW—for that, turn back to Chapter 4, which contains a detailed, step-by-step approach to the mechanics of importing. This chapter assumes you know how to import, but want more insight and strategy about the different methods and formats available to you.

This is rush hour on the Corel Freeway, and there are lots of on-ramps for you to choose....

Why Import?

Is this a dumb question? We think not. The usual reason—to bring in a piece of clip art—is not the only one. There are three reasons to import graphics into DRAW, and three distinct ways to do it:

To edit an existing graphic A graphic that is in a standard vector format (such as AI, CGM, or WMF) can be imported into DRAW and then edited. Once you import it into DRAW, you can then change it and integrate it into a larger drawing. A finished drawing can be imported and made to be one small component of a more complex project.

To incorporate an existing graphic We've chosen our words carefully: *edit* in the paragraph above, and *incorporate* here. Some graphic formats cannot be taken apart and edited by DRAW, but they can still be imported and printed by DRAW. These include all of the bitmap formats and placeable EPS files (EPS files imported via the PostScript Interpreted filter are an exception; we'll discuss them a little later).

To create a hot-link DRAW is a willing party to the Object Linking and Embedding phenomenon (you know it as OLE), in which graphics are sent across the Clipboard and are able to retrace their steps back to the original program that created them. We'll explore OLE in detail in this chapter and the next one.

Importing linked or embedded objects is not done through the File / Import command, but rather with the Edit / Paste Special or Edit / Insert New Object commands. However, this operation qualifies as an import, and we'll treat it as such. In broad categories, you could think of incoming graphics as being in vector or bitmap format. Imported vector art can be taken apart and edited; bitmap art cannot.

AUTHOR'S NOTE

Starting with version 5, DRAW has included a PostScript interpreter that can take PostScript print files and EPS files and attempt to replicate them with native DRAW objects. How well does it work? Has it improved since version 5? Stay tuned....

What Happens When You Import?

Importing (or pasting) graphics is not a one-size-fits-all proposition, although in all cases DRAW uses a *filter* to perform the task. Filters acts as translators. They enable DRAW to convert vector information from other file formats into its own internal objects, and to translate bitmap art into printable images. The key word here is *translate,* and it has implications for you: If DRAW has to translate graphic information from a format you can't read, how do you know whether DRAW got the translation right?

As recently as 1992, the answer to this question would have been "Cross your fingers, don't forget your mantra, and only import on Tuesday nights, when atmospheric conditions seem to be more favorable." Before today's file format standards were adopted and implemented, exchanging graphics information was all too often one big crapshoot. It required both parties (the exporting program and the importing program) to be on the same wavelength, and even then, elements such as hairlines, typeface names, and color mixes carried long odds of being interpreted correctly.

Today your prospects of accurate graphics exchange are much brighter, with the Windows Metafile (WMF) format taking hold and being recognized as an accurate and reliable format for translating graphical information. This bodes well for users of non-PostScript devices, as well as for those who want to take advantage of OLE.

Importing Clip Art

Getting clip art files remains the top reason that DRAW users go for the Import command. Whether these images come from an external source or from Corel's vast library of clip art, DRAW's defining characteristic for tens of thousands of users is its ability to ingest and digest clip art images from many different sources.

Our surveys show that most clip art is used for applications no more complicated than the one in Figure 30.1, which shows several cartoon figures, originally in CGM format, integrated into one composite drawing.

The clip art images that make up Figure 30.1 were not changed in any way, except for the addition of a slight skew to the man peeking over the desk. But most vector art that is imported into DRAW can be taken apart and edited, *just as if you had created the objects in DRAW initially.* This last point is important: When it imports vector art, DRAW uses its filter to translate all incoming objects into elements that it understands. Therefore, all objects are of a type that *you* understand—curves, lines, and text characters, with and without fills and outlines. Figure 30.2 shows Frosty, a longtime resident of Corel's clip art library, suffering from a breakdown—decidedly worse than a meltdown—into his DRAW components at the hands of the Arrange / Ungroup command.

Some graphic formats tax DRAW's filtering to the max. The CGM and GEM file types are notorious for being unruly with fills and outlines, and AI files often get typeface names wrong.

Other formats, such as CDR and CMX, need very little translation. In fact, Frosty needs no translation at all, as he is stored in DRAW's own CMX format. Note that you cannot make any changes to Frosty without first copying him to your hard drive (you can't write to a CD).

30.1

These pieces of clip art can be easily integrated into a single drawing.

Before Corel developed the CMX format, all clip art was saved and distributed in Corel's original file format, CDR. The ability to import CDR files is still an important function of DRAW 6. However, there is a subtle difference between *opening* and *importing* a CDR file. Using the Open command will start a new document or file. Using Import will

30.2

Disaster strikes
Frosty the Snow-
man in the form
of the Ungroup
command.

add the incoming CDR file contents to your currently active drawing.
In short, File / Open starts a new file; File / Import adds one file's contents to another.

NEW FOR 6

DRAW 6.0 is now an MDI (Multiple Document Interface) Windows
application. This means you can have more than one CDR file
open at a time. It enables you to drag objects from one opened
drawing and drop them into another. This dramatically eases the
tedious gymnastics of copying, pasting, opening, and closing that
used to be necessary to move elements from one CDR file to
another, and is one of the most welcome changes to DRAW 6.0.

Imported vector art always arrives on the page as one group of objects.
We're not sure whether this is an engineering requirement or just a decision on the part of the developers, but we like it. Generally, the first

thing you want to do to imported art is move it and resize it, and these two operations are eminently easier to do with a group. Once you have incorporated the group into your drawing, you can ungroup it and adjust its individual parts as needed. But remember, you can get to objects without ungrouping them. Just hold Ctrl when you click on them.

Because vector art can be disassembled and edited, it remains the most versatile form of clip art. The following paragraphs offer brief descriptions of the more popular vector flavors. For further notes on these and the other vector-based formats, get online assistance by choosing Help / Technical Support. Select the Import/Export File Transfer Information topic, and then search under the Import Filter Features & Limitations subtopic for the individual format name.

Adobe Illustrator Files

Few things are more frustrating for us while teaching or lecturing on these topics than having to try and explain how EPS files created by Adobe Illustrator are different from standard EPS files (even though it was Adobe that created the EPS format in the first place). The standard Encapsulated PostScript file was designed to be included in another container document, such as a PageMaker or Ventura file. The original concept was to provide a way to get the highest quality from an output from a printing device. Unlike the Illustrator brand of EPS, standard EPS was never intended to be opened and edited in a drawing program.

The Adobe Illustrator format is a special subset of the PostScript format. When you examine an Illustrator (AI) file in a text editor, they look like EPS (Encapsulated PostScript) files—they are stored in ASCII, and you can find in them a lot of the same unintelligible syntax as in standard EPS files (*gsave*, *annotatepage*, *grestore*, and *packedarray*, for instance). Illustrator files can be imported and placed in a CorelDRAW file as a group of editable objects. Though they generally produce highly refined, extremely accurate art, Illustrator files confuse the heck out of unsuspecting users who are led to believe that *all* EPS files can be imported and edited the way that AI files can.

To make matters even more interesting, DRAW *can* import standard EPS files, but not in the way it imports other vector formats (more on this shortly). To minimize confusion, in this chapter we will refer to Adobe's special flavor of EPS as *Illustrator format*, or as *AI files*. For your own sake, think of this format as completely distinct from standard EPS files.

AutoCAD

AutoCAD's DXF files can be imported into DRAW with relatively little fuss. Like Illustrator files, AutoCAD files are stored in ASCII format, making for an easier conversion. However, there are numerous features of AutoCAD that have no equivalents in DRAW, not the least of which is three-dimensionality. DRAW lives in only two dimensions and will force an incoming DXF file into the same narrow confines by simply stripping the 3D information out and discarding it.

AutoCAD continues to add features to the DXF format, and you will find that DRAW's filter may not be able to handle DXF files from recent releases of AutoCAD. For a complete discussion on the Auto-CAD/CorelDRAW connection, use DRAW's online Help. Choose Help / Technical Support, select Import/Export File Transfer Information, and then choose AutoCAD DXF found under the Import Filter Features & Limitations subtopic.

CorelDRAW's CDR Format

The CDR file format will forever be your friendliest, because it is DRAW's native language. Whatever is in the file—fountain fills, blends, unique typefaces, and so forth—will survive the trip into your current drawing unscathed (assuming you have installed the typefaces required by the incoming CDR file). CDR files created in earlier versions of DRAW might show some differences from the original; typical variations may include excess character and word spacing, which require some fine-tuning.

CorelDRAW's CMX Format

The CMX format is a hybrid of a full-fledged CDR file. If you export a drawing to CMX format and then reimport it, the integrity and quality of your drawing will be maintained. However, special effects such as contours, PowerLines, blends, and extrusions will be separated into their basic components and no longer editable using the various roll-ups that created them. The CMX format is intended to be an intermediate format that all Corel applications can read. Additionally, the CMX format creates smaller files than CDR. Corel has seized upon this as a good strategy for distributing its clip art on CDs.

Computer Graphics Metafile

The CGM format has come a long way, yet still has a ways to go. Commercial clip art stored in CGM format is usually simple enough to be low risk; trouble arises when you are forced to import a complex chart or image as a CGM file, perhaps because the originating program offers no other export choices. It takes two to tango here—DRAW's ability to *import* a CGM file will be no better than the originating program's ability to *export* a CGM file.

Compare Figure 30.3, a chart produced in Harvard Graphics, with the charts in Figure 30.4, which shows the same chart exported to CGM and imported to DRAW, and the same chart exported to WMF and imported to DRAW.

The original chart (Figure 30.3) features a smooth fountain-fill background and crisp text set in various weights of Eras, a classic Adobe Type 1 face. In the CGM file that Harvard exported and DRAW imported, the fountain has been replaced by a 25% shade, the text is all set in AvantGarde, and the labels running up the y-axis are misaligned. Also, there are many duplicate lines drawn on top of one another.

We're not sure what to blame here—DRAW's import filter or Harvard's export filter—and we're not sure if blame is necessarily warranted. After all, no objects disappeared during the transfer, the bars and the frame of the chart are all there, and the text came in as text, not a collection of

30.3

This chart, pro-
duced in Harvard
Graphics, will be
our guinea pig for
importing into
DRAW.

Original Harvard
Graphics chart

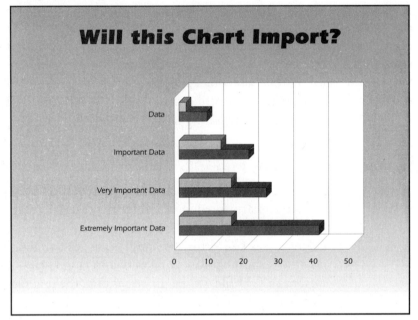

uneditable curves. The discrepancies can all be fixed in about 10 minutes. We would deem this an acceptable transfer, given the limitations
we have encountered with the CGM format. (We have certainly seen
worse. In fact, the first time we wrote about this topic in a CorelDRAW
book, a CGM file came into DRAW upside down and mirrored!)

Windows Metafile

The WMF format has enjoyed the most significant advances of any format, as more and more developers jump on this bandwagon. Though
we don't know beans about the inner workings of file formats and how
they are created, we can observe that WMF has become clean, accurate,
and very compact. The lower chart in Figure 30.4 shows the WMF file
imported into DRAW. The only imperfections are that the fountain fill

30.4

Importing CGM files to DRAW often produces less-than-perfect results (compare to Figure 30.3), but WMF files usually fare much better.

Chart imported to DRAW as .CGM file

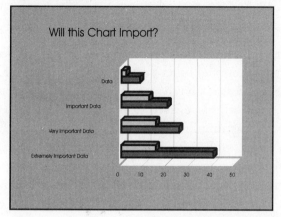

Chart imported to DRAW as .WMF file

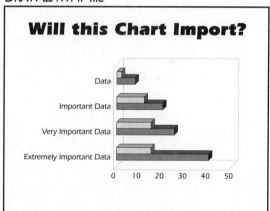

background came in solid white (a 30-second fix), and we got some duplicate lines (although not nearly as many as with the CGM import).

As you'll see in Chapter 31, the WMF format receives good marks in our Annual Export Torture Test, now in its fourth year.

Importing EPS Files

As of version 4, DRAW added EPS files to its list of importable files, and then 5 added yet another wrinkle to the PostScript import game. Allow us two paragraphs of background.

PostScript is a set of instructions, stored in plain ASCII text, that make sense to printers and other output devices having the ability to interpret it. PostScript instructions have one common objective: to describe a page. In fact, PostScript is referred to as a *page description language*. PostScript is really a programming language, similar to Pascal, Turbo C, and the various flavors of BASIC, but there is one big difference. With few exceptions, PostScript doesn't live inside your computer; it lives inside your printer. When PostScript instructions are sent to a PostScript printer, it begins building an image of the page. To get output from a service bureau that utilizes PostScript devices, you could deliver a file made on your computer containing the PostScript instructions your bureau's imagesetter needs to interpret and image your pages.

Encapsulated PostScript is a rigidly defined subset within the PostScript language. An EPS file is not designed to be sent directly to the printer (although, if you know how to manually modify the file, you can do it). Rather, it is intended to be incorporated into another document and then sent to the printer from there. An EPS file can be scaled up and down like any other graphic (that's what is meant by *encapsulated*). All of the output samples in this book (including Figures 30.3 and 30.4 earlier) were produced as EPS files and imported into Ventura Publisher for final publishing and printing.

Now here is the wrinkle that we mentioned earlier: In addition to what DRAW calls *placeable Encapsulated PostScript*—in other words, DRAW places the file on the page without trying to edit its components—DRAW 5 and 6.0 offer another import choice called *PostScript Interpreted* (PS). When using the PS filter, DRAW will try to do what your printer does—interpret the data and construct the image, using DRAW's native elements. In this case, the key word is *try*. This filter has proven to be quite amazing in its ability to interpret some PostScript information accurately, yet absolutely destroy other data.

Though we had no problems at all placing our Harvard Graphics chart as an EPS file (and getting a perfect printout from it), we didn't do so well with the Interpreted version. We did succeed in importing an EPS file made from the chart, but as Figure 30.5 shows, the results are flawed. The headline has been separated into individual characters in the wrong font, letter spacing is a joke, and many parts of the chart are

3 0 . 5

Results from the PostScript (Interpreted) filter are radically inferior to those of the EPS (placeable) filter.

Chart imported to DRAW
as Placeable .EPS file

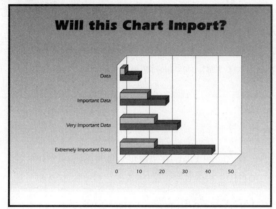

Chart imported to DRAW
as Interpreted PostScript file

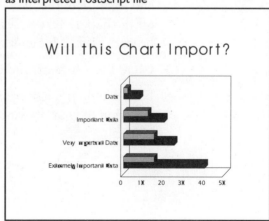

simply missing. The strangest change is that the chart labels have been converted to bitmaps, rather than characters or even curves. This result would serve us if, and only if, we were without the original file that produced the EPS file and desperately needed just a clue about what the image looked like. Our tests indicate that the PS filter cannot be counted on for any type of high-fidelity work. Think of it as an emergency measure.

WATCH OUT!

In version 5, it was quite common when using the PostScript Interpreted filter to get blown right out of CorelDRAW and Windows! We didn't encounter this phenomenon with version 6.0, but that won't stop us from continuing to warn you of the potential for some real fireworks when using the PS filter.

An EPS Test

If you have a PostScript printer, you can see how the two kinds of Post-Script importing work by following these steps:

1. Start DRAW and create a drawing. Anything will do; we created a gray oval with some text inside.

2. Use File / Export to create an EPS file. Make note of the name and location of the file. After clicking the Export button, turn off the Export Text as Text and Include Fonts options. Include a header: TIFF, 8-bit grayscale, with a resolution of 72 dpi.

3. Go to File / Import, and choose Encapsulated PostScript (EPS).

4. Find the file you just created and double-click on it. A representation of your drawing will appear as a single, uneditable object.

WATCH OUT!

Can't find EPS Export? Maybe you didn't install the filter when you installed CorelDRAW. Run Setup again and choose Custom. Uncheck everything except Import/Export Filters, click on Details, then select Vector Filters and click on the Details button again. Find the Encapsulated PostScript (EPS) and PostScript Interpreted import filters and add them to the Install list. Make sure you select all of the filters you want to use, not just the new ones you want to add. Any filters that were previously installed but are not selected when you rerun Setup will be deleted when you reinstall.

5. Return to File / Import, choose PostScript Interpreted (PS) as the format, and double-click the same file. A dialog asks you how to handle the incoming text. Select Import Text as Text and click OK. Another, more similar replication of the original appears on your screen.

You'll notice right away that the placeable EPS graphic looks different from the original object. (Actually, it looks a lot like an imported bitmap and for a very good reason, which we'll explain shortly.) Don't bother reaching for the Ungroup command; this graphic cannot be ungrouped, taken apart, or edited in any way. Why? Because DRAW's Encapsulated PostScript (EPS) filter doesn't really apply a filter to translate all the PostScript code contained in the file. When you import the file, DRAW says to itself, "Yup, that's an EPS file, all right—I'll just drop it on the page and let the printer worry about it later." And when it comes time to print, DRAW does just that. It includes the EPS file in the stream of data racing down the cable to the selected printer. At the other end of the cable, the printer interprets it and prints out the page with your beautiful EPS file intact.

You may wonder, if DRAW doesn't try to read the file, how come it can display the image on screen? The image you see on the screen is a low-resolution, bitmapped rendition of the way your image will look when actually printed, and nothing at all like the fidelity you are used to seeing from DRAW. Sometimes DRAW can't even show you this low-res image; sometimes it will just display a gray box (called a bounding box), which delineates the area the graphic will occupy. It's possible that the gray box will contain the name of the file and the application that created it.

Programs that include an export filter for creating placeable EPS files usually have a provision for including a bitmap image—a TIFF file (although some offer WMF as an alternative)—in the file itself. For instance, when you export an EPS file from DRAW 6.0, it asks whether you want to include an image header. You can choose between TIFF or WMF format. If you choose TIFF, you can further define the type—color, black and white, or grayscale—and the resolution of this bitmap representation. (Other programs call these *screen previews* or simply *headers.*) When you ask to have one included in an EPS file, the program creating the EPS file whips up a quick rendition of the drawing and tucks it away at the end of the EPS file data. Thanks to that image header, programs that receive EPS files have something to show you. The header serves only as a positioner, and generally contains little detail. But that is of no consequence to the end result, since the PostScript printer disregards the image header completely, concentrating instead on imaging only the good stuff.

So the reason EPS files look like imported bitmap images is because that's exactly what DRAW shows you. In Figure 30.6, the top oval and text were created in DRAW; these two objects were then exported as an Encapsulated PostScript file. This EPS file was imported twice, the first time using the Encapsulated PostScript (EPS) filter (middle oval) and the second time using the PostScript Interpreted (PS) filter (bottom). The figure illustrates the poor on-screen quality of the placeable EPS file. The PS file doesn't appear to have fared too badly, but upon closer inspection you will find that the text is now separated into single characters.

30.6

Looks can be deceiving: The placeable EPS file doesn't look very healthy in this on-screen image.

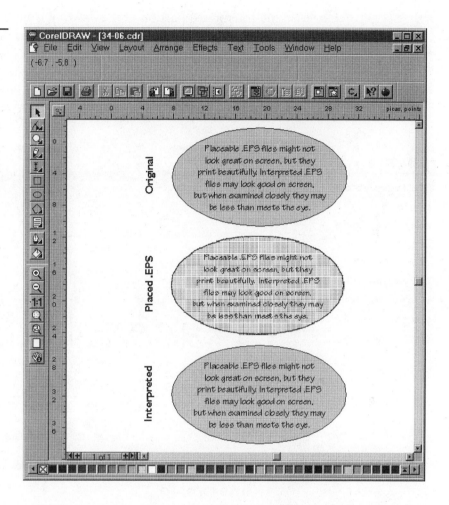

Whether printed from DRAW or exported as EPS and printed from PageMaker 5, the placeable EPS file prints beautifully, indistinguishable from the source. And, in this case, so does the Interpreted version. This is a great improvement over last year when the text in the Interpreted version was lost entirely.

However, the Interpreted portion of the drawing is *not* as perfect as the original. As Figure 30.7 illustrates, the text block is now separate characters rather than sentences. This will make any further text editing a royal pain. The figure also shows what happens if you were to choose to treat the text as curves when you import the file. Basically, you get what you ask for: curves rather than separate text characters.

30.7

The Interpreted portion is not exactly what it looks like. Whether you choose Text or Curves, you still won't be happy if you have to make any text changes.

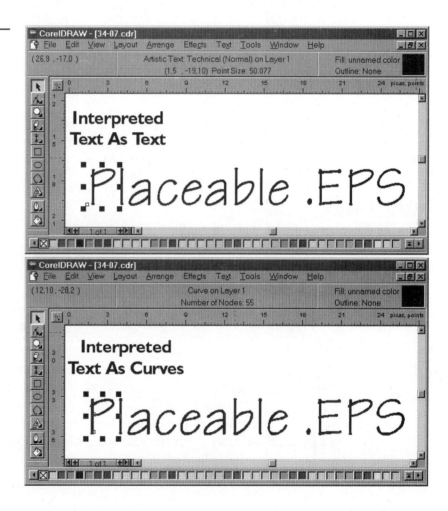

WATCH OUT!

As good as placeable EPS files are, they're not worth much more than their image headers if you intend to print them to a non-PostScript printer. The printer will just ignore all the PostScript code and print only the image header. If you are not sure whether your printer can print in PostScript mode, you can try looking in the manual, contacting the dealer you purchased the printer from, or calling the manufacturer.

Although you cannot take apart and edit the objects in a placeable EPS file, you can rotate, skew, stretch, and/or mirror them without loss of fidelity. The only exception to this is if your EPS file contains a bitmap image; scaling or stretching a bitmap image will cause major distortions and this could be hazardous to your career.

Importing Bitmap Images

DRAW can import many different bitmap formats, including the heavy-weights: TIFF, PCX, Scitex, and JPEG. Color, black and white, gray—DRAW doesn't care. To a large degree, DRAW treats these formats as it does EPS files, simply passing them on to the printer.

However, DRAW does speak bitmap to some extent. It can show you your imported bitmap images in considerable detail. If an imported bitmap contains 16 million colors, DRAW will show you an image of near television quality. Figure 30.8 shows off DRAW's screen rendering and printing prowess with bitmaps of various color depths. The printout from the 16-million color image is virtually lifelike.

You can't do much editing to bitmap images in DRAW, and what you can do, you do at your own risk. For instance:

You can scale a bitmap, but... Bitmap images are made up of dot matrices, which are extremely size-sensitive. Although you may get away with reducing a bitmap slightly, enlarging a bitmap file often results in a near-death experience.

30.8

If your bitmap image has the detail, **DRAW** will show it.

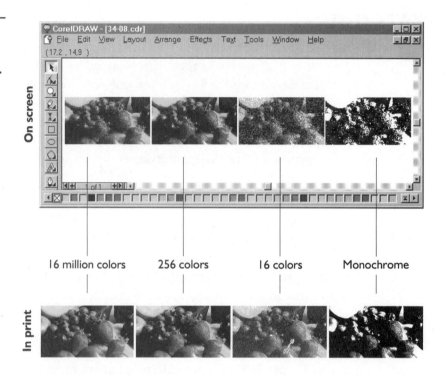

On screen

16 million colors   256 colors   16 colors   Monochrome

In print

You can rotate a bitmap, but… DRAW insists on showing you as much detail as it can, making for v-e-r-y s-l-o-w drawing times. So it's better to rotate the image before importing it. You can quell DRAW's high-resolution ways by toggling View / Bitmaps / High Resolution. Most DRAW users prefer to keep their display of bitmaps at high resolution and have their bitmaps rotated before they reach DRAW.

You can overlay objects on bitmaps, but… DRAW is not a paint program; it doesn't support transparent objects. Anything you place on top of a bitmap image covers that part of the image—the exception being objects that have transparent lenses applied.

Unless you have substantial field experience with color and grayscale printing, your best bet is to use bitmap images as backdrops to your drawings. Where bitmap images are concerned, the less fiddling, the better.

Bitmaps and Pieces

Here are a few odds and ends concerning bitmap images.

Lots of Dots, Lots of Data   Imported bitmaps can get big—in a hurry. Even if the file size isn't large, DRAW might need to move a mountain or two to import and display certain bitmap images. For instance, a TIFF file stored in the now-common compressed format might take up no more than 100K on your hard drive. But when you import it, DRAW uncompresses it, and the space requirements balloon to as much as four times the original size. The CDR file containing this bitmap will grow quite large, and DRAW will swipe an equally large chunk of space from your Windows TEMP directory.

Cropping with the Shape Tool   Bitmap images can be cropped in DRAW with no loss of fidelity. To crop a bitmap, select it and then choose the Shape tool. The selection handles around the image become cropping handles; by moving any one of them toward the middle of the image, you are essentially pulling a white window shade over the image. Cropping in CorelDRAW is not the same as cropping in PhotoPAINT. DRAW does not rescale the image; it only limits the portion that is visible.

Also, remember that you can apply a PowerClip to a bitmap, essentially stuffing it inside any other object. PowerClipping a bitmap inside of an irregular (nonrectangular) shape or inside of a piece of text is a very cool cropping effect, and to see it in action go to Chapter 12.

Cropping and clipping images in DRAW is convenient, but not efficient. It's not as if you have removed that part of the image—DRAW still holds it in memory and keeps track of all those dots. If you are working with large images, it would be better to crop the image in your image-editing program or use DRAW's Cropping option on the Import menu and then import the newly shorn image to DRAW. You'll get the most value out of cropping when you haven't yet decided how much image to use and are experimenting with different appearances. As we said, cropping is a tool of convenience.

Support for Separations   DRAW can import TIFF files that contain color-separation information. These so-called CMYK TIFF files are like ready-to-roll color files, with all process color information already separated. These special TIFF files used to be *persona non grata* with DRAW, but since 4.0, DRAW understands them and imports them.

Importing Linked Data

There's a more complete discussion about OLE in Chapter 31, but here is a preview and a look at how DRAW functions on the receiving end of the OLE operation.

It used to be simple—You copied from one program and pasted into another. That was all there was to the story. The data was perfectly content to travel hither and yon and drop itself into any program willing to accept it. Once it reached its destination, it completely forgot where it came from.

Not anymore. Today, data remembers its roots and can automatically return to its nest for a bit of rework. Data that remembers its source is the essence of OLE. Now things are more complicated, but also more powerful.

Servers and Clients

When a software manufacturer proclaims its program *OLE-compliant*, that means the program is able to function either as the source or the destination in an OLE exchange. In other words, it can supply data out across the Clipboard and be on call should the data need revising, or it can receive data from across the Clipboard and be able to make the call to the source program. Programs that can act as the source for linked data are called *servers;* these programs serve data to other programs. Programs that receive linked data are called *clients;* they are the programs to which data is served.

DRAW can function as a client or a server. It can be the source of hot-linked data, or it can receive the data. The dead giveaway of a program that is an OLE client is the Edit menu: If it offers a Paste Special command, then it is OLE-capable.

Creating an OLE Link

Creating an OLE link between two applications involves little more than a copy-and-paste across the Clipboard. To follow along with this procedure, you'll need to have Photo-PAINT installed on your system and have access to a bitmap file. If you can't readily locate one, you can use ROSE.PCX from the PRACTICE directory of the CD-ROM.

1. Start Photo-PAINT and open a bitmap image.

2. Using the Rectangular Masking tool (the tool second from the top in the PAINT toolbox), select a portion (any size) of the file.

3. Go to Edit / Copy to copy the selected part of the image to the Clipboard.

4. Close the image with File / Close, but don't exit PAINT. (This step isn't required, but it helps illustrate the OLE process; specifically, that the file is no longer open in PAINT.) Be sure to answer Yes when asked if you want to leave the contents of the Clipboard for other applications.

5. Next, start DRAW (or switch to DRAW if it is already running).

6. Go to Edit / Paste Special. You will see the dialog box shown in Figure 30.9. (If Paste Special is unavailable on your Edit menu, return to PAINT and repeat the first three steps of this procedure.)

7. Set the Paste Special options to match Figure 30.9 and click on OK in the dialog box.

Notice first that your image is shining out at you from DRAW, and second, that the status line refers to the image as a "CorelPhotoPaint-Image." In other words, DRAW understands that this object came from someplace else and, if necessary, knows how to get back there.

Editing a Linked Object

Once the link is established, setting OLE in motion involves nothing more than a double-click. If you decide that you need to make a change

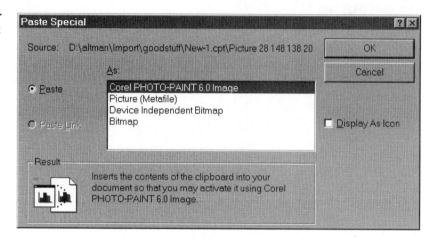

to your image, you don't have to bother reopening the file in Photo-PAINT and then reimporting it. Do this instead:

1. In DRAW, double-click on the image. DRAW starts to make a dramatic transformation. Notice that the title bar of the window now says Photo-PAINT 6 and displays the name of the DRAW file (or Graphic1 if you haven't saved yet). DRAW's menus, toolbars, and roll-ups have been replaced by the corresponding elements from PAINT. This is called *in-place editing*.

2. Make a change to the image, any change at all—even a big white eraser mark through it.

3. To get back to DRAW, click anywhere outside of the object.

PAINT knows that it is in the middle of an OLE operation, so it isn't interested in saving the file, but rather in *updating the object that is stored in the DRAW file* (a subtle distinction, we agree, but an important one to the OLE procedure). You now see all of DRAW's menus and toolbars and the change to the image.

Linked Files and Embedded Objects

There are two distinct types of data that an OLE client can receive: *linked files* and *embedded objects*. When DRAW received the image from Photo-PAINT in the foregoing exercise, DRAW gave you a choice (via the Paste Special dialog) of how it would treat the incoming data. DRAW can either swallow up a copy of the image for itself and be completely self-sufficient in handling this file, or it can link itself to the original file. Most programs call these two choices Paste Object and Paste Link; DRAW calls them Paste and Paste Link. If you select Edit / Paste or press Ctrl+V, you get the default, which is Paste Object. The Paste Special dialog, however, gives you all the possible choices of pasting an object into DRAW.

To understand OLE, you must first understand this: When an OLE server copies a picture to the Clipboard, it copies more than just the graphical information required by the client for printing. It also copies

- The name of the program that produced the graphic
- The name and full path to the graphic file
- The data that makes up the original file

On the receiving end, an OLE client provides you with several choices of how to accept the data (listed in the Paste Special dialog). You can always ask to paste just the picture with no link information at all; just switch the selection in the Paste Special dialog to Metafile, Device Independent Bitmap, or Bitmap.

Whereas the default choice Paste embeds an *object* into DRAW, choosing Paste Link creates a *link* between the image in DRAW and the original file. These two OLE choices are quite different, and their differences become especially apparent when you want to edit the image later.

If you paste the graphic image as a standard metafile or bitmap, the image comes in cold and limp, with no idea of its source. You can double-click on that graphic until the next solar eclipse and you won't get back to the source.

Editing a Linked File

When you double-click an image that was pasted as a linked file, you trigger a series of events for which Windows plays referee. Your double-click acts as an announcement:

> *DRAW (client):* "Hey Windows, I need to do some editing. Take care of this for me, will you?"

> *Windows:* "I'm checking my big black book, and I see here that the image you want to edit was pasted as a linked file. The file name is SCAN.TIF, it was produced in Photo-PAINT, and it was stored in your D:\IMAGES directory. I'll launch PAINT and open SCAN.TIF for you. When you're done editing, issue a Save command, and the image in your DRAW file will update immediately."

This is really no different from going through the motions yourself, but being spared those motions is a great convenience. When you are done editing the original file in the source program, a Save command performs the equivalent of your copying the image to the Clipboard, switching to DRAW, and pasting the image. OLE takes care of all of that for you automatically.

Editing an Embedded Object

This process is different from editing a linked file. An embedded object doesn't need an original file—everything needed to view, print, *and edit* the file is contained in the object: It's like a mini-original file. In this case, your double-click initiates the following dialogue:

> *DRAW (client):* "Hey Windows, I need to do some editing. Take care of this for me, will you?"

> *Windows:* "I'm checking my big black book, and I see here that the image you want to edit was pasted as an embedded object. Therefore, I won't try to find an original file; I just need to make sure I can open the program that created it. I'm switching to the Photo-PAINT in-place editing mode right now. There. When you're done, click anywhere outside of the embedded image in your drawing and I'll get you back to your DRAW session."

We like to think of it this way: With a linked file, Photo-PAINT still owns the image. Its fate is tied to that original file. But with an embedded object, DRAW owns the image. Everything necessary to view, print, and edit it is contained in the object.

Rules of Thumb for Linked vs. Embedded

Although both methods of using OLE offer you the editing convenience of the double-click, the rules of thumb for usage of the two techniques are different.

Use linked files when you want to maintain control of an original file. Perhaps you have an organization chart that you have pasted from VISIO into several drawings. The chart might change, and if it does, it's important that the change be reflected across all of the drawings that use it. If you have pasted the chart as a linked file, changing that original will automatically change every occurrence of it throughout your drawings.

Use embedded objects when you want independent control over an image. If you're going to paste 25 charts from VISIO and you want each one to have its own destiny, then paste them as objects. In this case there is no original file—changing one pasted image has no impact on any of the others, because each one is an independent object.

It's a good idea to use an embedded object when you are sending a drawing to users on different systems. If you gave a drawing with a linked file to a colleague, he or she would not be able to edit the linked image without also having the source file. But, as emphasized earlier, the embedded object needs no original file; everything required for editing is contained in the object. Your colleague would have to have the original application that created the object, but that's all.

DRAW's Role in OLE

You won't often need DRAW to act as the client in an OLE operation. Most graphics imported into DRAW can be changed from within

DRAW, obviating the need for DRAW to trace a graphic back to its source for changes. Just above, you stepped through the most common scenario under which DRAW plays client: when an imported *bitmap* image needs to go back for rework.

DRAW is more active as an OLE partner when it acts as server, not client. After all, one of DRAW's missions in life is to supply graphics to documents in other programs. That topic will be one of the highlights of the next freeway exit, "Exporting from DRAW"—but the news there is not all good.

CHAPTER

31

Exporting from DRAW

THIRTY-ONE

31

At long last, we've come to the final chapter in the CorelDRAW section of this book. Our guess is that after 30 chapters and some five gazillion pages, the last thing you want to read is a long, exhaustive treatise covering more than you care to know about exporting files. And after *writing* five gazillion pages, we don't particularly feel like throwing anything heavy at you, either.

That means we have chosen the perfect topic to end this book, because we think the best way to cover the topic of exporting is to show you, rather than just tell you. If you want to learn about the science of file filters, come to one of our conferences and corner an engineer. If you want to actually *write* a filter, you have our deepest sympathies. If you simply want to determine which format works best, read on.

Those of you who produce and print your artwork entirely within DRAW won't be interested in this chapter—thank you for coming, and please leave by the exits. The other 99% of you regularly, perhaps constantly, produce work that is designed to be incorporated into something else: a letter in your word processor, a brochure in PageMaker, a logo in Ventura Publisher, a background for a chart, or one of hundreds of other types of drawings that will find their way into other documents. The export questions you face are among the most salient of all, and this chapter is for you.

Choose Your Weapon

Here is the first question: What format should you use to export your work? At the risk of oversimplification, we intend to considerably narrow this field. If you're producing art designed to be used in another Windows program, we recommend you limit your choices to three:

- Encapsulated PostScript (EPS)
- Windows Metafile (WMF)
- The Clipboard

We maintain that there are few exceptions to this rule. If you have a PostScript printer, you can't go wrong with EPS. In our tests, EPS came in at or near the top in all categories: output quality, speed of export, size of file, time needed to spool to the printer, and time to print. Because of its flexibility in accommodating halftones, EPS is also the best equipped to handle such demanding elements as bitmap images, fine grays, fountain fills, and blends. If you read no further in this chapter—if you stop here and conclude that you will export all of your work as Encapsulated PostScript—then you will do just fine.

If you don't have a PostScript printer, there is still hope for you. In fact, DRAW 6.0 continues to offer the same "next-best solution" as version 5. This is the WMF format and, to a lesser degree, the various Clipboard options. All produce good results, each with its own benefits and drawbacks.

In general, use of all the other formats should be limited to specialty assignments—for example, CGM for sending files to some slide services, HPGL for creating work destined for a plotter, DXF files for work going into AutoCAD, and PCX or TIFF for sending artwork as bitmap images.

The Fourth Annual Export Torture Test

Submitted for your approval, the illustration in Figure 31.1 was created for our now-famous annual test of DRAW's exporting prowess. This is the fourth one; the first test was performed in late 1992 with DRAW 3, the second one in 1993 with DRAW 4, and the third in the DRAW 5 edition of this book in 1994.

3 I . I

**The subject of this
chapter's exporting
test**

The calendar design comes from artist Billie Gist and produced several elements that we think are indicative of a file filter's accuracy:

■ We blended the outlines around the month and year, to give them a glowing look. If an export format can't handle shifts in tone of at least 5%, the effect will be lost.

- For the days of the month, we changed to Geometric 231, a typeface with very fine lines and loopy curves—both potentially taxing on some file formats.

- Behind the calendar, we placed a conical fountain fill with several transitions between white and 20% black. These transitions are challenging to all file formats.

- The wheel is composed of .25-point hairlines. How well will they be rendered?

- The top and side of the cube are filled with graduated tones of gray. The top side has an extremely subtle shade that may be too subtle for many formats.

- The jet is an imported bitmap image; most formats simply ignore it.

- Finally, all these elements have been placed inside a PowerClip. Will the various file formats honor the clipping path?

If you would like to conduct your own tests, you will find this file (TORTURE1.CDR) in the PRACTICE directory. It is a 714K file, and requires that you install the Geometric 231 Heavy and Light typefaces from Corel's library (or you'll need to set the calendar days, dates, month, and year in different faces).

We exported this composite drawing from DRAW in nine different formats, including across the Clipboard, and recorded the size of the file and how long it took DRAW to create it. Then we printed each one from PageMaker 5.0 and from Ventura Publisher 5. Because there are fundamental differences between the two applications that are too numerous to go into here, we've decided to report the timing and file size results from PageMaker. This narrows the focus to comparing file format differences rather than on the performance of each page layout program. In general, we can say that each program did accept the various exported files, and each produced a printed page. If we found a drastic difference in the way one application handled a particular file format, we have made note of it in the paragraphs about that specific format. Unless otherwise noted, all output samples in this chapter are from PageMaker 5.0.

For each export, we recorded the time needed to send the print job to Print Manager; we refer to this as "Time to Spool" in the following table. This is the time elapsed between pressing the Print button and regaining control of your application. The "Time to Print" figure expresses how long it took from pressing the Print button until the printer started up, ready to image the page. Most importantly, of course, we evaluated the quality of the output. Table 31.1 lists the time and size statistics for each format.

Table 31.1: Export Formats and Their Performance Records

FORMAT	TIME TO EXPORT	FILE SIZE	TIME TO SPOOL	SIZE OF PRINTER DATA	TIME TO PRINT
CGM	:52	418K	:15	719K	1:43
AutoCAD	1:50	5,996K	:10	593K	1:35
EPS	:18	2,615K	:17	2,678K	2:03
GEM:	:24	537K	6:09	15,330K	33:15
HPGL	1:45	1,390K	1:00	732K	2:45
PCX	2:52	337K	:21	4,627K	3:04
TIF	2:50	6,761K	:20	4,647K	3:10
WMF	:13	362K	:45	2,153K	4:50
OLE	:05	2,421K	:50	2,144K	4:52

When copying across the Clipboard, we determined file size by saving the data as a CLP file, using the Clipboard utility supplied with Windows 95. All testing was performed on a 486-66 computer with 32MB of RAM, printing to a QMS 860 running in PostScript mode.

If you cross-reference the above information with the corresponding table from *Mastering CorelDRAW 5.0*, you'll notice that the majority of "Time to Export" times have increased and the resultant file sizes have grown larger. This is largely due to the "smarter" export functions that try to create the intermediate steps of the blend applied to the month and year of the calendar. Last year's "dumb" export functions didn't even attempt to render the steps. We'll leave it up to your eye as to which you prefer.

CGM

The first thing you'll notice about the CGM file, shown in Figure 31.2, is the missing picture of the jet. Most vector formats are unable to integrate bitmap images, so we were not particularly alarmed or shocked by the jet's absence. Though there is visible banding in the conical fill and the cube's shade, it is well within our definition of reasonable. This year the CGM file behaved much better compared to last year. Last year, the blend effect on the month and year came out completely black; this year they are much better represented.

Now take a look at Figure 31.3; this is the same CGM file brought into Corel Ventura 5.0. This demonstrates just how important it is that the importing functions of a receiving application are on the same wavelength as the exporting functions of CorelDRAW. In the Ventura printout, the month and year are a jumble of black outlines with no fills (this also explains why version 6's CGM file is drastically larger than version 5's), and the shaded fills in the cube have turned into a strange pattern. Only if you grew up in the seventies could you love the psychedelic effect applied to the conical fountain fill.

Our conclusion: From PageMaker 5, CGM survives the torture test and in fact performs better than in previous years. However, if you are using Ventura 5, it would be hard to give this file format a passing grade. On the plus side, there is no longer much need to use this format. Most professional slide services now work with PostScript files or original

3 1 . 2

This CGM file printed from Page-Maker produces acceptable fountain fills but distorted outlines.

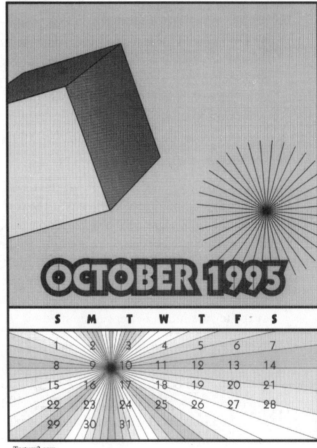

Torture2.cgm

application files. The only use we see for CGM is for communicating with an older slide shop that uses out-of-date equipment or for sending art to a non-Windows program that has limited import options.

DXF

This well-known AutoCAD flavor produced a much larger file than last year. After looking at Figure 31.4, we ask: What was gained?

31.3

This CGM file printed from Corel Ventura 5 is in pretty bad shape.

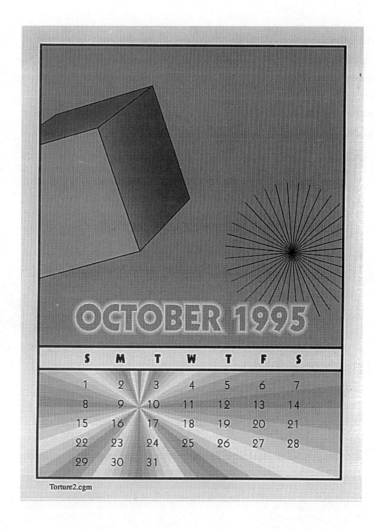

Torture2.cgm

We won't spend too much time harping on these imperfections, because in all fairness, the DXF filter is not designed for this type of use. Choose it only when you want to send a DRAW image directly into AutoCAD or a compatible program. Clearly, DXF is not designed for conventional work. Last year Ventura wouldn't even load the file; this year it swallowed it happily and took a little under four minutes to spit out almost the same disappointingly poor image as PageMaker.

3 1 . 4

The AutoCAD DXF format is not designed for exporting from DRAW to standard applications.

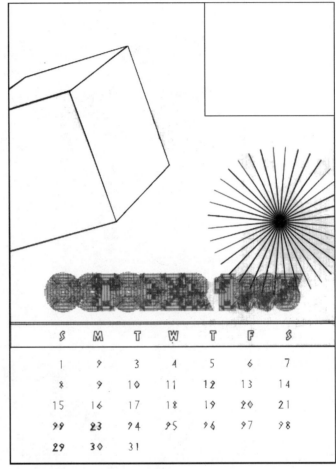

torture2.dxf

EPS

The overall winner, for the fourth year in a row, is Encapsulated Post-Script, and we won't be surprised if by the year 2000 it has stretched its string of victories to nine years in a row. The EPS filter produced 2.6MB of code in just 18 seconds, and the resultant file was equally efficient when making its way through Print Manager and to the laser printer. Amazingly, these are exactly the same timings that were recorded in last year's Torture test.

Again, output was crisp and superb from both programs, and as Figure 31.5 shows, the EPS file handled everything we threw at it, including the jet. It is the only vector-based format to accept bitmaps.

31.5

The winner and still champion: Encapsulated PostScript

As discussed in Chapter 30, applications such as PageMaker and Ventura cannot read an EPS file and produce an on-screen image from it; instead, they rely on a bitmap image that is commonly embedded within the EPS code. DRAW calls it an *image header*. You don't have to include a header, but if you do, DRAW 6.0 offers a wide variety of resolution and color-depth options. The options you select can have a significant effect on export time and file size. The times and sizes shown in the list below are for just the PostScript file with no preview image. Here is what happens if you include an image header:

Header	Time to Export	Size of File
72 dpi/black and white	0:28	2,632K
72 dpi/4-bit gray	0:47	2,680K
72dpi/4-bit color	0:50	2,680K
72dpi/8-bit gray	0:47	2,745K
72dpi/8-bit color	0:52	2,746K
150-dpi/8-bit color	1:20	3,192K

So what's the catch with EPS? There are two: You must have a PostScript printer in order to print these files, and screen clarity will be much poorer than what you get out of your printer. Last year, there were problems with preview images displaying in Ventura. Ventura 5 users will be happy to know that all the DRAW 6.0-generated EPS files with image headers show up fine. However, there are definite problems for PageMaker users. The only image previews that don't show up as gray or black bounding boxes are black-and-white and 8-bit gray.

Corel added another option to the EPS export functionality: incorporating an image header in the WMF file format rather than TIFF. This was very much requested, because the preview image provided by WMF objects is much better on the monitor. Well, Corel giveth and Corel taketh away, it seems. First, the file size of an EPS that incorporated a WMF header grew to 3.2MB. Then both PageMaker 5 and Ventura 5 had problems importing the file. Ventura rejected it completely and Page-Maker displayed only a gray box. Hopefully, Corel will have a maintenance release that fixes all these annoyances by the time you read this.

Our conclusion: PostScript printer owners should use EPS files for all conventional exporting to other applications. The only exception might be to take advantage of the convenience of OLE, discussed later in the chapter.

GEM

Our tests with the virtually obsolete GEM format were interesting, to say the least. Compared with last year's mediocre showing, this year the format is a disaster. Ventura handled the GEM file better than Page-Maker, but that's to be expected considering that GEM and Ventura started life together many years ago. One of the largest differences was the amount of data spooled off to Print Manager. Ventura kicked out 2,189K of instructions that took just under 5 minutes to image. Page-Maker didn't take the 8 hours it did last year, but it did take 33 minutes and 15MB of information to construct a really bad-looking image. We still conclude GEM is a huge time-waster. The resulting image shown in Figure 31.6 is from Ventura 5.

HPGL

Like DXF, the HPGL format is for specialty jobs, and the fact that the output from PageMaker and Ventura is unacceptable carries extenuating circumstances. As Figure 31.7 shows, all objects are rendered as outlines—there are no fill patterns at all. HPGL files are designed to be sent to plotters, and producing lines is exactly what a plotter is designed to do.

In other words, we can't blame the messenger for this bad news; the messenger was given a wrong street address and told to deliver the wrong package. Our torture test is simply not representative of the type of work you would send to a plotter. Plotters don't do fills, and they certainly don't do bitmaps. Therefore, we exonerate the HPGL format from all charges brought against it and, in conclusion, recommend you

31.6

**The old GEM
format, sunk to
a new low**

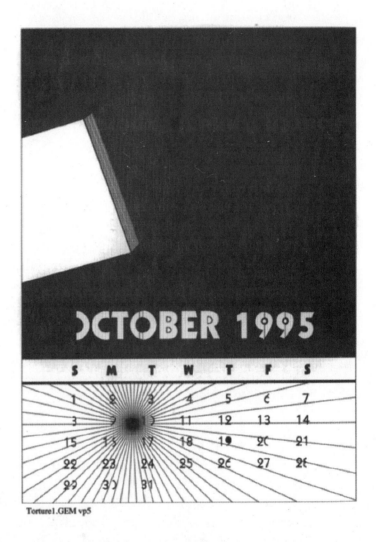

Torture1.GEM vp5

use HPGL files only when sending work directly to a plotter. One difference this year was that DRAW's HPGL filter attempted to render the
blends in the month and year. The attempt was honorable, but the result hardly justified the effort. It bloated the file significantly, yet the
output quality suffered anyway.

31.7

Use HPGL files when seeking output from a plotter.

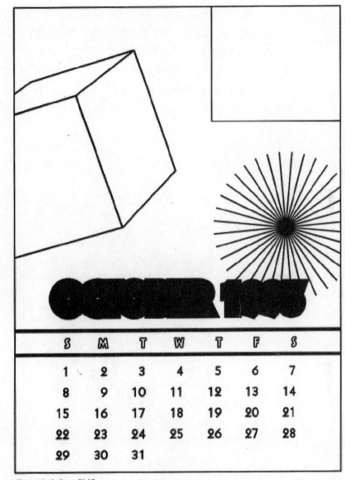

Torture1.plt from PM5

PCX and TIFF

We have heard stories of users exporting all of their work in bitmapped format, just to avoid using the more complex printer commands and instructions that have been known to produce printer errors. We understand that cutting off your nose to spite your face is also an option. Sorry, but the thought of producing vector images by describing every single dot that occurs on a page is too much for us to imagine.

Figure 31.8 shows the result of exporting a 256-color PCX file and printing it from PageMaker or Ventura. Ventura took its sweet time (over ten minutes), but PageMaker pumped it out in three. The secret to this discrepancy is the amount of data sent off by each app: Ventura's 18MB versus PageMaker's 4.6MB. The quality of the PCX export was better than that produced in DRAW 5. The previously lost shading in the blends and fountain fills is better now, but still exhibits extreme

3 1 . 8

As with all bitmaps, PCX files have finite resolution and number of colors. In this case, both sets of numbers are lacking.

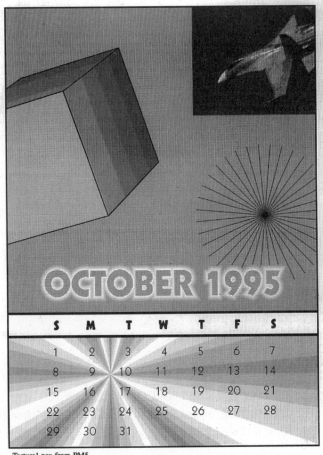

Torture1.pcx from PM5

banding. However, both of them fell down miserably in the calendar's fine type, which does not hold up to even moderate scrutiny. This is the result of a print file that is fixed at 300 dpi. When we created a 600-dpi bitmap instead, it took almost 19 minutes to export from DRAW 6.0 and the quality of the fountain fills and blends was no better!

We created the TIFF file with 16 million colors instead of 256, and the 6.7MB file that DRAW churned out gave us a hint that something voluminous was developing. Indeed, Figure 31.9 shows the dramatically better shading achieved by adding all of those colors, but alas, the text still looks like something a 300-dpi printer dragged in. We shudder to think of the file size had we created the image at 16 million colors *and* 600 dpi. Even then, the more curved parts of the drawing would not be much competition for the crisp 1,200-dpi (or even 2,500-dpi) output possible from the vector formats.

DRAW 6.0 also offers a 32-bit, CMYK TIFF option. Choosing this will increase your file size by 33% and it won't make your image look better, but it is necessary for getting proper CMYK color separations from programs like PageMaker 5. Sixteen million colors always equals an RGB TIFF (sometimes referred to as a *24-bit TIFF*). A CMYK TIFF is called a *32-bit TIFF*.

Our conclusion is that these two formats are best used for producing bitmap images that can then be brought into a paint program (not a page-layout program) for modification. There is no other legitimate value in converting high-resolution vector objects into fixed-resolution bitmap images.

WMF

We must start by pointing out that we prefer WMF over all other formats discussed so far (except EPS). Metafile is clean, compact, well supported, and widely embraced. Figure 31.10 is an example of what it can do. And if you don't have a PostScript printer, WMF files will help keep you from feeling like a second-class citizen.

31.9

This TIFF image has better tonal value than the PCX, but resolution is unimproved. The fine text does not survive close inspection.

Torture1.tif from PM5

Our primary disappointment with WMF this year is an echo of last year: the loss of bitmap support that we were delighted to find in 1993. With this one notable exception, we can recommend WMF as your export format of choice if you do not have a PostScript printer or you don't want to use the Clipboard. Overall, WMF passes our tests here with higher marks than any other file format, except EPS.

31.10

Output from the WMF file is very good, but alas, without support for bitmaps it's just not as universal as EPS.

tort256 wmf from pm5

The Promise of Object Linking and Embedding

In 1993, we wrote that OLE was a "major disappointment for us... PageMaker refused to print the test file, and Ventura printed only the large lettering and a black box where the [bitmap] is supposed to go."

Last year we were much more impressed, and so stated: "We had outstanding success moving our drawing back and forth between DRAW and PageMaker, Ventura, Word for Windows, and other applications, maintaining full editability and getting precisely the behavior we expected each time."

Well, this year has brought us Windows 95 and a set of new circumstances. We are much less enamored with OLE and DRAW 6.0 this time around. It's not that it doesn't work at all; it's just that it doesn't work consistently.

Figure 31.11 illustrates that Clipboard transfers still lack bitmap support, but also have a tendency to lose vital information, such as maintaining the highest number of shading levels in the conical fountain fill. There was one area where we did find consistency: whether we pasted a static Metafile, embedded an object, or created a link to a file, the output results were 50 seconds to spool from PageMaker, 2,187K of print data created, and 4.5 minutes to print.

They say that if you don't succeed, you've got to try, try again. Well, we did just that with OLE. Figure 31.12 demonstrates another route we took. We started in PageMaker and selected Insert Object from the Edit menu. Next, we chose CorelDRAW 6.0 Graphic from the list of eligible OLE objects and when DRAW 6.0 popped up, we chose to import TORTURE1.CDR (making sure that we specifically chose the CorelDRAW filter from the drop-down list). The image did arrive, but the results from OLE and DRAW 6.0 remained uneven and unreliable, no matter what we tried.

We tried OLE functions with Word for Windows 6.0. Again, we observed strange happenings that just couldn't be defined with any consistency. One of the oddest effects involved the color palette in DRAW, which was always getting corrupted. This corruption affected the palette, as well as other on-screen objects.

31.11

OLE enthusiasts will probably be disappointed with the Windows 95 Clipboard and **DRAW** 6.0 combination. This printout was the result of a copy-and-paste between **DRAW** and PageMaker 5. Take a look at the banding in the calendar area and the cube extrusion.

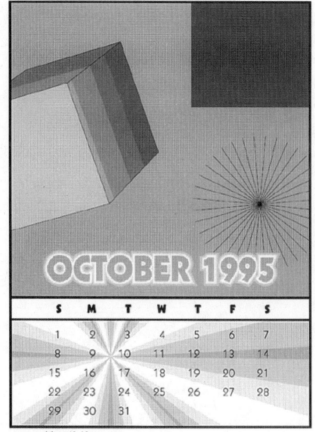

paste special as cd6 object

Will it be as unstable for you? We hope not. Would a different hardware and software configuration make it any better? Not that we can tell. We conducted this torture test on a PC with 32MB of RAM and allowed Windows 95 to manage its own swap file space. However, we think it's safe to say that OLE operations with DRAW 6.0 will probably not be reliable until Microsoft or Corel figures out who's at fault and then does something about it in the way of a maintenance release.

31.12

We really did try to give OLE the benefit of the doubt. This second attempt to embed a DRAW 6.0 object had even worse problems than copying and pasting via the Clipboard.

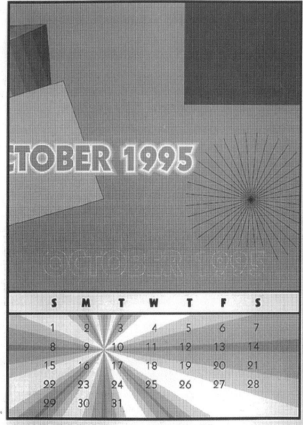

Insert object/Corel6 Graphic/Import/Torture1.cdr printedfrom PM5

| **What the Heck Is a CMX File?** | Since DRAW 5, Corel has created its own little information highway among the CorelDRAW applications, and the vehicles that travel this expressway are called *Presentation Exchange Data*. Logic would dictate that the file name extension for this creature should have been PED, but instead it is CMX. |

What the Heck Is a CMX File? (continued)

A CMX file resembles an efficient, compressed CDR file. It contains only the information necessary to render a drawing, without any of the layers, grid information, or other elements not crucial to the drawing. You may have already noticed that all of the clip art on the CorelDRAW CD is stored in CMX format.

There are two ways to interact with CMX data. The most obvious is to use the Export command and choose Corel Presentation Exchange to create a self-contained CMX file. You'll be able to import this into any Corel application that supports CMX. The second approach is less obvious: You may have noticed the Save Presentation Exchange Data option at the lower-right corner of the Save As dialog. With this option enabled, you save extra CMX data inside your CDR file.

Corel hopes to use CMX as the universal file-exchange language within CorelDRAW applications and, ideally, beyond. As the theory goes, if you include the extra Presentation Exchange Data in your drawing, then other Corel applications will be able to import your CDR files directly, pick out the essential graphical information, and produce a high-fidelity copy of your work.

Corel now has two versions of the CMX format: version 5 and version 6. The higher version is supposed to be a new 32-bit format and therefore is not readable by DRAW 5. So, be careful which format you export to if you want to bring the drawing into DRAW 5. DRAW 6.0 *can* read a version 5 CMX.

An exported CMX file is definitely smaller than a corresponding CDR. That's why Corel has chosen to distribute its clip art in CMX format. When we took our 714K TORTURE1.CDR file and exported it to CMX (6), the resulting

What the Heck Is a CMX File? (continued)

file was only 360K. Saving as a version 5 CMX gave us a 340K file. When we saved TORTURE1.CDR with the Presentation Exchange Data option turned off, the CDR file size shrank to a paltry 365K.

Before you think that saving as CMX rather than CDR is the key to capturing disk space, be warned. The CMX file disassembles some effects (such as blends) that are much, much easier to edit when left in CDR format. It's like trying to fix a spelling error in a passage of text that you have already converted to curves.

So how did other Corel 6.0 applications handle importing CMXs of our TORTURE1.CDR? PAINT did very well. PRESENTS failed badly. We threw both versions of CMX (5 and 6) and CDR (with and without PED) at PRESENTS, and nothing came in except the gray background. At this stage of the game, even DRAW had problems reimporting its own CMXs. One consistent offender was the control type on the month and year, which separated from the blends and moved out of position by a very noticeable amount.

Considering that most Corel 6.0 applications are now able to import the CDR format directly, it's hard to find a reason to enthusiastically recommend a situation where a CMX offers any unique value. Saving CDR files with PED consumes a lot more disk space and offers only two advantages that we could see. The first is that CDRs with PED import substantially faster than those without. The second is that Photo-PAINT can accurately tell the size of an incoming graphic and so creates a new bitmap image at optimal dimensions.

Summarizing the Torture Test

The safest, most reliable, and highest-fidelity method of transferring data from DRAW to other applications is via an Encapsulated Post-Script file. If you have a PostScript printer and you want to make sure you are working with peak accuracy, use EPS files—end of discussion.

If you do not have a PostScript printer, however, and you don't have bitmapped images contained in your DRAW files, export to WMF files. If you are staying within the Corel family of applications, or going out to one of the growing selection of programs offering a CMX import, try CMX as a non-PostScript option and see how it fares.

Last year we concluded this chapter with these words: "We certainly appreciate being able to finish the DRAW section of this book on a more upbeat note than in our 1993 book.... As of 5.0, DRAW's ability to communicate with the rest of the Windows community [via OLE] should earn it a good citizen award." It seems that things come in cycles, even the downside of advancing to new technologies; some call this "the bleeding edge." Most every export option available in DRAW 6.0 worked as reliably as in version 5; however the feeling of déjà vu we got regarding OLE's instability causes us to again end this year's Exporting chapter on a downbeat.

PART VIII

THE SUPPORTING CAST

We knew that this part of the book would be the source of much discussion and debate—among us authors, and between us and the publishers. The central question: What to do about the other modules in the CorelDRAW package—Photo-PAINT, DREAM3D, PRESENTS, et al. How much space do we devote to a collection of programs that see significantly less use than DRAW? (Some DRAW users have barely heard of the new PRESENTS, for instance, while others know it inside and out.)

Is it our responsibility to encourage Corel users to learn these other modules? If it's outside the scope of this book to cover the other modules in detail, then how do we handle them? Tutorials? Overviews? Coverage of new features? What good is a tutorial if you aren't interested in learning the program? And what good is an overview if you already know what the program does? There were lots of questions…

In the chapters of Part VIII, we attempt to give a little bit to everyone. With a solid overview, a bit of tutorial, and close attention to new features as of version 6.0, we hope to deliver to you an informed perspective of how these modules operate, who might use them, and how *you* might use them.

The New Photo-PAINT

Just as CorelDRAW puts some of the world's most powerful drawing and illustrating tools at your fingertips, Photo-PAINT gives you the power of a state-of-the-art photo lab combined with the tools and supplies of a university art department.

Here's an example: Within the Brush dialog and the Tool Settings roll-up for the Paint tool, you have access to a remarkable assortment of over 1,397,760,000,000,000,000,000,000 colored pencils. The selection of paintbrushes, airbrush nozzles, spray cans, chalks, pastels, pens, and markers is equally varied. And even if none of these suits a particular need, you can build even more tools on your own. You also have control over the type of paper or other medium on which you work. In addition, you can guide the interaction between your art and medium with their virtual universe, as well as all the elements in your images.

Digital images are composed of and defined by numbers. Each picture you see on your screen—from those nifty screensavers to every single dialog box in an application—is a collection of values and equations governing color, luminosity, hue, dimension, and so on. A vector image is defined in equations governing the shape, size, and color of objects; in a bitmapped image, on the other hand, the data quantifies the color and intensity of every pixel it contains. When you can control and alter that data, you can control and alter any picture in almost any conceivable way. The purpose of Photo-PAINT and of other paint and photo applications is to give you access to those equations and data in an understandable, easy-to-utilize environment.

First Things First

Before we begin, following are several definitions that we should get out of the way.

AUTHOR'S NOTE

If you need to increase your knowledge of concepts such as file formats, color models, and color theory—things that are very important to how PAINT does its work—they are well covered elsewhere in this book. Take a look at Part VII.

Tolerance is the term used whenever a tool, function, or effect is set for a color and mathematically similar colors. Tolerance is invariably a range. The software identifies the pixels that fall within the tolerance range by comparing the color of each pixel to the given color and evaluating their similarity. Tolerance values, when needed, are defined by entering the desired range or indicating it by moving a slide bar. The higher the tolerance, the more colors are included in the effect.

Paint mode is new in PAINT 6.0 and is also called Paint and Merge in some roll-ups. The paint mode is the way that your paint, line, or object is applied to the image. There are 20 paint modes available in a 24-bit image. The function of some, such as Normal, Inverse, If Darker, and If Lighter, are quite obvious. The Red, Green, or Blue modes add only in those channels. Experiment with the different modes to get familiar with them.

INSIDE INFO

You'll find that combining modes with variations of transparency can provide some great ghost and shadow effects.

Depth is the bit-depth of the image (1-, 4-, 8-, 24-, or 32-bit). The higher the bit-depth, the more colors the image can contain (and the larger the finished file is likely to be). In PAINT, 24-bit and 32-bit color images work best; 8-bit grayscale is best for black-and-white images. Although the 24- and 32-bit images give the best results when you're applying the tools and effects, PAINT works very well with other types of images, too. If you want to use special effects in an image that will ultimately be, say, an 8-bit, 256-color image, try converting it to 24-bit while you are working with it, and then back to 8-bit when you're done.

Channels are the individual color components used by a particular color model to define the color of each pixel in an image. An RGB image can be separated into red, green, and blue channels. In a CMYK image, each of the four channels are ultimately used to create a plate each for cyan, magenta, yellow, and black. For our purposes, a channel is also the graphical (image) representation of this data on the desktop. Channels used in this way can be altered much as a normal black-and-white image would be, and then recombined into a full-color image. RGB color is additive and CMYK color is subtractive, so an area of all red will show as white on an RGB red channel, and as black on the yellow and magenta channels of a CMYK image.

The *palette* is the collection of colors currently in use in the image. These may be the colors of the image set to palette form, PANTONE spot or process colors, or a custom palette taken from disk.

The *image* is the bitmapped or raster file currently open and selected on the desktop.

The *desktop*, for our purposes, is the active working area of the PAINT window, as shown in Figure 32.1.

The Raw Materials

As discussed in the very first chapter of this book, there are two types of computer graphics: vector objects and bitmapped images. A vector file is a series of equations that govern the size, color, and other particulars of each object in a drawing. This makes the objects easy to resize, allows use of standard and uniform shapes, and keeps the file size comparatively small. But it also makes fine, micro-alterations to the drawing more difficult.

3 2 . 1

The Photo-PAINT desktop

Bitmapped images, on the other hand, contain data for every pixel in the image. These images require more computer memory, but they are easier to alter and enhance on a small scale.

Of Formats and File Types

Bitmap images come in several formats and file types. The formats include

- 1-bit monochrome (2 colors; that is, 1 color and 1 no-color)

- 4-bit/16-color

- 8-bit grayscale (256 shades of gray)

- Duo-/tri-/quad-tone

- 24-bit, 256-color "truevision" or true-color (RGB model and others)

- 32-bit, high-depth images

With the smaller bit-depths, you trade less-realistic color for a smaller, more manageable file size, as shown in the following table:

Bits	Colors	Bytes in a 640x480 Image
1 (B & W)	2	37.5K
4	16	150K
8	256	300K
24 (True-color)	16,777,216	900K
32 (High-color)	4,294,967,296	1,200K

PAINT's File / Open dialog offers over 30 specific file types. Among the popular bitmap file types are

- Windows and OS/2 Bitmap (BMP)
- Paintbrush (PCX)
- CompuServe Graphics Interchange Format (GIF)
- Tagged Image File Format (TIF, TIFF)
- Targa (TGA)

Each file type has its own advantages and disadvantages, and the study of which type is best for what task has been the subject of more than one thick book. The most significant differences are in the types of image compression used and the resulting file size, detail, and/or color loss.

AUTHOR'S NOTE

For most of you, the most important consideration for your choice of file type is that not all of PAINT's effects will work on all file types or color depths. When you access the Effects menu and find all or many of its options grayed out and unavailable, you'll need to experiment with some other file types. Converting to RGB color (24-bit) from the Image menu gives you access to all the effects PAINT has to offer, but the image will usually look a little washed out on your screen.

Why Use PAINT?

Because of the differences between a vector file and a bitmap file, many effects and operations are impractical in a vector-based drawing program, no matter how powerful it might be. Enter Photo-PAINT.

Without argument, CorelDRAW's Lens, Blend, duplication, and manipulation tools give the program awesome imaging power, and a good deal of the world's most beautiful computer-based images come from the DRAW desktop. Many others, though, have been created with a combination of tools, including DRAW, Photo-PAINT, TRACE, natural media, and other software. Corel's alliance of tools and capabilities gives you creative force that few other graphics suites can approach, and that no other single application or suite of applications can match.

No small portion of the power in this alliance comes from PAINT and its broad array of image-editing and creative tools. DRAW illustrations can be made more photo-realistic in PAINT. Dynamic and fanciful effects can be added. Shadows, transparencies, softening of focus, color effects, and more are at your fingertips. Easily deserving of an entire book on its own, some of PAINT's most useful and fun abilities are covered here in this chapter.

What's New in Version 6.0

The migration of the Corel graphics suite to the 32-bit environment of Windows 95 and Windows NT brings a host of changes to most of the applications in the box. Right mouse-button support will save you hours in trips to the menus and toolbars. Substantial customization options for the work environment help you make the program truly your own. Go ahead and place those tools where you want them, remove some and add others, redefine keyboard shortcuts so you can remember them more easily…you can even change the function and tool names and buttons as you like. And, of course, there is the promise of better performance.

The changes made in PAINT version 6.0 not only enhance and increase its strengths as an image-editing tool, but go a long way toward making

PAINT a cutting-edge artist's tool for original creative work. Here are a few key items:

- Improved OLE 2 support
- Variable paint modes
- Movie and animation editing tools and controls
- Enhanced masking and object tools and controls
- Stronger image, format, and file conversion tools
- Grid and snap-to functions
- Text and word processing tools
- Over two dozen new Effects dialogs, bringing the total to 77
- Improved controls and preview functions for Effects
- A Paint Alchemy tool, with over 70 preset effects
- Fractal (Julia Set) Explorer 2.0 from HSC Inc. and Kai's Power Tools
- New lighting effects
- A new User-Defined effect

The remaining sections of this chapter give you first an overview of the tools and functions common to all PAINT tasks. Next is a section on some of the new special-effects capabilities, including examples. There's a section on using PAINT with DRAW or other applications, and finally a few notes on natural media emulation in electronic art.

AUTHOR'S NOTE

All of the images used in this chapter are available from either your CorelDRAW 6.0 CDs or this book's Companion CD (in the subdirectories of PRACTICE\IMAGES\PP). In addition, the CD contains some presets and canvases that you can import to your PAINT directories to give you even more options.

Welcome to the Studio

As you embark on this tour of the Photo-PAINT studio, remember that the user interface in PAINT is fully customizable—just as it is in DRAW and the other applications in the Corel suite. (See Chapter 15.)

The entire Toolbox can be "torn off" and "docked" anywhere on the screen. You can leave it at the left of the screen as usual, or dock it on top with the other toolbars, or on the right or bottom of the work area. The flyouts from the Mask, Zoom, Eraser, Line, and Primitives tools can be repositioned in the same way. Also, your favorite tools and functions can be assigned their own buttons and placed on a new or existing toolbar. Dock your new toolbars at any edge or let them float on the desktop. You can alter and customize keyboard shortcuts to suit your needs, and most pull-down menus can be rearranged or removed altogether.

Some Advice About Customization

The many interface personalization options make it a lot easier for you to work in an environment that you are comfortable with—but beware! It's easy to get so many elements on the table that you can't see your work. Before you know it you're down to a 2″×2″ working area for your picture!

In general, it's wise not to add anything to the Toolbox or toolbars until you are sure you will use it several times an hour. And don't float anything unless you plan to use it every few minutes. Above all, remember your options. There are at least three ways to get hold of any tool or function, and you can clear off your workspace just as easily as you can clutter it up. Don't be afraid to experiment, as we have done in Figure 32.2.

We predict that one of the first customizations you will want to perform is to alter the cursor's appearance for most of your tools. The default cursor is a nifty little picture of whatever tool you are using. Get rid of that just as soon as the novelty wears off—which will probably be one or two keystrokes after you try using it to apply a color or an effect with any accuracy at all. Go to Tools / Options, and choose Shape from the

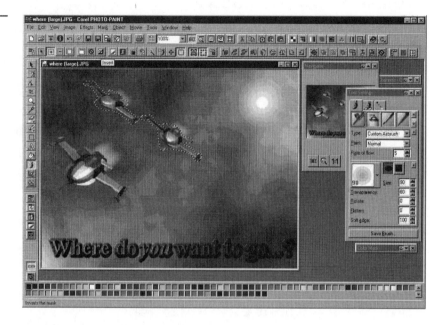

Cursors drop-down list. This produces a much less exciting cursor, but one that reflects the shape and size of the tool you are working with. You'll be able to see exactly where your magic will happen, saving you lots of trips to the Undo button. The Professional option gives you a crosshair at the center of the affected area. This allows extreme precision with small brush sizes and at high levels of magnification, but is often unsuitable for use with larger brushes.

Pull-Down Menus

The default menu bar presents the File, Edit, View, Image, Effects, Mask, Object, Movie, Tools, Window, and Help menus. Most of the functions on these menus are similar to those in other Windows menus. If you are unfamiliar with them, they're all explained in the online help. Simply search for the menu function title in the help index.

A few operations on the menus deserve special note. Let's take a look.

- **Undo,** in the Edit menu, reverses the last action performed. Undo List keeps a separate list of all the actions taken on each image and allows a linear undo, back to a certain point on the selected image. Using the Undo List function can be a time-consuming process, as it uses lots of memory. Watching the on-screen progress can be worrisome as well, because full screen refreshes may not be performed after each step. In addition, invoking a partial undo of a long series of actions may cause some unexpected results. By and large, however, the tool is very useful.

- **The View menu** offers several outlooks for what is on the desktop. It also offers controls for ruler and grid settings; these work the same as in DRAW. Later in the chapter we'll discuss all the roll-ups available from the View / Roll-Ups command.

- **In the Image menu** you get a host of image conversion operations. PAINT's image and file conversion suite is superior to that of many other graphics toolbox programs, particularly for color and size reduction. The Convert To selection brings up a flyout of the image options available to you. Unless you are very familiar with color, format, and dithering theory, you should experiment with the options that are offered after you choose a color reduction. PAINT has some of the best dithering controls available in any software, producing results that vary widely.

- **Calculations** is a new function in the Image menu. It lets you combine two images using one or all channels, and the paint mode and opacity options. The file CALCSTST.JPG in the PRACTICE directory of the Companion CD shows one possible effect, with an original image combined on all channels at 50% opacity, and a copy of the same image with the whirlpool effect added. Figure 32.3 shows this dialog in action.

- **The Movie menu** is new to PAINT and offers many movie editing tools. If you are doing extensive work on a movie, consider adding the Movie toolbar to the desktop (with View / Toolbars) to save mouse time.

■ **The Effects menu's** plentiful options are discussed in a later section, "The Desired Effect."

32.3

An overlay effect being produced with the Channel Calculations dialog

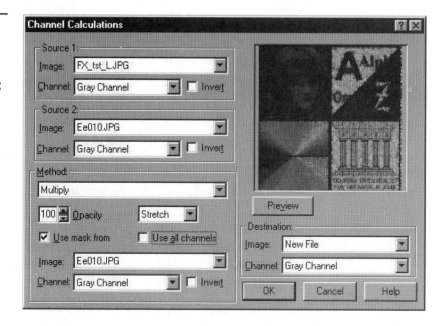

The Docked Toolbox

Every tool in the PAINT Toolbox can be altered and customized to some degree by the Tool Settings roll-up. It's smart to have it visible when you start experimenting with these tools. Open it with View / Roll-Ups or Ctrl+F8.

In addition to the familiar object picker tool, you'll find that the functions in the Toolbox are the same as they are in most other graphics applications, including DRAW.

The Mask Flyout In combination with the mask tools on the Standard toolbar, the items on the Mask flyout are arguably the most important equipment in any paint or photo manipulation program. Masking allows you to select a part of the whole image, either to affect that area alone, to protect that area from what you do to the rest of the image, or to create objects or copy areas.

The Rectangle and Circle mask tools work just like the tools of the same name in DRAW and elsewhere in PAINT. The Freehand mask tool helps you create a mask shape either by clicking from point to point or by clicking and dragging the cursor in the desired path. Double-click to close the mask path. All of these mask tools are useful for creating simple masks or object shapes, or for building the foundations of more complicated ones.

The Lasso and Magic Wand are for selecting areas of similar color within an image. Using tolerance levels in a normal or HSB mode lets you use these tools in either a general or very specific fashion.

Next in line is the Mask Brush tool, which will probably be the mask tool that you use most often. It allows you to mask using any one of PAINT's many brush sizes or shapes. This important utensil comes in handy for quickly masking out large, irregular areas that are not of the same color value, or for fine detail work around the edges of an object that you need to mask with precision.

Finally, you have the Mask Transform tool. This turns your mask into a sort of pseudo-object that you can resize, stretch, skew, rotate, or warp, much as you would an object in DRAW. Click repeatedly in the masked area to cycle through resizing and stretching handles first, then rotating and skewing handles, then warping or "perspective" handles.

The first two types of handles work just like DRAW's. The third set— the perspective handles—are used as in DRAW but with slightly different results. When you select a corner of your mask with the perspective transforming tools, you can drag that corner to any point on the screen. The mask is warped (its perspective is changed) by the new location of the selected corner. This result is different from that of PAINT's and DRAW's stretching and skewing tools, because with warping the other three corners remain in place. A double-click on any corner after warping has been added will "square" the mask to its new corners, effectively changing any warp to a stretch.

Node Edit Tool   The Node Edit tool, as well, works very much the same as it does in DRAW. Several types of objects, masks, lines, or paths may have nodes and Bézier handles to define their shape. These familiar aids will give you a good deal of control over the shape of PAINT objects.

Crop Tool   The Crop tool is a little like a very specialized masking device. Anything that can be done with it can also be done with the Mask tools, but not as conveniently.

With an image open, select the Crop tool, click on one area of the image, and then drag to another area and release the mouse button. You will see a cropping "mask" with eight control handles that you can use to stretch, squash, or resize the crop mask. Click and drag anywhere inside the crop mask to relocate it. Double-click anywhere inside it to quickly and easily crop the original image, which can then be altered and/or saved.

Zoom Flyout   Next up on the standard Toolbox is the Zoom flyout, which contains the Zoom tool and the Hand tool. Good zoom capability is absolutely crucial to image manipulation software, and there are excellent tools elsewhere in PAINT, such as the Navigator, to help you with that as well. Here, the magnifying glass lets you zoom in with a left-click or out with a right-click. The Hand tool controls a click-and-pan operation.

The Eyedropper   The Eyedropper is for sampling color, either from the mixing board or from the image itself. In an image with low bit-depth, you are limited to a sample size of one pixel, but the sample size can be customized in higher-color modes. The result of a larger color sample is an average of all the colors in that area, and the averaged color may not appear in the original image at all. The Eyedropper is often used in combination with the Color Replacer in the Undo flyout.

Undo Flyout   The flyout of Undo tools consists of the Local Undo, the Eraser tool, and the Color Replacer. Local Undo is for undoing part or all of the very last operation performed. It's very useful for touching up a brush stroke or smudge that you got a bit too enthusiastic about.

AUTHOR'S NOTE

> **If you undo too much, simply select another tool but don't do anything with it, and then select Local Undo again. You can now undo the Local Undo that you just did, and if you'd like, you can then come back and undo that undoing. You can keep that up until you can't remember who's on first.**

The Eraser tool removes all color from an area, bringing it back to the paper color. Double-clicking on the tool erases the entire image, leaving you a clean canvas. You can change the paper color by using the Ctrl key with either the Eyedropper or a click on the palette.

The Color Replacer replaces occurrences of the paint color, and other colors within the current tolerance, with the current paper color. Double-click to replace all instances of the target color range throughout the image.

The Line Tools Flyout   The Line flyout offers three tools for adding lines and line effects to an image.

The Line tool is used for point-to-point line drawing. By dragging, you create a line directly; by moving the mouse between clicks, you can preview the line before you double-click it into being. The width, transparency, and joints of the line are defined in the Tool Settings roll-up.

The Curve tool in PAINT 6.0—a combination pen and node editor—is much stronger than its version 5 counterpart. It creates a curved line made up of Bézier points that you can edit without switching tools. To complete the line, you either double-click, switch tools, or click on an area outside the line or its nodes.

The Pen tool draws a curved line directly on the image without any need (or allowance) for further editing.

The Shape Tools Flyout   Like DRAW's, PAINT's Shape tools fly-out provides quick rectangles and ellipses. It also produces irregular polygons. The settings, including outline color/width and fill specifics, are available in the Tool Settings roll-up. Note, for instance, that the way to achieve a rounded rectangle in PAINT is through Tool Settings. You can't alter the rectangle after it's drawn, as you can in DRAW.

The Text Tool   The Text tool will look quite familiar to users of DRAW. When you select it, the Tool Settings roll-up turns into a fairly standard text roll-up, and any text you create becomes an editable text object that's subject to the standard Text tools and the Object menu. Text objects take the selected paint color, and you can fill them using the Fill tool.

WATCH OUT!

> **Though you can still edit the text after you've added an effect (such as painting or distortion), the effect is lost, so get your text just right before you paint or shape it.**

To paint only your text using a brush, first make sure the Preserve Image option is enabled in the Image menu, and select the text object. Then you can click the Create Mask button on the Toolbar or in the Objects roll-up, or Create (Mask) from Object in the Mask menu. From there you can paint on the text without painting on the background as long as you don't move the text.

The Fill Tool   Another tool that is more powerful in PAINT 6.0 is the new Fill tool. It utilizes paint modes, tolerance levels, and transparency options. Otherwise it is very similar to the Fill tool in DRAW.

The Paint Tool   Discussed in detail later in this chapter, the Paint tool is rich in features and options. You'll want to use it in close conjunction with the Tool Settings and Color roll-ups.

The Effects Tool   The Effects tool replaces version 5's Smear tool. There are nine additional effects in the related Tool Settings roll-up, including smudge, brighten, contrast, hue, hue replacer, sponge, tint, blend, and sharpen. These are perhaps best thought of as quick area effects, and are very useful for altering or repairing small sections of images without the need for masking or accessing a menu. Experimentation and familiarity with the tool settings will mean the difference between your success and frustration when using these Effects operations.

The Clone Tool   The Clone tool also works with the Tool Settings roll-up. You'll find options for pointillism and impressionist cloning. There's also a custom effects tool that applies "in place" rather than at a given distance and bearing. This one includes an Eraser function for returning all effects back to the original saved image.

The Standard Toolbar

Along with the usual File, Print, Edit, Info, and Launch buttons, the default configuration for the Standard toolbar gives you a series of masking and object tools, marquee options, and zoom levels. (Especially helpful is the first setting on the Zoom pull-down, the To Fit option, for a quick overview of how your detail work is shaping up.)

Remember that you can extensively customize this toolbar to accommodate your own working style and maximize your productivity.

The Roll-ups

The View / Roll-ups command offers you eight roll-up dialogs: Channels, Color, Color Mask, Navigator, Nibs, Object, Recorder, and Tool Settings.

The Channels Roll-up   The Channels roll-up allows you to work directly with the RGB or CMYK channels of an image.

Channels can be altered, loaded from another image, saved to disk, or used as a mask. In this environment, paint and effects can be applied to one channel of an image and not the others. For example, in an RGB image try inverting only the red or the blue channel.

The Color Roll-up   This is your paint-mixing area. The Color roll-up's drop-down list will include all of the color models and palettes available for the selected image. This one is in RGB mode:

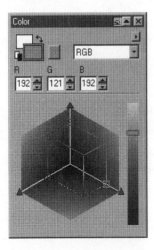

The flyout from this roll-up shows the configuration options and an option for adding the currently selected color to the palette. A color added to the custom palette will be placed at the end of the palette line-up. You can then "tear off" the color and place it elsewhere in the line-up, or delete it from the palette by right-clicking on the color and using the pop-up menu.

Identify your new colors by clicking on a blend point in the model, by dragging the mix handles inside the model, or by adjusting the color mix manually using the value boxes. Remember, there are 16,777,216 possible colors in an RGB palette. Experiment!

The Color Mask Roll-up   The Color Mask roll-up allows you to select areas of the image by color, and either change them or protect them from change. You can select or protect up to ten color bands. As is the case with many effects, Color Mask is only available in images with higher color depth.

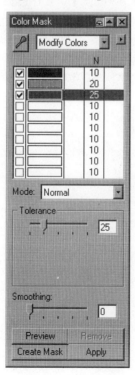

You select colors using the eyedropper button. Click on an area of the image to identify all instances of that color (or similar colors within tolerance) as part of the mask. You can alter the tolerance of each band individually to allow for the needed profile. When all your colors are selected, deactivate the eyedropper by clicking again on the button or by right-clicking anywhere. (Ignore the pop-up for now.)

Use the Preview button to check the color mask and see that it suits your needs. Adjust tolerances or reselect colors as needed. Next, create the mask with the Create Mask button. At this point you have a normal mask that is editable using all the regular Mask tools on the Mask flyout and pull-down menu.

Color mask is very useful for tricky projects such as masking around hair or other fine features, or for separating a DRAW or DREAM3D object from its background to add it into a PAINT image.

The Navigator Roll-up   This is perhaps the ultimate zoom tool for close-in image manipulations. With the Navigator roll-up you can see the results of your work on the "big picture" almost immediately—even in 1600:1 scale. You also get handy buttons for 100% Size, Best Fit, 1:1 Scale, Zoom In, and Zoom Out, along with grab-and-drag scrolling.

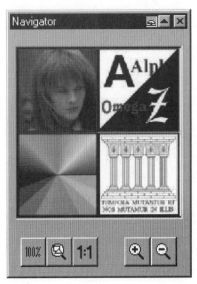

The Navigator's only drawback is the large amount of screen it takes up, but its value in micro-manipulation far outweighs this problem for most users.

The Nibs Roll-up   The Nibs roll-up is a stand-alone version of the Nibs selector from the Brushes page of the Tool Settings roll-up. This roll-up version lets you load, save, or append nibs to the nib files.

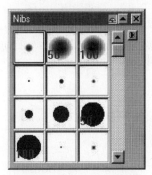

The Objects Roll-up   As you can see just below, this roll-up is in the same group with the Channels roll-up. It serves as a one-stop object management shop, a visual index of all objects in the active image.

Powerful capabilities such as variable paint modes and transparency are coupled with convenient buttons for creating masks from objects, objects from masks, and merging and deleting objects. With just a click of the mouse, you can select, lock or unlock the background or an object, and temporarily hide objects from view with the eye icon.

The Command Recorder   The Recorder roll-up is an extension of the CorelSCRIPT applet. Scripts are very much like macros, and most modern software provides extensive recording capability for these shortcut routines. You can learn more about scripts and their uses in the online help for the SCRIPTS application.

Tool Settings

The Tool Settings roll-up is the Grand Master of all PAINT roll-ups. Within its three pages you'll find settings to alter the behavior of almost every PAINT tool or function. You'll want to experiment freely with this one—it's full of possibilities, and its offerings change depending on which tool you've selected.

In this section we'll explore the Tool Settings as it would apply to the Paint tool. When the Paint tool is selected, the Tool Settings roll-up has three tabbed pages. These pages control (1) the brush itself, (2) the look and feel of the brush, and (3) the properties of the paint used.

Brush Choices   Click the first tab, the one with a brush on it, to get the first page of settings for the Paint tool:

- Pictures of a brush, pen, pencil, spray can, or other tools represent the brush presets. There is a scroll bar to page through the 15 different choices.

- The Type drop-down list offers brush presets. All of the qualities defined by these presets can be altered elsewhere in the roll-up. There is a flyout to the right of this drop box for resetting or deleting brush types.

- The Paint drop-down list lets you select the paint mode.

- On certain brushes, the Amount value box is active, for adjusting the amount or rate of flow. On a spraying brush, for instance, this value controls the amount of paint produced by a stroke; a low value gives a faint stroke, a high value a heavy one.

- Next comes a drop-down selection of shapes and sizes for the nib or nozzle used, binary buttons for selecting a round or square nib, and a flyout for creating a nib from an active mask.

- The five value boxes in the bottom third of the page are for controlling the brush size (1–100), transparency (0–99), rotation (0–360), flattening (0–99), and edge softening (0–100).

To get a feel for what these settings do, select the Paint tool. Open the Tool Settings roll-up and click the tab for the first page of settings. Select Custom Airbrush for the Type, and Normal for the Paint. Choose a round nib and give it the following values: Amount of flow 30, Size 98, Transparency 10, Rotate 0, Flatten 99, and Soft Edge 100. As you make these changes, watch how the brush changes in the nib. Then try a few quick up-and-down strokes. If you like the look you get, you can save this brush as "Blinds."

Brush Characteristics　The second page of Tool Settings for the Paint tool lets you control how your brush interacts with your canvas: brush texture, watercolors, and brush stroke.

The Texture settings are another way to alter the way paint gets applied to your image. Just about any bitmap can be used as a texture, but small, high-resolution, grayscale images work best.

The Watercolors settings control the blending of paint and colors in the canvas, and the Brush Stroke controls are for softening the edges of the stroke.

Paint Properties   The third page of Tools Settings for the Paint tool is for the load of paint in the brush and the color variation of the paint. You also get some additional controls on rate of flow.

First is the Dab variation. In PAINT, as in your high-school geometry class, a line is a series of points. For the purposes of this roll-up, those points are dabs of paint in the shape of the selected nib.

■ The Number of Dabs (1–25) governs how many dabs per click of the mouse button are applied to the image. A small round brush with a dab setting of 10, for example, will paint ten spots on the canvas with each click of the mouse. When you drag the mouse as a brush stroke, this value cycles so that a "line" is painted as a continuation of those ten spots.

- The Spacing of the dabs controls the solidity of the line in terms of the distance the mouse is dragged between applications of paint to the page. The Spacing value (1–999) is roughly a percentage of the actual brush size before soft-edging. Thus a value of 1 gives a solid line, and a value of 100 paints a series of dots that just touch (if Soft Edge on the Brush Settings page is set at 0). Higher values cause more and more space between spots.

- Spread (0–999) governs how closely the dabs follow the path of the mouse. A low value (under 50) places the paint quite close to the pointer. A higher value allows the paint to be placed anywhere in a large area near the pointer, producing anything from a pointillist effect to spatter.

INSIDE INFO

Like Spacing, the Spread value is based on a percentage, yet it is randomized—the paint can be applied anywhere in the given range. The Spread distribution pattern is cycled by the mouse click, but there's a trick! If Number of Dabs is 1, then the Spread will be randomized with each spot painted as you drag the mouse across the canvas; if Number of Dabs is set higher, the distribution of the first set of dabs will be continued throughout the stroke. So when you want a long brush stroke to be more randomized, you must click the mouse along the path of the stroke.

- Fade Out (0–100) is like the paint load in a brush. A low value carries more paint, and high values fade out more quickly.

The slide bars for Color Variation let you adjust the selected color's Hue, Saturation, and Luminance. Hue controls the amount of variation from the selected color; saturation controls intensity; and luminance controls brightness.

An Exercise in Color Variation   Try this exercise to see what can be done with a brush's color variation. On a clean, white, 24-bit RGB canvas, select a custom art brush with normal paint. Give it a size 20; leave transparency, rotation, and flattening at 0; set the soft edge at 25. Choose red as the paint color. Set number of dabs at 1, spacing at 125, and put both spread and fade out at 0. Try painting a few lines while the hue, saturation, and luminance are each set at 100 with the other two set at 0. Then toy around with intermixing the values.

AUTHOR'S NOTE

When the Effects tool is selected, the Tool Settings roll-up offers essentially the same options as in Brush mode. This gives you even more painting tools for such things as smearing, smudging, and blending your paint. You also get Effects-style tools for contrast, tint, hue, and sharpness.

The Desired Effect

The Effects menu is probably the single most famous and most used portion of PAINT. This toybox is bursting with possibilities in version 6.0—77 tools, with well over 150 subtools and presets. Each tool has variable (often many) values; the Alchemy tool, for instance, has 27, and the Julia Set Explorer, 11. This gives you around four thousand billion possibilities to consider, not to speak of what you'll be faced with when you begin to consider compound effects. We'll go over the mechanical possibilities here, as well as look at several examples, but in the end, you'll want to put on your mad scientist hat and immerse yourself.

Getting Familiar with the Effects

All of the effects work by manipulating a set of data in one way or another. The best way to get valuable insight into the way all of them work is to compare the results of one manipulation with another one. This also helps you to set up some signposts and landmarks for yourself, to use as you guide your images through the Effects menu in the future.

Load the image titled EFFECTS.TIF from the Companion CD, and watch how it is affected when you manipulate it. Try an effect, undo it, and try another one, or try the same one with slightly different settings. When you want to see the default values again, click the Reset button on the Effects dialog. Figure 32.4 shows the original EFFECTS.TIF image; all of the examples used in the following paragraphs are easy to re-create.

32.4

The unadulterated EFFECTS.TIF, B.E. (Before Effects)

When you look at the dialog for a particular effect, right-click around in different parts of the dialog. This provides you with a brief description of how each control will bear on the final effect. Dialogs with a Preview option also have a padlock button. When you activate this lock, the Preview window is automatically updated whenever you make a change in the effect's parameters. This is a handy little automation, but it can also be very time-consuming, as some of the effects are complex and require a lot of memory.

Now let's take a quick tour of the Effects menu. It has ten categories of effects: 2D, 3D, Adjust, Artistic, Blur, Color Adjust, Color Transform, Noise, Render, and Sharpen. From here, 77 different effects are accessed by flyout menus, and we'll go over some of the more interesting ones.

2D Effects

The 2D Effects include Band Pass, Displace, Edge Detect, Offset, Pixelate, Puzzle, Ripple, Shear, Swirl, Tile, Trace Contour, User Defined, Wet Paint, and Wind.

Band Pass is a very specialized focus tool. You can use it to isolate and eliminate unwanted noise or focal distortions in an image. This requires a good deal of experimentation to find which band frequencies have the problem data. Alter the inner, middle, and outer band sliders one at a time until you locate the problem area.

The **Displace** effect uses the mathematical values of a filter image to displace the areas of the subject image. Most bitmaps can be used as a filter image.

Edge Detect is one of several effects that use the differences between adjacent and nearby pixels to make assumptions about the image. Areas where two colors come together are defined as an edge. The background color of the image is changed, and the new edges are given exaggerated values to make them stand out. This is the best tool for achieving outlines of photographed images. To achieve the effect in Figure 32.5, use a

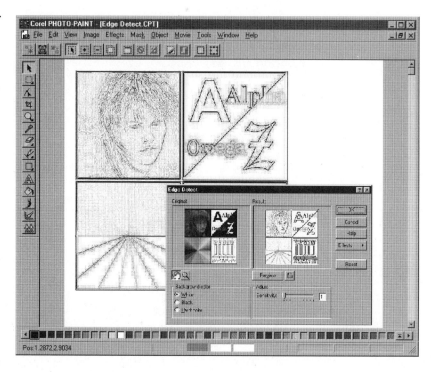

low Sensitivity setting with a white background, and then convert the result to 8-bit grayscale.

You can use **Offset** either to correct the position of an image on its "canvas," or to cause a large-scale tiling effect, as shown in Figure 32.6.

Pixelate causes an exaggeration of the gridlike pixel structure of an image. The colors within blocks of the image are averaged to a new value, which is then applied to the entire block. The Transparency option makes possible some very cool overlay effects.

Puzzle breaks the image down into smaller blocks, which are randomly offset from their original position. For the background that shows through the "cracks," you can choose either the original image or a solid color. If a solid color is selected, the new puzzle can be easily masked and turned into an object for overlay onto a new image.

32.6

Free image tiling, courtesy of the Offset controls

Use **Ripple** to make regular waves appear in an area of an image, like what you'd see in a fun-house mirror. Try masking just the woman's hair in the test image, with the mask brush. Then set Ripple for a horizontal effect, no distortion, with both period and amplitude of 5.

Shear gives you the same effect as the shearing handles that are available when you double-click on an object in DRAW or PAINT. You can also achieve other effects by manipulating the nodes in the graph-style box on the right side of the dialog. By selecting Freehand in the Edit Style drop-down box, the shear path can be drawn in (as in the .shr presets on the Companion CD). The Scale slider determines how exaggerated the shear will be. In Figure 32.7, it is *very* exaggerated.

32.7

Shear introduces curves into an image that used to be straight.

Swirl lets you add a nice "down-the-drain" look. Positive values on the slider give a clockwise swirl; negative goes counterclockwise. Figure 32.8 shows our attempt at psychodelia.

Tile reduces the image and repeats it a number of times vertically, horizontally, or both. The slider values go up as high as 100, which in our test image gives a tile size of 5×5 pixels. Kind of a nice houndstooth pattern…

32.8

Having fun with Swirl

Trace Contour is another difference-based effect. It has definable parameters to let you allow certain ranges to be traced. This filter works quite well in images with stark, easy-to-see color differences, but not so well with photographs.

Then there is the **User Defined** effect, which acts as a catch-all special effects control. By using the controls and settings, you determine the nature and degree of the effect, defining how many neighboring pixels are hit, how strongly, and in which direction. PAINT's documentation and online help provide very little assistance with this tool; you're really on your own. Nonetheless, it is a handy tool for relatively undramatic effects, like the blurring we produced in Figure 32.9.

32.9

Roll your own effects with the User Defined controls.

The User Defined effect is operated by entering values into a grid. Starting from the center of the grid, more filled-in squares means a larger neighborhood of effect. Higher positive or lower negative values produces a more pronounced effect. The User Defined effect comes with three presets for you to load and use, and you'll find two more in the PRACTICE\IMAGES\PP subdirectories on the Companion CD. Use those as a starting point for your experimentation.

Wet Paint gives a dripping effect to all or part of an image. Using this effect with a mask constrains the starting point for the dripping; unfortunately, it also limits the extent of the paint trails. If you want one part of an image to drip paint, try to mask below it a bit, to allow for a more realistic effect.

The **Wind** effect smears colors by defined amounts in a given direction. In the Blur flyout the Motion Blur effect does pretty much the same thing but allows you much more control.

3D Effects

The 3D Effects are 3D Rotate, Emboss, Glass, Map to Object, Mesh Warp, Page Curl, Perspective, Pinch/Punch, The Boss, Whirlpool, and Zigzag.

3D Rotate paints your image on the side of an imaginary cube so that you can look at it from another angle. From that point, it's easy to mask the new shaped image and turn it into an object, for importing to another image. Use the Preview button with this one, because some of the more extreme effects, such as an inverted image, won't be drawn.

Emboss is another of the difference-seeking effects. It makes light and dark areas appear to have height and depth, with a light source that you can place with direction buttons. PAINT 5's Emboss had more color options, but by altering the paper color before you emboss the image you can still get your emboss effect in any color in version 6.0. We think embossed effects look best in single colors with highlights and shadows, but setting the emboss color to gray, black, or paper color on a 24-bit color image will often leave behind color shadows. To get around this you can either convert the embossed image to 8-bit grayscale and then to 8-bit mono- or duotone; or you can convert the original image to 8-bit grayscale and then back to 24-bit and use a colored "paper." As shown in Figure 32.10, the effect is impressive.

Glass is the second embossing effect on the menu, and it is very similar to The Boss effect. It adds built-in color overlay and opacity tools, and refraction controls, but lacks the height control of the other effect. Both of these effects offer a great deal of possibility.

With **Map to Object** you can warp your image into one of three shapes. This effect doesn't have the background options included in the other

32.10

Embossing is one of the most flexible and easily produced of the special effects.

map distortion effects, but the background can easily be cropped out. Try adding a gradient fill at 100% tolerance and high transparency to finish the 3D effect. For an example of this, open DIALBALL.TIF from the PRACTICE\IMAGES\PP subdirectory of the Companion CD.

Mesh Warp lets you move an identified point in the image to another place. The filter extrapolates the stretching and compressing effects to the neighboring pixels. You can select grid sizes from 4×4 squares to 10×10, giving you up to 81 points to manipulate.

Remember as you use this filter that the lines on the Preview screen follow the main course of the "stress" on the image. The further a line gets from its original course, the more the actual effect is pushed beyond that line. Use the Preview button extensively as you work your way toward Figure 32.11.

3 2 . 1 1

Alka-Seltzer, anyone?

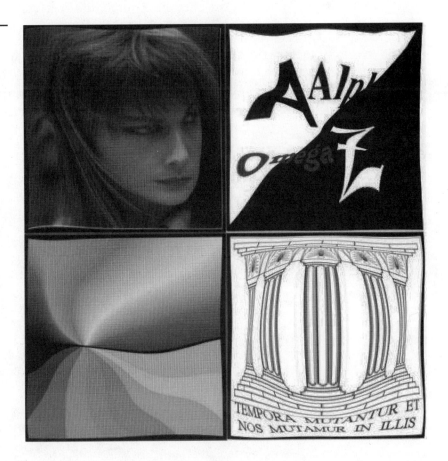

Page Curl applies either a vertical or horizontal effect that can be made opaque or transparent. If you apply the effect and then repeat it (by clicking the top item on the Effects menu), you can reduce the transparency. Unfortunately, there are no options for background or undefined areas, so the peeled area will be the paper color unless you further alter it.

Perspective is a lot like 3D Rotate, but you use handles instead of sliders—so you can achieve some pretty extreme or unreal results. You'll want to use the Preview button a lot, just as you do with 3D Rotate.

Pinch/Punch does just what it says. Imagine your image on a rubber sheet. This effect stretches the center of the image as if the sheet were being depressed (pinched) or punched out toward the viewer.

Whirlpool simulates several fluid, dynamic eddies and swirls or fountains placed into or over your image. With four slide bars and one check box for you to work with, this is another effect that is rich with possibilities (nearly 100 million)—one of which we show off in Figure 32.12.

32.12

One of the 100 million or so variations of **Whirlpool**

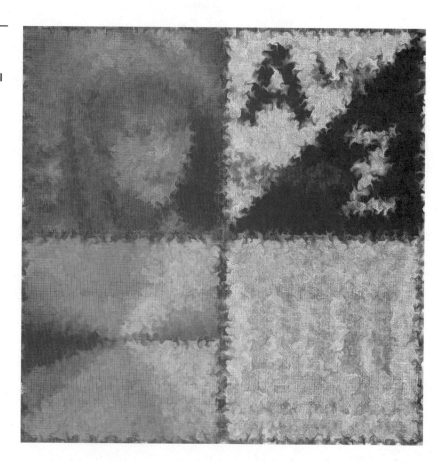

Adjust Effects

The Adjust Effects are Blur, Color Hue, Color Tone, Noise, and Sharpen.

Each dialog within the Adjust family is a virtual workshop for custom compound effects. You'll find windows for several types of effects within each category, a dedicated Undo button, intensity controls, and more. The effects of each window are compounded until you apply the full effect. This gives you substantially more flexibility than with the individual effects, but you'll need to do a little more trial and error until you've learned the techniques.

Artistic Effects

The Artistic Effects are Alchemy, Canvas, Glass Block, Impressionist, Smoked Glass, Terrazzo, and Vignette.

Alchemy is the most versatile of these in PAINT 6.0. Within its dialog (Figure 32.13) you have access to 27 variable controls, which provide roughly 4.33×10 to the 56th, or over 400 billion billion billion billion billion billion billion raw mathematical possibilities in a 24-bit image of 100×100 pixels.

32.13

The Alchemy workshop offers a dizzying array of possibilities.

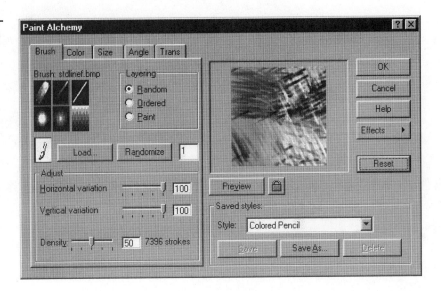

Alchemy will give you the strongest natural-media translation powers, as well as a virtually unlimited array of distortion and remapping techniques. The dialog is quite easy to understand, and it comes with 75 presets to help you get acquainted with it. Figure 32.14 shows one such preset.

32.14

We think this should be called the Sandstorm Preset.

The **Canvas** effect overlays a bitmapped texture on an image, giving it the look of having been painted on a natural (or unnatural!) surface.

You get several presets in the dialog's dedicated directory, but nearly any bitmap can be used—including the textures and other images on the CorelDRAW 6.0 CDs, after they are opened in PhotoPAINT and saved as bitmaps. Using an image as a canvas can also provide interesting results.

Glass Block makes the image look as though it's being viewed through textured glass or, at the higher values, in tiled mirrors.

The **Impressionist** effect is actually more like another textured glass effect—in the case of Figure 32.15, sand-textured windows.

3 2 . I 5

Impressionism is alive and well in PAINT 6.0.

Smoked Glass is another type of window through which your image can be viewed. You can control opacity and blur distortion.

The **Terrazzo** effect has lots of potential. Its basic operation is to take a portion of the image and create repeating tiles. The potential comes from its versatility. There are 17 different sampling/tiling patterns, and you can tile from the master image or from another. Controls let you alter the size, location, and often the shape of the sample. You can change the overlay's opacity, and pick from a short list of paint modes.

Try using the file PRACTICE\IMAGES\PP\SAMPLES\Fx_mask.JPG as a master image and experiment with the Terrazzo effect a bit. You can come up with some wonderful new canvas and brush-nib images just by playing with the Terrazzo effect and saving the results.

To save a canvas, crop or reduce the image to an area of 128×128 pixels and save it to PHOTOPNT\CANVAS\ in your main Corel directory (probably namedCOREL60). To create and save a nib, mask the area you want to make a nib from, select the Brush tool with the first page of the Tool Settings roll-up displayed, and click the arrow button to create a nib from the mask. On the Nibs roll-up, click the arrow button to add the currently used brush to the palette.

With **Vignette** you can create a black, white, or colored frame around the image. The Offset (how far into the image the frame reaches) and Softness of the frame's focus are configurable.

The **Blur, Color Adjust, Color Transform, Noise,** and **Sharpen** effect flyouts contain several tools for making mechanical adjustments to the appearance of an image. Many of them (the Blur and Sharpen families, for instance) may seem redundant, but the effects offered are subtly different in each case. Figure 32.16 shows a simple use of Color Adjust.

Render Effects

The Render Effects are 3D Stereo Noise, Julia Set Explorer, Lens Flare, and Lighting Effects.

3 2 . 1 6

Color Adjust, for those days when your mood is particularly dark

The **3D Stereo Noise** effect allows you to create stereograms of images with varying degrees of depth, and with or without "focus dots." The resulting image is black and white unless you use the Split Channels option in the Image menu and recombine the channels after applying the effect to each channel individually. You can also use Image / Calculations to overlay the stereogram to the original image. (By the way, this is the only way so far that we have been able to see the "picture" in a stereogram. Is that cheating?)

The **Lens Flare** simulates the sundog-like light flashes sometimes seen in natural-light photography. You can position the effect by clicking inside the Preview window. There are three lens settings, and a slide bar for adjusting brightness. This can add a new dimension to the idea of photorealistic graphics, as shown in Figure 32.17.

32.17

This image has its own solar flare.

The **Lighting Effects** dialog places the image on an imaginary wall or table so that you can add various spot, flood, ambient, or other lights. This is a gallery-style effect rather than an optical or remapping style.

Image Editing 101

The Photo side of PhotoPAINT is its state-of-the-art image manipulation tools. Special effects such as Sharpen, Blur, and Color Adjustment, and tools such as Masked Painting, Cloning, and Smudge/Smear are part of a formidable arsenal for changing and repairing images.

On the Companion CD under PRACTICE\IMAGES\PP\MANIP you'll find several images to acquaint you with the subject of image manipulation for fun and profit. We've taken these photographs from the CorelDRAW 6.0 CDs and altered them to simulate common image problems. There is also a Wordpad document giving step-by-step instructions for the exercises that go along with the images.

Using PAINT as a Partner to DRAW

Because of its wide array of powerful bitmap editing tools and special effects capabilities, PhotoPAINT is a perfect partner to CorelDRAW, DREAM3D, and many other artistic programs.

On the Companion CD under PRACTICE\IMAGES\PP\SAMPLES are several files that have been started in other applications and then imported to PAINT for the finishing touches. Each file has a Wordpad document of the same name, explaining what was done and why. Some files include the original images and step-by-step instructions so that you can reproduce the work done on the example. Some of the tools used include

- Sharpening for bitmaps where size was a crucial factor
- Dithering for use in 256-color environments
- Focus softening for a more photorealistic look
- Placement of drawn or rendered objects in a photo setting
- Addition of special backgrounds and visual effects

Both DREAM3D and DRAW are capable of producing very attractive artwork. For the addition of small details or sweeping "landscape" effects, however, you'll be better off using a bitmap editor. Take a look at the files on the Companion CD and try a few of the exercises. See what cross-application creativity can do for your work.

Natural Media Emulation

The personal computer has always promised to be a modern Genie in a bottle, both as a workhorse for performing tedious mathematical tasks and as an inexhaustible source of education and entertainment. One of the top cards in its hand has always been *simulation*. Your computer's simulation ability lets you quantify certain aspects of real life as a set of variables, giving you the opportunity to experiment with little or no risk. You can learn to fly a plane without the danger of a fatal crash. You can sit on the throne of a vast empire. Computer simulation promises you more than what might otherwise be possible in reality.

Some years ago people started realizing that only the bare surface of computer simulation had been explored. They began to see that even the tools and products of sports, music, and art can all be quantified. The effect of dragging an oil pastel across rough canvas can be defined by a set of equations. The amount of oil transferred, the depth and type of color the oil carries, the texture of the canvas, even the amount, direction, and color of light that strikes it—all of that can be expressed as mathematical values. And once you have the values and equations defined, it's a fairly simple matter to alter them or to apply them in different ways.

As a result, anything that can be done with natural tools (brushes, pencils, chalks, canvas, and so forth) can also be done with a computer. Sometimes the electronic equivalent of natural media is much more complicated, but often the reverse is true. Furthermore, many techniques are possible and even easy with a computer that are simply impossible otherwise. How easy would it be to find a can of spray paint that painted all colors of the spectrum, in bursts several tenths of an inch apart, in the shape of a musical quarter note, and with no drip or overspray? It's easy in PAINT.

The two strongest arguments against paint programs have always been (1) that the end result doesn't look "realistic" and (2) that the program's tools don't offer the artist the same "feel" of authentic tools.

The first argument has died a natural death: Art programs have come a long way from those early binary-style brushes. State-of-the-art creative software now takes into account the shape and angle of the brush; variances in color, cover, and opacity; even in some cases the amount of pressure applied to the canvas. With today's tools we can produce artwork that appears in many ways even more real than the real thing.

The second argument, concerning the feel of electronic tools, remains largely true. The mouse is awkward for drawing or painting, and the problem is worse because you're watching the results of your stroke on a screen several inches from your hand.

One way to get around this awkwardness is simply to practice. Just like anything else, working with electronic art media becomes easier and more natural with patience and serious use. Another answer to the problem is to get a digitizer tablet. These devices simulate traditional tools by using a pressure-sensitive pad and a penlike stylus. Many models are available, ranging from small 6″×6″ models to huge pads over 2′ per side; we have seen low-end pads advertised for just a little over $100. Getting good with a digitizer tablet takes plenty of practice, but many professional artists find them invaluable.

So what are the bottom-line benefits of computerized painting? First, you have unlimited supplies. You have all the chalks, paints, pens, and pencils in the world to choose from and then some. You never run out of any kind of paper, and clean-up is a snap (or, rather, a click!). Secondly, the computer is a much more forgiving partner than natural media. If you don't like what you've done, you simply undo it. No more of your potential masterpieces need be destroyed by one false brush stroke. On the other hand, if you really like what you've done, you can redo it! A favorite stroke or complex series of strokes can be saved, altered, and reapplied time and time again.

More and more professional artists are making the computer a key element of their studios, and many have all but forsaken natural tools altogether. Corel's Photo-PAINT module has grown stronger and more versatile with each version. And version 6.0 brings PAINT into the class of the industry's finest painting programs.

Try it yourself! You can use a sketch, drawing, or painting as the basis of your work. If you don't have a scanner, most cities have service bureaus that are convenient and inexpensive. Once you have your artwork on disk, you can import it into PAINT and let fly. Go crazy! Experiment with everything—after all, you have all the paint in the world at your disposal. When you do something you like, set a checkpoint or (if you have the disk space) save each iteration in a sequence of files. You can also use the Duplicate option in the Image menu to create a copy and shrink it to the bottom of the screen. In our opinion, that is the best (and most fun) way to learn Corel Photo-PAINT.

33

Show Business

THIRTY-THREE

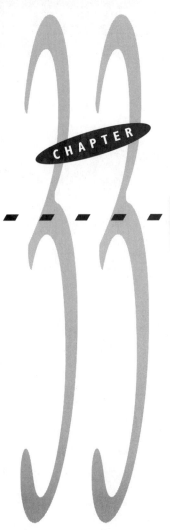

n CorelDRAW 6.0, the PRESENTS program comprises the features of CHART, MOVE, and SHOW from previous versions. Designed to produce presentations, PRESENTS lets you bring together text, graphics, charts, animation and sound. Whether you're creating overhead, 35mm slides, or a multimedia extravaganza with video and music, in PRESENTS you'll find a variety of impressive, timesaving, and practical tools for designing professional presentations.

Here are just a few of PRESENTS's powerful features:

- Robust OLE support enabling you to add objects from CorelDRAW, CorelMOTION and CorelMAP quickly and easily.

- Full text-formatting features, including character and paragraph spacing and bullet shapes.

- Filters for importing video, animation, and sound files.

- Libraries of slide backgrounds and layouts that streamline your work.

- An unparalleled selection of chart types. In addition to the standard bar, line, and pie charts, you'll find polar, scatter, and radar charting capabilities.

- Professional transition effects applicable to both slides and objects.

- Speaker notes and audience handouts

- On-screen annotation that lets you write on the screen during the presentation—like John Madden's coach's clicker.

- A runtime player application that lets you take your show on the road.

WATCH OUT!

After all the fanfare, here's a reality check: Though **PRESENTS** holds a lot of promise, at this writing it is unstable. For instance, the screen colors may go bonkers on you. So be sure to save your presentation file often and make a backup file occasionally. If the colors go berserk, exit **PRESENTS**, restart Windows, and try running **PRESENTS** again. Also, be patient—there may be times (working with templates and charts, for example) when you think **PRESENTS** has stalled, but actually it's still thinking.

Welcome to PRESENTS

When you first start PRESENTS, the start-up screen in Figure 33.1 appears.

33.1

The **PRESENTS** start-up screen includes options for selecting a background template and opening the last file you worked on.

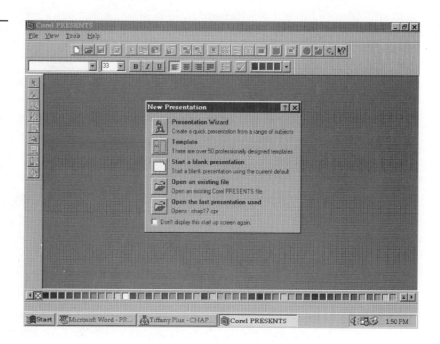

AUTHOR'S NOTE

If you are familiar with Corel 5's CHART, MOVE, and SHOW, or another presentation package such as PowerPoint, you're in luck. You should be able to pick your way through much of PRESENTS.

Selecting the Presentation Wizard prompts you to identify the subject matter of your presentation, such as Sales, Training, or Financial. Based on the topic selected, PRESENTS creates a new presentation complete with backgrounds, slide layouts, even sample contents. You can also reach the Presentation Wizard by selecting File / New / From Wizard.

Clicking on the Template button gets you an array of prepared slide backgrounds. The backgrounds are organized into categories for high-tech, scientific, funky, and much more. The Template option lets you choose a background as you begin building your presentation. You can also add a background at any time.

To build a new presentation from scratch, click on the Start a Blank Presentation button. You can add slides and backgrounds as you build the presentation.

The last two buttons in the start-up window allow you to open PRESENTS files.

Exploring the PRESENTS Interface

The PRESENTS screen has many tools and menus you'll recognize from other Corel applications. You can move and customize the tools and menus to fit your needs, just as you can in DRAW.

There are three views for your presentation—Slide view, Outline view, and Slide Sorter view (see Figure 33.2). You work with one slide at a time in Slide view, adding and formatting text and graphic objects. The Slide view is probably where you'll spend much of your PRESENTS time. In Outline view you can focus on the text content of your presentation. As discussed later in this chapter, the Outline view offers a quick way to create text slides. Slide Sorter view displays thumbnails of all of the slides in your presentation. You can rearrange the order of slides, control slide timings, and add transitions.

3 3 . 2

Three different views in PRESENTS help you to focus on a specific slide, text content, or overall slide organization (continued on next page).

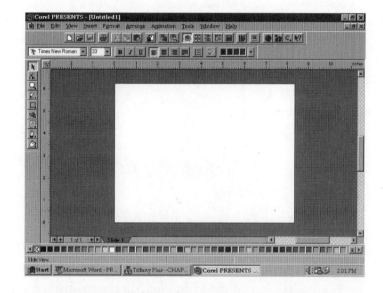

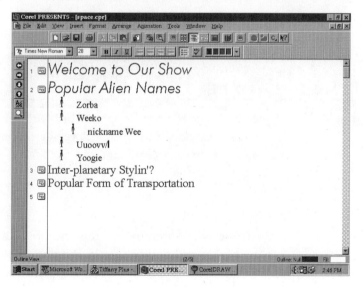

33.2

(continued)
**Three different
views in PRESENTS
help you to focus on
a specific slide, text
content, or overall
slide organization.**

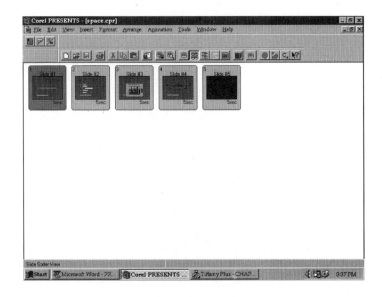

To move among the different views, select the desired view from the view menu or click on the appropriate view button.

The Standard toolbar and Text toolbar are displayed by default. As in DRAW, you can right-click on the toolbars to control their display. You can also right-click on the status bar to choose the types of information to display about the objects in your presentation, such as fill and outline attributes.

AUTHOR'S NOTE

Since the Text toolbar includes a button for selecting colors, you may want to close the Color Palette at the bottom of the screen to open up some screen space.

On the left, the PRESENTS Toolbox includes a Pick and Node tool, and a flyout with Zoom tools. Press and hold on the Rectangle tool to find the Ellipse and Polygon tools. Press and hold on the AutoShapes tool to display the flyout in Figure 33.3. After selecting a shape from

33.3

The AutoShapes tool makes it easy to add arrows, stars, and other shapes to your presentation.

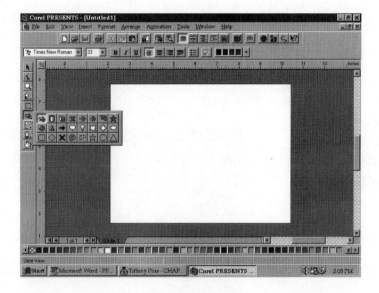

the flyout, you can draw the shape on the slide as you would draw a rectangle. Use the Node tool to edit these shapes, as you do in DRAW.

The Text, Outline, and Fill tools work as they do in DRAW. At the bottom of the screen are a slide counter and slide tabs that let you move through the slides in your presentation. Guidelines for aligning objects can be dragged from the rulers. (PRESENTS does not yet support diagonal guidelines.)

In the following sections, you'll find exercises that illustrate various features of PRESENTS. Each exercise builds on what the previous one accomplishes, so you'll want to do them in order. Follow along, and learn some tips and tricks for working with PRESENTS.

Setting Up Your Slides

Will your presentation be output to 35mm slides, letter-size paper, overhead transparencies, or shown on a computer screen? Before building the elements of your presentation, it's a good idea to specify the paper size, orientation, and margins, to ensure proper placement of text and objects on the slides. From the File menu, select Page Setup to display the Page Setup dialog (Figure 33.4). You'll find the necessary page settings in the Size/Margin page of this dialog. (By the way, don't be confused when slides in a presentation are sometimes referred to as pages. Slides and pages are the same thing.)

3 3 . 4

Use the Size/Margin settings in the Page Setup dialog to set up the slide.

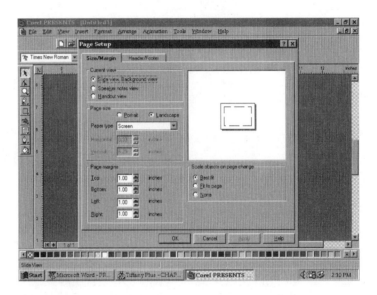

Adding Headers and Footers

PRESENTS includes options for adding header and footer text to every slide in your presentation. Click on the Header/Footer tab in the Page Setup dialog to display the header and footer settings. On the Header/Footer page, click Custom Header or Custom Footer to see even more header and footer options (Figure 33.5). Macro buttons make it easy to place the date, time, user name, company name, and slide number (for instance, "slide 2 of 10") as header and footer text.

Selecting Slide Backgrounds

You can create your own slide background with familiar effects such as fountain fills, patterns, and texture fills. PRESENTS also includes several libraries full of prepared slide backgrounds.

33.5

Click on a macro
button to insert
the date, time, and
other information
into header and
footer text.

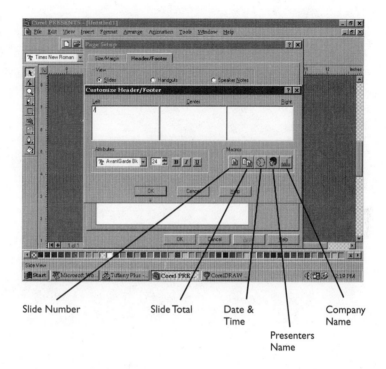

Slide Number   Slide Total   Date &   Company
                                        Time   Name

                                                  Presenters
                                                  Name

Use the Background view for creating slide backgrounds. To move to
Background view, click on the toolbar button that contains a gradient-
filled square. Objects added in this view appear on every slide.

To design your own slide background, select Edit / Background. A flyout appears with the various types of fills you can apply to a background. To choose one of the predesigned backgrounds, click on the
Libraries button in the Standard toolbar (it looks like books stacked side
by side). In the Libraries dialog (Figure 33.6), the libraries are divided
into groups. The background libraries offer backgrounds enhanced with
various fills and graphic objects.

In Background view, you can modify these supplied backgrounds to fit
your exact needs. For example, you might want to add your company
logo to an existing background. You cannot select background objects
in Slide view.

33.6

If you're looking for something new, try one of the prepared slide backgrounds from the background libraries.

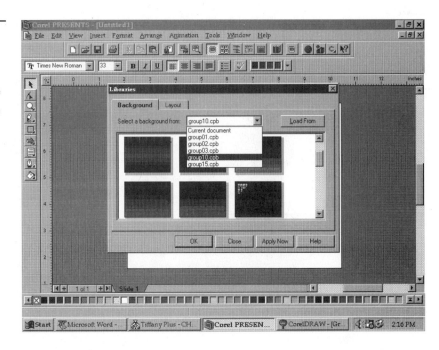

Selecting a Slide Layout

Slide layouts contain placeholders for text, charts, graphics, and animations. For instance, a slide layout for a title slide includes placeholders for a title and subtitle. The placeholders in a chart layout are for a title and a chart.

To select a slide layout, move to the slide where you want the layout to appear and click the Libraries button in the Standard toolbar. In the Libraries dialog, open the Layout page (Figure 33.7), and click the Preset Library button to display layouts for all kinds of slides.

The layouts that display a small chart will create chart slides. Layouts with a globe will create a placeholder for a map inserted by CorelMAP. Layouts with a small white square create a placeholder for OLE objects, such as a DRAW graphic or Excel spreadsheet.

33.7

A slide layout provides placeholders for building various types of slides.

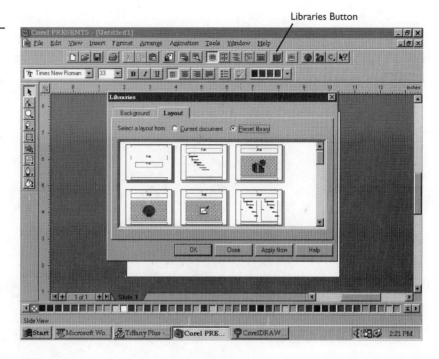

Exercise A

Here is the first of the chapter's series of exercises.

1. Select File / New / Document. A blank slide appears in Slide view.

2. Select File / Page Setup.

3. In the Page Setup dialog's Size/Margin page, open the Paper Type drop-down list and choose Screen to design a presentation for display on a computer screen. Keep the page margins at 1″.

4. Create the slide background. First click on the Background View button (see Figure 33.8). To select a predesigned background, click on the Libraries button. In the Background page, open the drop-down list of backgrounds. Choose a blue background from the group01.cpb library.

5. Using the Artistic Text tool, enter **Space Adventures, Inc.** Format the text in 20-point Futura (or whatever you like), fill it with white, and position it in the lower-left corner of the slide as shown in Figure 33.8.

33.8

You can add text and graphic objects to your backgrounds. These objects will be displayed on every slide in the presentation.

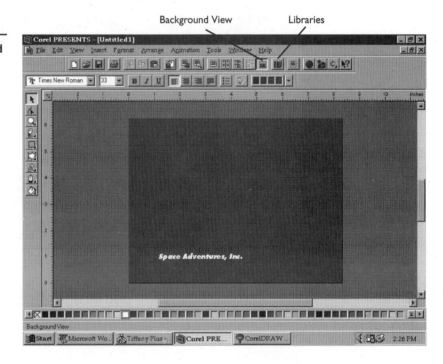

6. Click the Slide View button to return to the first slide.

7. Click the Libraries button again and open the Layout page. To view the layouts, click the Preset Library option, and choose the first layout (for a title slide).

8. Save the file and name it **SPACE.CPR**.

In the next exercise, you will insert new slides.

Inserting Slides: Off to See the Wizard...

The Insert Slides wizard helps you choose backgrounds and layouts for new slides. From the Insert menu, select Slide; or click on the Insert Slides button on the Standard toolbar (see Figure 33.9). The wizard first asks how many slides you want to insert. By default, new slides are inserted after the current slide, but there's also a Before Current Slide option if you need it. Type in or dial to the number you want, and click Next. In the next two windows, choose a slide layout and then a slide background. Click the Finish button to add the new slides to your presentation.

33.9

The Insert Slides wizard's first request of you is how many new slides you want.

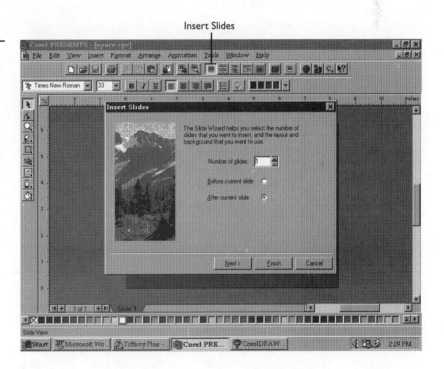

At this point, tabs for the new slides appear along the bottom of the PRESENTS work area. To move from slide to slide, you can click on the tabs or use the arrow buttons on the slide counter.

AUTHOR'S NOTE

> If you are inserting several slides, the layout you choose will be applied to all new slides. If you want more flexibility, choose the Blank layout; then you can apply a layout to each new slide individually.

Exercise B

Remember that the exercises in this chapter are connected. This exercise builds on what you did in Exercise A.

1. If it's not already open, open the SPACE.CPR file.

2. Click the Insert Slide button in the Standard toolbar. Type or dial up 4 as the number of new slides to create, and click Next.

3. At the top of the Select a Layout dialog, make sure the Current Document option is selected. Choose the Blank layout, and click Next.

4. By default, the last background selected is applied to the new slides. This is the one we want, so click the Finish button.

5. Display slide 2. Click the Libraries button in the Standard toolbar, open the Layout page, and choose the bulleted list layout (the second layout in the preset library).

6. Choose the Chart layout for slide 3, the OLE Object layout for slide 4, and leave slide 5 blank.

7. Save the file.

In the next exercise, you will enter and format text on the slides.

Working with Text

Text is a significant component of any presentation. The textual content and formatting are essential to making that good "first impression" that can make or break a deal. Fortunately, PRESENTS has many of the same helpful tools for entering, editing, and formatting text that are available in DRAW. You have tools for both Paragraph Text and Artistic Text. To enter text in a placeholder, select the Paragraph Text tool and click inside the placeholder. Use the Artistic Text tool to enter text where you don't have a placeholder. (You used the Artistic Text tool to enter the company name in Exercise A.) To edit text, click in the text with the same tool used to enter the text.

The proofing tools in PRESENTS—Spell Checker, Thesaurus, and Type Assist—work as they do in DRAW. These features are found in the Tools menu. To check spelling of the entire presentation, run the Spell Checker in Outline view.

Entering Text in Outline View

Though text can be entered in Slide view, you may find it convenient to add larger amounts of text in Outline view. Click the Outline View button to get a "text-only" look at your presentation (Figure 33.10). Use the Zoom tool to make the text in Outline view easier to read. An icon for each slide number appears in the left margin of the work area.

To enter a slide title, click beside the slide's icon on the left and begin typing. After the slide title, press Ctrl+Enter to add bulleted text. Press Enter again to add additional bullets at that level. To create a sub-bullet at the next level down from an existing bullet, press Tab or click on the Demote button in the toolbar; you can create up to five levels of bullets. Press Shift+Tab or click on the Promote button to move up one bullet level.

To add additional slides in Outline view, use the Insert Slides wizard.

When you return to Slide view, the text you've entered appears on each slide. If some of the text isn't visible, try enlarging the placeholders with the Pick tool. You may also need to reduce the type size. Any layouts and placeholders established in Slide view are not in effect in Outline view. In fact, the placeholders will be replaced by what is entered in Outline view.

3 3 . 1 0

In Outline view you can focus on the presentation's textual content.

Promote

Demote

Move Up

Move Down

Show/Hide Formatting

Zoom

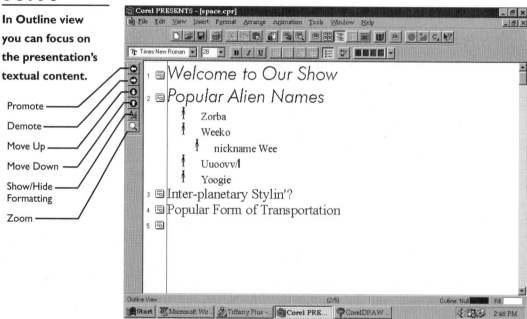

INSIDE INFO

You can also enter bullet text in Slide view. Just press Tab to "demote" the line to the next bullet level, or Shift+Tab to "promote" the line to the previous bullet level.

Importing Existing Text   To import text from a word processing application into the Outline view, use the File / Import command. If you are using a Windows program for word processing, you can also transfer the text through the Clipboard.

Formatting Text

Text can be formatted in either Slide or Outline view. Generally, text formatting is more efficiently done in Slide view because you get a better look at the layout and design of each slide. In fact, some attributes—such as color and alignment—are not available or not visible in Outline view.

Either the menus or the Text toolbar can be used for text formatting. To format a whole text string, select the text with the Pick tool; to format only selected text, drag to highlight the text. Then select Format / Character (Ctrl+T) to display the Character Attributes dialog (Figure 33.11). You can also format text using the Font, Size, Style and Alignment buttons on the Text toolbar.

When you enter text in a bulleted-text placeholder, the bullet appears automatically. To format the bullet, select the bulleted lines you want to edit and use Format / Bullet Style. In the Select Bullet dialog (Figure 33.12), you can designate the font and size of the bullet character. To change the color of the bullets, drag across them with the Paragraph Text tool. To remove the bullets, click on the Bullets button in the Text toolbar.

33.11

Text formatting in PRESENTS is done similarly to the way it's done in DRAW.

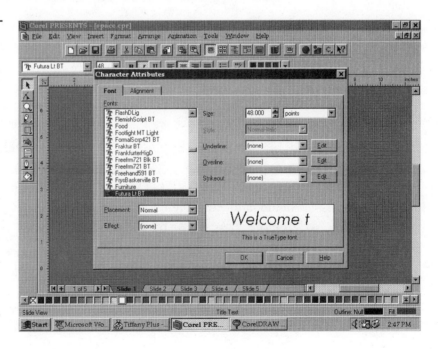

33.12

Choose the shape and size of bullets in the Select Bullet dialog.

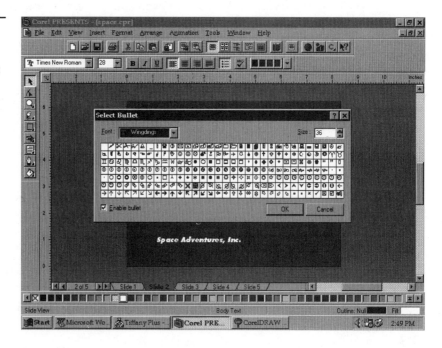

To adjust the default tab width and line spacing for bulleted text, select Tools / Options and click on the Text tab.

Exercise C

1. If necessary, open the SPACE.CPR file and display the first slide.

2. Using the Paragraph Text tool, click in the placeholder for the title. Enter **Welcome to Our Show.** Click in the subtitle placeholder and enter **Here's a Bunch of Stuff We Just Made Up.** You may have to enlarge the placeholder to see all of the subtitle.

3. Fill the title with red and format it in 48-point Futura Light (or whatever looks good). Fill the subtitle with yellow and format it in 24-point Times New Roman bold.

4. Switch to Outline view.

5. Click beside slide 2, and enter the title as displayed in Figure 33.13.

33.13

Press Tab or Click the Demote button to "demote" bullets to the next level. Press Shift+Tab or click the Promote button to return bullets to the previous level.

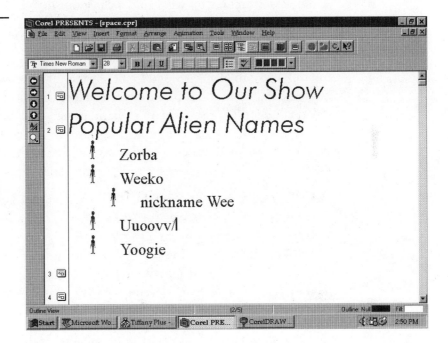

6. Press Ctrl+Enter to add the bullets. As you enter the bullets, use the Tab key to demote the bullets and Shift+Tab to promote the bullets.

7. Return to Slide view by double-clicking on the icon for slide 2.

8. Fill the title with red and format it in 48-point Futura Light. Then fill the text for all the bullets with white, and format them in 28-point Times New Roman.

9. With the bullet text still selected, choose Format / Bullet Shape. Change the font to Space (or whatever you like) and choose a new shape.

10. Using the Paragraph tool, drag across the first bullet and fill it with yellow. Repeat for the remaining bullets.

11. Save the file.

In the next exercise, you will build a chart on slide 3.

Creating Charts

You only have to glance through a newspaper or magazine to see how charted data has become an art form. You'll see graphs that illustrate which fast-food joint sells the most hamburgers, and charts depicting everything from stock values to minivan prices. These charts do much more than display numbers. They communicate with color and graphics, making the data interesting and easy to understand.

PRESENTS accesses the CorelCHART application to create charts. If you have selected a slide layout that includes a chart, simply double-click on the Chart icon in the toolbar. If the slide does not have a chart placeholder, click on the Insert a Chart button; the mouse shape changes to a crosshair with the Corel logo. On the slide, draw a rectangle to indicate the size and placement of the chart.

The Chart Type dialog appears after you've clicked on the chart placeholder or the Insert a Chart button (see Figure 33.14). Choose a chart type, and several variations of the chart appear on the right, with descriptions in the box just below.

Once you've designated a chart type, a chart with sample data is displayed. The menu bar and tools change, offering you new tools for building charts (see Figure 33.15). You replace the sample data with your own data to create your chart. Be careful—don't click outside the chart, or you'll return to PRESENTS.

To enter actual data, select Chart / Data or click on the Data button. The data sheet opens in spreadsheet form, and you can click in the cells and type in your data. Remove any unused data with Edit / Clear. You can also import data from Microsoft Excel. When you're ready, click OK to display the chart with your data.

33.14

PRESENTS has a wide range of chart types. After selecting the main chart type, choose the chart variation that will work best for your data.

33.15

New menus and tools appear when you add a chart.

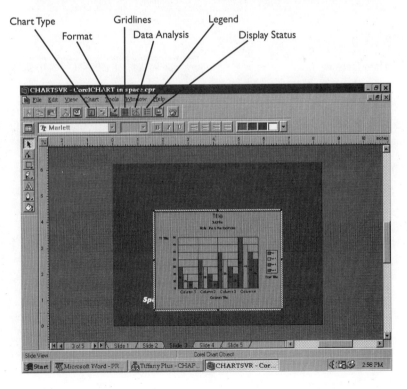

WATCH OUT!

> At this writing, the functions of clearing or adding chart categories and series are unstable; hopefully, this will be remedied soon.

Formatting Chart Data

This brief chapter doesn't allow detailed coverage of all the formatting options for charts. You'll want to explore the menus and toolbars to discover additional features. For instance, click on the Format button to work with the chart titles and axes. On the Titles page, you enter titles and control their display. The Data Axis page (Figure 33.16) contains options for adjusting the scale range and applying number formatting, such as currency symbols. Use the Category Axis page for the display of the axis and to add gridlines.

33.16

You can format many aspects of charts with the Format Chart dialog.

Format Chart

Titles | Data Axis | Category Axis

Axis
◉ Primary Data Axis   ○ Secondary Data Axis

Vertical / Hi-Low
☑ Display on Left
☐ Display on Right

Horizontal / Gantt
☐ Display on Top
☐ Display on Bottom

Scale
☑ Ascending
☐ Autofitted
☐ Staggered

◉ Linear
○ Logarithmic

Scale Range...   Number Format...

OK   Cancel   Apply   Help

The Legend button in the Standard toolbar helps you with the display and setup of the chart's legend, and the Gridlines button lets you format chart gridlines. The Data Analysis button lets you add lines representing the mean, standard deviation, and regression to your chart data.

If after creating the chart you need to change the chart type, click on the Chart Type button.

You can access the Fill and Outline tools to change the attributes of the chart frame, background, titles, lines, and other chart objects. For instance, to change a slice color in a pie chart, select the slice and apply the new fill, or use the color list in the toolbar to apply a fill color. Use the Text toolbar buttons to format chart text. You can also drag chart text and legends to new locations, if desired. After selecting a chart object, select Format / Selected Object to open a dialog with options for that object. You can also double-click on many chart elements to display dialogs with formatting options.

When you're finished creating the chart, click outside the chart area to return to PRESENTS. Whenever you need to make additional changes to the chart, just double-click on it to reopen the chart editing tools.

Exercise D

1. If necessary, open the SPACE.CPR file.

2. Move to slide 3 and enter the title **Alien Contact.**

3. Double-click on the chart placeholder on slide 3, and choose Vertical Bar as the chart type. Make sure the first vertical bar option is selected on the right, and click OK.

4. Once the chart appears, click on the Data button to view the sample data. Replace the sample data with the data displayed in Figure 33.17 and click OK.

5. Click on the Format button, and enter the chart title **Interplanetary Stylin'?**. For the subtitle, enter **People claiming to have had their hair styled by aliens.**

33.17

To quickly build a chart, replace the sample data with your data.

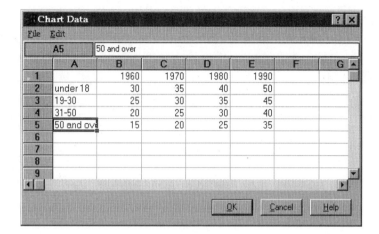

6. Turn off the display of the footnote, Y1 Title, Groups Title, and Series Title.

7. Add currency symbols to the numbers on the data axis. Carefully double-click *precisely* on the axis. In the Bar Chart Frame Properties dialog, click on the Data Axis page. Click again on the Number Format button and choose the $#,##0);($#,##0) format.

8. Select one of the bars and apply another color.

9. Select Chart / Selected Object to open the Bar Riser Properties dialog (see Figure 33.18). Set the Bar Thickness to Major, the Bar Spacing to Minimum, and turn off Show Data Values.

10. Click outside the chart to return to PRESENTS, and save the file.

In the next exercise you will import a DRAW graphic into the presentation.

33.18

PRESENTS provides many options for formatting charts, including bar thickness and spacing.

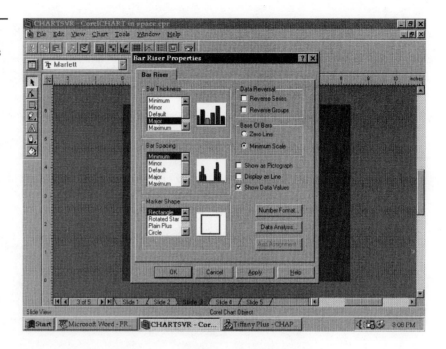

Working with Graphics, Video, Sound and OLE Objects

Like DRAW, PRESENTS can import many types of graphic file formats, such as EPS, CGM, and TIF. You can also import Corel's native file formats, including CDR from DRAW and CPT from PhotoPAINT. For even more pizzazz, you can incorporate video and sound files into your presentations. Video formats that can be imported include AVI and FLI files; sound formats include WAV and VOC.

If you have a microphone and a sound card, you can create your own sound files—for instance, a voice that explains slide information. To create a sound file, choose Insert / Sound and use the Wave Editor (Figure 33.19). Select File / Record, record the sound, and then select File / Stop.

33.19

Record your own
sound with the
Wave Editor.

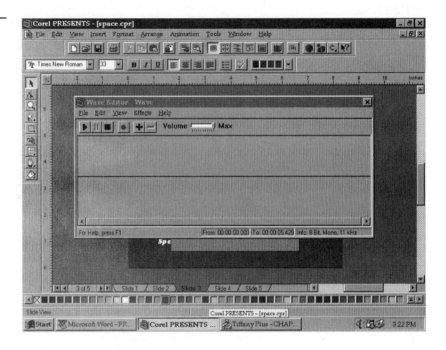

Working with OLE

PRESENTS supports OLE (Object Linking and Embedding), so you
can link or embed files from other OLE applications installed on your
system. You may want to add an Excel spreadsheet, keeping it linked
back to the original spreadsheet so it remains current. If you have selected a slide layout for adding OLE objects, simply double-click on the
OLE icon. If the slide does not have an OLE placeholder, select Insert /
New Object. From the Insert Object dialog (Figure 33.20), choose the
application in which you'll create the OLE object.

You'll find more information about OLE in CorelDRAW's on-line help
and your Windows 95 documentation.

The Launcher Button

PRESENTS also includes on the Standard toolbar a Corel Application
Launcher button for starting other Corel programs. Click on this

33.20

You can link or embed data from other Windows applications, because PRESENTS supports OLE.

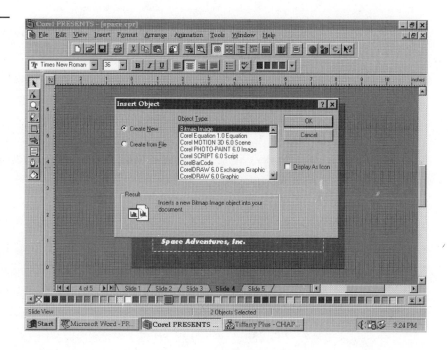

button to see a list of installed Corel applications, and then click on the application name to start the program. Unlike an OLE object, an object created in an application started with the Launcher button isn't automatically linked or embedded. Say you decide to add a DRAW graphic into a PRESENTS file. Clicking on the Launcher button lets you quickly start DRAW, where you can design a graphic and copy it to the Clipboard. You exit DRAW, return to PRESENTS, and paste in the graphic. If you don't want to embed the DRAW graphic, use the Paste Special command in PRESENTS and choose Metafile.

Exercise E

1. If necessary, open the SPACE.CPR file.

2. Move to slide 4, and enter the title **Popular Form of Transportation.** Format it using 36-point Futura Light.

3. Select the OLE placeholder and press Delete.

4. Click on the Corel Application Launcher button and start CorelDRAW.

5. In DRAW, get a spacecraft symbol from the Space category in the Symbols roll-up (if you don't have this category, find another symbol). Fill the spacecraft with green.

6. Copy the symbol to the Clipboard and exit DRAW. Click Yes when you're asked if the Clipboard data will be used with another program.

7. In PRESENTS, click the Paste button. The symbol is placed in slide 4. You can move and size it as you would in DRAW.

8. Display slide 5. You'll need to insert a black slide background here, so the presentation will fade to black at the end. Select Insert / Background / Uniform Fill and choose black from the Fill dialog.

9. When you're asked whether you want to edit the new background in Background view (this would cause it to be applied to all slides), click No.

10. Save the file.

In the next exercise you will apply transitions to your slides.

Lights, Camera, Action: Adding Movement to Slides

Presentations output to a computer screen or to video are often referred to as *desktop presentations*. By adding transition effects such as fades and wipes, you smooth the changes between slides and add movement and excitement to your presentation. With PRESENTS you can apply transitions to both slides and objects. For instance, you might make slide 2 "iris out" to cover slide 1. Slide 2 might have lines of bulleted text that "wipe on" one at a time.

You can apply transitions to slides in either Slide view or Slide Sorter view.

Working in Slide Sorter View

Slide Sorter offers several functions for adding movement to your slide presentations. Click on the Slide Sorter button on the Standard toolbar to view small thumbnails of the slides in your presentation (Figure 33.21). The Show/Hide Jacket button lets you hide the slide "jacket" surrounding each slide. With the Show/Hide Slide button, you can hide an entire slide during the presentation.

You can also use Slide Sorter view to adjust the order of slides in the presentation. Simply drag and drop the slide to the new location.

33.21

Slide Sorter view lets you preview your whole presentation, rearrange the order, delete slides, and apply transitions.

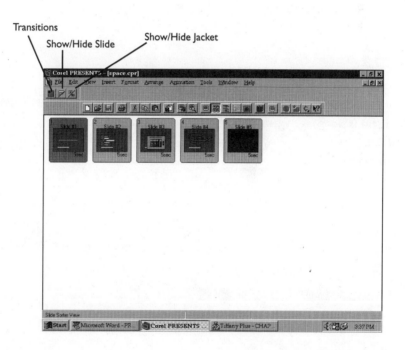

AUTHOR'S NOTE

You can add transitions in Slide view, as well. Right-click on the slide, and select Transitions from the pop-up menu.

Adding Transitions to Slides

The Slide Sorter view provides the Transition button (see Figure 33.22) for adding slide transitions. To add a transition, select the slide and click on the Transition button. In the Slide Properties dialog, shown in Figure 33.22, you can designate both opening and closing transitions to slides. Just open the drop-down list of transition effects and choose one. In the Duration and Steps boxes, specify how long you want the transition to last and how many steps it should take to complete. In a Vertical Blinds effect, for instance, you might specify a transition that lasts 2 seconds and builds in 10 steps. Use the Direction drop-down list to indicate the direction of the effect—for instance, a wipe transition that moves from top to bottom or left to right.

3 3 . 2 2

Select from a variety of opening and closing transitions to add movement to desktop presentations.

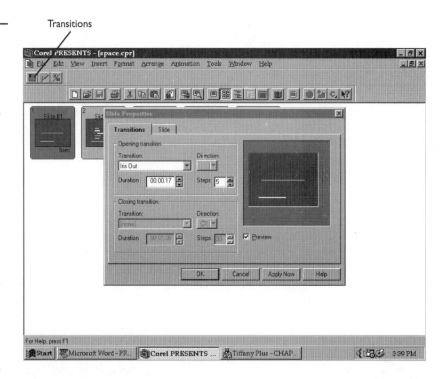

Transitions

WATCH OUT!

A transition effect cannot take longer than the slide timing. For instance, if the slide is only displayed for 2 seconds, the opening or closing effect cannot take 3 seconds to complete. If you get a message that the transition time surpasses the length of the slide timing, click OK. This does, however, cancel the effect you attempted and you will need to reapply the transition. Then, you can click on the Slide page in the Slide Properties dialog and increase the slide's timing. You'll find more information about slide timings later in this chapter.

Each slide can have a different opening and closing transition. To apply the same transition to multiple slides, select the desired slides before applying the transition. Use Shift to select a block of slides, or Ctrl to select individual slides.

Adding Transitions to Objects

Slide objects such as charts, graphics, and text can also be assigned transition effects. For instance, you might have your company logo fade out at the end of the presentation.

Object transitions are applied in Slide view. First, select the object to which you want to apply the transition. Right-click on the object and select Transitions from the pop-up menu. Then choose the desired opening and closing transitions, and specify duration and steps. The object transition begins immediately upon completion of the slide's opening transition. For instance, a transition applied to a logo would begin immediately after the slide transition.

We recommend you keep transition duration short. Two seconds may not seem very long, but to your audience it may be too long to wait for a transition to finish.

Previewing One Slide

Once you've added your transition effects, you can preview them. To preview the transitions applied to a single slide and its objects, click on the Preview Slide button in the Standard toolbar. The slide with the selected transitions will be displayed full screen.

Exercise F

1. If necessary, open the SPACE.CPR file.

2. Switch to Slide Sorter view.

3. Select slide 1 and click on the Transitions button. Choose Iris Out as the opening transition, and specify a duration of 00:00.17 and 5 steps. Click OK. Click on the Preview Slide button to see the effect.

4. Select slide 2 and click on the Transitions button. For the opening transition, choose Wipe Across. In the Direction box, choose Top to have the wipe go from top to bottom. Enter a duration of 00:00.17, 5 steps, and click OK.

5. Move to Slide view by double-clicking on slide 2.

6. Select the bulleted list, and right-click it. From the pop-up, select Transitions. Choose Wipe Across as the opening transition, with a duration of 00:00.17 and 3 steps. Click OK, and preview your work again.

7. Return to Slide Sorter view and add transitions of your choice to the rest of the slides. For the last slide, use the Fade In transition so the black background gradually fades in.

8. Save the file.

In the next exercise you will apply slide timings and preview the whole show.

It's Show Time: Running the Presentation

Will a speaker present your slides, or will the presentation run automatically? If it runs automatically, do you want it to loop back to the first slide when it reaches the end? Do you want to draw on the screen during the presentation? What about the timing of each slide? You need to address these options before the Big Show.

Adjusting Presentation Options

You have two options for running the presentation: manual advance or automatic advance. *Manual advance* allows a speaker or presenter to control how long each slide is on screen. The speaker presses the Enter key when it's time to advance to the next slide. With *automatic advance,* you can predetermine the amount of time you want each slide displayed. Slide timings are covered later in this section.

To run the show automatically, select Tools / Options. Open the Presentation page to display the dialog in Figure 33.23, and turn on Automatic Advance. The show runs manually unless this option is enabled. If you want the show to automatically loop back to the first slide when the show is over, turn on the Run Continuously option.

On-Screen Annotation   The ability to draw on a slide during a presentation enables the speaker to expound on certain points. For instance, in Figure 33.24, the presenter has drawn an arrow to lead the audience's attention to specific chart data.

To enable this on-screen annotation capability, you turn on the Display Pointer On Screen option for the presentation. Then use the Line Thickness and Pen Color buttons to format the Drawing tool.

33.23

Options for running your show include running it automatically with predetermined timing, looping back to the beginning, and using on-screen annotation.

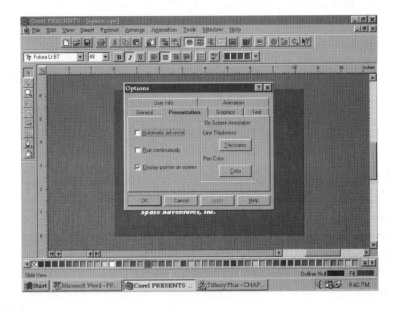

33.24

On-screen annotation is similar to what sports commentators do when they draw football plays on the TV screen.

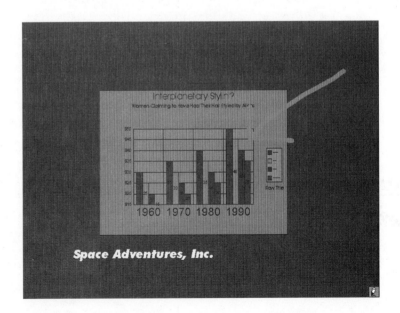

Setting Slide Timings

For automatic advance, you need to enter timings for the presentation's slides. In Slide Sorter view, select the slide and click on the Transitions button. Open the Slide page and enter a time for the slide in the Duration box (see Figure 33.25). You can also enter a slide name here. The "Welcome" being entered as the name for slide 1 in Figure 33.25 will appear on the tab at the bottom of the screen.

33.25

Timing is critical to presentations that advance automatically. Be sure to test the timings repeatedly.

AUTHOR'S NOTE

Thoroughly test the timings of your slides. You want the audience to have plenty of time to absorb the message.

Running Your Presentation

When you're ready to preview all of the slides and transitions, click on the Run Presentation button and select File / Run Presentation, or press F5. The first slide appears full screen. A show set for automatic advance will progress to subsequent slides on its own, or you'll need to press Enter to move to subsequent slides in a manual show. When you reach the last slide, press Enter to return to PRESENTS. At any time during the presentation, you can press Esc to return to PRESENTS.

To activate on-screen annotation while running the presentation, click the slide on which you want to draw. (You have to activate on-screen annotation for every slide.) An icon appears in the bottom-right corner of the slide. Now, you can draw with the mouse to highlight and emphasize elements in the presentation. Click again on the icon in the corner of the slide to deactivate the on-screen annotation.

WATCH OUT!

When you begin working with transitions and slide timings, be sure to save your file often. PRESENTS has been known to crash. Practice the presentation again and again, until you know it works without any problems.

Exercise G

1. If necessary, open the SPACE.CPR file.

2. Select Tools / Options. Make sure Automatic Advance is turned off and Display Pointer On Screen is turned on; then click OK.

3. Click on the Run Presentation button. When slide 1 is displayed, press Enter to move to slide 2.

4. Click the mouse to display the on-screen annotation icon. Click and drag the mouse to draw an × by the name "Yoogie."

5. Press Enter to display slide 3. Draw an arrow pointing to the last set of bars.

6. Continue previewing the rest of the presentation.

In the next section, you'll discover how to use CorelPRESENTS's Runtime Player.

Taking Your Show on the Road

Today many professionals are taking on-screen presentations with them for use with clients. Not all presenters want to take the time to load the PRESENTS program on their traveling PC, however—they just want to run the presentation. For this purpose, Corel provides the Runtime Player.

You must save the presentation as a Runtime Player file (.CPR) before you can display it with the Runtime Player. Select File / Save As, and choose Corel PRESENTS Runtime (*.cpr) for the file type. Choose the directory where you want to save the file, and enter a filename.

AUTHOR'S NOTE

Runtime Player files cannot be edited, so be sure to maintain your presentation in the PRESENTS .CPR file format, as well.

Using the Runtime Player

Click on the Runtime Player icon to start the program. (This icon is stored in the same folder as the icons for starting Corel applications.) Then select the file to be presented (Figure 33.26). You can preview the show and change the presentation options. (The option defaults are the ones you set up in PRESENTS.) When you're ready to run the presentation, click the Play button. After the last slide, press Enter to return to the Runtime Player screen.

33.26

Use the Runtime Player to display presentations on computers where PRESENTS is not installed.

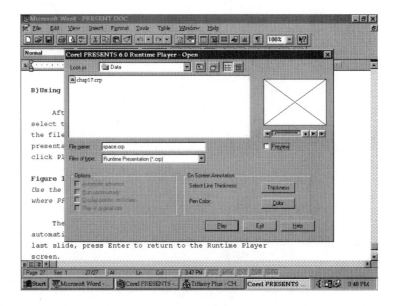

♣

Congratulations! If you have done all the exercises in this chapter, you've created a slide presentation complete with text, graphics, charts, and transitions.

Adding a Third Dimension: DREAM3D

CorelDRAW 6.0's new three-dimensional rendering application is called CorelDREAM3D (in this chapter we'll call it DREAM3D for short). DREAM3D provides the tools for creating three-dimensional renderings—complete with true perspective, lighting, shadows, and textures—to use in posters, packaging, advertisements, magazine and book covers, and other finished artwork. The program is also an alternative to photography for creating such items as book covers, product packages, and storefront displays.

DREAM3D is based on technology licensed from RayDream, Inc.; its predecessor program was Ray Dream Designer. The CorelDRAW 6.0 User's Guide provides a tutorial on DREAM3D—it's basically the same one that's in the RayDream Designer reference guide, with modifications to accommodate Corel's Windows 95-style interface. Corel's tutorial helps you acquire basic skills with DREAM3D, and you can do that on your own. Here in this chapter you'll get a chance to work with the real guts of the program, getting hands-on experience using DREAM3D's tools to create three-dimensional objects.

With DREAM3D, you create three-dimensional illustrations in five basic steps:

1. Build 3D objects

2. Apply colors and textures to your objects

3. Arrange the objects

4. Place lights and a camera

5. Render the scene

The Interface

Necessary to using DREAM3D is, naturally, some understanding of the interface. Figure 34.1 shows the DREAM3D interface as it appears when you first launch the program. You'll find its fundamental elements quite familiar; they are similar to those in all of Corel's applications. You can make a number of modifications to how DREAM3D operates and to its default appearance. We will discuss those options in the section on Preferences, but let's start by examining the main DREAM3D workspace as it appears when you first open the program.

34.1

The main view of DREAM3D when you first open the program

Display Plane Tool

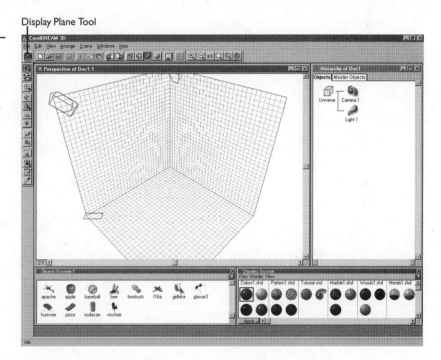

The Perspective Window: The Universe Explained

The Perspective window is where you get an overall view of your scene and objects through the camera of your choice. This view is what you are looking at most of the time when using DREAM3D. The Perspective window has three planes that represent the two back sides and bottom of a cube, referred to as *the universe*. The center or *zero point* of this universe is *not* where the three planes intersect; rather, it is the very center of the cube. In Figure 34.2, you can see a line passing through each of the visible planes of the universe, at the center of each of the planes and perpendicular to those planes. The spot where the three lines intersect is the zero point, the center of the universe.

34.2

The three inter-
secting bars shown
here intersect at
the zero point of
the three-
dimensional
universe.

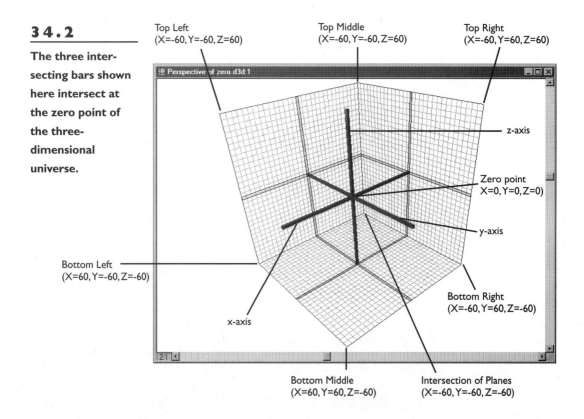

Top Left
(X=-60, Y=-60, Z=60)

Top Middle
(X=-60, Y=-60, Z=60)

Top Right
(X=-60, Y=60, Z=60)

z-axis

Zero point
X=0, Y=0, Z=0)

y-axis

Bottom Left
(X=60, Y=-60, Z=-60)

Bottom Right
(X=-60, Y=60, Z=-60)

x-axis

Bottom Middle
(X=60, Y=60, Z=-60)

Intersection of Planes
(X=-60, Y=-60, Z=-60)

With the installation defaults, the size of the universe is 120″ in all three dimensions (height, width, and depth). If you create objects that are larger than the known universe (somehow that sounds a little absurd, but see Figure 34.3), upon saving and reopening the file the universe will expand the same amount in all directions (see Figure 34.4) to accommodate those objects. The cube will remain a perfect cube, and thus the zero point will remain in the very center of the universe.

34.3

The x-axis has been lengthened from 120″ to 200″, so that 40″ on each end hangs outside the universe.

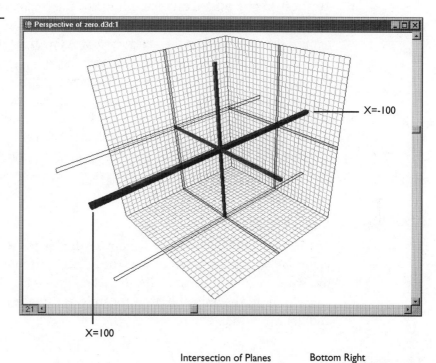

X=-100

X=100

34.4

After reopening the file in which the x-axis was lengthened, the universe has expanded by 40″ in each direction, outward from the center.

Intersection of Planes
(X=-100, Y=-100, Z=-100)

Bottom Right
(X=-100, Y=100, Z=-100)

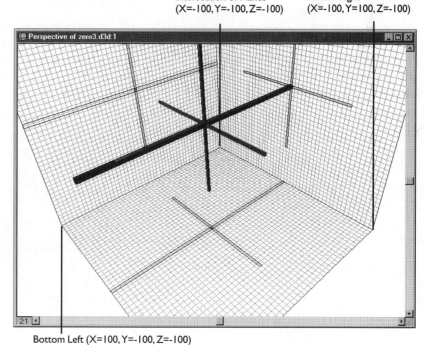

Bottom Left (X=100, Y=-100, Z=-100)

Default Light and Camera   Initially, the Perspective window's universe contains a single light and a single camera. You can see the single light in the upper-left of the Perspective window (it's there in Figure 34.1), but you cannot see the camera's location. That's because it's through the default camera that you are viewing this window. (Ever tried to look at your eyelids without a mirror?) You can only see the default camera in the Perspective window by adding another camera (in a different location) and switching the view to the new camera. You can, however, see the default camera in the Hierarchy window, which we'll examine next.

The Hierarchy Window

To the right of the Perspective window is the Hierarchy window (see Figure 34.5). Here you see a list of the objects currently in the Perspective window, as well as other details such as groupings. When you begin a new project, the only objects in the universe are the default camera and light.

34.5

The Hierarchy window contains a graphic representation of the universe and all objects that exist there.

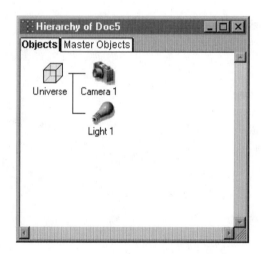

You can select objects from the Hierarchy window as well as from the Perspective window. Many of the manipulations you can do in the Perspective window can also be done in the Hierarchy window, and sometimes more easily. For instance, due to the number and complexity of objects in the Perspective window, it's far easier to select objects in the Hierarchy window. Then, if the desired functions must be performed in the Perspective window, you can click on the title bar of the Perspective window to activate it.

The Modeling Window

The Modeling window (Figure 34.6) does not appear when you first start DREAM3D or when you open a file. This window comes into play primarily when you're creating free-form objects with the Free Form tool or when you're using the Modeling Wizard (all explained later in the chapter). To get to the Modeling window, you click first on either of those tools and then in the Perspective window.

34.6

The Modeling window, accessed using the Free Form tool

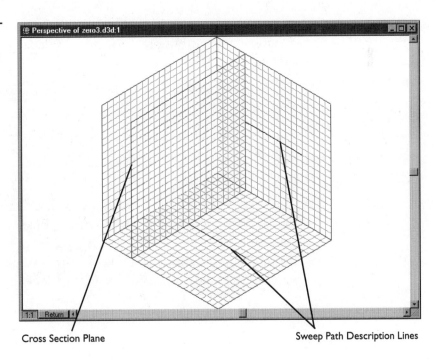

Perspective of zero3.d3d:1

Cross Section Plane

Sweep Path Description Lines

The Modeling window is where you'll do most of your work in DREAM3D, and you'll revisit it often as you work through this chapter.

The Toolbars

Immediately below the menu bar is the toolbar, shown in Figure 34.7. Actually, there two toolbars—the Standard toolbar and the Zoom toolbar. As in DRAW, the DREAM3D toolbars may be docked at any edge of the window, or floated in the workspace. If at any time you can't remember what a specific button does, pause the mouse cursor over the button and the balloon help will come to your aid.

34.7

DREAM3D's menu bar, Standard toolbar, and Zoom toolbar

As you can see, the buttons on the Standard toolbar are grouped by basic function.

- The first four are familiar to any Windows user: New, Open, Save, and Print.

- The next three buttons are the Clipboard functions: Cut, Copy, and Paste.

- Next are the file Import and file Export buttons.

- The next group of four buttons let you view your created objects at different quality levels: Bounding Box, Wireframe, Preview, and Better Preview. Better Preview shows actual color, lighting, and tile effects, but takes its time even on a fast computer. Wireframe is not available in the Modeling window.

- The Render Preview button is the one with the little monitor icon.

- The last button before the Zoom tools is the Group/Ungroup toggle. It works similarly to the grouping/ungrouping function in CorelDRAW.

The next group of six buttons constitute the Zoom toolbar. The Zoom In, Zoom Out, and Zoom to Actual Size tools are available in both the Perspective and Modeling windows. The last three are available in Perspective view only: Zoom to Selected, Zoom to All Objects, and Zoom to Working Box. (This last one is supposed to correspond to CorelDRAW's Zoom to Page tool but rarely works as expected.)

AUTHOR'S NOTE

The Zoom In tool does not allow you to marquee-select an area. You have to do that with the magnifier tool in the Toolbox.

When the Modeling window is open, certain tools in the toolbar are grayed out (not accessible); certain items in the menu bar are different, as well (see Figure 34.8). Once the Modeling window contains objects, the Clipboard functions (Cut and Copy, and Paste if you cut or copy an object) and the Group/Ungroup button become available.

34.8

When working in the Modeling window, not all tools are available in the toolbar.

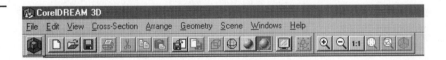

WATCH OUT!

If you return to the Perspective window from the Modeling window without creating an object, DREAM3D automatically places an object that consists of just one extrusion line. These objects are invisible and contribute nothing to your scene, but unless you conscientiously remove them, they will increase the complexity and the rendering time of your scenes. So get in the habit of deleting these "ghost" extrusions whenever you toggle between the Perspective and Modeling windows.

The Toolbox

The Toolbox, initially found at the left of the screen, is specific to the current window view. That is, the available tools depend on whether the Perspective or Modeling window is in use.

AUTHOR'S NOTE

For you RayDream users out there, the DREAM3D Toolbox includes a number of the tools formerly found in a window at the bottom of the RayDream screen.

The tools in the Toolbox, like those in the toolbars, are grouped roughly according to function. We'll start with the tools available in the Perspective window.

The Selection Tool   As its name indicates, the Selection tool is what you use to pick and manipulate (move or resize) objects. On the flyout is the Paint Shape Selection tool, used for picking and manipulating a painted area applied to the surface of an object.

Virtual Trackball   The Virtual Trackball allows you to freely rotate a selected object in multiple directions at once. The other tool on this flyout is the One-Axis Rotation tool, which rotates in a single plane only.

Zoom Tools   The Zoom flyout contains three tools that work much the same as in CorelDRAW, with some exceptions.

The Zoom In tool lets you simply click to obtain a 2X view, or you can marquee-select an area to be enlarged. However, be forewarned that the marquee magnification is not as refined as it is in CorelDRAW, and you may need some practice to get it to show the area you really want to see enlarged. The Zoom Out tool works identically to the one in Corel-DRAW. The Hand tool lets you "grab" the workspace and slide in around "behind" the view window. CorelDRAW 6.0 could take a lesson from this clever implementation of the Hand tool.

Object Creation Tools   Next are four tools whose purpose is object creation. To create and place an object in the Perspective window, you click on the desired tool and then click or drag in roughly the location you want the object positioned.

AUTHOR'S NOTE

You can seldom position objects accurately in the Perspective window. This is because the 2D workspace of a monitor cannot adequately represent 3D space. Just assume you'll have to relocate the objects, once placed.

The Free Form tool is used to create objects from scratch. The *form* is not as *free* as we would like, but perhaps in future versions we'll see some improvement.

The Primitive Objects tool—no, this is not for creating wooden clubs, flint arrowheads, and stone tablets—makes basic geometric shapes, including cones, cubes, cylinders, spheres and (for some unknown reason) icosahedrons:

These primitive objects can be moved, rotated, resized, or distorted. They may *not*, however, be taken apart into component pieces. In other words, you cannot take a sphere created with this tool and shear away half of it to make a hemisphere; you cannot remove any sides from a cube created with this tool. The *basic geometry* of a primitive object cannot be changed; this is an important factor to remember, as you will see later.

The Text tool:

needs little explanation, but it does need an apology (are you listening, Corel?). In comparison to its RayDream Designer counterpart, DREAM3D's Text tool has been hobbled. It does *not* support Type 1 fonts—only TrueType (contrary to the CorelDRAW User's Guide). So if you're a PostScript bigot, one of your next acquisitions will no doubt be a font-conversion utility such as FontMonger, from Ares Software.

Last of the object creations tools is the Modeling Wizard, which leads
you through the steps of creating Extrusion objects, Lathe objects, Pipeline objects, and Skin objects. The Modeling Wizard is covered in detail
in a later section.

Lights and Cameras   When you add Lights and Cameras:

they are added in roughly the position where you click the mouse (after
activating the tool). Just as it is with objects, positioning lights and cameras with the cursor is difficult in the 3D universe when you're using a
2D workspace (the screen). Count on having to reposition them using
the Object Properties dialog, which we'll discuss shortly.

Render Preview   The Render Preview tool:

enables you to marquee-select an area in the Perspective window, to be
rendered in nearly all the detail you would see if you went to a final rendering. Notably absent from a rendering done with this tool are shadow
effects.

The Paint Tools   Use the Paint Shape tool to apply a shade or texture map to a specific surface of an object. The flyout lets you select
whether the paint shape will be rectangular, polygonal, or elliptical
(oval):

Use the Brush tool to actually paint a specific portion of an object:

Use the Eyedropper tool to extract a shader or paint effect from another object, surface, or portion of an object, for use elsewhere:

Tools Specific to the Modeling Window

When you're viewing the Modeling window, the Toolbox changes. The object manipulation tools (Selection and Rotation), the Zoom tools, and the Paint tools all work the same as described above for the Perspective window. Tools specific to the Modeling window are as follows.

The Bézier Tool   The Bézier tool is used for creating lines and curves for initial shapes to be extruded, as well as for extrusion paths for those shapes.

The Point Tools Flyout   This flyout contains three tools:

With the Convert Point tool, you can change a corner point to a curve point or vice versa. You can also manipulate the Bézier handles of a curve point independently, thus creating a "cusp" point. The Delete Point tool does just that—deletes an existing point on a line or curve (á la Delete Node in CorelDRAW). And the Add Point tool adds a point (like Add Node in CorelDRAW) to an existing line or curve at the location where you click the mouse.

The Draw Shapes Flyout   The Draw Shapes flyout has four options:

- Draw Rectangle

- Draw Rounded Corners Rectangle; when you draw the "round rec," you get a dialog for specifying the width and height of the arc to be used for the round corners. DREAM3D does not remember this setting for the next "round rec," however.

- Draw Oval

- Draw Polygon; you get a dialog with this one, like "round rec." When you draw what is initially a hexagon, you then specify how many sides the polygon should have. The settings aren't retained for this one, either.

The Text Tool   The Text tool:

is much like the one in the Perspective window Toolbox. Text placed in the Modeling window using this tool, however, can be ungrouped and altered, point by point and curve by curve, as you can do in CorelDRAW by converting artistic text to curves.

The Display Planes Tool

The one tool remaining that is not really a part of either the toolbar or the Toolbox is the Display Planes tool. It's positioned at the "intersection" of the toolbars and the Toolbox. You use Display Planes to toggle on and off the display of any or all the grids in the Perspective window; just click on the corresponding grid in the tool. If you hold down the Alt key while clicking on a plane, that plane becomes the active one.

The active plane, shown in blue-green, controls the movement of objects when you use the mouse in the Perspective window.

The Object Properties Dialogs

The Object Properties dialog tells you general information about nearly any selected object in the Perspective, Hierarchy, or Modeling windows. It also provides you with a way of moving, scaling, and rotating objects—it's kind of a Swiss Army knife, as tools go.

To access the Object Properties dialog, just right-click on the object you're interested in, and select Properties from the pop-up menu. In Figure 34.9, the dialog reflects information about a sphere.

Here in this centralized location you can change many of the object's properties by typing in or dialing to new numbers (as opposed to, say, using the Virtual Trackball tool to rotate the sphere, or the cursor to move it). The X, Y, and Z values indicate the location of the object's *hot point*—an important element of an object's position that we'll study more in the section on moving and manipulating objects. You can even change the name of the object by simply typing over the name that's there. To make these new values take effect, you click on the Apply button.

Information reflected in Object Properties dialogs is, of course, based on the object itself. It is also based on the window being used to view the object, as described in the paragraphs that follow.

Properties for Objects in the Perspective and Hierarchy Windows

When you're viewing an object in the Perspective or Hierarchy window, the Object Properties dialog tells you the name of the object, the location of its *hot point*, its rotation values (Yaw, Pitch, and Roll) in degrees, and its size (SizeX, SizeY, and SizeZ). Notice the Keep Proportions

34.9

The Object Properties dialog contains a collection of dimensions, placement information, and angle of a selected object or group.

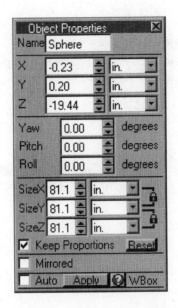

check box. This lets you maintain proportion as you resize. In our sphere example in Figure 34.9, let's say you want to change the sphere to an ovoid. You have to make sure that the Keep Proportions check box is *not* checked; otherwise, any value entered for SizeX, SizeY, or SizeZ will be applied to all three of these elements.

Properties for Objects in the Modeling Window

For objects in the Modeling window, the Properties dialog reflects data based on the object or portion of an object that is selected. Instead of having to resize or distort the object with the mouse, you can change values here in the Properties dialog. For instance, in Figure 34.10 you see the properties for the selected cross-section of the wireframe rectangle: the width and height of the object (provided it is still grouped, which it is upon first drawing); and the coordinate position of the top-left corner of the object's bounding area, relative to the center point of the Modeling window grid.

AUTHOR'S NOTE

> This figure also demonstrates the Drawing Plane view (available via View / Type), which is sometimes easier to use than the oblique perspective of the default Reference view.

34.10

This Properties dialog shows the position of a free-form object drawn in the Modeling window.

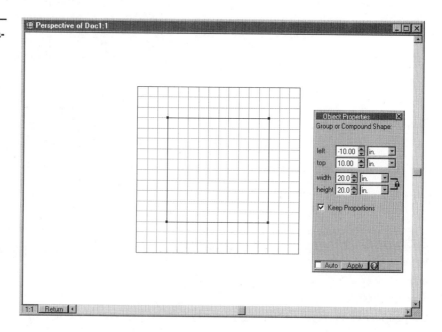

When objects in the Modeling window are ungrouped, the individual points making up the object become available for selection. (Use the Tab key to select a point on an ungrouped object.) Selecting these points causes the Properties dialog to show still different information.

■ *For cross-section corner points:* In the case of an individual corner point on an ungrouped object, the Properties dialog reflects the coordinates of the current position of that point, and you can modify these directly. The Properties dialog is a little flaky when it comes to individual points, however, and you may have to click on a point twice to update the window.

■ *For cross-section curve points:* In the case of an individual curve point (see Figure 34.11), the Properties dialog reflects not only the coordinates of the point itself, but the coordinates of the Bézier control points. These, too, may be modified in the Properties dialog. You also have the option to retract either of the Bézier control points.

■ *For points on extrusion or lathe paths:* In the case of corner and curve points on a lathe or extrusion path, the Properties dialog shows the coordinates of the points and the control points. However, despite the presence of an Apply button, these values cannot be modified here. (This bug was not created by Corel; it exists in the RayDream Designer ancestor, too—maybe this oversight will be rectified in a future version of DREAM3D.)

The Browsers

The Objects Browser, at the bottom-left of the screen (see Figure 34.12), is most useful for maintaining a library of objects and parts of objects that you use often. Its store of sample clip-art objects is vastly

34.11

When a curve point on a cross-section is selected, the Properties dialog reports (and lets you change) the position of the Bézier control points of that curve point.

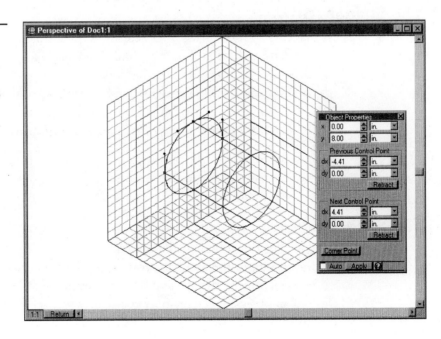

overrated, given the average person's need for such elements as a gigantic wasp or a miniature pizza. For the most part, you can probably close the Object Browser and never miss it.

34.12

Use the Object Browser to maintain a library of frequently used objects.

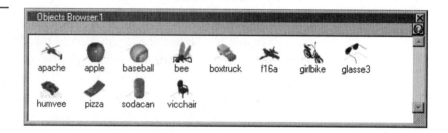

There's not much to say about the operation of the Objects Browser. It's fairly simple—to add an object to the browser, just drag an object over from the Hierarchy window. To use an object from the browser, just drag it over to the Perspective window.

The Shaders Browser

A shader is a set of surface characteristics, including qualities of color, texture, and reflection. Some prebuilt shaders are available in the Shaders Browser (Figure 34.13), at the bottom-right of the screen. Unlike the offerings in the Objects Browser, however, these shaders are actually *useful.* When a shader isn't directly applicable to your project, you can easily create duplicates and modify them to your heart's content.

The default shader—the one applied to objects as they are created—is the red one on the left in the top row.

The Shader Editor

The Shader Editor dialog (Figure 34.14), accessed by double-clicking on any shader in the Shaders Browser, is where you define the color and surface qualities of the specific shader, presumably for eventual application to an object. You can apply the shader to a selected object directly

34.13

The Shaders
Browser is a library
of shaders you can
use to apply sur-
face qualities to
objects.

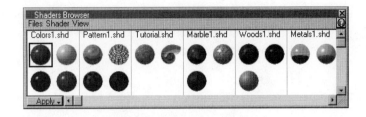

from within the Shader Editor, or you may do so from the Shaders
Browser once you've made your modifications.

34.14

Use the Shader Edi-
tor to define the
various surface
qualities for a
shader.

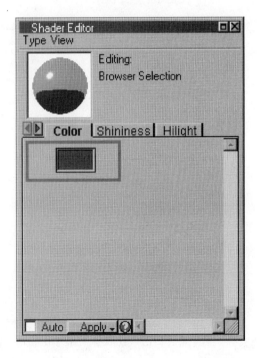

The Shader Editor contains tabbed pages of options that you can define
for a shader. Click a tab to open that page, and you'll see sliders and
buttons for adjusting that aspect of the shader. When you first open the

Shader Editor, you see only three tabs. To get to the others, click the right-arrow button at the left end of the row of tabs. Or you can use the small Maximize button in the upper-right corner to expand the Shader Editor and see all the tabs at once.

For any of these tabbed pages—Color, Shininess, Hilight, Bump, Reflection, Transparency, and Refraction—you can specify a type of setting: Value, Color, Texture Map, Operators, Patterns, or Natural Functions, all available in the Type menu. Some of these settings are not appropriate for some tabs, but DREAM3D warns you when you attempt to specify an inappropriate setting. Here's a closer look at the tabs:

- *Color.* The default color model is RGB, but you can change it to CMYK (in File / Preferences, which we'll discuss at length in an upcoming section).

- *Shininess.* Controls how much light is reflected (the light from any source within the scene).

- *Hilight.* Controls *how* light is reflected. It can be diffused when reflected; or highlights can be specular or concentrated points of light.

- *Bump.* Controls the texture of a shader. The texture itself is capable of casting shadows and thus contributes to the realism of an object.

- *Reflection.* Controls the degree to which a surface reflects other objects in the scene.

- *Transparency.* Controls the degree of "see-through" of an object.

- *Refraction.* Controls the degree to which light is distorted and/or redirected when passing through a transparent or semitransparent object. An example of use would be creation of a magnifying lens or, by using a texture map or bump values from the Type menu, creating the illusion of old glass that is of uneven thickness.

Customizing Shaders

The best way to grasp the concept of shaders is to experiment. Start by selecting a shader that comes closest to what you want, either in color or other qualities. Then open the Shader menu in the Shader Browser menu bar, and select Duplicate. (You typically have to scroll down the Shaders Browser to find the duplicate and select it before making changes. Unfortunately, DREAM3D does not switch the selection to the newly created duplicate.)

WATCH OUT!

Before you try adjusting any Shader Editor settings, be sure to read the sidebar, "Working with Channels in the Shader Editor."

Let's work with one of the popular effects. Select one of the metal shaders, the gold one, and duplicate it. Then access the Shader Editor, by double-clicking on the new duplicate shader or by right-clicking it and selecting Edit from the pop-up.

The default Bump setting for this gold shader makes an object look like gold foil rather than smooth gold, though you can't tell this by looking at the color in the shader sphere until you enter the Shader Editor and make a change to the Bump setting. By increasing the blending, the shader becomes more like polished gold.

Adjusting the Reflection Setting in Shaders   By increasing the Reflection setting for the gold shader—say, to 75%—you make the object appear to have more of a shiny, metallic surface. However, even in Better Preview mode, an object with this shader applied will look somewhat washed out in the Perspective window. This happens for a couple of reasons. For one thing, even the Better Preview mode doesn't show all aspects of lighting and shadows. Secondly, the Better Preview mode doesn't show any reflections of other objects in a scene containing this gold object. It is specifically other objects in a scene that cause a reflective object to appear reflective. Even if you rendered this scene, the gold object would still look washed out because there are no other objects to reflect except the surrounding white environment (referred to as *ambient light*, the color and brightness of which can be changed in the DREAM3D Scene menu).

If you add more objects to the scene, even if they're out of sight of the camera, the reflective object will appear more real. To add objects out of the camera's view, you need to turn on the production frame setting (under the View menu). The production frame shows what portion of your scene will appear in the rendering. If what the frame shows is not adequate, you can adjust the camera until it is correct.

You can then place objects either inside or outside the production frame, and then select Render / Preview from the Scene menu. You will then see that all the objects added to the scene have corresponding reflections in the gold sphere.

AUTHOR'S NOTE

Other functions of shaders are not covered in this chapter, and you'll want to explore them on your own.

Working with Channels in the Shader Editor

As you experiment with and learn about the workings of the Shader Editor, it's important to remember that each of the tabbed pages represents a *channel*. By default, when you apply a shader to an object, only *nonempty* channels—that is, channels with some setting—are applied. The empty channels of the shader are ignored, and if the object's existing shader had settings for those channels, those settings will be preserved. (This default can be changed, in the Preferences dialog, so that applying a shader defaults to applying it to *all* channels.)

For example, say you apply the shader called Concrete and select Apply All Channels (by clicking and holding on the Apply button until two choices drop down from it). Unless

Working with Channels in the Shader Editor (continued)

you are in Better Preview mode, you won't be able to discern much difference. To check the effect, you can use the Render Area tool in the Toolbox and marquee-select a specific area for rendering, or do a true Render Preview (Ctrl+R or click the Render Preview button). You can then see that your object has an obvious texture.

By double-clicking on the Concrete shader in the Shaders Browser and then clicking on each of the tabs, you can see why your object appears to have a texture: because the Concrete shader has settings for the Color and Bump channels. The Reflection, Transparency, and Refraction channels have no settings. By comparison, if you close the Shader Editor and then double-click on the red shader, you'll see that the Color channel has a value, but all the other channels are empty.

Now apply the red shader to your object again, this time selecting the Apply Non-Empty Channels choice in the Apply button's drop-down. When you apply only nonempty channels, your object retains the Concrete texture. That's because the red shader's Bump channel is empty. The Concrete shader changed the Bump texture of this object, and the red shader left that channel alone. Had you chosen Apply All Channels, the Bump channel would have been overwritten with null values.

Here's another example of how to use these options: Say you apply your polished gold shader, with Apply All Channels. Then, to make the object look like a blue-tinted metal object, you select the blue shader. (Or create your own shader with a Color setting only—no other channel settings.) Finally, you apply this other shader with the Apply Non-Empty Channels option. Your object becomes a shiny, reflective blue.

Moving/Manipulating Objects in the Perspective Window

We have already mentioned how difficult it is to accurately place an object when you first draw it, because of the fundamental differences between a 2D screen and a 3D environment. The mouse or other pointing device has no function for the third axis. (You could try lifting your mouse or pushing it into the table, but we doubt you'll get any satisfactory results.) So how *do* you move objects successfully? Look to the Object Properties dialog, and the all-important hot point.

Understanding Hot Points

An object's *hot point* is the single point of an object (or a set of grouped objects) that identifies its location in the 3D universe. Figure 34.15 shows the hot point for a cone.

Whenever an object is selected in the Perspective window, you can see the hot point. In addition, the object is shown with a *bounding box* that entirely surrounds the outermost dimensions of the object (see Figure 34.15). If you switch to the Bounding Box view by clicking on the Bounding Box Quality button in the toolbar, the bounding box is all you will see. In the Perspective window you can also see the 2D projects, or "shadows," on the grid planes of the universe, whether the object is selected or not.

You've already encountered some discussion of hot points in the section on the Object Properties dialog, so you already know that you can use the object's coordinates to see its position in relation to the center of your universe.

- For primitive objects, the hot point is at the exact center when the object is initially created.

- For free-form objects, it's a little more complicated. The hot point of a free-form object when it is first created corresponds

34.15

When an object is selected in the Perspective window, you can see the hot point and the bounding box.

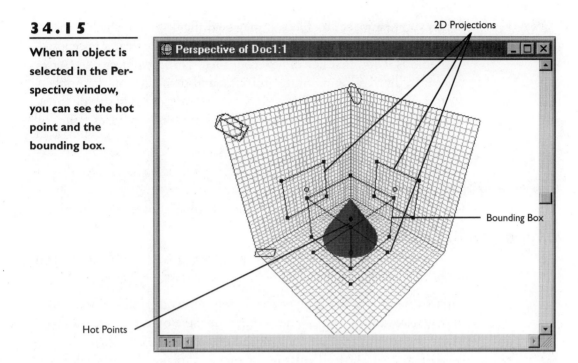

2D Projections

Perspective of Doc1:1

Bounding Box

Hot Points

to the center of the Modeling window's back plane. For instance, a small circle placed way up in the far-left corner of the back plane of the Modeling window will create a cylinder whose hot point is not even inside the cylinder.

When an object's hot point is *not* in the very center of the object, as in some free-form objects, or if you inadvertently move a hot point, you can easily return it to the object's center by selecting the object, pulling down the Arrange menu, and clicking on Center Hot Point.

Take a look at the X, Y, and Z coordinates of an object—its hot point—as expressed in the Object Properties dialog. The hot point appears in the Perspective window as a small 3D sphere (see Figure 34.15). In addition, there are three shadows (silhouettes) of the bounding box, one corresponding to each grid-plane of your universe. In DREAM3D, these are called *2D projections*.

When you first place an object, it may be difficult to tell which is the bounding box and which is the shadow. It is generally easiest to reposition objects if you first key in new coordinates for the object (0,0,0) to place it in the very center of the universe, and then click on the Apply button. With your object in the very center, you can easily see the three 2D projections on each of the planes. The hot point sphere, as well, casts 2D projections onto each plane.

Moving Objects

Quite a number of alternatives are available to you for moving objects in the Perspective window.

As described in the preceding section, you can specify new coordinates in the Object Properties dialog.

Another method is to simply grab the bounding box of the object and drag it around the screen. When you do this, the object moves parallel to the preferred plane (the background plane shown in a different color). To move perpendicular to the preferred plane, press the Alt key while dragging. To change the preferred plane, hold Alt and click the plane you want on the Display Planes icon.

Still another alternative is to move the object one plane at a time, by grabbing the 2D projection on one of the three planes and dragging it to the desired location. With this type of motion you are restricted to moving the object parallel to the plane from which you grabbed the 2D projection. In other words, the object remains exactly the same distance away from that plane, regardless of where you move the 2D projection; only the other two distances will change. You can then grab a 2D projection in *another* plane to relocate the object relative to the other two planes.

AUTHOR'S NOTE

If you move your object to the wrong place and lose the ability to grab it, remember that you can click on that object's icon in the Hierarchy window and use the Object Properties dialog to re-center the object in the universe.

Constrained Movement   If you want to move an object in one direction only, use the *constrain* function. By grabbing the 2D projection first and then pressing the Shift key, you can drag an object in a precisely horizontal or vertical direction, or at precisely a 45° angle from its original position.

Incidentally, this same constrain function works in the Modeling window with objects, corner points, curve points, and Bézier curve handles.

Using Grid Snap   The *working box*, yet another term for the universe, has a grid snap option like CorelDRAW's. Right-click anywhere away from an object in the Perspective window, and select Grid from the pop-up menu. In the Grid dialog:

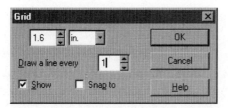

you can specify the unit value for the grid snap, as well as how many gridlines are actually drawn on screen on the planes of the universe. You can also turn on the Snap function so that all objects drawn or moved will snap into place according to the unit value set.

Rotating Objects

Initial placement of the primitive objects is always in the same orientation relative to the universe. For example, a cylinder's ends are always parallel to the "floor"—that is, the Z plane. A cone primitive object will always be placed with its base parallel to the bottom plane. A cube's faces will always be parallel to the planes of the working box. (The X, Y, and Z planes will be discussed further in a later section.)

When you want to rotate an object in the Perspective window, you have several ways of accomplishing this—just as you do for moving an object:

- The easiest but least controllable rotation method is the Virtual Trackball tool. This method is difficult to control because of the usual 2D vs. 3D conflict: You're trying to control motion in 3D space using a pointing device that only registers motion in two dimensions—up/down and left/right.

- Another method that gives you more control is the One Axis Rotation tool.

- You can also rotate an object by grabbing one of the points on the object's bounding box. This method, too, is somewhat difficult to control because the object rotates according to which point you grab.

- Sometimes it works better to grab one of the points on a 2D projection of the bounding box and rotate the object in a single plane.

- Of the rotation methods, by far the most accurate (if somewhat obtuse) is to type values into the Yaw, Pitch, and Roll settings in the Object Properties dialog. We'll discuss this in detail shortly.

No matter how you choose to rotate an object, the rotation occurs relative to the object's hot point. By default, a hot point is at the center of the object's bounding box. You can, however, move this hot point independent of the related object. You can move the hot point to any point in the object, on its surface, or some distance away from it. Thus you can rotate your object around any point in the universe. For example, an object with the hot point at its center will spin in place. An object with the hot point placed some distance away will orbit around that hot point. In this fashion, you can position items any way you like.

Remember, when you select the hot point, the Object Properties dialog reflects and allows you to change the coordinate position of the hot point. When you have the hot point selected, you can also snap it back to the center of the object simply by clicking the Send to Center button underneath the coordinate display in the Object Properties dialog. There's also a Lock to Object check box, just below the Send to Center button. When you enable this option, any new coordinates entered for the hot point in the Object Properties dialog will move not only the hot point but the object, as well. This allows you to maintain the current relationship of the hot point and its corresponding object. This does not work, however, when you move the hot point manually in the Perspective window. In that case, you have to move the object itself.

Constrained Rotation   Use the Shift key to constrain the object's rotation, and thereby control the angle of rotation in specific increments (degrees). The rotation increment that occurs with each "snap" is determined by the Rotation Angle in the Perspective section of the Preferences dialog. The default increment is typically too large; we prefer to set it at 5°. (Preferences are explained in a later section.)

Rotating Objects Using Yaw, Pitch, and Roll

Yaw, Pitch, and Roll are aviation terms, and in order to understand them, you need to know about the axes typically used to define three-dimensional space. The x-axis and y-axis are common to 2D representations; in 3D space, there is a third axis, as well—the z-axis. See Figure 34.16.

34.16

These three elongated cubes represent the three axes—x, y, and z—of the 3D universe.

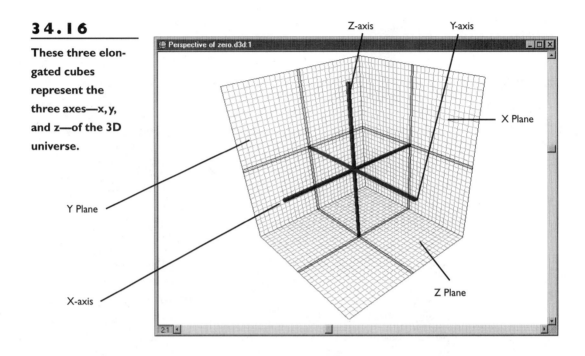

Z-axis

Y-axis

X Plane

Y Plane

X-axis

Z Plane

In DREAM3D, the z-axis is the vertical axis, perpendicular to the floor of this universe. That is, any movement on the z-axis changes the object's position up or down relative to the floor, or the *Z plane* of this universe. The x-axis is perpendicular to the right plane or *X plane* of the universe. And the y-axis is perpendicular to the left plane or *Y plane* of the universe.

Now, back to the rotation issue. If you were to use the Primitive Objects tool to create a cylinder (whose flat ends, by default, are parallel to the Z plane), and then change the Yaw of the cylinder, what would happen? Consider that Yaw rotates the object around the z-axis. If you rotate this cylinder around the z-axis, it's going to look exactly the same. In order to see that change, you would have to change the aspect ratio of the cylinder, so that its cross-section is not a perfect circle. See Figures 34.17 and 34.18.

34.17

Before: **To demonstrate the effect of the Yaw setting, this cylinder has had its aspect ratio changed so that the cross-section is not perfectly circular.**

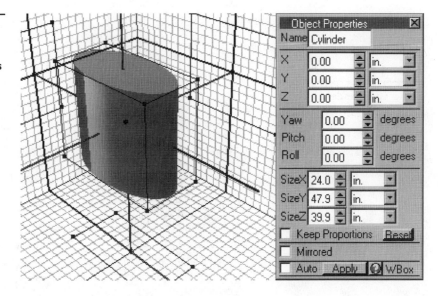

34.18

After: **This flattened cylinder has been rotated around the z-axis by 90°.**

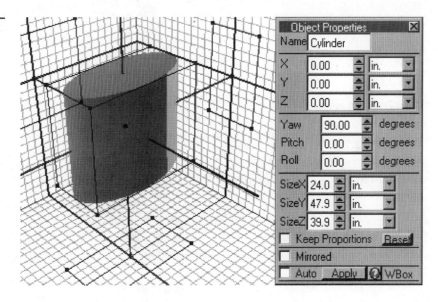

If you change just the Pitch value for the cylinder, it will rotate on the x-axis. See Figures 34.19 and 34.20.

34.19

Before: **The cylinder, as first created, before applying a new Pitch setting**

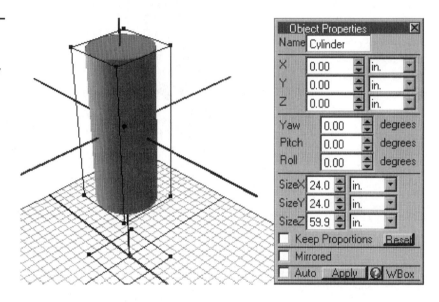

34.20

After: **The cylinder after changing the Pitch setting, which rotated it around the x-axis by 90°**

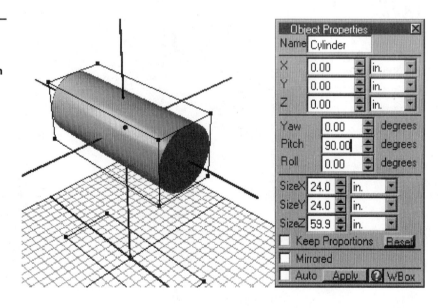

That leaves only Roll, which represents the one remaining axis, the y-axis. See Figures 34.21 and 34.22.

34.21

Before: **The cylinder, as first created, before applying a new Roll setting**

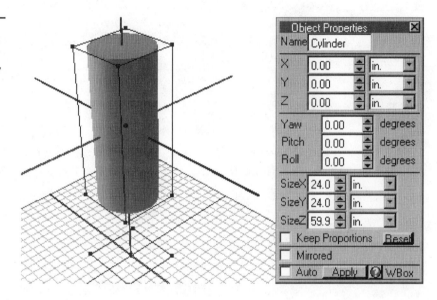

34.22

After: **The cylinder after applying the new Roll setting, which rotated it around the y-axis by 90°**

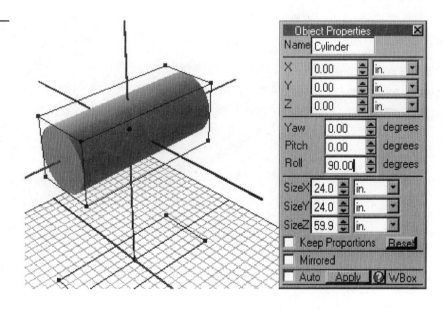

AUTHOR'S NOTE

Personally, we haven't figured out a way of committing the **Yaw,** **Pitch,** and **Roll** definitions to memory. Nearly every time we need to use them, we have to manually rotate the 2D projection for the object in the plane where we want the rotation, and then check the Properties dialog to see which setting changed.

Preferences

As mentioned earlier, you can customize the way DREAM3D works for you. The Preferences dialog is where you set the DREAM3D interface and operations to act and look just the way you want. Select Preferences in the File menu to get the dialog shown in Figure 34.23, and then in the drop-down list choose the category of settings you want to change.

34.23

The Preferences dialog's drop-down list presents the categories of DREAM3D's settings that you can change to suit your working environment.

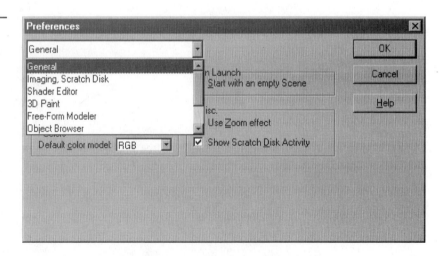

You need not exit the program to enable any preferences you have changed; your selections take effect immediately upon exiting the Preferences dialog, and they remain in effect until you change them.

AUTHOR'S NOTE

DREAM3D's on-line help for the Preferences dialog is quite detailed and complete, and you'll be able to find what you need to set up the application as desired. In this section we provide information on some options omitted from the help, and some recommendations.

Shader Editor Preferences

In the Default Apply Mode section of this dialog, you can choose whether you want all shaders channels, or nonempty channels only, applied to an object's primer. The default is nonempty channels only, but it is usually more convenient to have this set to Apply All Channels. For more information, see the sidebar, "Working with Channels in the Shader Editor."

Free-Form Modeler Preferences

By default, the Ask For Name When Creating A New Object option is turned on. With this setting enabled, you will be prompted for a name whenever you begin creating a new object. When this setting is off, DREAM3D names the objects Free Form 1, Free Form 2, and so on. Of course, you can rename objects at any time by clicking the name in the Hierarchy window when the object is selected, typing in a new name, and clicking Apply. Since the Free Form tool is difficult to learn, at first you'll probably make a lot of objects that you'll want to delete. There's no point wasting the time naming them until you know you've got them right, so we recommend you turn off this setting and name the objects later.

Object Browser Preferences

Turn on the Drop ClipArt As Master Object option to have clip art that is imported via the Object Browser treated as a single, grouped, master object, rather than handling its components as separate masters.

Most scenes use one or more duplicates (copies) of some particular object. Each duplicate is not a discrete object but rather another *instance* of an original *master* object. For example, the four legs of a table are typically not four separate objects, but four instances of a master table leg. The position, orientation, size, hot point, and shading of each object's instance may be unique; the *shape*, however, must be *common*.

If you change the geometry of an instance, you create a new master. If, on the other hand, you change the geometry of a master, you also change the geometry of all instances created from that master. This is very much like the Clone function in CorelDRAW.

Shading of instances may be unique or common. An example of common shading would be a dozen product packages on a shelf, all having the same label. Working at the master level, you can change the labels on all 12 packages in one operation. Working at the instance level, you can apply a special color to one of the labels; later, you could change the size of all of the labels without affecting the color applied to the one label.

Shader Browser Preferences

The two options under Default Apply Mode let you indicate whether you want to completely replace an object's primer with the shader you are applying or just replace the channels that have information in them. This setting, like the similar Shader Editor setting, is probably more convenient when set to Apply All Channels.

Creating Objects
Using the Modeling Wizard

DREAM3D's Modeling Wizard is one of the best ways to learn how to use the Free Form tool. You open it by clicking the Modeling Wizard tool in the Toolbox and clicking in the Perspective window.

The Wizard's opening screen presents a variety of choices (see Figure 34.24): Lathe Object, Extrusion, Pipeline, Skin Object, Spiral

Object, and Twisted Object. In the dialogs that appear when you make your choice, you'll make selections and provide information to help the Wizard construct your object.

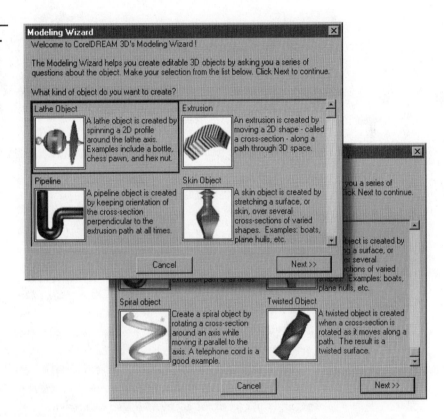

You can also independently create your own version of any of these six types of objects, rather than using one of the relatively useless examples provided by the Wizard. If you do choose the Create Your Own Object option for any of these objects, you will see, after all other specifications have been made, a final dialog for specifying the dimensions of your custom object (see Figure 34.25).

34.25

The Object Size
dialog

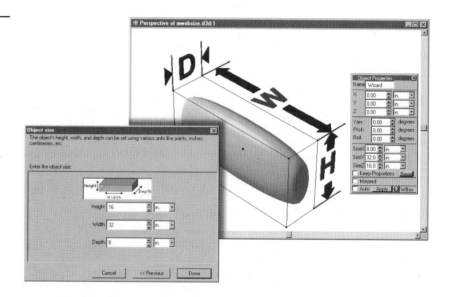

INSIDE INFO

Understanding Dimensions in the Object Size Dialog. **The Object Size dialog contains designations for Height, Width, and Depth. There is no indication, however, of how these dimensions correlate to the object itself or to the universe in the Perspective window. Here is the explanation: For objects with "ends," such as a cylinder with rounded ends, the dimensions of the ends are controlled by the Depth measurement, which is the dimension on the x-axis, and the Height measurement, which is the dimension on the z-axis. The length of the object—the length of any extrusion path—is specified with the Width measurement.**

Lathe Objects

A lathe object is created by spinning a 2D profile around a central axis (the *lathe axis*). Examples of lathe objects are a bottle, a chess pawn, and a hex nut. The Wizard's opening screen for a Lathe Object provides examples of a light bulb (boring), a vase (moderately boring), and a champagne glass (the most interesting of the three—more so, of course, were it to actually *contain* some champagne).

If you choose the Create Your Own Object option, the Profile Type dialog appears (Figure 34.26).

34.26

In the Profile Type dialog box, you choose the type of treatment for the front and back faces of the lathe object.

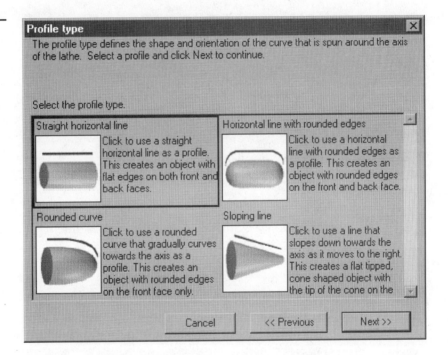

Selecting one of the four profile types—straight horizontal line, horizontal line with rounded edges (ends), rounded curve, or sloping line— leads you to the Lathe Shape dialog (Figure 34.27), where you choose either a polygonal lathe or a circular lathe for the 2D profile. The polygonal lathe follows a polygonal path when spun around the axis; the circular lathe spins around the axis always equidistant from the axis. If you choose the polygonal lathe, you get another dialog for designating the number of sides for the polygon.

34.27

The Lathe Shape
dialog

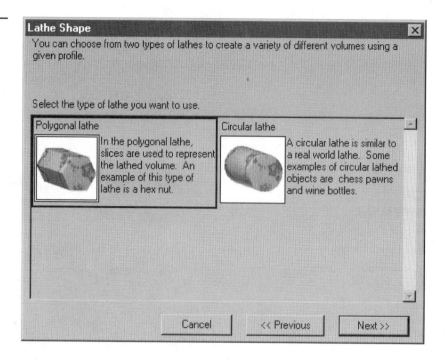

Finally, you see the last dialog box in the sequence, Object Size, shown earlier in Figure 34.25.

Extrusion Objects

An extrusion is created by moving a 2D shape (a "cross-section") along a path through 3D space. The Wizard's examples are a star, a flag, and 3D text.

If you select Create Your Own Object, a series of dialogs appear, where you specify your custom object's details—just as for the lathe object described in the preceding section. First, in the Cross-Section dialog, you choose the shape that will be moved along an extrusion path. Select Regular Polygon, and you will be presented with the same Polygon Specifications dialog that appears for polygonal lathe objects. Select

Square/Rectangle, Oval/Circle, or Rounded Rectangle, and you get the 3D Path dialog box. This dialog also comes up if you specify the number of sides for the regular polygon.

Next, in the 3D Path dialog, you designate that a particular cross-section will be moved along a straight, circular, angled, or wavy extrusion path. Last, you get the Object Size dialog box, illustrated previously.

Pipeline Objects

You create a pipeline object as you do an extrusion object, except that the orientation of the extruded cross-section is always perpendicular to the extrusion path. The Wizard provides examples of a chair frame, spaghetti (with sauce), and a bagel.

Selecting Create Your Own Object takes you to the same Cross-Section and subsequent dialogs that are used for an extrusion object.

Skin Objects

A skin object is created by stretching a surface (skin) over several cross-sections of the same or varied shapes. Real examples are boat hulls and airplane wings or fuselages. The Wizard's examples are a banana, a piece of candy in a wrapper with twisted ends, and a ketchup bottle.

If you choose to create your own object, you get the same Section dialog box used for pipeline and extrusion objects. Once you select your cross-section (and, if polygonal, specify the number of sides), the Number of Cross Sections dialog appears. Here is where you specify how many cross-sections are to be included in the extrusion.

WATCH OUT!

It's important to remember that if you require a sudden transition from one shape to another, you will need two cross-sections at that point along the extrusion path (see Figure 34.28).

34.28

This cylinder contains four cross-sections: one on each end, and two in the middle to create the sudden transition from the larger diameter to the smaller diameter.

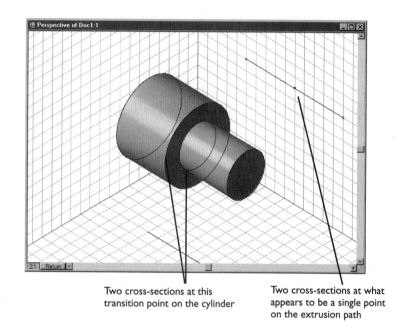

Two cross-sections at this transition point on the cylinder

Two cross-sections at what appears to be a single point on the extrusion path

Spiral Objects

A spiral object is created by rotating a cross-section around an axis while simultaneously moving it parallel to the axis. The Wizard provides examples of a corkscrew, a spiral seashell, and a telephone cord. But since these objects are difficult to modify, you'll probably just start out creating your own.

To create your own spiral object, begin by specifying the cross-section shape to be extruded along a spiral path. If you choose the polygon option, you are asked for the number of sides for the polygon.

In the next dialog, Spiral Rotation, you must enter the parameters for the spiral:

■ Number of Turns is the number of times the spiral will complete a full 360° path from the starting position of the path.

- Cross Section Scaling changes the size of the cross-section as it moves along the spiral path until, at the end of the spiral, it reaches the percentage of reduction or enlargement you've specified here.

- Spiral Scaling changes the diameter of the spiral from one end to the other, starting with the size you will later indicate with the Height and Depth specifications in the Object Size dialog, and ending with the percentage of reduction or enlargement you specify here.

The last stop is the Object Size dialog.

INSIDE INFO

> You may very well agree with our opinion that using the Modeling Wizard to create a spiral is an exercise in frustration. If so, here's a better way: Activate the Free Form tool and, while in the Modeling window, select the Extrusion Preset and use the Spiral option in the Geometry menu. It gives you much more control over the creation of spirals.

Twisted Objects

A twisted object is created by rotating a cross-section as it moves along the extrusion path. The Wizard's examples are a twisted column, a "twister" (tornado), and a screw.

If you create your own object, you'll first see the Cross-Section dialog. Next comes the Twist Rotation dialog, where you specify the twists (rotations). One twist equals a full 360° of rotation, and you can enter decimal increments of a full 360° rotation.

Next up is the Object Size dialog, and you're done.

Creating Objects in the Modeling Window

Custom objects are created in DREAM3D using the Free Form tool and the Modeling window. This section presents a series of exercises that give you hands-on experience in this process.

Remember: To activate the Free Form tool, you just click on the tool and click in the Perspective window. This brings up the Modeling window.

Tips on Working with the Grid in the Modeling Window

We recommend that before doing anything in the Modeling window, you change the grid size to be appropriate for the object you intend to create. The default is 32″ square. If the object you intend to draw is considerably smaller than this, reducing the size of the grid makes it much easier to work with your object. If the object you're going to create is larger than 32″, you should increase the size of the grid to encompass the entire object. You won't be able to see any gridlines for accuracy when you're drawing objects outside the grid.

The next step, if you require any accuracy whatsoever, is to turn on the grid snap (which is off by default) and change the grid frequency. The default grid frequency, as a carryover from RayDream Designer, is an inexplicable 1.6″. How many people do *you* know who work in increments of 1.6″? Might as well learn the keystrokes for this one (View / Grid or Ctrl+J or Alt+V+G). You'll probably use it a *lot*.

Exercise 1: Creating a Simple Free-form Object

In this first exercise you'll create a cylinder.

1. Open a new file, with File / New or the New button in the toolbar.

2. Select the Free Form tool in the Toolbox and click in the Perspective window. The Modeling window opens.

3. Select View / Grid or press Ctrl+J to get the Grid dialog box. Change the Grid Snap value to .5″. Change the setting for Draw A Line Every to 2, and turn on the Snap To option.

4. Change to Drawing Plane view (View / Type / Drawing Plane). While you're here, take a moment to look at all these shortcut keys—there's a lot to remember! If nothing else, just memorize the first two, Ctrl+0 for Reference view and Ctrl+5 for Drawing Plane view. For the rest, you may want to just drag out the ol' Post-It notes.

5. Pick the Oval tool and draw a perfect circle, 8″ in diameter. To do this, move the cursor to the drawing plane, and hold down the Shift key while dragging across the plane. This constrains the ellipse to be a perfect circle.

6. Now, before you go any further, establish in the Modeling window the location of the hot point of this new object you're creating. Bring up the Object Properties dialog. (Right-click on the circle you've drawn, and select Properties from the bottom of the pop-up menu.)

7. Using the Properties dialog, place this circle in the very center of the grid. Enter a Left value of -4″, which is negative half the circle's Width value. Enter a Right value of 4″, which is positive half the circle's Height value. See Figure 34.29.

By moving this object to the center of the drawing plane, you're predetermining the location of the object's hot point or point of reference (for positioning purposes in the Perspective window). Without this step, the hot point would be off-center with relation to the end of this object, making it difficult to position and align with other objects.

8. Return to Reference view (Ctrl+0).

9. To close the Modeling window, click the Return button at the bottom-left of the Modeling window.

34.29

After creating a free-form object, make sure the hot point is in the center. For this circle, the Left value is negative half the circle's Width value, and the Top value is positive half the circle's Height value.

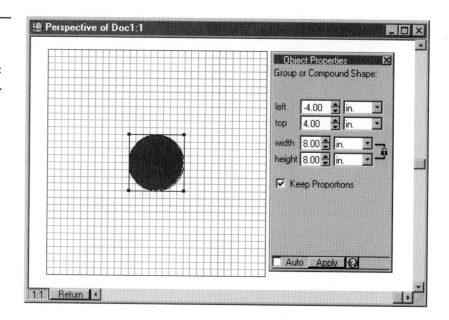

10. Now that you've successfully rendered this fantastic, extremely complex piece of artwork, assign it an appropriate name in the Hierarchy window: **My First Cylinder.** Click on the Apply button to have the change take effect.

11. Put this object in the center of the universe for later convenience. In the Properties dialog, change the X, Y, and Z values to 0, and click Apply.

12. You're going to use this cylinder for some of the other modeling exercises, so save this file now as Cylinder. (No need to include the file name extension. In fact, it's better if you don't—DREAM3D automatically provides the .d3d extension.)

Exercise 2: Duplicating Objects

In this exercise you'll work with the cylinder.d3d file you created in Exercise 1, and duplicate the cylinder.

1. Make sure the cylinder is still selected in the Perspective window.

2. Select Edit / Duplicate or press Ctrl+D.

Not much appears to have happened to the cylinder in the Perspective window. But in the Hierarchy window, you can see that there are now two Free Form objects bearing the same name. Note that this duplication process, unlike the Duplicate Shader command, leaves the duplicate selected. As discussed in the section on setting preferences for the Object Browser, the duplicate object is an *instance* of the first object (the *master*), and presently occupies exactly the same space as the master. Because objects in DREAM3D have no actual substance, no mass, they *can* occupy the same space.

3. To further demonstrate the principle of instance and master objects, rotate the cylinder on the z-axis. In the Properties dialog, change the Yaw value to 90°.

4. Click on the Better Preview button in the toolbar to get the best view of the junction of these two objects. Then, so that you can continue working more rapidly, turn off the Better Preview by clicking on the regular Preview button in the toolbar.

AUTHOR'S NOTE

This is a handy way to build a complex shape—by "overlapping" objects.

5. So that you can more easily keep track of the objects in this exercise, let's change the names of the cylinder objects to Master and Instance. In the Hierarchy window, click on the topmost free-form object (currently named My First Cylinder). In the Properties dialog, swipe the cursor across the name of the object, overtype the highlighted text with the new name **Master**, and click Apply.

6. Repeat the action in step 5, renaming the duplicate free-form object (also named My First Cylinder) to **Instance**.

Another example of this "shared space" construction would be if you wanted rounded ends—hemispheres, that is—on these cylinders. However, in DREAM3D, creating a hemisphere (or even a sphere, for that matter) with the Free Form tool is quite difficult. So in this case, you're going to use the sphere supplied in the Primitive Objects tool.

7. Open the Primitive Objects tool flyout and click the Sphere button (the rightmost one).

8. Move the cursor into the Perspective window and drag to create a sphere (any size will do for now).

9. With the newly created sphere still selected, open the Object Properties dialog (if necessary). Change the X value to 0, the Y value to 8, and the Z value to zero. Make sure the Keep Proportions box is checked, and change the SizeX value to 8. Click Apply.

10. What you have now is a rounded end on your Master cylinder. To get a better look at the results, click Zoom to All Objects in the toolbar (second tool from the right in the Zoom tool group). Then click Better Preview.

AUTHOR'S NOTE

If you do not have what is known as a Z-buffer on your video card, you may see a line where the sphere joins the cylinder. Don't worry about it; it probably won't appear in the rendering.

11. Once again, to allow you to work a little faster, return to regular Preview.

12. Now you can duplicate the Master sphere, placing three duplicates on the other three ends of the intersecting cylinders. With the sphere still selected, press Ctrl+D to make the first duplicate.

13. In the Properties dialog, change the Y value to −8. Click Apply. This places the duplicate on the other end of the same cylinder.

14. Press Ctrl+D again. Then click Zoom to All Objects button again.

Your Perspective window should now look like Figure 34.30. Note that the latest duplicate of the sphere is not in the same location as its immediate ancestor. That is because you changed a value in the Properties dialog right after making the last duplicate. Examine the Y value, and you'll see that it is −24, which is exactly the same distance from the Y position of the first duplicate (−8), and the same distance the Y position of the first duplicate was from the original (8), −16″.

34.30

If a location or rotation value is changed and applied as the first step following duplication of an object, subsequent duplicates made with Ctrl+D will have the same values.

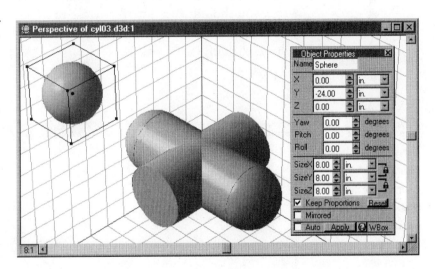

To create a series of objects, moved by the same amount in one or more directions and/or rotated the same way in one or more directions, change the appropriate values in the Properties dialog as the very next step after creating the first duplicate. Then click on the Apply button, and duplicate (Ctrl+D) as many times as needed. The subsequent duplicates will be moved and/or rotated by the same amount of difference between the original and the first duplicate.

For this exercise, you'll use this duplicating function to simultaneously create the duplicates *and* position them on all three of the remaining flat cylinder ends.

15. Delete the two sphere duplicates (Change to the Selection tool, click on each duplicate, and press Del.) You now have your two intersection cylinders, and a single rounded end (the sphere) on one of them.

16. Click on the original sphere. In the Object Properties dialog, make sure you didn't accidentally move the original from its X=0, Y=8, and Z=0 position.

17. Click on the Wireframe button in the toolbar, and then on Zoom to Selected Objects.

18. On the nearest corner of the bounding box surrounding the cylinder, you should see a dot. Very close to it, you should see second dot (see Figure 34.31). This is the sphere's hot point of the sphere; click on it.

34.31

The hot point of the sphere appears very close to the nearest corner of the box surrounding the sphere.

Hot point

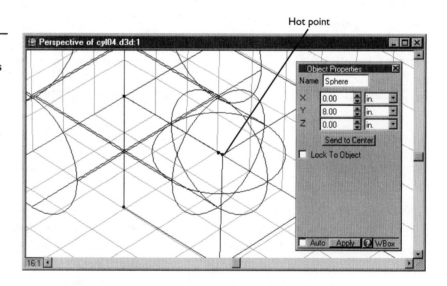

19. The Properties dialog now reflects the position of the hot point relative to the universe, X=0, Y=8, and Z=0. Change the Y value to 0, and click Apply. This places the hot point in the very center of the universe.

20. Switch back to regular Preview quality.

21. Click in an empty area of either the Perspective window or the Hierarchy window, to deselect the hot point. Then click on the sphere again to select it.

22. Create another duplicate of the sphere (Ctrl+D), change the Yaw value to 90°, and click Apply. Note that the sphere, instead of merely rotating on its *own* z-axis, rotated on the z-axis relative to the hot point.

23. Use Ctrl+D to create two more duplicates.

What you have just done is take advantage of Duplicate's ability to repli- cate not only an object, but movement and rotation as well. Because these spheres can be placed on the ends of the cylinders by rotating them around the center of the universe, by specifying the rotation only once you have duplicated the two remaining spheres and also rotated each around the z-axis by another 90° increment, placing them pre- cisely in the locations needed.

24. Click on Better Preview. This will take a little while to show on screen, but it's worth it to see the effect you've created. What you have is a self-replicating cold capsule that should look like Figure 34.32.

25. Change back to regular Preview, and save this file as **cylndr2**. (Don't save it to the original cylinder file because you'll be using that one for Exercise 4.)

Exercise 3: Changing Object Properties

Using the cylndr2.d3d file from Exercise 2, you're next going to change the sizes of the objects you have already created. You'll reduce the diame- ter (by half) of both cylinders and all four spheres.

1. In the Hierarchy window, right-click on the Master cylinder, and choose Properties.

2. In the Properties dialog, turn off the Keep Proportions option.

34.32

Self-replicating
cold capsule—the
results of Exercise 2

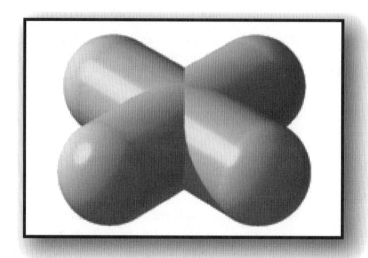

3. Change both the X and Z values from 8″ to 4″, and click Apply. Notice that only the Master cylinder has changed; the Instance cylinder remains unchanged.

4. Undo the last step (either select Edit / Undo or press Ctrl+Z).

5. Instead of independently changing the aspect ratio of *both* the Master and the Instance, you can change the *geometry* of the Master and have that change automatically applied to the Instance. In the Hierarchy window, click on the Master Objects tab, and then double-click on the free-form object (the Master cylinder) in the Hierarchy window. The Modeling window appears.

WATCH OUT!

If you don't first switch to the Master Objects tab before double-clicking on the Master cylinder, you will receive a dialog warning you that "you are about to open an object used more than once." In this case, you don't want to create a new master, so if you see this dialog, click the Cancel button.

6. Change to Drawing Plane view (View / Type / Drawing Plane, or Alt+V+T+D, or Ctrl+5).

7. Click on the circle (*carefully*—so you don't accidentally move it).

8. In the Properties dialog, turn off the Keep Proportions option. Change the Left value to −2″, the Top value to 2″, and both the Width and the Height to 4″. Click Apply.

9. Click on the Return button at the bottom-left of the Modeling window. Now the Master cylinder has been decreased in diameter, and so has the Instance cylinder—all with one modification to the Master (see Figure 34.33).

34.33

Modifying the Master cylinder has simultaneously modified the Instance cylinder.

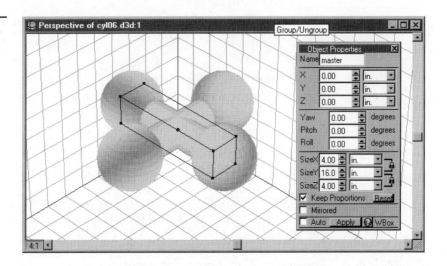

The key to using the master/instance relationship to change multiple objects with a single modification is that it gives you the ability to modify the *geometry* of the master object. The object becomes a different sort of object. The basic geometry of primitive objects cannot be changed, and the only way to modify the size or rotation of a primitive object is through the Properties dialog in the Perspective window. Therefore, you cannot change all three of the Instance spheres in our example by modifying the Master, even though the Master shows up in the Master Objects tab of the Hierarchy window. Instead, you must change each sphere's diameter individually.

Before changing the diameter of each sphere, you must also center the hot points of the spheres; otherwise, they will seem to move toward the center of the universe and will no longer even be visible (they'll be "inside" the cylinders).

10. In the Hierarchy window, click on the Objects tab.

11. For each of the spheres in the Hierarchy window, perform the following steps:

    a. Click on the sphere.
    b. Click on the title bar of the Perspective window.
    c. Center the hot point (Arrange / Center Hot Point, or Alt+A+C).
    d. In the Properties dialog, make sure the Keep Proportions check box is checked, change the SizeX value to 4, and click Apply.

12. If you like, turn on the Better Preview to check the results; your scene should now look similar to Figure 34.34. Be sure to turn off Better Preview when you're finished viewing.

13. If you want to keep it, save this file as **cylndr3**. Just make sure you don't save it to the original cylinder file because you'll be using that one for the following exercise.

Exercise 4: Creating Custom Shapes

In this exercise, you'll modify the basic geometry of the free-form object you created in Exercise 1. You'll change the basic circle cross-section to a crescent moon shape.

1. Open your original cylinder.d3d file.

2. In the Hierarchy window, double-click on My First Cylinder object. This brings up the Modeling window so you can modify the basic circle shape.

34.34

Complete scene
for Exercise 3 using
Better Preview to
show smooth
surfaces

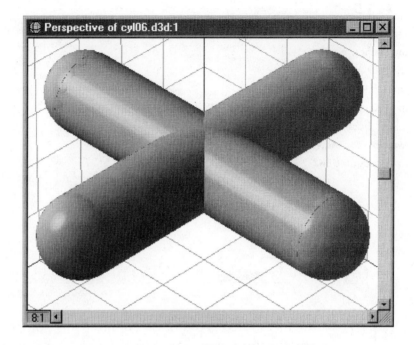

3. Change to Drawing Plane view (Ctrl+5) so you can work without the confusion of the extrusion.

4. Zoom in to the circle. (Click on the Zoom tool in the Toolbox, and then click in the center of the circle a couple of times.)

5. To modify this circle—other than by changing its properties or its location in the grid—you need to ungroup it. First, change to the Selection tool, and click on the circle.

6. Click on the Group/Ungroup button in the toolbar.

Now each point on the object becomes available for manipulation, along with the Bézier curve control points that dictate the curve used to generate the circle (see Figure 34.35). Working with these points takes a little getting used to. For instance, if you deselect the object and marquee-select an individual point, you might expect to see the Properties dialog immediately reflect the position of that point—but not so! Who knows why....

34.35

Once the circle is ungrouped, each of the four points, and the Bézier handles for each of those points, become available for individual manipulation.

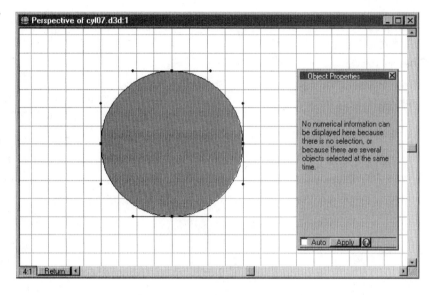

In order to see the coordinates of this point, you must *very carefully* position the cursor over that point and click, or marquee-select it a second time. If you decide to click on the point, you must do so carefully because it's all too easy to accidentally move the point—particularly if Snap to Grid is enabled and this point doesn't happen to fall on one of the snap grid increments. (But then, there's always Undo…)

Next you're going to change this circle to a crescent moon shape, by moving one of the points and modifying its curve handles, as well as those of the two adjacent points. You already turned on the snap grid for this object (in Exercise 1), so the points and curve handles will snap to half-inch increments.

7. With the Pick tool, start dragging the left node toward the right. After you start dragging, hold down the Shift key to prevent any vertical movement of this point. Drag over 1″ to the right of the horizontal center (the second snap point past the center), and release Shift only after you've released the mouse button.

8. Now you'll need to reduce the arc size for this point. Since you want this to be symmetrical, you'll use the Convert Point tool, and start over by dragging the handles out from the point. Select the Convert Point tool in the Toolbox. It's the fifth button down. (But if either the Add Point or Delete Point tool is showing, you can click and hold with the cursor over the Add Point or Delete Point button and pick the Convert Point tool from the resulting flyout.)

9. Place the cursor over the point you just moved, hold down the mouse button, and drag the Bézier handle downward by 1.5″ (three snaps from the point). If you see a "twist" occurring in the resulting curve, drag upward instead.

10. Now, for both the top and bottom points, you need to reduce the curvature slightly and change the angle dramatically. For this you'll use the Convert Point tool again because, by grabbing an individual curve control handle with this tool, you can manipulate one side of a pair of Bézier curve handles independently of the opposite side. This produces a *cusp* point—one that changes direction suddenly and sharply rather than smoothly and gradually. Using the Convert Point tool, grab the left end of the top Bézier curve handle, and drag it downward 1″ (two snaps) and to the right of center .5″ (one snap).

11. Repeat this with the bottom point's curve handle, only drag *up* and to the right. You should now have a moon shape like that in Figure 34.36.

12. Now we want the curve handles on the inside curve to be .75″ away from the point they control. Rather than going through the trouble of changing the snap grid just for this one modification, you can change the values for these curve handles in the Properties dialog. Deselect the object by clicking off to the side somewhere.

13. Carefully, so as not to move it, click on inside point.

34.36

Two snaps down, one snap over, and you've got yourself a moon.

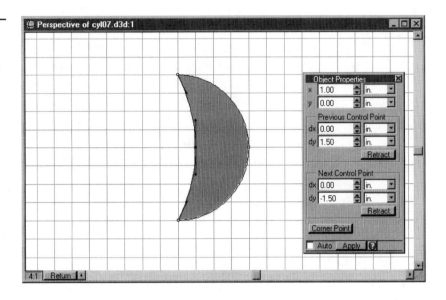

14. In the Properties dialog, change the Previous Control Point *dy* value to .75 and Next Control Point *dy* value to -.75, and click Apply.

15. Click the Return button in the Modeling window, and take a look at your object back in the Perspective window.

16. If you like, turn on the Better Preview; you'll see something like a very crude shoe-horn (see Figure 34.37). Remember to turn off Better Preview before continuing.

Additional Practice

You've now completed a basic introduction to the Modeling window and the creation of free-form objects in DREAM3D. You've learned how to create a simple free-form object in the Drawing Plane view, how to duplicate objects, and how to change the properties of objects. You've explored the benefits of the master and instance relationship, and seen how to customize free-form curve objects.

34.37

A better preview…

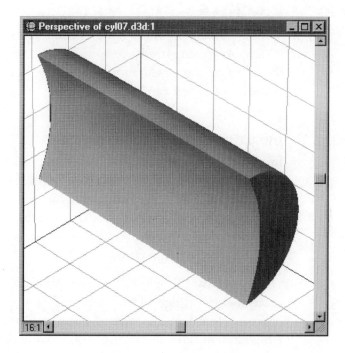

Before you launch into your own full-fledged 3D creation, however, you might want to further explore some other areas. Refer to the DREAM3D portion of your reference guide, and practice the following processes:

- Working with combined curves
- Working with multiple curves (not combined)
- Working with the sweep path
- Extruding with a symmetrical envelope
- Extruding with an envelope symmetrical in one plane
- Extruding with an asymmetrical envelope
- Adding points and cross-sections to the sweep path
- Working with lathe objects

When the Lights Come Up...

With the exception of the lighting parameters of a light source, working with lights is quite similar to working with other objects. Using either the Selection tool or the Properties dialog, you can resize, reposition, or rotate lights as you can any other object.

Adding, Duplicating, and Placing Lights

In addition to the single default light source in any file you create, you can easily add lights by clicking first on the Create Light tool in the Toolbox and then in the Perspective window. As with placement of other objects, you'll probably need to relocate the light once you've clicked in the Perspective window. For this, use the Properties dialog as described in the next section.

Once you have the light in the appropriate position, aiming it an object is easy. Select the light if necessary, and Shift-click on the object to be lighted. Select Arrange / Point At or press Alt+A+P. Or you can create a temporary object—a primitive object will do just fine—for aiming the light. In this case, once you've aimed it, deselect the light by Shift-clicking it, and then delete the temporary object.

Adjusting Light Parameters

To modify the parameters of a light, double-click on the light in either the Perspective window or the Hierarchy window. This brings up the Lighting Parameters dialog (Figure 34.38).

By default, all lights are *spot* lights, but you can change them to *distant* lights or *bulb* lights. Each type of light has a different set of parameters, all well described in the DREAM3D portion of the CorelDRAW 6.0 reference guide, Chapter 7.

34.38

Use this dialog to adjust the lights in the universe.

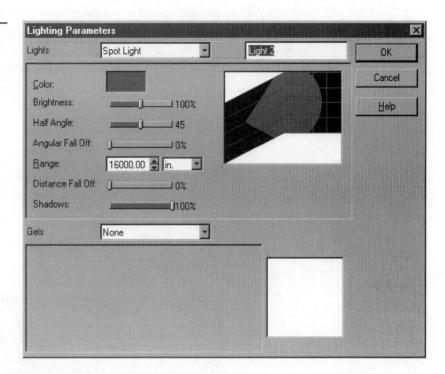

Roll the Camera

With the exception of the camera lens types, working with cameras is similar to working with lights and other objects. Either with the Selection tool or the Properties dialog, you can resize, reposition, or rotate cameras.

Adding, Duplicating, and Placing Cameras

The default camera in every DREAM3D file is what provides your view of the Perspective window. You can easily add cameras by clicking first on the Create Camera tool in the Toolbox and then in the Perspective window. As with placement of other objects, you'll probably need to relocate the camera once you've clicked in the Perspective window. For this, use the Properties dialog as described in the next section.

Once you have the camera in the appropriate position, aiming it an object is easy. Select the camera if necessary, and Shift-click on the object at which you're aiming the camera. Select Arrange / Point At or press Alt+A+P. Or you can create a temporary object—a primitive object will do just fine—for aiming the camera. In this case, once you've aimed it, deselect the camera by Shift-clicking it, and then delete the temporary object.

Adjusting Camera Settings

To modify the settings of a camera, double-click on the camera in either the Perspective window or the Hierarchy window. This brings up the Camera Parameters dialog (Figure 34.39).

34.39

Use this dialog to adjust the camera.

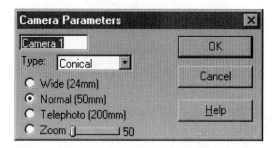

Another means of adjusting the camera is the Camera Settings choice in the Scene menu (Ctrl+E), which displays the Camera Settings dialog box (Figure 34.40). Here you can work with dynamic positioning and rotation of the camera, in addition to the same lens type settings that are in the Camera Parameters dialog.

The camera settings, as well, are thoroughly explained in the DREAM3D section of the CorelDRAW 6.0 reference guide.

34.40

The Camera Settings dialog is another means of adjusting the camera.

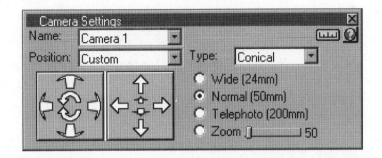

INSIDE INFO

Something that you may find helpful during the construction of a complex scene is the addition of many cameras, each pointing at some specific detail and from a specific angle. This lets you easily and quickly change viewpoints and zoom factors, without have to continually reposition the camera or use the Zoom tools. It's the virtual equivalent to being in more than one place at a time.

Action! (Well, Render, Anyway)

Chapter 8 of the DREAM3D portion of the CorelDRAW 6.0 reference guide gives a pretty good showing of all aspects of setting up and performing a rendering from your scene. Here are the salient points:

- *Production Frame* shows you, in your scene (the Perspective window), what area of your scene will appear in the rendering.

- *Rendering Settings,* such as Ambient Light, Background, and Atmosphere (Scene menu), control aspects of your rendering that do not appear in the Perspective window.

- *Render Preview* is for designating the values in a rendering used primarily for checking lighting, shadows, the rendering settings mentioned above, transparency, and reflections.

- *Batch Rendering* is for setting up an unattended rendering session for multiple scenes. (Watch out—this function may crash your computer.)

Life Is But a DREAM

CorelDREAM3D is a most complex program—nearly as complex as the premier product of the suite, CorelDRAW. Unfortunately, unlocking all of DREAM3D's mysteries in detail would require another book just as big as the one in your hand. Rather than risk rendering you muscle-bound from lifting another heavy book, we've offered you this abbreviated chapter.

After all, exploration is half the fun. DREAM on!

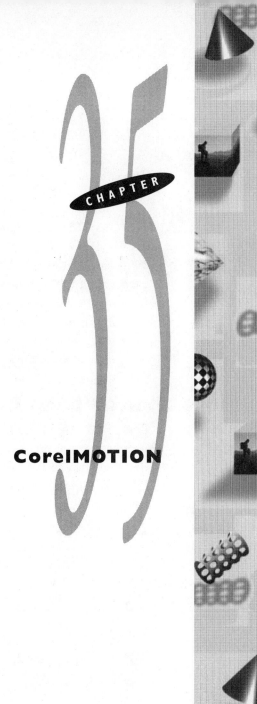

CHAPTER

35

CorelMOTION

THIRTY-FIVE

First CorelDREAM3D, then CorelDEPTH, now Corel-
MOTION3D! Why in the world did Corel include *three* 3D
applications in the CorelDRAW 6.0 suite? The answer is that
each program has its own specialty. And though CorelMOTION3D
has some limitations DREAM3D and DEPTH don't have, MOTION3D
provides a function that neither of its sister apps can: animation.
(Through the remainder of this chapter, we'll use the shortened name
MOTION for CorelMOTION3D.)

More Than a "Logo Animation" Tool

Corel bills MOTION as a "logo animation" program. That's a pretty
narrow description of MOTION's considerable abilities, but it does
describe one excellent use for the application. MOTION creates files
(.M3D) containing 3D objects, including a camera, lights, props, and
backgrounds.

MOTION's final product is an animation file, and you have your
choice of several popular formats:

- Video for Windows (.AVI)
- Quick Time Movie (.MOV)
- Autodesk FLIC (.FLC)
- MPEG Animation (.MPG)
- PICS Animation (.PCS)

Because the AVI format is a Windows standard, supported by Windows's own Media Player, in this chapter we'll refer to all animation files

generically as AVI files. These files can be played back with the Windows Media Player or incorporated in other Windows programs, including CorelPRESENTS.

MOTION provides two basic techniques for developing 3D shapes; one is called *extrusion*, the other is *lathing*. Figure 35.1 shows an example of these two types of three-dimensional (3D) shapes and the two-dimensional (2D) outline from which they were created. Notice how extrusion takes a flat, two-dimensional shape and "pulls" it to give it the third dimension of "depth." Lathing uses the two-dimensional curve or shape as the basis for the contour of a symmetrical object. It works by taking the 2D curve or shape and spinning it around an axis to create objects that are round.

3 5 . 1

The 2D shape on the left was used to make all of these 3D objects.

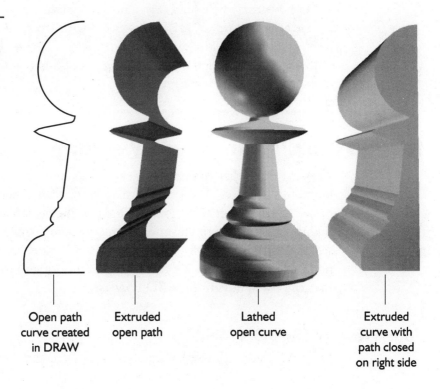

Open path
curve created
in DRAW

Extruded
open path

Lathed
open curve

Extruded
curve with
path closed
on right side

This chapter introduces you to several of the most commonly used functions of MOTION. Get comfortable with them—and with MOTION's somewhat unusual interface—and you'll soon be enjoying your work in this great 3D animation program.

INSIDE INFO

If you try to run CorelMOTION3D in 256-color video mode, you probably won't be happy with the quality of the screen rendering. You will see no real gradation in shadows, just black. This is disconcerting—not to mention that it doesn't at all help you visualize what your 3D animation will look like. Switching to a 16-bit Windows video driver (32K color or High color) will help, but the most accurate way to see your rendering is by working in 24-bit mode (16 million colors or True color). No matter what your video driver or how hideous your screen renderings, however, you'll be pleased with the final animation files. Your file will be rendered beautifully in either 16-bit or 24-bit mode, depending on the setting for Number Of Colors in File in Scene Setup / Rendering.

It's MOTION's World and Welcome to It

The first thing that you need to get used to about MOTION is the look of its interface. It doesn't resemble any of the other 3D applications or any of Corel's other programs. Don't let the default screen, predominantly black and bare, intimidate you; you can change this to suit yourself. A good metaphor for the empty screen is outer space: a void where nothing exists, and you are the one who will bring to life everything that will dwell in your little 3D universe.

Four Views of the 3D World

MOTION's default display gives you four different views of your universe: Camera, Top, Right, and Front (see Figure 35.2). Anyone familiar with blueprints and plan drawings will appreciate this representation of a complete 3D world on a two-dimensional device such as a computer monitor.

35.2

The Corel MOTION3D workspace

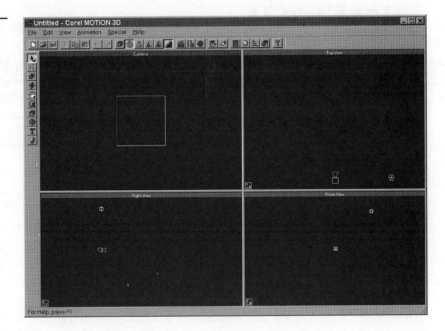

The upper-left window is the view from the camera. Think of looking through the viewfinder of a traditional camera. It can go wherever you want, and wherever it goes, you go. From a technical standpoint the camera is invisible and transparent. It can move like a ghost right through objects in your 3D world.

The other three views show you the arrangement of your universe's elements from the top, right side, and front. Note that the Front view (lower-right) is *not* the same as the Camera view, because in a 3D world the camera can be positioned anywhere. The major difference between these windows is that the objects in the Top, Right, and Front views are always represented as wireframe models. The Camera window has several ways to view your objects.

By using either Vertical Move or Horizontal Move, you can move and resize the elements in any one of MOTION's four view windows. Each window has a title bar that changes color to designate the active window —the one whose objects you are working on at the moment.

AUTHOR'S NOTE

It is the active window that gets rendered when it comes time to preview or produce your animation. If you really want to render an animation of one of the wireframe views, you can. But MOTION will warn you before it starts the rendering process, just in case.

Getting to Know the Camera View

Camera is by far the most flexible of MOTION's views. It has to be— because rendering and displaying 3D objects can be time consuming and tedious, and of course, the highest-quality rendering option takes the most time. Without some way to speed things up, developing 3D animations would be too laborious. That's why MOTION offers five different Camera view modes. All of these display modes can be set from the main toolbar or via View / Rendering Mode. Figure 35.3 illustrates the toolbar icons for each mode and a sample of the rendering quality you can expect from your monitor. The speeding-up process is a trade-off, of course: You give up some rendering details to get faster redraws.

Bounding Box   The most rudimentary viewing mode is called Bounding Box. It shows only a cube that represents the physical area your object takes up in 3D space. This cube shows no shape or surface details, except that it uses the assigned surface color for the bounding box lines.

3 5 . 3

MOTION's Camera view modes offer plenty of flexibility when it comes to viewing and rendering quality.

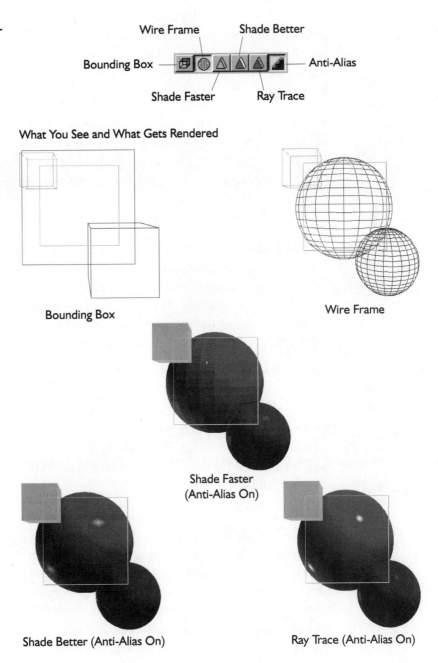

Wire Frame   Shade Better

Bounding Box

Shade Faster   Ray Trace

Anti-Alias

What You See and What Gets Rendered

Bounding Box

Wire Frame

Shade Faster
(Anti-Alias On)

Shade Better (Anti-Alias On)

Ray Trace (Anti-Alias On)

Bounding Box is the fastest mode for screen redraws, and you will appreciate this when your animations start to exceed a few seconds in length and contain several objects. This is the mode that is used when you select Preview from the Animation menu or click the Preview button on the main toolbar.

Wireframe   The second fastest rendering mode is Wireframe. Your 3D objects are displayed as shapes, but with only the surface color for the object's wireframe lines. You'll probably end up working in this mode most often, after you get some experience with MOTION and can better anticipate the effects of various surface shaders, camera angles, and light settings on your 3D scene.

Shade Faster   The fastest of the filled rendering modes, Shade Faster takes the wireframe model and "wraps" skin around it. You set the color and texture of the skin in the Edit / Surfaces dialog. Even though this view is crude compared to the other shaded modes, it gives you a good idea of the way your 3D scene is shaping up. You can even see the reflections from any lights that are in the scene.

Shade Better   The Shade Better rendering setting does just that—displays all objects with much more realism by smoothing out the angular wireframe shape and adding more detail to the surfaces. Unless you have a very fast computer, you will probably want to reserve this mode for use when you are close to finalizing your scene. You won't want to wait for MOTION to redraw the screen every time you change something or call up a dialog.

Ray Trace   The most spectacular rendering option is Ray Trace, which offers the most realistic depiction of your 3D scene. The most intriguing shading details, such as Surface Transparency and Reflection, are viewable only in Ray Trace mode. Of course, ray tracing is also the most strenuous for your computer, because it relies on complex mathematical computations to work its magic. Switching to this mode can make a computer seem to stand still. The only indication you'll have that anything at all is happening will be the slow advance of the Rendering status bar at the bottom of the window. Use Ray Trace for the final rendering, or for final checks just before making your animation file.

Anti-Alias Option   Another enhancement to the display and rendering of your 3D scene is the Anti-Alias option. When used in conjunction with the three Shade modes, anti-aliasing removes the "jaggies" from your renderings—and also slows down the rendering itself. Your decision to use this option will depend on the speed of your system and your selected preferences for the job. For maximum realism, we recommend that Anti-Alias be enabled before any finished renderings.

The Production Box   The white rectangle in the center of the Camera window has no official name that we can find. So, we'll borrow DREAM3D's name for a similar item found in that program: the "production box." This box shows you literally the area that will be rendered and saved in the Make Movie process—otherwise known as creating the .AVI file. You can adjust the size of this capture area by changing the window's Width and Height settings (in pixels), in the File / Scene Setup dialog. (In case you haven't got the message yet, remember: The larger you make the numbers, the larger the resulting .AVI file will be and the longer it will take to render the animation.)

You Always Need a Camera and Light

MOTION obligingly provides both of these elements when you start any new file. Without a camera to look through, you won't have any way to "see" and "capture" the images of your 3D objects. MOTION shows you the position of the camera in all the view windows except Camera.

Without at least one light, you can't see in your 3D universe. MOTION starts out with 1 Point light, which casts light out in every direction (as opposed to a Spot light, which acts like a flashlight casting a concentrated beam in one direction). You can add as many lights as you want to your scene; they are visible in all the viewing windows, including Camera.

The Tools of the Trade

Now that you've seen MOTION's fundamental screen presence, you need to know something about the tools and how to use them.

Notice the first icon on the toolbar (in its default arrangement); this is the Vertical Move tool, described just below. The small triangle in the lower-right corner of the tool button tells you that the tool is part of a flyout menu offering additional options (see Figure 35.4). To display a flyout, you point to the tool icon, hold down the mouse button, and the flyout appears to the right of the tool.

35.4

The toolbar, with
the Move tool fly-
out displayed

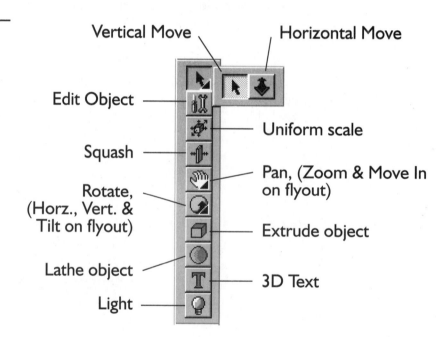

Vertical Move

Horizontal Move

Edit Object

Uniform scale

Squash

Pan, (Zoom & Move In
on flyout)

Rotate,
(Horz., Vert. &
Tilt on flyout)

Extrude object

Lathe object

3D Text

Light

The Move Tools

The Vertical Move tool positions any item in any of the viewing windows, in one direction only. The Horizontal Move tool (it's on the flyout) moves an object horizontally. In 3D space, moving objects is somewhat more complex than in the 2D drawing world. The first thing to remember is that for both Move tools, the point of reference in Camera view is different from the other three view windows.

- When working in the Camera window, use the Vertical Move tool to move objects side to side or up and down. Use Horizontal Move when you want to position something closer or farther away from the camera.

- In the Front, Right, or Top windows, the Horizontal Move tool always makes the object move horizontally. Vertical Move is more versatile and will move an object up or down or from side to side.

If all this sounds confusing, just keep practicing—most everyone finds they need some time to get used to positioning objects in 3D space.

The Object Editor Workspace

The next tool down is the Edit Object tool. When you select an object and click this icon, you open the Object Editor workspace shown in Figure 35.5. (You can also get into the Object Editor by double-clicking an object with one of the Move tools.) This workspace is where you modify the basic shapes that you create with the Extrude or Lathe Object tools.

The workspace has two areas: the 2D shape editing window and the 3D model window. The 2D window shows the shape or curve that is being edited. Exactly what you see will depend on whether you used the Extrude or Lathe Object tools to create the shape.

The Editor Toolbox   Tools in the Object Editor toolbox (see Figure 35.5) help you modify the shape, size, and construction of your shape outline. When you select the Shape tool, for instance, nodes appear on the outline, and the Node Edit box pops into view. Here are all the tools you need to modify your shapes, and working with these tools is similar to using DRAW's Node Edit roll-up. You can break an outline at a node point, add more nodes, delete nodes, and join two separate nodes to make a continuous line.

35.5

The Object Editor workspace showing the 2D shape editor with its tool-bars, and the 3D model window

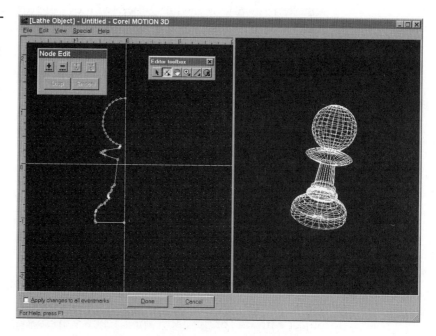

AUTHOR'S NOTE

The trick to importing a shape or curve drawn in CorelDRAW for use in MOTION is to first determine whether you want an extruded or lathed 3D item. Then use the correct object creation tool to create a dummy shape. Double-click the dummy shape to get into the Object Editor workspace, delete the shape, and use File / Import / Outline to bring in the CDR or CMX file.

Also in the Editor toolbox are the following useful items:

■ The familiar Pick tool; use it to move the shape around the Editor (this will dramatically change lathe objects, but not extruded ones) and to squeeze or stretch the basic outline.

- The Drawing tool (second tool from the right) has a flyout containing six different primitive shapes and line tools.

- The Zoom tool's flyout has three selections: the familiar Zoom In and Zoom Out, and the 1:1 tool that takes you back to actual size.

- The Pan tool (it looks like a hand) lets you move around the Editor. This is very handy after you have zoomed in to a higher magnification.

At the end of the Editor toolbar is the Rotate tool. It affects only the 3D wireframe representation of the shape in the 3D model window on the right. Depending on which mode you activated from the tool's flyout, the model will rotate in one of three directions as you drag it. This allows you to preview the results of modifying your shape in the Object Editor; the rotation does not change the shape's position in the 3D workspace.

Incidentally, you can remove the 3D model window if you like, leaving more room for the 2D window. Just turn off the 3D Model option in the View menu.

Object Editor Menus   The Object Editor menus offer several interesting items. One stop you'll want to make is the Special / Options dialog; it has quite a few options that will be of use to you. One of the functions most important to your MOTION projects is File / Import, which you'll use to bring in bitmaps for use as backgrounds, as well as the curves and closed-path objects that you create in CorelDRAW.

When you are finished editing your shape in the Object Editor, click Done to accept the changes you have made, or Cancel to retain your original outline. In either case, you will be back in the 3D work area.

Tools for Sizing

The next two tools in the main MOTION toolbox help you modify the size of your 3D elements. The third tool from the top is the Uniform

Scale tool; use it to scale an object up or down and keep it proportional at the same time. This means a globe will stay nice and round no matter what size you make it; likewise, a scaled cube will retain its equilateral sides.

On the other hand, if you want to make that globe into an egg or distort the cube into a rectangular box, then use the fourth tool down—the Squash tool. Your shape is distorted based on which side of the object you click and drag. The best way to get used to this tool is to experiment, and that's when you'll really appreciate Wireframe view the most.

Camera Positioning Tools

Next up (down, actually) on the toolbar is the hand icon that denotes the Zoom tool. Its flyout holds icons for Zoom In and Zoom Out, Pan, and Move In. Each of these tools affect the view or the position of the camera.

Zoom In and Zoom Out change the camera's lens, like using a zoom lens on a real camera. You don't move the camera, but the image seen through the lens appears to get either closer or farther away.

The other tools actually reposition the camera. Select the Pan tool, drag inside the Camera view port, and watch the position of the camera change in the Top, Right, and Front windows.

Use the Move In tool to reposition the camera closer to or farther away from your 3D elements. The name Move In is a bit of a misnomer, because you can move the camera away from your objects, too. When you drag upward with the Move tool, the camera moves back; drag downward, and it moves in.

Rotate Tool

The Rotate tool offers a flyout of several choices. You have a choice of Vertical, Horizontal, or Tilt modes. On your own, select each one and experiment to see how objects react when spun around these three different axes. Unlike the Rotate tool in the Object Editor, this Rotate tool really does change the shape's position in the 3D workspace.

Object Creation Tools

The last four tools are used to actually create 3D objects in the 3D viewing windows. When you activate any of these tools, you can click into any of the four viewing windows to place a new object.

Extrude   The Extrude Object tool looks like a cube. By default it makes a cube shape, but you can modify that shape. Use the Squash tool to make it a rectangle, for instance, or go into the Object Editor and completely change the shape to something much more complex.

The depth of an extruded object can be modified with the Squash tool.

Lathe   The icon that resembles a green globe is the Lathe Object tool. The default shape made by clicking any window is a globe—but looks can be deceiving! Click the Object Edit tool and you will see that the globe is actually made from a half-circle shape that is not a closed path at all. The Lathe function takes this outline shape and wraps it around the center axis until it makes a complete circuit of 360°.

The Lathe Object tool can only make symmetrical objects out of outline shapes. It does not matter whether the shape is a closed outline such as a circle, or an open path. In fact, you can get some pretty interesting results by experimenting with the kind of shape along with its position in relationship to the center vertical axis of the Object Editor.

3D Text Second from the bottom is the 3D Text tool, whose function is fairly self-explanatory. Figure 35.6 shows the Object Properties dialog that appears when you click the 3D Text tool in a window. Type your text string into the text box, set your extrusion depth, and press the Format Text button to get the Font dialog. There you can set the font, style, and size you want for your text string. When you are happy with your selections, OK your way out of the dialogs, and your text string will be rendered in the 3D viewing windows.

35.6

The Object Properties dialog for a 3D Text object

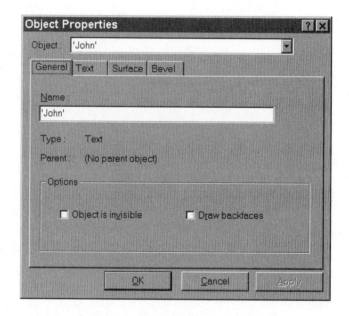

Light Source With the Light Source tool at the bottom of the toolbox, you can create lights to illuminate your 3D universe. The default start-up condition of a new MOTION file has one light positioned above the camera and to the right, at about 2 o'clock. This isn't nearly enough light to shine on a complex scene—although it does approximate what things look like in outer space— so we predict you'll be using this tool a lot to create additional light sources on your objects. Use the Vertical or Horizontal Move tools to position the light exactly where you like.

To customize the light source, right-click it and choose Properties from the pop-up menu. This gets you the Object Properties dialog with the appropriate settings displayed. Click the Light tab, and you'll be able to review and change the color of the light, its intensity, whether it should shine as a Point or Spot light, as well as other options.

INSIDE INFO

Getting a Spot light to shine in exactly the right direction can be tricky if you don't know the secret. Right-click the light and choose Point At from the pop-up. In the Point At dialog, pick your object from the Object To Point At list. It's that simple. Incidentally, this is also the quickest way to direct your camera toward a specific object in your 3D scene. First pick Camera from the Object To Direct list; then, from the bottom listing, choose the object to which the camera will point.

Working with the Camera

The camera is the last item that needs to be discussed to round out your tour of basic MOTION tools. We've already touched on a few of the tools that directly affect the camera and its view, including Pan, Move In/Out, and Zoom. Following are a few more pieces of camera trivia to guide you.

Bear in mind that the camera has no physical attributes in this 3D universe; when it comes to rendering your 3D images, the camera is quite invisible. With the camera placed right on top of an object, the effect will be as if you are passing right inside or through the object.

You will benefit greatly by making use of the Camera Navigation roll-up found under View menu (see Figure 35.7). Simply click the direction arrows to point the camera in another direction. These adjustments are very much like moving your head from side to side, looking up or down, or tilting your head to the right or left.

35.7

The Camera Navigation roll-up lets you easily point the camera in any direction desired.

Don't forget that the camera can move anywhere in your 3D workspace—as if it has wings. Combine this feature with MOTION's capability to change the size, position, and rotation of any object, and you'll start to realize the dramatic movement that's possible for your animations. This ability to create compound movements will certainly set your animations apart from those that simply vary the camera position and angle.

Color My World

MOTION assigns default colors to Extrude, Lathe, and Text objects—but this wouldn't be much of a 3D application if it didn't let you change those colors, would it? The easiest way to change color is in the Surfaces roll-up available from the View menu (see Figure 35.8). This roll-up contains a handful of predefined surface treatments, in which the colors and other aspects of a surface are already plugged in to get you going. So if you want your extruded object to have a metallic bronze color and finish, you can do it fast and easy by selecting Bronze from the roll-up and clicking Apply.

Another route to changing the attributes of your objects is the Object Properties dialog. Select the object if necessary, right-click to get the pop-up, and choose Properties. (Or use the Properties command from the Edit menu.) Figure 35.9 shows you the Surface page of the Object Properties dialog. Remember, the Object Properties dialog box is context sensitive, so it will display the appropriate tabbed pages containing the settings for the object you've selected.

35.8

The Surfaces roll-up offers preset colors and surface treatments that can be applied to any object with the click of a button.

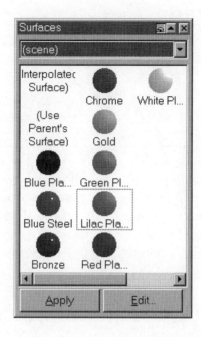

35.9

The Object Properties dialog for a Lathe object

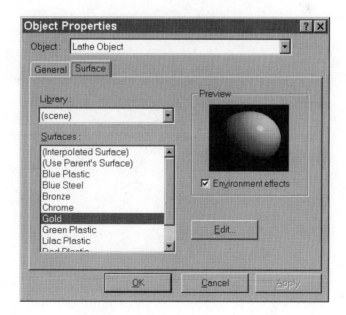

INSIDE INFO

> A very handy feature of the Object Properties dialog is that once it's displayed, you can choose which item in your current drawing you want to work with by selecting it from the Object drop-down list. The dialog's pages and settings will change to reflect only the properties available for the selected item.

Let's say you have a yellow globe and want it to be a particular red color. Go to the Object Properties dialog, open the Surface page, and choose a color from the Surfaces list. If you aren't happy with the color and other attributes of what you've chosen, click the Edit button. In the Edit Surfaces dialog (see Figure 35.10) you'll find a host of neat surface attributes to play with.

WATCH OUT!

> Before changing anything in the Surface Properties box in the Edit Surfaces dialog, be careful to first add a new color name to the Surfaces list on the left. Use the New button at the lower-left of the dialog. This will keep you from modifying and overwriting settings for the preset surfaces that come with MOTION.

When you're satisfied with the results of your changes, as seen in the preview window, click Update and then Close, and you'll be back in the Object Properties dialog. If you have created a new color name, pick that from the Surfaces list and click OK. Your selected object will now be colored and rendered.

For extruded objects and 3D text, the Object Properties dialog contains a Bevel page. Initially it's set to None, but you can select Straight, Double, or Convex from the Type drop-down list. When you choose a bevel type, the preview area to the right shows an approximation of the desired bevel effect. You can modify certain aspects of the bevel by changing the numbers in the Size and Depth boxes or by grabbing the small

35.10

The Edit Surfaces dialog gives you access to a host of options for all the aspects of a surface's visual appearance.

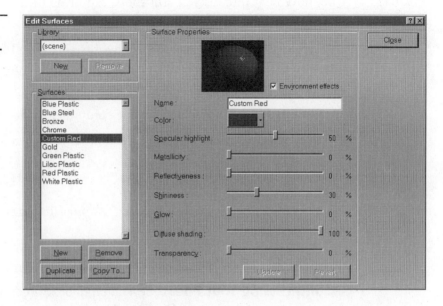

red circle on the preview and dragging it until it looks the way you want. There is also a check box that will apply this bevel to the back face of the extruded shape or text.

So You Say You Want to Make Movies?

So far we have discussed only the creation and manipulation of 3D shapes, but MOTION's secret weapon is its ability to make movies—animation files that can be played on your computer or incorporated into interactive presentations. So how do you make these animations?

Animation Files

First, let's start with a little background on what an animation file really is: a series of bitmaps displayed one after another, very quickly. These separate images are called *frames*. Elements or objects that are resized or repositioned slightly with each new frame appear to move, grow larger, shrink, and change shape. This is the process of animation—breaking up movement into discrete still-shots, capturing them, and replaying them at a high rate of speed.

With that in mind, it's easy to see why the animation files you create can grow quite large. Several things that are within your control will determine how large your files become:

- Size of the captured area (Scene Setup dialog, Render page)
- Number of colors your object will have when rendered (Scene Setup dialog, Render page)
- Length of the animation
- Frames rate (Scene Setup dialog, Animation page)

With all this to contend with, you'll need plenty of both time and hard disk space when it comes to rendering an animation.

Compressing Your Files   Several types of AVI compression schemes are available in MOTION. Using these will reduce your AVI file sizes—sometimes dramatically. But compression may cause blotchiness or other undesirable side-effects. You'll have to experiment to find the compression option that suits your purpose. To designate a compression type, select Scene Setup, open the Save page, and click the Compression button. The Compression Options dialog offers several compression types in the drop-down list. Pick one and then set any options that are available.

Making Your Movie with MOTION

MOTION really does make the animation process quite easy; but you have to do a bit of searching to find the appropriate tools for accomplishing this task. The most important tool you'll need is the Timelines window (Figure 35.11), available from the View menu. Of course, your own Timelines window will contain a list of the objects currently in your 3D workspace, including the camera and any lights.

35.11

The Timelines window is the control panel for all the functions necessary to producing animations.

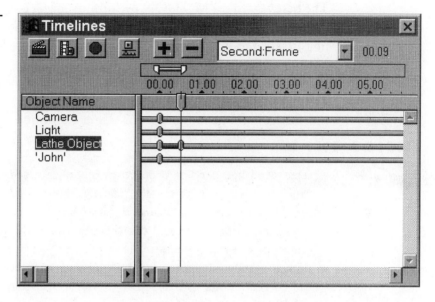

At this point, your animation is only one frame long—not much time for doing anything exciting, right? To add more frames, you need only click the Set Keyframe button (it's just to the left of the button with the big blue plus sign). Whether you realize it or not, you have just lengthened your animation by 1/2 second or nine frames—providing you've left the default value for Frames Rate at 18 and the Keyframe Increment at 1/2 second. Check the Rendering and Animation pages on the Scene Setup dialog to make sure.

A *keyframe* is a frame that contains a change from the previously set keyframe. A keyframe doesn't have to be every ninth one; it's any frame where a change has been made to any item in your 3D scene. What constitutes a change according to MOTION? Just about anything, including camera position changes, color adjustments, shape modifications, movements in lights, even importing a new shape.

The best way to see MOTION perform its magic is to try it out. If you are not already at frame 1, grab the sliding time marker that has the red line attached to it and drag it to the left until you reach the first frame. When you move the time marker, you are moving to and affecting the frame indicated by the number at the top, to the right of the drop-down box. Remember that the key to animating your 3D world and moving from frame to frame is this Timelines window.

INSIDE INFO

Frustrated because the drop-down box always seems to read "Second Frame"? It's actually "Second:Frame," meaning that the readout to the right indicates the number of seconds elapsed in the current animation and the current frame. This readout is a report of the red timeline marker position—not of the total time for your animation. There are several options for indicating the current frame or elapsed time in the drop-down list. For simplicity, you might want to change it to just "Frames."

Now activate the Lathe tool and click in the center of the Camera window to create a globe with the default size and color. Click the Set Keyframe button on the Timelines window to add more frames to the animation. Click anywhere on MOTION'S main window and press Ctrl+F to display the Edit / Surfaces dialog, choose Green Plastic, and click Apply. Next, with either Move tool, double-click the globe to get into the Object Editor workspace. Use the Shape tool and Node Edit to modify the amount or position of nodes and change the shape of the globe. As you can see in Figure 35.12, we chose to make some spikes here and there to create a kind of futuristic toy top. When you are finished editing the 2D outline, click the Done button to return to the 3D workspace and have the new shape rendered.

35.12

Our futuristic top, created in the Object Editor

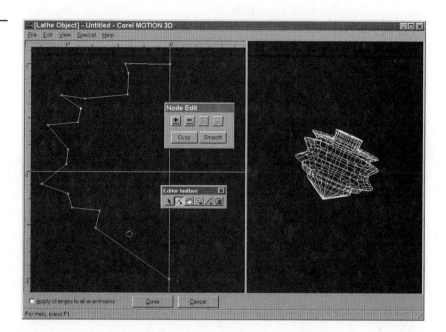

 WATCH OUT!

When rendering, make sure that (1) you have set the desired number of colors to render, on the Render page of the Scene Setup dialog; and (2) you are viewing the scene in the view mode in which you want the finished movie to be rendered. We like Shade Faster or Shade Better for most trial renderings, and Ray Trace for finished animations. Ray Trace mode can take forever, though, so save it for the very last step and only when you're sure you have the final version of the scene. It may even be necessary to let your computer run overnight for very lengthy Ray Traced renderings.

What have you accomplished at this point? You've created a globe, added nine frames (or 1/2 second of time), and changed both the shape and color of your original globe. Now let's see what MOTION does with all your hard work. Click the Make Movie button on the Timelines window (second icon from the left). When the dialog pops up, give your AVI file a name and a location on your hard disk. When you click Save, a Rendering preview window and Rendering Status dialog appear on screen to show you the progress of your animation sequence. Watch the Rendering preview window, and you'll see that MOTION is making all the intermediate changes needed to make your globe change shape and color. This rendering technique is called *morphing*.

When the animation rendering is complete, you can play the movie that you just made by selecting Play Movie from the Animation menu. MOTION launches the Windows Media Player application, loads the AVI file, and gives you control over playing it back. Press the Play button on the Media Player application and watch your animation do its thing. Congratulations—you're in the movie business!

Roll 'Em!

Where do you go from here? The possibilities are limitless. Well, not really, but we promise that you have only scratched the surface of MOTION's tools and capabilities. There are endless camera movements and object manipulations that you can employ. Besides the basics we've covered in this chapter, many more advanced features are waiting for you. You can add bitmap images for backgrounds and skies. How about altering the atmospheric conditions of your scene from a bright, clear day to a foggy one? You can even make objects completely or partially transparent. Just about anything your imagination can contrive is possible. You are the director, so go on and set the world of 3D animation in MOTION!

36

The Utilities

THIRTY-SIX

The concluding chapter in this book covers the programs in the CorelDRAW box that haven't quite reached "application" status, being referred to instead as "utilities." This might just be a matter of semantics to some, but we think the following programs are a lot like the support staff hired to ease the demands on company executives. We describe these "utilities" here according to our estimation of their relative importance.

OCR-TRACE

Considering all the features added to the newest incarnation of TRACE, it's only fitting that it be rewarded with a new name. Henceforth, from this day onward, ye ol' TRACE shall be known as OCR-TRACE.

The new name aptly indicates this program's new direction: the OCR stands for *Optical Character Recognition*. Earlier versions of TRACE also had this feature, but it wasn't really very strong. Many users may have missed or ignored it altogether. With version 6.0, things are different. And increased OCR capabilities are not the only area in which OCR-TRACE has improved dramatically. Here is a partial list of the new or enhanced features:

- Special-effects tracing methods, such as WoodCut, Sketch, Mosaic and 3D Mosaic
- Simplified tracing settings
- Ability to modify bitmaps before tracing
- Ability to edit nodes on a traced vector image before saving to a file

- A wide array of vector, text, and bitmap formats for saving files
- Ability to detect and trace graphics and text on the same original
- Templates, which can be designed and saved to accelerate tracing tasks on repetitive projects
- Ability to change text attributes, such as font and size, before saving recognized text to a file
- A Verify function, to check for spelling or other errors found in recognized text
- Multiple-page loading and tracing

With a redesigned interface, pumped-up optical character recognition (OCR) capabilities, and built-in scanning, OCR-TRACE is indeed a much more useful tool for the CorelDRAW user.

One of the best things about the current version of OCR-TRACE is its simplicity. The new special-effects tracing options allow plenty of room for flexibility and artistic flair. Yet, for the most common types of tracing assignments—black-and-white scans of drawings or signatures— you'll get workable results using the default settings without having to fiddle too much.

Our purpose here is to explain what OCR-TRACE can do, show you the controls, set up an example or two, and then encourage you to play. After all, it seems that the philosophy behind all of the CorelDRAW applications is that working with these tools can be fun.

Why OCR-TRACE?

If you are new to drawing programs, this is the first question you might ask. The answer lies in the differences between the two types of graphic images—bitmap and vector—created by software. These images are defined internally as either digital dots (bits or pixels) or mathematical instructions that describe how to draw lines and curves (vectors). Bitmap editors, generically called "paint" programs (including Photo-PAINT), manipulate pixels or bits. Graphics from these programs are called *bit-maps*. Drawing programs (including CorelDRAW) work with mathematical instructions and points of reference to draw *vectors* (lines and curves); their graphics are called vector graphics.

Although DRAW is able to import and display bitmap images, it is intended as a vector-based image creation and editing program. With this in mind, it's easy to understand why DRAW cannot edit a bitmap image's individual pixels. DRAW can only manipulate the bitmap image in limited ways, such as cropping, skewing, rotating, and flipping. In DRAW, a bitmap image is simply not as versatile as a vector object.

By now you may be lamenting, "If only that jumble of pixels could be converted into vector objects." This is where OCR-TRACE comes to the rescue. It *automatically* converts bitmap images into vector objects and text characters.

OCR-TRACE provides two basic functions. Let's take the TRACE portion first. TRACE takes bitmap graphics and converts them to lines and curves that are understood and editable by DRAW. The OCR part of the program attempts to recognize bitmap text and convert it into text characters easily understood by DRAW or any other word processor.

In Figure 36.1, you can see how OCR-TRACE works. The Image window (on the left) displays the original bitmap graphic, and the Vector window (on the right) displays the vector tracing. The Text window (lower-right) displays the results of any OCR function.

WATCH OUT!

Some of OCR-TRACE's commands are context-sensitive to the active window pane. How do you know which pane is currently active? Good question—we are annoyed that there are no obvious visual clues. The workaround is to make sure that you click somewhere in the pane you want to affect, before you select a command.

36.1

If you don't have all the toolbars seen in this arrangement of the **OCR-TRACE** workspace, right-click on any toolbar and select all the ones that are unchecked.

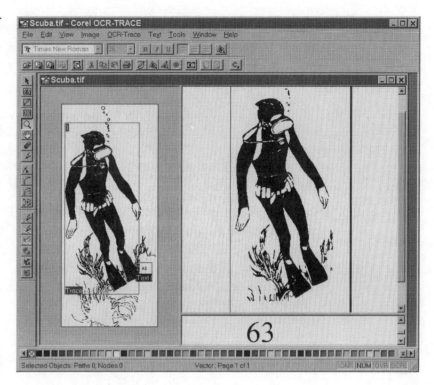

The Trace Settings dialog (Figure 36.2) is accessed via the OCR-TRACE menu. It contains a separate tabbed page for setting the options of each tracing mode. The OCR Settings dialog (Figure 36.3) is also accessed from the OCR-TRACE menu. It contains four pages of settings governing the OCR functions.

The Mechanics of OCR-TRACE

To put OCR-TRACE to work, you must first give it a bitmap image. There are two ways to do this: Open a bitmap file that you already have on disk, or select Acquire to use a scanner to digitize a piece of art or document. Both these options are on the File menu.

36.2

The Trace Settings dialog

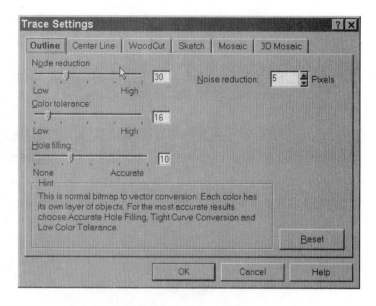

36.3

The OCR Settings dialog

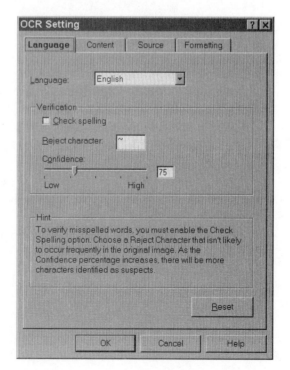

If you use a scanner, your sources for images are almost limitless. No longer must you rely on others to provide you with bitmap files, or have to create them yourself in a paint program. Now you can scan directly into OCR-TRACE, convert the image to vector, and send it to DRAW—without ever having a file on disk. (It is good practice, however, to keep backup files of your artwork.)

OCR-TRACE shares all of CorelDRAW's filters. That means OCR-TRACE can open files in any of the formats for which you have a filter installed. In addition, if you use File / Acquire to scan an image and then want to save it within OCR-TRACE, you can save it in any format for which you have installed a filter.

When you're scanning an image, the Acquire dialog will be specific to the scanner that you selected when you installed CorelDRAW. Detailed instructions on the use of this dialog and the care and feeding of your scanner will come from the scanner manufacturer.

INSIDE INFO

The popular **TWAIN** interface, which allows device manufacturers to write a single driver that will work with any Windows-based program, was not yet available in a 32-bit version at the time version 6.0 was developed, so Corel wrote its own 32-bit drivers for some of the most popular scanners. If your particular scanner model wasn't on the list of supported devices when you installed CorelDRAW 6, then you will not be able to use OCR-TRACE's Acquire function. Instead, you will need to load the 16-bit device driver supplied by your scanner manufacturer and use the accompanying software to save any scans to disk, then open them in **OCR-TRACE**. (It's a good idea to keep checking with Corel and your scanner manufacturer to see if a 32-bit device driver has become available.)

One of the reasons for converting bitmaps into vector images is that bitmaps are constructed of dots. Bitmap resolution is measured in *dpi*, dots per inch; the higher the number, the better the quality. If the resolution is not sufficient, the image may look jagged or grainy. When you enlarge a bitmap, the jagged or grainy appearance gets even worse. Once converted to a vector image, though, it looks much smoother, can be sized up or down with no loss in image quality, and can be printed at the highest possible resolution of your output device.

Figure 36.4 shows a typical application for OCR-TRACE. (This image consists of only black-and-white, although OCR-TRACE is perfectly capable of rendering color or grayscale images such as photographs.) The clip-art skin diver was scanned from an image about 3″ tall. To follow along, you can either scan the image from this book or open SCUBA.TIF in the PRACTICE directory.

36.4

This piece of clip art is an ideal candidate to be traced.

INSIDE INFO

> With small images, scan at a resolution one-half the maximum allowed by your scanner (300 dpi instead of 600 dpi, for example), and then scale to 200%.

Scanning images can be confusing. On the one hand, scanning color or grayscale photos at high resolutions may be a waste of effort if the image is ultimately destined to be imported and printed as a bitmap. Often, the extra data captured as a result of the higher resolution setting goes unused in the final output, causing the scanned files to be unnecessarily large.

On the other hand, when scanning images for tracing, the rules are completely different. Every dot you can cram into a given area will be useful during tracing, to get the most accurate representation. To see this graphically, scan an image into Photo-PAINT at both 300 and 600 dpi, and then enlarge both images. The 300-dpi scan quickly becomes jagged and then unrecognizable, but the 600-dpi scan can be enlarged to almost 200% before losing detail. Eliminating this jaggedness is the primary reason for tracing images and converting them to vector images in the first place. The rougher and more jagged the image, the more the manual clean-up work will be required later, so making the image less jagged before the trace will improve the accuracy and quality of the trace.

Finally, it is very important to work with an image large enough to allow OCR-TRACE to adequately turn corners. And because many scanning programs won't allow you to enlarge the image when scanning at the highest resolution of the scanner, it is often better to scan at a lower resolution and then set the scanner to scale the image to 200%.

Figure 36.5 shows the diver image after opening in OCR-TRACE.

3 6 . 5

This image is ready to be traced.

INSIDE INFO

If you're starting with a small piece of original black-and-white art, use a copy machine to enlarge it as much as possible before scanning.

Presto, Change-o

Ironically, the actual tracing is perhaps the easiest part of all: Just click the Outline Trace button, or select Perform Trace / By Outline from the OCR-Trace menu. Depending on the speed of your PC, you'll get a finished vector image in the right-hand window pane in a minute or two. You can modify how closely the trace fits the bitmap image by fiddling with the Node Reduction and Noise Reduction settings found on the Trace Settings dialog. As a jumping-off point, we recommend that you start by accepting the default Outline Trace settings. In many cases, that will be all you'll need.

Figure 36.6 shows the completed trace of the diver (on the right) alongside the original bitmap image (on the left). As you examine your traced image, you'll see obvious imperfections. If these flaws are not severe, you may be able to overlook them. If they are glaring, however, you'll undoubtedly have to bring the tracing into DRAW to clean it up. To minimize this clean-up procedure, remember our paraphrase of the adage, "An ounce of scanning prevention is worth a pound of clean-up cure."

36.6

OCR-TRACE studies the original bitmap image (left) and produces a collection of vector curves to replicate it (right).

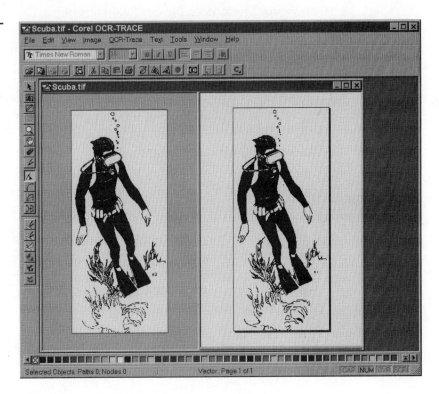

INSIDE INFO

> If you haven't done it already, enlarge the OCR-TRACE window to fill your screen. (Don't forget, though—this is just a low-resolution screen image, so the image will likely be jagged.) Enlarging the window makes it easier to work on part of the image, as well as to determine if the trace result is acceptable.

Tracing Only What You Need

OCR-TRACE offers several ways to convert only the portions of your images that you really need. You can select any portion, whether text or graphics. The key to this is using the Draw OCR block tools and the Draw Trace block tools. Simply load your bitmap, click on the appropriate block tool, and marquee-select the areas you want traced. You can place as many blocks as you like and even intermix the Trace and OCR block types on the same bitmap image. Figure 36.7 shows a form with a text block and a graphic block selected.

If you have intermixed the two types of Draw blocks, you must select Perform OCR-Trace from the OCR-Trace menu, or choose the OCR-Trace button from the Standard toolbar. Should you choose to initiate only a graphic trace or text recognition function from the menu or toolbars, the draw blocks of the other type will be ignored in the tracing pass.

If you find that you are repeatedly setting up complicated tracing blocks for the same kinds of documents, you can save each arrangement as a *template*. Templates can be reloaded whenever needed. This is ideal for projects such as forms, where several parts of the form, but not all of it, need to be traced. The functions for the saving and loading of templates are found under the File menu.

36.7

This image has a text block and a graphic block selected.

When experimenting with different tracing settings, you can easily remove the contents of the previous trace pass by clicking the mouse in the Vector window and selecting Edit / Clear All. To see the tracing in a wireframe view, select Objects / Wire Frame from the View Menu. From the same submenu you can select Show Bitmap, which superimposes the wireframe over the actual bitmap image.

Cleaning Up

There is one other check you can make before issuing your seal of approval on the trace operation. Right-click the Vector window and select Path Info from the pop-up. The Document Information dialog appears with the Path Info tab displayed, reporting the vital statistics of the vector paths in the tracing. When you click on a path, the dialog changes to display the particulars of the selected path.

Bear in mind that a complex drawing, with many paths and nodes, can bring a printer or imagesetter to its knees—not to mention that it can slow down the computer, cost you time and money at the service bureau, and above all, indicate sloppy work on your part.

Most tracing programs, OCR-TRACE included, have a tendency to create many paths with many nodes. There are several techniques that you can use, at different stages of your project, and using various programs, to produce the cleanest and most precise results.

NEW FOR 6

When you click on a path in the Vector window, the number of nodes on that path are shown on the bottom status bar. If you hold down the Shift key, you can select more than one path; the total number of nodes on all the selected paths will be displayed on the status bar. Remember that reducing the number of paths and nodes is your ultimate goal.

Begin with the highest resolution possible on the largest image possible. When it comes to text recognition, OCR-TRACE will warn you that it likes to work on scans that are at least 200 dpi. In addition, remember that in most situations the more contrast you have to begin with, the better off you'll be.

Don't set the Node Reduction setting to 0 unless you specifically want a stair-stepped look to your tracing.

Keep it simple. Sometimes it's easier to fix the bitmap *before* tracing. Take another look at Figure 36.6; in that trace of the original image there are hundreds of paths and thousands of nodes. Figure 36.8 shows how just erasing the seaweed made the final image much simpler. You can make these deletions in a bitmap editor like Photo-PAINT, or use the Eraser tool in OCR-TRACE. Simplicity can mean the difference between a dream job or a nightmare at the printer or service bureau.

INSIDE INFO

If the Eraser tool is too big to make fine edits to your bitmap image, try zooming in as close as possible. The Eraser will eventually work on a single pixel at a time.

36.8

A much simpler and more effective trace of the diver is accomplished by deleting the sea-weed before tracing.

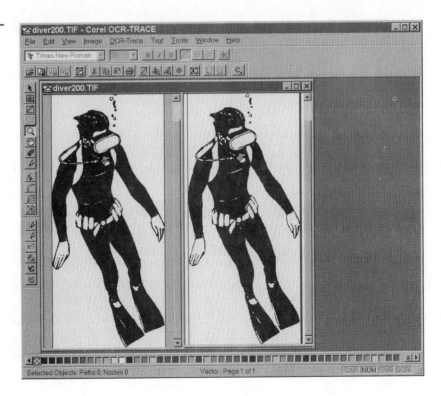

Fiddling with the Tracing Option Settings

Though it is true that the default settings for the Outline Trace option will serve for most images, if you find that your trace comes out with an unwieldy number of paths and nodes, it's time to start fiddling. Because the images you trace will be unique, there are no hard and fast fiddling rules to apply; generally, however, increasing the number in Node Reduction (the default is 30) and raising the Noise Reduction setting will reduce the complexity of the trace.

The following is a general description of the settings when using the Outline Trace mode.

- *Node Reduction* tells OCR-TRACE how tightly to follow the contour of the bitmap image. The lower the setting, the closer the trace will follow the pixels, and consequently, the more nodes in the final trace.

- *Noise Reduction* sets the amount of pixels that will be ignored by OCR-TRACE. To capture small details and fine lines, set this to 1 (the default is 5).

- *Color Tolerance* only works on grayscale and color images. It tells OCR-TRACE how many colors or gray shades to ignore when tracing. To render the most colors or shades available in the original bitmap, lower the setting. If you're after a posterized look, set the number higher (the default is 16).

- *Hole Filling* is available only when tracing grayscale or color images. It tells OCR-TRACE how to fill in gaps between shades or colors. For a realistic tracing with no white gaps, boost the setting toward Accurate.

Remember that for every Trace Setting adjustment you make, there will be compromises and trade-offs. Quite often, raising the Node Reduction and Noise Reduction settings produces a sloppy result and requires still more clean-up. Figure 36.9 shows the kind of changes to expect when you vary the Node Reduction settings. Changing the settings to the most accurate possible can make for long tracing times and curves with too many nodes.

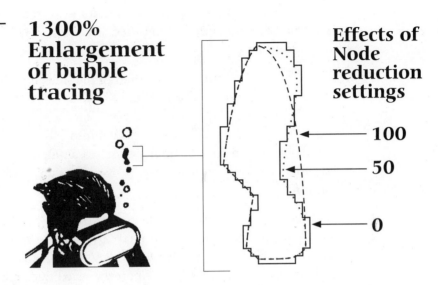

36.9

These are the kinds of changes you might get when varying the Node Reduction settings.

1300% Enlargement of bubble tracing

Effects of Node reduction settings

100

50

0

Fiddling with Nodes

OCR-TRACE does have built-in tools for moving and deleting nodes, and even for creating Bézier curves to modify and add to your tracing, but they are very rudimentary. When you factor in that these tools feel clumsy and slow, you'll understand why we recommend that most vector edits be made in DRAW instead of in OCR-TRACE.

Moving Uptown

Now that you have your traced image and recognized text, you'll undoubtedly want to bring them into DRAW so that they can be enhanced further or incorporated into other projects. There are three easy ways to accomplish this. Pick the one that best suits your needs.

- *Save to a file* by selecting File / Save / Vector or Text (there are equivalent buttons for these functions on the toolbar).

- *Drag and drop* by using the selection tool to click and drag the contents of the Vector or Text window and drop them into an opened DRAW document.

- *Copy to the Clipboard* by clicking in the Vector or Text window and choosing Edit / Copy, then activating DRAW and selecting Edit / Paste.

The safest and most flexible method of the three is saving the tracing as a file, which can be imported into DRAW at any time. Why do we say safest? Try this and learn the hard way: Trace something really complicated, copy it to the Clipboard, paste it into DRAW, and then hit the restart button on your computer. Stop screaming, I can't hear you. You say you'll lose all your hard work? OK, then, don't push the big red button.

This demonstrates just how vulnerable your work is should you suffer a crash or lock up. Basically, you'd have to start over from scratch. But save the tracing while inside OCR-TRACE, and it would be a simple matter to restart DRAW and import the saved tracing, right? Sure, it takes up some extra disk space, but this intermediate file can be deleted at a later time—when you're sure that it won't be needed as backup anymore.

Why do we say this method is flexible? Select Save / Vector from the File menu in OCR-TRACE. Now take a look at all the file format choices you have in the Save As Type drop-down list. That's a lot of flexibility. For saving graphics destined for DRAW, we like Corel-Trace (AI) or either of the two Corel Presentation Exchange (CMX) formats.

If you have used the OCR functions, then you have pretty much the same options for bringing the recognized text into DRAW. At this point in time, we can't recommend either the drag-and-drop or cut-and-paste methods. First, the drag-and-drop implementation is finicky…a real time-waster if you don't get it just right. Why bother? Second, both methods add an extra space at the end of lines. This means more wasted time finding and deleting extra spaces when you get your text into DRAW.

Saving in any of the word processing file formats for which you have a filter installed is easy and painless. This method is recommended because it allows you to make full use of OCR-TRACE's type-formatting functions. To customize any portion of recognized text, simply highlight it in the Text window and use the text tools on the toolbar to apply your formatting changes. This custom formatting will be saved when you use one of the word processing filters.

The last Save function applies to the original bitmap image. If you have made any changes to the image with the Eraser or Pencil tools and want to preserve them, you can select File / Save / Image. This is also a handy technique for converting the original image to another file format, should you desire.

When you use the Save function, OCR-TRACE will use the same file name as the original image, but will assign the appropriate file format extension. If you want to change the name, go ahead and enter whatever you like into the File Name field, but don't bother typing the extension or even trying to change it. OCR-TRACE is very insistent that *all* extensions end up exactly the way *it* wants them.

Mopping Up with DRAW

Now it's time to start DRAW and import your saved tracing (or select Paste if you've copied the tracing to the Clipboard while in OCR-TRACE). Before you can do any editing of this image, first ungroup it by selecting the group and choosing Arrange / Ungroup. Then use the Shape tool and the Node Edit roll-up to clean up the objects as necessary.

INSIDE INFO

If you have used an unusual typeface in your original bitmap and there is no exact match in your type library, you have a decision to make. In some cases, you can find a similar typeface from among the vast array included with DRAW, convert the text to curves, and reshape the letterforms as best as you can. If you can't find anything sufficiently similar, then you must use the scanned text and clean it up, pixel by pixel, in a bitmap editor like Photo-PAINT. Either way, it's a tedious job, to say the least.

By selecting objects in the drawing, you can see how OCR-TRACE went about its business of creating paths, curves, and fills to replicate a bitmap image. You will probably notice that there are many more nodes than necessary. Here is where DRAW 6.0's Auto-Reduce command, discussed in Chapter 7, can be a lifesaver.

The Finished Work

The remainder of your work on the traced image should be pretty routine at this point. You'll want to move nodes to straighten and reshape lines, and move control handles to smooth and reshape curves. (For a refresher on curve shaping and node editing, review Chapter 7, "As the Curve Turns.")

Figure 36.10 shows the original bitmap image (with the seaweed taken out) alongside the finished work.

36.10

**Before and After:
On the left, the ed-
ited bitmap image
before the trace.
On the right, the
high-quality vector
drawing after the
trace.**

Multimedia Manager

If you're like many CorelDRAW users who just upgraded to 6.0, you may have already burned several minutes searching for MOSAIC, the handy cataloging program that pops up from within DRAW versions 5 and earlier. MOSAIC now rests in peace, having been replaced by MULTIMEDIA MANAGER (hereafter to be called MM because we refuse to use all capital letters for a name that long).

As its name implies, MM does more than just catalog image files. Some of you are probably lonesome for MOSAIC's sleek and simple way of doing business—that was our first reaction, too. But we're glad that we gave MM a chance, because we have grown to like it. To summarize, we like the following:

- MM's new interface makes it much easier to drag and drop files into and out of *albums* (the new name for libraries).

- Albums are much more compact than MOSAIC's Library files and can contain intelligent links to files.

- MM's Print services are robust, capable of printing full images or just thumbnails, complete with file names, paths, and those cute frame borders.

- MM can produce quick-and-dirty slide shows from any files you add to an album.

- MM can read and understand many more types of files than MOSAIC.

You'll find operation of MM covered quite adequately in the CorelDRAW 6.0 User's Manual.

Extra, Extra, Read All About It: MM Tames Authoring Team

We used MM quite effectively for the production of this book. Its chapters contain numerous illustrations, artwork, printouts, and screen captures, and printing them out and passing them around to various authors and editors is always a daunting task. We know that in the age of electronic publishing, there should be a solution to this—perhaps a program like Adobe Acrobat—and theoretically, we could have created a portable document to send to everyone concerned. But a typical chapter from this book would produce an Acrobat file 15 to 20MB, so we'll keep this solution theoretical for the time being, thank you.

Instead, we used albums from MM for printing and for quick viewing purposes, and it worked great. In Figure 36.11 we are about to create an album for Chapter 20, the one on extrusions. We have navigated to the appropriate directory in the lower half of the dialog (which, incidentally, is a million times easier to do than it was in MOSAIC) and selected the files for this album. Notice that there are four different types of files.

Figure 36.12 shows how MM presents the files in its album once we dragged and dropped them there. We expected MM to be able to show us .CDR files and .TIF files, and we weren't surprised that it could sniff

36.11

Adding files to an MM album involves just one drag and one drop.

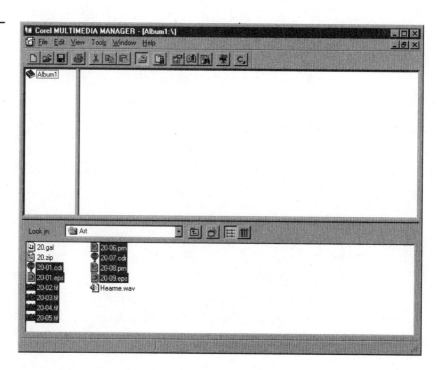

36.12

The ten files that comprise Chapter 20's artwork

out the image headers of .EPS files. But we were astonished to receive thumbnails from files 20-06 and 20-08, both print files with no embedded images at all. MM read those files and built thumbnails from the PostScript code!

We shot Figure 36.13 right after we saved the album, naming it Chapter 20.GAL (presumably short for "gallery"). After changing the view in the file window to show all file details (just as we would in Explorer), we found several items worthy of note:

■ The ten files for this chapter consume over 12MB of space (one of our smaller collections).

■ The .ZIP file containing all ten files consumes almost 5MB, so we could easily transport it electronically.

■ The .GAL file that we just created is only 21K!

36.13

With the album created and all file details shown, MM is dramatically thrifty.

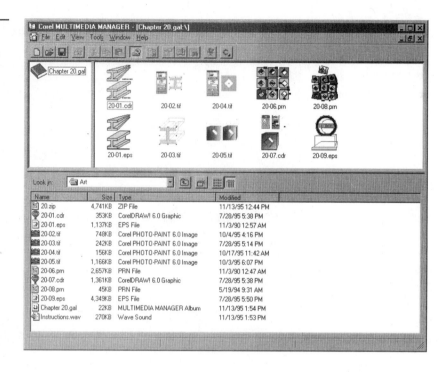

Sounds Good to Us

For many of this book's chapters, we created a sound clip of instructions about how certain files were to be handled. For this to be useful, we needed to include the actual wave file in the album, not just a thumbnail (a thumbnail of a sound clip would be pretty useless…). Figure 36.14 shows the results.

By right-clicking the sound file's icon and going to its Properties sheet, it was a simple matter to choose Update Data from the File Link page, thereby instructing MM to embed the data from the sound file instead of to create a link. The size of the album is up considerably—now over 242K—but that is well within transport limits, be it by diskette, direct connection, or e-mail. In Figure 36.14, we removed the Drive window, which is no longer needed once the files have been dropped into the album.

36.14

Double-click on
Instructions.WAV
to hear all about
these lovely images.

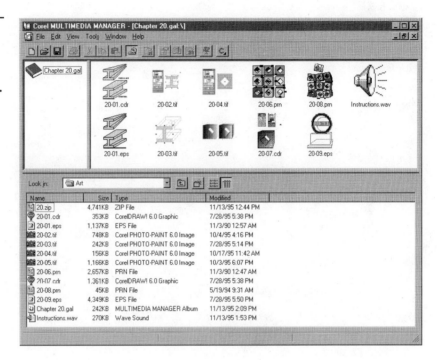

As you would expect from a program called MULTIMEDIA MAN-
AGER, all forms of video and audio files can be stored within an al-
bum. In fact, you can store anything there (just as you could with
MOSAIC). If MM doesn't know what to make of it, it creates a generic
icon for it. You could even throw in your AUTOEXEC.BAT and CON-
FIG.SYS files if you wanted to.

Printed Any Good Thumbs Lately?

From MM, you can print either thumbnails or the full images. For our
book project, to do quick printouts of images for proofing purposes,
this was a terrific tool. Figure 36.15 shows a page of thumbnails from
this chapter, and you'll see immediately that these images will win no
awards for their high fidelity. On the other hand, the entire page
printed in about 30 seconds, and for a quick look these thumbnails are
just what the doctor ordered.

3 6 . 1 5

Printed thumb-
nails, complete
with file names, can
be supplied from
MM in about
30 seconds.

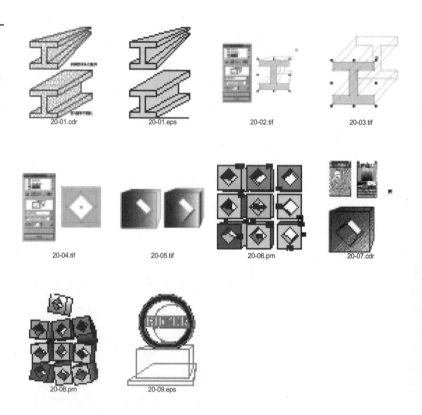

20-01.cdr   20-01.eps   20-02.tif   20-03.tif

20-04.tif   20-05.tif   20-06.prn   20-07.cdr

20-08.prn   20-09.eps

As you can tell, we like MULTIMEDIA MANAGER. Its interface has a few rough edges, and its Explorer window is a bit wimpy. (For instance, there is no Refresh command. So to refresh a directory, you must move to a different directory and then return to the first one.) But for a first-version application, it is quite impressive, and we have already made good use of it.

CorelDEPTH

From all respects, this new program appears to be Corel's answer to the automation that is being introduced into competitor's programs. Think of DEPTH as a super-duper, automated Extrude tool, and you won't be far off. Its job is to bring the feeling of 3D to flat objects. It does this by creating new surfaces where backs and sides would go (like Extrude), by determining how light would reflect off those surfaces (like Extrude), and by allowing you to rotate an object in 3D space (like Extrude). It can also bring depth to multiple objects and complete drawings (*un*like Extrude), and that is what distinguishes CorelDEPTH from a toy.

A Friendly Learning Curve

The fastest and easiest way to learn DEPTH is with its Step-by-Step wizard, which walks you through most of the essential steps. First, you are asked to choose the amount of depth you want for your object and the kind of edge it should have (regular or "beveled"). In Figure 36.16, we have chosen a medium depth and a beveled edge.

36.16

The first stop in the CorelDEPTH Wizard is choosing the amount of depth and the type of edge.

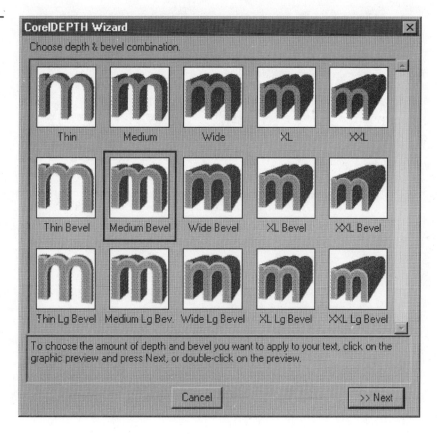

Next comes the rotation. DEPTH, like Extrude, provides an unlimited amount of rotation on all axes. We chose an extreme side view for our demo (Figure 36.17).

The second stop is rotation.

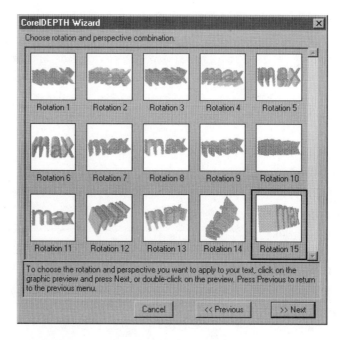

Next come colors, from which we chose a rather conservative combo of gray and blue (Figure 36.18), and then light source (Figure 36.19), for which we figured the top-left orientation would be best for the severe rotation that we had selected.

Finally, you enter some sample text and click Done. Figure 36.20 shows the result of our hand-held demo.

As you experiment with DEPTH, you'll probably spend most of your time fiddling with the Geometry Palette (from the Window menu), Light Source (from Arrange), and the rotation controls in the "Virtual Track Ball" (second icon down in the toolbox).

36.18

Then you choose colors for the front, back, and edges...

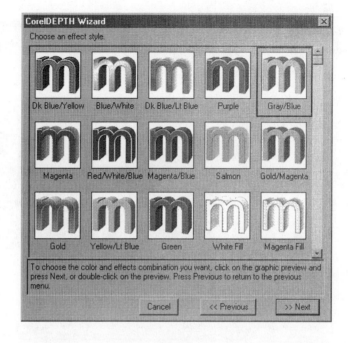

36.19

...and then you choose the direction of the light.

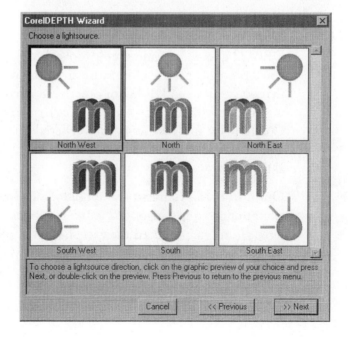

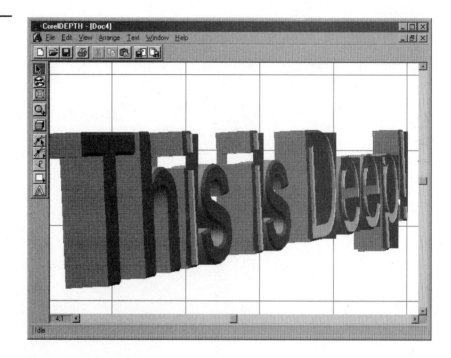

Extruding Your Own Creations

DEPTH does have some simple tools for object creation, but we think you'll probably get the most satisfactory results when you import work that you've done in DRAW or other vector-based programs. We are utterly dumbfounded by DEPTH's lack of an import filter for CorelDRAW files, and somewhat relieved that we could successfully copy and paste artwork from DRAW across the Clipboard into DEPTH.

Our own Byron Canfield (composer of Chapter 34) was the designer in charge of creating a logo for the International CorelDRAW User Conference, and he produced the very sharp monolithic image shown in Figure 36.21. He did this the old-fashioned way, using DRAW and manually drawn perspective lines. Because DEPTH can't do bitmaps, it would need help from another application to do the images that are clipped into each cube in this figure. Let's see how DEPTH and DRAW might work together on this project.

36.21

Can this nice logo be produced in DEPTH?

The Basic Shape   The basic shape is simply a collection of squares, containing shades of gray to mimic the rendition that we used for faxing and other low-resolution work. Figure 36.22 shows the logo as it looks in DRAW before migrating to DEPTH.

36.22

These squares are
the ingredients for
a recipe in **DEPTH**.

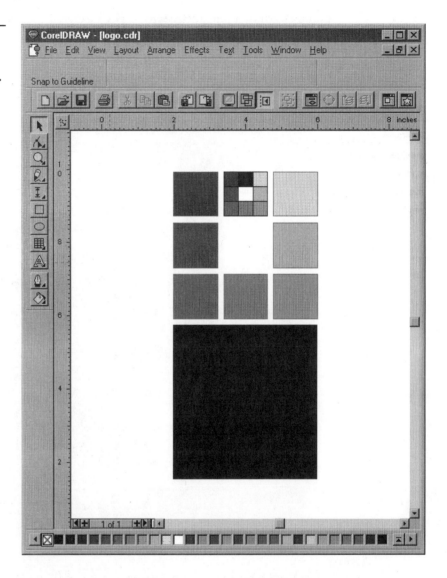

Once again, we had to schlep our logo across the Clipboard to get it
into DEPTH, and accomplished this without incident. (We still can't
believe that DEPTH won't allow us to import a .CDR file.) Once it was
in DEPTH, we sized it to taste, being careful to hold the Shift key to
maintain proportion while sizing.

Our first order of business was to go to View / Working Plane and toggle off the gridlines. Some jobs might be precise enough to require these; ours isn't. Our screen looked like Figure 36.23.

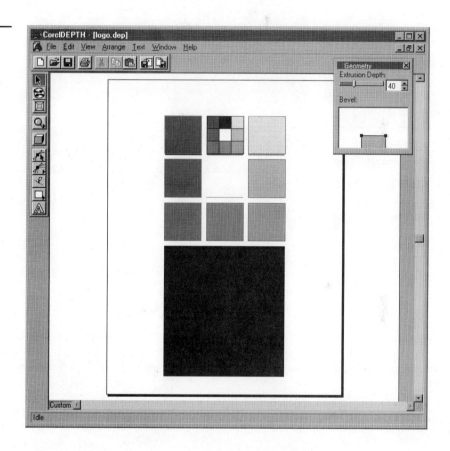

Unlike Extrude, there is no Apply button that turns on the effects of DEPTH; as soon as we pasted the logo into the program, the current specifications were applied to it. At first, we thought an extrusion depth of 40, as shown in the Geometry window in Figure 36.23, would be a lot...until we discovered that the unit of measure was points. So we cranked the value up to 120 and promptly got some depth to our monolith.

Rotate to the Max Rotation is similar to the new controls in DRAW's Extrude roll-up. In other words, they are way cool. With your mouse or pointing device, you can pitch the object forward or backward, rotate it around its lateral axis, around the circumference, turn it upside down, spin it like a top, you name it.

Our job was to simulate the angle and perspective of the original logo, so we pitched it forward a bit, and rotated it from left to right. The result is shown in Figure 36.24, and it was not what we had expected.

36.24

Hmmm, some sides appear to be missing...

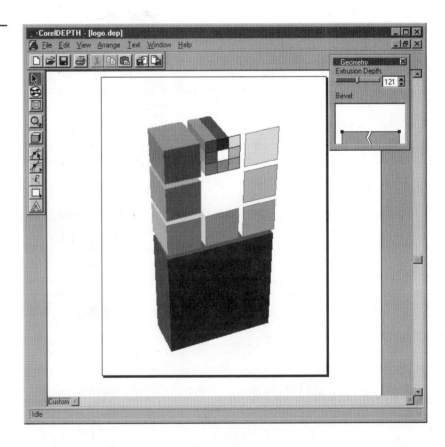

Indeed, we were unimpressed with DEPTH's less-than-precise interpretation—though we were able to work around it. We tried changing the light source, and quickly learned why DRAW's Extrude tool offers multiple light sources: It lets you make the light look more true-to-life. But we persevered and fiddled a lot with DEPTH's single light source until we found a position that was workable (shown in Figure 36.25).

Having created the right depth and perspective, DEPTH's job with this logo was now done. We were pleased to see an .EPS export option, assuring us that we could move our logo into virtually any page layout or

36.25

Adding light source makes this cube more believable. Not perfect, but believable.

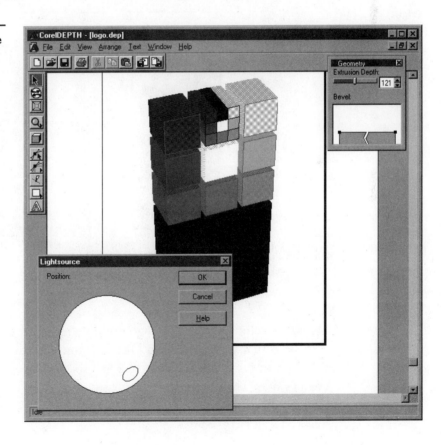

publishing program. There was Windows Metafile, too, and we also noticed the Illustrator format, which promised to be our gateway back to DRAW. We exported the file as Logo.AI, returned to DRAW, and imported it. Figure 36.26 shows the before and the after in DRAW.

36.26

DEPTH turned the original group of objects (left) into a 3D-like group (right).

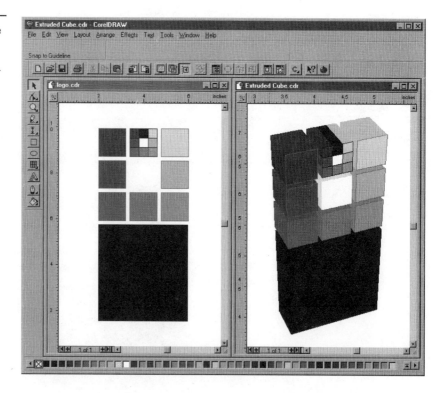

To our pleasant surprise, our logo not only returned to DRAW with the extrusions that we called for in DEPTH, but with the objects placed correctly. In other words, each cube had six four-sided closed objects, one per side. The object fills all got converted to RGB colors instead of CMYK, but on balance, the objects we wound up with were easily edited and well behaved.

In addition to exporting it as an Illustrator file, we also copied the object to the Clipboard and pasted it into DRAW. Interestingly, that yielded even better results, with fewer extraneous outlines and invisible objects. Figure 36.27 shows the project after five minutes of editing to provide the desired shading effects.

36.27

With all faces being separate objects, applying fills and outlines to specific parts of the final image (right) was easy.

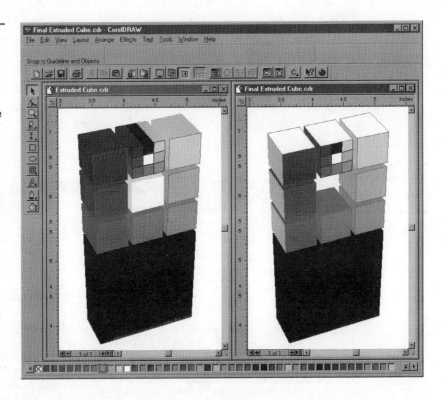

That's our short tour of DEPTH. Don't expect the world from it, and don't count on it for CAD-like precision. But it works as advertised—it creates nice, credible 3D effects, and it's easy to use.

CorelCAPTURE

So, you've got to write up some instructions on how to achieve a particular result on the computer. If only you could *show* how the screen is supposed to look, instead of having to put it into 12,000 difficult-to-follow words. The perfect tool for this job is CAPTURE, the venerable screen capture program that has been part of the CorelDRAW box since version 3.0. CAPTURE lets you save the screen to a graphics file that can then be incorporated into a document or presentation. If a picture is worth 1,000 words to your business, then this tool will earn some serious frequent-flier miles for you.

CAPTURE has been enhanced for version 6.0 in a number of ways. And there's a new tabbed page in the application window (Figure 36.28), refining the already good organization of the many available options.

36.28

CorelCAPTURE
is looking very
95-like in its cur-
rent incarnation.

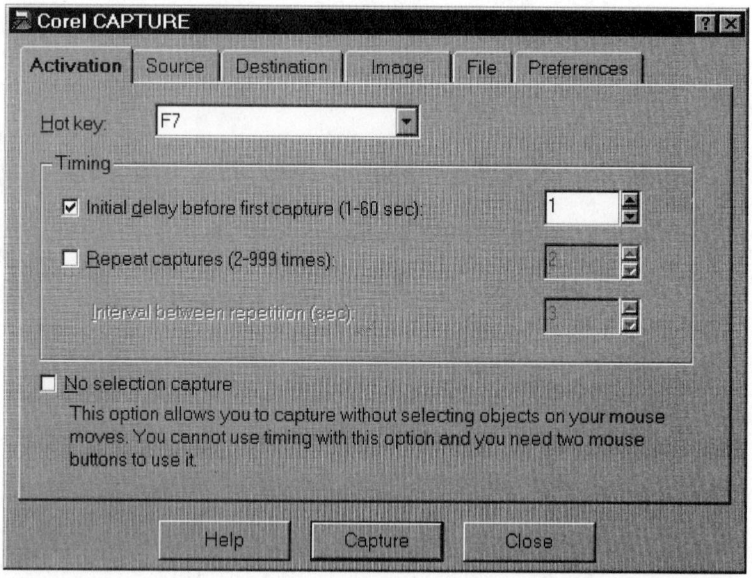

Activation

CAPTURE is activated by pressing a hotkey. After a delay is counted down, the capture is performed. You can specify the initial delay before the picture is taken, as well as the hotkey itself. (Hotkey determination is new to version 6; choose any Ctrl or Shift combination with the keys F2 through F10 or A through Z.) You can also choose the number of times to repeat the capture automatically (from 2 to 999), and the interval between repetitions.

The Activation page also sports a new No Selection Capture option that can capture a free-form area of the screen (rectangular, elliptical, or free-hand). You define this area by drawing it with your mouse, exactly as if you were using the Pencil tool in DRAW...well, *almost* exactly: You need to learn a new technique that involves drawing with both the left and the right mouse buttons pressed. We got the hang of it pretty quickly.

Source

The Source page (identical to that in version 5) helps you specify the area you want to capture. A graphical image representing the screen appears on this tab. As you select from the different options, colors change on the graphic to show which area will be captured:

- Full Screen capture is, as you'd expect, every pixel of your display.

- Current Window is the currently selected window or dialog.

- Client Window is the current document window without the application's caption, menu and toolbars, or border. If the document is not maximized in the application, Client Window is the entire document window.

- Rectangular Area or Elliptical Area is defined by you. You select the appropriate option, press the Capture button, and then press the hotkey. After the delay, the mouse cursor changes to a net. Click the left mouse button and drag to form a marquee around the area to be captured.

- With Freehand Area you use a technique similar to using the point-and-click technique with DRAW's Pencil tool, the result being a series of straight lines that define an area.

Destination

On the Destination page you select a storage place for the captured image to be stored. The options are a standard graphics file, an animation file (new in version 6.0), the Clipboard, the printer, or an OLE automated application (also new in this version). The OLE automated application is selected from a drop-down list box (which, as of this writing, includes only DRAW 6.0 and Photo-PAINT 6.0). The animation option assumes that you are capturing multiple images to create a cartoon effect.

Image

The Image page contains settings for the attributes of the saved image. Choose from Screen, Printer, and Custom. If you select screen, the image will not be altered. With Printer, you can change the color of the captured image to black and white, 16-color, grayscale, 256-color, or 24-bit color. And with Custom, you can change the color, image resolution, and image size.

File

When you elect to have images automatically saved to a file (in the Destination page), you specify the location of the saved files (the folder or directory) by clicking the Select Capture Directory button. This File page also allows you to specify the file name and type—including Windows bitmap (.BMP), Corel Photo-PAINT Image (.CPT), TIFF bitmap (.TIF), and PaintBrush (.PCX).

You can also choose to use file compression, which differs based on the file format chosen. Saved files can be automatically named; successive captures are named with sequential numbers added to the end of the file name. If you are creating an animation file, you set both the file name and frame rate here, as well.

Preferences

The Preferences dialog allows you to automatically add a border to the captured image, with your choice of border size (in pixels) and color. You can elect to have CAPTURE automatically hide its icon during a capture, to display a message box when a capture is completed, and to capture the area under the cursor. New to version 6.0, this Capture Under Cursor option highlights the window under the mouse cursor during the delay (set in the Activation tab). You move the mouse around until the desired window is highlighted. When the countdown reaches zero, the window currently highlighted will be captured.

CAPTURE has definitely grown up over the years and, in fact, lacks but one important feature, in our view: the ability to capture the mouse pointer. (Actually, few capture programs *can* do that because, technically speaking, the mouse pointer is not part of the screen.) Otherwise, all of the other bells and whistles are in there, including several that the competition never thought of.

FONT MASTER

Look as hard as you like, but you won't find FontMinder in the CorelDRAW 6.0 box. Corel has replaced it with its own font manager called FONT MASTER.

With the 1,000-plus fonts included in the 6.0 package, you definitely need some way to manage them—and just installing all of them at once isn't the answer. Not surprisingly, your system performance will suffer as a result. FONT MASTER takes the burden out of keeping track of fonts by helping you to arrange them in easy-to-manage groups that can then be easily installed, either permanently or temporarily. By creating an icon for a font group and placing it directly on the Windows 95 desktop, you make installation about as simple as it could possibly be.

A Question of Permanence

Using FONT MASTER will expose you to a new concept in font management: the notion of permanent and temporary fonts. A *permanent font* is one that is installed the conventional way and stays installed until you explicitly uninstall it. A *temporarily installed font* is one that is installed only for the current Windows session and is automatically removed when you shut down Windows. This arrangement makes child's play out of installing groups of fonts for specific customers or for particular jobs.

FONT MASTER helps you manage all of your fonts, both TrueType and Type 1, with simple drag-and-drop operation.

A Geography Lesson

FONT MASTER's workspace is divided into four windows, as shown in Figure 36.29. Following are descriptions of these windows, proceeding clockwise starting with the upper-left window.

36.29

FONT MASTER is a drag-and-drop maven for installing fonts, either permanently or just for the current Windows session.

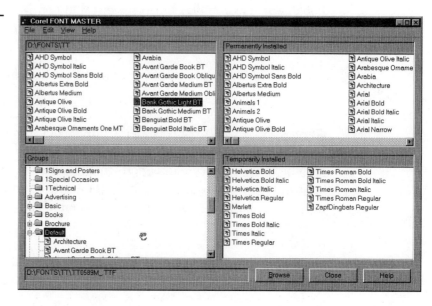

Source The Source window lists the fonts in the current folder (or directory), which is displayed in the window's title bar. Use the Browse button to change the folder this window looks at. You can display fonts by file name or font name. From this window, you can preview fonts, get detailed information about them, print samples of them, and delete them.

Permanently Installed Fonts listed in this window are considered permanent fonts. This includes fonts that are installed the conventional way, using the Fonts folder. To add fonts to this window—that is, to install them permanently—you can select fonts from any of the other windows and drag them here. Right-clicking in this window produces various context-sensitive services, such as Cut, which uninstalls a font but does not delete it; Copy, which copies a font to the Clipboard so it can be pasted into another FONT MASTER window; Paste, which pastes a font that has previously been copied; and Delete, which uninstalls the font and deletes it from the hard drive.

Temporarily Installed In this window are the fonts that have been installed for the current Windows session only. Adding to the convenience of temporary fonts is the fact that they don't have to consume hard drive space—they can stay on the CD. Furthermore, the CD only has to be in the drive during installation. Then you can remove it, use the fonts for the entire session, and know that they'll go away when you're done. Any font in this window can be dragged to the permanent window (or you can use File / Install to do the same thing).

Groups Entries in this window are displayed as folders. You can add fonts to folders by dragging and dropping them from one of the other FONT MASTER windows or by pasting a font that has previously been copied. Once you've grouped a set of fonts, you can easily install the entire group by dragging the folder to one of the Installed windows or by selecting one of the Install options from either the File menu or the context pop-up. And the handy Create Group Icon lets you make a desktop icon for an existing set of fonts, so installing them is only a mouse click away—you don't even have to start FONT MASTER. The Create Group Icon command is in both the File menu and the context pop-up.

When you create the group icon, you can specify whether the fonts should be installed permanently or temporarily, or you can designate that you want to be prompted for this information before installation. The New Group option—also in both the File menu and the pop-up—lets you create new folders.

We Miss Ares

We think FONT MASTER is a fine program, but we have difficulty welcoming it unreservedly into the CorelDRAW family. We can't help but feel that Corel has turned a cold shoulder toward Ares Software, Corel's former strategic partner and the makers of FontMinder, which was bundled with CorelDRAW 5. FontMinder 3.0 is one of the finest utilities available for Windows 95, and we don't hesitate to recommend it to DRAW 6.0 users. We do this as much out of loyalty as our belief that it's the best font-management tool available.

Corel's official response on this issue is that FontMinder wasn't ready when CorelDRAW 6.0 was ready to ship, but we don't accept that. As sure as the sun rises, Corel scheduled a maintenance release for version 6.0—but FontMinder was released well before then. Call us naive, but strategic partnerships like the one that existed between Corel and Ares helped us gauge the health of the graphics software business. With Ares out of the Corel orbit, at least temporarily, we think the CorelDRAW community has lost a good friend.

MEMO

CorelMEMO is new to version 6.0. It's one of the bundled applets that doesn't get mentioned in any of the related Corel literature. There's all of a page and a half devoted to it in the first section of the User's Manual; don't blink as you're turning pages, or you'll miss it.

MEMO is an OLE application, which means, first of all, that it can be utilized by any application that functions as an OLE client (that is, can receive OLE data). We've tried MEMO out in DRAW, Word for Windows, Excel, and other OLE client applications.

MEMO is meant to work much like the sticky notes we've all come to know and love. Even its default color is pale yellow, just like its paper Post-it counterpart. According to the User's Manual, this applet is designed to help you insert comments, notes, and bitmap images, and to leave reminders or note changes in a document. Once a memo is inserted into a drawing, it's quite noticeable, just like a real sticky note.

Inserting a memo is easy. In CorelDRAW you select either Insert MEMO or Insert New Object from the Edit menu. In other OLE client applications, you select the equivalent of the Insert Object option. Once you've activated MEMO from these various dialogs, the program springs to life in its own editing window, as shown in Figure 36.30.

A memo is divided into two sections: a single-line header that includes a small bitmap image and memo topic, and a body that contains the text of the memo. Even though the User's Manual says you can insert bitmap images in the memo, that applies only to the header—you can't paste an image in the body of the memo.

You can change the bitmap by selecting CorelMEMO Picture option; it's available from the Edit menu or by right-clicking on the bitmap and getting the pop-up. This brings up the Select Picture dialog, where you can pick from 16 standard pictures (bitmaps) included in MEMO. Or click the Browse button and choose your own bitmap image from anywhere on your system. Only standard BMP or DIB (Device Independent Bitmap) bitmap images are supported. The image you select will be automatically scaled to fit into the predefined image area.

MEMO's functionality is surprisingly complete, considering the relative austerity of this applet. You can change any aspect of the font for the header or body, the color of the memo paper, the header text color, and the body text color. You can choose to display the memo in the client

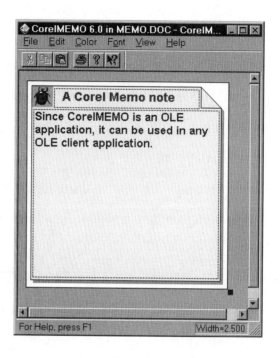

application as a picture (using the bitmap that you selected on the header line) or as a full-sized memo. The size of the memo paper is adjustable; the default is 2″ square.

Documentation for MEMO is included in the online help, although you won't need much help with this simple program. Move the mouse pointer to the header line, click to enter text, and either Tab to or click in the body to enter or edit text there. Rocket science, this is not.

You can print and preview directly from MEMO. The printed memo looks the same as the on-screen representation, whether it's printed from MEMO or from the client application. Once you add a memo to a drawing, it will always print unless you move it to a nonprinting layer. We think an option to prohibit printing the memo would be a nice addition.

We're not sure just how much stock to place in this cute little application, but we will end with the observation that when the memo is displayed full size in the client application, it really stands out, without being garish.

♣

Thirty-six chapters ago, we were discussing nodes, paths, and fountain fills; now we're finishing up by talking about electronic Post-it notes. Hmmm…

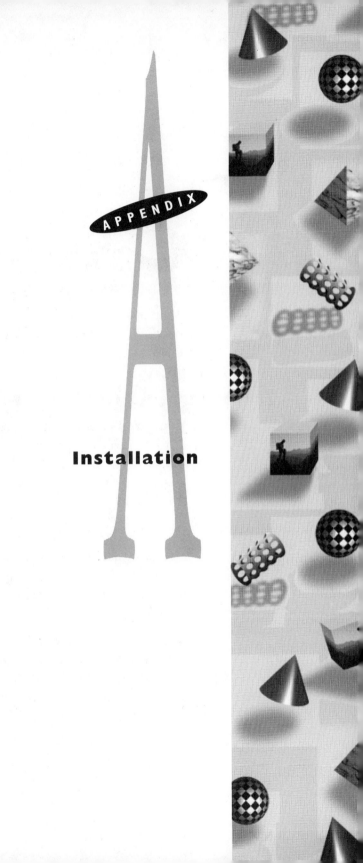

APPENDIX

A

Installation

CorelDRAW 6.0 is a suite of 32-bit applications. That means it will only run under a 32-bit operating system such as Windows 95 or Windows NT 3.51 or later. Installation of the program is not really rocket science, but it does have a number of options.

Begin by inserting CD Disk 1 into the CD drive. If you're running Windows 95, the CorelDRAW 6.0 Welcome screen will automatically appear.

The Infamous AUTORUN

Windows 95 has an Autorun feature that executes a program called Autorun every time a new CD is inserted. (To be more technically precise, a file called AUTORUN.INF is read from the root directory of the CD, and if there is an OPEN statement in an AUTORUN section in that file, the program named in the statement is executed.) Autorun was quite controversial among beta testers, many of whom wanted Corel to remove this "convenience" from the CD. These detractors made a good argument that users who had already installed DRAW would grow tired of this friendly but obtrusive greeting when all they wanted to do was install a font, check a README file, or some other housekeeping task. Corel decided to keep Autorun in place, however.

If you do want to omit the greeting, you can instruct Windows 95 to ignore the feature. To do this temporarily, hold down the Shift key when you insert the CD. To get rid of the greeting permanently, go to (deep breath) Control Panel / System / Device Manager / CD-ROM / (the CD-ROM drive name) / Settings and uncheck Auto Insert Notification.

AUTORUN.EXE displays the screen shown in Figure A.1. As you can see, there are three choices:

- The Setup button starts SETUP.EXE, which installs CorelDRAW 6.0. If you prefer, you can cut to the chase and simply start SETUP.EXE from the root directory of the CD and never even look at Autorun at all.
- Uninstall is covered at the end of this chapter.
- Cancel closes the Autorun program. Not much to that.

When you move the mouse cursor over one of the three buttons, a light-blue circle appears on the button indicating it is active. Click to select the option.

A . I

AUTORUN.EXE automatically starts when CorelDRAW CD Disk I is inserted into the CD-ROM drive.

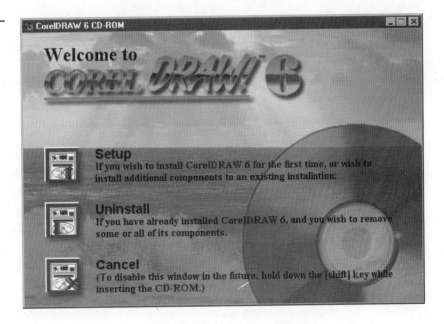

Setup

The Setup program is configured as a wizard that prompts you through installation options one step at a time. There is a Help button that invokes a help file, which very politely instructs you to refer to the User's Manual for more detailed information on Setup options. Thanks.

The first entry screen you encounter asks for your "full" name, company name if applicable, and your phone number. Once you've entered and confirmed that information, the next screen informs you of your serial number, which you are instructed to record in your User's Manual.

The next screen presents four installation options: Full, Custom, Minimum, and CD-ROM installation, as shown in Figure A.2. Click the radio button to see a description of the installation in the Setup Option Description box on the right. Click the Next button when you are ready to proceed.

The disk space estimates given in the description are accurate. Approximately 4MB of that space is consumed on the drive where Windows 95 is installed; the remaining space is taken up by CorelDRAW itself. Each option will prompt you for the target folder (directory) for the installation.

Full Installation

Full installation installs nearly all of the applications that come with CorelDRAW. (The exception is the BarCode utility, an OLE application that automates bar-code printing. You'll need to select the Custom installation option to load BarCode.) Full installation takes approximately 20 minutes on a 90-MHz Pentium machine with a double-speed CD-ROM and consumes a whopping 180MB disk space, just like the dialog box says. We remember when our hard drives didn't have that much storage space to begin with.

Full installation proceeds without a hitch and finishes up by adding a folder to the Start Menu. If you run the Registration Wizard (more on that later), approximately 20 items are added to the folder.

A.2

The four choices for installation. The most automatic choice, Full, is also the greediest, devouring almost 200MB of hard drive space.

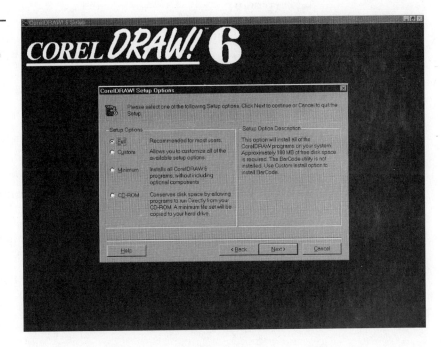

If you don't change anything, this setting installs exactly the same set of files as the full installation option above. With custom installation, however, you can pick and choose individually from among the following available applications and options:

- DRAW
- Photo-PAINT
- PRESENTS
- DREAM3D
- MOTION3D
- DEPTH
- MULTIMEDIA MANAGER
- OCR-TRACE
- FONT MASTER

- CAPTURE
- SCRIPT Editor
- SCRIPT Dialog Editor
- EQUATION Editor
- BarCode Wizard
- MEMO
- Twelve dictionaries for 11 different languages
- Labels (automates creation of labels, business cards, and envelopes)
- Import and export filters (default installs 89 import/export filters)
- TrueType Fonts (select from 1,029 fonts provided on the CD; default installs 12 fonts)
- Eleven scanner drivers

The dialog shows you a running total of the disk space required by the currently selected items, so if disk space is a concern, you can tailor your installation to meet current disk space availability. Duration of the installation procedure depends entirely on the items selected.

Custom installation adds a folder to the Start Menu, with shortcuts for each application that you choose.

CorelDRAW comes with about a gazillion symbols (in 58 libraries), but only six of the libraries are installed by default. If you want the full complement of symbols, you have to select them during the custom setup process.

Minimum Installation

The minimum installation option provides a bare bones installation, consuming "only" about 66MB. With this installation you can pick and choose import/export filters, as well as TrueType fonts. As with a custom installation, the default is to install all of the filters and 12 fonts.

The Minimum installation option automatically installs the following items:

- DRAW
- Photo-PAINT
- README
- CorelDRAW Uninstaller
- Corel Approved Partners
- Corel Color Manager Wizard
- Corel Tech Support help
- CorelDRAW Registration Wizard

CD-ROM Installation

The CD-ROM option consumes the least amount of disk space—only 32MB! This option requires that the CD be in the drive when you want to run any of the programs.

As with a Custom installation, you select the components you want to install, but only the most essential files for those components are placed on your hard drive; the rest stay on the CD.

The Rest of the Story

Once you choose one of the installation options, you are asked to select a drive with available disk space that Corel can use for temporary files. Finally, you choose a program folder where program shortcuts (used to start each of the applications) will be stored. You can add to an existing folder or create a new one.

The Setup program prompts you with a final Ready to Install dialog containing a summary of the selections you've made. It presents the destination directory, program folder, and disk space requirements so you can confirm or cancel your choices.

Setup displays the progress of the installation with the familiar Windows-style "Percentage Complete" status bar. Various bitmap images appear during the installation, with highlight information about the software that's being installed. When all the components are installed, a Setup Complete dialog comes up, sporting a Register button and a Finish button.

The Register button starts a Registration Wizard that prompts you for user information, the size of your business, what influenced you to buy CorelDRAW, and your choice of a charitable organization to which Corel will donate $1.00 when it receives your program registration. Once you've answered all of the registration questions, the wizard creates a text file containing your responses. You can then choose to print the information for postal mail to Corel, or use an installed fax modem to transmit your registration. If you run the Registration Wizard, a link to the text file it creates is added to the program folder so that you can easily access this file.

Once you've completed (or skipped over) registration, the only option that remains is the Finish button. Click that, and Setup exits and removes temporary files from your hard drive.

Uninstall

With the increasing size and complexity of today's programs, the numerous files that are installed in a variety of locations (including the WINDOWS directory and SYSTEM subdirectory), and the registration entries added by the installation program, manual removal of software is too complex for mere mortals. That's why most Windows programs include an Uninstall utility that is installed during setup.

CorelDRAW's Uninstall can be invoked from either Autorun, the Start Menu folder containing the Corel applications, or the Add/Remove Programs command in Control Panel. The Uninstall Wizard allows you to select everything or choose individual components to uninstall. We ran the program several times when testing the various Uninstall options, and it worked flawlessly every time.

Once you make your Uninstall selections, you get an Information window summarizing the components you wish to remove, followed by a final Ready to Remove Components dialog. A status window displays progress as each of the Uninstall steps is performed:

- Searching for installed components
- Removing files and directories
- Removing registry entries
- Removing shortcuts
- Updating current installation information

A final message box displays when Uninstall has completed its work. Press the Finish button to exit. You might notice that your Windows drive has a little less available disk space than before you installed CorelDRAW in the first place. This is because of shared components (called *redistributable files*) that CorelDRAW installs but cannot uninstall because they might be needed by other Windows programs.

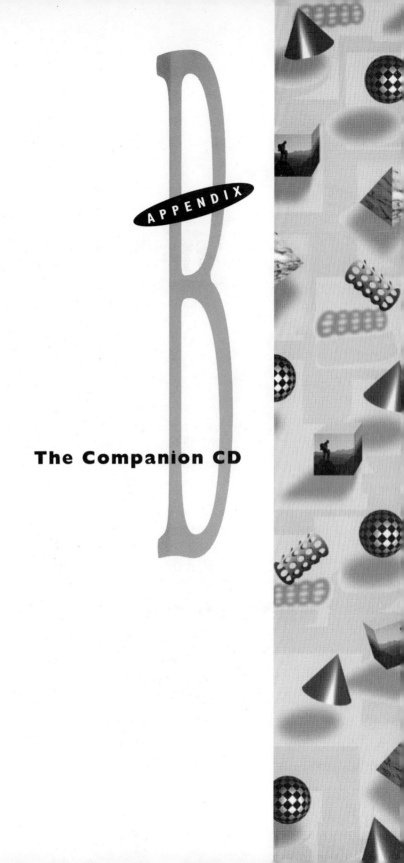

APPENDIX

B

The Companion CD

When we first decided to include a Companion CD with *Mastering CorelDRAW 4*, the decision was not made lightly. CDs were clearly the wave of the future, with Corel riding the crest of that wave as one of the first software publishers to release major programs on CDs as well as diskettes. And we knew that we could provide much more material to you on CD, including some programs that were too large to be included otherwise. But we also knew we would be leaving some of you out in the cold—namely, those of you who did not yet own CD players.

Today, a mere two years later, it's almost as difficult to buy a new PC system without a CD-ROM player as it is to find one that does not come with Windows 95 installed. If you don't already own a CD-ROM, chances are you will in the near future, and it's almost a certainty that you know someone who does.

CDs have become common adjuncts to books, magazines, and promotional campaigns, so we are no longer on the cutting edge of technology. But we are pleased to offer you the substantial collection of files included on this year's *Mastering CorelDRAW 6* Companion CD.

What You'll Find on the Companion CD

The Companion CD contains an assortment of practice files, sample images, utilities, product demonstrations, and other information designed to not only increase your productivity in and around CorelDRAW, but also to provide a bit of recreation. It includes

- Example and practice files for following along with many of the discussions and exercises throughout the book.

- A Gallery directory containing works created by various artists in CorelDRAW, including the images from this book's Color Galleries.

- A variety of free and shareware Windows programs culled from the Internet and other online sources, selected with the goal of simplifying and streamlining your use of CorelDRAW, Windows 95, and related software.

- Product samples and program demonstrations from commercial vendors, including a Working Model of CorelDRAW 6.0.

The CD contains four directories: DEMOS, PRACTICE, GALLERY, and PROGRAMS. The files and subdirectories for each are described below and in the README.TXT file located in the root directory of the CD.

DEMOS

The DEMOS directory contains working demonstration versions of CorelDRAW 6.0, Ares FontChameleon, and JIT's "Learning Windows 95," as well as sample images from several commercial specialty clip-art collections. The files from each vendor are located in separate subdirectories under \DEMOS, as follows.

Ares   The FontChameleon Starter Kit from Ares Software. Font-Chameleon allows you to create, modify, and blend Type 1 or TrueType fonts from master font outlines. This is a fully functional demo version of the program. It does everything except save descriptor files and actually build fonts.

Corel   A Working Model of CorelDRAW 6.0 that is fully functional except that output (file save/export, OLE, printing) is disabled. This Working Model requires Windows 95 or Windows NT. Install this demo using the Setup program in the DRAW6WM subdirectory.

JIT A working demo of the instructional CD "Learning Windows 95" from JIT Learning Products. All of JIT's demos and tutorials run under either Windows 95 or Windows 3.*x.* You'll need a sound card and speakers.

Periwinkle Images from Periwinkle Software's Past Tints Sampler and Garden Edition CDs. These are high-resolution digital images reproduced from antique originals. Included in this directory is a sample .CDR file that incorporates one of the images.

PhotoDisc Selected images from the PhotoDisc "Just Tools" collection. This directory also includes a sample .CDR file, a Gallery file with thumbnails of the entire collection, and an Acrobat .PDF file describing the product. See the README.TXT file for more information.

PIO Nostalgic, TIF-format "clip photos" from Classic PIO Partners, which can be used in DRAW or Photo-PAINT. There's also a sample .CDR file and a catalog in .PDF format. Details in README.TXT.

RT Vector art from three RT Graphics specialty collections—The Santa Fe Collection, The Plains Collection, and The Petrograph Collection. RT-GFX.TXT provides detailed descriptions of all three collections, and the accompanying .CDR file contains all the samples imported into DRAW 6.0.

GALLERY

The GALLERY directory is where you will find examples of professional artwork created with CorelDRAW, including the images from this book's Color Galleries. These works show off CorelDRAW's possibilities, and are good sources of ideas and inspiration. Some of the files here are winners in Corel's annual international art competition.

Several of the files include embedded sound clips of the artists discussing the creation of their work. The quality of playback will depend in large part on your system hardware.

PRACTICE

This book contains frequent references to material in the PRACTICE directory. We include here any files that you need to follow along with exercises, as well as some to help you better understand the function of a tool, command, or effect. Files that correspond to figures in the book have the figure numbers as their file names.

Many of the .CDR images used in this text were placed here in PRACTICE, so you can open them up, take them apart, and reverse-engineer the techniques used. All files can be opened straight from the CD, but in order to make changes and save those changes, you will need to copy the files to your hard drive.

AUTHOR'S NOTE

Some of the .CDR files on the CD may lead to Panose fontmatching messages when you open them. In the few files where the text is present and the font is important, we have generally converted it to curves. Your first response to any Panose message when opening these files should just be to OK it and see what you get. Generally, it will be just fine.

The Paint Subdirectory

The PRACTICE\PAINT directory contains files that accompany the exercises and discussions in the Photo-PAINT chapter (Chapter 32). The directory contains the following subdirectories:

- CANVAS
- EFFECTS
- MANIP
- SAMPLES
- SHEARMAP
- USERDEF

PROGRAMS

The PROGRAMS directory holds a variety of free and shareware programs for both Windows 3.1 and Windows 95. The majority of these are available on the Internet or other online sources. They are included here in their original distribution formats—most often, in the form of zipped archives. Archive files with a .ZIP extension must be unzipped with a file extraction utility such as PKUNZIP or WinZip (which is included on the CD). Files with .EXE extensions are self-extracting archives. Simply execute the file from the version of Windows where you want it installed.

Each utility is located in its own subdirectory under \PROGRAMS. For example, you can find Paint Shop Pro in PROGRAMS\PSPRO. Most of the programs include installation instructions and other basic documentation, usually in files with names like README.TXT or MANUAL.DOC.

Many of the programs included on this CD are *shareware*. Shareware is a method of software distribution that allows you to try out software before you pay for it. Each of the shareware programs on the CD has its own licensing terms. You should refer to the documentation that comes with each program to determine the restrictions on its use and how you can become a registered user.

Please support the shareware concept and the authors of these shareware programs by registering any program you use beyond the trial period.

AUTHOR'S NOTE

> Some of these programs will not run unless you have the appropriate Visual BASIC .DLL file in your WINDOWS\SYSTEM directory. Although some of the programs that require this file include a Setup program that copies the appropriate .DLL files as necessary, others do not. To circumvent this requirement while you're trying out these and other Visual BASIC programs, first copy the three files VBRUN100.DLL, VBRUN200.DLL, and VBRUN300.DLL from the \PROGRAMS_REDIST directory on the CD to your WINDOWS\SYSTEM directory. This will allow you to run any program written in Visual BASIC, regardless of whether it installs the proper .DLL file.

Following are brief descriptions of the utilities found in each of the PROGRAMS subdirectories on the Companion CD; for detailed information on each program, refer to its documentation or online help. As always with software distributed in this fashion, though all of the programs on the Companion CD have been thoroughly tested for reliability and safety, you do use them at your own risk.

ACCENT   This Windows program enables you to input special characters not normally found on a regular keyboard, including accented characters (diacritics) and other special symbols such as copyright or trademark signs. Accent is distributed as shareware.

Acrobat Reader   Version 2.1 of the Adobe Acrobat Reader is required to view the .PDF files included with some of the samples in the PRACTICE directory. ACROREAD.EXE is a self-extracting archive. This version of the Acrobat Reader may be freely distributed.

Color Clip (COLORCLP)   A collection of 95 .PCX clip-art images. You'll find a variety of subjects—animals, holidays, food, sports, and more. COLORCLP is distributed as shareware by Webfoot Technologies, and ordering information for the registered version is included in the archive.

Cubit Meister (CUBIT)   Cubit Meister is a shareware program that calculates proportions and converts units of measurement systems most prevalent in graphic arts (decimal and fractional inches, millimeters/centimeters, picas/points, and points). It requires the redistributable system files THREED.VBX (included in the archive) and VBRUN300.DLL (found in \PROGRAMS_REDIST).

DocMan (DOCMAN)   DocMan is a Windows 95 shareware program that enhances the Documents folder on the Start button, allowing you to add, delete, and create working lists of files.

Drag-and-File (DRGF32)   Drag-and-File is a shareware file manager for Windows 95 and NT 3.51. It lets you copy, view, move, and zip files from single or multiple windows. Features include file filtering and file association/dissociation, including the ability to associate data files with more than one program. This version includes a completely configurable toolbar, network support, formatting and disk copying functions, file descriptions, file icons, and a built-in DOS command line. Under Windows 95, Drag-and-File has full access to the Win 95 shell. You can bring up context menus, drag and drop with the right mouse button, and create shortcuts.

Fonter   Fonter is a Windows 3.1 program that allows you to view Type 1 or TrueType fonts, create printed lists with a text sample of each font, and print both sample sheets and character-set charts. The Preview/Install feature (TrueType only) lets you print a file list, compare fonts, and print font samples or specimens before actually installing the font. This is the shareware version of Fonter 7.0. Installation instructions are contained in FONTER.WRI. Fonter requires the file VBRUN300.DLL, found in the \PROGRAMS_REDIST directory.

Note: This program is not intended for use under Windows 95 and will not function properly in that environment.

Formula Graphics (FORMGFX)   Formula Graphics Multimedia System brings artwork, sounds, and animations together to create interactive multimedia titles. The system was designed to simplify the task of authoring on a production level, allow the creative content of a presentation to be as rich as possible, and make it possible to achieve an unlimited amount of interactivity. This 16-bit program will run under both Windows 3.1 and Windows 95, and a 32-bit version is now available. Formula Graphics is distributed as freeware; see the README.TXT file in the archive for program features and installation details.

Gang   GANG.CSC is a Corel script that "gangs" objects—takes whatever objects you have in DRAW and fits as many of them as possible on a page. GANG requires CorelDRAW 6.0 and Windows 95. Instructions for use are included in GANG.TXT.

Greek   Greek is a simple program that creates nonense or "greek" text for creating dummy layouts. It comes with no instructions, nor does it need any. Just run it and follow the prompts.

HotDog   HotDog is a Windows HTML editor that helps you create and maintain documents for the World Wide Web. HotDog provides quick access to tags and attributes, to assist in the creation of complex elements. It supports forms, HTML 3, and Netscape revisions. See the help file for more details. HotDog is not a WYSIWYG, desktop publishing-style editor and requires no word processing software to run. It's shareware, provided in a self-extracting archive.

Lview Pro (LVIEW)   LView Pro is a shareware image-file editor for Windows 95 and Windows NT 3.51 with NewShell. It loads/saves image files in JPEG JFIF; GIF 87a/89a; TIFF; Truevision Targa; Windows and OS/2 BMP; ZSoft's PCX; and PBMPLUS's PBM, PGM, and PPM formats. Excellent for creating interlaced GIFs with transparent backgrounds for Web pages. A Windows 3.*x* version of this program is also available from most online services.

MegaScan   MegaScan was designed to streamline mundane scanning tasks by scanning directly into CorelDRAW 3, 4, or 5. MegaScan was not designed to be an image-editing package, but rather a quick way to transfer camera-ready art or photos into DRAW. A detailed listing of program features is contained in MEGASCAN.TXT. Hardware/software requirements: Windows 3.1 or 95; CorelDRAW 3, 4, or 5; and a

100% TWAIN-compliant scanner or Video Capture system. Mega-Scan also requires the redistributable files VBRUN300.DLL and THREED.VBX, which are both included in the zipped archive. This 16-bit shareware version of MegaScan is compatible with Windows 95, and a 32-bit commercial version that works with DRAW 6.0 is also available.

MECN Tree Factory (MECNTREE)   The MECN Tree Factory is a modeling tool, designed for quick generation of "realistic" 3D polygon-based tree models. Once generated, these models can be exported in DXF, RAW, or LWO (Lightwave 3D object) file formats and used in your favorite 3D software for rendering and animating. The MECN Tree Factory is designed to allow experimentation and the immediate viewing of results, and includes an online tutorial. A self-extracting archive file.

Paint Shop Pro (PSPRO)   Version 3.11 of Paint Shop Pro, the popular shareware bitmap graphics program for image creation, viewing, and manipulation. Features include painting with eight brushes, photo retouching, image enhancement and editing, color enhancement, an image browser, batch conversion, and scanner support. The program includes 20 built-in filters, supports plug-in filters, and can handle over 34 file formats.

ROMCat   ROMCat provides a keyword-oriented search of the .CDR and .CMX clip art on your DRAW CDs. You can display thumbnails and direct import requests to DRAW. We have included prebuilt catalogs of keywords for DRAW 3, 4, 5 (release F1), and 6.0. ROMCat is distributed as freeware.

Scan95   The shareware version of McAfee's virus scanner for Windows 95. Detects and removes viruses. This is a self-extracting compressed file that should be executed under Windows 95.

Script   This is the 16-bit version of MegaScan/SCRIPT, a program by the author of MegaScan. SCRIPT allows you to scan files into

CorelDRAW 6.0 from a script written in CorelSCRIPT. Requires Windows 95, CorelDRAW 6.0, and a 100% TWAIN-compliant scanner or Video Capture system. MegaScan/SCRIPT is shareware, and requires the redistributable system files THREED.VBX (included in this archive) and VBRUN300.DLL (in the \PROGRAMS_REDIST directory).

Stereo Gram (STERGRMS)   A simple shareware stereogram program. Stereo Gram converts monochrome .BMP files into single-level, random-dot stereograms (two-dimensional graphics that appear three-dimensional) that can be viewed on screen or printed. This 16-bit program runs under Windows 3.1 or later, and a 32-bit version for Windows 95, Windows NT, and Win32S is also available.

Job Timer (TIMER)   Job Timer is an Art Charge tracking system for CorelDRAW. Timer displays art fees based on an hourly rate, with charges updated by the second. The program is integrated into DRAW to allow automatic reset of the timer when the user selects File / New in DRAW, and the timer is stopped during print time. A delay can be set before charges begin. The shareware version of Job Timer runs under Windows 3.1 or 95, and with any version of DRAW. A 32-bit commercial version designed to work specifically with CorelDRAW 6.0 is also available.

UltraClip (UCLIP)   UltraClip creates and manages a virtual clipboard for the Windows environment, allowing you to create mini-clipboards that store snapshots of the Windows Clipboard. You can also create mini-clips directly from several formats of graphic images stored on disk, and create and edit OLE objects with embedded or linked data. UltraClip is distributed as freeware; there is no registration fee.

WinQuilt (WINQ)   WinQuilt is a shareware utility that generates fractal-pattern bitmaps by running a random fractal equation through a given number of iterations. The shape of the bitmap, the number and pattern of its tiling, and the colors represented and their frequencies can all be set and modified. The process requires a good amount of memory, so if you have a slower machine you may want to set this utility to run overnight. WinQuilt will run on both Windows NT and 95. It requires at least a 486 PC and a graphics card using at least 32K colors. Under Windows 95, it requires a large amount of free memory when started.

WinZip   WinZip is the classic shareware Windows compression utility. Both a 16- and 32-bit version are included on the Companion CD. The install program in the \PROGRAMS\WINZIP directory will automatically detect your operating environment and install the appropriate version. In addition to .ZIP files, WinZip also includes built-in support for several popular Internet file formats. The 16-bit version includes an install/uninstall feature for archived programs.

XferPro   XferPro encodes and decodes binary files in formats commonly used for e-mail attachments. It includes support for the most common Internet formats (UU, XX, Mime, and BinHex). The program supports multiple enclosures and can automatically determine the type of encoding used. Shareware.

The REDIST Subdirectory   This directory contains the Visual Basic runtime modules VBRUN100.DLL, VBRUN200.DLL, and VBRUN300.DLL. VBRUN300.DLL is required by Windows programs written in Visual Basic 3.0, including several of the shareware programs on this disk.

NOTE TO THE READER: First level entries are in **bold**. **Boldfaced** numbers indicate pages where you will find the principal discussion of a topic or the definition of a term. *Italic* page numbers indicate pages where topics are illustrated in figures.

F

F2 key

Zoom In shortcut, 27

Shift + F2 key (Zoom On Selected), 27, 88

F3 key, Zoom Out shortcut, 27

F4 key, Fit In Window shortcut, 27, 88

F5 key

Pencil tool shortcut, 27

Ctrl + F5 (Style Manager), 381

F6 key, Rectangle tool shortcut, 29

F7 key, Ellipse tool shortcut, 29

F8 key

artistic text shortcut, 29, 313

Ctrl + F8 (PowerLines), 569

Shift + F8 key (paragraph text), 29, 313

F10 key

Shape tool shortcut, 26

Ctrl + F10 (Node Edit), 193

F11 key

Fountain Fill dialog box shortcut, 30

Ctrl + F11 (Symbols), 80

Shift + F11 (Uniform Fill dialog box), 30

F12 key

Outline Pen dialog box shortcut, 30

Shift + F12 (Outline Color dialog box), 30

Facing Pages printing option, 688

file compression

compressing CorelMOTION3D movie files, 1042

with WinZip, 1116

File Information button, Print Options dialog box Separations page, 730

File menu

Import command, 76–78, *77*

overview of, **32–33**, *32*

file name extensions. *See also* .CDR files; .EPS files

.ACL, 393

.AI, 819–820

.CDT, 398

.CGM, 816, 821–822, *822*, *823*, 847–848, *848*, *849*

.CMX, 816–818, 821, 862–864

.DXF, 820, 848–849, *850*

.GEM, 853, *854*

.M3D, 1022

.PAT, 268

.PCX, 831–834, 855–857, *856*

.PDF, 1111

.PRN, 694, 695–696, 755. *See also* print files

.PST, 405

.WMF, 822–823, *823*, 857–858, *859*

File page, in CorelCAPTURE, 1086

files. *See also* drawings; exporting; importing

animation files in CorelMOTION3D, 1041–1042

Color Clip (COLORCLIP) file, 1111

CORELDRW.CDT default template file, 383, 398–400

CORELDRW.CPL color palette file, 237

CORELDRW.END arrow style definition file, 210

CORELDRW.PST default preset file, 405, 406, 407

CorelMOTION3D file formats, 1022–1023

CORELPRN.INI file, 713

encoding and decoding software for binary files, 1116

importing

in logo exercise, 102, *102*

overview of, 76–78, *77*

opening multiple files, 51, 88, 818

print files

creating for color separations, 738–739, 777–778, *778*

creating Macintosh print files, 694–695

creating for service bureaus, 694–696, 738–739, 755, 777–778, *778*

downloading Type 1 fonts to, 755–756

What You'll Find on the CD

The *Mastering CorelDRAW 6* CD contains an assortment of practice files, sample images, utilities, product demonstrations, and other information designed not only to increase your productivity in and around CorelDRAW, but also to provide a bit of recreation. It includes:

- Example and practice files for following along with many of the discussions and exercises throughout the book.

- A Gallery directory containing works created by various artists in CorelDRAW, including the images from this book's Color Galleries.

- A variety of free and shareware Windows programs culled from the Internet and other online sources, selected with the goal of making your use of CorelDRAW, Windows 95, and related software easier and more productive.

- Product samples and program demonstrations from commercial vendors, including a Working Model of CorelDRAW 6.

The CD contains four directories: DEMOS, PRACTICE, GALLERY, and PROGRAMS. The files and subdirectories for each are described in Appendix B and in the readme.txt file located in the root directory of the CD.